LAW, JUSTICE, AND SOCIETY

LAW, JUSTICE, AND SOCIETY

A SOCIOLEGAL INTRODUCTION

Fifth Edition

Anthony Walsh
Boise State University

Craig Hemmens
Washington State University

New York   Oxford
OXFORD UNIVERSITY PRESS

Oxford University Press is a department of the University of Oxford.
It furthers the University's objective of excellence in research, scholarship,
and education by publishing worldwide. Oxford is a registered trade mark of
Oxford University Press in the UK and certain other countries.

Published in the United States of America by Oxford University Press
198 Madison Avenue, New York, NY 10016, United States of America.

Library of Congress Cataloging-in-Publication Data
Names: Walsh, Anthony, 1941- author. | Hemmens, Craig, author.
Title: Law, justice, and society : a sociolegal introduction / Anthony Walsh,
    Craig Hemmens.
Description: 5th edition. | Oxford ; New York, New York : Oxford University
    Press, [2019] | Includes bibliographical references and index.
Identifiers: LCCN 2019019355 (print) | LCCN 2019019774 (ebook) |
    ISBN 9780190843939 (online ebook) | ISBN 9780190084998 (online ebook) |
    ISBN 9780190843892 (pbk.) | ISBN 9780190843908 (instructor's manual) |
    ISBN 9780190843915 (powerpoint) | ISBN 9780190843922 (test bank) |
    ISBN 9780190843946 (loose leaf)
Subjects: LCSH: Law--Social aspects--United States. | Justice, Administration
    of--United States. | Sociological jurisprudence. | LCGFT: Textbooks.
Classification: LCC KF386 (ebook) | LCC KF386 .W325 2019 (print) |
    DDC 340/.115--dc23
LC record available at https://lccn.loc.gov/2019019355

Printing number: 9 8 7 6 5 4 3 2 1

Printed by LSC Communications, Inc., United States of America

Dedicated to my drop-dead gorgeous wife, Grace; my sons, Robert and Michael, my stepdaughters Heidi and Kasey; my grandchildren Robbie, Ryan, Mikey, Randy, Christopher, Ashlyn, Morgan, Stevie, Vivien, and Frankie; and my great grandchildren, Kaelyn, Logan, Keagan, Caleb, Luke, and Brayden. I should not forget the spouses that made this all possible: Patricia, Dianna, Sharon, Karen, Collette, Marcus, Michael, Amy, Jenna, and Mary Beth—A. W.

Dedicated to Mary, Emily, Sera, Amber, and Max, and to all my students—C. H.

*"What is hateful to you, do not to your fellow man.
This is the law: all the rest is commentary."
Talmud, Shabbat 31a.*

BRIEF CONTENTS

DETAILED CONTENTS

PREFACE

Law, Justice, and Society: A Sociolegal Introduction (fifth edition) is a text designed for use in courses such as Law and Justice, Introduction to Law, and Sociology of Law. Several aspects of this book are not found in competitive volumes. Many texts are written by authors with recognized expertise in only one or two of the areas covered, which results in very good chapters in those areas but also chapters that may contain errors and misunderstandings in others. *Law, Justice, and Society* is a collaborative effort that draws on the expertise of scholars with extensive track records in publishing, teaching, and actual field practice in the topics covered.

Law per se can be a dry topic when approached from a law school perspective. After all, law schools are in the business of turning out professionals who know how to navigate treacherous legal waters on behalf of their clients. This book is not a law book but rather a book *about* law for students wanting to learn the relationship of law to justice and to society. Law school classes focus on the law almost exclusively; our goal is to place the law in its social context. This is a book about how law as a social institution fits into and shapes other institutions. Most students who take a course such as Law and Justice or Sociology of Law have no intention of going to law school and just want to know the relationship of law to their own disciplines and to themselves as citizens, as well as the functions of law in their society. We are all potential witnesses, jurors, victims, or even offenders.

This Fifth Edition has been thoroughly updated in all respects. As usual, we have benefitted greatly from users and reviewers of this book and have incorporated most of the material they suggested to us. Each chapter now includes an "Issue Highlight" page that provides pro and con arguments surrounding a contemporary issue. These issues include sanctuary cities, bathroom laws, regulation reduction, religious accommodations, and so forth. These issues may lead to animated classroom discussions. Another improvement in the Fifth Edition is the inclusion of additional visual material. One of our reviewers of the Fourth Edition opined that the text needs to be broken up more with photos and graphs illustrating the points made in the text. We did just that, and the response was so positive that we added more in this edition.

Chapters 1 and 2 introduce the *idea* of law and justice. These chapters discuss the philosophy, history, and sociology of law. We even look at how some evolutionary biologists have viewed the law and its origin in nature, as opposed to the view that it is purely a social construction. In these chapters, we ask what law and justice are, where they come from, how they have been conceived in the past, and what their functions in society are. Readers will come away from these chapters realizing that few things in modern life are more important than the law.

Chapters 3 through 8 introduce the various aspects of modern American law and justice. Chapter 3 focuses on the process of making law and describes the Bill of Rights. Chapter 4 focuses on the federal and state court systems and the processes that occur within them. Chapter 5 examines criminal law, major crimes, and legal defenses. Chapter 6 looks at criminal procedure, such as the right to an attorney and the exclusionary rule. Chapter 7 covers various aspects of civil and administrative law, such as torts, family law, contract law, and white-collar crime. Chapter 8 focuses on the juvenile justice system.

Chapters 9 through 11 are more sociological and historical in orientation, focusing on how law affects the processes of social change and social control. Chapter 9 investigates the law as a formal method of social control, and focuses primarily on the criminal justice system. Chapter 10 concerns the limits of law as a social control mechanism and explores some so-called vice crimes and the law's differing approach to them across time and place. Chapter 11 explores how the law has been involved in momentous changes in the United States from before the American Revolution to the present day, with special emphasis on the role of the Supreme Court. We also examine the special role of the law in making society possible by its role in social control and the role of social movements in the process of social change.

Chapter 12 takes on a topic sorely lacking in competitive texts—women and the law. Its author, Dr. Mary K. Stohr, is a major figure in feminist criminal justice circles. She has had criminal justice field experience as a correctional officer and counselor and has served as an expert witness in court cases dealing with women's issues.

Chapter 13 provides an overview of the law as it has been applied to racial minorities in the United States from the earliest days of white settlement to the present. It documents the fight against slavery and the Indian fight to maintain cultural independence as well as touching on the Asian and Hispanic experience in the United States. As far as we are aware, this is the only law and society text that devotes a whole chapter to this important topic.

Chapter 14 focuses on comparative law. We learn far more about our own system of law if we know a little about other systems. The chapter looks at law in bands and tribes and in the four major legal traditions in the world today: common, civil, Islamic, and socialist. Students tend to become particularly interested in the practices of non–common law systems.

We hope that at the conclusion of a course based on this book students will have achieved the following primary objectives:

1. **An appreciation of the role of law in society.** Law is arguably the most important of all human inventions, based as it is on our innate sense of fairness, decency, and concern for a peaceable and orderly existence. We have tried to provide you with a "feel" for what law means and where it has come from (both in evolutionary and in cultural terms). Readers will come to a deeper understanding of the legal system as a basic social institution and of its relationship both to other institutions, such as the family, the economy, and government, and to social control and social change. The limits of the law in trying to prevent change and to police private morality also are discussed.

2. **A basic understanding of the courts, lawmaking, and criminal substantive and procedural law.** This book is an introduction to learning *about* law rather than learning law. Learning law is the process of becoming educated and socialized into the legal profession, whereas learning about law is the process of becoming an informed citizen. The student is given the details about the basics of law that every educated adult should know for participation in a democracy. These details are provided with as little legal jargon as possible.

3. **An appreciation of the concept of the rule of law.** The *rule of law* has been called the most important of all legal concepts. It is imperative that citizens of democracies know what it is, how it has evolved, and the mechanisms in place to ensure its survival. Imbedded in this rule is the relatively modern notion of due process, which involves procedural rules (the legal "dos and don'ts") that must be followed by criminal justice officials to ensure fairness and impartiality in the processing of criminal cases. The evolution of the once-absurd idea of due process is a fascinating story going back as far as the Magna Carta in 1215.

4. **An understanding of comparative law.** Understanding how other cultures view and implement law is one of the most interesting features of the study of law. It has been said that if you know only your own culture, you don't know your own culture. The process of understanding almost anything necessarily involves comparison and contrast. The law in the United States has English common law as its foundation. The most prevalent form of law in the world today is civil, or code, law, which differs in many interesting ways from the common law. However, it differs considerably less from the common law than do Islamic and socialist legal systems.

5. **Knowledge of the law's treatment of minorities and minors.** Racial/ethnic minorities, women, and minors have been excluded from full constitutional protection and historically have been treated in very different ways than have white male adults. This unequal treatment often has been sanctioned and even encouraged by the law. These specialized chapters document how the law has evolved to come to view unequal treatment as morally wrong and how it has gone about rectifying its earlier mistakes.

ACKNOWLEDGMENTS

We would first of all like to thank Executive Editor Steve Helba. Steve's commitment to the project and tremendous enthusiasm is greatly appreciated (as is his trips to the hinterlands to see his authors "in action"). Our fifth edition copyeditor, Wesley Morrison, spotted every errant comma, dangling participle, and missing reference in the manuscript, for which we are truly thankful, and production editor Jana MacIsaac made sure everything went quickly and smoothly thereafter. Thank you one and all.

We are also most grateful for the many reviewers who spent considerable time providing us with the benefit of their expertise as the text was revised. Attempting to please so many individuals is a trying task, but one that is ultimately satisfying, and one that undoubtedly made the book better than it would otherwise have been. These expert legal scholars include:

David Allender, Butler University

Susan Maggioni, MassBay Community College

Antoinette France-Harris, Clayton State University

Howard Smith, Penn State University

Lucas McMillan, Lander University

We also thank Marianne Hudson for helping with the test bank and for developing the excellent PowerPoint presentation that accompanies this text. Thanks especially to Michael Bogner of Chadron State College, who supplied Figures 1.1, 3.1, 3.2, and 6.2.

Finally, Anthony Walsh would like to acknowledge his most wonderful and lovely wife, Grace Jean, for her love and support during this and all the other projects that have taken him away from her. She is a real treasure, the pleasantest of persons, candy for his eye, and the center of his universe. He would also like to take the opportunity to once again berate his coauthor and his lovely wife for abandoning him and moving to Washington State University. It was so much easier co-authoring with them when they were in the next office.

Craig Hemmens would like to acknowledge the love and support of his wife and colleague, Mary Stohr, and his stepdaughter, Emily Stohr-Gillmore. He would also like to thank his former departmental colleague and once and future friend and coauthor, Tony Walsh, for encouraging him to avoid the trap of always thinking like a lawyer. Last, thanks to all the students who have listened and (hopefully) learned about the role of law in a just society.

LAW, JUSTICE, AND SOCIETY

CHAPTER 1

LAW: ITS FUNCTION AND PURPOSE

The bomb blast sent Jawad Sabah flying from his seat in Ali's tea shop in Baghdad. Jawad went there daily to seek the solace of relatives and friends following the gang rape and murder of his wife, Abeer, by a marauding militia gang six months earlier. Dusty but uninjured, he picked himself up, saw the flame-engulfed bus, and cried soulfully at the futility and wickedness of the world around him. Jawad wasn't thrilled with life under the brutal dictatorship of Saddam Hussein, but at least Baghdad had been relatively safe and he could drink his tea undisturbed. He remembered the jubilation he felt after the Americans overthrew Hussein in 2003 and his brutal police force melted from the scene. He also remembered the foreboding as looting and vengeance killings began to openly occur as Iraq plunged ever deeper into chaos. What law remained in Baghdad was imposed by the "infidel" Americans or by ineffectual and openly corrupt Iraqi police officers, neither of which could be considered legitimate by those whose behavior they were charged with regulating.

The Unites States' attempt to impose democracy on a country whose values, norms, and customs are at odds with it has not worked out well. The violence peaked in 2006 as Shiites and Sunnis continued to blow each other up, although things significantly improved after the troop surge of 2007. The American military finally withdrew from Iraq on December 15, 2011, ending an action that left thousands of American servicemen and many more thousands of Iraqis dead or wounded. Since the withdrawal of American forces, violence has again escalated across the country, and the Islamic State terrorist group captured large swathes of Iraqi territory, which has since been taken back.

If Iraq is to become a viable state, it must afford its people security, stability, and personal safety; these are the things that law is supposed to provide. The Iraqi Constitution is reasonably democratic for that area of the world, but as with all law, it is just a set of statements on paper without the will of human actors to give it life. For the law to be more than empty words, it needs the respect and awe of all individuals affected by its constraints and obligations.

It requires assurances that the police and judicial processes will be open to scrutiny and will provide equal protections for all citizens. Without such things, government loses its credibility, the economy languishes, organized crime flourishes, vigilantism emerges, and innocent people like Jawad are victimized. This chapter explores the cultural underpinnings and functions of law, describes how ancient philosophers and early sociologists viewed it, and introduces the idea of natural law.

INTRODUCTION

When most people think of law, images of the uniformed police officer or of the pomp and circumstance surrounding the criminal courts tend to dominate. If we ponder a little longer, we may conjure up images and smells of large, dusty books full of sterile rules and a multitude of archaic Latin terms and phrases and conclude that law is a pretty dull subject. Nothing could be further from the truth! Few topics are broader in scope than the law, and none is more important to social life—as Jawad Sabah would doubtless agree. For better or for worse, law insinuates itself into every aspect of social life, governing the relationship between person and person, between institution and institution, and between persons, institutions, and the state; we are all potential victims, witnesses, jurors, and even offenders. The point is that law is a social institution and to study it is to gain valuable understanding of one's society— its heritage, its values, and its day-to-day functioning.

Law has always been considered of the utmost importance in American life. The excerpt from Abraham Lincoln's Lyceum Address, given in 1838 when he was only 28 years old, makes this abundantly clear:

> Let reverence for the laws, be breathed by every American mother, to the lisping babe, that prattles on her lap—let it be taught in schools, in seminaries, and in colleges; let it be written in Primers, spelling books, and in Almanacs;—let it be preached from the pulpit, proclaimed in legislative halls, and enforced in courts of justice. And, in short, let it become the *political religion* of the nation; and let the old and the young, the rich and the poor, the grave and the gay, of all sexes and tongues, and colors and conditions, sacrifice unceasingly upon its altars. (Basler, 2007, p. 6)

Law justly promulgated and justly applied is the bedrock of individual liberty and social progress. Former legal counsel for the British government Phillip Allott (2001) augmented Lincoln's awe of the law when he wrote:

> In the making of the human world, nothing has been more important than what we call *law*. Law is the intermediary between human power and human ideas. Law transforms our national power into social power, transforms our self-interest into social interest, and transforms social interest into self-interest. (p. 19)

Allott is saying that law is a mechanism by which diverse individual and community interests become as close to being the same thing as possible. Law has been a study of endless fascination, and the subject of endless debate, for generations of philosophers and social scientists—let us join them.

WHAT IS LAW?

What is this thing called *law* of which Allott is so enamored? The question is a simple one with a variety of complex answers. The question also usually leads to others, such as "Where did it come from?" "How did it originate?" "What is it based on?" "Whom does it serve—everyone, or just those with the influence to get laws enacted and enforced?" The next two chapters attempt to answer these questions from a number of different perspectives. But let us first try to define law. The seventeenth-century English philosopher Thomas Hobbes (1952) defined law as "just a statute, commanding those things which are honest, and forbidding the contrary" (chap. 26.1). But law is much more than an aggregate of statutes that multiply promiscuously and then sometimes are sloughed off; "it is crucially the art and technique of applying these heterogeneous [statutes and] norms in the administration of justice" (Murphy, 2006, p. 106). We could provide other definitions that various thinkers have given, but we spare readers that and offer our own definition: **Law** is *a written body of general rules of conduct applicable to all members of a defined community, society, or culture, which emanate from a governing authority and which are enforced by its agents through the imposition of penalties for their violation.* This definition would not be acceptable to everyone. Nevertheless, it is offered as a working definition so that we may proceed with our endeavor.

Our definition is appropriate for all modern systems of law, but it does not completely fit preliterate societies. By definition, such societies do not possess writing, nor do they typically employ agents to enforce rules of conduct. However, law as a system of proscribed and prescribed behavior is certainly not unique to highly developed societies with written statutes and a formal system of law enforcement. All groups of people living together in organized groups have at least some type of rudimentary rules for governing conduct. They would not last very long as organized groups if they did not, for law is at the center of all organized social life. Indeed, the word *law* itself has come to us from a variety of Latin and Nordic words meaning "to bind" (people together). People who are "bound together" share a common culture, and all cultures share certain core elements. Our first task is to see how these common elements are related to law.

THE SIX PRIMARY CHARACTERISTICS OF CULTURE AND THEIR RELATIONSHIP TO LAW

Culture is the totality of learned socially transmitted behaviors, ideas, values, customs, artifacts, and technology of groups of people living in a common society. It is the transmission of all sorts of information from generation to generation by nongenetic means. All cultures possess six primary elements: beliefs, values, norms, symbols, technology, and language. These elements represent critical information that maintains and transmits culture across the generations. Without a general consensus about the nature of a shared culture in terms of the six primary elements, the socialization process would be a difficult task indeed. All of these elements are related to one another and, most centrally for our purposes, to the law. Let us take these elements one by one and see how they are related to the law.

1. Beliefs

Beliefs are ideas that we have about how the world operates and what is true and false. Beliefs may be about things that are tangible and observable and things that are not. Information that is observable or verifiable may be derived from scientific experimentation or some other type of experience. For example, although we can scientifically demonstrate that the earth is round and that it rotates around the sun, most people in Christopher Columbus's day were convinced that it was flat and that the sun rotated around the earth. However, scientists knew that the world was round long before Columbus's voyage; the Greek mathematician Eratosthenes had calculated its circumference with remarkable accuracy more than 1,000 years earlier. In those days, knowledge and news, and hence beliefs, traveled slowly.

Cultures also communicate shared beliefs about intangible, nonobservable phenomena such as religious and philosophical beliefs relating to "ultimate" questions like "Who am I?" "What is the purpose of life?" "Where will I go when I die?" and "How can I lead a just and good life?" These questions are not amenable to scientific answers, but they have been answered to the satisfaction of millions by religious, spiritual, and philosophical systems of belief that are even more important to understanding culture and law than are beliefs that are open to verification or falsification. They are more important because they are at the core of human concerns and meaning and because they appease the irritation of doubt.

Laws are often enacted to support our most deeply held beliefs, and as beliefs change over time, so do the laws that support them. When the established doctrine of the Roman Catholic Church was that the earth was the center of the universe and that the sun revolved around it, astronomers who held contrary beliefs were labeled heretics and had to tread lightly for fear of the possible consequences. Similarly, when slavery was permissible in the United States, laws were made to protect the "property rights" of slave owners. Now that we have ceased to believe in prescientific astronomical notions or in slavery, rules about heresy or property rights over human beings no longer exist in Western societies. Laws against heresy, however, continue to exist in many Islamic societies, and remnants of legally sanctioned slavery still exist in some African countries. The point is that if enough people believe something is real, the consequences are often real—regardless of the empirical validity of the belief. Witches do not exist (at least not in the stereotypical, broom-flying, spell-casting, potion-making sense), but this empirical truth was of no comfort to the many women legally burned over the centuries because people believed witches did exist.

2. Values

Values refer to normative standards shared by the culture about what is good and bad, correct and incorrect, moral and immoral, normal and deviant. Values are more general and abstract than specific beliefs, although values themselves differ in their generality and specificity. Shared values are an important binding force in culture and an important integrative mechanism that combines the disparate parts of our personalities into a coherent self-concept (Walsh, 2006). American values are based on transplanted and modified Western European values. Examples of broad and general "core" values in all Western societies include the Golden Rule, justice, equality, liberty, and the sanctity of life. Even though everyone defines these core values as good, people of different ideological persuasions may have quite different images in their heads when they talk about them. Take the different views of fairness and equality held by conservatives and liberals. Conservatives view fairness as an equal-opportunity *process*—a nondiscriminatory chance to enter the race; liberals tend to see fairness as equality of *outcome*, which implies that all should cross the finish line at the same time. If everyone is *equally* subjected to the same rules and *equally* judged by the same standards, fairness is achieved, according to conservatives, even if equality of outcome is not. Because they want to achieve greater equality of outcomes, liberals tend to believe in subjecting certain individuals whom they consider disadvantaged to different rules and then judging them by different standards in order to achieve fairness.

3. Norms

Rules governing appropriate conduct that are more specific than values known as norms. A **norm** is the action component of a value or a belief patterning social behavior in ways consistent with those values and beliefs. Some norms have serious moral connotations and are known as *mores* ("more-rays"). These standards are moral imperatives, and violations of them may be met with chastisement or serious punishment. Less serious norms are called *folkways*. Lacking the moral connotations of mores, folkways are habits that many people conform to automatically, such as the little rules of etiquette when meeting your fiancée's parents.

Laws always reflect the core values and mores of a culture. Western core values typically come from its Jewish/Christian heritage (think of the Ten Commandments and the criminal law: "Thou shalt not kill," "Thou shalt not steal," etc.). Few laws are ever passed that contravene deeply held cultural values without significant opposition from large segments of society. Laws assuring abortion rights, for instance, are so hotly debated because they involve conflicting core values: the sanctity of human life versus a woman's privacy and liberty to choose what happens to her body. Similarly, efforts to pass a constitutional amendment banning the burning of the American flag (exemplifying the value of patriotism) run up against the conflicting values of freedom of speech and political protest. Law is thus a social tool in which the norms reflecting a people's deepest values are put down in writing to assure the continuation of patterns of conduct that are deemed socially desirable.

Figure 1.1 illustrates the flow from values and beliefs to law. All societies have behaviors they encourage and behaviors they discourage through the use of informal rules. Discouraged behavior may eventually reach a point that society takes formal action by enacting laws against it and specifying punishments for those who engage in it.

Figure 1.1 The Progression from Informally Encouraged/Discouraged Behavior to Law

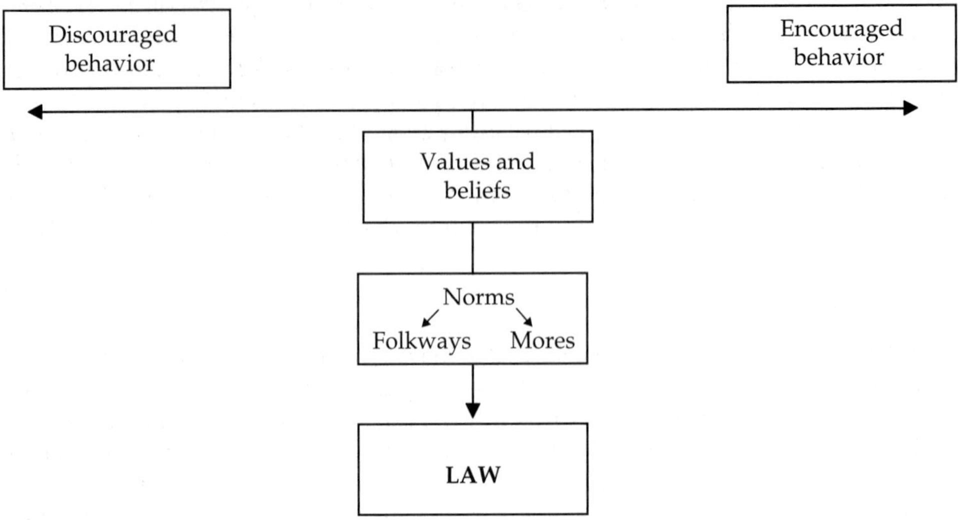

Figure provided by Professor Michael Bogner, Justice Studies Department, Chadron State College (2006).

Legal philosophers differentiate between laws that arise from the norms and customs of a given culture, which is known as **positive law**, and a hypothesized universal set of moral standards known as **natural law**. Legal positivism is a theory that explains law by examining its cultural context and studying the cultural sources of law as it *is*, without passing moral judgments. Natural law adherents philosophize about the law as it *ought* to be. Believers in natural law view it as standing above and placing limits on what is permissible in positive law, whereas positivists draw a distinction between law and morality. It is not that positivists divorce law from morality. Law and morality are always intertwined to some extent, but positivists aver that it is not necessarily so and that law is law if it has the appropriate authority behind it—even if it offends moral sensibilities. Positivists insist that all law is morally relative and must be judged according to the cultural context in which it was made. That is, there are no "good" or "bad" laws judgeable as such outside of their cultural context. The essential feature of law for most positivists is its coerciveness or authoritative power to command compliance, not its moral quality (Leiter, 2001). Legal positivists may well agree that law should be moral but that we should study law as we find it rather than as we would like it to be.

Natural law theorists counter that if everything is relative and no absolute standards exist for deciding among conflicting beliefs of right and wrong, then all cultural value systems are equally valid. This limits discussion of issues of morality and truth to descriptive and nonnormative discourse. It amounts to intellectual laziness hiding behind the mask of tolerance of diversity because we can rest content with "truth" being whatever happens to be true for us or for the culture in question. Since there is no objective way of determining truth and error, relativism relieves us of the burden of being in error. Such a position, according to natural law adherents, is incoherent because it provides relativists with no defensible grounds for criticizing obnoxious cultural practices (the Holocaust, slavery, the execution of homosexuals, female genital mutilation, torture, cannibalism, and so on). For natural law proponents, we must have bedrock universal moral principles on which to base our law or else "laws" are simply the commands of a sovereign state backed by force. The great British legal philosopher H. L. A. Hart, although an ardent positivist, praised the US Constitution for incorporating moral principles, thus making "morality relevant to determining the law in a manner consistent with positivism" (Soper, 1992, p. 2408).

4. Symbols

Anthropologists and sociologists often refer to nonmaterial culture as symbolic culture. Although the totality of symbolic culture includes nonphysical things such as gestures, language, values, and norms, we concentrate here on physical and tangible **symbols** that are identified with something less tangible. Symbols are concrete physical signs that "stand for" and signify abstractions that range from the mundane and specific, such as the little man or woman painted on the restroom door, to those that are suffused with meaning and can evoke the deepest of feelings, such as a nation's flag. While the figures on the restroom doors point to something useful, they do not capture our emotions. A flag, while less useful in a day-to-day sense, expresses all that it means to be a part of the nation signified by that piece of cloth. A symbol such as a flag may transcend many cultures so that persons living in different ones may understand the symbol within their own cultural context. Think of the different emotional responses evoked in Washington, Paris, and Tehran by seeing a mob burning the American flag. The American flag is recognized as a symbol representative of the American nation in each of those cities, although this recognition has vastly different emotional meanings to their citizens.

Symbols are of vast importance to the law, which is a rather abstract and intangible notion itself. Think of the symbolic meanings involved inside an imposing courtroom, viewing robed (and sometimes bewigged) judges sitting on elevated stages flanked by flags and uniformed law officers. Think of the "sacred" text of the nation's constitution, the pomp, the ritualism, the old-fashioned terminology sometimes used ("Hear ye!"), the formal oaths sworn, all of which symbolically support the notion that the law is of great importance and above any individual. The law must "stand for something" (which is what *symbol* means) that is agreeable to at least the majority of society's members if it is to be considered legitimate.

Finally, we have the symbol of justice in the Greek goddess *Themis* (*Justitia* for the Romans) personifying the divine law established by the gods, whose familiar statue is found atop many courthouses. She is usually depicted carrying scales to weigh truth and fairness in one hand and a sword depicting the state's power to enforce its legal rulings in the other. She is also usually portrayed wearing a blindfold to symbolize the idea that justice should be neutral and meted out objectively, with no concern for the respective status, power, or identity of the parties involved. The symbolism surrounding the law helps those who observe it to "feel" its majesty and awesome power and thus helps to legitimize and sustain it.

5. Technology

Technology is the totality of the knowledge and techniques a people employ to create the material objects of their sustenance and comfort. As Karl Marx was fond of telling us, the different forms of technology employed by a culture (hunting and gathering, agriculture, industrial, postindustrial) create different physical, social, and psychological environments. It should be obvious to everyone that the way we live and work has profound effects on all aspects of our lives, including our beliefs, values, and symbolic interpretations. The material trappings associated with life in a technologically advanced culture connote a special significance to its members that would not be evident to persons in preliterate societies. The more technologically advanced a society, the more complex the relationships among its parts—and the more that society relies on law to monitor those relationships.

Different stages of technology affect the law in at least three ways (Vago, 1991). First, it supplies technical inventions and refinements (fingerprinting, DNA testing, polygraphy, computerized databanks, and closed-circuit TV cameras) that change ways in which criminal investigations are conducted and the law is applied. Second, technological advances in the media (the ability to televise congressional hearings and courtroom dramas, videotapes of police officers beating suspects) may change the intellectual climate in which the legal process is executed. Third, new technology presents the law with new conditions with which it must wrestle. For instance, modern practices such as artificial insemination and surrogate motherhood bring up issues never dreamt about 50 years ago. If a man donates his sperm, or if a woman carries the fertilized egg of another woman, what are their legal claims to the child? How about other technology-driven issues such as surgical and chemical "cures" for criminals, pornography and fraud on the Internet, human cloning, and the possible uses and misuses of DNA profiling? How about freedom of expression in semipublic venues like Facebook and Twitter? In 2009, bad-girl rocker Courtney Love was sued for libel by a fashion designer for defaming her on Twitter; Love settled out of court. In 2016, Donald Trump ran an "underground" presidential campaign on Twitter, delighting his followers and infuriating his opposition. So what can one say on Twitter?

The challenges that scientific and technological advances present for the law are different from past challenges because many of these advances (nuclear power, genetic engineering, chemical plants, and so on) have potentially catastrophic risks attached to them. In the past, catastrophes (disease, natural disasters, and foreign invasion) came overwhelmingly from events external to the affected society and were accepted as normal, inevitable, and beyond the society's control. Modernization and globalization, however, have brought potential catastrophes that are internally manufactured and have global reach (Giddens, Duneier, & Applebaum, 2005). The nuclear accident in Chernobyl, Ukraine, in 1986; the chemical leakage in Bhopal, India, in 1984; and the toxic waste incident in Love Canal, New York, in 1978 are examples of huge manufactured disasters with consequences that extended beyond national boundaries.

Because these and a host of other potential hazards are manufactured and internal rather than natural and external, we have evolved a **risk society**, meaning a society "increasingly preoccupied with the future (and also with safety), which generates the notion of risk" (Giddens, 1999, p. 3). This does not mean that there are more risks today than in the past, although arguably there are, but rather that we are more aware that we can do something about them. *Risk* is thus conceptually different from *danger* or *hazard* in the sense that it is bound up with human control and "particularly with the idea of controlling the future" (Giddens, 1999, p. 3). Automobiles are not going to stop pouring excessive carbon dioxide into the air unless the law mandates lower emission levels; the ozone layer will grow and global warming increase unless the law mandates control of chlorofluorocarbons and stops to deforestation. But since these things occur cross-nationally, there is little that the legal system of a single country can do except tend to the problems in its own backyard. The point is that whether problems/risks/hazards are addressed by local, national, or international law, law has an increasingly central role in our lives.

6. Language

Language is a vast repository of information about culture; it is in effect the "storehouse of culture." To develop any kind of culture as we know it without language would be practically impossible. Language is a terribly complex thing, but children learn it almost effortlessly, thanks to Mother Nature's "technology" built in over eons of evolutionary time. Human communication enables us to discuss the simple and the profound, to talk about events and ideas from the past, and to plan for the future, and it provides a way to convey a wide array of ideas and events to others. Language is part of the great biological leap that separates the human species from other species. Although animals communicate with one another and some primates can even be taught to communicate vocally in a rudimentary, humanlike way, only humans are able to express and understand abstract ideas and to communicate them through language.

Words mean what they mean because culture defines the meanings they denote. In cultures with writing—a symbolic representation of the language—information can be recorded and transmitted to future generations. Language thus becomes the vehicle for cultural evolution and transmission across the generations. In a very real sense, cultural definitions existing in the language help to create reality for the members of a culture.

Language is related to law in the most obvious way; it provides us with the ability to formulate, articulate, and understand rules of conduct. Without language, none of the other characteristics of culture would be possible, and our behavior would be regulated only by vague, visceral feelings of right and wrong impinging on us through anger, fear, anxiety, joy, and empathy. Written language is absolutely necessary to the idea of law because written law warns everyone in advance about what is forbidden conduct and what is not. Although preliterate cultures have rules, the simplicity of such cultures necessitates only a few simple ones that everyone understands. The more complex a culture becomes, the more it relies on written codes of conduct. This is a general principle of legal philosophy upheld by all anthropological, historical, and sociopolitical data available to us.

Law, then, is integral to all aspects of culture. Since the dawn of civilization, there has been some form of rules and sanctions designed to ensure socially desirable conduct and thereby bring order to a culture, to define authority and its limits, and to clarify the responsibilities, duties, and obligations members owe to one another. Given the great importance of law, it is not surprising that philosophers, historians, sociologists, and scholars from many other disciplines have debated the nature and function of law for centuries. The ideas of some of these men are discussed in the following sections. We limit ourselves to what these scholars had to say about topics that have the greatest bearing on the content of other chapters in this book and to a brief discussion of one of the earliest and most famous legal codes.

THE CODE OF HAMMURABI

The first legal codes showed that there were well-advanced societies exhibiting signs of mature civilization many centuries ago. The **Code of Hammurabi** (Hammurabi was a King of Babylonia who lived from 1810 BC to 1750 BC) was long acknowledged as the oldest known written code of law. We now know, however, that other documents of this type existed in the area of the Middle East called Mesopotamia, but no other was so broad in its scope. The code was discovered inscribed on a round pillar, seven feet four inches high. On the top of the pillar was Shamash, the sun god, handing the legal code to Hammurabi. The code of King Hammurabi was not law in the sense that law is understood today—that is, a set of abstract principles applicable to all. Rather, it was a set of judgments originally pronounced to solve particular cases (Bottero, 1973). Nor was it an attempt to cover all possible situations as modern codes are, and as far as we know, it was never copied and distributed to those officials charged with the day-to-day administration of Hammurabi's vast kingdom (Sinha, 1990). Nevertheless, the system of justice contained in the code showed signs of mature rule development in that it governed relationships pertaining to sexual behavior, property rights, theft, and acts of violence. The law forbade retaliatory actions and deadly blood feuds among the people, leaving punishments to be dispensed by the king's agents. The "eye for an eye, tooth for a tooth" (*lex talionis*) concept of justice stated in the code predates the Old Testament passage familiar to Jews, Christians, and Muslims. The law introduced specified standards of conduct and remediation by independent third parties to settle disputes. A written code, theoretically impartial in its application, represented a tremendous advance for society in general and the administration of justice in particular.

Although the laws contained in the code were secular in nature, the law's administration was almost exclusively in the hands of the priesthood. Hammurabi was wise enough to buttress the codes (and his own) authority with the approval of the gods. The linking of the code to an honored deity was a powerful piece of psychological gilding employed by many others before and after Hammurabi. The prologue to the code reads,

> Then Anu and Bel delighted the flesh of mankind by calling me, the renowned prince, the god-fearing Hammurabi, to establish justice in the earth, to destroy the base and the wicked, and to hold back the strong from oppressing the feeble: to shine like the Sun-god upon the black-haired men, and to illuminate the land. (Edwards, 1971, p. 23)

EARLY THINKERS ABOUT LAW

The extent to which law has been deemed important in the affairs of humans can be gauged by noting that every social and political philosopher of any stature has felt compelled to comment on it at some length. They have attempted to come to grips with such topics as where law comes from, what its nature is, what it is for, why it is necessary, whom it serves, and what human life would be without it. Philosophical insights have been important in every field of inquiry as a beginning point, as a basis for examining what may or may not be possible, and as a method by which we clarify our terms and organize our thinking. We begin with Plato and his thoughts about natural law and how it is related to positivist law.

Plato

Plato (427–347 BCE) stands as one of the most influential thinkers in the history of the world. Not only do his writings affect all Western legal systems, but his approach to thinking about legal concepts influences how law is taught and learned in most Western universities. This method of inquiry, known as the "Socratic method," was named after Plato's mentor, Socrates. Rather than define the concepts to be discussed at the outset, Plato's definitions and ideas slowly unfolded in "dialogue" form as he debated them in his imagination with Socrates.

Perhaps Plato's best-known contribution to philosophy is his *theory of forms*. This theory is of interest because it helps us to understand the ideas of natural law and of justice developed by later philosophers and legal theorists. For Plato, all philosophy is an attempt to come to grips with **forms**. Plato's forms are not subjective mental images confined to our minds but are real essences wholly independent of our knowledge about them, which contain the only true and ultimate realities. The things that we perceive through our five senses are corrupt and transitory copies of these ultimate and eternal realities of the forms. Among the imperfect objects we possess is the law. Only by apprehending the nature and substance of the eternal forms can humans act with wisdom, and only by conforming to universal principles (the forms) can the rules of rightful conduct be determined. The task of lawmakers is thus to understand the *form* or *idea* of law so that they can fashion the best possible resemblance of it that humans are capable of making (Lavine, 1989).

Although never wavering from his theory of forms, Plato did not neglect to analyze and dissect the tangible world and the imperfect reality it contained. Because human beings as they exist in the transitory world are imperfect copies of the idea of humanness, their behavior is less than perfect. And to regulate the self-interested, contentious, and sometimes evil mortals, law is necessary even if it is also less than perfect, as all man-made things are. Plato (1952) offered one of the most comprehensive ideas of law in ancient times in a treatise on government:

> When men have done and suffered injustice and have had experience of
> both, not being able to avoid the one and obtain the other, they think that
> they had better agree among themselves to have neither, hence there arise

Plato and Aristotle

laws and mutual covenants; and that which is ordained by law is termed by them lawful and just. This they affirm to be the origin and nature of justice—it is a mean or compromise, between the best of all, which is to do injustice and not be punished, and the worst of all, which is to suffer injustice without the power of retaliation; and justice being at a middle point between the two, is tolerated not as good but as the lesser evil, and honored by reason of the inability of men to do injustice. (p. 311)

Plato further argued that the state was virtuous, and that only through the state could the behavior of the citizenry be regulated. The state was superior to the individual because only it could lay down a set of workable rules to govern the complex behaviors of human beings. Anarchy and chaos would be the inevitable result if law was not present to restrain the insatiable desires of the citizenry. Without the law, human nature would run amok, since it always sought to satisfy its appetites without much regard for the concerns of others. Plato felt that humans lacked the power to distinguish good from evil, for if they had the power to comprehend the difference, there would be no need for law. Plato's concept of positivist law and of its necessity due to the insatiable and selfish appetites of human nature would be given its greatest impetus by the British philosopher Thomas Hobbes many centuries later—and later yet by the French sociologist Émile Durkheim.

Aristotle

Aristotle (384–322 BCE), who was a pupil of Plato, assumed that the state was created not only so that individuals could simply live but so that they could live well, and he agreed with his master that law must be something more than mere convention, a simple codification of custom. Aristotle disagreed with Plato on a number of other law-related issues, however. Whereas Plato was an elitist who favored the rule of an elite class (*philosopher-kings* and *guardians*) whose great wisdom would guide the city state, Aristotle favored an egalitarian system in which the rulers would be subservient to the law. This faith in the common person and in the ultimate authority of the law was a very radical idea, one that is difficult to find in the writings of any other legal philosopher until John Locke's work 2,000 years later. Aristotle knew that laws passed by rulers tended to favor the interests of their own class, and he warned that legislators must guard against these tendencies. Accordingly, the goal of the legislature must be to provide for the greatest happiness of the greatest number (Aristotle, 1952). Aristotle's ideas were given impetus by British philosopher and lawyer Jeremy Bentham, who popularized the "greatest happiness for the greatest number" principle in the early nineteenth century.

Aristotle (1952) equated the concept of law with justice:

> Since the lawless man was seen to be unjust and the lawful man just, evidently all lawful acts are in a sense just acts; for the acts laid down by the legislative art are lawful, and each of these we say is just. (p. 377)

Persons acting unlawfully receive "too much" from society, and victims of their behavior receive "too little." The goal of law was to see that everyone receives what they justly deserve by their actions. These just desserts may be in the form of rewards, if acting justly, or punishments, if acting unjustly. Aristotle's ideas of justice are expanded in the next chapter.

Thomas Hobbes

English philosopher Thomas Hobbes (1588–1679) was perhaps the most important of the seventeenth-century legal philosophers. In his famous book *Leviathan* ("commonwealth" or "state"), we see Hobbes's view of human nature lead him to ideas of law quite different from those of Plato and Aristotle, although he mirrored Plato in advocating an all-powerful sovereign. Hobbes considered humans to be a selfish lot concerned only with their own interests. According to Hobbes, the "state of nature" (i.e., precivilized life) was a "war of all against all" and was "nasty, brutish, and short." Fear of violence and death under such conditions drove human beings to devise a **social contract** with one another to create a state that could protect them from predation and exploitation.

Hobbes had a great concern for order in society (he had witnessed the bloody English civil wars of 1642–1645 and 1648–1649) and argued for a strong sovereign capable of enforcing the social contract and thus providing security from disorder and anarchy. Hobbes (1952) disavowed any notion of natural law and was very much

a legal positivist, arguing that there are no laws until a government is formed: "When a Commonwealth is once settled, then are there actually laws, and not before; as being then the commands of the Commonwealth; and therefore also civil laws: for it is the sovereign power that obliges men to obey" (p. 131). Justice is thus identified with positive law, the form of which was to be determined by a strong sovereign (in the modern sense, the state), rather than with some set of universal principles, as in the natural law of Plato and Aristotle. Laws are the commands of the sovereign—nothing more, nothing less. The sovereign's subjects are morally obliged to obey because they are parties to the social contract.

Thomas Hobbes

Hobbes's overweening concern for order and security can be gauged by his opinion that *any* government providing these things for its citizens, by whatever means, was just. According to Deininger (1965):

> The theme in Hobbes's *Leviathan* is that men are normally better off even in a despotic state than they would be in the absence of a political organization. Hobbes believes men are weak and cowardly, even subject to moments of sheer irrationality—thus needing for their protection a political structure which, by its coercive might, can minimize disorder by restraining the rash actions of individuals and groups as well as by laying an obligation to act when security is at stake. (p. 153)

Hobbes's defense of absolutist monarchy was published in 1661, just 12 years after Charles I was beheaded by the English Parliament for trying to practice what he preached. In many ways, Hobbes served to galvanize the thoughts of the Parliamentarians about what it was they were fighting for. Hobbes's liking for unquestioned obedience to authority and for peace at any cost provided them with an articulated agenda they could oppose item by item. One person whose work can be construed as a response to Hobbes is fellow English philosopher John Locke.

John Locke

John Locke (1632–1704) held a much more optimistic view of human nature than Hobbes. Because of his views about the common person and the law, Locke's writings have been interpreted by a number of individuals as providing justification for the Glorious (English) Revolution of 1688, the American Revolution of 1776, and the French Revolution of 1789 (Lavine, 1989). In *The Second Treatise on Government*, originally published in 1690, Locke described the state of nature as inferior to the organized political state only because of its lack of law, not because it was "nasty" and "brutish." Locke believed that our minds and personalities are like "blank slates" when we arrive in this world; what we become and how we behave is entirely the result of our past experiences interacting with our present circumstances. Locke's (1952) conception of the state of nature, human nature, and the necessity of law is captured in the following passage:

> Though man in that state [of nature] has an uncontrollable liberty to dispose of his person or possessions, yet he has not liberty to destroy himself, or so much as any creature in his possession, but where some nobler use than its bare preservation calls for. The state of nature has a law of nature to govern it, which obliges every one; and reason, which is that law, teaches all mankind who will but consult it that, being all equal and independent, no one ought to harm another in his life, health, liberty, or possessions; for men being all the workmanship of one omnipotent and infinitely wise Maker—all the servants of one sovereign master, sent into the world by his order, and about his business. (p. 5)

Contrary to Hobbes, Locke postulated that this state of nature had natural laws based on moral obligations that governed conduct and logically preceded an established political system. This led Locke to one of his most important conclusions regarding the state of nature and the formation of a government. The central question of his *Second Treatise* is "Why would men, living in a state of nature with harmonious relationships form a political system to govern them?"

John Locke

> Men being, as has been said, by nature all free, equal, and independent, no one can be put out of this estate and subjected to the political power of another without his own consent. The only way whereby any one divests himself of his natural liberty and puts on the bonds of civil society is by agreeing with other men to join and unite into a community for their comfortable, safe, and peaceable living one amongst another, in a secure enjoyment of their properties and a greater security against any that are not of it. This any number of men may do, because it injures not the freedom of the rest; they are left as they were in the liberty of the state of nature. (Locke, 1952, p. 54)

For Locke, human beings enjoy freedom and independence in the prepolitical state of nature, and they do not have to surrender their liberty in order to live in a political community, as Hobbes supposed. Like Hobbes, Locke assumed that individuals enter into a social contract with the government to be governed, but the government must protect individual freedoms, not curtail them in the name of security and order. Furthermore, since the social contract is entered into freely, it can be broken by the governed if the state does not maintain its part—that is, if it acts despotically and arbitrarily. This principle became extremely important to the American colonists, and later to the framers of the US Constitution, who were trying to deal legally with what they considered to be the oppressive laws, policies, and decrees of the British Parliament. The influence of Locke on the writing of such American authors of the Constitution and the Bill of Rights as Thomas Jefferson and James Madison was great (Pojman, 1989).

John Rawls

The eminent American legal philosopher John Rawls (1921–2002) theorized broadly about justice from a liberal position without being explicit about natural law. However, he did allude to it when he compared law to a scientific theory: "A theory however elegant and economical must be rejected or revised if it is untrue; likewise laws and institutions no matter how efficient and well-arranged must be reformed or abolished if they are unjust" (1999, p. 3). Laws and institutions must thus be evaluated according to the principles of justice, as scientific theories are judged by truth. Of course, both truth and justice are intangible and open to subjective interpretation.

What is justice for Rawls? Just like the social contract theorists we have discussed, he found it necessary to propose a time in history during which humans did not live in organized political societies. Rawls shapes his theory of justice with the use of a thought experiment conjuring up a hypothetical situation he called the **original position**. In Rawls's state of nature, individuals were neither brutal beasts nor noble savages, but were equal, rational, and self-interested with "a capacity for a sense of justice and for a conception of the good" (Rawls, 1996, p. 19). He wanted to go beyond thinkers like Hobbes and Locke to describe in some detail the nature of the contract in terms of the kind of society the contract would specify. In elucidating the terms of the contract, Rawls strongly favored equality over meritocracy, but without belittling the latter. He envisioned a just society as one that arranged social institutions so that even the least advantaged members of society would reap fair benefits (without spelling out exactly what "fair" means in this context) and in which all social positions would be open to all people under conditions of equal opportunity.

Rawls was uneasy with the idea of equal opportunity as a nondiscriminatory *process* because, as he points out, some individuals have greater natural talents than others and, according to him, that is unfair. He asserted that we have done nothing to earn our natural talents, and thus we are not fairly entitled to all the benefits that those talents could bring us. Rawls was aware that in coming together to write this hypothetical social contract, rational self-interested individuals will try to do so in such a fashion as to privilege themselves and their descendants.

How might it be possible to prevent them from doing this? Rawls asks which principles of justice would rational and self-interested individuals choose to regulate social institutions if they had to make that choice behind a **veil of ignorance**. By the veil of ignorance, Rawls means that in determining the nature of their society, individuals would not know what their ascribed roles (race, class, gender), or even their personal characteristics (intelligence, strength, conscientiousness, etc.), would be. In other words, what kind of society would people endeavor to make in complete ignorance of their future place within it? Rawls argues that they would choose exactly the same liberties and opportunities for everyone because each of them would be that "everyone." They would choose a society in which the most disadvantaged would be afforded special help and opportunities because they just might be one of the disadvantaged. We expand on Rawls's ideas of justice and equality when we debate the concept of "social justice" in chapter 11.

SOCIOLOGICAL PERSPECTIVES OF LAW

The law is one of the six social institutions (the others are the family, education, religion, the economy, and the polity). All institutions make rules regulating conduct within them, but in modern democratic and secular states, only the rules contained in the law enjoy the enforcement power of the state. In many ways, law serves the purposes of the other institutions, such as regulating what constitutes a legal marriage, defining what is permissible in schools, defining the relationship between

Max Weber

Émile Durkheim

Karl Marx

church and state, making sure contracts are adhered to, and determining voter eligibility. Because the law serves these purposes, sociologists specializing in the study of these other institutions should have an understanding of the law. Sociologists also recognize that law is written by humans who bring ideological biases and personal baggage to the task and thus recognize that laws should be critically analyzed.

Early sociological luminaries such as Karl Marx, Émile Durkheim, and Max Weber were steeped in law and "regarded the sociology of law as an integral part of social theory" (Schluchter, 2002, p. 257). They all wrote at times when other social institutions appeared to be radically changing, and they sought to understand why. All three saw law as a method of redefining relationships between persons and institutions. But according to their own ideological leanings, they viewed law as either greasing the squeaky wheels of change to make the passage quieter for everyone or as a weapon to maintain the power and privilege of the few. These early social thinkers saw law as both a product and a producer of social change as well as a response to, and sometimes a cause of, social unrest. In fact, nineteenth-century sociology was so immersed in the law that Donald Kelly (1990) has characterized modern sociology as "the ghost of jurisprudence past" (p. 275).

Max Weber

Few scholars have had greater influence on contemporary legal thinking than German sociologist and lawyer Max Weber (1864–1920). In his most famous work, *Economy and Society* (1905/1978), Weber argued that the law was different from other kinds of rule-following behavior in three fundamental ways. First, regardless of whether or not persons want to and habitually do or do not obey the law, they face external pressures to do so. Second, these external pressures involve the threat of coercion and force. Third, these threats are carried out by agents of the state charged with that specific duty. Nowhere in Weber's writings do we see allusions to natural law by which unjust laws may be invalidated.

Weber's major interest was in the increasing rationalization of the world. He wanted to explain how the world had changed from a hierarchical model of lords

Table 1.1 *Summary of Max Weber's Decision-Making Typology*

	Irrationality	Rationality
Substantive	Decisions made subjectively by nonlegally trained individuals on a case-by-case basis.	Decisions made on a case-by-case basis guided by logically consistent principles (bureaucratic rules, religion, ideology) other than law.
Formal	Decisions based on formal rules that are not based on logic (superstition, magic, ordeals, oath-swearing, etc.).	Decisions based on formal logical rules and principles made by legally trained persons bound by those rules but with a high degree of independence.

and peasants overwhelmingly concerned with the afterlife to a one of technical progress and capitalism firmly planted in this life (Collins & Makowsky, 1993). The progress and expansion he saw around him was possible only if the people responsible for it could plan ahead secure in the knowledge that if all citizens followed certain binding rules, things would happen in a relatively predictable fashion. Without such predictability, economic progress and expansion cannot happen, and the economy is destined to remain at the level of barter. Predictability and progress can only occur under a binding code of conduct rationally derived from the minds of individuals schooled in legal and administrative theory and practice and enforced by a cadre of honest and professional state agents. As Robert Gordon (2012) sees it:

> The rule of law then came to be seen as crucial to modernization and the building of viable capitalist societies. The difference between dynamism and stagnation, prosperity and poverty boiled down to a few simple variables—*legal* variables regulating a free and competitive market. (p. 211)

Weber was very interested in how authorities in various cultures made decisions when confronted with issues of contention and how the decision-making process that was employed accelerated or retarded modernization (rationalization) in those cultures. Weber is perhaps best known in legal circles for his fourfold typology of legal decision-making. As expected, the two fundamentals of Weber's typology are the *rationality* or *irrationality* of legal procedure. Rational procedures rely on logic; nonrational procedures rest on mysticism, faith, or superstitions. Rational or irrational procedures may be either *formal* or *substantive*. *Formal* refers to decision-making on the basis of established and inflexible rules and implies the independence of the legal system from other social institutions. *Substantive* refers to decision-making that takes the substance of individual cases into consideration rather than relying on general legal principles (Turkel, 1996). Table 1.1 presents a summary of Max Weber's decision-making typology.

The four methods of legal decision-making derived from these elements can be described in more detail as follows:

1. **Substantive irrationality**: This method is the least rational of the four types. It is based on case-by-case political, religious, or emotional reactions on the

part of a nonlegally trained person acting without a set of legal principles. The biblical story of King Solomon, who was asked to solve the dilemma of two women claiming maternity and possession of the same infant, is an example of substantive rationality. Solomon ordered the baby to be sliced into two and divided between the women. One woman agreed to this solution, while the other begged Solomon to give the infant to her rival. Solomon reasoned that the second woman must be the true mother and that the first woman could not possibly be and made his decision in favor of the second woman. Because Solomon's decision was shorn of any legal rules, it was irrational, and because it was decided on a case-by-case basis, it was substantive. However, the decision was the essence of justice and wisdom.

2. **Formal irrationality**: This method is based on such concepts as religious dogma, magic, oath-swearing, and trial by combat or ordeal. There are certain formal rules to be followed, but they are not based on reason or logic. The process of oath-swearing (discussed in chapter 14), used to settle cases in some Islamic countries, is an example of formal irrationality.

3. **Substantive rationality**: This method is guided by a set of internally consistent general principles other than law. Examples of this type would be decision-making applied on a case-by-case basis according to the logic of some religious, ideological, or bureaucratic set of rules. The principles that are seen in the Code of Hammurabi indicate that substantive rationality was the method of legal decision-making used. Much of American administrative law is of this type when dealing with issues involving complex technological issues (see chapter 7).

4. **Formal rationality**: This is the most rational and ideal of all four types. It combines a high degree of independence of legal institutions with a set of general rules and procedures applicable to all. Those who make the decisions on these grounds are monitored by others trained in the law. All Western legal systems fall into this category (Evan, 1990). Table 1.1 presents a summary table of Max Weber's decision-making typology.

Although Weber clearly favors Western formal rationality, the other three methods are not necessarily "wrong" or unjust; all four methods must be evaluated in the context of the culture in which they are being used. Weber was primarily concerned with identifying the kind of legal reasoning best suited to modern capitalism and not necessarily passing judgment on these decision-making methods as functional or dysfunctional in the cultural contexts in which they were employed. As we shall see in the next chapter, cases settled exclusively on the basis of formal rationality may sometimes be at odds with justice.

Émile Durkheim

French sociologist Émile Durkheim (1858–1917), a contemporary of Weber's, was interested in the relationship between types of law and types of society. Durkheim's basic theme is that all societies exist on the basis of a common moral order, not on the basis of rational self-interest as implied in the "social contract" theses of Hobbes or Locke. In his famous book *Division of Labor in Society* (Durkheim, 1893/1960), he set out to examine the effects of the division of labor on social solidarity. By *social solidarity*, Durkheim meant the degree to which people feel an emotional sense of belonging to their groups. The strength of social solidarity depends to a great extent on the kind of economic system a society has and on the stage of its development. Durkheim divided societies into two types: the nonindustrial societies of earlier times, characterized by what he called **mechanical solidarity**, and modern or industrial societies, characterized by **organic solidarity**.

In nonindustrial societies, social relations were based mostly on primary group interactions (frequent face-to-face contact with the same people), which tended to result in strong emotional bonds. Such societies had only a simple and limited division of labor; individual differences were minimized. Since people were involved in a limited range of occupations, most looked at life in the same predictable way. Social relations were personal and uncomplicated for the most part, with strong norms leaving little leeway for deviant behavior. Mechanical solidarity thus grows out of sameness—out of a commonality of experience—and produces a very strong *collective conscience* or *collective consciousness* (in French, they mean the same thing; Collins & Makowsky, 1993).

With the onset of the Industrial Revolution and the factory system came a broad division of labor, which resulted in a shift from mechanical to organic solidarity. Durkheim chose the term *organic* to illustrate this type of solidarity because it was consistent with his functionalist view of society as an organism consisting of interdependent parts. Organic solidarity is characterized by *secondary* relationships in which people interact for brief periods to accomplish specific goals such as exchanging services (workers in factories, students in schools, shoppers in stores, repairmen in homes, etc.). The collective consciousness is weakened because of this basically unemotional pattern of temporary and goal-directed interaction. Additionally, because of occupational specialization, people began to conceive of themselves less in terms of the groups to which they belong and more as individuals. Organic solidarity thus grows out of differences and a sense of social interdependence rather than from shared experiences and a common identity.

With changes in patterns of interaction came changes in the form of social solidarity, which in turn generated changes in the law. The greater the complexity of a society and the greater the shift from predominantly primary to secondary interaction, the more laws are required to regulate the different kinds of relationships among citizens. Growth in social and economic complexity almost by definition requires growth in legal complexity. For instance, the efforts of the Chinese government to modernize and to develop a market economy resulted in thousands of new laws, and the number of lawyers in the country more than doubled (Turkel, 1996).

Different types of social solidarity generate changes in the criminal law as well. In preindustrial societies, the community exercised great power over the life of the individual. Because of the strong collective conscience, norm violations generated great moral outrage, and punishments were extremely harsh. Durkheim called this pattern of response to violations of the collective conscience *retributive* or *repressive* justice (Durkheim was too Eurocentric here; many preliterate cultures stressed arbitration and reconciliation over harsh punishments). Punishments, according to Durkheim, functioned to reaffirm the righteousness of the moral norms that had been violated. But as the collective conscience became weaker under the increased division of labor in industrial societies, so did the strength of collective moral outrage. The lessening of moral outrage led to more tolerant attitudes toward minor rule breakers and to a more humanitarian form of justice that was *restitutive* rather than retributive. The old notions of retributive justice, however, are still in evidence in some Islamic countries that continue to lop off the hands of thieves, stone adulterers to death, and apply the lash to users of alcohol (Fairchild & Dammer, 2001).

ISSUE HIGHLIGHT

American Civil Liberties Union: Good or Bad for America?

It is great to have a trusted and allegedly neutral legal system, but it might be even better if we also had an organization not officially a part of that system to monitor it—guarding the guardians, so to speak. The American Civil Liberties Union (ACLU) sees itself in that role. Founded in 1920, its stated mission is "to defend and preserve the individual rights and liberties guaranteed to every person in this country by the Constitution of the United States."

The ACLU is either loved or hated. The major criticisms are its involvement with cases in which it represents peoples and organizations that promote offensive behaviors and views and its efforts to purge religion from the public square. Is the ACLU—on balance—good or bad for America?

Bad

At the beginning of the ACLU, Roger Nash Baldwin its primary founder, said, "Communism, of course, is the goal." The ACLU is not communist today, but it is decidedly leftist in its implicit opposition to the family and to Christianity by its muscular defense of atheism. It is the biggest legal advocate for pornography, claiming that it is a form of free speech, yet rarely defends Christian speech and never defends speech that is critical of homosexuality or that advocates intelligent design (a supposed alternative to Darwinian evolution). The ACLU has been a major player in every federal court case on the side of those seeking to eliminate religion completely from the public square. It has defended the Man/Boy Love Association that advocates "Sex before eight, or else it's too late," but has fought against the Boy Scouts of America holding their Jamborees on government property because they have the audacity to pray and swear an oath of "duty to God." It has defended illegal immigrants and terrorists and has done everything it can to undermine the Patriot Act designed to protect Americans after 9/11. Famous liberal lawyer Alan Dershowitz (2018) claims that the ACLU has become a hyperpartisan political advocacy group and has become involved in supporting hard-left candidates and agendas. The list could go on for pages, but we'll let the ACLU's primary opponent, Alliance Defending Freedom, have the last word: "Far from the noble protector of our constitutional rights many Americans believe it to be, the ACLU has from its earliest days deliberately and patiently chipped away at the legal, moral, and religious foundations of our Republic."

Good

The ACLU is indeed composed mostly of leftist liberals, but it is conservative in the sense that it fights to preserve civil liberties for everyone. It did begin with communist aspirations, but as Roger Baldwin became disillusioned with it, he led a campaign to purge the ACLU of communists. It defends some very unpopular causes and speech, but free speech should not be just for views that are popular. Who will speak up for despised people's rights if not the ACLU? It has been accused of attempting to rob America of its Judeo-Christian heritage but does not attack Christianity; rather, it believes that religion should be confined to the home and to the places of worship and has no place in the public square. The ACLU's position is that although religion is important for social morality, it violates the Establishment Clause of the First Amendment to have prayer or "moments of silence" in schools and to display crosses and the Ten Commandments on government property. Following the lead of our opponents, we will let the ACLU speak for itself: "For nearly 100 years, the ACLU has been our nation's guardian of liberty, working in courts, legislatures, and communities to defend and preserve the individual rights and liberties that the Constitution and the laws of the United States guarantee everyone in this country."

TWO OPPOSING PERSPECTIVES: CONSENSUS AND CONFLICT

Sociologists who study the law as a social institution and its function as a social control mechanism tend to view it in terms of one of two broad perspectives. Which perspective a scholar favors tends to depend on his or her more fundamental perspective on society. Some scholars view society as basically good, just, and providing equal opportunity for all individuals; this is the consensus view of society. Others view society as basically unjust, unequal, and discriminatory; this is the conflict view of society.

Consensus theorists emphasize how society is structured to maintain its stability and view it as an integrated network of institutions (the family, church, school, economy, government) that function to maintain social order and the system as a whole. Social stability is also achieved in this view through cooperation, shared values, and the cohesion and solidarity that people feel by being part of a shared culture. Consensus theorists are aware that conflicts often arise in social life, but they stress that such conflicts are temporary and both can be and are solved within the framework of shared fundamental values as exemplified by a neutral legal system.

Conflict theorists consider society to be composed of individuals and groups with sharply different interests and to be characterized by conflict and dissension. People and groups everywhere, these theorists maintain, seek to maximize their interests. Since resources are limited, conflict between different individuals and groups is inevitable and continuous. The stability and order that consensus theorists see is only temporary and is maintained by coercion rather than consensus—that is, by the ability of more powerful people and groups to impose their will upon the less powerful.

Which view is correct? The simple answer is that it is impossible to say without specifying what society we are talking about. All societies are characterized by both consensus and conflict; it is almost impossible to imagine any society in which they are absent. Max Weber recognized the dual nature of society when he defined law in a manner that encompasses both consensus and coercion: "Laws are 'consensually valid in a group' and are 'guaranteed through a coercive apparatus'" (Turkel, 1996,

p. 8). We have to remember that these two competing models are examples of what sociologists call *ideal types*. Ideal types are abstract conceptual tools that accentuate, purely for analytical purposes, the phenomenon being studied; they lay no claims to mirror the day-to-day reality of any concrete example of that phenomenon. Let us examine law in the context of these two ideal-type models of society.

The Consensus Perspective

All of the legal theorists we have encountered thus far have been proponents of the consensus perspective. The **consensus perspective** views law as basically a neutral framework for patching up conflicts between individuals and groups who primarily share the same set of fundamental values. Law is viewed in a manner analogous to the immune system of the body in that it identifies and neutralizes potential dangers to the social body before they can do too much damage. Thus, law is a just and necessary mechanism for controlling behavior detrimental to peace, order, predictability, and stability and for maintaining social integration. Specific legal codes are assumed to express compromises between various interest groups regarding issues that have been contentious in the past, not to codify the victories of some groups over others. Law is also seen as reflecting the community's deeply held values and as defining the rights and responsibilities of all those within it, and it is considered a legitimate expression of morality and custom. If coercion is sometimes needed to bolster conscience, it is because the individual, not the law, is flawed. The law is obeyed by the vast majority of people not out of fear but out of respect, and it is willingly supported by all good people.

Perhaps the main reason we have not yet encountered any theorist with a conflict view of the law in this chapter so far is that these theorists were all members of privileged classes, which naturally endears the status quo to them. Except for Aristotle's brief note of concern that legislators should guard against laws favoring their own class, any hint in the works of these writers that the law could unfairly serve the needs of the elite comes percolating from below the surface. We see this in Thrasymachus, Plato's antagonist in the dialogue on justice contained in *The Republic* (1960, book 1). Thrasymachus argues that the law is merely the legalizing of the interests of the stronger. For the conflict perspective to be given full voice, it had to wait for writers arising from the less privileged classes, which could only come after education became more widespread.

The Conflict Perspective

Underlying the **conflict perspective** of the law is the view that law functions to preserve the power and privilege of the most exploitive and duplicitous, not to protect the weak and helpless. As we have seen, although thinking of social processes in terms of conflict between rival factions (usually between social classes) goes back as far as Plato, the more formal treatment of conflict as a concept traces its origin to the thought of the nineteenth-century German philosopher Karl Marx. Marxist legal scholars agree that law exists to settle conflicts and restore social peace but insist that conflicts are always settled in favor of the ruling class in any society, even if it may sometimes look like other segments of society also benefit (e.g., a general tax cut in which the wealthy gain millions while the working person gains a dollar or two every paycheck). The basic proposition of the conflict perspective was set down by Marx and his coauthor Friedrich Engels (1888/1972) in *The German Ideology*: "The ideas of the ruling class are in every epoch the ruling ideas; i.e., the class, which is the ruling material force of society, is at the same time its ruling intellectual force" (p. 136).

For Marx and Engels, society is divided into two classes: the rulers and the ruled. The ruling class, by which Marx and Engels meant the owners of the means of production (factory owners and entrepreneurs), control the "ruling material force of society." Because these individuals control the means of production, they are able to buy politicians, the media, the church, and all other social institutions that mold social values and attitudes and thus law. The relationship between power and law-making has been described (perhaps cynically) as the "Golden Rule," which posits that "those with the gold make the rules."

Marx and Engels explain why "the exploited" do not recognize their exploitation with reference to the idea of **false consciousness**, by which they mean that the working classes have accepted an ideological worldview that is contrary to their best interests. Workers have been duped into accepting the legitimacy of the law by the ruling classes and are not aware that the law does not serve them. They blindly and docilely obey the law and believe that they are behaving morally by doing so. The ruling class is able to generate the false consciousness of the workers by virtue of its control over key institutions such as education, religion, the media, and of course, the law itself. These institutions define what is right and what is wrong, and they control the flow of information so that it conforms to the worldview of the ruling class.

A school of legal thought premised on Marxist/conflict views is **critical legal studies** (CLS) or critical legal theory. CLS emerged during the tumultuous years of the late 1960s and early 1970s in law schools that challenged the status quo and rejected much of positive and natural law. This school of thought claims that law is politics by other means in the sense that it is a way the "privileged classes" maintain their favored place in society and a way to "legitimately" keep the working class down. Legal rules are not the codification of cultural custom, as positivists claim, but rather a series of statutes legitimizing exploitation and designed to maximize economic growth and efficiency, which is a bad thing for CLS theorists because they believe it is done to the detriment of the workers. CLS theorists look almost exclusively at what they consider defects in the law and ask "how law legitimates power in both senses of the word: how it shapes, channels and restrains power and how it mystifies, disguises, and apologizes for it" (Balkin, 2008, p. 1).

A sort of radical left-wing legal realism (a system of thought we will meet in the next chapter), CLS maintains that judges do not simply apply logic to the law as written but rather seek to impose rulings that support and reinforce the status quo by looking for provisions in the law that will support their interpretation. Today, CLS has more or less vacated the legal academy, with the space being rented out to a variety of other radically critical legal schools such as critical race; critical gender; and critical lesbian, gay, bisexual, and transgender studies (Gordon, 2012). Needless to say, these offshoots of CLS have strong views of their own that look for examples of how the law has thwarted their agendas, at least according to them, and they are definitely not supporters of the status quo.

We do not have to be Marxists, or even liberals, to agree that great wealth confers special privilege on its possessors or that history is replete with class struggles. In Athens in 594 BCE, Plutarch wrote of the great disparity of wealth between classes and the dangerous conflict it generated (Durant & Durant, 1968, p. 55), and President John Adams (1778/1971) wrote that American society was divided into a small group of rich people and a large mass of poor people engaged in a constant class struggle. Neither do we have to be conservatives to realize that any society without a fairly strong moral consensus will not last very long.

Because both consensus and conflict are ubiquitous and integral facts of social life, we must address both processes in this book while attempting to remain agnostic with respect to which process "really" characterizes social life in a general sense. In reality, conflict and consensus/cooperation resemble the Chinese concept of the interdependent unity of yin and yang; we cannot have one without the other. Hopefully, it will become clear to the reader that the consensus perspective is most suitable for explaining certain sets of facts and the conflict perspective is better suited to explaining other sets of facts. We hope that it will also become plain that conflict is as necessary as consensus to maintain the viability of a free society. In fact, conflict may form the very foundation of later consensus in pluralistic societies such as the United States, since justice for all is usually unattainable unless the oppressed agitate strongly for it (Rawls, 2003). This principle is illustrated in subsequent chapters discussing the rights of workers, racial minorities, and women.

SUMMARY

Law is a written body of rules of conduct applicable to all members of a defined community, society, or culture that emanate from a governing authority and are enforced by its agents through the imposition of penalties for their violation. We looked at the six primary characteristics of culture and their relationship to law. These characteristics are beliefs, values, norms, symbols, technology, and language. Our discussion of these characteristics showed that law is, and always has been, an integral part of culture. Examining law as a social construct is known as legal positivism.

We traced thinking across the centuries about various aspects of the law from Hammurabi to the more recent sociological writing of Weber and Durkheim. The law was relatively well developed in Hammurabi's Code, replacing a system of personal vengeance with a system in which a neutral third party was charged with making decisions in both criminal matters and business transactions.

Plato felt that although justice and wisdom were part of the perfect order of the universe, humans could approach these ideals only through reason. Humans had the capacity to emulate the good and the just, but they rarely did. Plato thus reasoned that if law did not exist, society would degenerate into chaos. To some extent, he articulated an idea that was given its greatest impetus about 2,000 years later by Thomas Hobbes.

Aristotle equated the concept of law with justice. He assumed a very strong utilitarian interpretation of the law, going much further than Plato in terms of arguing for the rights of ordinary people. For Aristotle, the most important goal of the legislature was to provide for "the greatest happiness of the greatest number" in society.

He also offered the "radical" notion that even the rulers of a nation should not be above the law.

Thomas Hobbes disavowed any belief in natural law or justice. He saw the "state of nature" as a warlike state where only the strong survive. Because of this warlike state, people agree to engage in a social contract in which they surrender many of their freedoms in exchange for protection. Hobbes argued that the main goal of government under this contract was to provide for the security of the individual and that any state doing so was just by definition. Hobbes believed that the sovereign was an absolute ruler who could employ oppressive tactics in the service of obtaining an orderly society.

The work of John Locke stands in sharp contrast to the work of Thomas Hobbes. Locke both refuted the absolute right of monarchs and reconciled strong government with the liberty of the individual. In contrast with Hobbes's brutish state of nature, Locke's was one in which individuals enjoyed liberty and harmony and was only inferior because it lacked law. States or governments develop and exist by virtue of the social contract, according to the terms of which individuals maintain most of their liberties while voluntarily surrendering to a civil government their power to punish transgressors themselves. Locke also wrote that when governments overstep their powers, individuals have the right to reconstitute that civil government based on the moral force of natural law. Locke's version of natural law, liberty of individuals, and the proper role of civil society provided the ideas and justifications for the British, American, and French revolutions.

Max Weber asserted that if a society is to advance into a more modern and complex structure, it must be governed by rational law. For the modern capitalistic economy to develop, it needed a predictable and dependable legal system. Natural law may be the philosophical "touchstone" of a society in terms of individual rights and responsibilities, but the development of any complex capitalistic economy depends on a predictable, rational system of law. Weber's four types of legal decision-making, ranked from the least to the most rational, are substantive irrationality, formal irrationality, substantive rationality, and formal rationality.

Émile Durkheim was interested in the relationship between law and social solidarity. He postulated two types of social solidarity: mechanical and organic. Mechanical solidarity is associated with preindustrial societies and grows out of the sameness of everyone's experiences; organic solidarity is associated with industrial societies and develops from the interdependence of individuals that exists due to an advanced division of labor. The growing complexity of industrialized societies required the increasing reach of civil law to regulate the great variety of transactions that occurred in such societies.

Criminal law also changes with the type of solidarity within a society. Societies characterized by mechanical solidarity have a very strong collective conscience, which leads to great moral outrage when norms are violated and to a retributive or repressive form of justice. A weakening of the collective conscience follows a change to organic solidarity, which leads to the more tolerant and humanitarian restitutive form of justice.

Most sociological students of the law conduct their analyses from one of the two general sociological models of society: the consensus model or the conflict model. The consensus model views society as an integrated network of institutions held together by a common set of values. The law is seen as a neutral protector of the continuity and stability of these institutions and values. This perspective also views society as basically good and just. The conflict model holds the opposite view: conflict rather than consensus is the main characteristic of society, and the law serves the purposes of the ruling classes. This view is presented most forcefully in the works of Marx and Engels. We indicated that all societies are characterized by both conflict and consensus, with one process dominating at one time and the other at another time.

DISCUSSION QUESTIONS

1. What do you think are the main differences between legal rules and other kinds of rules?
2. Give one or two examples of how changing values and/or technologies have led to changes in the law.
3. In what ways are (a) Plato and Hobbes and (b) Aristotle and Locke alike in terms of their views of human nature and the law?
4. Do you believe that the "ruling class" (decide for yourselves who these people may be) unfairly pass laws favorable to themselves and detrimental to the rest of us? If they do, what can we do about it?
5. In what ways can conflict be beneficial to a society? Can conflict actually support consensus?
6. Would you choose to live under a brutal dictator such as Hitler, Stalin, or Saddam Hussein or suffer the chaos of a society without any kind of law?

CHAPTER TERMS

Beliefs	Language	Social contract
Code of Hammurabi	Law	Substantive irrationality
Conflict perspective	Mechanical solidarity	Substantive rationality
Consensus perspective	Natural law	Symbols
Critical legal studies	Norm	Technology
False consciousness	Organic solidarity	Values
Formal irrationality	Original position	Veil of ignorance
Formal rationality	Positive law	
Forms	Risk society	

References

Adams, J. (1971). *In defence of the Constitution of the United States* (Vol. 1). New York, NY: De Capo Press. (Original work published 1778)

Allott, P. (2001). Law and the remaking of humanity. In N. Dorsen (Ed.), *Democracy and the rule of law* (pp. 19–30). Washington, DC: CQ Press.

Aristotle. (1952). *Nicomachean ethics*. Chicago, IL: William Benton.

Balkin, J. (2008). Critical legal theory today. In F. J. Mootz (Ed.), *On philosophy in American law* (pp. 64–72). Cambridge, England: Cambridge University Press.

Basler, R. (2007). Lyceum address. *Abraham Lincoln Online*. Retrieved from http://www.abrahamlincolnonline.org/lincoln/speeches/lyceum.htm

Bottero, J. (1973). The first law code. In S. Brandon (Ed.), *Ancient empires* (pp. 22–28). New York, NY: Newsweek Books.

Collins, R., & Makowsky, M. (1993). *The discovery of society* (5th ed.). New York, NY: McGraw-Hill.

Deininger, W. (1965). *Problems in social and political thought*. New York, NY: Macmillan.

Dershowitz, A. (2018, June 6). The final nail in the ACLU's coffin. *The Hill*. Retrieved from http://thehill.com/opinion/civil-rights/391682-the-final-nail-in-the-aclus-coffin.

Durant, W., & Durant, A. (1968). *The lessons of history*. New York, NY: Simon & Schuster.

Durkheim, É. (1960). *The division of labor in society*. Translated by G. Simpson. New York, NY: Free Press. (Original work published 1893)

Edwards, C. (1971). *Hammurabi, King of Babylonia*. Port Washington, NY: Kennikat Press.

Evan, W. (1990). *Social structure and the law: Theoretical and empirical approaches*. Newbury Park, CA: SAGE.

Fairchild, E., & Dammer, H. (2001). *Comparative criminal justice systems*. Belmont, CA: Wadsworth.

Giddens, A. (1999). Risk and responsibility. *Modern Law Review, 62,* 1–10.

Giddens, A., Duneier, M., & Applebaum, R. (2005). *Introduction to sociology*. New York, NY: Norton.

Gordon, R. (2012). Critical legal histories revisited: A response. *Law & Social Inquiry, 37,* 200–215.

Hobbes, T. (1952). *Leviathan*. Chicago, IL: William Benton.

Kelly, D. (1990). *The human measure: Social thought in the Western legal tradition*. Cambridge, MA: Harvard University Press.

Lavine, T. (1989). *From Socrates to Sartre: The philosophic quest*. New York, NY: Bantam.

Leiter, B. (2001). Legal realism and legal positivism reconsidered. *Ethics, 111,* 278–301.

Locke, J. (1952). *The second treatise of government*. Indianapolis, IN: Liberal Arts.

Marx, K., & Engels, F. (1972). The German ideology. In R. Tucker (Ed.), *The Marx–Engels reader*. New York, NY: Norton. (Original work published 1888)

Murphy, J. (2006). The lawyer and the layman: Two perspectives on the rule of law. *Review of Politics, 68,* 101–131.

Plato. (1952). *The dialogues of Plato*. Chicago, IL: William Benton.

Plato. (1960). *The republic and other works*. Garden City, NY: Doubleday.

Pojman, L. (1989). *Philosophy: The quest for truth*. Belmont, CA: Wadsworth.

Rawls, A. (2003). Conflict as a foundation for consensus: Contradictions of industrial capitalism in Book III of Durkheim's *Division of labor*. *Critical Sociology, 29,* 295–335.

Rawls, J. (1996). *Political liberalism*. New York, NY: Columbia University Press.

Rawls, J. (1999). *A theory of justice*. Oxford, England: Oxford University Press.

Schluchter, W. (2002). The sociology of law as an empirical theory of validity. *Journal of Classical Sociology, 2,* 257–280.

Sinha, S. (1990). *What is law? The differing theories of jurisprudence*. New York, NY: Paragon House.

Soper, P. (1992). Some natural confusions about natural law. *Michigan Law Review, 90,* 2393–2423.

Turkel, G. (1996). *Law and society: Critical approaches*. Boston, MA: Allyn & Bacon.

Vago, S. (1991). *Law and society* (3rd ed.). Englewood Cliffs, NJ: Prentice Hall.

Walsh, A. (2006). *Correctional assessment, casework, and counseling* (4th ed.). Lanham, MD: American Correctional Association.

Weber, M. (1978). *Economy and society: An outline of interpretative sociology* (Vol. 2). Edited by G. Roth and C. Wittich. Berkeley: University of California Press. (Original work published 1905)

CHAPTER 2

JUSTICE
AND THE LAW

After Adolf Hitler came into power in 1933, he decided that there would be no more flirtation in Germany with such nonsense as individual rights. The law would exist only to serve his vision of the state. Nazi Germany would live under the law of power, not the power of law. Just three months later, Jews were dismissed from the civil service, and over the following months and years, they were deprived of everything, even their lives in the death camps scattered across Europe. These acts took place under the cloak of law after 1935 with the implementation of the Nuremberg Laws, which stripped Jews of all legal, civil, social, and political rights and defined them as a separate race under the *Law for the Protection of German Blood and Honor.*

Do we have a moral right to pass judgment on the customs and laws of another culture that we find repugnant? Because Nazi law met every rational criteria for lawmaking by a sovereign nation, by what standards would legal relativists condemn such laws? Despite their belief in the relativity of morals, these theorists would have to turn to the ideas of justice embedded in natural law as the basis of their condemnation. This is exactly what the victorious Allies did when they tried Nazi war criminals at Nuremberg. The crimes committed by the Nazis, although legal under positivist Nazi law, violated universal principles of civilized behavior and human dignity.

Other legal theorists at the time, while not denying that the Nazis deserved punishment, felt that the Nuremberg trials were a travesty, a "victor's justice" conducted in ways that violated many principles of law. For instance, the charge of "crimes against humanity" did not exist prior to the trials; hence, the Allies created an ex post facto (retroactive) crime. The Nazi defendants relied on positivist legal principles to defend themselves by rightfully claiming that they were operating under German law as it existed at the time (because of the Nazi experience, modern German law is very much influenced by natural law).

The tensions between positivism and natural law are evident. Positivists claim that the Allies cloaked their desire for revenge using the language of natural justice and, by so doing, had violated the rule of law. Believers in natural justice replied that moral standards cried out for retribution and that the Nuremberg trials established a needed international standard of conduct. After reading this chapter, decide whether it is wise to posit "universal standards" with which all cultures must comply. If so, who gets to define those standards, and how might they be enforced?

INTRODUCTION

This chapter discusses questions that philosophers, theologians, and legal scholars have pondered for millennia: "What is justice?" "Where does it come from?" and "What is its relationship to the law?" Justice is one of those great intangibles, like truth, beauty, and love, all recognizable in their particular manifestation but awkward to define. Justice (like truth, beauty, and love) is an *ideal*, not an objective "thing" that we can lay our hands on in the sense that the written law is. It is above all a *moral* ideal that persons and social institutions owe one another; it is something we must strive to understand and practice as the ultimate goal of the legal endeavor. Let us first try to come to grips with the first question: "What is justice?"

WHAT IS JUSTICE?

The definition of *justice* in Webster's dictionary goes around in circles. *Justice* is: "The maintenance or administration of what is just." The dictionary previously defines *just* as "Conforming to a standard of correctness; righteous; merited; deserved" and gives as synonyms the terms *fair* and *upright*. Nevertheless, we are beginning to get an idea of what a general definition might look like, and you are probably thinking that justice is a very desirable thing, which of course it is.

Perhaps the definition of justice that has gained the widest acceptance over the centuries is the one offered by Aristotle 300 years before the birth of Christ: "**Justice consists of treating equals equally and unequals unequally according to relevant differences**" (Walsh, & Stohr, 2010, p. 133). Similarly, the great Roman Jurist Dometius Ulpanius defined justice as "the constant and perpetual will to allot everyman his due" (Day, 1968, p. 31). Justice is thus about how we behave toward and treat others and how decisions are made about what type of behavior and treatment is appropriate given our perceptions about what others deserve. The equally balanced scales weighing conflicting claims and the sword of retribution are an internationally recognized symbol ("Lady Justice").

With Aristotle's definition in mind, we look at what various legal scholars have considered as the two components of justice with which Aristotle was most concerned: distributive justice and retributive justice.

Distributive Justice

Distributive justice relates to how a political entity such as a nation-state distributes resources to its members. If there are no good reasons to distribute resources unequally (in the Aristotelian sense, meaning there are no *relevant* differences), then resources should be equally distributed. But of course there are relevant differences

Lady Justice on Top of the Old Bailey in London

with respect to resource distribution, although there may be arguments about just how relevant they are. Distributive justice is about rightful, merited, deserved distribution; it is not about need. A just distribution depends on the individual's contributions and value to the community.

The Marxist principle "From each according to his ability, to each according to his need" does not sit well with Aristotelians. They may agree that it is excellent advice for parents to apply to their children, but it is not a recipe for just government. Two people may have identical needs, but one of them may *deserve* a much greater proportion because of his or her contributions to the community. Dividing the resource pie equally, regardless of people's differing contributions to its existence, is unjust (although folks like John Rawls might disagree). A simple example will give you the idea of what we mean. Think how students who have done work worthy of an A grade would feel if required to donate their extra points to pull up other students with Ds and Fs because they "need" the points. Is giving each student a C grade regardless of their efforts because they need to pass the class just? What consequences do you think it would have on the future efforts of students? According to Aristotle's definition, because their differing scores reflect some mixture of talent and effort, they are a relevant difference; grading students unequally is thus just.

What if rather than talking about test grades we talk about more basic things, such as food, clothing, and shelter? For example, is the provision of welfare for the "have-nots" of society just? We are not asking if it is decent or compassionate—we are only asking if it is just. Welfare means that the government has taken money from productive members of society and given it to nonproductive members on the basis of the need of the latter. Help for the disabled, the temporarily unemployed, and the formerly productive who by no fault of their own lack the capacity to function independently is considered just according to Aristotelian criteria because such people have earned it by their past efforts. On the other hand, what about a woman who has three or four children out of wedlock by different men and who has never contributed anything to society? Her need is real, but it is self-induced and thus exploitive of those whose money is taken to support it. Providing such a person with needed resources may be compassionate, but it is not, according to Aristotle's definition, just. Compassion may be a strong component of justice, although it is not always necessarily so.

Some argue that there are times when certain people get less than they deserve because others have acquired more than their share. For instance, according to Elizabeth Palermo (2014), the average annual compensation for a CEO of a company in the United States in 2012 was a whopping $9.6 million, while the average US worker made a little more than $44,000 in the same year. The main reason for this is that CEO compensation has changed from being based on salary and bonus to based predominately on stock options. She cites researchers who maintain that CEOs deserve such compensation because this method means that they must do well for their companies (reflected in the value of company stocks) and what is good for a company is good for its employees. While we can all agree that a CEO's worth to a company is greater than that of any line worker, we have to ask what relevant difference makes him or her 218 times more valuable? We will see later that stock-based compensation has led to some of the worst corporate scandals in American history and thus may not be a good way to compensate CEOs.

How about athletes and actors, who contribute nothing to the community except frivolous entertainment, with some making more each year than an entire 400-person police force, whose contributions to the community are enormous, and many times more than any much maligned CEO? While such a situation is reflective of some bizarre values, a market economy allows these kinds of discrepancies in resource distribution. The invisible hand of market capitalism "decides" that someone playing on screen or in a sports stadium is worth more than 400 individuals putting their lives on the line trying to keep our streets safe, and like it or not, by the logic of a market economy, he or she deserves it. According to Aristotle's concept of justice, it is only when the accumulation of resources is exploitive that it becomes unjust. Athletes and entertainers do not obtain their inflated incomes by exploiting others: the public freely pays to watch them perform, and we freely purchase the goods and services provided by the captains of industry. It is the scarcity of something that people want rather than its intrinsic value that determines market price. Water, which is absolutely vital to all life, is far more intrinsically valuable than gold, but it is the abundance of water and the rarity of gold that determines their market value. Likewise, line workers and police officers are far more easily replaced than are the rare talents of a corporate CEO or an NBA star.

Exploitation has been a constant feature in the history of humankind, as have attempts to justify it by claiming that its fruits were the due of "naturally superior" people. Anatole France's well-known declaration "Justice is made to give everyone his due; to the rich his richness, to the poor his poverty" was his caustic reply to Aristotle's "to each his due" concept of justice. However, this is unfair to Aristotle, who condemned *undeserved* richness and poverty alike. Democratic governments have long recognized the unjustness of exploitive concentrations of wealth and have taken legislative steps to correct it. As we will see in chapter 11, most democracies have encouraged (or at least allowed) the formation of trade unions to fight work-place exploitation; they have regulated business; and they have sought a more equitable distribution of wealth by implementing a progressive income tax. Because the privileged classes have stoutly resisted such things, none of them occurred without great struggles. However, each of these reforms moved the economic systems of the democracies involved closer to the ideals of distributive justice as most philosophers and social theorists have viewed it.

Retributive Justice

Retributive justice is concerned with *how* a society's system of law goes about determining guilt or innocence (procedural retributive justice) and then how it goes about determining the proper (just) punishment (substantive retributive justice) for the guilty. We concern ourselves for the moment only with substantive retributive justice. (We discuss substantive and procedural law at length in a later chapter, but for now, it is sufficient to say that substantive law places limits on the actions of individuals by defining acts that are and are not permissible and procedural law places limits on the agents of the state as they go about the business of enforcing substantive law.) Like distributive justice, substantive retributive justice involves people getting what they rightly deserve according to their behavior. To be just, a society must punish with fairness and impartiality, which means that equals must be punished equally and unequals must be punished unequally according to relevant differences.

The criminal justice system recognizes that one relevant difference in terms of deciding punishment is the amount of harm done by a criminal act. Thus murder, rape, and robbery are punished more severely than petty theft, receiving stolen property, and simple assault. The first three crimes are punished more severely because justice tries to seek a balance between the harm done to the victim and the pain the criminal must suffer.

But is the severity of the crime the only relevant difference that should determine punishment—that is, should all people committing the same crime receive equal punishment? Do you believe that a cardiologist and a laborer are punished equally if they are both fined $100 for speeding? Is there any relevant difference that justifies treating one differently from the other? Although $100 is still $100, it is pocket change to the cardiologist but may be a big chunk of the laborer's weekly take-home pay. Just punishment is about equality of pain, not the equality of the instrument (the amount of the fine) used to inflict it, because the pain itself is what supposedly provides the deterrent effect. Thus, when financially unequal offenders are *fined* equally, they are not being *punished* equally and therefore not justly. A just punishment would be one that hurt both parties roughly equally. The day-fine system used in some European countries might accomplish this. Under this system, a convicted person pays a fine equal to a day's pay, which could be $500 per day or $50 per day, depending on his or her daily salary. For instance, a Finnish billionaire was fined the equivalent of $216,900 for speeding in 2004, which beat the former Finnish record speeding fine of \$148,000 ("Finland Millionaire," 2004). This record was beaten a billionaire in Switzerland who was fined \$290,000 for driving his Ferrari at twice the speed limit (Jordans, 2010).

There are many issues related to punishment and justice, one of which is sentencing disparity among convicted criminals. If the statutory penalty for a given crime is open ended (say, from "2 to 10 years"), the actual punishment an offender receives will depend on the judge's exercise of discretion guided by legal and extralegal factors. However, the subjective opinions of individual judges as to what constitutes deserved punishment naturally leads to wide sentencing disparities, with "hanging" judges at one extreme and "bleeding heart" judges at the other. Temperamental and ideological differences among judges hardly constitute a relevant difference for determining different penalties for defendants who are roughly similarly situated in terms of the crimes they committed and their criminal records.

One solution tried in various jurisdictions to minimize sentencing disparities has been the use of sentencing guidelines. Sentencing guidelines are a way of numerically defining Aristotle's definition of justice by assigning numbers both to various aspects of the crime and to characteristics of the offender. The crime seriousness or "offense rating" section of the Felony Sentencing Worksheet (FSW) shown in Figure 2.1 assigns points according to (a) the statutory gravity of the crime; (b) whether or not the crime was committed while the defendant was on probation, parole, or bail; (c) the amount of monetary loss; and (d) a series of aggravating ("shocking and deliberate cruelty?") or mitigating (did the victim contribute to his or her victimization?) circumstances. The prior record section is concerned with (a) number of prior felony and misdemeanor offenses; (b) previous probation, parole, or bail violations; (c) whether the defendant has previously served prison time; and (d) a series of mitigating factors, such as voluntary restitution, being a family breadwinner, or being substantially law abiding over a certain period prior to the present offense. Points on both sections are added and applied to a sentencing grid at the point at which the scores intersect. These grids indicate a sentence that may be presumptive or advisory, depending on the jurisdiction.

How do the designers of guidelines know what the important aspects of the crime and the defendant's character are? The FSW from Ohio was designed following a two-year study of the sentencing practices of 60 percent of Ohio's felony judges (Walsh, 2006). The study determined what these judges *as a whole* considered relevant, thus ruling out any idiosyncratic opinions that individual judges may have. The study also determined what sentences these judges gave *on average* to defendants similarly situated in terms of the FSW's criteria. Averaging sentences pulled the sentences of the overly lenient and overly severe judges into the middle of the distribution of sentencing possibilities. Averaging the sentences of a state's judges combines their wisdom, promotes consistency, and provides other judges with sentencing norms based on the past practices of their peers. Sentencing according to these criteria provides a mean between two equally unjust extremes. Such a practice is probably as close as we can get to the ideal of retributive justice as it is applied to the punishment of wrongdoers.

Figure 2.1 Felony Sentencing Worksheet

Defendant's Name: _____ Case No. _____

<u>OFFENSE RATING</u>

1. Degree of Offense
Assess points for the one most serious offense or its equivalent for which offender is being sentenced, as follows: 1st degree felony = 4 points; 2nd degree felony = 3 points; 3rd degree felony = 2 points; 4th degree felony = 1 point. ___

2. Multiple Offenses
Assess 2 points if one or more of the following applies: (A) offender is being sentenced for two or more offenses committed in different incidents; (B) offender is currently under a misdemeanor or felony sentence imposed by any court; or (C) present offense was committed while offender on probation or parole.

3. Actual or Potential Harm
Assess 2 points if one or more of the following applies: (A) serious physical harm to a person was caused; (B) property damage or loss of $300 or more was caused; (C) there was a high risk of any such harm, damage, or loss, though not caused; (D) the gain or potential gain from theft offense(s) was $300 or more, or (E) dangerous ordinance or a deadly weapon was actually used in the incident, or tis use was attempted or threatened.

4. Culpability
Assess 2 points if one or more of the following applies: (A) offender was engaging in continuing criminal activity as asource of income or livelihood, (B) offense was part of a continuing conspiracy to which offender was party, or (C) offense included shocking and deliberate cruelty in which offender participated or acquiesced.

5. Mitigation
Deduct 1 point for each of the following, as applicable: (A) there was substantial provocation, justification, or excuse for offense; (B) victim induced or facilitated offense; (C) offense was committed in the heat of anger; and (D) the property damaged, lost, or stolen was restored or recovered without significant cost to the victim.

Net Total = Offense Rating

<u>OFFENDER RATING</u>

1. Prior Convictions
Assess 2 points for each verified prior conviction, any jurisdiction. Count adjudications of delinquency for felony as convictions.

Assess 1 point for each verified prior misdemeanor conviction and jurisdiction; count adjudications of delinquency for misdemeanor as convictions. Do not count traffic or intoxication offenses as disorderly conduct, disturbing the peace, or equivalent offenses.

2. Repeat Offenses
Assess 2 points if present offense is offense of violence, sex offense, theft offense, or drug abuse offense, and offender has one or more prior convictions for same type of offense.

3. Prison Commitments
Assess 2 points if offender was committed one or more times to a penitentiary, reformatory, or equivalent institution in any jurisdiction. Count commitments to state youth commission or similar commitments in other jurisdictions.

4. Parole and Similar Violations
Assess 2 points if one or more of the following applies: (A) offender has previously had probation or parole for misdemeanor or felony revoked; (B) present offense committed while offender on probation or parole; (C) present offense committed while offender free on bail; or (D) present offense committed while offender in custody.

5. Credits
Deduct 1 point for each of the following, as applicable: (A) offender has voluntarily made bona fide, realistic arrangements for at least partial restitution; (B) offender was age 25 or older at time of first felony conviction; (C) offender has been substantially law-abiding for at least 3 years; and (D) offender lives with his or her spouse or minor children or both and is either a breadwinner for the family or, if there are minor children, a housewife.

Net Total = Offender Rating

INDICATED SENTENCE   -Circle the box on the chart where the offense and offender ratings determined on the previous page intersect. This indicates a normal sentencing package.

			OFFENDER RATING		
		0-2	3-5	6-8	9-11	12 or more
Offense Rating	6 or More	Impose one of three lowest minimum terms No probation	Impose one of three highest minimum terms No probation	Impose one of three highest minimum terms No probation	Impose one of two highest minimum terms. Make at least part of multiple sentences consecutive. No probation	Impose highest minimum term. Make at least part of multiple sentences consecutive. No probation
	5	Impose one of three lowest minimum terms Some form of probation indicated only with special mitigation	Impose one of three lowest minimum terms No probation	Impose one of three highest minimum terms No probation	Impose one of three highest minimum terms No probation	Impose one of two highest minimum terms. Make at least part of multiple sentences consecutive. No probation
	4	Impose one of two lowest minimum terms Some form of probation indicated	Impose one of three lowest terms Some form of probation indicated only with special mitigation	Impose one of three lowest minimum terms No probation	Impose one of three highest minimum terms No probation	Impose one of three highest minimum terms No probation
	3	Impose one of two lowest minimum terms Some form of probation indicated	Impose one of two lowest terms Some form of probation indicated	Impose one of three lowest minimum terms Some form of probation indicated only with special mitigation	Impose one of three lowest minimum terms No probation	Impose one of three highest minimum terms No probation
	0-2	Impose lowest minimum term Some form of probation indicated	Impose one of two lowest minimum terms Some form of probation indicated	Impose one of two lowest minimum terms Some form of probation indicated	Impose one of three lowest minimum terms Some form of probation indicated only with special mitigation	Impose one of three lowest minimum terms No probation

Aristotle

PROBLEMS WITH ARISTOTLE'S DEFINITION OF JUSTICE

Although we have shown a positive attitude about Aristotle's definition of justice as "treating equals equally and unequals unequally according to relevant differences," can you spot a potential problem with it? The big problem rests with defining what *relevant* differences are. Is skin color a relevant difference? If so, we can justify slavery by asserting that we are treating unequals unequally. How about gender, religion, nationality, and sexual orientation? All these statuses have been—and still are, in some countries—considered at one time or another to be relevant differences, thus granting people permission to treat the disvalued group badly. Justice will be more fully realized when we view relevant differences exclusively as differences of conduct, not as differences of ascribed statuses such as those just mentioned.

Conflict theorists would point out a further problem with Aristotle's view in that even if the *process* of justice is identical for every person brought before the courts, the *result* in terms of equal treatment and probability of favorable outcome is impossible under the present legal systems. Conflict theorists would point out that in an adversarial system of law, "justice" is just another commodity, the quality of which depends on its price. Everyone is entitled to legal counsel in the United States, even paid for by the state if the person is indigent, but only the privileged few can afford the legal superstars of the world. With the aid of great lawyers, the factually guilty may be set free; with poor lawyers, or even good lawyers lacking the incentive of a big fee, the innocent may be found guilty. Both outcomes are perversions of justice.

ISSUE HIGHLIGHT

Positivist Law v. Natural Law: King Creon and Antigone

We have said that positivist law and natural law are often at odds. The problem is that while positivist law is objective in the sense that it is written down and practiced, natural law is not written down and can be quite subjective. No better illustration of the tension between positivist and natural law exists than law than the Greek tragedy *Antigone* written by Sophocles around 441 BCE. As you read this, try to understand the positions of both King Creon and Antigone, and who you think was right.

In this play, Antigone's standards of natural justice clash with King Creon's positivist law. The story revolves around two brothers leading opposite sides in Thebes' civil war: Polyneices and Eteocles. Both brothers were killed in battle, and Creon, the new ruler of Thebes, declared that Eteocles would be honored and Polyneices disgraced. Polyneices had rebelled against the rightful ruler of Thebes. Creon therefore decreed that Polyneices was a traitor undeserving of a decent burial according to the law, and that anyone attempting to give him one should be punished as a traitor. This is a problem because in Greek culture, the spirit of a body not buried by sundown on the day of death is doomed to walk the earth for eternity. Antigone was the sister of both brothers. Her position was that the gods have commanded the living to give the dead a proper burial, and that she had a greater duty to the gods and to her brother than to the man-made law forbidding his burial, hence for her natural law outweighs man-made positivist law. In defiance of Creon, Antigone buries her brother and is arrested and condemned to death.

Haemon, Creon's son and Antigone's fiancé, tries to persuade his father to spare Antigone, and when Creon refuses, Haemon vows never to see his father again. Creon then imprisons Antigone in a cave, but a blind prophet tells him that the gods side with Antigone, that he will lose one child because of his actions, and that the sacrificial offerings of Thebes will not be accepted by the gods. Creon then relents and says that he will bury Polyneices and free Antigone. Before he can do this, however, he is informed that Haemon has killed himself, and that so has Antigone. Another messenger informs him that his grief-stricken wife has killed herself, cursing Creon with her last breath. Thus chastened, Creon abdicates the throne a broken man, although he believes that the actions he had taken were in fact the right ones under the law as written.

Who do you think was right in this situation? It's easy to favor the tragic figure of Antigone for her heroic stand against Creon, but Polyneices did commit treason against the state and would have been justly punished had he survived the battle. According to Greek belief, the gods had placed Creon on the throne, and thus we can argue that Creon had a divine right to rule according to the laws as written. In this sense, natural law and positivist law were one and the same. Issues such as those in *Antigone* assure that there will always be a tension between ideas of natural and positivist law—what we feel is unwritten justice and what is contained in written law that may be considered unjust.

LEGAL REALISM

Unlike natural law and legal positivism, **legal realism** is not a theory or philosophy of law but rather the study of legal decision-making. Legal realists examine how law is actually applied and the implications of that application. They evaluate law not "as written" but "as practiced." After all, law becomes "real" only in the hands of judges and administrators, and obviously, lawyers must understand law as it is understood and applied by decision-makers. For legal realists, law is indeterminate; that is, law by itself does not fully determine the outcome of a legal action. Legal rules certainly "influence" judicial decisions, but they do not determine them in any absolute way. While legal positivism is a theory of society's legal norms from which the decision in a case can be logically deduced like a mathematical theorem, legal realism is about what judges really do (Leiter, 2001). Chief Justice Oliver Wendell Holmes's succinct definition of law sums legal realism up nicely: "The prophecies of what the courts will do in fact, nothing more pretentious, is what I mean by law" (Kidder, 1983, p. 21).

Legal realists maintain that nonlegal reasons such as a subjective judgment of fairness often explain judicial decisions and by doing so can introduce justice (or injustice) into law. This does not mean that judges can make arbitrary decisions or that legal realism and positivism are incompatible. The former obviously needs the latter for judges not to stumble into Weber's substantive irrationality. Judges' decisions are guided by positive law even if they are not completely determined by it. Note how the great eighteenth-century American judge Chancellor Kent cleverly made use of positive law to make decisions he felt were just:

> My practice was first to make myself . . . master of the facts. . . . [B]y the time I had done this slow and tedious process I was master of the cause [case] & ready to decide it. I saw where justice lay and the moral sense decided the cause half the time, & I then set down to search the authorities until I had exhausted my books, & I might once & a while be embarrassed by a technical rule, but I most always found principles to suit my views of the case. (Kaye, 1998, pp. 13–14)

Kent's strategy amounts to judges sending their clerks to the legal parking lot to find a vehicle that will take them from where they are to wherever it is they want to be without breaking down. A more recent admission of subjective feelings justice trumping positivist law is that of Thurgood Marshall, the first African American Supreme Court Justice who once said when asked his judicial philosophy: "You do what you think is right and let the law catch up" (Rhode, 1992, p. 1259). Many studies show that judges' decisions are frequently predictable by their political ideology, race, gender, and religion, depending on the nature of the case before them. Judges sitting on appeals courts are also frequently subjected to ideological dampening (a Democrat sitting with two Republicans, or vice versa, will move ideologically toward his or her two colleagues) or amplification (if all judges on a panel are of the same political persuasion, their ideology will be amplified; Miles & Sunstein, 2008).

Of course, if judges go too far in injecting their subjective interpretations into the law as written in order to rationalize their decisions, there are layers of appeals courts to set the matter "right." Thus, only the US Supreme Court has the luxury of deciding cases after the fashion of Chancellor Kent or Thurgood Marshall and being assured that those decisions will not be overturned. For instance, in *Bush v. Gore* (2000), the case that gave the presidency to George W. Bush, the justices came up with a novel interpretation of the Fourteenth Amendment's equal protection clause (all Florida counties did not count votes in the same way, thus Bush's equal protection rights were violated). Even here, a decision is based on a majority vote rather than on the interpretation of a single judge, and it has to have at least the appearance of following the Constitution (notwithstanding that the Constitution is what the majority of justices say it is). However, the point is: even when mangling the law beyond recognition, most judges are presumably convinced that they are dispensing justice, despite the fact that in *Bush v. Gore* the Court made the decision strictly along party lines and thus was unable to disguise its politics. In addition, in this case, liberal justices adopted what would normally be considered a conservative interpretation of the Constitution and conservative justices a liberal interpretation (Upham, 2011, p. 264). The Court's mask of impartial positivism dispassionately interpreting the Constitution was completely demolished in this case.

We do not wish to be overly cynical by giving the impression that it is only characteristics of judges that influence their decisions. It is generally considered that *Muller v. Oregon* (1908) was the first time that the US Supreme Court openly acknowledged social science data in rendering its decision (Tomkins & Oursland, 1991). This case involved a woman who was required to work in excess of 10 hours in one day at Muller's laundry, in violation of an Oregon law forbidding excessive hours for women. Muller was convicted of violating the law and fined. His appeal eventually was heard by the US Supreme Court, which upheld the Oregon statute despite of the fact that three years earlier it had upheld the rights of a bakery to work its bakers (all males) 16 hours per day (*Lochner v. New York*, 1905). In *Muller*, the Court "distinguished" the two cases on the basis of the difference between the sexes. Part of the ruling stated:

> That woman's physical structure and the performance of maternal functions place her at a disadvantage in the struggle for subsistence is obvious. This is especially true when the burdens of motherhood are upon her. Even when they are not, by abundant testimony of the medical fraternity continuance for a long time on her feet at work, repeating this from day to day, tends to injurious effects upon the body, and as healthy mothers are essential to vigorous offspring, the physical well-being of woman becomes an object of public interest and care in order to preserve the strength and vigor of the race. . . . [H]istory discloses the fact that woman has always been dependent upon man. He established his control at the outset by superior physical strength, and this control in various forms, with diminishing intensity, has continued to the present.

This ruling was hailed by women at the time, but modern feminists have criticized it for its alleged sexist assumptions, as well as on the grounds that it protected only women, not all workers (Tomkins & Oursland, 1991).

Legal realism belies the claim that the United States is "a country of law, not men." The hearings on the nomination of Sonia Sotomayor to the US Supreme Court in 2009 made it plain that decisions of social importance are not made by objective judges devoid of passion for one side of an issue or the other. As an appeals court judge, Sotomayor dismissed a discrimination claim by white firefighters who were denied promotion after passing the required exams because no black firefighters passed them. Opponents of Sotomayor's nomination made much of her claims of empathy with the less fortunate. We are not saying that this is right or wrong—only that some level of judicial emotional bias is inevitable. The critical issue is not whether judges should rely on their emotions but rather whether they can empathize with diverse groups of people, not only groups with whom they identify.

WHERE DOES JUSTICE COME FROM? TWO PERSPECTIVES OF LAW AND JUSTICE AS NATURAL

In this section, we explore two perspectives on why and how law and justice exist in the first place. Do we discover law like physicists discover new scientific facts about the physical world, or do we make it up as we go along like novelists make up their plots? Obviously, we make up specific laws relating to given issues as they arise, but what about the more abstract concepts of law and justice, the inner urge that makes people everywhere *want* to apply rules to conduct?

People everywhere not only want to apply rules to conduct, they want to apply rules that are just, if for no other reason than because they themselves want to be treated fairly. Is justice inherent in the very nature of humanity in the same sense that physical laws are inherent in the universe? Think of the physical laws that are the bases for sciences such as physics and chemistry. These laws create harmony and predictability in the universe. They operated long before humans discovered them, and they continue to operate whether or not we are aware of them. Physical laws are not invented, nor do they evolve from earlier, incomplete versions of themselves: they are simply *there*, waiting to be discovered, understood, and applied. The more we understand about the nature of these physical laws, the more we can harness them for human good. Likewise, the more we search for and understand moral laws, the more just and harmonious our societies will be.

Philosophers have long contemplated the question of whether natural laws govern human behavior in the same sense that physical laws govern the physical world. The great philosopher Immanuel Kant thought there were when he spoke of the two things he could be absolutely sure of: "The starry heavens above, and the moral law within" (Thomas, 1962, p. 255). Consider that the first moral statement children make, and often with some force, is "That's not fair!" How do children arrive at that conclusion so readily, and why is it so immediately compelling if the sense of fairness is not somehow within them? Finkel, Harré, and Rodriguez Lopez (2001) call these "not fair" complaints "commonsense justice" because they "are uttered long before children come into contact with any formal introduction to general moral principles" (p. 7).

If there is a natural law, we have to ask ourselves if it is the product of a deity concerned with our well-being or the product of blind evolutionary processes. We are concerned here with the concept of law as an instinct for rule-making that is as natural to the human species as thought and emotion. Proponents of natural law believe in a natural basis for law based on an inner voice yearning for justice, although they differ on its source. One perspective is the *transcendental perspective*, and the other is the *evolutionary perspective*. The first words of the Declaration of Independence shows that the Framers hedged their bets by making reference to both the transcendental and natural perspectives of natural law:

> When in the Course of human events, it becomes necessary for one people to dissolve the political bands which have connected them with another, and to assume among the powers of the earth, the separate and equal station to which the Laws of Nature and of Nature's God entitle them, a decent respect to the opinions of mankind requires that they should declare the causes which impel them to the separation.

The Transcendental Natural Law Perspective

A moral relativist basically believes that whatever is considered right and proper in any given society is morally right even if outsiders might consider some practices of that society (e.g., cannibalism, wife beating, widow burning, the mutilation of young girls by clitorectomy) to be morally repugnant. Social scientists warn against passing moral judgment on cultures other than our own because doing so implies that we are asserting the superiority of our own culture, and to do that supposedly makes us bigots, racists, and ethnocentrics. Since few people like to be called such names, many social scientists are moral relativists (at least publicly). However, there are those who believe absolute moral standards of right and wrong that transcend time and culture and are universally applicable exist.

Transcendentalism is a philosophical position that emphasizes the primacy and superiority of the spiritual over the material. It does not deny the reality of the physical world and its human constructs, such as positive law, but asserts that the transcendental (meaning "above," "beyond," and "exceeding normal human knowledge") realm is more fundamental. Transcendentalists believe in timeless universalistic **natural laws** that transcend the legal interests of a particular society at a particular time in history. The **transcendentalist perspective** is that the *ought* of law runs downward from some transcendental realm (wherever that may be) through jurisprudence (the philosophy of law) and education to the individual (Wilson, 1998). This perspective agrees with Plato's assertion (remember his theory of the forms?) that as humanity becomes more civilized, learned, and wise, it will discover the nature of this law and apply it for the benefit of all, just as we discover and apply physical laws.

Natural law is not a formal set of statutes or procedures. No country has a natural law system in the sense that it has a common law or socialist law system, although some natural law principles may be woven into them. Many of the precepts contained in the Ten Commandments, considered to be elements of natural law because they are God-given, have been incorporated into most of the world's legal systems.

Natural law may be considered "law within the law," a set of moral precepts that tempers positivist law with concerns of fairness and justice that are absolutist principles morally binding on all societies and individuals. The international legal community even has a name for something quite close to this called *jus cogens*, which literally means "compelling" or "higher" law. Although this principle does not explicitly appeal to natural law, it obviously is strongly influenced by it and has been an accepted doctrine in international law since 1986 (Caplan, 2003). Advocates of *jus cogens*, like advocates of natural law, insist that any positive law contrary to it is not valid and may even constitute a corruption of law (Danilenko, 2003).

The ringing passage of the Declaration of Independence that asserts "We hold these truths to be self-evident, that all men are created equal; they are endowed by their Creator with certain inalienable rights" is a well-known example of the use of natural law to invalidate legally constituted English colonial laws of the period. These words make plain that the US Constitution did not *grant* rights to the people but rather established a government of laws in order to *secure* each person's rights to life, liberty, and property "to which the laws of Nature and Nature's God entitle them." In this sense, the function of law is not to create justice; rather, it is to prevent injustice by guarding natural rights from predation. In 1775, Alexander Hamilton wrote his vision of natural rights contained in the First Amendment: "The sacred rights of mankind are not to be rummaged for, among old parchments, or musty records. They are written, as with a sun beam, in the whole volume of human nature, by the hand of the divinity itself; and can never be erased or obscured by mortal power" (2012, pp. 97–98). In this view, the rights laid out in the First Amendment (see chapter 3) were not dreamt up in the human mind, but are rights demanded by our human DNA, planted therein by the Creator.

So who decides when human law is in conflict with natural law? The quick and dirty answer is: "those with the power to do so." Because natural law is not a set of written statutes and procedures, its advocates must turn to ideas of morality set down in the texts of the various religions in the world or in constitutions modeled on them. And as with any idea or principle, transcendental natural law can be used for ends less than fair and noble. Transcendental natural law fits Weber's substantive-irrational law and has been employed by monarchs and their champions to support the so-called "divine right of kings." According to this philosophy, the king's law-making powers come from God, so his decisions could no more be questioned than the will of God himself. Because the issue of whether Parliament's positive, formal-rationality lawmaking power or the king's substantive-irrational, "divine" power should prevail produced much turmoil in England during the seventeenth century, there has always been a certain distrust of the concept of natural law in the English-speaking world (Friedrich, 1963).

Natural law has also been used against the idea of the divine right of kings. We may assume that much of the quest for natural law is embedded in the desire to limit the absolute power of the sovereign (or the state). Those seeking limitations of state power have searched beyond positive law (which is, after all, the product of the state) by searching for authoritative principles by which these limitations can be legitimized.

Although many of the early proponents of natural law saw it as God-given, it is not necessary to believe in a deity to believe in the concept. For secular believers in natural law, the "higher" nature of natural law means that its principles are derived from the nature of human beings. In a general sense, natural law means that humans everywhere should be treated with dignity and respect and viewed as intrinsically valuable "ends-in-themselves," not as means to some other end. This is the idea behind the Golden Rule, versions of which exist in all of the world's major religions. Humans are assumed to have an innate sense of justice and to know deep inside when those principles are being violated, even when it is they who are violating them.

The Evolutionary Perspective

The **evolutionary perspective** attempts to explain the origins of law and justice with reference to the principles of evolutionary biology. From this perspective, law may be considered "natural" because it flows from the evolved nature of *Homo sapiens*. As one evolutionary legal theorist put it: "The ability to formulate, articulate and understand rules, like other regularities that characterize successful species, undoubtedly had a significant impact on subsequent hominid [*hominid* refers to any bipedal primate such as modern humans] evolution" (Gruter, 1991, p. 61).

The primary difference between the two natural law positions is that evolutionists seek empirical support for their views through studying the behavior of human and other social species. Rather than viewing natural law as something from above and molding human choice to its bidding via positivist law, the evolutionary position begins with human choice. That is, humans are biologically predisposed to make certain choices because those choices promoted the survival and reproductive success (the goal of all living things) of our distant ancestors. Because they were functional, these choices became norms and were eventually codified into positive law. Ancient lawmakers then attempted to impress on the people that the law originated in some transcendental realm (as we saw with Hammurabi; Wilson, 1998).

We do not want to give the impression that this perspective enjoys a privileged position because it is "scientific." Laws are value statements about what *ought* to be, and scientists are in the business of trying to discover what *is*, without investing it with moral overtones. Evolutionary legal theorists do not engage in searches for "law genes," but they do seek to explain law as a by-product of evolved human desires for peace, order, fairness, and predictability. The evolutionary perspective thus attempts to illuminate why law is necessary by focusing on the evolutionary origins of humanity's more offensive traits. (Of course, humans have many nice traits too, but we do not need laws to regulate those.)

When evolutionary theorists refer to something as "natural," they do not use the word as a synonym for "good" or "desirable." Philosophers use the term **naturalistic fallacy** to describe the common practice of confusing *is* with *ought* (Jones & Goldsmith, 2005). What *is* represents a scientific observation; what *ought to be* is a moral hope. Many disagreeable traits and behaviors were adaptive in the sense that individuals possessing them tended to be more successful in securing mating opportunities and thus passing on those traits to offspring, which is what biologists mean by *reproductive success*. The most successful reproducers contribute disproportionately to any species' gene pool, and over time, their genes (and hence the traits they promote) came to dominate it. These biological truisms point only to what is, not to moral statements about what ought to be.

Evolutionists view any behavior that is found in all cultures at all times to be natural ("arising from nature"). Moral sensibility is a universal trait, although the things that offend it may vary considerably from culture to culture and from time to time. This moral sensibility probably developed in our species as a counterstrategy to evolved exploitive strategies, and the rules of conduct we have come to call "law" are manifestations of this moral sensibility. Without a sense of moral outrage, we would not react against, and therefore not deter, the murderer, rapist, thief, cheater, and free rider, and any genes inclining individuals to such behavior would have proliferated. Without the evolved sense of moral outrage, we would all be conscienceless psychopaths (Walsh, 2006; Wiebe, 2004).

Moral outrage is probably also the basis for the desire for revenge, which may be considered a necessary evil for humans to make credible threats. If we threaten to break someone's legs if he steals our bananas but do not carry out the threat when he does, the miscreant has no rational reason for not stealing them again in the future. If our distant ancestors made nothing but idle threats, the impulse to take what is not ours would be far stronger than it is today. The more the potential for retaliation is a reality, the less likely we are to actually harm one another, as the would-be miscreant will take the potential of being hurt seriously. Thus, moral outrage buttressed by retaliatory action is a plausible candidate as the basis of our sense of justice.

As with any universal desire, the desire to punish has a built-in physiological basis. We recognize justice because we recognize injustice, and we recognize injustice not by reference to standards of law but by *felt* outrage at experiencing injustice.

We thus *feel* justice by virtue of our evolved physiology prior to articulating conceptions of it. As Walsh (2000) put it, "The positive feelings accompanying the punishment of those who have wronged us, coupled with the reduction of negative feelings [evoked when we are wronged], provides powerful reinforcement [for punishing], as suggested by the popular saying 'Vengeance is sweet'" (p. 853).

There is evidence for this from imaging studies showing increased blood flow to areas of the brain that respond to reward when miscreants are punished. This suggests that punishing those who have wronged us provides emotional relief and reward for the punisher (de Quervain et al., 2004). Similar research has provided strong evidence for Durkheim's insight about the functional role of punishment discussed in chapter 1. This body of research has also concluded that what is called "altruistic punishment" has been crucial for the evolution of cooperation among humans (Fehr & Gachter, 2002). For the evolutionary biologist, altruistic punishment is punishment applied by someone who has not been personally wronged for the benefit of those who have. For the rest of us, it is punishment applied by agents of the state on behalf of those who have been wronged.

Humans assuredly have an innate wish for harmony, peace, predictability, fairness, and control in their environments, and a desire to establish ways in which these things can be accomplished. According to the evolutionary perspective, these ways are designed and implemented by human beings and are thus socially constructed, but the motivations behind them are innate. As Fikentscher (1991) put it, "If there is a human drive, and instinct for the just, it cannot be separated from the idea of justice and its material contents [the law]" (p. 317).

This does *not* mean that cultural ideas of justice are irrelevant unless they conform to the will of a deity as manifested in holy writings, as in the transcendental perspective. The evolutionary perspective posits a moral *universality*, which implies generality but recognizes the possibility of exceptions, as compared to the absolutism of the transcendental perspective (Wilson, 1998). The evolutionary position asserts that the emotional and intellectual equipment for moral outrage has evolved; it does not specify all the behaviors that will evoke it. If a cultural norm forbids public urination (as in the United States) or the slaughter of cattle (as in India), then people in those cultures will be rightly outraged when these things occur. They will also feel emotionally reassured that justice is done when offending parties are punished. Different cultures shape different expectations and will thus elicit different emotional responses to what seems wrong (Walsh, 2000).

Not all moral outrage is arbitrary and culture-bound. Some actions generate moral outrage at any time or in any place, which is what we mean by "universality." These are the actions that most threatened the survival and reproductive success of our distant ancestors. Public urination and irreverent attitudes toward cattle had absolutely no reproductive consequences in evolutionary environments (nor do they today, of course), and thus outrage about such things is purely culturally conditioned. However, behaviors such as murder, rape, and theft evoke outrage everywhere because these were the most evolutionarily relevant threats our distant ancestors faced.

Numerous fascinating examples of evolutionary thinking applied to various aspects of law can be found in the literature (e.g., Browne, 1997; Cosmides & Tooby, 2006); there is even an organization headquartered at Vanderbilt University called the Society for the Evolutionary Analysis of Law, with an agenda made obvious by its name. However, to appreciate the nuances of such thinking requires a solid background in evolutionary biology, which we cannot provide here. Suffice it say that this is one of the perspectives attempting to account for the "ultimate" origins of law. Its basic ideas are that laws have been devised by all societies as cultural counterstrategies to aspects of human nature conducive to exploitation and that our evolved moral sensibilities provide the basic biological motivation to formulate them.

WHAT IS THE RELATIONSHIP OF LAW TO JUSTICE?

When most people think of justice, they probably think of law, but law and justice are not identical. In fact, law professors often get a bit testy if someone mentions justice, and it is difficult to find the term even indexed in most law books. Because it is easier and consistent with their objectives to describe law as it is (legal positivism) rather than to evaluate its moral content, most law professors are quite happy to be legal positivists. Law *can* be in accordance with justice, but it can also be the furthest thing from it. Law is in accordance with justice when it respects, cultivates, and protects the dignity of even the lowliest person living under it; law violates justice when it does not. Believers in natural law maintain that the goal of positive law should be to bring itself into conformity with what is just. We have to be confident that we can find justice and that we can harness it and put it to practical use for the benefit of humankind, just as scientists seek to harness the laws of nature and put them to practical use. After all, it is only through law that justice can be achieved.

Equity

Equity is a term derived from the Latin word for "just" and refers to remedies for wrongs that were not recognized under English common law. In many respects, equity is at the heart of the relationship between justice and law in the English-speaking world, and it illustrates what we said earlier about law becoming more just as our standards of morality evolve to a higher plane. Equity principles are heavily used in family and contract law, since they allow judges to fashion necessary remedies not readily apparent from a reading of legal statutes. The judicial philosophy of Chancellor Kent described earlier is an example of one man's efforts to make law and justice the same thing.

The idea of equity in law in medieval England evolved in parallel with the evolution of the role of the king's chancellor, who was essentially the king's most important minister (his "prime" minister). One of the chancellor's responsibilities was to handle petitions from the king's subjects seeking relief from rulings in common law courts. By the thirteenth century, the common law had become a very inflexible system. Judges frequently applied the same abstract principles and procedural rules rigidly to every case, regardless of the issues involved, and often failed to see the intent behind precedent as they sought to follow the letter of an ancient ruling rather than its spirit. Judges also failed to realize that ever-changing social circumstances and mores require a dynamic, "living" system of law.

Westminster Hall

As a result of the rigidity of common law, many people felt unjustly treated by the courts and turned to the king (through his chancellor and his staff) to seek justice. This does not mean that the common law of the time was inherently unfair. The law was more incomplete and inflexible than purposely unfair, and equity was conceived of as a corrective for this. With an increasing number of petitions, an entirely independent court system with its own distinct set of principles and procedures was eventually implemented, known as the **Courts of Chancery**. The first mention of such a court was in 1280, during the reign of Edward I (r. 1272–1307). Judges presiding in these courts were directed to view each case as unique, to be flexible and empathetic, and to think in terms of *standards* or *principles* of fairness rather than *rules* of law. Because common law was a corrective, many equity decisions were contrary to its principles as a rational and predictable legal system (Reichel, 2005). It is important to note that equity supplemented, not replaced, common law: equity "begins where the law ends; it supplies justice in circumstances not covered by the law" (McDowell, 1982, p. xii). In other words, if justice were to be served in England, the cold formality of common law alone would not suffice. Courts of Chancery were a necessary "add-on" because of the equity defects apparent in the rigid common law at the time. Westminster Hall, the oldest existing part of the Palace of Westminster (the Houses of Parliament), was erected in 1097 and was the main Court of Chancery for more than 500 years (Horwitz & Polden, 1996).

English monarchs welcomed a court system separate from that of the common law because judges were becoming too independent for their liking, and these separate courts reasserted royal power in legal matters (Fairchild & Dammer, 2001). Nevertheless, over the centuries common law and equity engaged in dynamic cross-pollination to the benefit of both. The common law became fairer and more flexible, and the judges of the chancery courts began relying on rational legal principles and precedent to make equity more predictable. Some of the benefits to each system are given by Reichel (2005): "Common law judges learned that technicalities were not an excuse for reaching obviously wrong decisions, and the chancellors came to understand better the law and its application" (p. 116). The two courts eventually became so alike that formal distinctions between them were removed in 1875, although there are still provisions for separate courts of law and equity in England. Some states in the United States (notably Delaware) have chancery courts, but US judges are empowered to hear cases of both law and equity (Abadinsky, 2003).

An Example of an Equity Decision

What kinds of legal decisions violate equity, and what exactly is an equity decision? Civil law (i.e., noncriminal law) in the United States throughout most of the nineteenth century was very much oriented toward protecting the legality of contracts between individuals. As long as no specific contract was violated, the defrauding, maiming, and killing of innocent consumers and workers by defective products and dangerous working conditions were not cause for legal action. Victims of defective and/or dangerous products could not sue the manufacturers because the guiding legal principle was *caveat emptor* (let the buyer beware). Companies had no legal duty to be concerned with the welfare of those to whom they sold their products; it was incumbent on buyers to be concerned with their own welfare. Similarly, unhealthy and dangerous working conditions in mines, mills, and factories were excused under the freedom of contract clause of the US Constitution. Companies and individuals had entered into a contract to exchange work for wages, with no contractual provisions made for the conditions under which the work was to be done (Abadinsky, 2003). American law in this period was as rigid as twelfth-century English law, as judges mechanistically applied legal rules without concern for standards of equity. Equity became more and more a consideration of American courts in the late nineteenth and early twentieth centuries, however, as laws were passed making companies liable for defective products and protecting workers from unsafe working conditions.

The classic American equity case is *Riggs v. Palmer* (1889) because it illustrates the tension between the *rules* of law and the *principles* of equity. Elmer Palmer was to be the major recipient of his grandfather Francis Palmer's large estate upon Francis's death. Fearing that his grandfather was about to disinherit him, Elmer poisoned him. Elmer was arrested, convicted for murder, and sentenced to 10 years' imprisonment. Since the will in question had not been changed, Elmer laid claim to the estate, a claim contested by two of Francis's daughters. The law was clear: "No will in writing, not any part thereof, shall be revoked or otherwise altered," and thus the New York Court of Appeals was obliged to uphold the will's validity.

However, the majority of the court reasoned that to allow someone to profit from his crime violated principles of justice and ruled in favor of Mrs. Riggs (daughter of Francis Palmer). Two dissenting judges (clearly legal positivists) argued that judges must look to the law, not moral principles, when making decisions. They also argued that the murder was irrelevant to the issue before them because it had already been addressed in other courts, and that to deny Elmer the estate that was legally his amounted to additional punishment. Many other legal positivists railed against the decision, declaring it a dangerous precedent because the primary purpose of law is predictability and predictability is lost if principles trump rules. Nothing is precedent until it is done for the first time, however, and now every state has so-called "slayer statutes" that prevent killers from profiting from their crimes. What was once a hotly contested equity *principle* now has evolved into a commonsense *rule* of positivist law.

GAROFALO AND NATURAL CRIME

Perhaps the best example of a specific attempt to "naturalize" elements of the law was Raffaele Garofalo's formulation of a natural definition of crime. Garofalo (1851–1934), an Italian criminologist and legal scholar, was dissatisfied with the positivistic definition of crime ("crime is what the law says it is"), which to him appeared arbitrary and "unscientific." Garofalo wanted to anchor the definition of crime in something natural and "real," like tying linear measurement to the circumference of the earth using the metric system rather than relying on the arbitrary Anglo-American method of measurement in feet, inches, and miles. Garofalo's definition of crime was to be anchored in human nature, by which he meant that an act should be considered a crime only if it was universally condemned. He reasoned that an act would be universally condemned if it offended the natural sentiments of probity (integrity, honesty) and pity (compassion, sympathy). We see here how Garofalo anticipated many of the points made by evolutionary scientists regarding universal evolved emotional responses to wrongdoing. Natural crimes are evil in themselves (*mala in se*), whereas "man-made" crimes (*mala prohibita*) are wrong only because they have been made wrong by positive law.

Crimes such as prostitution, drug usage, and gambling are *mala prohibita* because they are not universally condemned. Not only are they not universally condemned—people actually seek to be "victimized" by prostitutes, drug dealers, and gambling operators. On the other hand, no one ever seeks to be murdered, raped, assaulted, or robbed. These crimes are intrinsically evil, and the litmus test for determining *mala in se* status is that no one (except in the most bizarre of circumstances) wants to be a victim of them. These kinds of arguments are often made today by those who would like to see "victimless" (*mala prohibita*) crimes legalized because criminalizing behavior and services that many people want tends to lead to organized crime, police corruption, and a general disrespect for the law.

THE RULE OF LAW

The only way we can be reasonably assured of integrating important aspects of justice with a legal system is to declare strict adherence to what is called the **rule of law**. The idea of the rule of law appears to have originated with Plato in *Laws* (2000):

> For that state in which the law is subject and has no authority, I perceive to be on the highway to ruin; but I see that the state in which the law is above the rulers, and the rulers are the inferiors of the law, has salvation, and the very blessings which the Gods can confer. (p. 89)

This idea of the rule of law, not of men, evolved in the English-speaking world from the time of the Magna Carta (1215) through the English civil wars (1642–1646 and 1648–1649) and the Glorious Revolution (1688–1689) of the seventeenth century. These struggles of the English people were efforts to gain freedom from arbitrary government power and oppressive sovereigns. Struggles for freedom and liberty continued with the American Revolution and Civil War and are still going on today around the world. For this reason, Samuel Donnelly (2006) asserts that "the English-speaking countries of the world are renowned citadels of the rule of law" (p. 42). Donnelly also makes the point that the notion of natural law has been essential for the "advance of the rule of law and the promotion of human rights" (p. 51).

Philip Reichel (2005) expresses the idea of the rule of law in the phrase "laws change but the *Law* must remain" (p. 175). He illustrates the point by saying that when the English king put people to death (presumably, Reichel meant people innocent of any criminal act), he broke the law, but when the Russian tsar did the same thing, he created law. What Reichel meant by this is that the English king was acting within a system that recognized a set of fundamental values and principles that were supposed to be supreme. By violating these principles, the king had set himself above the law and therefore violated it. The Russian tsar was not operating within such a system of fundamental values and principles, however, and therefore there were no laws to break. He, not the law, was supreme, and thus the law could be bent and twisted to his will. The English king violated both justice and law; the Russian tsar violated only justice.

Although the rule of law can be violated, the fact that it exists serves as a rallying point and source of legitimacy for those who would oppose individuals and governments who violate it. It is primarily for this reason that the rule of law has been called "the most important legal principle in the world" (Chieveley, 1997, p. 760).

According to Reichel (2005), the rule of law contains three irreducible elements:

It requires a nation to recognize the supremacy of certain fundamental values and principles.

These values and principles must be committed to writing.

A system of procedures that hold the government to these principles and values must be in place.

The first element is relatively unproblematic. It is difficult to imagine a modern organized society without a set of fundamental values (secular or religious) that it holds supreme. The second element is also relatively straightforward. Any culture possessing a written language would be expected to put such important guiding principles into writing so that all may refer to them. Documents containing these principles may be the culture's holy books or a nation's constitution. The third element is much more problematic because it determines if a country honors its fundamental values in practice as well as in theory. At bottom, law is a set of lifeless statements; it has no life apart from human actors. If the law is to be consistent with justice, it can only be so if the procedures followed by the servants of the law are, and are perceived as being, fair and equal.

The system of procedures to hold the government to its principles is articulated by the concept of **due process**. When we speak about something that is due to us, we usually refer to something that we feel we are rightly entitled to. Due process is procedural justice that is due to all persons whenever they are threatened with the loss of life, liberty, or property at the hands of the state. Due process is essentially a set of instructions informing agents of the state how they must proceed in their investigation, arrest, questioning, prosecution, and punishment of individuals who are suspected of committing crimes. Due process rules attempt to assure that people are treated justly by the state. Unlike distributive justice, due process is not something a person earns by his or her actions; it is something that is due (hence the term) to everyone, without exception, simply because of their humanity.

To appreciate due process and how far we have come in implementing it, it is instructive to examine times when the idea was completely alien. Imagine you are in

France 300 years ago. Soldiers come to your house in the dead of night, batter down your door, arrest you, and lodge you in a filthy dungeon. Furthermore, imagine that you genuinely do not know why this is happening. You try to find out for years while rotting in that dungeon, but no one you ask has the slightest idea. All you and they know is that you are the victim of one of the infamous *lettres de cachet* ("sealed letters"). Purchased from the king, his ministers, or some other high-ranking aristocrat, these letters ordered authorities to seize and imprison anyone who had in any way offended them. And when (or if) you were finally released, there would be nothing you could do about what had happened because it was all perfectly legal under the Code Louis of 1670, which governed France until the implementation of the Code Napoléon in 1804 (Durant & Durant, 1963, p. 16). The Code Louis is a perfect example of a system of positivist law being at odds with justice.

JUSTICE EVOLVING: CESARE BECCARIA AND REFORM

Such injustices found all around Europe did not go unnoticed by many influential thinkers of the period. During the Enlightenment (a historical period typically considered to have begun with the Glorious Revolution in England in 1688 and ended with the French Revolution of 1789), a wave of reform sentiment swept Europe. The man considered most responsible for this sentiment invading the law and the criminal justice system was an Italian nobleman and professor of law named Cesare Bonesana, Marchese di Beccaria. In 1764, Beccaria published what was to become the manifesto for the reform of judicial and penal systems throughout Europe—*Dei Delitti e della Pene (On Crimes and Punishment)*. The book constituted an impassioned plea to humanize and rationalize the law and to make punishment more reasonable. In other words, it was a plea for both substantive and procedural justice.

Beccaria did not question the need for punishment, but he did believe that laws should be designed to preserve public safety and order, not to avenge crime. He also took issue with the practice of secret accusations (*lettres de cachet*) and of keeping the accused ignorant of the charges brought against them, asserting that such practices led to general deceit and alienation in society. He argued that persons should be able to confront their accusers, to know the charges brought against them, and to enjoy the benefit of a speedy public trial before an impartial judge. If guilty, the criminals' punishment should fit the crime (i.e., be proportionate to the harm done to society), should be identical for identical crimes, and should be applied without reference to the social status of either the offender or the victim.

Beccaria also championed the abolition of the death penalty and the cause of mild and merciful punishment (relative to the barbarous practices of the day, for he did approve of various forms of corporal punishment). According to Beccaria, such punishments should only just exceed the level of damage done to society. To ensure a rational and fair penal structure, punishments for specific crimes

Cesare Beccaria

must be decreed by written criminal codes and the unbounded discretionary powers of judges severely curtailed. The judge's task was to determine guilt or innocence and then to impose the legislatively prescribed punishment if the accused was found guilty. Many of the reforms were implemented in Europe during Beccaria's lifetime (Durant & Durant, 1967, p. 321).

Beccaria's greatest influence was on the European continent. As we have seen many of the due process rights of today have been slowly evolving in England since at least the early thirteenth century. Although we discuss due process rights contained in the Fourth, Fifth, Sixth, and Eighth Amendments to the Constitution in their modern American context in much greater detail in chapter 6, here we give brief coverage to their origins.

Due process rights involve everything that was denied to the victims of the *lettres de cachet*: the right to be secure in one's home, to confront one's accuser, to know the charges, to secure counsel, to be tried by a jury of peers, and to be free of excessive bail as well as from cruel and unusual punishment. These rights are guaranteed in the United States by the Bill of Rights. The Bill of Rights did not, of course, arise from nothing; it has a history. As legal historian Bernard Schwartz (1980) put it, "To understand the history of the federal Bill of Rights, one must understand the development of constitutional guarantees of liberty which led up to the 1791 document" (p. 3). The most relevant documents enunciating these guarantees prior to the adoption of the US Bill of Rights in 1791 are the Magna Carta (1215), the Statute of Winchester (1275), the Petition of Right (1628), and the Bill of Rights (1689). The great colonial charters of early America were built on the foundation of these documents and contributed considerably to what was eventually to become the US Bill of Rights as we know it today. The relationship of these documents to the various due process rights is briefly touched on as we discuss the various rights in a criminal justice context.

Note that these various rights have been constantly violated over the centuries by the state and its agents of social control. If they had not been, there would not have been the necessity to continually add to the documents that supposedly guaranteed them for all time. When violations became particularly egregious, however, brave and moral individuals have been able to point to those guarantees to legitimize their complaints and outrage at these violations. Sir Edward Coke (1552–1634) is a major figure in the evolution of common law because of his many writings about such issues as the rule of law and procedural law. Coke (pronounced "Cook") was solicitor general under Elizabeth I and Lord Chief Justice under James I. James dismissed Coke as chief justice and had him imprisoned in the Tower of London for nine months for reminding him once too often that the king was not above the law and that Parliament was not subservient to him. After his release, Coke was elected to Parliament, where he was most influential in clipping the monarchy's wings; James I had died by this time and was succeeded by Charles I. In response to excessive taxation, many people had been imprisoned by Charles. This gravely upset Parliament, which responded by having Coke draft the Petition of Right,

Sir Edward Coke

which asserted the right of habeas corpus and the right to a trial by one's peers, among other things. Although Charles refused to acknowledge the Petition of Right at first, he finally yielded to Parliamentary pressure. Coke was the first person to suggest a series of written procedures for implementing substantive criminal law; thus. he is often called the "father of due process" (Boyer, 2004). But in the final analysis, these revered documents are only as good as the people entrusted with implementing the principles written therein. A firm commitment to the rule of law on the part of the government, coupled with the people's sense of justice and their political empowerment, makes these precious guarantees more secure than they have ever been before.

HERBERT PACKER'S MODELS OF CRIMINAL JUSTICE

In 1964, Professor Herbert Packer wrote an article that has influenced just about everyone who has written about the operation of the criminal justice system since then. Packer's two models of the criminal justice system provide a framework to explore the relationship between the everyday operation of that system and justice itself, and as we will see, equally moral individuals and societies can hold very different conceptions of justice. The major tension between these two models is between an emphasis on justice for an offended community and a focus on justice for those who offend against it. These alternative conceptions of where the emphasis should lay often clash, but out of these clashes sometimes come compromises that elevate standards of justice.

Packer (1964/1997) proposed two "ideal-type" models reflecting different value choices that undergird the operation of the criminal justice system. These two models are the *crime control* and the *due process* models. Ideologically, the crime control model embodies traditional conservative values, and the due process model embodies traditional liberal values.

The Crime Control Model

The **crime control model** emphasizes community protection and argues that civil liberties can only have real meaning in a safe, well-ordered society. To achieve such a society, it is necessary to suppress criminal activity swiftly, efficiently, and with finality. Swiftness and efficiency demand a well-oiled criminal justice system in which cases are handled informally and uniformly in "assembly-line" fashion. Police officers must arrest suspects, prosecutors must prosecute them, and judges must sentence them "uncluttered with ceremonious rituals that do not advance the progress of the case" (Packer, 1964, p. 4). To achieve finality, the appeals must be kept to a minimum. The assumption is that such a process will more efficiently screen out the innocent— and that those who are not may be considered "probably guilty." Packer does not want us to think of a presumption of guilt as the conceptual opposite of the presumption of innocence; the crime control model does not advocate a return to the days of *lettres de cachet*. As Packer puts it, "reduced to its barest essentials and when operating at its most successful pitch," the crime control model consists of two elements: "(a) an administrative fact-finding process leading to the exoneration of the suspect, or to (b) the entry of a plea of guilty" (p. 5).

The Due Process Model

If the crime control model can be likened to an assembly line, the **due process model** can be likened to an obstacle course in which impediments to carrying the accused's case further are encountered at every stage of his or her processing. Police officers must obtain warrants when possible and not interrogate suspects without the suspect's consent; evidence may be suppressed; and various motions may be filed that may free a factually guilty person. These and other obstacles prevent the efficient and speedy processing of cases. Convicted persons may file numerous appeals, and it may take years to gain closure of the case. The due process model is more concerned with the integrity of the legal process than with its efficiency, and with legal rather than with factual guilt. Successful defenses can and have been mounted that have had nothing to do with factual guilt. Factual guilt translates into legal guilt only if the evidence used to determine it was obtained in a procedurally correct fashion. Advocates of the due process model do not place the same degree of trust in agents of the criminal justice system (sometimes with good reason) that crime control advocates do.

Which model do you think best exemplifies the ideals of justice? It is probably correct to say that under a crime control model, more innocent people may be convicted, and that under a due process model, more (factually) guilty people will be set free. In the first instance, the individual has been unjustly victimized, and in the second, the community has been unjustly victimized. Clearly, both models have their faults as well as their strengths. The danger of a runaway crime control model is a return to the days when due process was nonexistent; the danger of a runaway due process model is that truth and justice get lost in a maze of legal ritualism. But these are ideal-type models that do not exist in their extreme form anywhere in the world where which the rule of law is respected. They lie on a continuum, with the United States characterized as operating with a due process model and Canada with more of a crime control model (Ellis & Walsh, 2000). The underlying values of these two common law countries that help to determine where they sit on the criminal justice continuum are exemplified in the objectives of "life, liberty, and the pursuit of happiness" in the American Declaration of Independence and "peace, order, and good government" in Canada's British North America Act. Both countries have respected civil liberties better than most others throughout their histories, but it is fair to say that Canada has been more conservative in its insistence that civil liberties can have meaning only in an orderly society (Hagan & Leon, 1977).

An Illustration of the Models in Action

A series of US Supreme Court cases illustrating the "tinkering" that goes on to modify the excesses that might arise with exclusive use of either model involves an escaped mental patient, Robert Williams, who kidnapped, raped, and murdered a 10-year-old girl, Pamela Powers, on Christmas Eve 1968. Two days after the crime, Williams turned himself in to the police in Davenport, Iowa. Because the crime took place in Des Moines, a detective was dispatched to transport Williams from Davenport. Williams's lawyer secured the detective's agreement not to question Williams during the trip, but the officer was concerned that Pamela's body be found before the snow fell, after which it may not have been discovered until the following spring. The officer engaged Williams in conversation during which the officer made statements, but did not ask questions, about how important it was to the family to find Pamela's body so that they could give her a proper Christian burial. This "Christian burial speech" touched whatever spark of decency remained in Williams, who then directed the detective to the girl's frozen body. On the basis of this evidence, Williams was convicted of murder in 1969.

After going through a series of appeals, the case reached the Supreme Court in 1977 (*Brewer v. Williams,* 1977). The Court overturned Williams's conviction by a 5-4 vote, stating that Williams had not waived his right to counsel during questioning and that the officer's "Christian burial speech" constituted custodial interrogation. It was reasoned that since Williams's confession was obtained in violation of his right to counsel, any evidence obtained on the basis of it (Pamela's body) was inadmissible under the exclusionary rule (we will talk about this more in the next chapter). The majority of the justices were obviously more enamored with legal ritualism than with justice and discounted the mental anguish such a decision would cause Pamela's family. Their blind obedience to legal rules and technicalities remind us of the common law courts in thirteenth-century England. As Chief Justice Warren Burger put it in his strong dissenting opinion, "The result reached by the Court in this case ought to be intolerable in any society which purports to call itself an organized society" (Robin & Anson, 1990, p. 188).

Brewer v. Williams is an example of the excesses of the due process model. However, this case was one of a number involving the boundaries of custodial interrogation from a time when the crime control model ran amok. The most famous of these cases, *Brown v. Mississippi* (1936), involved the alleged murder of a white man by three black men. All three men were sentenced to death on the basis of confessions obtained under torture (they were whipped and told that the whippings would not stop until they confessed). The injustice to the community inherent in the *Brewer* case can be viewed as one of a number of correctives to the injustices suffered by defendants typified in the *Brown* case.

The "golden mean" between the contending views of justice relative to the issue of confessions was probably reached in *Nix v. Williams* (1984), which enunciated the *inevitable discovery* exception to the exclusionary rule. In affirming Williams's 1969 conviction upon retrial, the Court ruled that search parties looking for Pamela's body would have found it by legal means sooner or later, and thus the fact that it was found because of Williams's confession was irrelevant. Thus, almost 16 years after the murder, Pamela's family could finally obtain some closure. We might say that the Court had corrected a corrective, and that this process of tinkering by successive approximations to broad-reaching justice is the best that mere mortals can hope for.

SUMMARY

Aristotle's definition of justice as consisting of treating equals equally and unequals unequally according to relevant differences serves as our conception of justice. In this chapter, we examined distributive justice, which is about the fair distribution of resources. A fair distribution of resources is determined not by what persons need but what they deserve by virtue of their efforts and contributions. Retributive justice is concerned with how a society determines guilt or innocence of accused persons (procedural restitutive justice) and the determination of proper punishment for those found guilty (substantive retributive justice). The latter concern involves punishing with fairness and impartiality according to the amount of damage the defendant has done to the community. Sentencing guidelines, which seek to balance the severity of the crime and the defendant's criminal history, can be viewed as instruments designed to decrease sentencing disparity and thereby make punishments more equitable.

We also addressed the idea of legal realism, a study of law as practiced rather than as written. We saw how legal decision-making is not fully determined by written law but often by judges' subjective interpretations of what is just in a case. Judges may decide the way they are going to rule and then seek justification for their decision in the statutes after the fact.

We then addressed the origins of justice, focusing on the transcendental and evolutionary perspectives. Both perspectives assert the existence of a "natural law" that may be at odds with positivist law and that can be discovered. The transcendental perspective emphasizes the primacy and superiority of the spiritual over the natural. It posits an absolutist system of natural laws that are binding on all persons at all times. These laws are usually considered "God-given" and found in the holy books of the world's religions. The evolutionary perspective views natural law as originating in our evolved human nature. Because humans have acquired a number of deceptive and exploitive traits to achieve goals, we have also developed a set of counterstrategies for detecting and punishing such behavior. The major difference between the two perspectives is that the transcendental perspective views natural law as God-given and a set of absolutes. The evolutionary perspective asserts that natural law evolved to formalize our moral sensibilities, and although universal, it allows exceptions regarding what specific behaviors might evoke them.

In discussing the relationship between law and justice, we noted that only through law can justice be achieved. We began by discussing the role of equity in the evolution of the common law. Separate courts of equity evolved in England in the thirteenth century because the common law had become overly rigid and often at odds with justice. These courts of equity, or Courts of Chancery, were directed to be flexible and to decide cases based on standards of fairness rather than on rigid rules of law. It is important to note that equity supplemented rather than replaced common law, and that both systems benefited from the cross-pollination of ideas over the centuries.

The rule of law is the only way we can reasonably assure that we are integrating important aspects of justice into our legal systems. The rule of law contains three irreducible elements: (a) a nation must recognize the supremacy of certain fundamental values and principles, (b) these values must be committed to writing, and (c) a system of procedures holding the government to these principles and values must be in place. The first two principles are relatively unproblematic, but the third, requiring a nation to honor the first two in practice as well as in theory, is much more problematic. The third principle is best articulated by the concept of due process, which is procedural restitutive justice in practice. Due process is not something one earns by exemplary behavior but rather something that is due to everyone by virtue of their humanity. We contrasted due process with its complete absence under the infamous Code Louis that existed in France from 1670 to 1804, when ordinary people had no rights whatsoever. The efforts of Cesare Beccaria to humanize European law by instituting rules of due process were noted, as were the precursors of the due process rights we enjoy in the United States today under the Bill of Rights.

Herbert Packer's two "ideal-type" models of criminal justice are the *crime control* and *due process* models. The former emphasizes the protection of the community from the criminal, and the latter focuses on the protection of the accused from the state. No modern legal system completely conforms to either of these ideal types. Rather, each system lies on a continuum somewhere between the extremes. Both models can take their positions too far, requiring some legal adjustment. We illustrated this in terms of the crime control model with the torture-confession case of *Brown v. Mississippi* and in terms of the due process model with *Brewer v. Williams*. The excesses of both were eventually righted in subsequent Supreme Court decisions.

DISCUSSION QUESTIONS

1. What do you think Aristotle would say regarding the justice/injustice of race- and gender-based quotas in education and employment? Do you agree or disagree with him?
2. Do you find the tremendous inequalities in wealth and salary structure in our society to be just or unjust? Should salary be based on social usefulness rather than on the market? If so, what would be the economic and social consequences?
3. Do you believe in natural law and natural justice? If so, which of the two positions (transcendental or evolutionary) most convinces you? If you do not believe in either position, from where do you think humans gained their sense of justice?
4. Why is law sometimes at odds with justice? Give an example.
5. Relate the rule of law to Packer's models of criminal justice.
6. Go to the *Brewer v. Williams* case at http://www.law.cornell.edu/supct/html/historics/USSC_CR_0430_0387_ZS.html and read Justice Stewart's majority opinion and Justice White's dissent. Choose one position or the other, and debate the issue in terms of justice as you understand the concept.

CHAPTER TERMS

Courts of Chancery
Crime control model
Distributive justice
Due process
Due process model
Equity

Evolutionary perspective
Justice
Legal realism
Natural law
Naturalist fallacy
Retributive justice

Rule of law
Transcendentalism
Transcendentalist
perspective

References

Abadinsky, H. (2003). *Law and justice: An introduction to the American legal system*. Upper Saddle River, NJ: Prentice Hall.

Boyer, A. (2004). *Law, liberty, and Parliament: Selected essays on the writings of Sir Edward Coke*. Indianapolis, IN: Liberty Fund.

Browne, K. (1997). An evolutionary perspective on sexual harassment: Seeking roots in biology rather than ideology. *Journal of Contemporary Legal Issues, 8*, 5–77.

Caplan, L. (2003). State immunity, human rights, and *jus cogens*: A critique of the normative hierarchy theory. *American Journal of International Law, 97*, 741–781.

Chieveley, Lord Goff. (1997). The future of the common law. *International and Comparative Law Quarterly, 46*, 745–760.

Cosmides, L., & Tooby, J. (2006). Evolutionary psychology, moral heuristics, and the law. In G. Gigerenzer & C. Engel (Eds.), *Heuristics and the law* (pp. 181–212). Cambridge, MA: MIT Press.

Danilenko, G. (2003). International *jus cogens*: Issues of law-making. *European Journal of International Law, 2*, 42–65. Retrieved from http://www.ejil.org/article.php?article=2025&issue=101

Day, F. (1968). *Criminal law and society*. Springfield, IL: Charles C. Thomas.

de Quervain, D., Fischbacher, U., Valerie, T., Schellhammer, M., Schnyder, U., Buch, A., & Fehr, E. (2004). The neural basis of altruistic punishment. *Science, 305*, 1254–1259.

Donnelly, S. (2006). Reflecting on the rule of law: Its reciprocal relations with rights, legitimacy, and other concepts and institutions. *Annals of the American Academy of Political and Social Sciences, 603*, 37–53.

Durant, W., & Durant, A. (1963). *The age of Louis XIV*. New York, NY: Simon & Schuster.

Durant, W., & Durant, A. (1967). *Rousseau and revolution*. New York, NY: Simon & Schuster.

Ellis, L., & Walsh, A. (2000). *Criminology: A global perspective*. Boston, MA: Allyn & Bacon.

Fairchild, E., & Dammer, H. (2001). *Comparative criminal justice systems*. Belmont, CA: Wadsworth.

Fehr, E., & Gachter, S. (2002). Altruistic punishment in humans. *Nature, 415*, 137–140.

Fikentscher, W. (1991). The sense of justice and the concept of cultural justice. *American Behavioral Scientist, 34*, 314–334.

Finkel, N., Harré, R., & Rodriguez Lopez, J. (2001). Commonsense morality across cultures: Notions of fairness, justice, honor and equity. *Discourse Studies, 3*, 5–27.

Finland millionaire gets $216,900 speeding fine. (2004, February 11). *Idaho Statesman*, p. 2.

Friedrich, C. (1963). *The philosophy of law in historical perspective*. Chicago, IL: University of Chicago Press.

Gruter, M. (1991). *Law and the mind: Biological origins of human behavior*. Newbury Park, CA: SAGE.

Hagan, J., & Leon, J. (1977). Philosophy and sociology of crime control: Canadian–American comparisons. *Sociological Inquiry, 47*, 181–208.

Hamilton, A. (2012). The farmer refuted. In Hillsdale College Politics Department (Ed.), *The U.S. Constitution: A reader* (pp. 95–98). Hillsdale, MI: Hillsdale College Press.

Horwitz, H., & Polden, P. (1996). Continuity or change in the Court of Chancery in the seventeenth and eighteenth centuries? *Journal of British Studies, 35*, 24–57.

Jones, O., & Goldsmith, T. (2005). Law and behavioral biology. *Columbia Law Review, 105*, 405–498.

Jordans, F. (2010). Europe slapping the rich with massive traffic fines. Retrieved from https://www.glocktalk.com/threads/europe-slapping-the-rich-with-massive-traffic-fines.1168841/

Kaye, J. (1998). Commentaries on Chancellor Kent. *Chicago-Kent Law Review*. Retrieved from http://www.nycourts.gov/history/legal-history-new-york/luminaries-supreme-court/documents/kaye-on-kent.pdf

Kidder, R. (1983). *Connecting law to society*. Englewood Cliffs, NJ: Prentice Hall.

Leiter, B. (2001). Legal realism and legal positivism reconsidered. *Ethics, 111*, 278–301.

McDowell, G. (1982). *Equity and the Constitution: The Supreme Court, equitable relief, and public policy*. Chicago, IL: University of Chicago Press.

Miles, T., & Sunstein, C. (2008). The new legal realism. *University of Chicago Law Review, 75*, 831–851.

Packer, H. (1997). Two models of the criminal process. In S. Wasserman & C. Snyder (Eds.), *A criminal procedure anthology* (pp. 3–9). Cincinnati, OH: Anderson. (Original work published 1964)

Palermo, E. (2014, May 21). Top CEOs deserve high salaries, researchers say. *Business News Daily*. Retrieved from http://www.businessnewsdaily.com/6453-ceo-pay-is-rising-heres-why.html

Plato. (2000). *Laws*. Edited and translated by B. Jowett. Amherst, NY: Prometheus.

Reichel, P. (2005). *Comparative criminal justice systems: A topical approach* (4th ed.). Upper Saddle River, NJ: Prentice Hall.

Rhode, D. (1992). Letting the law catch up. *Stanford Law Review, 44*, 1259–1265.

Robin, G., & Anson, R. (1990). *Introduction to the criminal justice system* (4th ed.). New York, NY: Harper & Row.

Schwartz, B. (1980). *The roots of the Bill of Rights* (Vol. 1). New York, NY: Chelsea House.

Thomas, H. (1962). *Understanding the great philosophers*. New York, NY: Doubleday.

Tomkins, A., & Oursland, K. (1991). Social and scientific perspectives in judicial interpretations of the Constitution. *Law and Human Behavior, 15*, 101–120.

Upham, F. (2011). Reflections on the rule of law in China. *National Taiwan University Law Review, 6*, 251–267.

Walsh, A. (2000). Evolutionary psychology and the origins of justice. *Justice Quarterly, 17*, 841–864.

Walsh, A. (2006). Evolutionary psychology and criminal behavior. In J. Barkow (Ed.), *Missing the revolution: Darwinism for social scientists* (pp. 225–268). Oxford, England: Oxford University Press.

Walsh, A. & Stohr, M. (2010). Correctional assessment, casework, and counseling (5th ed.) Alexabdria, VA: American Correctional Association,

Wiebe, R. (2004). Expanding the model of human nature underlying self-control theory: Implications of the constructs of self-control and opportunity. *Australian and New Zealand Journal of Criminology, 37*, 64–84.

Wilson, E. (1998). The biological basis of morality. *Atlantic Monthly, 281*, 53–70.

Cases Cited

Brewer v. Williams, 430 U.S. 387 (1977)

Brown v. Mississippi, 297 U.S. 278 (1936)

Bush v. Gore, 531 U.S. 98 (2000)

Lochner v. New York, 198 U.S. 45 (1905)

Muller v. Oregon, 208 U.S. 214 (1908)

Nix v. Williams, 467 U.S. 431 (1984)

Riggs v. Palmer, 115 N.Y. 506 (1889)

CHAPTER 3

MAKING LAW

Dollree Mapp was at home early one spring morning in 1957 when Cleveland, Ohio, police officers stormed into her office without a search warrant. They were looking for a suspect in a recent bombing, but all they found were some pornographic books and pictures. Mapp was charged with possession of obscene materials and convicted despite her protest that the search of her home violated her Fourth Amendment right to be free from "unreasonable" searches and seizures and that the evidence seized during the search should be excluded from trial. The trial and appeals courts denied her claim, noting that the US Supreme Court had previously held, in *Wolf v. Colorado* (1949), that while the Fourth Amendment applied to the states through the due process clause of the Fourteenth Amendment, the remedy for violations of the Fourth Amendment—namely, exclusion of the unlawfully seized evidence—did not apply to the states.

In *Mapp v. Ohio* (1961), however, the US Supreme Court overruled *Wolf v. Colorado* and held that the remedy of the exclusionary rule should in fact be applied to the states, along with the right to be free from unreasonable searches and seizures. The Court admitted this decision meant it was ignoring the principle of stare decisis, which says that prior decisions should govern future decisions and that courts should be consistent in their interpretation of the law. But the Court felt it had to do this because in the decade after *Wolf v. Colorado* was decided, the states had refused to apply other remedies for violations of the Fourth Amendment, thus rendering, for all practical purposes, the protections of that provision of the Bill of Rights meaningless.

INTRODUCTION

We have previously explored why law exists and explained its existence by noting that people need a mechanism for enforcing order and resolving disputes peacefully. Laws are created by a legislature, provide rules to guide conduct, and are a

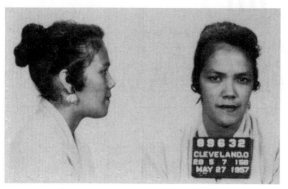

Dollree Mapp

means of resolving disputes and maintaining order through the medium of the courts. In this chapter, we discuss the historical development of the law, focusing on the Anglo-American concepts of the common law (defined later), much of which had been developed in England by the fifteenth century, and the related concepts of precedent, stare decisis, and the role of the judge in creating, interpreting, and applying the law.

The Western legal tradition may be traced to the **Code of Hammurabi**. This is the first known written legal code, and it expressed a retributivist "eye for an eye" philosophy. Roman law, the next major codified set of legal principles, was influenced heavily by Babylonian legal principles in the Code of Hammurabi. The Roman Laws of the Twelve Tables (450 BCE) was the first entirely secular written legal code (the Code of Hammurabi was very much a religious as well as secular code). During this time, law began to change its focus from acting as a mechanism for resolving private disputes to viewing crimes as offenses against society as well as against the victim.

COMMON LAW

The spread of the Roman Empire brought Roman law to Western Europe, but it had minimal impact on English common law. The Norman Conquest of England in 1066 brought feudal law, which provided the basis for the common law, to England. During the following several hundred years, England slowly developed what came to be known as the common law system. After the Norman Conquest, the new rulers established new forms of government, including courts of law. By the reign of Henry II (r. 1154–1189), who is often referred to as the "father of the common law," a body of law had been developed and applied nationally. Decisions were written down, circulated, and summarized. The first systematic attempt to collect and explain these decisions was compiled under the supervision of Henry's Chief Justice Ranulf de Glanvill in a book titled *Treatise on the Laws and Customs of the Realm of England*, which appeared around 1188. This book details the transition from what was essentially the irrational decision-making of pre–Norman England to adherence to formal legal rules (Turner, 1990). The result was a more unified body of law, which came to be known as the **common law** because it was in force throughout the country.

The next important document in the evolution of common law was the **Magna Carta** (or "Great Charter") of 1215. The Magna Carta was a document drawn up by English barons to limit the power of the sovereign (specifically, the notorious King John, who persecuted Robin Hood) and to assert certain rights. Contained in the document are the first dim glimpses of many of the rights we take for granted today, such as the right to trial by jury, proportionality of punishment, and the privilege against self-incrimination. Although King John's acquiescence to the provisions of the charter was a victory for the barons, it meant little at the time for the common person.

Henry de Bracton's *On the Laws and Customs of England,* written between 1250 and 1260, built on Glanvill's work and furthered the "commonality" of common law. Bracton was a high-ranking judge in England who was enamored of the idea that common law was based on case law decided using ancient custom rather than authoritative codes imposed on people from above. The common law was thus judge-made law. That is, it was law created by judges as they heard cases and settled disputes. Judges wrote down their decisions and, in so doing, justified them by reference to custom, tradition, history, and prior judicial decisions. *On the Laws and Customs of England* was essentially a compilation of these judicial rulings made over the previous decades, arranged to show how precedent may guide future rulings. For this reason, Bracton is often referred to as the father of case law (Stramignoni, 2002).

As judges began to rely on previous judgments, they developed the concepts of stare decisis and precedent. Of course, for there to be precedent, there must be prior decisions. At first, judges made decisions without referring to previously decided cases or other courts. They simply heard the case and decided the appropriate outcome based on their understanding of the law as they had learned it through the reading of legal treatises. But as time went by, judges came to rely on prior decisions as a means of justifying their decision in the cases before them.

PRECEDENT AND STARE DECISIS

Under the common law system developed in England, every final decision by a court creates a **precedent**. This precedent governs the court issuing the decision as well as any lower, or inferior, courts. The common law system was brought to America by the early colonists, so many of its principles, including precedent and a belief in stare decisis, remain in force today in American courts. Thus, all courts in a state are bound to follow the decisions of the highest court in that state, usually known as the state supreme court. All courts in the federal court system are bound to follow the decisions of the US Supreme Court. This is the notion of precedent.

Precedent is binding only on those courts within the jurisdiction of the court issuing the opinion. Thus, a decision of the California Supreme Court is not binding on any court in Alabama. Alabama courts are not subject to the jurisdiction or control of California courts and thus are free to interpret the law differently from California courts. However, decisions from courts in other jurisdictions, while not binding, may be persuasive. This simply means that a court may give consideration and weight to the opinion of other courts. Thus, an Alabama court may consider the judgment of an Idaho court, or an American court can consider the judgment of a British, Australian, New Zealand, or any other common law court (although it is quite rare for American courts to consider the rulings of the courts of other countries). Courts may do this when faced with an issue that they have not dealt with before but that other courts have examined.

Stare decisis means "let the decision stand" (Black, 2001). Under the principle of stare decisis, if there is a prior decision on a legal issue that applies to a current case, the court will be guided by that prior decision and apply the same legal principles in the current case. Stare decisis, then, is the principle behind establishing the value of prior decisions, or precedent. It is a principle that assures us that if an issue has been decided one way, it will continue to be decided that way in future cases. Through a reliance on precedent and the principle of stare decisis, common law courts were able to provide litigants with some degree of predictability regarding the courts' decisions.

Precedent establishes a legal principle, but not every pronouncement that a court makes in a ruling establishes precedent. Pronouncements that do are known as *ratio decidendi* ("the reason for the decision"). *Ratio decidendi* is the legal principle, or rationale, used by the courts to arrive at their decisions. Additional supporting statements are called *obiter dicta* ("things said by the way"), or simply **dicta**. These statements are other legal or nonlegal arguments used to support the ratio decidendi and do not constitute precedent.

Precedent is not necessarily unchangeable. Judge-made law may be set aside, or overruled, by an act of the legislature if the constitution permits the legislature to do so. Additionally, the court that issued the precedent may overrule it, or a higher court may reverse the decision of a lower court. If an intermediate-level appeals court decides an issue one way and the losing party appeals to a higher appeals court, such as a state supreme court, that higher court may reverse the decision of the lower court. Higher-level courts are not bound by the judgments of lower courts; they are bound only by the decisions of courts above them in the court structure. Chapter 4 contains a discussion of the federal and state court systems.

Stare decisis, then, involves a respect for and belief in the validity of precedent, and precedent is simply the influence of prior cases on current cases. Understandably, courts are reluctant to reverse decisions they made previously, as this is akin to a tacit admission of error. Courts do so, however, when presented with a compelling justification. Thus, stare decisis is not an inflexible doctrine but merely a general rule. There are always exceptions, as with most areas of the law.

Alternatively, rather than expressly overrule a prior decision, a court may instead seek to *distinguish* the prior case from the present case on grounds that the facts are slightly different. By doing so, the court can avoid overruling a prior decision while coming to what it considers the proper result in the present case. Until a decision is expressly overruled, it stands as an accurate statement of legal principles or "good law."

No history of the evolution of common law is complete without a discussion of English judge and philosopher William Blackstone. For Blackstone, laws were creations of God waiting to be discovered via the use of reason. Blackstone's four-volume *Commentaries on the Laws of England* (1765–1769) was the definitive work on the common law for at least the next century. In these volumes, Blackstone organized the common

William Blackstone

law into four parts: (a) the rights of individuals (procedural law), (b) public wrongs (substantive criminal law), (c) private wrongs (torts), and (d) property rights (law of contracts).

Blackstone had a tremendous influence on the Founding Fathers and on the philosophy behind the Declaration of Independence. The rights of Englishmen, indictment of the Crown, the prohibition of taxation without representation, and natural law phases such as "self-evident" and "unalienable rights"—all were from Blackstone (Bailey, 1997). Blackstone's works were so influential in the shaping of the United States that the American historian Daniel Bernstein commented, "No other book except the Bible played a greater role in the history of American institutions" (Bailey, 2006, p. 5).

SOURCES OF LAW

There are several primary sources of law. These include judge-made law (the common law) and legislative law (the Constitution, statutes, ordinances, and administrative regulations). Other sources for what constitutes appropriate conduct, such as religion and ethics, were discussed in chapter 1. The focus here, however, is on the forms of the law. Note from Figure 3.1 that the US Constitution sits above and governs all lawmaking beneath it. The Constitution overrides a statute if the two are in conflict.

Legislation is enacted by the legislature under the authority granted to it by the Constitution. A constitution creates a government—it literally *constitutes* the government. Legislatures are given authority to act in certain areas, and within these areas, they may pass legislative enactments or bills, often referred to as statutes, which are collected into codes, such as the penal code.

Legislators, sometimes referred to as lawmakers, quite literally make law. Acts of the legislature are not, however, lawful per se. In other words, just because a legislature passes a bill does not mean the bill is a lawful exercise of the legislature's authority. Acts of the legislature may not limit the constitution under which the legislation was created. For instance, the US Congress may not lawfully pass legislation that abridges the Fourth Amendment.

Figure 3.1 The Sources and Types of Law

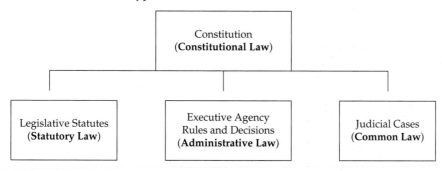

Figure provided by Professor Michael Bogner, Justice Studies Department, Chadron State College (2006).

Who decides when the legislature has acted beyond the scope of its authority? In the United States, the Supreme Court has the final say as to the constitutionality of statutes passed by either state or federal legislatures. This is known as the power of judicial review and is discussed in greater detail later in this chapter.

Administrative regulations are another form of legislation that under certain circumstances may have the force of law. This means that they will be enforced by the courts just like a statute. Administrative regulations are issued either by agencies of the executive branch, which derive their authority from a delegation of power by the executive branch, or by independent agencies created through a delegation of power from the legislature. Examples include regulations affecting food and drugs and occupational safety requirements. Both the federal government and state governments issue administrative regulations. Administrative law is discussed in more detail in chapter 7.

Statutes are frequently written broadly, leaving administrative agencies with the task of filling in the blanks. For instance, a statute may prohibit the sale of margarine but leave the definition of what constitutes margarine unclear (a Supreme Court case in the 1930s actually dealt in part with this issue!). Agencies are empowered to do this through the delegation of authority to them by the executive or legislative branch. Common examples include the Department of Health and Human Services and the Department of Veterans Affairs. Violation of an administrative regulation generally is not treated as a crime but rather as a civil violation (see chapter 7). Like broadly written statutes, the US Constitution leaves much room for interpretation. For example, the Fourth Amendment prohibits "unreasonable searches and seizures." But what is unreasonable? What constitutes a search or a seizure? There are no easy answers to these questions, and the US Supreme Court has struggled to define the terms, as we will see in chapter 6.

Why are statutes ambiguous? Why does the legislature not write more clearly and explain exactly what it means? First, it is difficult to define, in a few sentences, something involving human conduct—there is an almost infinite range of possible actions by individuals. Second, legislators are politicians, and politics involves compromise. Thus, a statute may be written so that it appeals to the greatest possible number of legislators, but in doing this, the language of the statute may be watered down and made less, rather than more, precise. This is particularly likely when dealing with controversial issues. Politicians may decide to leave it to the courts to define more clearly the terms of a statute. While judges in some jurisdictions hold office for life and cannot be removed simply for declaring legislation void, in many states judges are elected and thus are subject to removal if the electorate does not approve of their interpretation of legislation.

SOURCES OF INDIVIDUAL RIGHTS

There are several sources of individual rights in the United States. These include federal and state constitutions, case law, court rules, and legislation. Individual rights are those possessed by the individual, which protect him or her from others as well as from the government. Examples include freedom of speech, freedom of religion, and the right to counsel. The US Constitution, particularly the Bill of Rights, is the primary source of individual rights. While states are free to provide more individual rights than the Constitution does, neither Congress nor a state may enact a law that abridges a federal constitutional right. This is because the Constitution is paramount; it is the supreme law of the United States.

THE CONSTITUTION

The Continental Congress (the colonists' first attempt to form a unified national government) was formed through the adoption of a document called the **Articles of Confederation** in 1781. This attempt was a failure, in large part because the national government created by the Articles of Confederation lacked the ability to require states to work together for the common good. It lacked the authority to tax, to raise an army, or to force the states to comply with any mandate. The states were more akin to countries, acting in their own self-interest, than states that were part of a union. The first president of the Continental Congress, John Hanson, held the title of "President of the United States" yet was little more than a chairperson, and he is now essentially a footnote to history.

In 1787, the Continental Congress invited delegates from the 13 original states (Rhode Island declined to attend) to meet in Philadelphia and write a new constitution to replace its Articles of Confederation. If the national governing body's lack of power was to be rectified and a truly *United* States realized, the delegates knew that the new nation would need a strong central government. Supporters of a strong centralized government were called Federalists, and supporters of a weak central government were called Antifederalists or "states rightists."

The result of the convention in Philadelphia was the creation of the US Constitution. The Constitution is different from ordinary legislation in that it is primarily concerned with establishing the powers of the federal government, both between the branches of government and between the government and the individual citizen (Amar, 1998). The Constitution itself contains few protections of individual rights. The only individual rights mentioned in the Constitution are the right to seek a writ of habeas corpus (a document challenging the legality of a person's detention), the prohibition on bills of attainder (legislation imposing punishment without trial), and the prohibition on ex post facto laws (legislation making prior conduct criminal). These are discussed more fully in chapter 5.

When the Constitution was submitted to the states for ratification, several states were reluctant to approve it without specific protections of individual rights. In response to these concerns, the **Bill of Rights** was added. These provisions were initially drawn up by James Madison. His proposals were condensed into the 10 amendments we know today. With the addition of these amendments, the Constitution

James Madison

was ratified by the original 13 states in 1791. The complete texts of the Constitution and the Bill of Rights are provided in Appendix A.

THE BILL OF RIGHTS

The first eight amendments in the Bill of Rights set out 23 individual rights. These rights include protections against government action of all kinds and originally were intended to apply only to actions by the federal government. As mentioned, the Bill of Rights was added to reduce the apprehension of states' rights supporters who feared a strong central government would infringe on the rights of citizens of the states (Anastaplo, 1995). Not until the twentieth century were the provisions of the Bill of Rights applied to actions of state governments through a process referred to as incorporation, which is discussed later in the chapter after an examination of the most significant provisions of the Bill of Rights, beginning with the first amendment. (See Table 3.1.)

First Amendment

Congress shall make no law respecting an establishment of religion, or prohibiting the free exercise thereof; or abridging the freedom of speech, or of the press; or the right of the people peaceably to assemble, and to petition the Government for a redress of grievances.

The First Amendment covers the freedoms of religion, speech, press, and assembly. It is not surprising that the first provision of the Bill of Rights deals with these topics. Freedom of speech and the press as well as the freedom to assemble peacefully were all issues of great concern for the colonists prior to the American Revolution, and religion had been a primary force in the settling of America and held a central position in people's lives in England during the 1500s and 1600s. Many bloody conflicts were waged over which religion should be the official religion of England. The colonists sought both to avoid such conflicts and to avoid persecution for their own religious beliefs. A number of colonies had their own established or quasi-established religion (Feldman, 2005), and they believed that if their particular colony's religion could not be established as the official religion of the whole nation, then it was best not to have any religion established as the nation's official religion.

With respect to religion, there are two guarantees in the First Amendment: the government shall not establish an official, state-supported religion, nor shall the government interfere with individuals' religious practices. The essence of these two clauses is that the government is not to be in the business of either promoting or destroying religion. Whereas the state was heavily involved in religion in England, the founding fathers wanted the US government to stay out of the religion issue entirely (Anastaplo, 1995).

The first guarantee is often referred to as the **establishment clause**. This creates what the Supreme Court has referred to as a "wall of separation between

Table 3.1 *Constitutional Rights*

Constitutional Article or Amendment	Rights
Article I, Section 9	Habeas corpus, no bills of attainder, no ex post facto laws
First Amendment	Freedom of speech, press, and assembly; freedom of and from religion
Second Amendment	Right to bear arms
Third Amendment	Freedom from quartering soldiers
Fourth Amendment	Freedom from unreasonable searches and seizures; warrants must be based on probable cause and stated with specificity
Fifth Amendment	Grand jury indictment; freedom from double jeopardy and self-incrimination; rights to face accusers, to due process, and to just compensation for takings
Sixth Amendment	Rights to speedy trial, to impartial jury, to be informed of charges, to obtain witnesses on one's behalf, and to an attorney
Eighth Amendment	Freedom from excessive bail or fines and from cruel and unusual punishment
Ninth Amendment	Listing of rights in the Bill of Rights does not imply the absence of other rights (e.g., the right to privacy)
Thirteenth Amendment	Freedom from slavery
Fourteenth Amendment	Right to citizenship of native-born people, to equal protection of the law, to be free of laws that abridge the privileges and immunities of citizens, and to due process from the states (rather than the federal government)
Fifteenth Amendment	Right to vote regardless of race
Seventeenth Amendment	Right to vote for senators
Nineteenth Amendment	Right to vote regardless of gender
Twenty-Sixth Amendment	Right to vote by persons 18 years old or older

church and state" (*Everson v. Board of Education*, 1947). This does not mean the government cannot be involved in religion to some degree, but the Court has stated that any statute affecting religion is valid only if three conditions are met: (a) the statute must have a secular (nonreligious) purpose, (b) the primary purpose of the statute must be neither pro- nor anti-religion, and (c) the statute must not foster "excessive" government entanglement with religion (*Lemon v. Kurtzman*, 1971).

This does not mean the freedom to worship is absolute. Valid government regulations, which incidentally restrict religious practices, are permitted. For example, a state may ban polygamy under its authority to enact health and safety regulations, even though this at one time imposed a restriction on the religious practices of some Mormon sects, or it can forbid the use of mind-altering substances in prisons, notwithstanding that by doing so it may infringe on religious practices of some Native American inmates.

The freedom of speech is one of the most treasured rights possessed by Americans. This right has been accorded great, but not total, weight by the Supreme Court. Thus, the Court has held that the freedom of speech in some instances includes the right to say things that may anger others, including so-called hate speech, or speech directed at minority groups. The Court also has held that the freedom of speech includes not just verbal statements but written statements and some physical acts. These physical acts, when intended to make a point, are referred to as "symbolic speech" or "expressive conduct." Examples include signs, picketing, and the burning of the American flag to protest government conduct (*Texas v. Johnson*, 1989).

Freedom of speech is not absolute, however. The Supreme Court has held that the government can regulate obscenity (*Miller v. California*, 1973), and that speech that is likely to provoke a violent response is referred to as "fighting words" (*Chaplinsky v. New Hampshire*, 1942). Commercial speech (advertising, song lyrics, books and magazines, and so forth) may be regulated to a greater degree than so-called "political" speech (*Virginia State Board of Pharmacy v. Virginia Citizens Consumers Council, Inc.*, 1976). In general, however, the Supreme Court looks with disfavor on attempts to curb any kind of speech. Instead, it has repeatedly endorsed the view of Justice Oliver Wendell Holmes that society is improved by permitting a "free marketplace of ideas."

In a very real sense, the First Amendment forms the nucleus of the other rights found in the Bill of Rights. The Framers went beyond their English ancestors in drafting the American Bill of Rights in the areas of freedom of religion, speech, and the press. Although virtually everything in the Bill of Rights having to do with criminal justice was taken from the various English documents discussed in chapter 2, there was nothing analogous to these three freedoms contained in them.

Second Amendment

> *A well regulated Militia, being necessary to the security of a free State, the right of the people to keep and bear Arms, shall not be infringed.*

The Second Amendment provides citizens with the right to "keep and bear arms" and states that this right shall not be "infringed." The right to bear arms was one of only two "individual" rights (the other was the right to petition) contained in the English Bill of Rights that the Framers took as their guideline for crafting the American Bill of Rights. Opponents of gun control legislation use this amendment as support for their claim that the state may not limit the use and possession of firearms (Kates, 1983; Williams, 1991).

The history behind this amendment suggests it was intended, at least in part, not to allow individuals to possess any weapons they wanted as protection against other individuals but to allow the states and groups of citizens (a militia) to have weapons to protect themselves against oppression by the federal government (Levinson, 1989).

When the Bill of Rights was passed, there was great concern that the federal government might become oppressive, and allowing states to form militias would not be of much use if the federal government had outlawed weapons. At the time, there were no public stores of weapons, so if the federal government were to prohibit private ownership, states would be unable to fight back, as their citizens all would be unarmed to some degree.

In 2008, in *District of Columbia v. Heller*, the Supreme Court held that the Second Amendment protects the rights of *individual* gun owners and is not just a right of states or the people to create and arm militias. The case arose after the District of Columbia, in response to a tremendous amount of gun violence, enacted what its supporters acknowledged was the strictest gun control law in the country. It placed stringent restrictions on the ownership of firearms, including requiring persons who lawfully owned guns to keep those guns unloaded and disassembled or locked in their homes. Dick Heller and several others brought suit, claiming the law violated their Second Amendment right to bear arms.

Justice Antonin Scalia, writing for a narrow 5-4 majority, asserted that the opening clause of the Second Amendment referring to the need of militias to be armed was merely one of the reasons for an individual right to bear arms. Justice Scalia focused a portion of his opinion on the role of handguns in self-defense, suggesting that self-defense was a fundamental right as well. The decision raised more questions than it answered, however. It will take further litigation to determine just what the decision means for state efforts to regulate the purchase of firearms and handguns and for firearm registration policies. The decision appears to allow regulation but sets no standard for evaluating that regulation. Justice Scalia said the decision is not meant to cast doubt on the constitutionality of laws prohibiting gun ownership by felons or the possession of firearms in sensitive areas such as schools.

Third Amendment

> *No Soldier shall, in time of peace be quartered in any house, without the consent of the Owner, nor in time of war, but in a manner to be prescribed by law.*

The Third Amendment was a product of its times. Prior to and during the American Revolution, English troops sometimes were housed in the homes of private citizens against the wishes of the homes' owners. The Third Amendment makes such a practice unconstitutional by expressly forbidding the quartering of soldiers in private homes against the wishes of the owner at any time. A similar clause prohibiting the billeting of soldiers and sailors is contained in the English Petition of Right of 1628.

Fourth Amendment

> *The right of the people to be secure in their persons, houses, papers, and effects, against unreasonable searches and seizures, shall not be violated, and no Warrants shall issue, but upon probable cause, supported by Oath or affirmation, and particularly describing the place to be searched, and the persons or things to be seized.*

The Fourth Amendment is the provision of the Constitution that stands most directly between the individual citizen and the police. This amendment forbids "unreasonable" searches and seizures and requires the existence of "probable cause" before warrants may be issued or a search or seizure may take place. Warrants are required to describe the subject of their search with "particularity." The particularity requirement was a response to the British practice in colonial times of issuing general warrants, which allowed British customs inspectors to search for virtually anything, anywhere, at any time (Cuddihy, 1990). The colonists (especially those engaged in smuggling) found this practice most distressing, and it was one of the prime precipitating factors in the American Revolution.

Requiring probable cause to search or seize was the Founding Fathers' attempt to limit the ability of the police to interfere at will in the lives of individual citizens. Instead, the police must have some reasonable amount of evidence that the person has engaged in criminal activity. We refer to this degree of proof as **probable cause**, which means a fair probability that a crime has occurred. Probably cause is less than proof beyond a reasonable doubt but more than a simple hunch.

The Fourth Amendment does not forbid all searches and seizures but rather requires they be reasonable. The obvious question, then, is what is reasonable? Courts have struggled mightily to define this phrase, and much of the law of criminal procedure is devoted to its explication. Criminal procedure is discussed in detail in chapter 6.

Fifth Amendment

> *No person shall be held to answer for a capital, or otherwise infamous crime, unless on a presentment or indictment of a Grand Jury, except in cases arising in the land or naval forces, or in the Militia, when in actual service in time of War or public danger; nor shall any person be subject for the same offence to be twice put in jeopardy of life or limb; nor shall be compelled in any criminal case to be a witness against himself, nor be deprived of life, liberty, or property, without due process of law; nor shall private property be taken for public use, without just compensation.*

The Fifth Amendment provides a number of protections for individual citizens. These include the right to an indictment by a grand jury, freedom from double jeopardy, the right to due process and just compensation, and the privilege against self-incrimination. These rights are all associated with the criminal trial. Many of the provisions of the Fifth Amendment were born out of reaction to practices in Europe during the Middle Ages. The Star Chamber (a notorious and oppressive court in England that was characterized by secrecy and torture, devoted to obtaining self-incrimination by confession, and abolished by Parliament in 1641) and the Spanish Inquisition are examples of intrusive activities by governments during this time, when arrested individuals had few rights and torture and forced confessions were common. Such practices made their way to American shores as well, as evidenced by the Salem witch trials.

The Fifth Amendment requires that a person be indicted by a grand jury before he or she may be tried on a criminal charge. A **grand jury** is a group of citizens, selected in a fashion similar to a **petit** (trial) **jury**, who listen to the case presented by a

---

ISSUE HIGHLIGHT

The Police and the Fourth Amendment

The Fourth Amendment governs law enforcement searches and seizures. It does not prohibit all searches and seizures, however—it prohibits only those that are "unreasonable." That seems like a pretty reasonable (pun intended!) distinction, right? But if the police are not allowed to conduct unreasonable searches and seizures, how do we determine *what* is unreasonable? And *who* gets to decide? And what do we *do* if a search or seizure is found to be unreasonable? The Fourth Amendment, like much of the Bill of Rights, answers one question. but the answer leads to further questions. As you will see in future chapters, the answers to these questions remain hotly debated today. For example:

1. *What* constitutes an unreasonable search or seizure? The US Supreme Court has held, at different times in its history, that only those searches/seizures that violate a person's property rights can be unreasonable. More recently, the Court has held that for a search/seizure to be unreasonable, the suspect's "reasonable expectation of privacy" must have been violated (and then, of course, "reasonable expectation of privacy" has to be defined).

2. *Who* gets to decide if a search or seizure is unreasonable? The US Supreme Court, thanks to its decision in *Marbury v. Madison* (1803), has the final say in determining the meaning of the Constitution and its amendments, including the provisions of the Bill of Rights. Over the years, however, critics have argued that the police, or the legislature, or the executive (governor or president) should have the final say.

3. If a search or seizure is found to be unreasonable, what do we *do* about it? The US Supreme Court adopted the exclusionary rule in *Weeks v. United States* (1914) and *Mapp v. Ohio* (1961). Under this approach, evidence seized in violation of the Fourth Amendment is excluded from a criminal trial—it cannot be used to prove the defendant's guilt. Many countries do not use the exclusionary rule and instead allow the evidence to be admitted and find other ways to punish police misconduct. The US Supreme Court in recent years has been reluctant to apply the exclusionary rule and has suggested, in multiple cases, that a better approach might be to punish officers administratively, or to allow lawsuits by suspects who have had their Fourth Amendment rights violated. This remains a contentious issue in criminal procedure.

---

prosecutor and determine whether there is sufficient evidence to bind the defendant over for trial. The purpose of the grand jury is to ensure the government does not prosecute individuals without some proof of guilt. Thus, the grand jury is meant to serve as a check on the power of the government and as a barrier between the individual citizen and the government.

An **indictment** is a document formally charging the defendant with a crime and is handed down by a grand jury after hearing the evidence presented by the prosecutor. The requirement of an indictment before criminal prosecution is one of a handful of provisions in the Bill of Rights that has not been incorporated into the Fourteenth Amendment and applied to the states. In *Hurtado v. California* (1884), the Supreme Court expressly held that the right does not apply to state criminal trials, and this decision has never been overruled. Nonetheless, a number of states either require indictment by statute or state constitutional provision or provide prosecutors with the choice of seeking an indictment or proceeding through an information. A substitute for an indictment, an **information** is a document filed directly with the court by the prosecutor, thus bypassing the grand jury.

The Fifth Amendment also prohibits placing someone in **double jeopardy**. This means a jurisdiction may not (a) prosecute someone again for the same crime after the person has been acquitted, (b) prosecute someone again for the same crime after the person has been convicted, and (c) punish someone twice for the same offense. This does not mean a state may not try someone again if the first trial ends in a mistrial or a hung jury. A mistrial may be declared if a legal error that unfairly prejudices the defendant occurs during a trial. The trial is then thrown out, and a new one is held at a later date. A hung jury occurs when the trial jury is unable to reach a unanimous verdict in a case that requires unanimity. Not all jurisdictions require a unanimous verdict in civil or criminal cases. In those states where the verdict must be unanimous, however, if the jury is deadlocked and the judge believes that further deliberations would be pointless, he or she may excuse the jury and order a new trial. This is similar to a declaration of mistrial. In these situations, there has been neither an acquittal nor a conviction. An acquittal occurs when a jury votes unanimously that the defendant has not been proven guilty "beyond a reasonable doubt," which is the burden of proof in a criminal case. An acquittal, or "not guilty" verdict, does not necessarily mean that the defendant did not commit the crime for which he or she was charged; it simply means that the state was unable to meet the high burden of proof necessary for conviction. Additionally, if a conviction is overturned on appeal, the state may retry the person, as the reversal on appeal is not an acquittal but merely an acknowledgement that the trial was not fair and must be redone.

While the double jeopardy clause bars multiple punishments for the same offense, there are exceptions. Under the **dual sovereignty doctrine**, a person can be prosecuted in both federal and state court for the same offense, or in the courts of different states for the same offense if certain circumstances surrounding the offense occurred in more than one state. An example of this might be a person who is kidnapped in Ohio but then taken to Michigan. In this case, the offender can be tried for kidnapping in both Ohio and Michigan, as the offense occurred in both states. Double jeopardy does not apply in these situations because a different sovereign, or jurisdiction, is prosecuting the person. However, a person may not be tried for the same crime in both a municipal court and a state court, as these two courts derive their authority from the same source—the same state constitution.

The Fifth Amendment also protects individuals from being forced to incriminate themselves. The **privilege against self-incrimination**, so familiar to those who have watched television shows and seen police officers read *Miranda* warnings to suspects, is a right we often take for granted today but that did not exist in early common law. The privilege allows a defendant to refuse to speak to police about the crime charged and to refuse to testify at trial. Furthermore, the prosecution is barred from commenting on a defendant's refusal to testify, as the Supreme Court has determined that doing so would limit the privilege against self-incrimination by suggesting that asserting a constitutional right was somehow evidence of something to hide (*Griffin v. California*, 1965).

The privilege against self-incrimination is not total, however. The Supreme Court has held that the privilege protects a person from compelled testimonial communications, which is a fancy legal phrase meaning "spoken admissions" (*Malloy v. Hogan*, 1964). The privilege does not apply to the obtaining of evidence from a suspect by other means, such as taking blood samples, fingerprints, or requiring his or her presence in a lineup.

The Fifth Amendment also provides for due process of law. Exactly what constitutes due process of law, however, is much debated. Essentially, due process means the state must follow certain procedures, designed to protect individual rights, before they deprive an individual of his or her liberty or property.

The "taking clause" of the Fifth Amendment involves the circumstances in which the state or federal governments can seize private property for public use under the principle of eminent domain. "Public use" is usually thought of in terms of building needed roads, bridges, and parks, which are literally for the use of the public. In a classic conservative–liberal issue, state and local governments across the country have been seizing private property (with just compensation) and selling it to private developers for nominal sums. Conservatives see this as violation of sacred property rights, and liberals see it as a justifiable use of government power to fit a broader definition of "public use." Liberals believe private development of seized land increases property values and provides work, both of which increases a government's tax revenues and therefore can be considered a public benefit. The most famous of such cases decided by the Supreme Court is *Kelo v. City of New London* (2005), in which the Court ruled in favor of New London's right to condemn homes in a 90-acre, blue-collar neighborhood and sell the land to a private developer for a building that would provide jobs and help revitalize the area.

Sixth Amendment

> *In all criminal prosecutions, the accused shall enjoy the right to a speedy and public trial, by an impartial jury of the State and district wherein the crime shall have been committed, which district shall have been previously ascertained by law, and to be informed of the nature and cause of the accusation; to be confronted with the witnesses against him; to have compulsory process for obtaining witnesses in his favor, and to have the Assistance of Counsel for his defence.*

The Sixth Amendment, like the Fifth Amendment, contains a laundry list of rights. These rights are associated with the criminal trial and include the right to a speedy trial, the right to a public trial, the right to a trial by an impartial jury, the right to notice of the charges against oneself, the right to representation by counsel, and the right to confront the witnesses against oneself.

The right to a speedy trial means that the defendant must be brought to trial without "unnecessary delay" (*Barker v. Wingo*, 1972). In the Barker case, there was a five-year delay between Willie Barker's indictment and trial. A five-year delay is hardly "speedy," but in upholding his conviction, the Supreme Court ruled that "speedy" is determined on "an ad hoc balancing basis, in which the conduct of the prosecution and that of the defendant are weighed." In other words, there is no inflexible rule defining "unnecessary delay." A whole host of factors, such as the reason for the delay and its length, must be considered on a case-by-case basis. In Barker's case, the Court essentially said that five years was not excessive because Barker had not actually asked for a speedy trial!

In response to the concerns of civil libertarians following the *Barker* decision, the US Congress passed the Speedy Trial Act of 1974, which set a specific time limit of 100 days from arrest to trial. This act applies only to federal cases, but most states have enacted similar legislation. However, considerable "wriggle room" still exists, and if push comes to shove, states can always fall back on the less stringent constitutional law provided by *Barker* that trumps statutory law.

The right to a public trial means that defendants have a right to have the public attend the trial if they so wish. The right to notice of the charges against the defendant simply means the prosecution must inform the defendant prior to trial what it is he or she is accused of so that a defense may be prepared. This can occur through the filing of an information or the handing down of an indictment by the grand jury. Both these rights emanate from the traditional Anglo-Saxon distrust of secrecy in government as a menace to liberty (again, think of the Code Louis, *lettres de cachet*, the Star Chamber, and the Spanish Inquisition).

The right to a trial by an impartial jury means the right to a jury, selected from the community where the crime occurred, that is not predisposed to believe the defendant is guilty. In other words, the members of the jury may be aware of the events that led to the trial, but they must not have formed an opinion as to the guilt (or innocence) of the accused: this is the presumption of innocence so valued by common law legal tradition. Trial by jury is an ancient right, mentioned in the Assize of Clarendon (1166) and affirmed in the Magna Carta (1215; Anastaplo, 1995).

The Sixth Amendment also provides for the assistance of counsel. The Supreme Court has interpreted this to include the right to assistance of counsel at any proceeding deemed to be a "critical stage" in the fact-finding process prior to trial, not only at the actual trial (*Kirby v. Illinois*, 1972). Precisely what constitutes a critical stage is subject to some dispute, but it includes the preliminary hearing, the arraignment, the trial itself, and the right of appeal.

The Supreme Court also has determined that the right to counsel means indigent persons who cannot afford to hire a lawyer must be provided one at the state's expense, so long as the defendant faces the possibility of incarceration for six months or more. Additionally, the Court has held that the right to counsel includes the right to the *effective* assistance of counsel (*Strickland v. Washington*, 1984).

The right to counsel was first recognized in the Statute of Merton in 1236. Of course, this right was not nearly as useful to the accused then as it is today. At the time, accused persons were permitted to have relatives or friends counsel them, and free men had the right to an attorney (such as there were in those days) unless charged with a felony or with treason.

Seventh Amendment

> *In Suits at common law, where the value in controversy shall exceed twenty dollars, the right of trial by jury shall be preserved, and no fact tried by a jury, shall be otherwise re-examined in any Court of the United States, than according to the rules of the common law.*

The Seventh Amendment provides for the right to a trial by jury in federal civil trials. This amendment applies only to federal trials; it has not been incorporated into the Fourteenth Amendment by the Supreme Court.

Eighth Amendment

> *Excessive bail shall not be required, nor excessive fines imposed, nor cruel and unusual punishments inflicted.*

The Eighth Amendment prohibits several things, including excessive bail and cruel and unusual punishment. Both of these prohibitions are written broadly, and the courts have struggled with interpreting them.

For example, the prohibition on excessive bail does not expressly state that bail must be set in all cases—it just says bail cannot be excessive. What constitutes excessive bail varies widely, but according to the Supreme Court, it is bail set at a figure higher than necessary to ensure the presence of the defendant at trial (*Stack v. Boyle*, 1951). While the Eighth Amendment does not clearly provide for a right to bail, such a right existed in common law and has been codified in state statutes. Bail does not have to be granted, and the Court has ruled that a person considered to be a threat to public safety may be denied bail (*United States v. Salerno*, 1987).

The prohibition on cruel and unusual punishment limits the type and form of punishment imposed by a state or the federal government after conviction of a crime. It prohibits torture as well as punishment that is disproportionate to the offense. The cruel and unusual punishment clause does not prohibit the death penalty, as it is deemed to be in accord with contemporary standards of decency and as the death penalty existed at the time of the passage of the Eighth Amendment.

Ninth Amendment

> *The enumeration in the Constitution, of certain rights, shall not be construed to deny or disparage others retained by the people.*

The Ninth Amendment simply states that the listing of some rights in the Constitution should not be construed as a listing of all the rights retained by individual citizens. In other words, the rights provided in the Bill of Rights should not be taken as the *only* rights that citizens have—they are merely *some* of the rights retained by the people (Massey, 1995). This is similar to the natural law or natural rights approach discussed in chapter 2.

The obvious question is, of course, that if the Bill of Rights is not all inclusive, what exactly are the other rights retained by the people? The Supreme Court has struggled to provide a framework for delineating these rights, as the discussion on incorporation that follows indicates.

In at least one case, the Supreme Court expressly mentioned the Ninth Amendment as providing a basis for giving individual citizens other, unenumerated rights, such as a right to privacy (*Griswold v. Connecticut*, 1965). Estelle Griswold was the director of the Planned Parenthood League of Connecticut, and she and the league's medical director had been found guilty of dispensing birth control advice and devices (both then illegal in Connecticut), for which they were fined $100 each. In overturning their conviction, the Court affirmed that the right to privacy is very important while also acknowledging that it is not specifically mentioned anywhere in the Constitution. In their ruling, the Justices discussed an old English case (*Entick v. Carrington*, 1765) in which the British High Court's opinion rested heavily on a "natural" right to privacy. Justice William Douglas, who delivered the Court's majority opinion in *Griswold*, stated that the specific constitutional guarantees of the Bill of Rights "have penumbras [incompletely lighted areas] formed by emanations from these guarantees that help give them life and substance." In other words, although the right to privacy is not specifically mentioned in the Constitution, such a right can be logically deduced from the rights that are. *Griswold* was a very important step to *Roe v. Wade* (1973), which granted abortion rights to women under the principle of privacy, and to *Lawrence v. Texas* (2003), which outlawed sodomy statutes under the same principle. Thus, the Ninth Amendment has more social importance than it is often given credit for.

Tenth Amendment

> *The powers not delegated to the United States by the Constitution, nor prohibited by it to the States, are reserved to the States respectively, or to the people.*

The Tenth Amendment has been largely ignored by the Supreme Court. It simply states that the rights not delegated to the federal government by the Constitution are reserved for the states or individual citizens. This is simply the principle of federalism and constitutionalism; the federal government is a government of enumerated powers. This means it has no authority unless so granted by the Constitution, and where the federal government has no authority, the states and individual citizens retain the authority.

OTHER AMENDMENTS

In addition to the individual rights enumerated in the Bill of Rights, several other, later constitutional amendments directly implicate individual rights. For example, the Reconstruction Amendments, passed shortly after the Civil War, were intended to protect the recently freed slaves from abuse at the hands of state governments. The Reconstruction Amendments include the Thirteenth, Fourteenth, and Fifteenth Amendments. While initially intended to prevent the southern states from limiting the rights of the recently freed slaves, today these amendments, particularly the Fourteenth Amendment, are used to protect all citizens from state actions that impinge on constitutional rights.

Thirteenth Amendment

> *Neither slavery nor involuntary servitude, except as a punishment for crime whereof the party shall have been duly convicted, shall exist within the United States, or any place subject to their jurisdiction. Congress shall have power to enforce this article by appropriate legislation.*

The Thirteenth Amendment prohibits slavery in the United States. Since its enactment, it also has been used to uphold civil rights legislation passed by Congress to prevent racial discrimination by private citizens. Where other amendments prohibit discrimination by state governments, there is no such limiting language in the Thirteenth Amendment. Courts have interpreted it as not merely outlawing slavery but forbidding so-called "badges of slavery," or practices intended to keep blacks at lower social and economic levels than whites (Tribe, 1988).

Fourteenth Amendment

All persons born or naturalized in the United States, and subject to the jurisdiction thereof, are citizens of the United States and of the State wherein they reside. No State shall make or enforce any law which shall abridge the privileges or immunities of citizens of the United States; nor shall any State deprive any person of life, liberty, or property, without due process of law; nor deny to any person within its jurisdiction the equal protection of the laws.

The Fourteenth Amendment is very long, containing five sections. Here, we include only the first section, which has to do with individual rights. This is an important amendment because it is the first that specifically forbids states from mistreating their citizens. Although the Bill of Rights was intended to apply only to actions of the federal government, after the Civil War congressional leaders realized that individual states were just as capable of oppressing individual citizens as was the federal government (Klarman, 2004). They responded by enacting the Fourteenth Amendment, which forbids states from denying citizens due process of law or equal protection of the law. These two clauses have dramatically altered the way that states deal with citizens. (The privileges and immunities clause is discussed later in the chapter.)

The **due process clause** is identical to the clause in the Fifth Amendment, except that it applies to the actions of state governments rather than the federal government. It has been interpreted to incorporate most of the various provisions of the Bill of Rights, making them applicable to the states. The **equal protection clause** has been interpreted to preclude states from making unequal, arbitrary distinctions between people. It does not ban reasonable classifications, but it does prohibit classifications that are either without reason or based on race, gender, national origin, or religion. These are sometimes referred to as *suspect classifications* (Tribe, 1988). In other words, where the law limits the liberty of *all* persons, it is a due process question; where the law treats *certain classes* of people differently, it is an equal protection question.

Not all classifications are a violation of equal protection. States may treat people differently if they have a legitimate reason to do so. For example, states may refuse to issue a driver's license to a minor or limit the age at which a person may lawfully consume alcoholic beverages. Classifications based on age are not suspect (meaning likely illegal) if (a) the state can demonstrate an interest in the health and safety of minors who are a peculiarly vulnerable segment of society and (b) there is no history of "invidious" discrimination against minors, as there is for minorities and women. Furthermore, juveniles are seen as possessing fewer rights, or lesser rights, than adults. Thus, a juvenile curfew might be upheld, whereas a general curfew including adults would be struck down.

STANDARD OF REVIEW

In constitutional law, the outcome of a case is often determined as much by the standard of review the court employs as by the facts of the case. Not all of the individual protections set forth in the Bill of Rights are accorded the same respect. Rather, there is a hierarchy of rights. The court usually employs either a *strict scrutiny* or *rational basis* review, depending on whether a *fundamental right* is implicated or a *suspect classification* is impacted (Tribe, 1988).

Fundamental rights are those freedoms the Supreme Court has determined are "essential to the concept of ordered liberty," rights without which neither liberty nor justice would exist (*Palko v. Connecticut*, 1937). Examples include virtually all of the various provisions of the Bill of Rights as well as the Fourteenth Amendment guarantees of due process and equal protection. To date, the Court has held that only race and religion are suspect classifications in all circumstances, although gender, illegitimacy, and poverty occasionally have been treated as suspect classifications (Tribe, 1988).

Under **strict scrutiny review**, the state may not enact legislation that abridges a fundamental right unless (a) it has a compelling interest that justifies restricting a fundamental right and (b) the legislation is "narrowly tailored" so that the fundamental right is not abridged any more than absolutely necessary to effectuate the state's compelling interest. An example of a compelling interest is the state's interest in the health and safety of its citizens. Additionally, the Supreme Court requires that for legislation to be narrowly tailored, a sufficient nexus must exist between the legislative body's stated interest and either the classification drawn or the means chosen to advance the state's compelling interest.

This standard of review is referred to as the strict scrutiny test because the Court looks closely at the purpose and effect of the legislation rather than merely accepting the claims of the legislature that the legislation is needed or accepting the legislation as presumptively valid (Tribe, 1988). The reason for employing a higher standard of review when legislation impacts on a fundamental right or suspect classification is that closer analysis is required when individual liberties are threatened. The burden is on the government to prove the constitutionality and necessity of legislation exposed to a strict scrutiny test.

Laws involving quasi-suspect classifications such as gender and legitimacy are reviewed under the **intermediate scrutiny standard**. A law is upheld (passes constitutional muster) if the Court finds that it is *substantially related* to an *important* government purpose. The burden of proof lies primarily with the state under this standard of review.

If neither a fundamental right nor a suspect classification is implicated, a state may enact legislation abridging that right or impacting that class so long as there is a rational basis for the legislation. This standard of review generally is referred to as **rational basis review**, since under it the Court will not strike down legislation that appears to have some rational basis. The Court does not look closely at the effects of the legislation, unlike in the strict scrutiny test. Under this standard of review, state actions are presumptively valid (Tribe, 1988). This standard of review is obviously a much easier one to pass. The legislature need not choose the best possible means;

Figure 3.2 Standards of Judicial Review

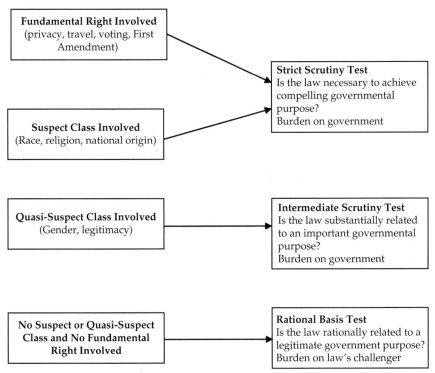

Figure provided by Professor Michael Bogner, Justice Studies Department, Chadron State College (2006).

it merely must appear that it has chosen means that are not wholly unrelated to the achievement of the legislative purpose. Figure 3.2 differentiates between the standards of review.

INCORPORATION OF THE BILL OF RIGHTS IN THE FOURTEENTH AMENDMENT

As previously stated, originally the Bill of Rights applied only to the federal government, and state and local governments were not bound by its various provisions. This was because at the time the Constitution was adopted, people feared a strong centralized government. State governments were viewed much more favorably, and many state constitutions contained protections of individual rights similar to those in the Bill of Rights. In 1833, the Supreme Court in *Barron v. Baltimore* (1833)—the first Bill of Rights case, coming a surprising 42 years after its ratification—expressly held that the Bill of Rights applied only to the federal government.

The *Barron* case involved the clause of the Fifth Amendment that forbids governmental taking of private property without just compensation. John Barron wanted this clause applied to the states, since the city of Baltimore had essentially taken his property without compensation. The Supreme Court dismissed his claim, stating that the amendment did not apply to the states and therefore that the Court lacked jurisdiction in the matter. This case showed that without the application of the Bill of Rights to the states, individuals would have no recourse to higher authority if the states violated their rights.

After the Civil War and the failed attempt by the southern states to secede from the Union, federal legislators felt it was necessary to amend the Constitution to provide greater protections for individuals from the actions of state governments. There was in particular a fear that the southern states would attempt to limit the ability of the recently freed slaves to become equal citizens. The result was the passage in 1868 of the Fourteenth Amendment.

The Fourteenth Amendment, as discussed earlier, contains three clauses: the privileges and immunities clause, the due process clause, and the equal protection clause. The essence of each of these clauses is that they bar states, not the federal government, from infringing on individual rights. The amendment was expressly intended to control state action, but it was unclear exactly how far it went. As mentioned, the original spur for it was a desire to protect the rights of the freed slaves, but the language of the amendment was broad and not specifically limited to state actions infringing on the rights of blacks.

An early attempt to apply the language of the privileges and immunities clause to persons other than the recently frees slaves failed in the *Slaughterhouse Cases* (1873). At issue was a Louisiana state statute, passed by a highly corrupt state legislature, granting one corporation a monopoly on the slaughterhouse business. The petitioners (the person or persons bringing the suit) argued that the privileges and immunities clause should be interpreted as prohibiting unreasonable restrictions on business because the restriction in question deprived them of their right to pursue their lawful trades. The Supreme Court sided with the monopoly, emphasizing that the due process clause should not be a source enabling judges to nullify laws they considered unreasonable (despite the financial gain some legislators realized from the monopoly, there were genuine public health concerns involved). It has been argued that the Court's decision was intended to protect black citizens by emphasizing that the Fourteenth Amendment was meant specifically for them (Ross, 2003), but the Court's "hands-off" stance regarding state legislation actually left them at its mercy (see chapter 13).

During the latter part of the nineteenth century, however, the Court began to use the due process clause of the Fourteenth Amendment to strike down state action involving economic regulation. Due process rights are said to extend beyond procedural rights (discussed fully in chapter 5) to encompass substantive due process as well. Under the principle of **substantive due process**, legislatures cannot pass laws that infringe on substantive rights such as free speech and privacy (this is the legal theory under which the privacy rights applied in *Griswold*, *Roe*, and *Johnson* were based). This all sounds very liberal until we realize that the Court has used the principle repeatedly to hold that states could not impose regulations such as minimum wage laws and child labor laws on private businesses because doing so violated due process. The violation of due process consisted of the regulation or taking of a right such as the right to work or to enter into a contract (even if the "right" meant having to work long hours for low wages).

During the 1930s, the use of the due process clause to protect economic interests fell into disfavor, in part because the Supreme Court used it to strike down much of President Franklin Delano Roosevelt's New Deal legislation, which was intended to ease the burden of the Great Depression. At the same time, however, the Court began to use the due process clause of the Fourteenth Amendment to protect individual rights from state action. Beginning in the late 1930s, the Court incorporated most of the provisions of the Bill of Rights into the Fourteenth Amendment's due process clause and applied them to the states. Many of the criminal law provisions were applied to the states during the 1960s by the Court under the leadership of Chief Justice Earl Warren (Domino, 1994).

By **incorporation** we mean that the justices interpreted the due process clause of the Fourteenth Amendment, which says no state shall deprive a person of life, liberty, or property without "due process of law," as prohibiting states from abridging certain individual rights. Many of these rights are included in the Bill of Rights, hence these rights were included (or incorporated) in the definition of due process. Various Supreme Court justices have advocated different approaches to incorporation during the twentieth century. These are discussed next.

Total Incorporation

Under the total incorporation approach, the due process clause of the Fourteenth Amendment made the entire Bill of Rights applicable to the states. In essence, the phrase "due process of law" was interpreted to mean "all of the provisions of the Bill of Rights." This approach has never commanded a majority of justices on the Court. However, a prominent supporter of this approach was Justice Hugo Black.

Total Incorporation Plus

As the name implies, the total incorporation plus approach goes a step further than the total incorporation approach. Under total incorporation plus, the due process clause of the Fourteenth Amendment includes all of the Bill of Rights and, in addition, other unspecified rights. A principal advocate of this approach was Justice William Douglas, who argued that the various provisions of the Bill of Rights created a "penumbra" (*Griswold v. Connecticut*, 1965) in which the whole was greater than the sum of the parts. That is, the individual rights contained in the Bill of Rights, when examined together, create other rights. Thus, he argued that the various provisions limiting the ability of the government to intrude into a person's private life (e.g., the Fourth Amendment prohibition on unreasonable searches and the Third Amendment prohibition on quartering troops in private residences) created a general right to privacy.

Fundamental Rights

In *Twining v. New Jersey* (1908), the Supreme Court suggested that some of the individual rights in the Bill of Rights might be protected from state action not because the Bill of Rights applied to the states but because these rights "are of such a nature that they are included in the conception of due process of law." This became known as the fundamental rights approach. Under this approach, there is no necessary relationship between the due process clause of the Fourteenth Amendment and the Bill of Rights. The due process clause has an independent meaning that prohibits state action that violates rights "implicit in the concept of ordered liberty" or those rights that are "fundamental" (*Palko v. Connecticut*, 1937). Exactly what constitutes a fundamental right is left to the justices who consider the history and tradition of the law. Additionally, justices consider the "totality of the circumstances" of each case in determining whether a right is fundamental. This approach provides justices with greater discretion, and they may interpret it either narrowly or broadly. This approach enjoyed strong support in the Supreme Court until the late 1960s. A principal advocate of this approach was Justice Felix Frankfurter.

Selective Incorporation

The selective incorporation approach combines elements of the fundamental rights and total incorporation approaches in modified form and is the approach that seems to predominate in most Supreme Court cases. This approach favors a piecemeal, gradual, and selective method of incorporation. Selective incorporation rejects the notion that all of the rights in the Bill of Rights are automatically incorporated in the due process clause of the Fourteenth Amendment, but it does look to the Bill of Rights as a guide to the meaning of due process. Selective incorporation rejects the "totality of the circumstances" component of the fundamental rights approach and instead incorporates rights deemed fundamental to the same extent and in the same manner as applied to the federal government.

As an example, the Supreme Court in *Wolf v. Colorado* (1949) held that the Fourth Amendment was fundamental and applied it to the states, but the Court also decided that the exclusionary rule was not fundamental and therefore did not apply it to the states. Thus, state law enforcement officials were told by the Court that while they must obey the Fourth Amendment, a failure to do so would not result in the exclusion of evidence obtained through a violation of the Fourth Amendment. In *Mapp v. Ohio* (1961), under selective incorporation, the Court held both the right (freedom from unreasonable searches) and the means of enforcing the right (the exclusionary rule) were part of the due process clause of the Fourteenth Amendment.

Selective incorporation became popular in the 1960s with the Warren Court. A principal advocate was Justice William Brennan. While selective incorporation accepted the idea that the due process clause protects only "fundamental rights" and that not every right in the Bill of Rights is necessarily fundamental, over time it has led to the incorporation of virtually everything in the Bill of Rights. The criminal protections not yet included are the right to an indictment by a grand jury and the prohibition on excessive bail. The Second and Seventh Amendments have not been incorporated.

It should be noted that just because the Supreme Court has deemed incorporation necessary does not mean that most of these rights did not already exist in the states. Many states had rights in their state constitutions that in some instances were even more protective of individual rights than those in the Bill of Rights. For

Table 3.2 *Summary of Incorporation Theories*

Total Incorporation	Total Incorporation Plus	Selective Incorporation
Intent: To make all provisions of the Bill of Rights applicable to the states	**Intent:** To protect rights enumerated in the Bill of Rights plus certain unenumerated rights	**Intent:** To incorporate provisions of the Bill of Rights in a careful and discriminative way
Justification: Due process clause of the Fourteenth Amendment	**Justification:** The totality of the rights in the Bill of Rights created a penumbra over the law	**Justification:** Only fundamental rights should be incorporated; nonfundamental rights should be left as state concerns

example, a number of states had privacy rights in such matters as abortion and the bearing of arms long before the Court's "discovery" of "penumbras."

Table 3.2 presents a summary of incorporation theories.

JUDICIAL REVIEW

Given the varied sources of law and the ambiguous language of many statutes and constitutional provisions, it is inevitable that laws will come into conflict or that interpretations of statutes will differ. When this happens, who decides which law is paramount? In the United States, the answer to that question is the courts, through the power of judicial review.

Judicial review simply means the court has the power to examine a law and determine whether it is constitutional. To make this determination, judges must examine the law and compare it with the Constitution. This requires them to interpret the language of both the statute and the Constitution. If the judge determines the law is constitutional, he or she upholds the law; if not, he or she declares the law unconstitutional and therefore void.

For example, the Fourth Amendment prohibits "unreasonable" searches. Suppose a state legislature passes a law allowing police officers to search anyone they encounter on a public street. Is this law constitutional, or does it violate the prohibition on unreasonable searches? To answer this question, judges must examine the history and meaning of "unreasonable" as contained in the Fourth Amendment. They do this by examining precedent.

Judicial review is not specifically provided for in the Constitution. Rather, judicial review is judge-made law. *Marbury v. Madison* (1803) established the authority of the US Supreme Court to engage in judicial review of the acts of the other branches of government. The Court stated in *Marbury* that it was the duty of the judiciary (rather than the president or Congress) to interpret the Constitution and apply it to particular fact situations. The Court also said that it was the job of the courts to decide when other laws (acts of Congress or state laws) were in violation of the Constitution and to declare these laws null and void if they were. This is the doctrine of judicial review.

One fact of which we must be aware is that the law is not like mathematics, in which all students who apply the correct algorithm with care will inevitably arrive at the correct solution to the problem. Law is preeminently a human endeavor, and the "correct" solution to a legal problem depends on all kinds of human foibles, eccentricities, and interests. For this reason, the existence and extent of judicial review has been hotly debated from the very beginning of the United States, as we shall see in future chapters.

Marbury v. Madison

Marbury v. Madison is perhaps the most important case ever decided by the Supreme Court because it established the authority of the high court. Article III of the Constitution created the Supreme Court, but it did not discuss whether the Court could review legislation or interpret the Constitution.

At the time the Constitution was adopted, there was heated debate concerning which branch of government had the authority to declare an act void. There were three suggestions on how to handle such a situation: (a) each branch within its sphere of authorized power has the final say; (b) the Supreme Court has the final say, but only as to the parties in cases before the Court; and (c) the Supreme Court has the final say. This controversy was finally resolved by the opinion in *Marbury*. An examination of the case provides insight into this controversy and how the Court handled the situation.

The facts of *Marbury v. Madison* were as follows:

> President John Adams, a Federalist, appointed 42 of his fellow Federalists as justices of the peace for the District of Columbia just days before turning over the office to incoming President Thomas Jefferson, a Democrat. Adams's Secretary of State, John Marshall, delivered most of the commissions to the newly appointed justices of the peace but failed to deliver Marbury's.

> The newly elected president's secretary of state, James Madison, refused to deliver Marbury's commission, so Marbury applied directly to the Supreme Court for a writ of mandamus (a writ compelling public officials to perform their duty). The Court was granted original jurisdiction in such matters by the Judiciary Act of 1789. The Court agreed to hear the case but was unable to do so for 14 months because Congress passed a law that stopped the Court from meeting.

> In 1803, the Supreme Court reconvened, heard the case, and decided Marbury was entitled to his commission but that it could not issue a writ of mandamus. Chief Justice John Marshall (formerly Adams's secretary of state!) wrote the opinion of the court.

John Marshall

> Marshall said:
>
> (a) Marbury was entitled to his commission, as he had a legal right that was not extinguished by the change in office of president or the failure to deliver the already-signed commission;
>
> (b) a writ of mandamus was a proper legal remedy for enforcing Marbury's right;
>
> (c) however, the Supreme Court lacked the constitutional authority to issue such a writ. This was because the Judiciary Act of 1789 gave the Supreme Court original jurisdiction in such cases, but this grant of authority to the

Supreme Court was unconstitutional because Article III of the Constitution defined Supreme Court jurisdiction.

The Judiciary Act of 1789 had the effect of changing (by enlarging) the jurisdiction of the Supreme Court, but Congress cannot pass a statute that changes the Constitution. The only way to change the Constitution is through a constitutional amendment (see next section). As stated by Chief Justice Marshall, "an act of the legislature, repugnant to the Constitution, is void." In other words, the Constitution is superior to congressional legislation.

Prior to the decision in *Marbury*, Democrats argued that the Supreme Court lacked the authority to declare acts of other branches of the federal government unconstitutional, while Federalists supported judicial review. If the Court had issued a writ of mandamus, it could not have forced Madison to honor it. Thus, the Court was faced with a serious challenge to its authority. Marshall's opinion saved the Court's prestige while allowing the Democrats to claim a political victory (they did not have to appoint any more Federalists as justices of the peace). What was more important in the long term, however, was that the decision established as law the idea that the Supreme Court has the authority to review the constitutionality of congressional activity (and presidential acts)—this is judicial review.

This was obviously a major victory for the Supreme Court, and although opposed at the time, it was accepted, at least in part, because the result in the case was satisfactory to opponents of a strong Supreme Court. The Court did not use the power of judicial review to invalidate congressional legislation again until the *Dred Scott* case in 1857, when it held that slaves were not citizens of the United States (see *Scott v. Sandford*, discussed in chapter 13), so Congress had little reason to complain.

THE PROCESS OF AMENDING THE CONSTITUTION

In this chapter, we have discussed at some length the most important amendments that impact individual liberty, but without touching on the process by which these amendments come into being. The Constitution may be changed—or a Supreme Court ruling interpreting the Constitution overturned if the Court does not itself overturn it—only by a constitutional amendment. And a constitutional amendment may be passed only by following one of two procedures set forth in Article V of the Constitution. The first process involves two-thirds of both houses of Congress passing a resolution calling for an amendment. If the resolution passes both houses, the proposed amendment must be ratified (approved) within seven years by three-fourths of the states. The second method involves two-thirds of the states voting to call for a convention at which a constitutional amendment can be proposed. All 27 amendments (out of thousands that have been proposed) have been added to the Constitution using the first process.

The Eleventh Amendment, passed in 1795, is particularly interesting for a number of reasons, not the least of which is that it was passed in response to the Supreme Court's very first constitutional decision (*Chisholm v. Georgia*, 1793). The issue before the Court was whether the state of Georgia was subject to the jurisdiction of the US Supreme Court and the federal government. The case involved a citizen of South Carolina suing Georgia for payment of goods supplied to the state during the Revolutionary War. Georgia refused to appear before the Court, claiming sovereign immunity (a doctrine precluding a suit against a sovereign government without its consent), which meant that it thus was not liable to be sued. Article III of the Constitution plainly states that federal courts have jurisdiction to decide cases "between a State and citizens of another State," and therefore the Court ruled against Georgia's sovereign immunity claim and for Chisholm's claim for compensation.

Many states objected to this ruling, claiming that if they were held liable for debts incurred during the Revolutionary War, they would face financial ruin. The Eleventh Amendment was therefore passed both to prevent further such suits and, perhaps more important, to assert the sovereignty of the states. This amendment reads:

> The Judicial power of the United States shall not be construed to extend to any suit in law or equity, commenced or prosecuted against one of the United States by Citizens of another State, or by Citizens or Subjects of any Foreign State.

Nevertheless, both the federal government and the states may, and often do, waive their right not to be sued. Whenever the issue has arisen in Supreme Court cases, the ruling has always favored the sovereign immunity of the states, although dissenting opinions have consistently asserted that the states surrendered their sovereign immunity when they ratified the US Constitution.

SUMMARY

In this chapter, we discussed the historical development of the law with a particular focus on the concepts of common law, precedent, stare decisis, and judicial review. We also examined the sources of law, focusing primarily on the US Constitution and the Bill of Rights. The Bill of Rights provides many of the individual rights that American citizens enjoy today. We also discussed the means by which the Bill of Rights, originally applicable only to the federal government, has been applied to the states through the due process clause of the Fourteenth Amendment.

Associated with incorporation is the concept of judicial review. This is a tremendously important concept in the law, for it is judicial review that gives to the courts the power to declare acts of other branches of government void as unconstitutional. Without this power, the courts would be unable to provide an important check on the action of the executive and legislative branches of government.

The American system of government was designed by the Founding Fathers with checks and balances among the branches of government. Nonetheless, judicial review is a controversial subject. Many feel it gives the courts too much power vis-à-vis the other branches of government, and it allows democratically elected leaders to be obstructed by unelected judges. The question students should ask in deciding whether they support the concept of judicial review is: "Who else can provide a check on the other branches of government?"

The law, in the end, is what we in society make it. Whether written by judges or legislators, it can be changed in one way or another. It is the responsibility of individual citizens to be aware of their rights and the law and to ensure that no branch of government is too powerful at the expense of the others.

DISCUSSION QUESTIONS

1. What is common law, and what role do precedent and stare decisis play in the development of the law?
2. How did the Bill of Rights come to be applied to the individual states?
3. What is the power of judicial review, and how was it developed?
4. Why was the Bill of Rights adopted, and what rights are contained in it?
5. What are the different standards of review in constitutional law, and when are they used?
6. Given the Supreme Court's "discovery" of penumbras in the Bill of Rights, should the right to privacy be extended to assisted suicide for terminally ill patients and/or access to marijuana for medical purposes? Why or why not?
7. Go to http://www.earlyamerica.com/review/spring97/blackstone.html and read about Sir William Blackstone. What was his impact on American institutions?
8. What are the primary sources of the law, and how do they differ from one another?
9. How has the equal protection clause of the Fourteenth Amendment been applied by the Supreme Court?
10. Using strict scrutiny review, under what circumstances can a state abridge fundamental rights?

CHAPTER TERMS

Administrative regulations
Articles of Confederation
Bill of Rights
Code of Hammurabi
Common law
Dicta
Double jeopardy
Dual sovereignty doctrine
Due process clause

Equal protection clause
Establishment clause
Fundamental rights
Grand jury
Incorporation
Indictment
Information
Intermediate scrutiny standard
Judicial review
Legislation

Magna Carta
Petit jury
Precedent
Privilege against self-incrimination
Probable cause
Rational basis review
Stare decisis
Strict scrutiny review
Substantive due process

References

Amar, A. (1998). *The Bill of Rights.* New Haven, CT: Yale University Press.
Anastaplo, G. (1995). *The amendments to the Constitution: A commentary.* Baltimore, MD: Johns Hopkins University Press.
Bailey, G. (1997). Blackstone in America: Lectures by an English lawyer become the blueprint for a new nation's laws and leaders. *Early American Review.* Retrieved from http://www.earlyamerica.com/review/spring97/blackstone.html

Black, H. (2001). *Black's law dictionary* (5th ed.). Minneapolis, MN: West.

Blackstone, W. (1765–1769). *Commentaries on the law of England*. 4 vols. London, England: Routledge.

Cuddihy, W. (1990). *The Fourth Amendment: Origin and original meaning* (Unpublished doctoral dissertation). Claremont College, Claremont, CA.

Domino, J. (1994). *Civil rights and liberties*. New York, NY: HarperCollins.

Feldman, N. (2005). *Divided by God: America's church–state problem—and what she should do about it*. New York, NY: Farrar, Straus and Giroux.

Kates, D. (1983). Handgun prohibition and the original meaning of the Second Amendment. *Michigan Law Review, 82*, 204–279.

Klarman, M. (2004). *From Jim Crow to civil rights: The Supreme Court and the struggle for racial equality*. New York, NY: Oxford University Press.

Levinson, S. (1989). The embarrassing Second Amendment. *Yale Law Journal, 99*, 637–709.

Massey, C. (1995). *Silent rights: The Ninth Amendment and the Constitution's unenumerated rights*. Philadelphia, PA: Temple University Press.

Ross, M. (2003). *Justice of shattered dreams: Samuel Freeman Miller and the Supreme Court during the Civil War era*. Baton Rouge: University of Louisiana Press.

Stramignoni, I. (2002). At the margins of the history of English law: The institutional, the socio-political and the "blotted out." *Legal Studies, 22*, 420–447.

Tribe, L. (1988). *American constitutional law*. Mineola, NY: Foundation Press.

Turner, R. (1990). Who was the author of Glanvill? Reflections of the education of Henry II's common layers. *Law and History Review, 8*, 97–130.

Williams, D. (1991). Civic Republicanism and the citizen militia: The terrifying Second Amendment. *Yale Law Journal, 101*, 550–623.

Cases Cited

Barker v. Wingo, 407 U.S. 514 (1972)

Barron v. Baltimore, 32 U.S. 243 (1833)

Chaplinsky v. New Hampshire, 315 U.S. 568 (1942)

Chisholm v. Georgia, 2 U.S. 419 (1793)

District of Columbia v. Heller, 554 U.S. 570 (2008)

Entick v. Carrington, 19 Howell's State Trials 1029 (1765)

Everson v. Board of Education, 330 U.S. 1 (1947)

Griffin v. California, 380 U.S. 609 (1965)

Griswold v. Connecticut, 381 U.S. 479 (1965)

Hurtado v. California, 110 U.S. 516 (1884)

Kelo v. City of New London, 545 U.S. 108 (2005)

Kirby v. Illinois, 406 U.S. 682 (1972)

Lawrence v. Texas, 539 U.S. 558 (2003)

Lemon v. Kurtzman, 403 U.S. 602 (1971)

Malloy v. Hogan, 378 U.S. 1 (1964)

Mapp v. Ohio, 367 U.S. 643 (1961)

Marbury v. Madison, 1 Cranch 137 (1803)

Miller v. California, 413 U.S. 15 (1973)

Palko v. Connecticut, 302 U.S. 319 (1937)

Roe v. Wade, 410 U.S. 113 (1973)

Scott v. Sandford, 60 U.S. 393 (1857)

Slaughterhouse Cases, 83 U.S. 36 (1873)

Stack v. Boyle, 342 U.S. 1 (1951)

Strickland v. Washington, 466 U.S. 668 (1984)

Texas v. Johnson, 491 U.S. 397 (1989)

Twining v. New Jersey, 211 U.S. 78 (1908)

United States v. Salerno, 481 U.S. 739 (1987)

Virginia State Board of Pharmacy v. Virginia Citizens Consumers Council, Inc., 425 U.S. 748 (1976)

Weeks v. United States, 232 U.S. 383 (1914)

Wolf v. Colorado, 338 U.S. 25 (1949)

CHAPTER 4

FEDERAL AND STATE COURTS

The Supreme Court comprises eight associate justices and the chief justice. The justices are nominated by the president, confirmed by the Senate, and serve for life or until they choose to retire. There is no standard career path that one can follow to become a justice. Many Supreme Court justices served as judges in the US Courts of Appeal, while others served as judges on state supreme courts. Others came to the high court without any prior judicial experience. Some were law professors, and others senators with a great deal of political experience.

One of the most unique justices, in terms of background and life experiences, was Justice William O. Douglas. He served on the Court longer than any other justice, from 1939 to 1975. Prior to joining the Supreme Court, he was a distinguished law professor at Columbia and Yale, and he served as chairman of the Securities and Exchange Commission under President Franklin Roosevelt. His experience in academe and in politics provided him with fairly typical credentials for a Supreme Court justice. What made him stand out from others was his approach to life. Douglas grew up poor in Yakima, Washington, and was one of the first Supreme Court appointees to come from the West. Throughout his life, he maintained a love for the West and the outdoors, leaving Washington, DC, immediately after the close of the Supreme Court's term in June to spend the summer months in the mountains of Washington state, near Mt. Rainier. Because Supreme Court justices have duties that require them to review documents throughout the summer months, this meant the Court clerk's office had to find a way to deliver documents to Justice Douglas, often very quickly. Today, with ATVs, the Internet, and cell phones, getting in touch with someone—even someone living in a cabin in a remote area of Washington state—is not that difficult. But in the 1940s and 1950s, this sometimes meant sending Supreme Court clerks on horseback into the wilds to find Justice Douglas, who on more than one occasion reviewed important Court documents in front of a campfire while clerks waited to obtain his decision and signature on the paperwork.

INTRODUCTION

Justice is something we all seek for ourselves and for others, and while we may have different ideas about what constitutes justice, in America the place people go to obtain it is the court system. Everyone has heard someone say "I'll sue you!" or "I'll take this case all the way to the Supreme Court!" The many different types of courts all share the feature of being intended to provide justice. Courts fulfill several functions while dispensing justice, depending on the case.

Justice William O. Douglas

First, and most important, the courts "do justice" by providing all parties with due process of law. Courts settle disputes by providing a forum for obtaining justice and resolving disputes through the application of law (Meador, 1991). In the courts, injured parties may be heard, and the state may seek to punish wrongdoers; private parties may seek redress in civil court, and the state may seek to punish violators of the criminal law in criminal court. While the courtroom is obviously not the only place people may go to settle disputes, Americans traditionally have not been reluctant to turn to the courts for redress. The courts are used much less frequently in other cultures, such as in China, where social control is exercised less formally (we explore this in chapter 14).

Second, courts make public policy decisions. Policy-making involves the allocation of limited resources (e.g., money, property, or rights) to competing interests. The United States has a long tradition of settling difficult policy questions in the courtroom rather than in the legislature (Perry, 1994). This is because politicians, fearful of harming their reelection prospects, often avoid settling complex and/or difficult problems. Additionally, the rights of minorities often are unprotected by the legislature, so courts are forced to step into the breach. Finally, there is an acceptance of litigation as a tool for social change. Examples of how the US Supreme Court has shaped social policy include those involving economic reforms during the Great Depression, the extension of criminal procedure rights to defendants, race relations and school desegregation, reapportionment, and abortion (Wasby, 1993). Law and social change is the subject of chapter 11.

Third, courts clarify the law through the interpretation of statutes and the application of general principles to specific fact patterns (Abraham, 1987). Courts are different from the other branches of government in many ways, but perhaps the most significant difference is that courts are reactive: courts do not initiate cases but rather serve to settle controversies brought to them by others—"plaintiffs and defendants," in legal parlance.

In this chapter, we discuss the role and structure of the federal and state courts with an emphasis on the role of the US Supreme Court, the court of last resort. The court systems of the various states and the federal court system share a number of characteristics but also can be quite different. Some examples of different court systems are provided to illustrate these similarities and differences. We discuss trial and appeals courts as well as courts of limited jurisdiction. Frequently, issues arise concerning the interplay of federal and state courts as well. After our explanation of court structure, we discuss the trial process, focusing on the criminal trial.

JURISDICTION

To appreciate how and why court systems are set up the way they are, it is important to understand the concept of jurisdiction. The term **jurisdiction** comes from the Latin *juris* ("law") and *dicere* ("to speak") and denotes the legal authority or power of a court to hear, pronounce on, and decide a case. A court's jurisdiction is conferred by statute or constitution. There are four primary types of jurisdiction: personal, subject matter, geographical, and hierarchical (Shreve & Raven-Hansen, 1994).

Personal jurisdiction involves the authority of the court over the person. A court may acquire personal jurisdiction over someone if that person comes in contact with the court, either by being a citizen of the state or by committing an act or acts that contravene the laws of that state.

Subject matter jurisdiction involves the authority conferred on a court to hear a particular type of case. Some courts may hear only a specified type of case. Examples include traffic court, juvenile court, and probate court. Thus, a juvenile court would hear only matters involving juveniles. Smaller jurisdictions often do not have such courts, instead combining all of the specialized courts into one court because of limited resources.

Geographical jurisdiction refers to the authority of courts to hear cases that arise within specified boundaries, such as a city, county, state, or country. This is sometimes is referred to as *venue*. For a court to have jurisdiction over an event, that event must have taken place, either in whole or in part, within the geographical jurisdiction of the court. Thus, a person who kills someone in California could not be prosecuted in North Carolina for that murder. The proper forum would be in California.

Precisely where a crime occurs is not always clear-cut. For instance, a person may be kidnapped in Mississippi and then taken to Texas. In this case, the kidnapping is a "continuing offense"—meaning that it can occur in more than one place, and that each state into which the victim is taken could charge the kidnapper with the crime. Furthermore, both states may prosecute without violating the prohibition on double jeopardy, as they are each separate sovereign governments. This means that each state derives its authority from a different source—its own state constitution. While two states can prosecute a person for the same offense, a state and a county in that state cannot, as the county derives its jurisdiction from the same source as the state (that state's constitution). Most crimes, however, take place in only one jurisdiction—where the crime occurred. An example is murder—a person can be killed only once, and the state in which the killing occurs has the jurisdiction to prosecute the killer.

Within each state there are also jurisdictions, usually defined by county boundaries. A state crime must be tried both within the proper state and the proper district within the state. The proper court within California for a murder, for example, would be the county in which the killing occurred. Occasionally, a defendant in a criminal case may request a change of venue. Such a request must be based on evidence that it is impossible for the defendant to obtain a fair trial in the original court, perhaps because of substantial adverse publicity.

Hierarchical jurisdiction involves the division of responsibilities and functions among the various courts. There is both original and appellate jurisdiction, as well as limited and general jurisdiction, as follows.

Limited jurisdiction means that a court is limited to hearing only a particular class of cases, often dealing with a particular topic, such as a small claims court or a misdemeanor court. Smaller jurisdictions often do not have such courts, instead combining all of the specialized courts in one court because of limited resources, as previously mentioned.

General jurisdiction means a court has the authority to hear a variety of cases. An example is the state trial court, which often has the authority to hear all manner of civil and criminal cases. *Civil cases* involve a dispute between two private parties, such as over contract or property law. *Criminal cases* involve prosecution of an individual by the state for violating state criminal law.

Original jurisdiction means the court has the power to hear the case initially. For example, in federal court, all felony cases begin in the district court, while a suit between two states would start at the Supreme Court level. The court of original jurisdiction is where the trial takes place.

Appellate jurisdiction means the court has the power to review a decision of a lower court. Appeals courts may affirm or reverse lower court judgments and either enter a new judgment or send the case back to the lower court for reconsideration in light of its decision. Appellate courts do not conduct a retrial; rather, they generally are limited to a review of the trial record to determine if any significant legal errors occurred. The court hears oral arguments by the attorneys for each side and reads legal briefs filed with the court, then bases its decision on these materials rather than on new evidence.

THE FEDERAL COURTS

Essentially, there are two court systems in the United States: the court systems of the 50 states and the federal court system. Federal courts are sometimes referred to as **Article III Courts** because they are established by Congress pursuant to its authority to create "inferior" (meaning lower) courts under Article III of the US Constitution. The jurisdiction of federal and state courts frequently overlap, as when an act that is a crime in a state is also punishable under federal law (e.g., bank robbery). The Constitution drawn up by the Framers in 1787 created a government with three branches—the legislature, the executive, and the judicial. The duties of each branch were set forth in separate articles of the Constitution. The duties of the judicial branch were listed in Article III, which established the Supreme Court and authorized "such inferior courts as Congress" chose to create. Neither the number of justices of the Supreme Court nor the form of any potential "inferior" courts was described.

At first, the idea of creating a system of federal courts met with much resistance from supporters of states' rights, who were afraid that federal courts would infringe on the jurisdiction and authority of state courts. Antifederalists sought limitations on Article III for the same reason they sought a Bill of Rights: they feared a strong central government. On the other hand, several contributors to the *Federalist Papers* (a series of articles written by James Madison, Alexander Hamilton, and John Jay supporting ratification of the Constitution) argued for a strong federal court system as a bulwark against the actions of a democratically elected legislature. These writers saw the Constitution as the paramount law of the land and believed it the job of the courts to interpret it and prevent the legislature from passing laws that may infringe on constitutional rights, which they saw primarily as property rights (Kelly, Harbison, & Belz, 1983).

With the independence of the United States, one of the first acts of the newly elected Congress was to pass the Judiciary Act of 1789. This act established Supreme Court membership at six justices. The act also created three federal circuit courts and 13 district courts, one in each of the original states. From this, an entire federal system has grown that today encompasses some 13 federal circuit courts and over 100 district courts. The first set of intermediate-level appellate courts with purely appellate jurisdiction was established more than 100 years later, in 1891.

The federal court system today consists of three primary tiers: district courts, courts of appeal, and the Supreme Court. Each of these courts has different functions. These are discussed in the following sections.

District Courts

The district court is the trial court—the court of original jurisdiction—for the federal court system. There are currently 94 federal judicial districts in the 50 states (including several in US territories). Each state has at least one district court. Some, such as California and Texas, have as many as four (see Figure 4.1). With one exception (Wyoming, whose district court includes all of Yellowstone National Park, even the portion in Montana), no judicial district crosses state lines.

Figure 4.1 The Federal Judicial Circuits

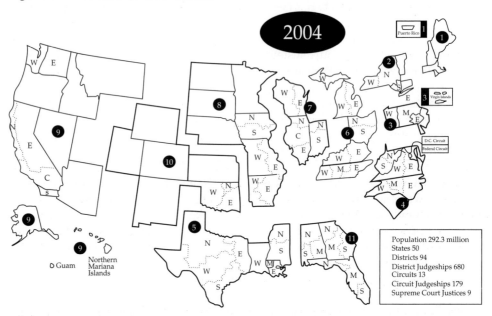

Source: Wheeler R. & C. Harrison: Creating the Federal Judicial System (3rd Edition). Washington, D.C. Federal Judicial Center, 2005.

In each district, there is a US District Court. In total, there are more than 670 federal district judges, all of whom are appointed for life and hold office "during good behavior." Furthermore, their salary cannot be reduced during their term of office. This protects the independence of the federal judiciary and sets it apart from state court judges, most of whom are appointed or elected to a defined term of years.

Also within each district court are subordinate judicial officers referred to as federal magistrates. These officers conduct preliminary proceedings in cases before the district court and issue warrants. Judgments entered by magistrates are considered judgments of the district court. Federal magistrate courts are similar to courts of limited jurisdiction in state courts (Smith, 1992).

Federal district courts are not courts of general jurisdiction. Rather, they have original jurisdiction to hear only those types of cases specified by acts of Congress, and Congress may authorize the district court to hear only those cases and controversies specified in Article III of the Constitution. The majority of cases in federal court deal with claims arising out of federal law, either civil or criminal. These may be based on federal statutes or the Constitution. District courts conduct trials for all federal criminal offenses and hear civil cases where there is diversity of citizenship between the parties. **Diversity of citizenship** refers to the situation in which the opposing parties are from different states.

Until recently, much of the federal court docket was comprised of civil cases, but in recent years, this balance has begun to shift. Congress has greatly increased the number of federal crimes in the past few years. Consequently, while civil cases filed in federal district court still far outnumber criminal cases, criminal trials take up a significant portion of the district court's time. In 2017, there were 367,937 cases filed with the federal district courts. Crimes tried in federal courts include many types of white-collar crimes, kidnapping, bank robbery, mail fraud, and civil rights abuses. The current "war on drugs" and the illegal immigration crisis have added greatly to the federal courts' burdens, together comprising about 60 percent of criminal cases heard by them. Mainly because of these two issues, some jurisdictions have been forced to postpone all civil proceedings to deal with the backlog of criminal cases. The Constitution requires a "speedy trial" in criminal cases, and consequently, criminal cases take precedence, often delaying civil cases significantly.

The other major category of cases in federal courts are civil cases arising out of the court's diversity jurisdiction. District courts are authorized to hear any civil matter, even if it involves state law, if the amount in question exceeds $75,000 and the parties are diverse—that is, if they are citizens of different states. Federal courts were given diversity jurisdiction originally because the Founding Fathers feared state courts would be biased in favor of their residents when presented with a suit between a resident and a nonresident. Allowing the nonresident to shift the case to federal court was originally seen as a means of ensuring a fair trial (Kelly et al., 1983).

Courts of Appeals

The next level in the federal system comprises the courts of appeals. These courts also are referred to as circuit courts. There are 13 courts of appeals: 11 for the 50 states, 1 for the District of Columbia, and 1 for the federal circuit (see Figure 4.2).

Figure 4.2 The Federal Court System

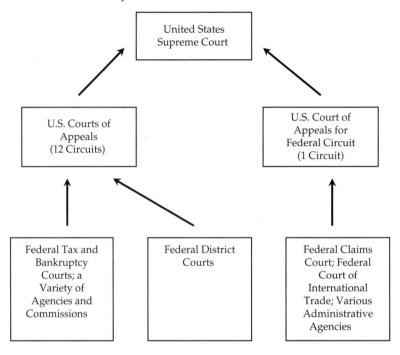

Ninth Circuit Court of Appeals

The jurisdiction of the Court of Appeals for the Federal Circuit is defined by statute to include appeals from several federal administrative agencies, patent claims, and decisions of the Claims Court and the Court of International Trade (two specialized federal trial courts). The District of Columbia has its own appeals court in part because of the large volume of cases filed there. The 11 remaining courts of appeals are organized on a territorial basis, with each covering several states. For instance, the Eleventh Circuit encompasses the states of Florida, Georgia, and Alabama, while the Ninth Circuit, the largest of the courts of appeals, includes the states of Alaska, Hawaii, California, Nevada, Arizona, Idaho, Oregon, Washington, and Montana, as well as Guam and the Northern Marianas Islands.

The number of judges on each of the courts of appeals varies from 6 in the First Circuit to 29 in the Ninth Circuit. Appeals are heard by three-judge panels. The makeup of these panels is constantly changing so that Judge X does not repeatedly sit with Judge Y. If there are conflicting decisions involving the same legal issue between two panels, the entire circuit may sit *en banc* (meaning "as a group") and rehear the case.

ISSUE HIGHLIGHT

Break up the Ninth Circuit?

The Ninth Circuit is by far the largest of the 13 federal courts of appeal, both in terms of geographical area covered (Alaska, Arizona, California, Guam, Hawaii, Idaho, Montana, Northern Mariana Islands, Nevada, and Washington), number of judges (29 active judges and 16 senior judges as of 2018), and number of appeals (over 12,000 annually as of 2017). It has a reputation for being a "liberal" circuit that is frequently overturned by the US Supreme Court. Critics of the court have argued for years that it does not accurately reflect the more conservative mindset of many of the states, such as Idaho and Montana, in the region, and a number of critics have advocated for splitting the Ninth Circuit into two or more circuits, both to better distribute the workload and to allow the liberal-leaning states and conservative-leaning states to separate. What do you think of this proposal?

Reasons to Break Up the Ninth Circuit

1. Reduce the geographical size of the circuit.
2. Reduce the number of judges in one circuit.
3. Divide up the states so the "liberal" states and "conservative" states are gathered together with like-minded states.
4. Reduce the influence of California, the state with the most appeals heard by the Ninth Circuit.

Reasons Not to Break Up the Ninth Circuit

1. The workload, not the geographical size, of the circuit is what matters—and this can be addressed by adding more judges.
2. It is difficult to determine if a state is "liberal" or "conservative" depending on the issue, and no other circuit was created expressly on ideological grounds.
3. While the Ninth Circuit is reversed most often by the US Supreme Court, that does not mean it is doing a poor job—it just means it decides more cases, and so more of its cases get selected for consideration by the US Supreme Court.

This obviously can be a bit unwieldy in those circuits that have a large number of judges; consequently, federal law permits courts of appeals with more than 15 active judges to sit en banc with fewer than all of their members (Meador, 1991). The Ninth Circuit may hold en banc hearings with as few as 11 of its 29 judges. As with district court judges, Courts of Appeals' judges are appointed for life.

Supreme Court

The third and final tier in the federal court system is the Supreme Court. This is the court of last resort for all cases arising in the federal system as well as all cases in state courts that involve a federal constitutional issue. All Supreme Court decisions regarding constitutional law are precedents that bind all lower federal and state courts. Only future Supreme Court decisions or a constitutional amendment can overturn a Supreme Court decision, although the Court usually respects its own precedents. The Supreme Court has original jurisdiction over a very small number of situations, including suits between states, suits between the United States and a state, and suits between a state and a foreign citizen. These rarely occur, and when they do, they typically involve a dispute between states. The bulk of the Court's docket is comprised of cases taken on appeal from either a federal court of appeals or a state supreme court (Wasby, 1993).

The Court's appellate docket is almost entirely discretionary—that is, the Court may choose which cases it takes and which it refuses to hear. This is very different from trial courts and lower appeals courts, which must hear cases brought before them. Parties seeking to appeal to the Supreme Court petition for a **writ of certiorari**, which an order to the lower court to send the record of the case up to the Supreme Court. The justices vote whether to accept a case. If four or more justices vote to accept a case, it is placed on the Court's docket. This is known as the **rule of four** (Wasby, 1993). If the Court elects to hear an appeal, it issues the writ to the lower court, requesting the case be sent up. If four votes to accept are not obtained, the petition for a writ of certiorari is denied, and the decision of the lower court is left as is. Typically, when the Court refuses to grant certiorari, it does so because there is no difference of opinion on the issue that is the subject of the case among the circuit courts or because no federal constitutional issue is raised. Refusal to accept an appeal is not considered a decision on the merits of the case and has no binding precedential value. It simply means that the Court has chosen not to hear the case, for whatever reason (Brigham, 1987). Only about 2 percent of petitions to the Court are granted certiorari.

The Supreme Court Justices

The law is inherently conservative, and so are most of its servants. The conservatism of the law is plain in its respect for precedent and predictability (and hence the status quo). The conservatism of the Court is also apparent in the composition of its members since the Court's beginning. As of 2018, there have been 113 justices, of whom 93 have been white, Protestant, and male. Forty-six years after its inception, the Court had its first Catholic, Roger Taney, appointed in 1835. It was not until 1916 that the first Jew, Louis Brandeis, was appointed and not until 1965 that the first black man, Thurgood Marshall, was appointed. Upon Marshall's retirement, the second black justice, Clarence Thomas, was appointed. The first female, Sandra Day O'Connor, was appointed to the Court in 1981. She was joined in 1993 by the Court's second female member, Ruth Bader Ginsburg. Sonia Sotomayor became the third female and the first Hispanic to serve on the Supreme Court when she was appointed in 2009.

Currently, the Court is composed of nine justices, one of whom is designated the chief justice. John Roberts became chief justice in 2005 following the death of former Chief Justice William H. Rehnquist. Congress has the authority either to enlarge or reduce the number of justices on the Supreme Court and has done so in the past. Congress has not changed the number of justices in more than 100 years, however, and it seems unlikely it may try to do so now in the face of a long-standing tradition of having nine justices on the Court.

Supreme Court Justices 2018

While created as a third branch of the federal government, the Supreme Court did not immediately establish a significant presence in the affairs of the country. In fact, there was so little for the Court to do that the first chief justice, John Jay, resigned to take a position as an ambassador. Not until the term of John Marshall (1801–1835) was the Supreme Court able to establish its role in the government. Today, the Supreme Court plays a significant role in public affairs (Cooper, 1988).

THE STATE COURTS

While the federal courts (particularly the Supreme Court) capture most of the attention of the media and the general public, the state courts are the true work-horses of the American judicial system. State courts currently process in excess of 100 million cases a year. These range from the most serious of criminal offenses to complex civil litigation to the run-of-the-mill divorce case or traffic ticket.

The structure of state courts is much more varied than that of the federal court system. The 50 states have created a variety of court structures. Some court systems are unified and clearly organized; others are a jumble of overlapping jurisdiction and confusion. In this section, we present a "typical" state court system.

The most common state court system is comprised of four levels, or tiers, of courts. There are courts of limited jurisdiction, courts of general jurisdiction, inter-mediate appellate courts, and a final appellate court or court of last resort. Although most states have only one court of last resort, Oklahoma and Texas have two. Texas has one for civil appeals (Texas Supreme Court) and one for criminal appeals (Court of Criminal Appeals). The Texas court hierarchy is presented in Figure 4.3.

Figure 4.3 The Texas State Court System

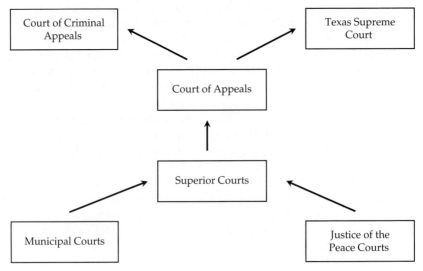

Courts of limited jurisdiction are those courts that deal with the less serious offenses and civil cases. These courts are referred to by a variety of names, including justice of the peace court, magistrate's court, municipal court, and county court. These lower courts handle a wide variety of matters, including minor criminal cases, traffic offenses, violations of municipal ordinances, and civil disputes under a certain amount, usually $1,000. On the criminal side, these courts also may be responsible for issuing search and arrest warrants and conducting the preliminary stages of felony cases, such as the preliminary hearing and arraignment. On the civil side, these courts may handle a variety of matters, including juvenile delinquency, family law, and probate.

Proceedings in lower courts are often more informal in nature than they are in appellate or trial courts. Generally, there is no right to trial provided in these courts. If losing parties wish to appeal adverse decisions, they must do so through a **trial de novo** in the court of original jurisdiction. A trial de novo is not like a standard appeal, where the higher court concerns itself only with a review of the trial record and consideration of any possible legal errors. Instead, it is an entirely new trial. Lower courts are not "courts of record"—that is, there is no constitutional requirement to provide an official, verbatim recording or transcript of the proceedings. The only official document is the judgment of the court.

While courts of limited jurisdiction receive very little attention, they are important for several reasons. First, these courts are the only experience that many citizens will ever have with the court system. Second, they process a tremendous number of cases, and there are many of these courts. The National Center for State Courts reports that there are almost 14,000 lower courts, which process more than 80 million cases each year. Third, these courts often are involved in the crucial early stages of criminal cases, the issuance of search and arrest warrants, and the determination of whether to set bail and to hold the suspect over for trial.

The next level in a typical state court system is the courts of general jurisdiction. These are the trial courts for civil and criminal matters. They are also courts of original jurisdiction in that trials for felonies are held in them. A **felony** is defined as a crime for which the possible punishment includes a sentence of imprisonment for at least one year. Generally, these courts are authorized to hear any matters not exclusively designated for courts of limited jurisdiction. In some states, they even may have concurrent jurisdiction with lower courts on some matters such as misdemeanors. They also may hear appeals, in the form of a trial de novo, from lower courts.

A trial court usually is referred to as the district court, circuit court, or superior court, although at least one state (New York) refers to its trial court as the supreme court and its court of last resort as the court of appeals. The precise workload of the trial courts varies by jurisdiction. In less populous areas, the trial court may hear all manner of cases, including civil and criminal. In more populated areas, there may be a greater specialization, with one court handling only felony trials and another handling only civil matters.

To date, 39 states have two levels of appellate courts, consisting of an intermediate appellate court and a court of last resort. Intermediate appellate courts are largely a creation of the twentieth century. As jurisdictions became more crowded and court dockets increased, officials saw a need to relieve the state supreme court of the burden of hearing all appeals of right. The states that have not created an intermediate court tend to be either very small or not very densely populated.

The intermediate appellate courts are referred to by a variety of names, but by far the most common is the court of appeals. The primary purpose of the intermediate court of appeals is to hear felony appeals of right. An appeal of right is an appeal that state legislatures permit all criminal defendants as a matter of law and occurs after a final order has been entered by the trial court. There is no constitutional right to appeal a guilty verdict, but all 50 states and the federal government provide for an appeal of right by either statute or state constitutional provision. The number of judges on the intermediate appellate court varies, and many states have more than one intermediate appellate court.

The court of last resort is in most states called the state supreme court, and the number of judges on this court varies by state from three to nine. The court of last resort usually hears the majority of appeals on a discretionary basis, similar to the US Supreme Court. This allows them to control their docket and focus on cases involving significant legal issues. Exceptions are those states that do not have an intermediate appellate court and states with the death penalty. In states without an intermediate appellate court (usually the smaller, less populous states), the state supreme court is the only appellate court and thus is mandated by law to hear all appeals. Most states also require their supreme court to hear all appeals in cases involving the death penalty. This is provided as an extra safeguard, as the punishment in these cases is obviously the most severe and the states want to be absolutely sure the defendant has received a fair trial.

For most cases, the state supreme court is the end of the line, the final arbiter of the dispute. The only option for a losing party in the state supreme court is to appeal directly to the US Supreme Court, and to do so, the party must be able to identify a legal issue that involves the US Constitution or a federal law. While it is common for a litigant to proclaim "I'll take my case all the way to the US Supreme Court," it is very unlikely that the case will actually get there, as the Supreme Court decides fewer than one case a year.

OVERVIEW OF THE CRIMINAL PROCESS

The criminal process begins with either the filing of a complaint or an arrest. A **complaint** is simply an accusation on a formal document that may be filled out by an officer or a private citizen accusing a specified person or persons of committing a specified criminal act or acts. If an arrest is made first, a complaint will be sworn out afterward, usually by the arresting officer. The complaint serves as the charging document for the preliminary hearing.

Search and arrest warrants are obtained by police officers who first must fill out an affidavit stating the facts relied on to create probable cause. **Probable cause** is a legal concept referring to the amount of proof a police officer must have to search or arrest someone. This is discussed further in chapter 6. After individuals are arrested, they are booked. **Booking** is an administrative procedure, and it involves making an entry in the police blotter at the station indicating the suspect's name, arrest time, and offense and taking the suspect's fingerprints and photographs.

The first court appearance is referred to as the **initial appearance** and takes place in a municipal or justice of the peace court. Once a person is arrested, the individual must be brought before a magistrate "without unnecessary delay." It is here that suspects are informed of their constitutional rights as well as the nature of the charges against them, and a bail decision is made as to whether it will be granted and, if so, at how much it will be set.

The next stage in the proceedings is the preliminary examination or **preliminary hearing**. Here, the magistrate determines if there is probable cause to believe that an offense was committed and that it was the defendant who committed it. If probable cause is established, the defendant is "bound over" for trial, meaning that a trial date is set and the defendant is notified of the pending charges. The preliminary examination is a formal adversarial proceeding conducted in open court. The Supreme Court has defined it as a "critical stage" of the prosecution, which means the defendant has a right to have his or her lawyer present.

Charges may be filed against a defendant either by an **information** or by an indictment. An **information** is prepared and signed for by the prosecutor. It informs the defendant of the facts and the elements of the offense for which he or she is and is a more efficient way to proceed, as it eliminates the need to organize a grand jury and present evidence. The Fifth Amendment requires the federal government to proceed through an **indictment** handed down by a grand jury. This clause of the Fifth Amendment is one of the few that has not been applied to the states, so states may use an information instead (*Hurtado v. California*, 1884). A little less than half of the states require an indictment. Twelve states require indictment by a grand jury only for felonies, while three states require indictment by a grand jury only for capital offenses. Four states require indictment by a grand jury for all felonies and misdemeanors (del Carmen, 2009).

The typical grand jury has 23 people, and proceedings are not open to the public. The only persons present aside from the members of the grand jury are the district attorney and any witnesses whom the attorney calls. Some states follow the federal model and seat grand juries of 23 members; other states seat anywhere from 6 to

23 members. Few states require grand juries in all felony cases, and in some states, a grand jury is formed only at the discretion of the prosecutor. The rationale behind requiring an indictment by a grand jury is that this body can act as a check on an overzealous prosecutor, preventing him or her from prosecuting cases for which there is not sufficient evidence. Since the grand jury hears only evidence presented by the state and the defense does not have the opportunity to challenge the information, rarely does a grand jury not return an indictment. This does not necessarily mean it is not achieving its purpose of preventing improper prosecutions, however, as its very existence may prevent prosecutors from taking shaky cases to the grand jury. In this way, the grand jury does check the prosecutor's power.

The next step in the process is the **arraignment**, a formal hearing before a felony court where defendants are again informed of the charges against them and advised of their rights. At this time, the defendant enters a **plea**, which is the defendant's response to the charge against him or her. Possible pleas include guilty (by far the most common plea), not guilty, standing mute, and no contest. **Standing mute** means that the defendant is refusing to plead. In these instances, the court enters a plea of not guilty on behalf of defendant, thus preserving the constitutional right to trial. A plea of no contest, also referred to as **nolo contendere**, means the defendant accepts whatever punishment the court would impose on a guilty defendant but refuses to admit liability. A no contest plea is frequently used by defendants who fear being exposed to civil liability for their criminal misdeeds, and a guilty plea would so expose them.

A fourth possible plea, not accepted as a valid option in all states and only rarely allowed in the federal system, is the Alford plea. An **Alford plea** is one in which the defendant enters a guilty plea but denies having committed the crime to which he or she is pleading. The reason that the Alford plea is not recognized in some states, and only reluctantly accepted in special circumstances in others, is that when a defendant enters a plea of guilty, he or she is expected to so state on the record. Judges do not take it lightly when defendants say they are guilty on the one hand and then assert their innocence on the other. As famous British jurist Lord Birkett responded to a defendant who said, "As God is my judge, I'm innocent": "He isn't. I am. You're not."

✳ THE JURY AND ITS SELECTION

Juries have played a crucial role in the common law almost from its beginnings. Its modern form started to take shape during the reign of Henry II, when the ecclesiastical (church) courts banned trial by combat and trial by ordeal in their courts (Macnair, 2006). Trial by combat meant that the parties literally fought each other, and trial by ordeal meant ordeals such as carrying hot coals for a certain distance. Victorious combatants and ordeal sufferers whose wounds did not fester within three days were said to have been favored by God, the ultimate judge, and thus innocent (Shapiro, 2002).

Early jurors were composed of what were known as "knowledgeable witnesses." These were "good and lawful" men who could provide testimony relating to what they knew about the events and persons involved in the case. They also sat in judgment, so the outcome of a case was the result of collective "witness/judgment" wisdom

Jury (1881)

(Macnair, 2006). The number of jurors necessary for a case to be heard was settled in favor of the old Anglo-Saxon custom of 12 men. Why the number 12 was chosen has been the topic of much speculation, but Horowitz and Willging (1984) supply a rationale that we find satisfying: "Twelve apostles, twelve tribes of Israel, twelve patriarchs, twelve officers in Solomon's court, twelve months in a year, are among the credentials it has as a number of unusual potency" (p. 165).

Gradually juries began to be composed of disinterested parties rather than individuals with special knowledge of the case or of the parties involved. Unlike the continental systems of law, in which professional judges were finders of both law and fact, the common law system since the time of Edward I (1239–1307) has been one in which matters of law were the domain of the judge while matters of fact were the domain of juries, although there are exceptions. That is, judges made sure that the trial process followed legal rules and procedures and instructed jurors on the law, but only jurors could be finders of fact; in other words, only jurors were to determine the meaning of the evidence provided by both sides of a dispute (Shapiro, 2002). This is the concept of the jury that was imported into the United States by the early colonists, and we continue to view it this way today.

Jury Selection

When defendants (suspects become defendants once they have been officially indicted) plead not guilty, the next step in the process is the trial itself. Once a trial date is set, jury selection begins. The jury is selected from the eligible members of the community who are selected at random, usually from voting or automobile registration records. These records are used to obtain as complete a list as possible of all the residents of a community. The legal term for summoning jurors is the **venire**, which is Latin for "to cause" or to "make come" (to the courthouse). Prospective jurors are examined by the judge and/or the attorneys for the prosecution and defense to determine whether they have any bias, prejudice, or interest that would prevent them from being impartial. This process of questioning the jurors is referred to as the **voir dire**, which literally means "to speak the truth."

While the stated purpose of the voir dire is to obtain an unbiased jury, in reality each side seeks not only to excuse potential jurors who are biased against their side but also to keep on potential jurors who are biased toward their side. Many attorneys are so averse to impartial juries that they even employ the services of professional **jury consultants** to make sure they do not get one. These consultants use the theories and methods of social science to help them determine what type of person is more likely to favor their side. Jury consultants are expensive and are mainly used in civil cases involving millions of dollars. In criminal cases, their use is confined to the very rich and/or celebrity defendants, such as Robert Blake and O. J. Simpson (both of whom beat strong cases against them).

Both the prosecution and the defense may seek to remove potential jurors they feel may be biased against them. Jurors may be removed by a **challenge for cause**, in which a valid reason for wanting to dismiss an individual is shown to the court's satisfaction, or they may be removed through the use of a **peremptory challenge**, for which no reason need be given. While challenges for cause are unlimited, peremptory challenges are usually limited to a certain number (most commonly 6 or 12). The Supreme Court has held that peremptory challenges may not be used to exclude potential jurors on the basis of race (*Batson v. Kentucky,* 1986) or gender (*J.E.B. v. Alabama,* 1994).

The Supreme Court also has held that a jury need not be composed of the traditional 12 members, since there is no constitutional requirement for such a number. Juries with as few as six members have been approved for both civil and criminal trials (*Williams v. Florida,* 1970). Furthermore, there is no constitutional requirement that the jury verdict be unanimous, even in criminal cases. The Supreme Court has approved verdicts of 10-2 (*Apodaca v. Oregon,* 1972) and 9-3 (*Johnson v. Louisiana,* 1972); however, juries consisting of six members must render unanimous verdicts (*Burch v. Louisiana,* 1979). Finally, the requirement for a "jury of one's peers" has been interpreted simply as requiring that the jury be selected from the community where the crime takes place. It does not mean the jury must share any other similarities with the defendant. (Initially, the principle of a trial by one's peers proclaimed in the Magna Carta meant that nobles should be tried by nobles and commoners by commoners. Today, there is no such requirement.)

The Trial

Once the jury is selected and sworn in, various motions may be filed by attorneys for each side. A **motion** is simply a request made to the court asking it for something, such as granting a continuance, suppressing evidence, or dismissing the case. After any motions have been granted or denied, the next step in a jury trial is the making of opening statements—first by the prosecution, because it has the burden of proof, and then by the defense. The defense may choose to reserve its opening statement until after the prosecution has presented its evidence. This is referred to as the prosecution's case-in-chief. During this phase, the prosecution must establish each element of the crime charged beyond a reasonable doubt.

Once the prosecution has presented its evidence and called its witnesses, the defense has an opportunity to present its case-in-chief. The defense is not required to put on any evidence or witnesses, but if the defense chooses, it may raise several types of defenses. These include an alibi or an affirmative defense such as insanity or self-defense (these defenses are addressed in chapter 5). The prosecution may then choose to rebut the defense's case.

Next are closing arguments, in which each side has the opportunity to sum up its case. Here, the prosecution gets to go last, since it has the burden of proof. After closing arguments, or in some jurisdictions before them, the judge will give the jury instructions on the applicable law. These include instructions on the elements of the crime charged, the presumption of innocence, and the burden of proof—which in criminal trials is proof beyond a reasonable doubt.

Once the jury has received its instructions, it retires to the jury room to deliberate, and it remains there until a verdict is reached. In most jurisdictions, criminal verdicts must be unanimous, despite the Supreme Court's ruling that unanimity is not constitutionally required. In these jurisdictions, failure to achieve a unanimous verdict (a "hung jury") means that a **mistrial** is declared. If this occurs, the defendant may be retried without violating the prohibition against double jeopardy because the case never reached a verdict. Alternatively, the prosecutor may decide that the state cannot win its case and dismiss the charges.

Sentencing

If a jury returns a verdict of not guilty, the defendant is set free, and the constitutional prohibition on double jeopardy prevents the state from prosecuting the defendant again for the same act or appealing the not guilty verdict. If the verdict is guilty, then a sentence must be imposed. In most instances, the judge imposes the sentence. An interesting case strictly affirming the separation of roles between judges and jurors was handed down by the Supreme Court in *Ring v. Arizona* (2002). Timothy Ring was convicted by the jury of killing an armored-car driver in a robbery. A separate hearing called the penalty phase, which is constitutionally required in a death penalty case, was then held before the judge alone to determine sentencing. After hearing testimony, the judge found that the aggravated circumstances of the murder warranted the death penalty. The problem the Supreme Court found was that the aggravated circumstances heard by the judge constituted facts, and the finding of matters of fact is the domain of juries. The Court thus vacated Ring's death sentence and required that the jury determine the appropriate sentence. This ruling affected only the eight states in which judges alone impose the death penalty.

In other kinds of cases, the sentence is usually not handed down immediately after the verdict. Instead, the judge orders a presentence investigation report (PSI) written by officers in a probation department. This report contains information about the offense, the offender's personal and criminal histories, medical and psychological information, and any other pertinent information used to aid the officer in making his or her sentencing recommendation and to guide the judge in actually imposing the sentence. The PSI thus contains facts discovered by the PSI investigator, which are then conveyed to the sentencing judge along with a sentencing recommendation based on them. These facts are not available to a jury, so unless the PSI is written on a case that was plea bargained and thus no jury is involved, this opens the door for another *Ring*-type ruling by the Supreme Court in the future.

A number of different sentences are possible. These include probation, a suspended sentence, or a fine. Factors influencing the sentence include the information contained in the PSI, the attitude of the defendant, and the defendant's prior criminal and personal histories. In recent years, there has been a move to increase sentence length and require incarceration, with the result being a tremendous growth in the number of persons imprisoned. However, probation, which may be paired with fines and some jail time, is still the most common sentence in the United States.

Appeals

Once a person has been convicted and sentenced, there are two ways to challenge the trial outcome. A defendant may file either a direct appeal or an indirect appeal, also known as a writ of habeas corpus. **Habeas corpus** translates as "you have the body," and the writ requires the person to whom it is directed to either justify the confinement of the person named in the writ or release that person from custody. There is no federal constitutional right to an appeal, but every state allows a direct appeal, either by statute or state constitutional provision.

Habeas corpus is an ancient legal remedy, dating back at least to the Magna Carta, and is often referred to as the "Great Writ." The writ of habeas corpus is considered an indirect appeal because it does not directly challenge the defendant's conviction but instead challenges the authority of the state to incarcerate the defendant. The state defense to a habeas writ, however, is based on the conviction—that is why the defendant has been incarcerated.

There is no time limit for filing a habeas petition, unlike for a direct appeal, which in most jurisdictions must be filed within a set period, usually several months. However, Congress has restricted the use of habeas corpus by imposing time limits on federal habeas petitions if there is evidence of intentional delay by the defendant that injures the prosecution's case. Additionally, Congress and the Supreme Court have restricted habeas corpus by imposing limits on how such appeals are filed and pursued, such as requiring that inmates include all their appealable issues in one writ rather than doing separate, consecutive writs for each issue (Maahs & Hemmens, 1998).

COURT ACTORS

There are three key actors in court: judges, prosecutors, and defense attorneys. It is important to understand what they do and how they do it so that we can better understand why courts function the way they do and how they can be improved.

Judges

The judge serves as a sort of referee, responsible for enforcing court rules, instructing the jury on the law, and determining the law. Judges are expected to be completely impartial. Trial judges have tremendous power to control a case, although they do not actively participate in the trial by questioning witnesses or the defendant, unlike judges in many non–common law legal systems.

As a whole, judges are not representative of American society. Just like their counterparts on the Supreme Court, they are frequently white, male, and upper middle class. Women and minorities are underrepresented, not only with respect to their numbers in American society but to their proportion in the legal community. A number of commentators have argued that this results in bias, either intentional or unintentional. Others have suggested that even if bias does not exist, there is a perception among many segments of the population that justice is not obtainable because minorities and women are underrepresented on the bench (Graham, 1990; Slotnick, 1988).

There are three common methods of selecting judges: appointment, election, and the merit system. Different jurisdictions use different methods of selecting judges. Some jurisdictions use more than one method, while others, such as the federal system, use only one.

Appointment by the chief executive of the jurisdiction (the president of the United States or the governor of an individual state) is the oldest method of selecting judges. All 13 of the original colonies used it, and it is used today in the federal system and about 20 states. Table 4.1 presents methods of selecting judges for courts of general jurisdiction in all 50 states and the name that each state employs for their courts of general jurisdiction.

Election of judges became popular during the 1830s, when Democrats under the leadership of Andrew Jackson gained control of Congress from the Federalists. Jackson and his supporters believed wholeheartedly in popular democracy and thought that appointment of judges was undemocratic (Slotnick, 1988). Georgia (1824) was the first state to implement judicial elections. As seen in Table 4.1, currently 29 states use popular elections to select judges.

These elections take one of two forms. Some states have *partisan* (meaning aligned with a particular party) elections in which candidates for judicial office run in the party primary and their political affiliation is listed on the ballot. Thirteen states use this method. In 16 other states, judges are selected by nonpartisan elections in which no political affiliation is listed. In two states, South Carolina and Georgia, judges are elected by the legislature.

The third method of selecting judges is the merit system. This system is based on one originally developed by the American Judicature Society in 1909 and endorsed by the American Bar Association in 1937. It was first adopted by Missouri in 1940; consequently, it sometimes is referred to as the *Missouri plan* (Slotnick, 1988).

The merit system has become popular only recently. In 1960, only four states used the system, but by 1998, about half the states used it. The merit system has three parts. First, a nonpartisan nominating commission selects a list of potential candidates based on the candidates' legal qualifications. Second, the governor makes a selection from this list. Finally, the person selected as a judge stands for election (this is referred to as *retention*) within a short time after he or she is selected, usually within one year.

Prosecutors

Under the early common law, there were no public prosecutors. Instead, private citizens were responsible for litigating their criminal cases. Private prosecution gave way to public prosecution as society came to view crime as an offense not just against the person but against society as well. Today, private prosecution is no longer permitted in any state. In its place are prosecutor's offices. There are more

Table 4.1 *Methods of Selecting Judges for Courts of General Jurisdiction and Names Given to Courts of General Jurisdiction by State*

Election	Name	Nominating commission	Name	Appointed by governor	Name
Alabama (P)	Circuit	Alaska	Superior	Maine	Superior
Arkansas (P)	Circuit	Arizona	Superior	New Hampshire	Superior
California (N)	Superior	Colorado	District	New Jersey	Superior
Florida (N)	Circuit	Connecticut	Superior	Rhode Island	Superior
Georgia (N)	Superior	Delaware	Superior		
Idaho (N)	District	Hawaii	Circuit		
Illinois (P)	Circuit	Iowa	District		
Indiana (P)	Circuit	Kansas	District		
Kentucky (N)	Circuit	Maryland	Circuit		
Louisiana (P)	District	Massachusetts	Superior		
Michigan (N)	Circuit	Nebraska	District		
Minnesota (N)	District	New Mexico	District		
Mississippi (P)	Circuit	Utah	District		
Missouri (P)	Circuit	Vermont	Superior		
Montana (N)	District	Wyoming	District		
Nevada (N)	District				
New York (P)	Supreme				
North Carolina (P)	Superior				
North Dakota (N)	District				
Ohio (N)	Common Pleas				
Oklahoma (N)	District				
Oregon (N)	Circuit				
Pennsylvania (P)	Common Pleas				
South Carolina (L)	Circuit				
South Dakota (N)	Circuit				
Tennessee (P)	Circuit				
Texas (P)	District				
Virginia (L)	Circuit				
Washington (N)	Superior				
West Virginia (P)	Circuit				
Wisconsin (N)	Circuit				

Note: P = partisan election; N = nonpartisan election; L = election by legislature. Election, $N = 31$ (13 partisan, 16 nonpartisan, 2 legislature); nominating commission, $N = 15$; appointment by governor, $N = 4$.

than 25,000 prosecutors today, although about half of them are part-time (primarily in small jurisdictions).

The Judiciary Act of 1789 provided for a US attorney for each court district who was appointed by the president. In 1870, Congress authorized the creation of the Department of Justice, with an attorney general and assistants. The attorney general, a political appointee, is an administrator who sets prosecution priorities for deputy attorney generals. Deputy attorney generals are appointed by the president, are confirmed by the Senate, and serve at the pleasure of the president. Assistant US attorneys are not political appointments.

State prosecutors are called by various names, such as district attorney, solicitor, county attorney, state's attorney, and commonwealth attorney. State prosecutors are usually elected officials with appointed assistants who do most of the trial work. Only four states (Alaska, Connecticut, Delaware, and New Jersey) do not have an elected district attorney. The district attorney's duty is to prosecute cases in the name of the people but also to do justice by pursuing only those who have committed crimes. District attorneys have tremendous power to decide whether or not to prosecute, and this power is largely unreviewable, meaning that there are few real or meaningful restrictions on prosecutorial discretion.

Defense Attorneys

Defense attorneys are expected to represent their client as effectively as possible while acting within the rules of court. The right to counsel existed in common law and in state constitutions. The Sixth Amendment codified this right. The Supreme Court has interpreted the Sixth Amendment requiring the right to counsel as applying at any "critical stage" of the prosecution, not just at trial. Thus, a defendant has been held to have the right to counsel at a lineup, which takes place after indictment; at the preliminary hearing; and during pretrial discovery.

The role of defense counsel is primarily (a) to ensure that the defendants' rights are not violated (intentionally or in error); (b) to ensure the defendants know all their options before they make a decision; (c) to provide the defendants with the best possible defense, without violating ethical and legal obligations; (d) to investigate and prepare the defense; and (e) to argue for lowest possible sentence or best possible plea bargain (Uphoff, 1992).

There are several types of defense counsel. These include privately retained counsel, public defenders, and court-appointed counsel. Private attorneys are selected and paid for by the defendant. Public defenders are hired full-time by the state but work for defendants who cannot afford to hire their own lawyer. A court-appointed counsel is a private attorney who is paid by the state on a case-by-case basis to represent indigent defendants.

A fourth method of providing indigent offenders with counsel is the contract system. Under this system, a number of private law firms may enter bids to serve as a sort of subcontractor in the area covered by the court's jurisdiction. This system is usually utilized in lightly populated counties, and the contract typically goes to the lowest bidder.

While the Supreme Court has held that there is a right to counsel, the Court has not held that this means a right to the counsel of one's choice in all cases. A person who can afford to hire a lawyer may do so. Those who cannot afford a lawyer will be provided one, but there are limits on when the appointment will occur and the defendants have little or no say in who is selected to represent them.

THE LEGAL PROFESSION

Prosecutors, defense attorneys, and judges have one thing in common—they are all lawyers. They have graduated from a law school, passed a state bar examination, and are members of the legal profession, or "bar." The legal profession has a long and colorful history, both in the United States and around the world. Originally, one became a lawyer in the United States by reading the law and serving as an apprentice for several years with an established attorney. After a period of work and study by the potential lawyer, he (only men were lawyers for much of early American history) could be sponsored by his supervising lawyer.

Until the 1870s, there was little control over who could call themselves a lawyer and engage in the practice of law. Several states created **bar associations**, groups of lawyers who attempted to regulate the practice of law, and in 1878, a national organization, the American Bar Association, was created and tasked with promulgating regulations and standards for the practice of law. Eventually, each state developed its own bar association and took responsibility for regulating the practice of law in that state.

Membership in a bar association today requires, at minimum, a degree from an American Bar Association–accredited (or approved) law school, passage of a **bar examination**, and a background check. Each state has its own bar association and bar examination; passage of the bar exam in one state does not allow a person to practice law in other states.

Legal education developed at approximately the same time that state bar associations began to proliferate. While law schools had existed since the 1780s, it was not until the 1870s that the modern approach to legal education was developed. Christopher Columbus Langdell, the dean of Harvard Law School from 1870 to 1895, is often credited with the development of the legal education model that focuses on the study of appellate opinions (often referred to as the **casebook approach**) and the use of the so-called Socratic method in the classroom. The **Socratic method** is intended to model the dialogue between Socrates and his students—the professor asks the law student a series of questions intended to force the student to identify key legal principles and doctrines and to apply them to hypothetical situations. Law schools today still employ the Socratic method and the legal casebook, but many have moved beyond this approach and added courses that emphasize the daily practice of law—the "nuts and bolts" of the law—as opposed to legal theory and doctrine.

Once a person has passed a state bar exam, he or she is eligible to practice law in that particular jurisdiction. While all attorneys take the bar exam, not all attorneys practice the same law. Some lawyers focus on criminal law; others focus on some aspect of the civil law, such as contracts, family law, or personal injury law. Some lawyers spend much of their day in court working as litigators. Other attorneys rarely enter the courtroom and focus their practice on research. Some attorneys work in the public sector and others in the private sector. The popular image of the lawyer is someone who works in a large law firm, but in reality, most lawyers work in very small law firms or as solo practitioners.

SUMMARY

In this chapter, we have provided an overview of both the federal and state court systems, and we have examined the key actors in the court system (judges, prosecutors, and defense attorneys). We also have provided an overview of the trial process from arrest to sentencing. While these may seem like "basic" materials to some, they are crucial components of the legal system. One cannot understand how justice is done if one does not understand how cases are dealt with and who is involved in the justice process. It is crucial that students understand not only the stages in the process but also the roles played by those involved at each stage.

The United States has essentially 51 court systems—1 federal system and 50 state systems. While there are many similarities between these systems, there are also differences in both how the process works and how the participants in the process are selected. Different states have different court arrangements. Some states have elected judges, while others (and the federal system) rely on appointed judges. These differences are important factors in how justice is distributed in the courts.

The criminal trial process has many stages, and each stage is important. At each stage, the prosecution is called upon to demonstrate to the court that there exists sufficient evidence to hold the defendant over for further proceedings; this burden increases from "probable cause" to, eventually, "proof beyond a reasonable doubt." At each stage, the prosecution and defense reveal some of the information they have; by the time the trial is through, both sides have had the opportunity to present to the fact finder (usually a jury) all the evidence in their possession. The jury is then called upon to render a verdict. The appeals process provides a degree of protection for defendants who have been convicted—this close scrutiny of the trial process is unparalleled in the world. The appeals process is set up to determine whether mistakes were made at trial that caused a miscarriage of justice.

While justice may be an elusive concept, and one with different meanings for different people in the United States, the court system clearly is intended to provide a forum for doing justice. There are many different types of courts, but all share this common feature. Courts serve as a forum for settling disputes between private parties, as a means of prosecuting individuals who break the law, and as a place where public policy sometimes is made. The common refrains "I'll sue you" and "I'll take it all the way to the Supreme Court" are evidence that courts are a popular forum.

DISCUSSION QUESTIONS

1. What are the different types of jurisdiction?
2. What are the different stages in the criminal trial process, and why is each important?

3. What are the different methods for selecting judges, and what are the advantages and disadvantages of each?
4. What are the ethical problems involved in the use of jury consultants? Does the use of jury consultants result in one system of justice for the rich and another for the poor?
5. If a jury verdict of guilty is not unanimous, does that mean that there was reasonable doubt? If so, do you think non-unanimous verdicts violate the Sixth Amendment?
6. Should Supreme Court justices be elected and therefore responsible to the people for their rulings? Why or why not?
7. What is the role of the defense attorney?
8. What are the different types of pleas a defendant may enter?
9. What is the difference between a challenge for cause and a peremptory challenge?
10. What role does the grand jury serve?

CHAPTER TERMS

Alford plea
Appellate jurisdiction
Arraignment
Article III courts
Bar associations
Bar examination
Booking
Casebook approach
Challenge for cause
Complaint
Diversity of citizenship
Felony
General jurisdiction

Geographical jurisdiction
Habeas corpus
Hierarchical jurisdiction
Indictment
Information
Initial appearance
Jurisdiction
Jury consultants
Limited jurisdiction
Mistrial
Motion
Nolo contendere
Original jurisdiction

Peremptory challenge
Personal jurisdiction
Plea
Preliminary hearing
Probable cause
Rule of four
Socratic method
Standing mute
Subject matter jurisdiction
Trial de novo
Venire
Voir dire
Writ of certiorari

References

Abraham, H. (1987). *The judiciary: The Supreme Court in the governmental process* (7th ed.). Boston, MA: Allyn & Bacon.

Brigham, J. (1987). *The cult of the court.* Philadelphia, PA: Temple University Press.

Cooper, P. (1988). *Hard judicial choices.* New York, NY: Oxford University Press.

del Carmen, R. (2009). *Criminal procedure: Law and practice.* Belmont, CA: Wadsworth.

Graham, B. (1990). Judicial recruitment and racial diversity on state courts. *Judicature, 74,* 28–34.

Horowitz, I., & Willging, T. (1984). *The psychology of law: Integrations and applications.* Boston, MA: Little, Brown.

Kelly, A., Harbison, W., & Belz, H. (1983). *The American Constitution: Its origins and development* (6th ed.). New York, NY: Norton.

Maahs, J., & Hemmens, C. (1998). The Prison Litigation Reform Act and frivolous section 1983 suits. *Corrections Management Quarterly, 2,* 90–94.

Macnair, M. (2006). Vicinage and the antecedents of the jury. *Law and History Review, 17*(1), 24–41.

Meador, D. (1991). *American courts.* St. Paul, MN: West.

Perry, M. (1994). *The Constitution in the courts.* New York, NY: Oxford University Press.

Shapiro, B. (2002). Testimony in seventeenth-century English natural philosophy: Legal origins and early development. *Studies in History and Philosophy of Science, 33,* 243–263.

Shreve, G., & Raven-Hansen, P. (1994). *Understanding civil procedure* (2nd ed.). New York, NY: Matthew Bender.

Slotnick, E. (1988). Review essay on judicial recruitment and selection. *Justice System Journal, 13,* 109–124.

Smith, C. (1992). From U.S. magistrates to U.S. magistrate judges: Developments affecting the federal district courts' lower tier of judicial officers. *Judicature, 75,* 210–215.

Uphoff, R. (1992). The criminal defense lawyer: Zealous advocate, double agent, or beleaguered dealer? *Criminal Law Bulletin, 28,* 419–456.

Wasby, S. (1993). *The Supreme Court in the federal judicial system.* Chicago, IL: Nelson-Hall.

Cases Cited

Apodaca v. Oregon, 406 U.S. 404 (1972)

Batson v. Kentucky, 476 U.S. 79 (1986)

Burch v. Louisiana, 441 U.S. 130 (1979)

Hurtado v. California, 110 U.S. 516 (1884)

J.E.B. v. Alabama ex rel T.B., 511 U.S. 127 (1994)

Johnson v. Louisiana, 406 U.S. 356 (1972)

Ring v. Arizona, 536 U.S. 584 (2002)

Williams v. Florida, 399 U.S. 78 (1970)

CHAPTER 5

CRIME
AND
CRIMINAL LAW

Ms. Cogdon suffered from occasional bouts of sleepwalking and night-mares. She had spoken to her doctor about these events, and he had prescribed her a sedative and suggested she consider psychiatric counseling. One night, Ms. Cogdon talked with her daughter, Pat, about the possibility that the country would get involved in the war in Korea. She then went to bed. That night, Ms. Cogdon dreamed that there was a war going on around her house and that soldiers had entered the house and were attacking her daughter. When Ms. Cogdon awoke, she was in her neighbor's house. When she returned home, she discovered that her daughter Pat was dead. It turned out Ms. Cogdon had been sleepwalking and had gone outside to the wood-pile, picked up an axe, come back into the house, gone into Pat's room, and struck her twice in the head with the axe, killing her.

Ms. Cogdon was arrested and tried for the murder of her daughter. She admitted administering the blows that killed her daughter and did not claim that she suffered from a mental disease or insanity. Instead, her defense to the charge was that she did not "act" in killing her daughter because she was asleep. The criminal law generally requires that to hold a person liable for committing a crime, there must be evidence that that person committed a voluntary act. Ms. Cogdon argued that because she was asleep, her obtain-ing the axe and striking her daughter with it were not voluntary acts. Rather, they were involuntary, products of her dream and her sleepwalking. The jury accepted Ms. Cogdon's account and voted to acquit her on the grounds that her actions were not truly voluntary.

INTRODUCTION

In this chapter, we discuss the basic elements of criminal law, sometimes referred to as substantive law. **Substantive law** is the law of crimes, as compared to **procedural law** (discussed in chapter 6), which contains the rules the state must follow when investi-gating suspects or prosecuting someone who has committed a crime. Substantive law is defined by statute, and it *prescribes* (tells us what we should do) and *proscribes* (tells us what we should not do) various types of conduct. It is a code of conduct that everyone in a society is expected to follow and includes such items as prohibitions on murder, assault, and burglary. Criminal laws are enforced by the state, and violation of the criminal law is treated as an act against the state as well as the individual victim. The primary purpose of criminal law is thus to protect the public from harm by punishing harmful acts that have occurred and forbidding conduct that may lead to it.

WHAT IS CRIME?

A frequently quoted definition of crime is that of Paul Tappan, who defined it as "an intentional act in violation of the criminal law committed without defense or excuse, and penalized by the state" (Walsh & Ellis, 2007, p. 3). This is a legal definition with five components: **crime** is an (a) *act* in violation of (b) a *criminal law* for which (c) a *punishment* is prescribed, and the person committing it must have (d) *intended* to do so and to have done so without a legally acceptable (e) *defense or* justification (see Table 5.1). Defining *crime* is not the same as defining *gravity* or *photosynthesis* because unlike these natural phenomena crime is defined into existence rather than discovered. By this we mean that crimes can be defined into and pass out of existence by human beings. This does not mean that they have no harmful substance independent of human definitions of them as such, but we must remember that what are crimes at one time or in other cultures may be considered virtues at other times or in other cultures.

For instance, the Harrison Narcotics Act of 1914 created a large class of criminals overnight by in effect criminalizing the sale, possession, or use of "narcotics." Although the wording of this act clearly states that it was intended to ensure the orderly marketing of narcotics, it was soon interpreted and acted upon as prohibiting them (Goode, 2005). Prior to the act, there were few restrictions on these substances, many of which were sold in pharmacies and elsewhere as cures for all kinds of ailments. Crimes also pass out of existence. People could be imprisoned in many states for committing sodomy or burning the American flag until recently. Statutes criminalizing sodomy were ruled unconstitutional by the US Supreme Court in *Lawrence v. Texas* (2003); statues criminalizing flag burning were struck down in *Texas v. Johnson* (1989).

Despite the arbitrariness of many criminal statues, a core of acts are universally condemned and criminalized. According to the International Criminal Police

Table 5.1 *The Five Components of a Criminal Act*

1. An *act*, which is in violation of
2. a *criminal law*, for which
3. a *punishment* is prescribed and
4. for which the person committing the act must have *intended* to do so
5. and to have done so without legally acceptable *defense or justification*.

Organization (Interpol), acts such as murder, rape, assault, and theft are criminalized in every one of its 125 member nations (Ellis & Walsh, 2000). These are crimes we defined in chapter 2 as *mala in se* crimes, or crimes that are inherently harmful because they generate strong emotional responses in all victims of them. Acts not considered *mala in se* may or may not be criminalized in a particular place at a particular time according to the social attitudes surrounding those acts at the time. All socially harmful acts run the risk of criminalization, but not all are so classified.

A crime is a subcategory of all harmful acts. Figure 5.1 helps to distinguish between the various subcategories. The largest circle contains all harms, personal and social, criminal and noncriminal. Some harmful acts, such as drinking to excess, are considered no one else's business except the person engaging in them unless that person creates a public annoyance or endangers public safety. The next largest circle contains all social harms that are regulated by the state but not by the criminal justice system. These acts are typically regulated by civil law or administrative bodies (see chapter 7). The next circle contains all crimes, both *mala prohibita* and *mala in se*, and the final circle contains the "core" *mala in se* crimes.

Walsh and Ellis (2007) differentiate *mala in se* from *mala prohibita* in terms of three concepts that are arrayed on continua from low to high: consensus, seriousness (corresponding to severity of penalty), and harm. There is little consensus among people on the seriousness of crimes such as prostitution and smoking marijuana: for some, the social harm is regarded as minor, and penalties are consequently relatively light. There is universal consensus, however, that *mala in se* crimes such as murder and rape are wrong. It is also obvious that such crimes cause high levels of social harm and are extremely serious offenses, and therefore they carry severe penalties.

Part I offenses in the Federal Bureau of Investigation's annual report known as the **Uniform Crime Reports** (UCR) are major *mala in se* crimes. The UCR defines these eight crimes (murder, rape, robbery, aggravated assault, burglary, larceny/theft, motor

Figure 5.1 *Mala in Se* and *Mala Prohibita* Crimes as Subsets of all Harms

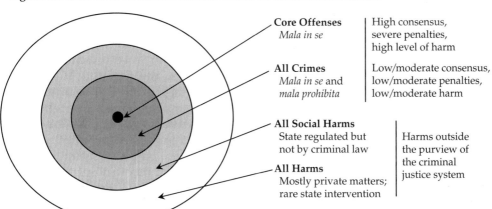

Source: A. Walsh and L. Ellis (2007). *Criminology: An Interdisciplinary Approach*. Thousand Oaks, California: Sage/Pine Forge Press. Reprinted with permission.

vehicle theft, and arson) and reports their annual incidence. A large number of other offenses, known as Part II offenses, also are reported in the UCR. These are a mixture of *mala prohibita* offenses, such as gambling and prostitution, and a number of other offenses that are less serious *mala in se* offenses, such as simple assault. Part I offenses include those known to the police, whether or not an arrest was made for them; the much more numerous Part II offenses are reported only if an arrest was made.

While different jurisdictions define criminal acts, defenses, and penalties differently, there are similarities that traverse jurisdictional boundaries. Common characteristics of criminal law include a description of prohibited conduct, a list of the penalties prescribed for those who violate the law, and the provision of certain defenses to criminal liability. Conviction carries with it the community's formal condemnation. This final element is what sets criminal law apart from civil law, which involves disputes between private parties.

 ## SOURCES OF CRIMINAL LAW

Criminal law is derived from a variety of sources, including state and federal constitutions, state and federal statutes, and common law. Treason is the only crime specifically mentioned in the US Constitution. The bulk of criminal law is located in state statutes, variously referred to as the penal code or the criminal code. Much of the states' criminal codes are derived from common law crimes. New crimes are added as circumstances warrant, however, and definitions of crimes may be modified over time.

Around the middle of the nineteenth century, states began to codify the common law, enacting criminal codes that set forth in one location the law of crimes. Statutes define the elements (the various parts) of a crime more specifically than was the case under common law, and some states still recognize as crimes those acts defined as such by common law even though they have not seen fit to codify them. A growing source of criminal law is federal criminal law. Traditionally, law enforcement has been left largely to the states, but as criminals become more sophisticated and their actions impact others outside of their local community, Congress criminalized additional activities, including selling drugs and kidnapping. Of course, these acts are crimes under state law as well.

LIMITATIONS ON CRIMINAL LAW

A state cannot criminalize any conduct it chooses. The due process clause of the Fourteenth Amendment has been interpreted by the Supreme Court to include both procedural and substantive due process. Substantive due process essentially means that there are limits to what conduct the law may seek to prohibit. Specifically, the due process clause forbids the passage of laws that infringe on the substantive rights of individuals, such as the rights to free speech and assembly, because such rights are fundamental and necessary for what the Court has termed "ordered liberty."

The legal theory of substantive due process is the underlying theory for the privacy rights extended in *Griswold v. Connecticut* (1965; access to birth control information and devices), *Roe v. Wade* (1973; abortion), and *Lawrence v. Texas* (2003; sexual practices). As with the concept of crime, however, what does and does not come under the umbrella of substantive due process has changed over time.

There are a number of other legal limitations on criminal law. Criminal laws that are either overly broad or vague (e.g., a law that prohibits anyone from "being about in public without a clear purpose") may be declared unconstitutional. A criminal law violates the **overbreadth doctrine** when it fails to narrowly define the specific behavior to be restricted. For instance, banning the sale of obscene materials is permitted, but a statute banning the sale of all material related to sexual activity would be overly broad.

A statute is **void for vagueness** if it fails to clearly define both the act prohibited and the appropriate punishment in advance. A statute must give fair notice to both law enforcement and citizens on exactly what conduct is forbidden so as to limit arbitrary enforcement and provide individuals with fair warning of what they lawfully may do (*Papachristou v. City of Jacksonville,* 1972). Fair notice simply means letting people know what is (and is not) permitted.

Criminal statutes also must not restrict due process or equal protection. Due process refers to the idea that laws must be enforced in a fair and nonarbitrary manner. Equal protection means that the state cannot enact or enforce laws aimed at restricting the rights of individuals who are members of "suspect classifications," or groups that historically have been ill-treated. According to the Supreme Court, these groups include racial minorities and, in some circumstances, women (*J.E.B. v. Alabama ex rel T.B.,* 1994).

The Eighth Amendment bars "cruel and unusual punishment." This has been read by the Supreme Court to require that a punishment be proportionate to the crime committed. Hence, the death penalty is appropriate only in cases where a murder has been committed (*Gregg v. Georgia,* 1976). The Eighth Amendment does not require that each jurisdiction punish an offense in precisely the same manner, nor does the concept of proportionality mean what it seems. The Court has allowed states to impose sentences of life in prison for habitual felons even when the underlying felonies involve nothing more serious than obtaining a total of less than $230 over a 15-year period by false pretenses (fraudulent use of a credit card and writing bad checks) in three separate incidents (*Rummel v. Estelle,* 1980). Needless to say, many would define this draconian sentence for such a trivial set of offenses as cruel and unusual.

Other constitutional limitations on criminal law that are raised less frequently include a prohibition on *ex post facto* laws and *bills of attainder.* **Ex post facto laws** are those passed "after the fact," meaning that the event occurs first and then it is criminalized. For example, if abortion becomes illegal in a state after September 5th, an abortion provider could not be prosecuted for performing one on September 4th but could if he or she performed one on September 6th. The ex post facto provision also forbids increasing the penalties for a crime after it has already been committed. Ex post facto laws that benefit the defendant are applied retroactively, however. Hence, a person sentenced to death in a state that subsequently abolishes the death penalty will benefit from having his or her sentence commuted to life imprisonment. **Bills of attainder** are laws that impose punishment without a trial. Such bills were issued under old English common law for crimes against the state, such as treason, and marked the accused as "attainted" (morally contaminated).

ELEMENTS OF CRIMINAL LIABILITY

Criminal law does not punish individuals for all harms done, nor does it prohibit certain acts and thoughts that many consider reprehensible, such as refusing to aid a drowning person or hating someone for the color of his or her skin. Criminal liability attaches, in most instances, only when there exists both a criminal act and the intent to commit the act, which together are the cause of harm to another. There are five elements of criminal liability, each of which must be established beyond a reasonable doubt. Taken together, these comprise the body of the crime, or **corpus delicti**.

1. *Actus Reus* (Criminal Act)

There must be an act for criminal liability to attach. The law does not punish evil thoughts alone—only when these thoughts are acted on may they be punished. There are three forms of the criminal act, or *actus reus*, meaning a guilty act: (a) voluntary bodily movements, (b) an omission in the face of a duty to act, and (c) possession.

Voluntary movements occur by virtue of the actor's free will, without coercion and with awareness of the actor's conduct. This excludes involuntary bodily movements such as reflexive actions or unconscious activity (e.g., sleepwalking). Words may constitute acts in some cases, such as solicitation to commit a crime or threatening someone. The state may not punish someone on the basis of his or her status alone. For example, the Supreme Court has said that it is unconstitutional to punish someone for being a drug addict, which is a status (*Robinson v. California,* 1962), but lawful to punish someone for being drunk in public, which is an act, even if the person suffers from chronic alcoholism (*Powell v. Texas,* 1968).

A failure to act, or an omission, is generally not subject to sanction even if it is morally reprehensible. However, there are two narrow circumstances where failing to act may result in criminal liability. These include a failure to perform a legal duty (e.g., failing to register a handgun when the law requires it or failure to pay income taxes) and failure to intervene to prevent serious harm when there exists a *special relationship* between the parties (as in the case of parents and children).

Possession itself may constitute a criminal act if the person has some knowledge that what he or she possesses, such as a weapon or child pornography, is illegal. While possession is passive, acquiring possession requires action, and retaining possession in the face of awareness that it is unlawful to possess the item is similar to an omission.

2. *Mens Rea* (Criminal Intent)

Criminal liability generally does not attach based on actions alone. There also must exist some sort of guilty mind, or **mens rea.** The rationale for this requirement is that society does not wish to punish unavoidable accidents. Modern criminal law recognizes several levels of intent, and varying levels of punishment associated with them. While the language varies by jurisdiction, many states track the language of the Model Penal Code, promulgated by the American Law Institute (1962). *Mens rea* is a sticky concept, however, for how can one person know what is in the mind of another? Nevertheless, *mens rea* must be proven, so the existence of a guilty mind is inferred from the circumstances surrounding the criminal act.

Model Penal Code

Criminal motive and criminal intent are different things. *Intent* refers to the mental purpose or desire to commit a certain act; *motive* refers to the cause, or the reason why the act was committed. While some degree of intent is required for criminal liability to attach, there is no requirement that the prosecution prove motive, although it is commonly done as a means of explaining the act to the jury because it helps to clarify intent. Thus, prosecutors will frequently not only prove all the elements of an offense (e.g., murder) but also provide a reason or motive why the defendant would want to kill the victim (e.g., anger or greed).

The **Model Penal Code** sets forth four levels of intent: purposeful, knowing, reckless, and negligent. A person who acts *purposefully* does so consciously, with the intent to commit a certain act or produce a certain result. This person is virtually certain of the results of his or her conduct. A person acts *knowingly* when he or she is practically certain of the result to follow from this conduct. This person possesses knowledge of what he or she is doing but lacks the premeditation and determination of one who acts purposefully. A person acts *recklessly* when he or she operates with awareness of the risk involved but without the certainty of knowledge that harm will follow.

Criminal culpability is based on the conscious creation of a risk of harm rather than an intent to harm, and **negligence** is the unconscious creation of a risk of harm. Negligent actors are those who should have been aware that they were creating a substantial and unjustifiable risk of harm. This standard is an objective one—if the "reasonable" person would have been aware of the risk of harm, then the negligent person is responsible for being aware of his or her conduct.

There is one other form of intent developed in common law, known as the doctrine of transferred intent. This doctrine of **transferred intent** applies to situations where someone intended to harm person A but in error harmed person B. To prevent the defendant from escaping liability by claiming that he or she did not intend to hurt person B, and that therefore the element of intent is missing, courts developed the concept of transferred intent. This concept means that the intent to harm a person who is not actually harmed is transferred to the person who is. Thus, if Pat shoots at Brett with the intention of harming him but misses and kills Victor instead, under the doctrine of transferred intent Pat's intent (to kill Brett) is transferred to Victor, so Pat cannot claim he is not guilty of a crime because he did not intend to kill Victor.

3. Concurrence

Concurrence is simply the union of the criminal act (*actus reus*) and criminal intent (*mens rea*). The criminal intent must set the criminal act in motion. Acts not generated by criminal intent do not constitute criminal conduct. For instance, Dick and Jane live in the same apartment complex and are in the habit of walking into each other's apartment unannounced to visit. One day. Dick walks into Jane's apartment to ask her if she has any spare marijuana since he is all out. He finds that Jane is not home, so he rummages around looking for her stash of pot. Finding none, he decides to take her new stereo and pawn it for drug money. In this case, Dick could not be charged with burglary because burglary requires that a person enter a structure by "force or fraud." Since he had consent to enter Jane's home at any time, he did not enter by force or fraud. The criminal intent to steal Jane's stereo occurred only after he had entered and found her not at home, not before, as required to prove the crime of burglary. Dick could only be prosecuted for larceny/theft, which carries a less severe penalty than burglary, because *mens rea* was formed only after entry into Jane's apartment.

4. Causation

Causation is the legal principle that the criminal act is the act that is the cause of the harm. There are two types of causation: factual and legal.

Factual cause refers to the idea that "but for" the actor's conduct, the harm would not have occurred. It is an initial act that sets a series of other acts in motion that leads to some harm. Factual causation is a necessary, but not a sufficient, element for the imposition of criminal liability. A legal cause also must exist.

Legal cause, also referred to as **proximate cause**, is not as straightforward as factual cause. For all practical purposes, in the vast majority of criminal cases, they are the same thing. The issue of proximate causation becomes relevant only when some additional acts not under the accused person's control or that he or she could not reasonably foresee intervene between the factual cause and the harm ultimately inflicted. Another way to view proximate cause is the proximity ("nearness") in time between the accused's actions and the ultimate degree of harm caused to the victim. The question often asked in such cases is: "For which act does it seem fair and just to hold the actor accountable?" Consequences of an act that are not reasonably foreseeable to the actor are "intervening causes" and serve to relieve the actor of some degree of criminal liability.

An example might be if Joe punches his friend Bob in the face and breaks his tooth. When Bob goes in to have his tooth replaced, the dentist, drunk from having too many margaritas at lunch, accidentally gives Bob too many drugs, and Bob dies as a result. While it is true that Joe is in some ways the "cause" of his friend's untimely demise, since if he had not punched his friend Bob would not have gone to the dentist, most would agree that the dentist's behavior was not reasonably foreseeable to Joe. Therefore, Joe is not be liable for Bob's death simply for setting in motion an unlikely chain of events. He could, of course, be held liable for assault (for punching Bob).

5. Harm

Harm is simply the result of the act or the injury to another. Harm occurs in all crimes, even so-called "victimless" crimes. Harm may be physical, as in murder, or mental, as in threatening someone. There can be no liability without harm, although this harm may be to society in general rather than to a specific individual. The state may even criminalize acts that ostensibly harm only the actor, such as suicide, prostitution, or drug abuse. Such acts, of course, can harm others involved with the actor (spouses, parents, children) far more seriously than many other criminal acts such as robbery or assault.

 ## LIABILITY WITHOUT FAULT

There are a few instances in which criminal liability may attach without proof of criminal intent. These include strict liability and vicarious liability.

Strict liability is an important concept in tort law (discussed in chapter 7) but also is used in the criminal arena when there is a strong public interest involved to justify eliminating the *mens rea* requirement. **Strict liability** imposes accountability without proof of criminal intent in situations where society deems it fair to do so. Statutory rape (sexual intercourse between an adult and a minor) provides an example. It does not matter whether the adult knew the correct age of the minor, or even if the minor told the adult that he or she was of consenting age—criminal liability still attaches to the adult. Minors are considered not legally capable of giving sexual consent, and society has deemed it important to protect minors from exploitation, even at the expense of eliminating the *mens rea* requirement for the commission of a crime. The age of consent varies across nations and across states, but the most typical age of consent is 16.

Vicarious liability refers to the imputation of accountability from one person to another, usually the individual's superior/supervisor. Here, liability is based not on a person's act but on the individual's relationship to the person who committed an illegal act. It eliminates the criminal act requirement for the second actor by imputing the first actor's intent to this second individual and is different from strict liability, which eliminates the necessity of proving *mens rea*. An example would be the liability of correctional administrators for the actions of the officers they are supervising; in some instances, a supervisor may be held accountable for the actions of his or her subordinates. It is important to note this form of liability attaches only in civil cases, never in criminal cases.

INCHOATE CRIMES

Crimes that occur in preparation for an offense are called **inchoate crimes**. The adjective *inchoate* means "to begin" or "to partially put into operation." Although in reality inchoate crimes are anticipatory and incomplete crimes, legally they are crimes in which criminal liability exists even if the contemplated act or actions never take place. There are three types of inchoate crimes: attempt, solicitation, and conspiracy.

Attempt

In early common law, it was not a crime to attempt but fail to complete a criminal act. As the law developed, however, the doctrine of **attempt** developed as a means of controlling potentially dangerous persons and activities. To be liable for attempting to commit a crime, there must be proof of the specific intent to carry out an act that constitutes a crime. General intent, or the person's general tendency to commit criminal acts at any time or against any person when the opportunity arises, is not sufficient. As criminal law does not punish evil thoughts alone, there must be some evidence of a specific intention to commit an overt act in the pursuance of the intended crime. Courts generally require evidence of "some step" or "substantial steps" (see Model Penal Code; American Law Institute, 1962) that constitute perpetration of the criminal act. An example of "some step" might be driving to the bank with a handgun and a mask in the vehicle. An example of a "substantial step" might be walking into a bank with a handgun.

Solicitation

Solicitation involves the intent to induce another to commit a crime. There must be words or some action of inducing, accompanied by the intention to induce—joking about a crime is not enough. The solicited crime need not actually be committed for there to be solicitation. Thus, a crime has occurred as soon as Jane asks Dick to kill her husband. Dick need not actually kill Jane's husband—or take any steps at all to do so—for Jane to have committed a crime. The crime is in Jane's asking Dick to commit a crime. (Dick has not committed any crime if he refuses the solicitation.)

Conspiracy

A **conspiracy** is an agreement between two or more people for the purpose of committing a crime. If Jane and Dick seriously make plans to kill Jane's husband, then both are guilty of conspiracy to commit murder. As with solicitation, the intended crime need not occur for the conspiracy to be committed—in most jurisdictions, an agreement for an unlawful purpose is enough. Some jurisdictions also require some act in furtherance of the conspiracy. A co-conspirator may be held liable for the actions of others in the conspiracy, even if he or she is unaware of their offenses.

PARTIES TO CRIME

The doctrine of **complicity** sets forth the situations in which more than one person may be held liable for criminal activity. Complicity still requires all the elements of criminal liability but allows liability to attach for someone else's conduct.

The common law recognized four parties to a crime:

1. Principles in the first degree (those who commit the act).

2. Principles in the second degree (present when the crime occurred, acting as lookouts, getaway drivers, etc.).

3. Accessories before the fact.

4. Accessories after the fact.

Complicity includes accessories both before and after the fact, so long as they are aware that a crime will occur or has occurred.

Accessories before the fact are individuals who were not present at the crime but who facilitated it in some way, such as by providing plans, information, or weapons. Accessories after the fact are individuals who aided the principles in some way after the crime was committed, such as by hiding them or their criminal gains or by providing them with information useful in avoiding capture.

Modern statutes have eliminated the distinction between principles and now make them, as well as accessories before the fact, equally culpable accomplices. The statutes do retain the distinction between principles and accessories after the fact, however.

DEFENSES TO CRIMINAL LIABILITY

There are several defenses to criminal liability. A **defense** is a response made by a defendant to the complaint, which if successful allows the defendant to avoid criminal liability. For example, a defense may take the form of an **alibi**, whereby the defendant asserts he or she is not the person who committed the act charged. An alibi is different from the other defenses because the defendant is claiming innocence, whereas the other defenses admit committing the act. In the latter, the defendant raises one of two affirmative defenses—justification or excuse.

Affirmative defenses are those in which the defendant has the burden of production and the burden of persuasion. The **burden of production** refers to the duty to produce evidence. In every criminal case, the prosecution must introduce evidence showing that the defendant, in all likelihood, committed the crime with which he or she has been charged. Failure to produce such evidence results in a dismissal of the case. The **burden of persuasion** refers to which side must "prove" its case. Again, in criminal cases, the prosecution has the burden of persuasion and must prove its case to the jury beyond a reasonable doubt. When the defense is asserting an affirmative defense, however, both burdens shift from the prosecution to the defense. Generally, the burden of persuasion for affirmative defenses is by a preponderance of the evidence, although in some states a higher burden is imposed for certain defenses, such as the insanity defense. Affirmative defenses may result in acquittal, cause a reduction of the charge, or serve to mitigate the punishment.

Justification Defenses

A **justification defense** is one in which the defendant admits responsibility for the act that occurred but claims that, under the circumstances, the act was not criminal. Examples of common justification defenses include self-defense, consent, and execution of public duties.

Self-Defense

Self-defense may be successfully claimed if the defendant can demonstrate that he or she used force to repel an imminent, unprovoked attack in the reasonable belief that he or she was about to be seriously injured. The defendant may use only as much force as is necessary to repel the attack. There are a number of limitations and exceptions to the general rules of self-defense. These include the **retreat doctrine**, which states that a person must retreat rather than use deadly force if doing so is possible without endangering the person's life. The **castle doctrine**, on the other hand, states that persons attacked in their home need not retreat from a potentially deadly invasion and/or attack. States differ as to which doctrine defines their stance vis-à-vis self-defense claims. Self-defense also may apply to the defense of others and in some circumstances to the defense of property.

Consent

Consent is a defense, albeit a controversial one, to some crimes. Most jurisdictions provide that persons may consent to suffer what otherwise would be an actionable injury. What acts a person can consent to suffer are limited, however, and it must be demonstrated that the consent was voluntary, knowing, and intelligent. As we have seen, the consent of a minor to have sex with an adult is not considered voluntary, knowing, and intelligent and would therefore not be a legally permissible consent defense. An example of voluntary, knowing, and intelligent consent is that of the professional athlete who chooses to engage in activity where injury similar to an assault may occur, such as a football player who suffers a broken arm when he is tackled and falls awkwardly to the ground.

Execution of Public Duties

Agents of the state, such as police officers or soldiers, are permitted to use reasonable force in the lawful execution of their duties. This defense, called **execution of public duties,** allows the use of deadly force under the proper circumstances and police to engage in activities that otherwise would be criminal if they are doing so as part of their law enforcement efforts, such as posing as a drug dealer. The most controversial element of this defense is police killings, since officers are limited to the circumstances under which deadly force can be used (*Tennessee v. Garner*, 1984).

Excuse Defenses

An **excuse defense** is one in which a defendant admits that what he or she did was wrong but argues that, under the circumstances, he or she was not responsible for the improper conduct. Examples include duress, intoxication, age, and insanity.

Duress

Duress may be raised as a defense in a limited number of situations. These vary by jurisdiction but generally include situations involving the threat of serious, imminent harm to oneself where the act is less serious than the threatened harm. Thus, a person is acting under duress when he commits theft to avoid being killed by the person holding him or her hostage. Duress is allowed as a defense under the rationale that those forced to commit a crime in such circumstances do not act voluntarily, so there is no *actus reus* component. Another explanation is that subjugation to the will of another removes the *mens rea* component (Dressler, 1995). In some states, the duress defense excuses only minor crimes, whereas in others, it excuses all crimes except murder.

Intoxication

There are two forms of intoxication: voluntary and involuntary. Voluntary intoxication never provides a complete defense but may negate the *mens rea* component for an offense requiring specific intent in some states by reducing the degree of the crime charged. In other states, the rule is that the voluntary act of drinking establishes voluntariness and thus cannot be used as any kind of mitigation. Voluntary intoxication also may be used in mitigation of the penalty. Involuntary intoxication may provide a defense if it can be shown that the actor was unaware that he or she was being drugged. In such cases, the actor is excused because he or she is not responsible for becoming intoxicated; consequently, it would be unfair to hold him or her liable for the resulting uncontrollable action. The Supreme Court has held that due process does not require states to allow the defense of intoxication (*Montana v. Egelhoff*, 1996).

Age

Historically, youth has been treated as a defense to criminal liability on the grounds that persons below a certain **age** lack the requisite mental capability to form *mens rea*. Under the common law, there was a presumption that children under the age of seven years were incompetent. Today, various jurisdictions define the age of majority (when one becomes an adult) at varying ages. Those classified as juveniles are generally dealt with not in the criminal justice system but in the juvenile justice system. The *parens patriae* doctrine of the juvenile court, which essentially means that the state acts as a parent to the child (discussed further in chapter 8), is giving way to an increased desire to treat juveniles similarly to adult offenders.

Insanity

Insanity is a legal term to describe mental illness that excuses criminal liability by impairing *mens rea*. Mental illness and legal insanity are not the same thing. A person can be judged mentally ill by medical standards but sane by legal standards, and vice versa. The insanity claim is probably the most controversial of all defense strategies, although it is rarely used. There are several different legal tests for insanity, all of which have been criticized as either too difficult or too easy to establish.

The first case in which the modern insanity defense was successfully mounted was in *Rex v. Hadfield* (1800) in England. John Hadfield was an ex-British soldier who had received a head wound and had a great dislike of King George. Convinced that King George was preventing the second coming of Jesus, Hadfield took a shot at the king, missed him,

Daniel M'Naghten

and was tried for high treason. Upon hearing testimony of expert witness, the judge halted the trial and ordered Hadfield sent to a mental institution (Hawthorn, 2000).

Another British case, *Rex v. M'Naghten* (1843), cemented the modern insanity defense. This time, the intended target of an assassination attempt was Prime Minister Robert Peel. Daniel M'Naghten missed Peel and hit the prime minister's secretary, Edward Drummond, who subsequently died. M'Naghten was found not guilty by reason of insanity and sent to a mental institution. This case became the foundation for insanity defenses around the world. The **M'Naghten rule** is also known as the **right–wrong test**, meaning that the M'Naghten standard for insanity is realized if a defendant did not know either what he or she was doing or that it was wrong.

Other tests for insanity are as follows:

- **Durham rule:** Also known as the *product test*, the Durham standard is met when the act was the product of the defendant's mental illness. Note that it goes beyond the right–wrong test to include mental disease or defects. Almost all states have abandoned the Durham test as too broad.

- **Irresistible impulse test:** An irresistible impulse is defined as the inability to control one's conduct even though one is aware that the conduct is wrong.

- **Substantial capacity test:** The substantial capacity test is met when the defendant lacks substantial capacity to appreciate the wrongfulness of his or her conduct or the ability to control it. It is a combination and modification of the right–wrong test and the irresistible impulse test.

Following the uproar over the 1982 acquittal by reason of insanity of John Hinckley, who had wounded President Ronald Reagan and several others in an assassination attempt, Congress passed the Insanity Defense Reform Act of 1984, and the states made a variety of changes to their insanity laws. These included dropping the defense altogether, shifting the burden of proof, changing their commitment and release rules, and more generally, adopting a "guilty but mentally ill" (GBMI) defense. The GBMI verdict maintains the defendants' criminal liability, and hence criminal sentence, but mandates psychiatric treatment for them. Several states and the federal courts have limited the use of the insanity defense or altered the burden of proof in establishing the defense. Federal courts, for instance, require that the defense establish insanity by clear and convincing evidence rather than by the standard usually applied to affirmative defense, a preponderance of the evidence.

Procedural Defenses: Entrapment

There are a number of other defenses against liability that are called **procedural defenses**. In these defenses, it is claimed that somewhere along the line in processing the case, the criminal justice system violated the defendant's due process rights. These defenses include double jeopardy, denial of a speedy trial, and use of illegally seized evidence. These issues are discussed elsewhere in the text, so we do not go into them here. We do, however, discuss entrapment, a defense that is increasingly being raised by defendants caught in drug and Internet sexual enticement stings (Johnson, 2006).

ISSUE HIGHLIGHT

Abolish the Insanity Defense?

The insanity defense, if it is successful, allows a defendant who has committed what is considered a criminal act to escape criminal liability. This is what excuse defenses do—remove criminal liability from those who under normal circumstances would be found guilty of committing a crime and then punished accordingly. The use of the insanity defense in some high-profile cases, such as John Hinckley's, and the "get tough on crime" movement of the 1980s and 1990s led some to advocate for abolition of the insanity defense. While these abolitionists have not been generally successful (only four states [Idaho, Kansas, Montana, and Utah] have eliminated the insanity defense), a number of states and the federal system have modified the insanity defense, making it more difficult to establish. Should the insanity defense be abolished?

Reasons Why the Insanity Defense Should Be Abolished

1. It allows "guilty" people to avoid criminal liability.
2. It is difficult to determine what constitutes insanity.
3. It sends a message that the government is "soft" on crime.
4. It prevents victims and their families from obtaining closure through seeing the person who hurt them punished.

Reasons Why the Insanity Defense Should Not Be Abolished

1. Persons with mental disabilities should not be treated the same as those without mental problems.
2. The criminal law is designed to hold responsible for wrongdoing only those individuals who intended to commit a crime, not those who could not control their conduct or understand the consequences of their actions.
3. Those found not guilty by reason of insanity do necessarily return to society—most are civilly committed on the basis of their mental disability so they can receive appropriate treatment in a secure setting.
4. The insanity defense is rarely used, and even more rarely successful, so it is very limited in application. Thus, this debate is much ado about nothing.

The Supreme Court laid out two rules of entrapment in *Sherman v. United States* (1958), stating that **entrapment** occurs when (a) the crime is the result of "the creative activity" of law enforcement and (b) the prosecutor cannot prove beyond a reasonable doubt that the defendant was "independently predisposed" to commit the crime. Creative activity, such as stings and decoy operations, is therefore permissible if used to trap individuals who were predisposed (i.e., had a preexisting inclination) to commit the crime for which they were arrested. If a person steals money from the pocket of a police officer acting as a drunk lying in the gutter, or if he or she consistently sells stolen property at a pawnshop operated by the police, that person has demonstrated predisposition. As one judge was famously heard to remark, "Traps must distinguish between the unwary innocent and the unwary guilty."

CRIMES AGAINST THE PERSON

Crimes are frequently categorized on the basis of the type of act. Under this approach, there are crimes against the person, crimes against property, crimes against society, and crimes against public order and morality. Each of these categories encompasses a wide range of conduct. Crimes against the person often are ranked among the most serious offenses.

Murder

The Federal Bureau of Investigation (FBI; 2015) defines **murder** as "the willful (non-negligent) killing of one human being by another" (p. 15). There were 14,196 murders in the United States in 2013. Murder is a subcategory of homicide—a broad, all-inclusive term for any killing of another human being. Definitional issues include what is a human being, when is someone alive (or dead), and what types of homicide deserve punishment. The issues of when life begins and ends are difficult moral and ethical questions, and they pose legal problems as well. Some states criminalize the killing of an unborn fetus, while others require the baby be born alive and then die before a killing is considered to have occurred. Determining when life ends is made more difficult as medical science has made it possible for severely injured persons to live indefinitely while hooked up to life-support devices. Under the common law, death was defined as when the heartbeat stopped, but many states now define death as occurring when there is an irreversible cessation of brain function.

The Model Penal Code distinguishes between lawful killings (e.g., those committed in self-defense) and unlawful killings, or **criminal homicides**. There are three forms of criminal homicide: murder, manslaughter, and negligent homicide. Under the common law, murder generally was defined as the killing of another person with **malice aforethought**, which means an intentional, premeditated (i.e., planned) killing. Murder is today defined by the Model Penal Code as a killing that occurs (a) purposefully, (b) knowingly, or (c) recklessly under circumstances exhibiting extreme indifference to human life. As these comprise three distinct levels of intent, murder is graded into first degree and second degree. First-degree murder encompasses those killings that are deliberate and premeditated. Second-degree murder includes any killings that are intentional but not premeditated or planned.

American Law Institute

States and courts differ on how planned and how premeditated a crime must be in order for it to be considered first-degree murder. Some regard it as a period of careful and thoughtful consideration that includes the formulation of some preconceived design for carrying out the crime, while others hold that premeditation may be formed in a matter of minutes. Many such "instantly premeditated" murders can actually be worse than a murder that takes place after months of planning. For instance, someone who forms a sudden urge to rape and kill a child for no other reason than sheer wanton bloodlust and then does so has surely committed a more atrocious act than an abused wife who carefully plans how to do away with her husband and does so.

Manslaughter is a second category of criminal homicides and includes both involuntary and voluntary manslaughter. **Involuntary manslaughter** is a criminal homicide in which an unintentional killing results from a reckless act. **Voluntary manslaughter** is an intentional killing that occurs either (a) under a mistaken belief that self-defense required the use of deadly force or (b) in response to adequate provocation, while in the sudden heat of passion. Adequate provocation under the common law included instances such as a husband catching his wife in the act of committing adultery. Today, **adequate provocation** is defined as a killing that occurs after such provocation as the law deems sufficient—namely, that which could cause a reasonable person to react violently. Examples include catching a spouse committing adultery, being assaulted, and coming upon someone trespassing in one's home. Words alone are not considered sufficient to create adequate provocation. Additionally, the existence of adequate provocation does not eliminate criminal liability for a homicide, but it does reduce the charge (and associated punishment) from first-degree murder to voluntary manslaughter.

Negligent homicide, the third category of criminal homicide, is an unintentional killing in which the defendant should have known that he or she was creating a substantial risk of death by his or her conduct, which itself deviated from the ordinary level of care owed to others (American Law Institute, 1962). The most common example is negligent driving, and in some jurisdictions, there is a separate offense, such as vehicular homicide.

Another type of murder is felony murder, a category ranked as first-degree murder in some states but as second-degree murder in most. Under the **felony murder rule**, an individual may be held liable for an unintended killing that occurs during the commission of a dangerous felony, such as robbery or rape. There is no requirement of intent to either kill or inflict serious injury. It is enough if the person was engaged in a dangerous felony or a felony in which serious injury was a reasonably foreseeable outcome.

There are a number of offenses against the person aside from murder and manslaughter. These offenses, while less serious than killing, nonetheless are treated seriously in criminal law, as they involve harm of one form or another to a person. Among these are assault and battery, robbery, and a myriad of sexual offenses, including rape, sexual assault, and child sexual abuse. These offenses, while different in form, all share the common denominator of direct harm to a person inflicted by the actor.

Rape

The FBI (2015) defines forcible **rape** as "the carnal knowledge of a female forcibly and against her will" (p. 27). This definition includes attempts to commit rape but excludes statutory rape (i.e., sex with an underage female) and the rape of males. Rapes of males are classified as either assaults or other sex offenses, depending on the circumstances of the crime and the extent of physical injury. Under the common law, rape was defined as "carnal knowledge by a man of a woman who is not his wife, forcibly and without her consent." This definition created several interesting holes in the law: only men were capable of rape, only women could be raped, men could not rape their wives, the only act that constituted rape was vaginal intercourse, and there must be evidence of both force and resistance to force. All 50 states have formally abolished the so-called *marital rape exception*, although in some states, if a rape takes place within the context of marriage, it is considered a factor mitigating the seriousness of the charge and the severity of the punishment (Belknap, 2001).

Many states have rewritten their statutes using gender-neutral language so that the crime applies to acts committed by men and women and to acts committed against men and children. Many states also have relaxed the common law requirement that a woman physically resist her attacker on the grounds that requiring her to do so may simply put her at risk of additional harm. Additionally, there has been an attempt to limit the sort of evidence that can be introduced at trial. Rape shield statutes restrict the introduction into evidence of a victim's sexual history. The Model Penal Code follows this approach, focusing instead on the conduct of the defendant. This aligns the elements of rape law more closely with the elements of modern assault law, which does not focus on the conduct of the victim. Some states no longer even classify the crime as rape but instead use the phrase "sexual assault" (Texas Penal Code, 2005).

Other sexual offenses, which are currently the subject of much public debate, include child sexual assault. Recent highly publicized cases involving allegations of child sexual abuse and the increase in the number of reports of sexual assaults on children by both family and strangers have heightened public awareness and led to a toughening of child sexual abuse laws. While the elements of these laws track closely the elements of rape law, the punishment accorded them is often even more severe.

Aggravated Assault

The FBI (2015) defines **aggravated assault** as "an unlawful attack by one person upon another for the purpose of inflicting severe or aggravated bodily injury" (p. 37). As opposed to simple assault, aggravated assault is an assault in which a weapon such as a knife or a gun is used, although the use of personal weapons such as hands and feet can result in a charge of aggravated assault if they cause great bodily harm. Aggravated assault is the most common violent felony. Each incident of aggravated assault carries the potential threat of becoming a murder. It has been claimed that without the speedy access to modern medicine we enjoy today, many aggravated assault victims would end up as murder victims (Harris, Thomas, Fisher, & Hirsch, 2002).

Under the common law, there was a clear distinction between the offense of assault and the offense of battery. **Assault** was either (a) an attempt or (b) a threat to inflict immediate harm by a person with the present means of carrying out the attempt or threat. No physical contact was necessary for an assault to take place—it was enough if the assailant attempted to complete the assault or even if the victim reasonably feared for his or her safety. A completed assault in which there was actual bodily contact was considered a battery. Under the common law, a **battery** was defined as unjustified, offensive, and intentional physical contact of some sort. It could be a blow from a fist, being spit upon, or being shot. Today, many jurisdictions have merged the offenses of assault and battery, referring to both as assault and grading what was assault under common law as a less serious form of the offense.

Robbery

The FBI (2015) defines **robbery** as "the taking or attempted taking of anything of value from the care, custody, or control of a person or persons by force or threat of force or violence and/or putting the victim in fear" (p. 31). Robbery is thus larceny by force and is classified as a violent rather than a property offense. It is the most serious form of larceny, as it involves an offense against both property and person. Any force or threat of force constitutes "force" for purposes of imposing criminal liability for robbery. A taking of property accomplished by the threat of future harm to person, property, or reputation is **extortion**.

Robbery carries a more serious penalty than any other crime except murder and rape in every state because the act of taking property from someone entails a strong risk of violence. Note that while a pickpocket takes personal assets from another's care, custody, or control, there is no force or threat of force because the person is not usually aware of the theft until later. The offense of pocket-picking is classified as a larceny/theft, a crime against property.

CRIMES AGAINST PROPERTY

Crimes against property encompass a broad spectrum of activities. The most common include burglary, trespass, arson, theft in its myriad forms, forgery and uttering, and receiving stolen property. While crimes against the person receive the bulk of media and public attention, crimes against property are far more common. The 2014 UCR reports that over 88 percent of crimes reported to the police were property crimes. Early common law recognized only the crime of larceny, but as society developed and criminals devised new ways to deprive people of their possessions, the law responded by creating new offenses. Because the law of theft developed so haphazardly, these theft offenses were confusing and hard to distinguish from one another. Today, many states have done away with the variety of theft offenses and lump together all crimes involving the unlawful obtaining of property as larceny.

Arson

Arson is defined by the FBI (2015) as "any willful or malicious burning or attempting to burn, with or without intent to defraud, a dwelling house, public building, motor vehicle or aircraft, personal property of another, etc." (p. 61). In other words, arson is setting fire to a structure with the intent to burn the structure, either in whole or in part. Under early common law, arson applied only to the burning of the dwelling of another. The definition of the crime was soon expanded to cover any structure, including one's own home and nonresidential buildings. Most jurisdictions grade arson so that the burning of an occupied structure is first-degree arson and the burning of an unoccupied structure is second-degree arson. Some jurisdictions have expanded arson to cover the burning of personal property (e.g., vehicles) as well as structures, and this is generally treated as third-degree arson. There must exist an intent to burn, which excludes negligent acts but includes reckless conduct.

Burglary

The FBI (2015) defines **burglary** as "the unlawful entry of a structure to commit a felony or theft" (p. 45). Burglary is a crime committed against the home. Since the earliest common law, dwellings have been afforded special protection from entry by both agents of the state and uninvited guests.

The definition of burglary has changed over time as society has developed and conditions have changed. In early common law, burglary could take place anywhere that was likely to attract people, including public places. Gradually, burglary was limited to home invasions, and by the seventeenth century, it was defined as the breaking and entering of the dwelling of another at night with the intention of committing a felony inside. Burglary was restricted to nocturnal home invasions on the theory that invasions at such times were more likely to result in greater harm to the occupants, who were more likely to be home at the time. Nighttime entry is no longer a necessary element, although almost all states differentiate between burglaries of a home taking place at night (aggravated, or first-degree, burglary) and those that take place during the day or of a structure other than the home.

It is important to note that burglary is not entry alone—there must be an *unlawful* entry accompanied by the present intent to commit another crime once inside. Thus, stealing a television from your neighbor's house is not necessarily burglary unless you had the intent to remove the television *before* entering the house (the concurrence of *actus reus* and *mens rea*). The unauthorized taking of the television set would still be a form of larceny, of course. Going into someone's house or simply onto their property unlawfully without the intent to commit any additional acts is trespass.

Today, burglary is much more broadly defined in most jurisdictions. It may occur at all hours of the day and is not limited to dwellings but applies in virtually any structure. In fact, burglary statutes across the country are such a confusing mixture of laws covering such a wide variety of conduct that many acts are considered burglary. The element of "unlawful entry" enables shoplifting to be classified as burglary if the suspect is unwise enough to admit that he or she entered the store for the specific purpose of stealing. A variety of incidents that have actually resulted in burglary charges and convictions include pumping gas and leaving without paying, stealing popcorn from a sidewalk stand, stealing from a locked glove compartment, and taking a few coins from a vending machine. Regardless of state statutes, "burglaries" (e.g., shoplifting) that do not fit the FBI definition must be reported to the FBI as larcenies.

Larceny/Theft

The FBI (2015) defines larceny/theft as "the unlawful taking, leading, or riding away from the possession or constructive possession of another" (p. 49). The unwieldy phrase and concept of "constructive possession" refers to circumstances in which the victim may still have possession of the item in question (e.g., a credit card) but someone else has stolen the number and thus can use it without the victim's consent.

Under the common law, **larceny** was the unlawful taking and carrying away of another's personal property, with the intent to permanently deprive the rightful owner of its possession. This definition encompassed takings that occurred by force and those that occurred without the knowledge of the owner. It was not larceny if someone deprived another person of property under any other circumstance. As society evolved and people began to rely on others to do business, personal property was placed in the custody of another for a limited purpose. Thus, Mary might give a bank clerk $100 to deposit in her bank account, and if the clerk kept the money for himself instead, it was not larceny as there was no wrongful taking—Mary willingly handed over the money to the clerk. Courts soon responded to this strange situation by enlarging the definition of larceny, which today is defined broadly and includes taking by stealth, by fraud, and by false pretenses. Under the common law, each of these was a separate offense, but in many jurisdictions, they now all are classified as larceny. This trend follows the Model Penal Code approach of consolidating common law theft offenses.

All elements of larceny have been significantly broadened over the years. The "taking" element is satisfied when an actor gains brief control over an item, either directly or indirectly. The "carrying away" element is satisfied if the item is moved even a slight distance from its original location. The "personal property" element has been expanded to cover both personal and real property (*personal* property is anything that is movable; *real* property is land and anything growing out of or affixed to it). There still must be intent to deprive a person permanently of his or her property. A temporary misappropriation of the property of another is not larceny but is punishable as a lesser offense. Teenagers who steal a car and then abandon it (thus showing no intent to gain permanent possession of it) will probably be charged with joyriding rather than with larceny. Motor vehicle theft is a larceny, but it is considered different enough from other larceny/thefts to warrant a separate classification in the UCR. Most jurisdictions now grade larceny based on either the method of taking or the value of the property taken.

According to the value of the item(s) stolen, larceny/theft is classified either as grand theft or as petty theft; the former is a felony and the latter a misdemeanor. The distinction varies from state to state, but the cutoff amount is under $1,000 in every state. The value of the property is its value at the time it was stolen, not its replacement value. Because of the wide variation among the states regarding the grand/petty cutoff point, the FBI does not make that distinction in its annual report of the number of larceny/thefts.

CRIMES AGAINST PUBLIC ORDER AND MORALITY

Crimes against persons and property have readily identifiable victims, but other acts for which the victim is less readily identifiable also are classified as crimes. These acts fall into one of two categories: crimes against public order and crimes against morality. Crimes against public order are those in which the injury is to the peace and order of society. These include disorderly conduct, unlawful assembly, and vagrancy. Crimes against morality, or public morals crimes, are those in which the moral health of society is injured. These include consensual sexual acts such as fornication and adultery as well as prostitution and obscenity.

People who commit public order offenses generally do not direct their conduct at specific individuals. Public order offenses are frequently challenged as constitutionally invalid because they place limits on cherished individual rights such as freedom of assembly and privacy. States must take care to craft public order legislation carefully so that it does not impermissibly limit constitutionally protected conduct. Statutes that do so often are struck down by courts on the grounds of vagueness or overbreadth.

According to early common law decisions, it was a crime to disturb the public tranquility. This was referred to as breach of the peace. Today, many states have codified it as **disorderly conduct**, a catch-all phrase that has been held to include acts as diverse as public drunkenness, vagrancy, playing loud music, and fighting. Disorderly conduct in a group setting generally is referred to as **unlawful assembly**. This includes groups assembled in public without the necessary permits as well as riots. Vagrancy is a crime that developed in feudal England after the Black Death to control the peasants and tie them to their lords. Vagrancy laws made it a crime to move about the country without proof of employment. Today, courts often determine vagrancy statutes to be unconstitutionally overbroad (*Papachristou v. City of Jacksonville*, 1972).

Public morals offenses involve acts committed by consenting adults that society has nonetheless chosen to prohibit. Examples include fornication, adultery, bigamy, and prostitution. Most public morals offenses involve the regulation of sexual activity in some form. While these acts all involve consenting adults, some argue that in fact consent is not freely given by some (as in the case of prostitution) or that such conduct diminishes the moral capacity of society and hence is deserving of criminalization as a means of eliminating or at least reducing such activity.

SUMMARY

In this chapter, we discussed the basic elements of criminal law as well as the purposes of criminal law and its sources and limitations. Criminal law governs much of human activity today. According to social contract theory, when human beings abandoned their solitary existence for the benefits of living among others, they gave up some of their individual rights to the state in return for the benefits gained from living in society. Criminal law is the formal means by which society attempts to control the conduct of individuals. Informal means of social control still exist and are often effective, but when informal means fail, criminal law exists to deal with society's transgressors.

Criminal law has developed as society has developed. Definitions of crimes have changed, and new offenses have been created in an attempt to maintain a rational set of rules by which society can function and individuals within society can be protected from others. What is legal may vary across the years and by culture, but all societies with a written criminal law share many similarities.

The issues with which scholars, judges, and juries continue to struggle involve the limits of the criminal sanction. How much can society expect the criminal to accomplish? When is it fair and just to hold individuals accountable for their conduct and to subject them to criminal sanctions? Determining not only when liability should attach but also the appropriate level of punishment are difficult issues involving policy considerations, legal doctrine, and morality.

In this chapter, we attempted to explain not only what constitutes a particular crime, such as murder or arson, but also why certain acts are crimes but others are not and why we assess blame differently depending on the circumstances of each event and the mental state of the defendant. There are no easy answers in this area.

DISCUSSION QUESTIONS

1. What are some of the prominent limitations on criminal law?
2. What are the five elements of the corpus delicti, and why must each be proven?
3. What are the five elements of criminal liability?
4. What is the difference between an excuse defense and a justification defense?
5. What are the major categories of crimes, and how are crimes classified?
6. What are the four levels of intent in the Model Penal Code, and how do they differ from one another?
7. What are the three forms of criminal homicide, and how do they differ from one another?
8. What is the difference between the M'Naghten test for insanity and the irresistible impulse test for insanity?
9. What are the three types of inchoate crimes?
10. One day Mr. Smith receives an e-mail from an unknown person named "Julie" who writes that she has viewed his website and found him to be very attractive. After several e-mail exchanges, Smith asks "Julie" to meet him and have sex. She agrees but then informs him that she is only 15 years old. Upon hearing this, Smith calls the meeting off. "Julie" then sends several more e-mails imploring Smith to meet her and have sex. He finally agrees, but when he arrives at the meeting place and identifies himself, he finds that "Julie" is a police officer, who then arrests him for soliciting sex from an underage minor. Does Smith have a good entrapment defense? Was he predisposed to engage in sex with a minor?

CHAPTER TERMS

Actus reus	Assault	Burglary
Adequate provocation	Attempt	Castle doctrine
Affirmative defenses	Battery	Causation
Aggravated assault	Bills of attainder	Complicity
Alibi	Burden of persuasion	Concurrence
Arson	Burden of production	Consent

Conspiracy
Corpus delicti
Crime
Criminal homicides
Defense
Disorderly conduct
Durham rule
Entrapment
Ex post facto laws
Excuse defense
Execution of public duties
Extortion
Factual cause
Felony murder rule
Harm
Inchoate crimes

Insanity
Involuntary manslaughter
Irresistible impulse test
Justification defense
Larceny
Legal cause
Malice aforethought
Manslaughter
Mens rea
M'Naghten rule
Model Penal Code
Murder
Negligence
Negligent homicide
Overbreadth doctrine
Procedural defense

Procedural law
Proximate cause
Rape
Retreat doctrine
Right–wrong test
Robbery
Self-defense
Solicitation
Strict liability
Substantial capacity test
Substantive law
Transferred intent
Uniform Crime Reports
Unlawful assembly
Vicarious liability
Void for vagueness
Voluntary manslaughter

References

American Law Institute. (1962). *Model penal code*. Philadelphia, PA: Author.

Belknap, J. (2001). *The invisible woman: Gender, crime, and justice*. Belmont, CA: Wadsworth.

Dressler, J. (1995). *Understanding criminal law* (2nd ed.). New York, NY: Matthew Bender.

Ellis, L., & Walsh, A. (2000). *Criminology: A global perspective*. Boston, MA: Allyn & Bacon.

Federal Bureau of Investigation. (2015). *Crime in the United States, 2013: Uniform crime reports*. Washington, DC: US Government Printing Office.

Goode, E. (2005). *Drugs in American society* (6th ed.). Boston, MA: McGraw-Hill.

Harris, A., Thomas, S., Fisher, G., & Hirsch, D. (2002). Murder and medicine: The lethality of criminal assault 1960–1999. *Homicide Studies, 6*, 128–166.

Hawthorn, C. (2000). "Deific decree": The short, happy life of a pseudo-doctrine. *Loyola of Los Angeles Law Review, 33*, 1755–1810.

Johnson, J. (2006). The entrapment debate: Are undercover investigations egregious conduct of law enforcement? Retrieved from http://www.grayarea.com/entrap.htm

Texas Penal Code. (2005). Chapter 22 (Assaultive Offenses). Longwood, FL: Gould.

Walsh, A., & Ellis, L. (2007). *Criminology: An interdisciplinary approach*. Thousand Oaks, CA: SAGE.

Cases Cited

Gregg v. Georgia, 428 U.S. 153 (1976)

Griswold v. Connecticut, 381 U.S. 479 (1965)

J.E.B. v. Alabama, 511 U.S. 127 1419 (1994)

Lawrence v. Texas, 539 U.S. 558 (2003)

Montana v. Egelhoff, 518 U.S. 37 (1996)

Papachristou v. City of Jacksonville, 410 U.S. 156 (1972)

Powell v. Texas, 392 U.S. 514 (1968)

Rex v. Hadfield, 27 Howell's State Trials 1281 (1800)

Rex v. M'Naghten, 8 Eng. Rep. 718 (1843)

Robinson v. California, 370 U.S. 660 (1962)

Roe v. Wade, 410 U.S. 113 (1973)

Rummel v. Estelle, 445 U.S. 263 (1980)

Sherman v. United States, 356 U.S. 369 (1958)

Tennessee v. Garner, 471 U.S. 1 (1984)

Texas v. Johnson, 491 U.S. 397 (1989)

CHAPTER 6
CRIMINAL PROCEDURE

Police officers in Wisconsin received information that Steiney Richards was selling large quantities of cocaine out of a hotel room. They obtained a search warrant for Richards's hotel room and went to execute it in the middle of the night. A police officer, dressed as a maintenance worker, knocked on Richards's door and asked to come in. Richards refused to admit the officer and shut the door. The police then broke down the door and entered the room, where they apprehended Richards and discovered a large amount of cocaine hidden in the ceiling of the bathroom. Richards was charged with drug possession.

At trial, Richards claimed the police entry of his hotel room without any notice of who they were or why there were there violated the Fourth Amendment, which prohibits "unreasonable" searches and seizures. He argued that the common law "knock and announce" rule requires police to give notice of their presence and purpose before entering a dwelling to conduct a search. The police in this case admitted they did not knock and announce but argued the search was nonetheless reasonable, however, because Richards was suspected of selling drugs and experience indicated that drug dealers were dangerous. Thus, telling Richards they were police officers might cause him to try harming them in order to prevent their entry into his hotel room. The Supreme Court has held that when police obtain evidence in violation of the Fourth Amendment, that evidence is inadmissible at trial, but the trial court in this case held that the police entry without notice was reasonable.

Richards appealed all the way to the Supreme Court, which noted that the common law knock and announce rule was part of the "reasonableness" requirement of the Fourth Amendment and that police must generally knock and announce before entering a dwelling to execute a search warrant. The Court upheld the search, but refused to create a blanket exception to the knock and announce rule for drug search warrants, however, for fear that doing so would essentially eliminate the knock and announce requirement in all drug cases, without proof that all drug dealers were inherently dangerous. In this case, they balanced the competing interests of law enforcement and civil liberties of citizens.

INTRODUCTION

Whereas criminal law sets forth the appropriate code of conduct for all citizens, criminal procedure comprises the rules that govern the manner in which the state may go about depriving an individual of his or her liberty. More simply put, criminal law comprises the rules for all in society; criminal procedure comprises the rules for the police and the prosecutor. Balancing the rights of the individual with the authority of the state and its agents is a difficult but crucial process. Procedural rights are derived primarily from the due process clause in the Fifth and Fourteenth Amendments. Due process is a tremendously important legal concept, and perhaps the single most powerful phrase in the law used to prevent governments from unjustly depriving individuals of liberty.

A question that concerns all democratic societies is how much authority to grant the state vis-à-vis the individual citizen. Both the state and the individual are imperfect entities that need controlling. Human nature being what it is, people will offend against one another to the overall detriment of the state, and power being what it is, the state will abuse it to the detriment of all. Social contract theory, as enunciated by Thomas Hobbes and John Locke, posits that by choosing to live among others, individuals give up some of their liberties and permit the state to intervene in their lives. But how much intervention and in what manner the state may do so are vital questions with which the courts have struggled over the centuries.

PURPOSE OF CRIMINAL PROCEDURE LAW

As we saw in chapter 2, there are two competing models of the criminal justice system: the due process model and the crime control model. The history of criminal procedure law has been a constant pendulum swing between these two models. Recall that the due process model is concerned primarily with the protection of individual privacy even at the expense of factually guilty parties occasionally evading justice. The due process model emphasizes the importance of the formal legal process as a means of ensuring mistakes are kept to a minimum, and it operates on the presumption of innocence. The underlying premise of this model is that truth at any price is too costly for liberty to endure. The crime control model primarily is concerned with the reduction of crime and the protection of public order. It emphasizes the use of discretion and police power as a means of quickly and efficiently investigating and screening cases, and it operates on the presumption that a defendant is most likely guilty.

Criminal procedure law attempts to balance the differing goals of these two models, but it is a zero-sum game. Granting the police greater power to investigate crime means reducing individual liberty and privacy, while increasing individual rights may result in suspects who are factually guilty going free because the state is unable to prove legal guilt beyond a reasonable doubt (the burden of proof in criminal cases). The words of the famed English legal scholar Sir William Blackstone sum up the primary sentiment shared by advocates of the due process model: "It is better that ten guilty persons escape, than that one innocent suffer."

SOURCES OF CRIMINAL PROCEDURE LAW

The legal foundation for most criminal procedure law is the US Constitution, including the Bill of Rights and the Fourteenth Amendment. The Bill of Rights sets forth 23 individual rights, and as we pointed out in chapter 3, the Bill of Rights originally was conceived as applying only to the federal government. During the twentieth century, however, the Court interpreted the due process clause of the Fourteenth Amendment as including, or incorporating, many of the individual rights contained in the Bill of Rights, thus making these rights applicable to the states.

Other sources for criminal procedure law are state constitutions and federal and state statutes. States are free to provide more individual rights than the federal constitution, but states cannot deny or diminish any federal constitutional rights. In the past, states were seen as generally being less protective of the rights of criminal suspects than the federal government, but in the past few decades, a number of state courts have interpreted their state constitutions as providing greater protections of individual liberties than the federal government.

Still other sources of criminal procedure come from the provisions of the Bill of Rights, in particular the Fourth, Fifth, and Sixth Amendments. Courts frequently are asked to interpret the meaning of these amendments and to apply them to current fact situations. The Fifth Amendment prohibits self-incrimination, but does requiring a person to take a breathalyzer test or give a blood sample constitute self-incrimination when the results may be used against that person at trial? The Fourth Amendment prohibits the unreasonable seizure and search of persons, places, and effects, but what is an "effect"? And what is "unreasonable"? Courts must answer these questions to determine when the police have exceeded the scope of their authority, either intentionally or unintentionally.

The Supreme Court has the final word on the constitutionality of any state action that is challenged as violating a constitutional right. Consequently, much of criminal procedure law comes from Supreme Court decisions. As courts decide only the case before them and do not issue policy directives, criminal procedure law has developed fitfully, on a case-by-case basis. Much of criminal procedure has been written in the past 60 years, since the Supreme Court began to apply the provisions of the Bill of Rights to the states, which conduct the bulk of criminal investigation and prosecution.

SEARCH AND SEIZURE LAW
AND THE FOURTH AMENDMENT

Search and seizure law is governed in large part by the Fourth Amendment, which states that citizens have a right to be free from "unreasonable" searches and seizure and that warrants shall be issued only upon a showing of "probable cause." These two portions of the amendment sometimes are referred to as the reasonableness clause and the warrant clause, respectively.

The Warrant and Reasonableness Clauses

The **warrant clause** of the Fourth Amendment states that all warrants must be based on probable cause and must describe the place to be searched or the person to be seized with "particularity." *Particularity* means that the warrant must make clear on its face who or what is to be searched or seized so as to limit the discretion of the police officer.

The Supreme Court has interpreted the **reasonableness clause** of the Fourth Amendment to allow searches without warrants provided there exists both probable cause and an *exigent circumstance* (meaning a critical or urgent situation) that justifies the failure to obtain a warrant. These exigent circumstances, or exceptions to the warrant requirement, have been spelled out by the Court on a case-by-case basis and apply to a variety of situations. Examples of such situations might be officers chasing a suspect into the suspect's home to apprehend him before he can initiate actions that might make an arrest more problematic, such as obtaining a weapon or destroying evidence.

Probable Cause

Probable cause exists when "the facts and circumstances within the officers' knowledge and of which they had reasonably trustworthy information are sufficient in themselves to warrant a man of reasonable caution in the belief that an offense has been committed" (*Brinegar v. United States*, 1949). The Supreme Court has acknowledged that probable cause is a "fluid concept," meaning that it can ebb and flow to meet a variety of specific circumstances (*Illinois v. Gates*, 1983). Probable cause does not require absolute certainty or even a great likelihood—a "fair probability" of criminal activity is enough.

To compare, the burden of proof in a criminal trial is "beyond a reasonable doubt," which often is equated with near certainty, while the burden of proof in a civil trial is a "preponderance of the evidence," which simply means more likely than not. While it is difficult to accurately quantify or precisely define the levels of proof (Hemmens, del Carmen, & Scarborough, 1997), probable cause is similar to the "preponderance of the evidence" standard in civil trials and significantly less than what is necessary to obtain a criminal conviction.

ARREST

The Fourth Amendment prohibits unreasonable seizures, but *seizure* is a broader term than *arrest*, which does not encompass all detentions. **Seizure** involves the exercise of dominion or control by the police over a person or item. So what standards determine when a detention has occurred? According to the Supreme Court, a **detention** occurs when a reasonable person, viewing the particular police conduct as a whole and within the setting of all the surrounding circumstances, would have concluded that the police in some way had restrained his or her liberty so that the person was not free to leave (*Michigan v. Chesternutt*, 1988).

When an Officer May Arrest

Individuals may be arrested pursuant to an arrest warrant, or a police officer may arrest an individual without a warrant if that officer has probable cause to believe a criminal act has occurred. Warrantless arrests generally are allowed only for misdemeanors committed in the presence of the officer and for felonies either when the crime is committed in the presence of the officer or the arrest occurs in public. Police may not make a warrantless arrest in a private dwelling that is not the suspect's unless there are exigent circumstances or they have consent to enter (*Payton v. New York*, 1980). This consent to enter must be given by a person who has the legal authority to do so, such as an adult resident of the dwelling.

Manner of Arrest

Police officers may use whatever force is reasonable under the circumstances to make an arrest. Deadly force is permitted only when it is necessary to protect life. Deadly force may be used to prevent escape only if the officer has probable cause to believe the suspect poses an immediate threat of serious harm to the officer or others (*Tennessee v. Garner*, 1985).

Police officers executing an arrest (or search) warrant at a private dwelling are required to "knock and announce" their presence and purpose and to provide occupants of the dwelling a reasonable amount of time to answer the door. This common law principle has been endorsed by the Supreme Court, which also has indicated that the common law exceptions to the knock and announce rule apply (*Wilson v. Arkansas*, 1995). These exceptions, or instances when the police may ignore the rule of announcement, are when reason exists to believe escape is likely, evidence will be destroyed, or officers may be injured if notice is given (Hemmens, 1997).

Types of Seizures

Police may ask questions of anyone in public, and doing so does not constitute an arrest or even a seizure. In such "on-the-street encounters," citizens remain free to leave and even ignore the police officer's question. While doing so may arouse police suspicion and/or resentment, it does not create probable cause for an arrest.

Some encounters with the police do not rise to the level of an arrest but are more intrusive than mere on-the-street encounters. These types of detentions, sometimes characterized as "seizure tantamount to arrest," do not require probable cause but do require more than mere suspicion. These encounters are classified as seizures but not full arrests. Examples include traffic stops and stop and frisks on the street.

Stop and Frisk

A **stop and frisk** involves a police officer stopping people in public and questioning them as to their identity and activity, followed in some circumstances by a limited "pat-down" search of their outer clothing. Stop and frisk procedures were endorsed by the US Supreme Court in *Terry v. Ohio* (1968) and sometimes are referred to as "Terry stops" or "investigative detentions." In *Terry,* the Court attempted to balance the interests of law enforcement with individual rights in situations where police do not have probable cause to arrest but do have some inkling of criminal activity based on their observation of the suspect and their experience. This level of proof is referred to as

> "reasonable suspicion" and has been defined by the Court as "a less demanding standard than probable cause . . . that can be established with information that is different in quantity or content . . . [and it] can arise from information that is less reliable." (*Alabama v. White*, 1990)

While a stop and frisk is not an arrest, it is a form of search and seizure. Consequently, the Fourth Amendment applies. However, because the stop is not an arrest and the frisk is not a full search, the Court has determined that probable cause is not necessary. Rather, all that is needed is "reasonable suspicion."

There are two distinct parts of the encounter: the stop and the frisk. To stop an individual, a police officer must have reasonable suspicion, in light of his or her experience and observations, that a crime has occurred or is about to occur. Such an "investigatory stop" must be temporary and no longer than necessary under the circumstances to achieve its purpose. Police officers may ask questions intended to dispel any suspicions and alleviate any fears they may have during these investigatory stops.

A frisk does not automatically follow from a stop. If—and only if—the investigatory stop does not allay an officer's reasonable fear about his or her safety or the safety of others, then the officer may conduct a frisk of the detained individual. The Supreme Court has made clear that the sole purpose of a frisk is for the protection of the officer. It is not meant to be a fishing expedition to ferret out evidence of criminal activity.

The frisk is defined as a pat-down of the suspect's outer clothing. Any object that the officer reasonably believes might be a weapon may be removed and seized and may provide probable cause for arrest on the charge of carrying a concealed weapon. The Supreme Court has referred to this as the "plain feel" doctrine (*Minnesota v. Dickerson*, 1993). If the object is not a weapon but rather something that is typically used in the commission of some crime (e.g., burglary tools), the item would be admissible evidence. Officers may not, however, manipulate items they feel in or under the outer clothing to discern what those items are when they are plainly not weapons. If an officer seizes contraband without following these guidelines, the contraband cannot be used as evidence at trial. The officer does not have to return the contraband to the suspect, however, but may keep it and turn it over to his or her superior officer.

Stop and Frisk

Vehicle Stops

Vehicles, by virtue of their mobility, present a particularly difficult situation for both law enforcement and the courts. A seizure occurs every time a vehicle is stopped, even if the purpose of the stop is limited (*Delaware v. Prouse*, 1979). While every vehicle stop is a seizure, not every seizure of a vehicle necessitates either probable cause or a warrant because the nature of most routine traffic stops is not very intrusive. Generally, police must have at least reasonable suspicion of criminal activity to stop a vehicle. Exceptions are roadblocks to check for drunk driving or illegal aliens and to check licenses and registration papers. In these instances, the Supreme Court has allowed police to stop cars absent any individualized suspicion of wrongdoing has and justified this determination by balancing the "slight" intrusion of the stop against the public interest served by the seizure (*Michigan Department of State Police v. Sitz*, 1990).

Once an officer has stopped a vehicle, he or she is authorized to ask the driver to exit the vehicle. This is true even if the stop is for a minor traffic violation. Additionally, if the officer reasonably fears for his or her safety after the driver has exited the vehicle, the officer may conduct a frisk for weapons (*Pennsylvania v. Mimms*, 1977). Officers may order passengers out of the vehicle as well, even when there is absolutely no indication of wrongdoing on the part of the passenger (*Maryland v. Wilson*, 1997). The officer may request vehicle registration and other licensing documents, examine the vehicle identification number, and ask questions of both the driver and the occupants. If the person legally stopped by a police officer refuses to identify himself or herself, that person may be arrested. The officer also may seek consent to search the vehicle without informing the driver that the initial stop is over and that the driver is free to leave (*Ohio v. Robinette*, 1997).

SEARCHES

A **search** is the examination of an individual's house, person, or effects to discover items related to criminal activity. *Effects* include papers, purses, cars, and other like items. Items sought may include contraband; fruits of the crime; instrumentalities of the crime, such as weapons, burglar's tools, or the getaway car; or evidence of the crime. The Fourth Amendment applies only to areas where persons have a reasonable expectation of privacy, such as in their homes; Fourth Amendment rights do not generally apply with the same force in public locations because people have a lesser expectation of privacy in public (*Katz v. United States*, 1967).

Reasonable Expectation of Privacy

The concept of reasonable expectation of privacy is a relatively recent addition to criminal procedure, beginning with the decision in *Katz v. United States* (1967). Before the *Katz* decision, courts seeking to determine when a "search" had occurred focused on whether police conduct infringed on a property interest (meaning an area afforded constitutional protection). If so, then the police conduct constituted a search, and the protections of the Fourth Amendment applied. The decision in *Katz* abandoned the focus on property interests in favor of considering the expectation of privacy that the individual and society had in a given situation.

A **reasonable expectation of privacy** has subjective and objective components: (a) the subject of the search must have a subjective expectation of privacy, and (b) society must view that expectation as reasonable. The fact that a person believes he or she has an expectation of privacy is not sufficient—this expectation of privacy must be objectively reasonable, meaning it is one that society, not just the individual, accepts.

Exceptions to the Search Warrant Requirement

While police generally are required to obtain a search warrant, the Supreme Court has held that a variety of exigent circumstances justify a warrantless search. There are also several actions that are not considered to be searches, so the Fourth Amendment does not apply. These exceptions have been developed by the Court on a case-by-case basis. Each is discussed in turn.

Search Incident to Arrest

Police officers executing a valid arrest of a suspect may conduct a full search both of the suspect and of the area within the suspect's immediate control (*Chimel v. California*, 1969). Known as the **search incident to arrest** exception, this search must occur at the same time as the arrest. The scope of the search includes anywhere on the person and the so-called "lunge area," or immediate vicinity of the suspect. For instance, police arresting someone in a house may search the room in which the arrest occurs but cannot search other rooms in the house.

The justifications for this exception include officer safety, prevention of evidence destruction, and prevention of escape. The search incident exception applies to all custodial arrests regardless of the severity of the offense for which the person is being arrested. So long as the person is being taken into custody, a search incident may be performed. This exception does not apply to situations such as traffic stops, which are detentions but ones in which no arrest occurs.

Consent to Search

If police obtain an individual's **consent to search**, there is no need for probable cause or a search warrant. A search conducted pursuant to consent is not a search for Fourth Amendment purposes—that is, the Fourth Amendment simply does not apply. Police may ask anyone for consent to search without any basis for doing so, but there are some limitations on consent searches. First, consent must be both voluntary and intelligent. That is, the police must demonstrate that a suspect's consent was not obtained as the result of coercion or force and that the suspect knew what he or she was doing. Police are not required to inform suspects of their right to refuse consent, however. Second, consent may be limited to a particular area or time and may be withdrawn at any time. Third, valid consent to search may be obtained only from a person with the apparent authority to consent, such as the owner and resident (not absent landlord) of a home or driver of a car (Hemmens & Maahs, 1996).

For a long time, courts applied the so-called "co-occupant consent rule." This rule meant that police could conduct warrantless searches and seize contraband belonging to a resident of a home who was someone other than the person granting consent if the person granting consent was an adult validly residing in the home. This rule was overturned by the Supreme Court in *Georgia v. Randolph* (2006), in which it ruled that a co-occupant could not give consent to search over the objections of another co-occupant who is present. The *Randolph* decision was narrowly scripted on the physical presence of a co-occupant who is objecting to the search. It does not necessarily apply to a co-occupant who is absent from the premises at the time his or her co-resident grants consent (*Fernandez v. California*, 2014).

Vehicles

The Supreme Court has ruled that the inherent mobility of vehicles eliminates the necessity of obtaining a search warrant in many instances (*Carroll v. United States*, 1925). The Court also has noted that there is a lessened expectation of privacy in a vehicle that is in public. However, while the warrant requirement is relaxed, the probable cause requirement is not. To search a vehicle without a warrant, the police must be able to: (a) demonstrate that there exists probable cause to search and (b) establish that the vehicle is mobile. This mobility creates the exigency justifying relaxation of the warrant requirement.

For many years, the Supreme Court rule regarding search incident to arrest in motor vehicles was that when a police officer arrested the driver of a car, that officer could conduct a warrantless search of the passenger compartment of the car, including any containers, that reasonably might hold a weapon or evidence of the crime for which the driver has been arrested, and that this search could be conducted after the officer has placed the driver in the police cruiser for transport to the police station (*Chimel v. California*, 1969). After years of criticism that this rule was illogical, the Supreme Court finally changed course. In *Arizona v. Gant* (2009), the Court held that search incident of a vehicle after an arrestee has been secured is *not* permitted under the search incident exception unless the search is for evidence related to the arrest. The Court noted that the rationale for the search incident exception (prevention of evidence destruction and officer safety) was not present when the arrestee was secured.

Vehicle Search

Many police departments as a matter of policy impound and/or inventory vehicles after the driver is arrested. This procedure is intended to guard the property of the arrestee as well as to protect the department from lawsuits alleging theft of personal property within the vehicle. The Supreme Court has upheld warrantless inventory searches as long as they are routinely conducted by the department and not done as a pretext to search for evidence or contraband (*Florida v. Wells,* 1990). The Court also has upheld warrantless searches of impounded vehicles even when the driver has not been arrested (*South Dakota v. Opperman,* 1976).

Finally, the installation of electronic tracking devices on a vehicle in a public area is not permissible without a search warrant because the installation constitutes a trespass (*United States v. Jones,* 2012). Installation of a tracking device is possible, however, if police have probable cause and obtain a search warrant. Monitoring of these devices is not permissible when the vehicle is in a private dwelling, however, as there is a heightened expectation of privacy in a dwelling or on private property (*United States v. Karo,* 1984).

Plain View

According to the **plain view doctrine**, objects are subject to seizure if they are in the plain view of an officer who has a legal right to be in a position to see them (*Harris v. United States,* 1968). The plain view doctrine is not actually an exception to the Fourth Amendment but rather another instance in which the protections of that amendment simply do not apply—when officers lawfully observe something, they are not conducting a "search" for Fourth Amendment purposes. Hence, no warrant or probable cause is required. The Supreme Court at one time suggested such observations must be "inadvertent" (accidental rather than purposeful) but has retreated from that requirement (*Horton v. California,* 1990).

The plain view doctrine is just that—it is limited to the seizure of items that an officer sees. It does not apply to items discovered by touch, smell, or any sense other than sight. Evidence discovered by the other senses may be admitted under one of the other exceptions to the warrant requirement. For instance, if an officer smells evidence of methamphetamine being cooked in someone's house, he or she must obtain a warrant to search for the methamphetamine the officer knows to be there on the basis of olfactory evidence. Because the meth lab is not in plain view, it cannot be seized in the absence of a warrant.

Police may use tools that aid them in their observation, such as a flashlight (*Texas v. Brown,* 1983). Furthermore, the officer must be lawfully present at the spot where he or she observes the item. If an officer enters a dwelling illegally, he or she may not take advantage of the plain view doctrine. Finally, it must be "immediately apparent" that the item observed is seizable, either as contraband, evidence of a crime, or the fruits of a crime (*Arizona v. Hicks,* 1987). Police cannot move or manipulate the item to learn more about it.

Open Fields

Certain areas outside the home are classified as "open fields." Items in open fields do not fall under the protection of the Fourth Amendment, as they are not "house, papers and effects" (*Hester v. United States,* 1924). As with items in plain view, items in open fields may be seized without a warrant or probable cause. Unlike the plain view doctrine, police need not be lawfully in an area considered open fields to seize an item observed there—under this doctrine, officers may seize and use in court evidence they obtain while trespassing.

Open fields is a misleading term, as these areas need not be either open or a field. Rather, **open fields** simply refers to everything that is *not* defined as being within the *curtilage*, which is the land and buildings immediately surrounding and intimately associated with a dwelling. The curtilage includes fenced areas incorporating the house, garages, and other buildings used primarily for domestic purposes, such as a shop or washroom. Curtilage is, essentially, an extension of the home. Any land that is deemed outside of the curtilage is "open fields." This doctrine applies to fields, forests, and other land formations equally (LaFave, 1996). While the curtilage is considered protected by the Fourth Amendment, it does not receive the same level of protection afforded the interior of the home. The Supreme Court has permitted aerial surveillance of the curtilage on the theory that there is not the same expectation of privacy in the curtilage as inside the home (*California v. Ciraolo,* 1986).

Abandoned Property

Abandoned property is not protected by the Fourth Amendment, as the person abandoning it has demonstrated a willingness to give up possession and control of the item. It belongs to no one. Consequently, **abandoned property** may be seized without a warrant or probable cause. The key is determining when abandonment has occurred. This depends on where the item is discarded and the intent of the person discarding the item.

Intent to abandon may be inferred from the manner in which the item is discarded. Items tossed to the ground accompanied by a statement such as "I don't want this" clearly have been abandoned, as have items left behind and not retrieved for a substantial period of time. Intent to abandon also may be inferred from the location of the abandonment. A textbook left behind on a desk in a classroom may have been abandoned, but it is unclear without further information if it was left there intentionally. If the textbook is in the trash can in the classroom, however, this more clearly suggests an intent to abandon. Items thrown in the trash in public are considered abandoned, but items thrown in the trash on private property are not considered abandoned until the trash is placed outside the curtilage of the home for regular collection (*California v. Greenwood,* 1988).

Special Needs of Law Enforcement

The **special needs of law enforcement exception** is actually a series of exceptions to the search warrant requirement. It is applied in cases that are a mixture of criminal investigation and conduct by other public agencies not related to the police. Examples include searches of students by school authorities, searches of closely regulated businesses, and searches of probationers and parolees. In these instances, the Supreme Court has held that searches may be conducted without a warrant, on less than probable cause, and without individualized suspicion (e.g., having focused suspicion on a particular individual). These types of searches are frequently referred to as **administrative searches**.

Because individuals on probation or parole waive their Fourth Amendment rights, probation and parole officers may conduct searches at any time without a warrant and without the probable cause needed by police officers. However, the Supreme Court has stated that if a probation order is written in such a way that provides for submission to a search "by a probation officer or any other law enforcement officer," then the police gain the same rights as probation and parole officers to conduct warrantless searches and searches based on less than probable cause (*United States v. Knights*, 2001). The justification for such searches varies according to the subject of the search, but the common factor is the Court's willingness to balance the limited intrusion on individual rights against the heightened public interest in the subject (e.g., school security and product safety), with the governmental interest outweighing the principle of *de minimis* (literally, "the least"), or negligible, intrusion on individual liberty (Stuntz, 1992).

Figure 6.1 shows the flow of procedural reasoning expected in search and seizure cases. Stage 1 consists of asking if a reasonable expectation of privacy exists, and Stage 2 asks if warrant requirements were met.

Figure 6.1 Flow of Procedural Reasoning in Search and Seizure

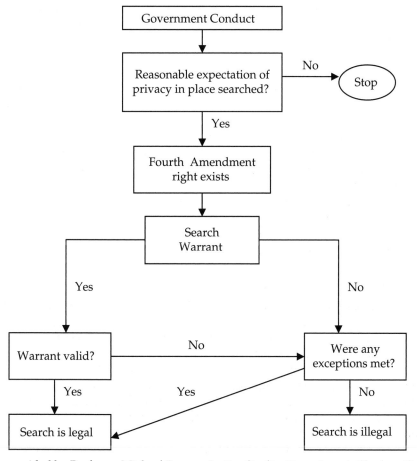

Figure provided by Professor Michael Bogner, Justice Studies Department, Chadron State College (2006).

RIGHT TO THE ASSISTANCE OF COUNSEL

Criminal procedure laws would not be very helpful to suspects and defendants without some mechanism in place for assuring that these laws were followed by the police. Accused individuals who are both knowledgeable about the nature and extent of their rights and competent enough to assert and protect them are few and far between. This is why the right to the assistance of legal counsel is specifically enumerated in the Sixth Amendment.

This right was long interpreted as a prohibition against the government denying defendants who wanted and could afford the services of a lawyer to assist them in their defense rather than as an affirmative right. Beginning with *Powell v. Alabama* (1932), however, the Supreme Court started to expand the meaning of the assistance clause. In this case, Ozie Powell and eight other black youths—the so-called "Scottsboro Boys"—were charged with raping two white women. No defense attorney was assigned to the case until the day of the trial, which took place only 12 days after the youths' arrest. The youths were represented by Stephen Roddy and Milo Moody. According to Linder (1999), "Roddy was an unpaid and unprepared real estate attorney who, on the first day of trial, was so stewed he could hardly walk straight. Moody was a forgetful seventy-year-old local attorney who hadn't tried a case in decades" (p. 1). Eight of the nine youths were convicted and sentenced to death; the ninth, a 12-year-old, was sentenced to life imprisonment.

The case eventually reached the Supreme Court on the basis that the youths were effectively denied their liberty interests by virtue of receiving essentially no legal assistance at trial. The Court reversed their convictions on Fourteenth Amendment due process grounds because, at the time, the Sixth Amendment did not apply to state proceedings (the Sixth Amendment had not yet been incorporated; Hemmens, Thompson, & Nored, 2013). The *Powell* decision held that due process requires the appointment at government expense of defense attorneys for indigent defendants facing capital charges. Although *Powell* was limited to death penalty cases, it provided the groundwork for extending the right to counsel for all indigent defendants facing serious felony charges in federal courts in *Johnson v. Zerbst* (1938).

The *Johnson* ruling was not made applicable to the states, although by this time many states did provide legal counsel for indigent defendants. In *Gideon v. Wainwright* (1963), the Supreme Court ruled that the right to counsel was so fundamental to the American system of justice that it should be applied to the states based squarely on the Sixth Amendment. Clarence Earl Gideon was charged with burglary of a pool hall, and he requested that an attorney be appointed to assist him in his defense because he was indigent. The trial court refused his request, stating that Florida law required the appointment of government-funded lawyers only to indigent defendants facing the death penalty. The Supreme Court remanded the case, stating that "any person haled [sic] into court, who is too poor to hire a lawyer, cannot be assured of a fair trial unless counsel is provided for him." Gideon was acquitted in the retrial, where he was represented by a competent attorney provided by the state.

In *Argersinger v. Hamlin* (1972), the Supreme Court further clarified the circumstances under which an accused indigent defendant has the right to government-provided counsel. Indigent defendant Jon Argersinger was convicted in Florida of carrying a concealed weapon (a misdemeanor) without the assistance of counsel. On vacating Argersinger's conviction, the Court established that any indigent defendant facing incarceration for a felony or a misdemeanor with a possible sentence of more than six months must be represented by counsel.

RIGHT TO COUNSEL DURING INTERROGATIONS AND PRETRIAL IDENTIFICATION PROCEDURES

One of the most important sources of evidence in a criminal investigation is the suspect. A significant number of cases are solved through obtaining a confession from the suspect; many others are solved in large part through the use of eyewitness identifications of the perpetrator. While the Fourth Amendment governs most search and seizure situations, the Fifth and Sixth Amendments regulate situations involving interrogation of criminal suspects and identification procedures.

The Fifth Amendment provides that persons shall not be compelled to incriminate themselves, but while self-incrimination cannot be compelled, it is permitted. The standard for admissibility of a confession has historically been voluntariness. Precisely what constituted a voluntary statement has developed over the years. The Supreme Court has determined that police use of physical force to obtain a confession renders that confession involuntary. Later, the Court declared involuntary those confessions obtained after extended interrogation in isolation and those obtained through the use of mental coercion. In 1964, the Court held that a criminal defendant had a right to counsel once the police investigation "is no longer a general inquiry, but has begun to focus on the defendant" (*Escobedo v. Illinois*, 1964).

Two years later, in *Miranda v. Arizona* (1966), the Supreme Court held that evidence obtained by the police during a custodial interrogation could not be used at trial unless suspects first were informed of both their privilege against self-incrimination and their right to counsel. *Miranda* is probably the most controversial criminal procedure decision ever handed down by the Supreme Court, in part because police feared it would lead to a dramatic reduction in confessions and because the decision went beyond just declaring one particular police practice unconstitutional.

The Court did not merely hold that police must inform

Interrogation

Figure 6.2 The *Miranda* Warnings

1. The person being arrested has a right to remain silent;
2. anything the person says can be used against them in court;
3. the person being arrested has a right to have an attorney present during any questioning;
4. if the person being arrested cannot afford an attorney, one will be appointed for them prior to any questioning.

suspects of their rights: it set forth exactly what the police should say. This became known as the *Miranda* **warnings** and is detailed in Figure 6.2.

Custody

Miranda warnings are required when there is a *custodial interrogation*. **Custody** has been defined as when the suspect "has been subjected to a formal arrest or equivalent restraints on his freedom of movement" (*California v. Beheler,* 1983). It is fairly obvious when an arrest has occurred—police say so or place handcuffs on the suspect and transport him or her to jail. The more difficult situation is determining when a person has been deprived of his or her freedom in a significant way. The test here is whether a reasonable person in the suspect's position would conclude that he or she is not free to leave. Factors considered by the courts in this determination include the actions of the police, the location of the encounter, and the time of the encounter.

Interrogation

Miranda warnings are not triggered by custody alone, however. The warnings are required only when there is both custody and interrogation. What. then, is interrogation? **Interrogation** occurs (a) when police are asking questions the answers to which may incriminate and (b) in circumstances in which the police, through their actions, create the "functional equivalent" of an interrogation. The police create the functional equivalent of an interrogation when they engage in activity they "should know is reasonably likely to evoke an incriminating response from a suspect" (*Rhode Island v. Innis,* 1980).

Circumstances in Which *Miranda* Is Not Required

In a number of situations, *Miranda* warnings need not be given. If there is not both custody and interrogation, *Miranda* warnings are not required. Examples of situations the Supreme Court has held do not constitute custody include routine traffic stops (*Berkemer v. McCarty,* 1984) and sobriety checkpoints (*Michigan Department of State Police v. Sitz,* 1990). Examples of situations the Court has held do not constitute interrogation include conversations between two officers in the vicinity of the suspect, situations in which someone volunteers a statement without prompting, routine questioning of persons at the scene of a crime, questions intended to clarify an ambiguous response, questions that are part of a stop and frisk, and when there is a threat to public safety (*New York v. Quarles*, 1984).

Extension and Application of the *Miranda* Warnings

The Supreme Court has decided a number of cases involving the *Miranda* warnings. The Court has held that once suspects have invoked their right to remain silent, police may not question them further until they meet with a lawyer or unless the suspects initiate further communication (*Edwards v. Arizona*, 1981). The Court also has held that once suspects invoke their right to counsel, they may not be questioned about any other offense unrelated to the one for which they were arrested and about which they have asserted their right to remain silent (*Arizona v. Roberson*, 1988).

While these decisions clarify and extend *Miranda*, most of the decisions have restricted the reach of *Miranda* as originally interpreted. The failure of the police to inform a suspect that an attorney, retained without his or her knowledge by a family member, was attempting to reach him or her does not invalidate a confession obtained by the police because the suspect did not know he or she had a lawyer (*Moran v. Burbine*, 1986). A police officer posing as an inmate need not provide *Miranda* warnings to a suspect in jail before asking him or her incriminating questions because the location of this questioning is assumed to have no coercive atmosphere (*Illinois v. Perkins*, 1990).

Requesting a lawyer at a bail hearing is not considered an invocation of the right to counsel for crimes with which the suspect had not yet been charged because the request is construed as limited to the Sixth Amendment right to counsel at trial, not as an invocation of the Fifth Amendment right to counsel prior to questioning (*McNeil v. Wisconsin*, 1991). If police obtain a voluntary, but unwarned, confession, they may remedy any possible problems with the confession by giving proper *Miranda* warnings, procuring a waiver of rights signed by the suspect, and then obtaining the confession again, even though the suspect may not realize the initial confession was inadmissible (*Oregon v. Elstad*, 1985).

An illegally obtained confession also may be admitted at trial if it is used solely to impeach the testimony of the defendant (*Harris v. New York*, 1971). In other words, if during a trial the defendant asserts his or her innocence, an illegally obtained confession in which the defendant admits guilt may be used as evidence that the defendant's trial testimony is not to be trusted. However, it may not be used as evidence of the defendant's guilt.

Finally, the rights mentioned in the *Miranda* warnings may be waived by the suspect so long as the written waiver is "knowing, intelligent, and voluntary." This means that the suspect is fully informed and understands the possible consequences of waiving his or her rights and does so free of any form of coercion in the form of threats or promises.

Figure 6.3 Summary of Steps in the Evolution of the Right to the Assistance of Counsel

Powell v. Alabama **(1932)** Indigent defendants have right to free counsel in capital cases.	*Johnson v. Zerbst* **(1938)** Indigent defendants charged with serious felonies in federal courts have right to free counsel.	*Gideon v. Wainwright* **(1963)** Sixth Amendment applied to the states. Indigent defendants have right to free counsel in all felony cases.
Argersinger v. Hamlin **(1972)** Indigent defendants have right to free counsel in misdemeanor cases as well as felony cases if facing incarceration.	*Escobedo v. Illinois* **(1964)** Suspects have right to counsel when the police cease making general inquiries and focus on a particular individual.	*Miranda v. Arizona* **(1966)** Suspects must be informed of right to counsel, as well as other rights, before custodial interrogation.

ISSUE HIGHLIGHT

Abolish the *Miranda* Warnings?

The *Miranda* warnings were first set forth by the US Supreme Court in 1966. In the 50 years since, the warnings have become a part of popular culture—repeated *ad infinitum* in countless movies and television shows and discussed in high-profile cases. Some critics have argued that the warnings should no longer be required as everyone (police, suspects, criminals, and ordinary law-abiding citizens) already knows them. Thus, punishing the police for failing to read a suspect the warnings serves no real purpose and can result in a confession being excluded from trial.

Other critics have asserted the *Miranda* warnings should no longer be required because the warnings are not working as expected—that is, suspects continue to waive their rights and unintentionally implicate themselves. These critics argue the *Miranda* warnings have become a "form of words" with no real meaning, just something that police officers say when they make an arrest. What do you think? Should the *Miranda* warnings be abolished?

Reasons Why the *Miranda* Warnings Should Be Abolished

1. Since everyone already knows them, they serve no valid purpose.
2. The *Miranda* warnings have become rote, and suspects do not realize how important the warnings are.
3. The cost for failure to read a suspect the *Miranda* warnings (the exclusion of important evidence) is too great.

Reasons Why the *Miranda* Warnings Should Not Be Abolished

1. Not everyone knows their rights, and being arrested is a stressful event wherein one could easily forget these rights. Thus, a reminder is worthwhile.
2. The warnings reduce (but do not eliminate) the possibility that suspects will falsely confess or implicate themselves.
3. Requiring the police to tell people their rights is a sign of a strong democracy that values individual rights over results.

Figure 6.3 summarizes the major cases in the evolution of the right to the assistance of counsel.

Lineup

Pretrial Identification Procedures

Police have long acknowledged that a pretrial confrontation of a criminal suspect and the witness is a common and effective investigatory tool. Eyewitness identifications are notoriously unreliable, however, and the Supreme Court has held that a criminal defendant has a right to counsel not only at trial but at any "critical stage" in the criminal proceedings, including most pretrial events. Reconciling the competing interests of individual liberty and crime investigation has led to some unusual results in this area. According to two decisions, decided five years apart, the Supreme Court held that a suspect has a right to counsel at a lineup if it occurs after criminal charges have been filed (*United States v. Wade*, 1967) but that no right to counsel exists if the lineup takes place prior to charges being filed (*Kirby v. Illinois*, 1972). The rationale for providing the right to counsel at a postindictment lineup is that such an event now constitutes a "critical stage" in the prosecution. Because there is the potential for prejudicial error at such events, a lawyer can ensure the procedure is conducted properly, and if it is not, the defendant then has a record with which to challenge the identification procedure at trial (Grano, 1974).

THE CONFRONTATION OF WITNESSES CLAUSE

The **confrontation clause** in the Sixth Amendment states that the accused has the right "to be confronted with the witnesses against him"—that is, to challenge via cross-examination any witnesses hostile to him or her. This affords the defense the opportunity to test the credibility of hostile witnesses and prevents the use of hearsay statements made outside of the courtroom (*ex parte* evidence). *Ex parte* witness statements are common in civil law but generally prohibited in criminal trials.

The right to confrontation was the issue in *Pointer v. Texas* (1965). Bob Pointer was charged with the "robbery with violence" of Kenneth Phillips. During the course of the proceedings, Phillips left Texas and indicated that he would not return. During the trial, the state offered Phillips's written testimony into evidence, to which the defense objected on the grounds that it was being denied the opportunity to confront Phillips. The judge overruled the objection, stating that the defense had had an opportunity to confront Phillips at the preliminary hearing. Pointer was convicted, and the Texas Court of Appeals affirmed. The US Supreme Court disagreed, however, when it remanded the case and made the confrontation clause obligatory on the states.

The Court further clarified the interpretation of the clause in *Crawford v. Washington* (2004). Michael Crawford stabbed Kenneth Lee during an argument. Both Crawford and his wife, Sylvia, corroborated each other's story initially, but in a second interview, Sylvia's statement differed as to her husband's self-defense claim. During the trial, Crawford invoked his marital exception privilege, which prevented Sylvia from testifying at the trial, but the state was allowed to introduce her *ex parte* statements into evidence because of the "unavailability" (as a result of the marital exception) of Sylvia as a witness. Crawford was convicted of assault with a deadly weapon, and the Washington Supreme Court affirmed.

The US Supreme Court reversed Crawford's conviction, declaring that statements of absent witnesses may be admitted only when the witness is unavailable (which Sylvia was if the marital exception rule was to be honored) or if the defense had prior opportunity to cross-examine (recall that in *Pointer,* the Court brushed aside the fact that the defense had had such an opportunity). The Court ruled that "unavailable" should be read to mean that the witness is "demonstrably unable to testify in person."

The confrontation clause does not absolutely guarantee the right to face-to-face confrontation at trial even if the hostile witness is fully capable of being there. The right can be denied when denial serves an important policy and where reliability is otherwise assured. An example of this would be in cases involving the sexual molestation of very young children where the children's testimony is corroborated by an examining physician or social worker following strict procedural guidelines.

THE EXCLUSIONARY RULE

The **exclusionary rule** provides that any evidence obtained by the government in violation of the Fourth Amendment guarantee against unreasonable searches and seizures is not admissible in a criminal trial for the purpose of proving guilt. It is a judicially created remedy for violations of the Fourth Amendment, not an explicitly provided part of that amendment. The rule, the reason for its existence, the method and scope of its implementation, its social consequences, and the exceptions to it all have long been the subjects of fiery legal debate. Opponents of the rule feel it absurd to throw out valid evidence because of the manner in which it was obtained. On the other hand, proponents feel that without a means of enforcing the Fourth Amendment guarantee, the amendment is reduced to a "form of words," as Justice Tom Clark said in *Mapp v. Ohio* (1961).

Advancing Toward the Exclusionary Rule

The first hint of something like an exclusionary rule from the Supreme Court came in *Boyd v. United States* (1886). This case involved the compulsory production of some business papers that revealed a conspiracy to defraud the customs revenue service rather than a search and seizure, although the Court likened it to one. Boyd's conviction was overturned and the case remanded to the lower courts, where the evidence provided by Boyd's papers was to be excluded. The Court reasoned that Boyd had been compelled to be a witness against himself (by being forced to produce the papers in question) based on the prohibition of such in the Fifth Amendment.

In *Adams v. New York* (1904), the plaintiff was arrested for possessing illegal lottery tickets and relied on *Boyd* to have his conviction overturned. The Supreme Court, however, held that the circumstances of *Boyd* did not apply and stated that the fact the materials were seized illegally "is no legal objection to the admission of the evidence." The Court further stated that how the evidence was obtained was a collateral matter for which the trespasser (the arresting officer) "may be held responsible civilly, and perhaps criminally, but his testimony is not thereby rendered incompetent." In its decision, the Court upheld the guiding principle of the common law that "evidence is evidence is evidence." This is still the guiding principle in most other common law systems in which the judiciary is reluctant to police the police, considering such action to be an unwarranted intrusion into the business of a separate branch of government. Unlike American judges who today *must* exclude illegally obtained evidence (with the exceptions noted later), judges in these countries have discretionary power to exclude evidence obtained under questionable circumstances. However, it is not unusual for them to do so since they apparently feel, in common with the justices in *Adams,* that other remedies would best serve the interests of justice (Reichel, 2005).

Boyd came up again in *Weeks v. United States* (1914). Fremont Weeks had been convicted on the basis of evidence (as in *Adams,* the evidence was related to illegal lotteries as well as seizing a number of private items) seized in two warrantless searches of his home, and he sought to have his conviction overturned. On this occasion, the unanimous decision of the Supreme Court held that the evidence seized in an illegal manner should have been excluded by the trial court and remanded the case. Thus, the exclusionary rule was born.

The exclusionary rule, however, applied only to evidence illegally obtained by federal law enforcement officers for use in federal criminal prosecutions. Because of this limitation, state law enforcement officers were still free to seize evidence illegally without fear of its exclusion in state criminal proceedings. Additionally, evidence seized illegally by state police could be turned over to federal law enforcement officers for use in federal prosecutions, as the federal law enforcement officers were not directly involved in the illegal seizure. The fruits of illegal activities of federal officers could likewise be turned over to state law enforcement for prosecution. This was known as the *"silver platter" doctrine*, meaning that evidence was simply being given to law enforcement agencies unencumbered by the rule (LaFave, 1996).

An offspring doctrine of the exclusionary rule that further aggravated its critics is known as the **fruit of the poisonous tree**. This metaphorical phrase denotes that just as evidence discovered during an illegal search, arrest, or interrogation is inadmissible because of the exclusionary rule, any later evidence derived from these illegal procedures must also be excluded. For instance, if Tony is interrogated illegally and, on the basis of that illegal interrogation, officers obtain a warrant to search his home and find incriminating evidence, that evidence is inadmissible even though the search was conducted with a valid warrant. The idea behind the concept is that if the tree (the original illegality) is "poisoned," then the fruit (the subsequent evidence derived from it) is "tainted" (*Nardone v. United States*, 1939). As with the exclusionary rule itself, at the time this rule applied only to the federal courts.

The next important case in the evolution of the exclusionary rule was *Wolf v. Colorado* (1949). Julius Wolf, a practicing physician, was convicted of performing illegal abortions on the basis of evidence taken from his office in a warrantless search. In *Wolf*, the Supreme Court applied the Fourth Amendment against the states, incorporating it into the Fourteenth Amendment. However, the Court refused to apply the remedy of the exclusionary rule, leaving the enforcement of the Fourth Amendment up to the individual states. Thus, Wolf's conviction was affirmed.

Twelve years later, in *Mapp v. Ohio* (1961), the Court took the step it had failed to take in *Wolf* and applied the exclusionary rule to the states. As discussed in chapter 3, the home of Dollree Mapp had been searched without a warrant because she was suspected of harboring a bombing suspect. The police did not find the suspect but did find a number of obscene materials in a trunk, and Mapp was arrested, convicted, and imprisoned. She appealed her conviction on her First Amendment rights to free expression, but the Court ignored this in favor of her Fourth Amendment rights. The Court reversed her conviction and applied the exclusionary rule to the states because it acknowledged the states had failed to provide adequate remedies for Fourth Amendment violations committed by state police officers.

The Court also stated that the exclusionary rule is designed to serve at least two purposes: (a) the deterrence of police misconduct and (b) the protection of judicial integrity. In recent years, however, the Court has emphasized almost exclusively the deterrence of police misconduct, leading to the creation of several exceptions to the rule. While courts and commentators have suggested alternate means of enforcing the Fourth Amendment, such as civil suits for damages, criminal prosecutions of police engaged in illegal activity, and administrative sanctions, the Supreme Court concluded in *Mapp* that these means of enforcing the Fourth Amendment were ineffectual. Note that the term *illegal* in this context does not necessarily mean a criminal act; rather, it usually means a violation (knowingly or unknowingly) of some constitutional procedural rule.

Curtailing the Exclusionary Rule

As previously noted, the exclusionary rule has been severely criticized by a number of courts and commentators. Prior to its application to the states in *Mapp*, Justice Benjamin Cardozo voiced the most quoted critical opinion of it in *People v. Defoe* (1926): "There has been no blinking at the consequences [of applying the exclusionary rule]. The criminal is to go free because the constable blundered." Despite its many critics, the exclusionary rule has not been overruled. The Supreme Court has carved out several exceptions to the rule over the years, however, and has held that the exclusionary rule does not apply in a number of proceedings.

Proceedings in Which the Exclusionary Rule Is Not Used

The *Weeks* and *Mapp* decisions both involved criminal trials. The Supreme Court has been reluctant to extend the exclusionary rule to other proceedings, even if there is a potential for loss of liberty. The Court has held that the exclusionary rule does not apply in civil cases and grand jury investigations, and a number of lower courts have concluded that the rule does not apply to probation and parole revocation hearings. Furthermore, illegally seized evidence may be admitted in a criminal trial if the purpose for admitting the evidence is not to prove guilt but rather to impeach a defendant's testimony (Hemmens & del Carmen, 1997).

The Standing Exception

In *Rakas v. Illinois* (1978), the Supreme Court held that to claim Fourth Amendment protection, a defendant must have standing. To have **standing** means that a person has the right to bring legal action by virtue of being personally harmed. For instance, if Otto is legally present in someone else's home (but is not a resident) when the police conduct an illegal search and discover incriminating evidence belonging to him, he does not have standing to seek redress in the courts because he cannot claim a legitimate expectation of privacy in another person's home. Otto does, of course, have an expectation of privacy with regard to searches of his person in that home.

In *Rakas*, the petitioner appealed his conviction on armed robbery charges on the basis that police had illegally searched a car in which he was the passenger and found shells in the glove compartment and a sawed-off rifle that was under the front passenger seat and therefore not in plain view. Rakas moved to suppress the rifle and shells on Fourth Amendment grounds, but the trial court denied the motion because Rakas lacked standing to object to the lawfulness of the search because he did not own either the car or the rifle and shells. The Supreme Court upheld the finding of the Illinois court.

Independent Source Exception

Under the **independent source exception**, evidence may be admitted if knowledge of that evidence is gained from a source that is entirely independent from a source tainted by illegality. In *Segura v United States* (1984), police illegally entered Segura's apartment, conducted a warrantless search, and remained there for 19 hours awaiting a search warrant. When the warrant arrived, the police conducted a search and found cocaine and evidence of trafficking. The state court disallowed evidence derived from the initial illegal search but allowed evidence found during the execution of the warrant. The Supreme Court ruled that the information on which the warrant was secured came from sources independent of what the officers had seen upon illegal entry, and that it was known to them well before their entry (it had come from an informant previously arrested who told police he had bought drugs from Segura). The Court affirmed Segura's conviction.

Attenuation Exception

Under the **attenuation exception**, illegally obtained evidence is admissible if there is a less-than-clear causal connection between the illegal police action and the evidence—that is, if the means of obtaining the evidence is sufficiently remote from the illegality. In *Wong Sun v. United States* (1963), there was a convoluted chain of events starting with illegal police entry into a laundry. The owner of the laundry told the police that another person had been selling drugs; this person in turn implicated the laundry owner and another person, Wong Sun. Wong Sun was illegally arrested (his arrest was a fruit of the poisonous tree since the laundry had been entered illegally), arraigned, and released on his own recognizance. Several days later, Wong Sun voluntarily returned to the police station, confessed, and was subsequently convicted. Later, Wong Sun claimed that because the entry into the laundry was illegal and the evidence seized there inadmissible as poisoned fruit, and since his own arrest was therefore illegal and had he not been arrested he would never have confessed, his conviction should be overturned. The Supreme Court disagreed, saying that the connection between the arrest and Wong Sun's confession had "become so attenuated as to dissipate the taint." In other words, the impact of the initial illegality on Wong Sun's confession had been weakened (attenuated) by time and subsequent events and was therefore allowable (see Figure 6.4).

Good Faith Exception

The exceptions we have looked at so far have been essentially about the admissibility of evidence obtained indirectly from police misconduct and may be considered exceptions to the fruit of the poisonous tree doctrine rather than to the exclusionary rule per se, which deals with evidence directly obtained by such conduct. The **good faith exception**, on the other hand, is an exception to the exclusionary rule proper.

In *United States v. Leon* (1984), the Supreme Court held that evidence obtained by the police acting in *good faith* is admissible. Based on an anonymous informant's tip, police officers applied for and received a search warrant to search Alberto Leon's home, where they found large quantities of illegal drugs. Leon was arrested, but a judge concluded that the affidavit for the search warrant did not establish the probable cause necessary to issue the warrant, and that the evidence obtained could not be used at Leon's trial (it was the fruit of the poisonous tree). The government appealed,

Figure 6.4 Summary of the Evolution of the Exclusionary Rule

Advance of the Exclusionary Rule

Boyd v. U.S. (1886)	*Adams v. N.Y.* (1904)	*Weeks v. U.S.* (1914)	*Nardone v. U.S.* (1939)	*Wolf v. Colorado* (1949)	*Mapp v. Ohio* (1961)
Hint of an exclusionary rule based on the Fifth Amendment.	Affirmed common law principle that evidence is evidence.	Formulated the exclusionary rule for federal cases.	Fruit of the poisonous tree first announced.	Applied the Fourth Amendment to states but not the exclusionary rule.	Applied the exclusionary rule to states.

Retreat from the Exclusionary Rule

Wong Sun v. U.S. (1963)	*Rakas v. Illinois* (1978)	*Segura v. U.S.* (1984)	*U.S. v. Leon* (1984)	*Nix v. Williams* (1984)
Evidence is admissible if it is attenuated by it being sufficiently remote from the initial illegality.	Defendant must have standing to claim Fourth Amendment protection.	Evidence is admissible if obtained from a source independent of any initial police illegality.	Evidence is admissible if officers acted in good faith based on the actions of others (i.e., judges, legislators, etc.)	Evidence is admissible if it would have inevitably been discovered by legal means.

claiming that the police had acted in good faith. The Court agreed, stating that the exclusionary rule is not a right but a remedy intended to deter illegal police conduct. In cases such as *Leon*, the majority argued, the rule cannot deter where the police act in good faith based on a warrant issued by a judge since an officer cannot reasonably be expected to question the judge's probable cause determination.

The Court has extended this rationale to allow the introduction of evidence obtained by the police acting in good faith reliance on an arrest warrant issued that is later discovered to be void. For instance, in *Arizona v. Evans* (1994), Isaac Evans was pulled over for a traffic offense and found to have an outstanding arrest warrant. Based on this, the officer arrested Evans, performed a search incident to arrest, and found drugs on him. Unbeknownst to the officer, the arrest warrant had been voided, but the clerk had failed to remove it from the computer. Thus, the arrest was invalid, as was the subsequent search arising from that arrest. The Court admitted the evidence, however, despite the fact that it was obtained by an unlawful search because the officer did not know that the warrant was invalid and had relied in "good faith" on the computer records.

The rationale for the good faith exception is that excluding evidence obtained by police who have not knowingly violated the Fourth Amendment and relied in "good faith" on other actors in the criminal justice system does not serve the purpose of deterring police misconduct, the primary goal of the exclusionary rule. The good faith exception does not apply to errors made by the police themselves, even if the errors were entirely inadvertent—it applies only to situations where the police relied on others such as magistrates and clerks who, it later turns out, made a mistake.

Inevitable Discovery Exception

Another exception to the exclusionary rule proper, the **inevitable discovery exception** permits the introduction at trial of evidence that was illegally obtained by police officers if the police can demonstrate they would have eventually discovered the evidence by legal means. This ruling was based on the murder/rape case discussed in chapter 2 to illustrate the interplay between the due process and crime control models of criminal justice (*Nix v. Williams*, 1984). The burden is on the police to prove they would, in fact, have discovered the evidence lawfully even if they had not acted illegally.

SUMMARY

In this chapter, we discussed the sources of criminal procedure and the various protections afforded criminal defendants by the US Constitution and the Bill of Rights. In particular, we focused on the Fourth, Fifth, and Sixth Amendments. We discussed the meaning of "unreasonable" in the Fourth Amendment as well as that of "search" and of "seizure." These terms sometimes mean something different legally than they do in general usage. The Supreme Court has carved out a vast body of law dealing with the meaning of the Fourth, Fifth, and Sixth Amendments. There are exceptions to virtually everything, however, and law enforcement officers are expected to be familiar with the nuances of the law. Individual citizens also would do well to know their rights.

Due process of law is a very important legal concept. It is one of the strongest defenses that individual citizens have against their government. Criminal procedure, the rules the government must obey when it seeks to deprive a person of his or her liberty, is a direct outgrowth of the concept of due process.

Criminal procedure law is constantly evolving as police resort to new tactics and technologies in their war on crime. The courts, as interpreters of the Constitution, are continually struggling to maintain the proper balance between the competing interests of law enforcement and individual privacy. The Bill of Rights provides a number of broad individual protections, and the Supreme Court has endeavored to develop more precise, understandable parameters of these protections.

The Fourth Amendment prohibits unreasonable searches and seizures, but the Court has not applied this standard blindly, developing the concepts of "reasonable suspicion" and permitting techniques such as stop and frisk. In some instances, the Court has created clear, specific rules for police conduct, such as the exclusionary rule and the *Miranda* warnings. In other instances, the Court has resorted to a case-by-case mode of analysis, sometimes leaving law enforcement unsure of what is permitted. This confusion to some degree is unavoidable, as the abstract legal doctrines that comprise criminal procedure law are constantly challenged by new technologies, new fact patterns, and a changing political climate. The Supreme Court is both a legal and a political institution, and its decisions invariably are affected to some degree by public opinion about crime—what is "unreasonable" today may not have been unreasonable 50 years ago.

DISCUSSION QUESTIONS

1. What is the meaning of due process of law?
2. What is the difference between the crime control model and the due process model of criminal justice?
3. What is the meaning of probable cause?
4. What is the difference between an arrest and a seizure?
5. What are the major exceptions to the search warrant requirement, and what do they allow a police officer to do?
6. What is the exclusionary rule, and why does it exist?
7. Discuss the evolution of the exclusionary rule and its subsequent curtailment in light of the court cases that deal with it.
8. What are the *Miranda* warnings, and when must they be read? When are they not required?
9. What are the limitations imposed by the US Supreme Court on lineups conducted by the police?
10. Under what circumstances may a police officer be justified in using deadly force?

CHAPTER TERMS

Abandoned property

Administrative searches

Attenuation exception

Confrontation clause

Consent to search

Custody

Detention

Exclusionary rule

Fruit of the poisonous
tree

Good faith exception

Independent source
exception

Inevitable discovery
exception

Interrogation

Miranda warnings

Open fields

Plain view doctrine

Reasonable expectation
of privacy

Reasonableness clause

Search

Search incident to arrest

Seizure

Special needs of law
enforcement exception

Standing

Stop and frisk

Warrant clause

References

Grano, J. (1974). *Kirby, Biggers* and *Ash*: Do any constitutional safeguards remain against the danger of convicting the innocent? *Michigan Law Review, 72,* 717–755.

Hemmens, C. (1997). The police, the Fourth Amendment, and unannounced entry: *Wilson v. Arkansas. Criminal Law Bulletin, 33*(1), 29–53.

Hemmens, C., & del Carmen, R. (1997). The exclusionary rule in probation and parole revocation proceedings: Does it apply? *Federal Probation, 61*(3), 32–46.

Hemmens, C., del Carmen, R. V., & Scarborough, K. E. (1997). Grave doubts about "reasonable doubt": Confusion in state and federal courts. *Journal of Criminal Justice, 25*(3), 231–251.

Hemmens, C., & Maahs, J. (1996). Reason to believe: When does detention end and a consensual encounter begin? An analysis of *Ohio v. Robinette. Ohio Northern Law Review, 23*(2), 309.

Hemmens, C., Thompson, A., & Nored, L. (2013). *Significant cases in criminal procedure.* New York, NY: Oxford University Press.

LaFave, W. R. (1996). *Search and seizure: A treatise on the Fourth Amendment* (3rd ed.). Minneapolis, MN: West.

Linder, D. (1999). The trials of the "Scottsboro Boys." Retrieved from http://law2.umkc.edu/faculty/projects/FTrials/scottsboro/SB_acct.html

Reichel, P. (2005). *Comparative criminal justice systems: A topical approach* (4th ed.). Upper Saddle River, NJ: Prentice Hall.

Stuntz, W. J. (1992). Implicit bargains, government power, and the Fourth Amendment. *Stanford Law Review, 44,* 553–617.

Cases Cited

Adams v. New York, 192 U.S. (1904)

Alabama v. White, 496 U.S. 325 (1990)

Argersinger v. Hamlin, 407 U.S. 25 (1972)

Arizona v. Evans, 514 U.S. 1 (1994)

Arizona v. Gant, 556 U.S. 332 (2009)

Arizona v. Hicks, 480 U.S. 321 (1987)

Ohio v. Robinette, 117 519 U.S. 33 (1997)

Oregon v. Elstad, 470 U.S. 298 (1985)

Payton v. New York, 445 U.S. 573 (1980)

Pennsylvania v. Mimms, 434 U.S. 106 (1977)

People v. Defoe, 150 N.E. 585 (1926)

Pointer v. Texas, 380 U.S. 400 (1965)

Powell v. Alabama, 287 U.S. 45 (1932)

Rakas v. Illinois, 439 U.S. 128 (1978)

Rhode Island v. Innis, 446 U.S. 291 (1980)

Segura v. United States, 468 U.S. 796 (1984)

South Dakota v. Opperman, 428 U.S. 364 (1976)

Tennessee v. Garner, 471 U.S. 1 (1985)

Terry v. Ohio, 392 U.S. 1 (1968)

Texas v. Brown, 460 U.S. 730 (1983)

United States v. Jones, 132 S. Ct. 945 (2012)

United States v. Karo, 468 U.S. 705 (1984)

United States v. Knights, 534 U.S. 112 (2001)

United States v. Leon, 468 U.S. 897 (1984)

United States v. Wade, 388 U.S. 218 (1967)

Washington v. Texas, 388 U.S. 14 (1967)

Weeks v. United States, 232 U.S. 383 (1914)

Wilson v. Arkansas, 514 U.S. 927 (1995)

Wolf v. Colorado, 338 U.S. 25 (1949)

Wong Sun v. United States, 371 U.S. 471 (1963)

CHAPTER 7

CIVIL AND ADMINISTRATIVE LAW

In 1978, three teenage girls, Judy and Lyn Ulrich and their cousin Donna, were driving to church in Indiana when their Ford Pinto was rear-ended. Gas spilled out and caught fire, condemning the trapped girls to horrible deaths. Ford knew its Pintos had gas tanks that easily ruptured in rear-end collisions of over 25 miles per hour. The company also knew that the problem could have been fixed for $11 per vehicle but decided against doing so. Why? Accountants estimated that not fixing it would result in about 180 burn deaths and 1,200 serious burn injuries, which would cost Ford $49.5 million dollars in lawsuits and other claims. In comparison, fixing the problem would cost $137 million, so Ford reasoned that to do so would be fiscally unsound and bad business.

A former Ford engineer claimed that 95 percent of the people who died in Pinto crashes would have survived had the problem been fixed. The Ford executives who made the decision to ignore the problem may be the worst serial murderers in history (remember, by their own calculations, they knew a certain number would die because of their decision). Yet no Ford executive was ever imprisoned for this reckless disregard for human life; their cost–benefit analysis was even used to lobby against federal fuel leakage standards to show how unprofitable those would be!

Ford Motor Company was criminally charged with the deaths of the Ulrich girls, but Ford won its case on a technicality (Ford subsequently paid the Ulrich family $22,500 in a civil suit). This was the only time the criminal courts were involved because corporate wrongdoing falls under the rubric of administrative law, and complaints about corporations by individuals are decided in civil courts. In this chapter, we will see how civil and administrative law complements criminal law. The assumption of civil law is that noncriminal acts can also be harmful and need a venue to be adjudicated. The changing legal climate of today would probably see Ford being charged criminally, civilly, and administratively.

INTRODUCTION

So far, we have concentrated on law and justice as they pertain to criminal matters, but social justice requires that the law also concern itself with other harmful, or potentially harmful, acts that society has seen fit to regulate but that are outside the purview of the criminal justice system. Law is not only about redressing harms already done; it is also about trying to prevent them and to ensure fairness and predictability in everyday life. Law provides rules about how individuals, agencies, and corporations should conduct themselves. Law protects individuals and society from harmful things such as defective products and polluted air and water. Law tells us how to conduct business; it monitors the contractual promises we make; it regulates business practices; it tells us who we may or may not marry, who gets what if the marriage breaks up, and myriad other things, all of which fall under the broad umbrella of civil law. Whereas public law involves the regulation of the various relationships between and among the government and nongovernmental entities, such as corporations and private individuals, **civil law** is private law; it governs transactions between nongovernmental entities.

DIFFERENTIATING CRIMINAL AND CIVIL LAW

Many disagreements arise between and among citizens and institutions concerning matters such as property rights, contract disagreements, and personal injuries. These disputes are resolved through civil law, although certain harms may fall into both criminal and civil categories. As the social contract theorists argued, participants in the social contract must be willing to sacrifice some personal interests to achieve an environment conducive to the protection of important liberties for all. Civil law joins criminal law in serving this important end, designed as it is to provide remedies for individuals harmed by others, to manage social conflict, and to restore social harmony. Reduced to its bare bones, civil law defines and governs the rights and duties that all individuals owe to all other individuals.

Civil law is divided into five major categories: torts, property, contract, family, and juvenile law. While there is a great deal of overlap among these categories, each contains their own substantive law and procedures. *Tort law* involves injury to persons or property are called torts. *Property law* focuses on the ownership and acquisition of property through conveyances and inheritances. *Contract law* deals with the enforceability of private agreements between individuals and organizations. *Family law* is the set of laws involving marriage, child custody, and other issues arising in personal relationships, and *juvenile law* applies to laws regulating the behavior of minors. This chapter focuses on four of the five major fields of civil law (juvenile law is covered separately in the chapter 8). These subjects, along with criminal law and criminal procedure, are typically covered during the first year of law school as they are the foundation of civil law in the United States.

Like the criminal justice system, the civil justice system relies on substantive and procedural law forged by both legislative action and judicial decisions. However, a variety of important distinctions make civil law different from criminal law. Table 7.1 summarizes distinctions between criminal and civil law. In a civil case, a complaint is filed by a private party, known as the **plaintiff,** rather than by a prosecutor because the injured party is a private citizen, not the state. Occasionally, however, the government may be involved in a civil suit, either as a plaintiff or a defendant. At the termination of a civil trial decided in favor of the plaintiff, redress may be in the form of monetary damages, injunctions, or **specific performance** (particular actions the defendant must perform). There can be no penalty inflicted by the state, such as imprisonment or probation, in a civil action. However, the court may order the sheriff to execute the judgment order by seizing and selling a losing defendant's property to satisfy the judgment. The defendant, of course, may appeal the verdict or the judgment to a higher court.

The cases against football and movie star O. J. Simpson provide us with many examples of the differences between the criminal and civil law. In 1994, Simpson was arrested and criminally charged with the murders of his former wife, Nicole Brown-Simpson, and Ronald Goldman. Simpson was acquitted after a lengthy and highly publicized criminal trial. However, the victims' families (the plaintiffs) filed a wrongful death suit against Simpson in civil court. Simpson was found by the jury in the civil trial to be "responsible" for the deaths of Brown and Goldman.

Why was Simpson found culpable in the civil case but acquitted in the criminal case? Much of the reason has to do with the different standard of proof requirements in criminal and civil law. A conviction in a criminal trial requires proof beyond a reasonable doubt, while civil courts require proof by a preponderance of the evidence. **Preponderance of the evidence** simply means that the evidence indicates it is more likely than not that the defendant committed the wrongful act. This is a much lower standard of proof than required in a criminal trial. This lower standard of proof is justified on the grounds that the defendant does not stand to lose a fundamental right (life or liberty) in the event of an adverse decision.

The standard of proof is ratcheted up a few notches in some states, under certain circumstances, to a standard known as **clear and convincing evidence**. This standard establishes proof falling somewhere between the traditional standards of preponderance of the evidence and beyond a reasonable doubt. The cases in which this standard is applied are typically those in which punitive as well as compensatory damages are being sought or in cases of involuntary civil commitment.

Punitive damages, also known as exemplary damages, are damages awarded in excess of compensatory damages and are intended to serve as a punishment and to discourage the conduct of the type the defendant displayed. For instance, the jury in the Simpson civil case awarded the Brown and Goldman families millions of dollars in punitive damages because the jurors found Simpson to be responsible for the deaths of Brown and Goldman.

Involuntary commitment is the use of legal means to commit someone to a mental institution against his or her will. Both punitive damages and involuntary commitment decisions against a civil defendant can be seen as quasi-criminal penalties in that persons are being deprived of liberty or property, and thus some states reason that a standard of proof closer to the criminal law standard is warranted.

Table 7.1 *Summary of Major Distinctions Between Criminal and Civil Law*

Distinction	Criminal Law	Civil Law
Who is the legal victim?	The state	The individual
Who initiates action?	State or federal prosecutor	Private party or parties known as plaintiffs
Issue before the courts	Did the defendant violate a criminal code?	Did the defendant cause harm to the plaintiff(s)?
Standard of proof	Beyond a reasonable doubt	Generally, preponderance of evidence, sometimes extended to clear and convincing evidence
Who has the burden of proof?	The prosecution	Initially the plaintiff, but both parties must "prove" their cases
What is the remedy sought?	Punishment—probation, jail, prison, death	Money or other compensation, punitive damages, resolution of conflict
Rights of the defendant	All rights enumerated under the Fourth, Fifth, Sixth, Eighth, and Fourteenth Amendments	Amendments do not apply to private matters; they are rights owed only by the state to individuals
Who has the right to appeal an adverse decision?	The defendant	Both the plaintiff and the defendant

Another difference is that in criminal cases, the burden of proof is always on the state, whereas in a civil case, the burden is initially on the plaintiff to prove the allegation. If the plaintiff has made a prima facie case, the burden of proof then shifts to the defendant. A prima facie (literally, "at first look") case means enough evidence exists for there to be a case to answer. A prima facie case may be rebutted by contrary evidence, but some cases may be beyond rebuttal. For example, suppose you are having some work done by a contractor during the winter in your unheated garage while you are away. The workers use a heater to heat up the garage while working but forget to turn it off when they leave. As a consequence, your garage catches fire, causing considerable damage. This may be covered by a common law doctrine known as *res ipsa loquitor* (literally, "the thing speaks for itself"). In such cases, facts are self-evident that negligence lies with the defendant, and it is not necessary to provide additional details, since to any reasonable person it is obvious that the defendant is liable. Only about 6 percent of civil cases go before a jury, and when they do, there are fewer hung juries than in criminal cases, both because of the lower standard of evidence and because more states allow non-unanimous jury verdicts in civil cases (Melone & Karnes, 2003).

The rights afforded criminal defendants under the Fourth, Fifth, and Sixth Amendments do not apply to civil defendants. Evidence excluded in a criminal trial can usually be introduced in civil cases, such as the DNA and other physical evidence excluded in Simpson's criminal trial but included in his civil trial. Defendants can remain silent, but doing so is tantamount to forfeiting the case. The right to cross-examine witnesses hostile to the defendant's case is diminished in that a witness's deposition (recorded verbal evidence sworn under oath for later use in court) may be read into evidence in his or her absence. There is no obligation for the state to provide an attorney for indigent defendants in civil cases, since the state is not bringing the case to court. A final important difference is that whereas only the defendant can appeal an adverse decision in a criminal case, in civil law either party can appeal given the presence of adequate legal grounds to do so.

TORT LAW

The term *tort* comes from the Latin *tortus*, meaning "a wrong," and it refers to an act that is illegal but not criminal. **Tort law** is the body of law associated with harm caused to plaintiffs by the action or inaction of defendants other than breaches of contract, which are dealt with in contract law. A wide range of harms is covered under the tort rubric, such as invasion of privacy, personal injury, medical or legal malpractice, product liability, and simple trespassing. Many torts had their origins in criminal law and may still overlap with it, in that a wrong may be remedied in both criminal and civil courts. Tort law is thus similar to criminal law as it deals with persons who have been harmed by other persons. Unlike criminal law, however, tort law does not seek to punish the wrongdoer but rather to help the injured party gain financial recompense, even if the wrongdoer has already been punished for the same wrong in criminal court. The purpose of tort law is to determine what harm has been done to someone, and how best to remedy that harm, in order to put the person harmed back as close as possible to the position he or she was in before that harm occurred. Damages are awarded to those harmed by wrongdoers. These damages are typically monetary but in some situations may include a court order to perform or cease performing certain acts.

Tort law is the bread and butter of most lawyers because torts constitute by far the majority of cases brought before American courts. Tort cases are even more likely than criminal cases to be settled prior to trial. One study of almost 397,000 civil cases (about 67 percent tort cases) in state courts located in 75 of the nation's most populous counties found that a mere 3 percent went to trial (Cohen & Smith, 2004; see Figure 7.1). Another study found that only 2 percent of the 98,786 tort cases in federal courts in fiscal year 2002–2003 went to trial (Cohen, 2005).

Tort cases are not as "sexy" as criminal cases, and we hear about them only when we find huge amounts being awarded to plaintiffs on the basis of what are ostensibly dubious claims. Such claims included the woman who sued McDonald's for millions of dollars because she spilled a cup of their hot coffee on herself, the woman who sued the estate of her psychotherapist because he did not refer her to an alternate therapist before he committed suicide, or the overly sensitive bank robber who sued police for humiliating him by laughing at his purple penis, made that way when the booby-trapped bag carrying his swag exploded and deposited purpled dye thereon.

Figure 7.1 Highlights of Jury Trial Outcomes of Tort, Contract, and Real Property Cases in 2001

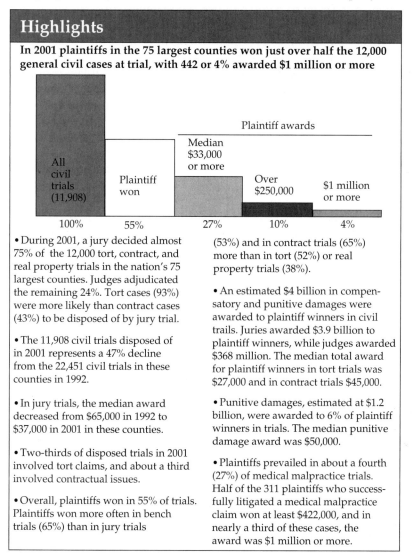

Highlights

In 2001 plaintiffs in the 75 largest counties won just over half the 12,000 general civil cases at trial, with 442 or 4% awarded $1 million or more

Plaintiff awards

All civil trials (11,908) — Plaintiff won — Median $33,000 or more — Over $250,000 — $1 million or more

100%   55%   27%   10%   4%

• During 2001, a jury decided almost 75% of the 12,000 tort, contract, and real property trials in the nation's 75 largest counties. Judges adjudicated the remaining 24%. Tort cases (93%) were more likely than contract cases (43%) to be disposed of by jury trial.

• The 11,908 civil trials disposed of in 2001 represents a 47% decline from the 22,451 civil trials in these counties in 1992.

• In jury trials, the median award decreased from $65,000 in 1992 to $37,000 in 2001 in these counties.

• Two-thirds of disposed trials in 2001 involved tort claims, and about a third involved contractual issues.

• Overall, plaintiffs won in 55% of trials. Plaintiffs won more often in bench trials (65%) than in jury trials

(53%) and in contract trials (65%) more than in tort (52%) or real property trials (38%).

• An estimated $4 billion in compensatory and punitive damages were awarded to plaintiff winners in civil trails. Juries awarded $3.9 billion to plaintiff winners, while judges awarded $368 million. The median total award for plaintiff winners in tort trials was $27,000 and in contract trials $45,000.

• Punitive damages, estimated at $1.2 billion, were awarded to 6% of plaintiff winners in trials. The median punitive damage award was $50,000.

• Plaintiffs prevailed in about a fourth (27%) of medical malpractice trials. Half of the 311 plaintiffs who successfully litigated a medical malpractice claim won at least $422,000, and in nearly a third of these cases, the award was $1 million or more.

Source: T. Cohen and S. Smith 2004. *Civil trial cases and verdicts in large counties, 2001 (April).* Bureau of Justice Statistics.

A person can be held liable for a harm both in civil and criminal courts regardless of the outcome of the criminal case. This does not constitute double jeopardy, which applies to the prospect of additional criminal trials leading to additional punishments (loss of life or liberty). For example, because only the state can legitimately punish a person and the state was not a party in the O. J. Simpson civil case, there is no danger of punishment (defendants may face punishment, however, if they ignore the judgment of the court). Certainly, the award of several million dollars to the plaintiffs was painful to Simpson, and certainly, the plaintiff relied on the power of the state to enforce the verdict. However, there is never a question of double jeopardy in civil cases following an acquittal because civil cases concern private matters.

This does not mean that plaintiffs can again bring suit against the same person for the same tort if they did not prevail in the case. The civil law protection corresponding to the double jeopardy protection in criminal law is known as *res judicata* (literally, "thing decided"). This principle means that once the case has been through all possible appeals, it is decided forever. Circumstances in which *res judicata* do not apply include those in which perjury or witness tampering affected the verdict or in cases where it can be shown that all legal issues involved were not fully litigated. Since no such exceptions apply to double jeopardy, *res judicata* is not fully equivalent.

Tort Categories

There are three primary categories of torts: *intentional* acts, *negligent* acts, and acts for which there is *strict liability*. These categories are defined based on the intent of the defendant. The O. J. Simpson civil suit tort case was based on the claim of "wrongful death" caused by Simpson. In tort cases, *intent* is presumed when an action takes place and is differentiated from *motive* (the term used in criminal cases) because *civil intent* is simply the desire to cause the consequences, not the reason for having that desire. However, many of the defenses to criminal intent also serve as defenses to civil intent (e.g., self-defense).

Intentional torts include acts in which the defendant (referred to as the *tortfeasor*) deliberately causes harm to another person or their property. An example of an intentional tort is assault and battery (again, a criminal matter that also may be pursued in civil court by victims seeking monetary compensation).

Negligence is "conduct which falls below the standard established by law for the protection of others against unreasonable risks of harm" (Kionka, 1988, p. 19). For negligence to exist, the plaintiff must prove that (a) the defendant had a duty to act in a certain way, (b) the defendant breached that duty, and (c) this breach of duty was the cause of the plaintiff's injury or loss.

The typical standard of care is referred to as **ordinary care**. This is the degree of care expected from the "reasonable person." Negligence cases often hinge on the "reasonable person" standard. That is, did the defendant act the way a reasonable person should have acted to prevent the harm from occurring?

Another important element in tort cases is *causation*. In addition to the requirement that the tortfeasor (the person who commits a wrong) owes a duty to the victim, the victim must be able to show that the tortfeasor's actions were the cause of the victim's injuries. As in criminal law, there are two types of causation—*actual cause* and *proximate cause*. Actual cause is also called *"but for"* cause. If the injury would not have occurred but for the defendant's action, then there exists actual cause. Proximate cause is also called legal cause (i.e., the requirement that the defendant's action be not only the actual cause also legally responsible). There can usually be no intervening causes; that is, the acts of a third person that come between the original negligent act and the harm do not excuse the original act.

The 1955 case of *Lubitz v. Wells* is a good example of a failed negligence claim. In this case, James Wells left one of his golf clubs in his backyard. His son, while playing with his neighbor, Judith Lubitz, picked up the golf club and swung it at a rock. In doing so, he accidentally struck Judith's chin with the club. Suit was brought against Wells for negligently leaving a dangerous instrument in a place where children might find and play with it. The court held that a golf club did not constitute an "intrinsically dangerous" item such that a reasonable person should not leave one lying in his or her own backyard and found for the defendant.

Strict liability torts are cases in which the plaintiff need not prove that the defendant acted intentionally or negligently. Liability is established if it can be shown that the plaintiff was injured and the defendant was the cause of the injury. Strict liability typically is applied to situations where a person chooses an activity that creates a risk of harm to others. For instance, torts concerning injuries sustained due to drunk drivers are included in this category. The courts have ruled in a number of cases that drunk drivers are strictly liable for the harm caused by their actions while driving drunk. In these cases, there is no need to prove intent or negligence. Another example in which strict liability has been applied is in the ownership of animals. Generally, the owners of domestic animals are strictly liable for any injuries that their animals may cause, even if they took all precautions against an animal getting loose.

Defenses to Liability

In addition to challenging issues such as causation and duty of care, tort defendants may raise other, affirmative defenses. These include contributory negligence, comparative negligence, and several other defenses. **Contributory negligence** is a doctrine holding that if an injured party was in any way partially responsible for his or her injuries, then he or she is barred from recovering from a tortfeasor. So if two parties are both negligent, neither may sue the other. Once preeminent, this doctrine has fallen out of favor as society has come to recognize that a tortfeasor should not get a "free pass" simply because the injured person was partially to blame.

Comparative negligence is a doctrine that attempts to apportion the responsibility among each party. For instance, if Frank is injured by Bill's negligent conduct but the court determines Frank was also negligent (say, 25 percent responsible), then Frank may recover only the percentage of his injuries caused by Bill—in this case, 75 percent.

Defenses to torts include **consent** and **immunity**. A person may consent to being harmed by another person (boxers, etc.), although the law typically does not allow a person to give valid consent to serious harm. As we discussed in chapter 3, under the doctrine of sovereign immunity, governments could not be sued by their citizens. Most governments have relaxed this defense, however, and now allow citizens to sue the government in many (but not all) circumstances. Judges are also immune from civil suits for judicial actions such as placing a dangerous man on probation who subsequently kills someone. Judges can, of course, be sued for actions that fall outside of their judicial duties. Some other court officials also enjoy limited immunity when performing quasi-judicial duties, such as a probation officer performing a presentence investigation inadvertently omitting information that would have precluded the judge from placing the dangerous man on probation.

Tort Reform

Tort reform is essentially about efforts of insurance companies and their clients to get Congress to pass laws severely limiting what they see as frivolous lawsuits and exorbitant punitive damages awarded by jurors who see civil trials as *"poor David"* v. *"deep-pocket Goliath"* battles. Tort reform has been a hot-button social issue for the past two decades that has pitted lawyers against insurance companies, Republicans against Democrats, and pundits of all persuasions against one another. Each side plants its flag on the moral high ground by claiming that their position on the issue is in accordance with a more just system of civil law.

One of the first things we should note is that the tort reform issue is driven by "headline" cases, such as the McDonald's coffee spill case mentioned earlier. In this case, the woman in question was burned so badly as to require skin grafts, the coffee was being served 40 to 50 degrees hotter than in most other establishments, and McDonald's knew this because it had received numerous previous complaints (Melone & Karnes, 2003). The case of the woman wanting to sue her therapist was thrown out, and the "purple penis" case is apparently an urban legend dreamt up (like many others) in e-mail land (Mencimer, 2004). Judges have discretion to throw out cases without merit, and huge awards are extremely rare. Figure 7.1 provides highlights from a nationwide study of jury trial outcomes of tort, contract, and real property cases in the year 2001. As seen in the figure 7.1, if a plaintiff won (the outcome 55 percent of the time), the median (half above and half below the stated figure) compensatory award was $27,000, and punitive damages were awarded to a mere 6 percent of the winning plaintiffs, who received a median award of $50,000.

Further, the golden age of the American "sue the bastards" tradition appears to have passed. The 2001 data presented in Figure 7.1 represent a 48 percent decrease from data for the same 75 counties obtained in 1992 (Cohen & Smith, 2004), and tort trials declined 79 percent in federal courts from 1983 to 2003 (Cohen, 2005). This can be attributed to a number of factors. The "golden age" included the asbestos cases in the 1980s, the Dalkon Shield (an intrauterine birth control device), silicone breast implants, and tobacco cases in the 1990s. Anti-tort reformers argue that the declining number of tort cases shows that civil litigation is effective in forcing business to take greater care regarding the products it puts on the market.

Proponents of tort reform insist that all they want is to place caps on excessive punitive damages, claiming that they drive businesses and medical professionals out of business, force insurance premiums up, and generally increase prices for everyone. For instance, physicians in high-risk specialties such as obstetrics and neurosurgery may pay as much as $133,000 per year for malpractice insurance, which has led to a number of them leaving the profession or moving to states or countries with punitive damage caps and lower insurance premiums ("Insurance Loss," 2003). This leaves patients without physicians and/or drives the prices charged by these physicians sky-high. A number of studies have shown that states with caps on malpractice awards have lower health care expenditures for patients with no corresponding loss of medical efficiency (see Hellinger & Encinosa, 2006).

PROPERTY LAW

Property law in the United States is largely a product of the English common law. Many of the legal doctrines used to decide property cases were first developed by the English courts in the seventeenth and eighteenth centuries, although many changes have since been made. Justice, in the case of property law, most often is defined as the protection of ownership rights. The law has been written and used to protect the owners and possessors of property.

The legal term *property* varies somewhat from the common usage. In a legal sense, **property** means the right of possession or ownership. Property includes personal property, such as an automobile or a television; real property, defined as land or permanent attachments to land; and intellectual property, defined as ideas or concepts developed by an individual or group. In each case, legal property refers to the right of ownership or control over the item, land, or idea in question (Dukeminier & Krier, 1988). The following two cases are examples of property law in action.

The case of *Pierson v. Post* (1805) shows that even 200 years ago Americans were willing to litigate almost anything. In 1804, Lodowick Post took his hounds hunting in New York. After a short time, his dogs found and gave chase to a fox. As Post was approaching the fox in the final stages of the chase, a man named Jesse Pierson shot the animal and carried it away in full sight of Post. The question that came before the Supreme Court of New York in 1805 concerned the point at which a hunter gains property rights over the hunted animal. This question turned on the legal issue of control. Did Post have control over the fox, or was it still "fair game"? According to the court, property rights over wild animals begin only at the time of absolute control. In this case, Post did not have absolute control over the fox, and therefore Pierson's act, however discourteous, did not violate any property rights that Post could claim.

The issue in the *City of Oakland v. The Oakland Raiders* (1982) was the 1980 decision by the owner of the Oakland Raiders football team to move that team to Los Angeles. The City of Oakland fought the move by arguing the city had a property right in the team. A California statute authorized cities to acquire, through the power of eminent domain, any property necessary to carry out any of its powers or functions; this primarily includes items that have a valid public use, such as land for building roads and highways. The City of Oakland argued that the Raiders football franchise served the valid public purposes of recreation and commerce and on this basis claimed that it could seize the team through the power of eminent domain. The California Supreme Court determined that allowing the city to the take ownership of the football team would unnecessarily restrict business owners in the enjoyment of their property. The court determined that it would be unjust to constrict business in such a fashion regardless of the claims of the city, and the Raiders moved to Los Angeles. (The Raiders moved back to Oakland in 1995.)

Interests in Real Property

In common law, a number of different types of interests (or rights) in real property were developed by the courts, largely in response to changes in how people used the land. These interests include freehold estates. A **freehold estate** is one wherein a person owns a piece of property and is distinguished from a nonfreehold estate, which typically involves only a right to use property (as in a rental agreement). Types of freehold estates include a fee simple estate and a life estate. A **fee simple estate** is an interest in real property that ends when the person dies, at which time the interest reverts to the original owner of the property. A **fee simple absolute estate** is one in which the property interest does not revert to the original owner. This is the type of property interest most commonly used in the United States.

It is of course possible for more than one person to own an interest in real property, as when a husband and wife both own their home. When multiple parties each own an equal share of a piece of real property, they have a **tenancy in common**. If one of the parties dies, under the right of survivorship that person's interest in the property may be transferred to the surviving party.

There are a number of other issues involving real property, such as air and sub-surface rights. It is possible for a landowner to sell the rights to the air above his or her land or the right to use or extract materials from below the land (e.g., minerals or water). A landowner also may grant an **easement** to someone, which is a limited right to use the property for a particular purpose. For example, if William owned some land that surrounded land owned by Dawson, Dawson could not legally cross William's land to get to his property. Williams could grant Dawson an easement to cross his land, which could prescribe where Dawson was allowed cross his land and for how long such a right would continue.

While real property is typically transferred either by gift or sale, it is possible for a person to acquire an interest in another's property simply by using it. Under the doctrine of **adverse possession**, if Smith openly and exclusively uses all or a portion of land owned by Jones for a specific period of time (traditionally, at least seven years), then at the end of that time period he may file suit to obtain the land. The purpose of adverse possession is to encourage people to use their property and take steps to protect it from encroachment.

Property owners are generally well protected by the law, however. While the doctrine of adverse possession exists, it is very easy to prevent a claim of adverse possession, and it affects only property that has been abandoned by the original owner. However, the law does impose some duties on owners of real property.

Under the nuisance doctrine, a property owner may not use his or her property in such a way that it has an unreasonable, adverse effect on other property owners. Thus, a homeowner may be prevented from operating a slaughterhouse in a residential area, as such a use of the property does not comport with surrounding uses.

Property owners also have a duty to keep their property in reasonably safe condition and take reasonable steps to protect those who come onto the property—including trespassers—from harm. Until the twentieth century, trespassers had no rights, and if they were injured while trespassing on another's property, they could not sue for damages. Today, however, courts recognize that landowners have a duty to keep their property free of dangers that a trespasser could not be expected to discover.

Interests in Personal Property

Personal property includes any tangible item not connected to the land, such as automobiles, books, televisions, money, and the like. These are sometimes referred to as *movables.* Personal property does not include land or items permanently attached to the land (e.g., trees or buildings) or intangible items (e.g., patents or copyrights). A person may of course own personal property and transfer that personal property permanently to another, either by sale or gift.

Personal property also may be the subject of a temporary transfer of possession to another for a particular purpose, with the understanding that the property will be returned at a later time. This is called a **bailment,** which involves the transfer of possession but not ownership. When Marlene takes her skirts to the cleaners, for example, she gives the skirts to the counterperson, who gives Marlene a receipt. When Marlene returns, she presents the receipt, pays the bill, and is given her skirts. Marlene did not transfer ownership of her skirts to the cleaners, nor does she give the skirts to the cleaners to use as they see fit. She merely transfers possession of the skirts to the cleaners for the limited purpose of having them cleaned.

CONTRACT LAW

Contract law is the law governing the conduct of business. **Contracts** are defined as legally enforceable promises. They are formal agreements between two or more parties, voluntarily undertaken, that make certain promises in exchange for other specified promises. Thus, contract law is concerned with determining the legality of written and spoken agreements between citizens, groups, agencies, and corporations. Fundamental to the operation of any business is the ability to conduct business transactions. Imagine the chaos of a world with no expectations about business agreements and what constitutes a legally binding contract. It would be very difficult to conduct any type of arranged deal without some common understanding of contracts. Contract law provides this common understanding.

Much of the law concerning contracts is now guided by the **Uniform Commercial Code** (UCC). The UCC is designed to standardize trade and contract practices among merchants and businesses. Historically, law concerning the trade and sales of goods and property fell under the governance of common law in the English-speaking world. Until the nineteenth century, merchant law was the standard for legal practice. This law was the result of merchant dealings and common law precedent concerning fairness. In 1893, the British Law of Sales was introduced as statute. In the United States, work began on a code of commerce separate from the British Law of Sales in the 1940s, which resulted in the first version of the UCC in 1952. Since then, the code has been adopted in all states except Louisiana, which has a civil (or code) law system similar to that of France. The UCC codifies a variety of principles already established by common law.

Elements of a Valid Contract

Every contract has similar elements. These include at least two parties to the contract, both of whom are capable of signing it (meaning they have legal capacity). In addition, both parties must agree to the terms of the contract, and there must be a promise supported by consideration. Promises are the backbones of contracts and become legally binding when supported by legal considerations. Consideration is essentially the *reliance* by a party to the agreement. Put simply, a contract generally consists of two or more parties making promises to one another. It becomes legally binding when one or more of the parties relies on the promise of the other. Contracts can be either written or verbal and must meet the following requirements:

- *Two-party requirement:* There must be two parties to a contract. A person cannot make a contract with himself or herself. While this may seem obvious, it is nonetheless a requirement of contract law.

- *Legal capacity requirement:* Only the person whom the law recognizes as capable of being a party to a contract may sign. This means a person must be mentally competent and be an adult. A person who is "underage" cannot sign a binding contract. The same is true for persons who suffer from a mental problem that limits their ability to understand what they are doing, regardless of age.

- *Assent requirement:* Both parties to a contract must agree to the terms of the contract and must indicate this assent. This requirement is intended to ensure that both parties understand the terms and are aware that a contract is being created. Assent may be given verbally or in writing and must be objectively reasonable. This means that an agreement made in jest is not a valid contract; likewise, negotiations do not, in and of themselves, constitute a contract.

Assent is often described as involving an *offer* and an *acceptance*. One party makes an offer to be bound by a contract; if the other party agrees, then a valid contract may be created. If a promise is made in exchange for performance, a unilateral *contract* is created. If a promise is made by both parties, then a *bilateral contract* is created.

- *Legality requirement*: Fraudulent contracts, in which one party clearly intends to defraud the other, or illegal contracts, such as the promise to pay a certain amount of money for the delivery of contraband goods, are not legally enforceable.

Another concept crucial to the study of contract law is the notion of *good faith*. In most contract negotiations, there is an assumption that all parties are making promises that they mean to keep, and that these promises are made based on a common understanding of what will be required to meet the obligations incurred according to standards of fair dealing in trade. It is considered a *breach of contract* when the terms of a contract are not met.

The 1973 Massachusetts case of *Sullivan v. O'Connor* is an example of contract law in action. Alice Sullivan was an entertainer who relied on her appearance for her living. She entered into a contract with James O'Connor, a plastic surgeon, for reconstructive surgery on her nose to enhance her beauty and improve her public appeal. Originally, the contract called for Sullivan to have two surgeries performed by O'Connor to have her prominent nose shortened. Sullivan actually had to go through three surgeries, and the end result was not satisfactory to her. It was determined that further surgery could not repair the nose. Sullivan sued O'Connor for breach of contract. O'Connor made a "good faith argument," asserting that he had done the best he could with the "resources" (Sullivan's nose) provided and thus fulfilled his part of the bargain. Nevertheless, the Massachusetts Supreme Court held that the promise made by the surgeon to make Sullivan's nose appealing was enforceable and that Sullivan could recover not only the costs of the failed surgeries but also damages based on the worsening of the condition after the contractual breach.

Legal contracts can be voided without penalty under certain circumstances. In a classic "rich man/poor man" case (*National Labor Relations Board v. Bildisco & Bildisco,* 1984), the US Supreme Court ruled that a business could relieve itself of a labor contract (i.e., breach the contract) if a Chapter 11 bankruptcy petition had been filed, even before a bankruptcy court had approved or rejected the petition. Chapter 11 bankruptcy laws are designed to limit business failures by allowing the reorganization of business debts toward this end. In itself, this is a positive thing, but the additional uses it was put to after *Bildisco* had tremendous social impact. Numerous other companies found the Court's permitting of employers to unilaterally breach a collective bargaining contract to be extremely attractive. The threat of such contract breaches left union employees with few protections against loss of their collectively bargained contract rights, and companies all over the United States engaged in an orgy of union busting armed with the Court's *Bildisco* ruling (Walsh, 1988).

Family Law

The family is the basic institution of any society, and therefore the state is a third party in every marriage. Thus, we should expect all societies to have laws designed to protect the integrity of marriage. **Family law** is conciliatory rather than accusatory, in that there is no necessary judgment of right or wrong in spousal disputes but rather an effort to arrange an outcome that comes as close as possible to pleasing everyone involved. Family law is focused largely on the entering into and the dissolution of marriages and other interpersonal relationships and the resultant changes in fiscal and personal responsibilities between the parties. There are no national family laws but rather a number of different state laws with different implications for married couples. Nevertheless, there are several requirements for a valid marriage everywhere, such as obtaining of a marriage license from the state. Included with the license may be a blood test and a waiting period. Additionally, marriage vows must be exchanged in the presence of someone who is legally permitted to acknowledge the marriage, such as a minister or judge, and the marriage vows must be witnessed.

Who May Marry Whom?

Marriage is a legal contract that carries with it rights and responsibilities for both parties. As a contract, it must meet certain requirements to be considered legal, as with any other contract. A person must be 18 years of age or older to get married without parental permission in almost all states. Certain exceptions may apply, such as pregnancy, but this is the general rule. A person under legal age is considered incompetent to enter into a marriage contract. Other incompetencies precluding the issuance of a marriage license include mental deficiencies, such as insanity, and being under the influence of intoxicating substances at the time of application. Closely related persons, such as brothers and sisters, parents and children, or cousins, may not enter into a marital contract. Any such marriages fraudulently entered into would make the parties eligible for the criminal charge of incest. The final requirement is that neither party be currently married to someone else. If a person already married marries someone else, he or she is guilty of bigamy, which carries a penalty of up to five years' imprisonment in most states.

The Supreme Court and the Right to Marry

The first of the few cases involving the scope of the right to marry came before the Supreme Court in *Reynolds v. United States* (1878). George Reynolds, a Mormon, had been convicted of bigamy in Utah. Reynolds claimed the right to multiple simultaneous marriages as his religious duty, but the Court ruled that religious duty was not a valid defense against a criminal indictment.

In *Skinner v. State of Oklahoma, Ex. Rel. Williamson* (1942) the Supreme Court stated that the right to marry was a "basic civil right." However, in adding that "[m]arriage and procreation are fundamental to the very existence and survival of the race," the Court was implicitly defining marriage as something that only opposite-sex partners can enter into. (*Skinner* was actually a case about castration for an inveterate criminal offender; marriage came into it only because castration would prevent procreation.)

Loving v. Virginia (1967) is an important case because it overturned a number of state statutes banning interracial marriage. Richard Loving, a white man, and Mildred Jeter, a black woman, were residents of Virginia but had to leave the state to get married. On their return, they were arrested for violating Virginia's anti-miscegenation law (a law against interbreeding involving persons of different races) and sentenced to one year of imprisonment, which was suspended on the condition that the Lovings leave Virginia. The Supreme Court eventually heard the case and ruled that distinctions based on race were "odious" and must be subject to "the most rigid scrutiny" under the equal protection clause of the Fourteenth Amendment.

In *Zablocki v. Redhail* (1978), the Court ruled that "deadbeat dads" had a right to marry (Roger Redhail was denied a marriage license based on the fact that he was seriously in arrears with his child support payments from a previous marriage), and in *Turner v. Safley* (1987), the Court ruled that even prison inmates have a fundamental right to marry. Yet while *Skinner, Loving, Zablocki,* and *Turner* invalidated marriage prohibitions against certain people, none of the cases changed the core definition of marriage as a union between a man and a woman.

Figure 7.2 Trends in Public Opinion of Same-Sex Marriage

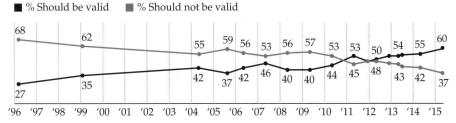

Do you think marriages between same-sex couples should or should not be recognized by the law as valid, with the same rights as traditional marriages?

■ % Should be valid   ■ % Should not be valid

Source: Gallup Poll (2015). http://www.gallup.com/poll/1651/gay-lesbian-rights.aspx. Copyright © 2015 Gallup, Inc. All rights reserved. The content is used with permission; however, Gallup retains all rights of republication.

The Road to Same-Sex Marriage

At the turn of the twenty-first century, not a single country in the world allowed same-sex marriage. The Netherlands was the first country to allow it in 2001, and on June 26, 2015, the United States became the twentieth country to make it legal nationwide. The road to same-sex marriage was difficult but proceeded with rapidity considering that the US Supreme Court struck down state laws that criminalized sodomy a mere 12 years earlier (see chapter 10). Note also from Figure 7.2 that public opinion in favor of the validity of same-sex marriage more than doubled from 27 percent in 1996 to 60 percent in 2015.

We have seen how the Supreme Court has consistently declared that the right to marry is part of the fundamental "right of privacy." In 1996, concerned about the supposed threat to traditional marriage posed by the growing demand for same-sex marriage, 342 representatives and 85 senators voted to pass the **Defense of Marriage Act** (DOMA), which was signed into law by President Bill Clinton. Section 3 of DOMA provides the following definition of marriage:

> In determining the meaning of any Act of Congress, or of any ruling, regulation, or interpretation of the various administrative bureaus and agencies of the United States, the word "marriage" means only a legal union between one man and one woman as husband and wife, and the word "spouse" refers only to a person of the opposite sex who is a husband or a wife.

Almost all states that did not already have laws prohibiting same-sex marriage initiated such laws modeled on DOMA. Yet the California Supreme Court ruled that same-sex marriage was constitutionally permissible in 2008, and Arthur Smelt married Christopher Hammer. In that same year, however, the voters in California passed Proposition 8, amending the California Constitution to end the right of same-sex couples to marry there. In 2009, Smelt and Hammer filed a lawsuit against California and the United States, arguing that both DOMA and Proposition 8 were unconstitutional. The suit alleged that DOMA violated due process and equal protection rights, free speech, privacy, and one that we have not yet addressed, called the *full faith and credit clause* of Article IV of the Constitution. This clause states: "Full Faith and Credit shall be given in each State to the public Acts, Records, and judicial Proceedings of every other State." In other words, Smelt and Hammer alleged that because other states were not required to recognize another state's same-sex marriage, this clause was violated, as was their right to travel as a married couple. In August 2009, a federal district judge dismissed the case on jurisdictional grounds without ruling on the constitutional merits of DOMA.

On February 7, 2012, a federal appeals court struck down California's ban on gay marriage, and on May 30, 2012, a three-judge panel of the US Court of Appeals for the First Circuit (Boston) unanimously declared DOMA unconstitutional. In a 5-4 decision in June 2013, the US Supreme Court struck down the pivotal Section 3 of DOMA restricting the terms *marriage* and *spouse* to heterosexual unions as unconstitutional under the due process clause of the Fifth Amendment. The case (*United States v. Windsor*, 2013) involved a claim for federal tax exemption for surviving spouses brought by Edith Windsor, who was 84 years old at the time and had married Thea Spyer, another women, in Canada in 2007. Spyer died in 2009, leaving her entire estate to Windsor, who claimed the federal estate tax exemption for surviving spouses but was barred from doing so by Section 3 of DOMA. Although the case settled a narrow claim for estate tax exemption and applied to federal tax law, it set the terms for challenges to state bans on same-sex marriage. That is, while *Windsor* did not establish a constitutional right for same-sex marriage, it was a clear indication that the Court was trending in favor of it. The conclusion of the majority opinion written by Justice Anthony Kennedy reads as follows:

> DOMA instructs all federal officials, and indeed all persons with whom same-sex couples interact, including their own children, that their marriage is less worthy than the marriages of others. The federal statute is invalid, for no legitimate purpose overcomes the purpose and effect to disparage and to injure those whom the State, by its marriage laws, sought to protect in personhood and dignity. By seeking to displace this protection and treating those persons as living in marriages less respected than others, the federal statute is in violation of the Fifth Amendment.

Only two years later, the Supreme Court, in another 5-4 decision, ruled in *Obergefell v. Hodges* (2015) that homosexual marriages are legal in every state. There were two issues before the Court in *Obergefell*. First, does the Fourteenth Amendment require a state to license a marriage between two people of the same sex? And second, does the Fourteenth Amendment require a state to recognize a marriage between two people of the same sex when their marriage was lawfully licensed and performed in another state? The case combined cases from Kentucky, Michigan, Ohio, and Tennessee and included more than 20 plaintiffs.

The basic facts of the case are that Ohioans James Obergefell and John Arthur were married in another state. When Arthur died, the state of Ohio would not list Obergefell as his spouse on his death certificate. Obergefell sought an injunction to require the state to do so. The funeral director joined the lawsuit, asking the court to protect his right to recognize same-sex marriages on other death certificates. In the other cases combined with *Obergefell*, the plaintiffs raised a broader challenge, arguing that Ohio's refusal to recognize out-of-state marriages between same-sex couples violates the Fourteenth Amendment regardless of what marital benefit is affected. The plaintiffs in the case involved four same-sex couples, all married in other states, who wanted Ohio to recognize their marriages on their adopted children's birth certificates. Writing for the majority in *Obergefell,* Justice Anthony Kennedy concluded:

> The Court, in this decision, holds same-sex couples may exercise the fundamental right to marry in all States. It follows that the Court also must hold—and it now does hold—that there is no lawful basis for a State to refuse to recognize a lawful same-sex marriage performed in another State on the ground of its same-sex character. No union is more profound than marriage, for it embodies the highest ideals of love, fidelity, devotion, sacrifice, and family. In forming a marital union, two people become something greater than once they were. As some of the petitioners in these cases demonstrate, marriage embodies a love that may endure even past death. It would misunderstand these men and women to say they disrespect the idea of marriage. Their plea is that they do respect it, respect it so deeply that they seek to find its fulfillment for themselves. Their hope is not to be condemned to live in loneliness, excluded from one of civilization's oldest institutions. They ask for equal dignity in the eyes of the law. The Constitution grants them that right.

Like so many other decisions, this one was based on the slimmest of margins, and the four dissenting justices were scathing in their remarks. Dissenting opinions by Justices John Roberts, Antonin Scalia, Clarence Thomas, and Samuel Alito claimed the Court was undermining the democratic process. It was noted that of the 35 states that had put the issue to the electorate, 32 opted to retain the traditional definition of marriage. Justice Scalia called the decision "a naked claim [by the Court] to legislative—indeed, super-legislative—power; a claim fundamentally at odds with our system of government."

The other major concern addressed was religious liberty. In Justice Thomas's dissent, he wrote:

> In our society, marriage is not simply a governmental institution; it is a religious institution as well. Today's decision might change the former, but it cannot change the latter. It appears all but inevitable that the two will come into conflict, particularly as individuals and churches are confronted with demands to participate in and endorse civil marriages between same-sex couples . . . [and this has] potentially ruinous consequences for religious liberty.

See chapter 10 for a discussion of gay rights versus religious liberty.

Common Law Marriage

Common law marriage may be established by couples cohabiting and acting in every way as though married (owning property in common, filing joint income taxes, etc.) even though they have not been through a formal wedding ceremony and have no license. These marriages are recognized as valid if established in states allowing them, but 39 states have abolished such marriages. The primary reason is that states recognize marriage to be a legal contract that carries with it rights and responsibilities for both parties, and too many opportunities exist for evading responsibilities, fraud, and all manner of legal complications if one of the couple dies, deserts, or defaults on the implied contract. For instance, common law spouses may have to go to court to establish that all the elements of a common law marriage existed in their relationship before he or she may gain access to a spousal right, such as access to the other spouse's pension or inheritance of his or her property.

Divorce and Annulment

Just as there are licensing requirements for marriage, the dissolution of the marital contract by divorce or annulment requires legal grounds. Grounds (legally acceptable reasons) for divorce are divided into *no-fault* (e.g., irreconcilable differences) and *fault* categories. All states now have **no-fault divorce**, meaning there is no assumption of fault by either marriage partner for the marital breakup. Some states retain fault-based divorce in addition to their no-fault grounds. Fault grounds, which were traditionally such things as adultery, cruelty, desertion, insanity, and alcoholism, are used in states retaining fault for issues such as child custody and financial settlements even if a no-fault divorce has already been granted.

Marriages may also be annulled. An **annulment** is a legal declaration that a marriage never existed because the legal requirements for a valid marriage were not met. An annulment can be obtained if someone lacked the legal ability to consent to marriage (underage, mentally incompetent, drugged, already married, etc.). Other grounds include impotence and concealing a sexually transmitted disease or pregnancy from a union with some other person.

Dividing Property, Child Custody, and Spousal Support

Marriage is a partnership in the same sense that a Smith and Jones landscaping business is, and the dissolution of the partnership requires a determination of who gets what out of that partnership. Statutes governing property division vary by state, but two types dominate: *dual-property* and *all-property* models. In the **dual-property model**, which is followed by most states, the courts consider assets held jointly (i.e., acquired during the marriage) by the spouses and separate assets each brought with them to the marriage, inherited, or received as gifts during the marriage. If separate property is not commingled with joint assets, courts will typically recognize the separate ownership of the individual spouse, and that property will not be divided along with joint marital assets. In the **all-property model**, the courts typically divide all property owned by either spouse at the time of the divorce equally.

In marriages with children that end in divorce, the courts also have to decide the emotional and often acrimonious issue of child custody. In some cases, one spouse (usually the husband) voluntarily gives up custody to his former wife, but when a battle ensues, the courts in all 50 states are charged with making their decisions with the preeminent concern being the best interests of the child.

Child support is an area of family law that has grown in scope and consequence. Child support is based on the custodial status of the parents. That is, after the legal breakup of a family with children, the courts often are asked to require that the parent without primary physical custody assist with the financial burden placed on the parent with primary physical custody. Most often, the amount of support is based on a calculation of income and the costs associated with child-rearing. Many states have established complex formulas to determine an equitable settlement that includes aggregate family income and time spent with each parent.

The twentieth century was a time of growth and change in the realm of family law. The traditional patriarchal family was challenged by a variety of social shifts. The role of women changed in US society, as well as throughout the Western world, and this has had an impact on expectations about the nature of family structures and responsibilities. Divorce is more common in the United States than ever before, which has resulted in child custody and support issues that have been, until recently, largely left untouched by legal code or statute.

ADMINISTRATIVE LAW

Administrative law (or regulatory law) is a branch of public law involving governmental administrative agencies whose activities include the making, enforcing, and adjudicating of specific regulatory agendas, such as clean air, health standards, and occupational safety. In essence, this means that administrative agencies combine the governmental roles of the legislative, executive, and judicial branches of government in one agency. These agencies have a huge impact on people's lives because they regulate just about everything we see, hear, taste, touch, smell, or breathe. For this reason, administrative agencies have been termed the "shadow government" (Samuels, 2006, p. 232).

Article I, Section 8 of the US Constitution grants Congress the plenary (complete) power to regulate commerce. Prior to the twentieth century, the operating principles of the US government vis-à-vis business were *laissez-faire* (literally, "leave do"; i.e., leave business alone) and *caveat emptor* ("let the buyer beware"). Both of these principles essentially amounted to injunctions against governmental interference with business on behalf of public interests. During the twentieth century, however, things turned around dramatically, to the point that for better or for worse, the government's unofficial operating principles may be defined as *interférez tout* ("interfere with everything") and *caveat venditor* ("let the seller beware").

Origins and Growth of Administrative Agencies

The United States has seen explosive growth in administrative/regulatory agencies since 1789, when they were more like executive branch bureaucracies such as the Bureau of Customs or the Bureau of Indian Affairs. According to the US Attorney General's Committee *Final Report* (1941, p. 8), there were just 11 administrative agencies in existence prior to the close of the Civil War. The first regulatory agency in the modern sense of an agency making, enforcing, and adjudicating its own rules independent of the executive branch of government was the Interstate Commerce Commission (ICC), created in 1887 in response to supposedly unfair railroad tariffs. However, this agency protected businesses against other businesses; the interests of the general public tended to be ignored. (The ICC was abolished in 1995, with the Surface Transportation Board taking on many of its functions.)

Administrative agencies grew rapidly in number under President Franklin Roosevelt's New Deal legislative programs in the 1930s "to address the vast economic and social crises wrought by the Depression" (Fenster, 2005, p. 70). The *Final Report* listed 51 such agencies in 1941. New Deal legislation, and the agencies created to oversee it, came up against fierce opposition from Republicans and business interests. George Shepard (1996) called this fight "a pitched political battle for the life of the New Deal" (p. 1562). The issue fought over was the expansiveness of the federal government: Should the government intervene supposedly on behalf of its people, or would such an extension of its already considerable power eventually lead to a centrally planned economy and the dictatorship that implies? We revisit this issue in chapter 11.

New Deal opponents saw regulatory agencies as rapacious bureaucrats who made decisions on a case-by-case (substantive rationality) basis rather than on the foundation of precedent and formal/rational rules (Schiller, 2005). In response to this criticism, Congress passed the **Administrative Procedure Act** (APA) of 1946, which established the basic procedural standards for federal agencies, letting them know how they may propose and establish their regulations and go about adjudicating violations of them. The APA also outlined the process for the federal courts to review agency decisions should the occasion arise. These procedures formalized what previously was rather arbitrary and "placed many courtlike procedural requirements (cross-examination, rules of evidence, formal records) on agency adjudication" (Schiller, 2005, p. 112). In essence, the APA represented a compromise allowing the expansion of governmental power while quieting conservative concerns about federal dictatorship. Most people today would probably agree that government regulation is a good thing in terms of protecting their health and safety, but many others view it as having gone much too far, becoming intrusive and economically detrimental.

The White House website listed 170 federal agencies (a 233 percent increase from the 1941 total) and commissions as of 2006. Many of these agencies are duplicated at the state level, and altogether, these state and federal agencies employ almost 20 million people (Samuels, 2006). It is no wonder that administrative law touches most of us more intimately than criminal or civil law. The alphabet soup of agencies regulate the gas or electricity we perk our coffee with (Federal Energy Regulation Commission [FERC]); the food we eat for breakfast and the pills we take afterward are grown, raised, manufactured, and packaged under the regulations of the Food and Drug Administration (FDA); the car we drive to work must conform to Environmental Protection Agency (EPA) standards; and the highway we drive on is overseen in general terms by the National Highway Traffic Safety Administration (NHTSA). We could go on for pages, but the picture is clear—administrative law is everywhere. It drowns new businesses in regulations, and it is expensive. The latest estimate is provided by Crain and Crain (2010): "The annual cost of federal regulations in the United States increased to more than $1.75 trillion in 2008. Had every U.S. household paid an equal share of the federal regulatory burden, each would have owed $15,586 in 2008" (p. iv). This burden on business is, of course, passed on to consumers as a "hidden tax"—there is no free lunch.

ISSUE HIGHLIGHT

How Much Regulation Is Too Much?

We have seen the tremendous reach of regulatory bodies in the contemporary United States. With the election of Donald Trump to the presidency, the issue of how much regulation is too much has come to the forefront. President Trump announced that for every new regulation proposed, two others should be cut, and he has aggressively driven his agenda to undo the rules and regulations of his predecessor, Barack Obama, who was as seemingly fond of government regulations as Donald Trump is hostile to them. Both President Obama and President Trump know that a certain amount of regulation is necessary, but how much is too much? Are you inclined to be more regulation friendly, like Obama, or are you regulation hostile, like Trump?

Trump

We are glad to see Donald Trump aggressively attacking and eliminating costly, job-killing regulations that stifle the economy. Obama seemed intent on suffocating business with all kinds of regulations. Clyde Crews (2015) tells us that "of six all-time-high *Federal Register* page counts, five have occurred during the Obama administration" (p. 144). For instance, the page count of regulatory rules in the 2014 *Federal Register* was 78,978. If you stack that many pages up, you get a pile 14 feet 8 inches tall. Anyone could fall afoul of some obscure rule lurking in that huge pile. But don't cry for big business; it actually likes regulation because it can afford to hire teams of lawyers and Washington lobbyists to look after their demands and monitor their compliance with complex regulations. It is the small and medium-sized enterprises that hate it. Big business delights in regulation because competition, not regulation, is what eats into their profits. The big guys are less worried about complying with regulations than they are with "upstart" businesses that may find a better way of doing what they are doing. Complex regulations means fewer upstarts entering "their" market, and the less competition, the better it is for them and their bottom line. Government regulation is the dear friend of crony capitalism and the enemy of entrepreneurial capitalism. Both politicians and big business benefit from it: politicians get power and campaign contributions, and business gets protection from competition. Regulatory agencies proliferate like rabbits, thus increasing big government's control of the economy. Progressives favor them because it means a more active role for the government in the economy, and politicians love them because it concentrates more power in their hands, which shudder at calls for limited government that would make them less relevant.

Obama

Who wants to go back to the days when businesses were unregulated, and who wants their food and medications adulterated and dangerously defective products endangering the public? President Obama may have gone overboard with his regulatory agenda, but a number of the regulations President Trump is eliminating are needed to protect the health of the population and prevent people from being victimized by fraud. For instance, coal companies have been relieved of a lot of anti-pollution rules, and financial advisers are relieved of certain rules designed to prevent conflict of interest issues. Yes, regulations are costly and in some instances hinder economic growth, but deregulation can have devastating effects on the economy as well. The deregulation of the savings and loan (S&L) companies in the 1980s and 1990s led to widespread fraud and had a hugely negative impact on the economy. Some scholars also blame lax US banking regulations for the global financial crisis of 2008, which had devastating consequences for most while others lined their pockets. Human nature being what it is, when restraints are relaxed we will tend to pursue our immediate interests with little care for others. There must always be a watchful eye with the power to impose punishment on those individuals and businesses selling goods and services to others or otherwise dealing with the public. Without this oversight, we get a return to *laissez-faire* capitalism in which anything goes as long as a profit is made. Yes, President Obama went too far in his efforts to micromanage the economy, but we are afraid that Trump will go to the opposite extreme. What any economy needs is a system of honest regulation that does not hobble new enterprises and is free of politicians looking to line their pockets.

Legislative Function of Administrative Agencies

Administrative law is law created by the administrative agencies themselves based on authority granted them by Congress. These laws are the rules, regulations, procedures, orders, and previous decisions of agency courts. They apply only to the businesses and activities that fall under the specific areas of responsibility and expertise of the agency; for instance, the Securities and Exchange Commission (SEC) has the power only to regulate activities related to the stock exchange and securities markets. Congress has authorized regulatory agencies to create their own rules because the legislature has realized that it lacks the knowledge to create specific rules pertaining to highly technical subject matter with which many agencies deal. Congress makes broad laws (e.g., employers must not discriminate, companies may not pollute the air, and automobiles must be safer) and delegates the specific details to agencies with personnel who have a professional knowledge of their agency's area of responsibility. However, as the Supreme Court has held, filling in the details of law is not lawmaking per se, and thus Congress and state legislatures have oversight powers regarding the decisions of the agencies operating under their mandates (Friedrichs, 2001).

Investigatory and Enforcement Functions of Administrative Agencies

Congress also has empowered regulatory agencies to investigate violations of agency rules and to devise ways of enforcing them. Agencies may go about these functions by requiring annual reports from the businesses they regulate, conducting on-site inspections, or investigating complaints from workers or competing businesses. For example, the SEC requires companies to report profits and losses that may lead to the uncovering of fraud, the Occupational Safety and Health Administration (OSHA) may visit dangerous work sites for signs of unsafe working conditions, and the Office of Equal Opportunity will investigate charges of workplace discrimination when members of protected categories (racial minorities and women) complain that they are victims of it. OSHA, for instance, with a 2004 budget of $468 million, has 1,100 inspectors and claims to have cut workplace fatalities by 60 percent and occupational injuries/illness rates by 40 percent since its inception in 1971. In 2004, OSHA reported that its inspectors identified 86,708 violations, for which violators were fined a total of $85,192,940 (Occupational Safety and Health Administration, 2005).

Judicial Function of Administrative Agencies

Most disputes and regulatory infractions are settled informally by voluntary settlements. Agencies prefer such settlements because they relieve the agency of expensive investigations and court hearings. If matters cannot be settled informally, the regulatory agency holds a hearing presided over by an administrative judge, who is an expert on, or at least substantially knowledgeable about, the substantive matter at hand. Although more informal than a criminal or civil trial, the proceedings of an administrative hearing are governed by the APA's procedural rules. Both parties to a dispute are entitled to be represented by attorneys, but hearings take place without juries. The administrative judge (or examiner) is thus the finder of both fact and the administrative law to be applied.

If losing parties in such a hearing so choose, they can appeal their case to the more formal civil law system. However, because they lack the often complex and technical substantive knowledge of an administrative examiner, judges are reluctant to preside over such cases. If an administrative ruling is overturned by the courts, it is based on points of law (e.g., the administrative law was not correctly interpreted or the examiner exceeded his or her authority or was obviously biased) rather than on fact. Courts are extremely reluctant to overrule administrative judges, however, and almost always defer to their special expertise. In *National Cable & Telecommunications v. Brand X Internet Services* (2005), the Supreme Court even went as far as to hold that federal agencies are free to "overturn" federal court rulings bearing on interpretations of regulatory statutes unless the court's interpretation is the only one possible.

Since 1984, courts have applied what is known as **Chevron deference** to appeals from administrative court hearings. *Chevron deference* is a phrase that originated from a Supreme Court case (*Chevron U.S.A., Inc. v. Natural Resources Defense Council, Inc.*, 1984) in which the Court was asked to clear up an ambiguity in some provisions of the federal Clean Air Act. The Natural Resources Defense Council (NRDC), a private environmental protection group, challenged the EPA's interpretation of the Clean Air Act when it allowed Chevron Oil to use equipment that did not meet the NRDC's interpretation of the act. The Court held in this case that courts must defer to an administrative agency's interpretation of its own rules because Congress has granted them such authority. If there is ambiguity or gaps in the statutes, however, the federal courts may then decide if an agency's interpretation is "reasonable."

Administrative Law and Corporate Crime

Because regulatory agencies do not come under the jurisdiction of the US Department of Justice, they lack criminal enforcement powers beyond assessing fines. If an agency's investigation uncovers criminal violations as opposed to merely regulatory violations, it can refer cases for criminal prosecution. There are many complications and practical difficulties in recognizing and reporting corporate crime, however. As Walsh and Ellis (2007) point out:

> With common street crime we have a body lying in the street, a house burgled, a dazed mugging victim, or a car stolen. These easily understood and defined discrete events quickly come to the attention of the police, who then record them and set out to find the perpetrators . . . many victims [of white-collar crimes] do not even know they have been victimized, and the sequence of events is often quite the opposite. (p. 398)

In other words, with white-collar crime, investigators may start with a suspicion that something has happened, then try to find out what, and then try to find out who is responsible. Serious corporate crimes, such as the Enron, WorldCom, and Adelphi Communication frauds prosecuted in the early 2000s, are incredibly complex and require thousands of hours and millions of dollars to unravel.

In its annual UCC, the Federal Bureau of Investigation (FBI) provides the nation with a count of the mayhem that occurred on the streets of America the previous year. Except for forgery/counterfeiting, fraud, and embezzlement (usually relatively minor crimes committed by individuals), white-collar crimes are conspicuously absent from the annual crime tally. The FBI has a Congressional mandate to collect and report the "in your face" crimes committed on America's streets, but there is no mandate to collect and report crimes that occur in America's suites.

A separate accounting of major white-collar crimes, however, is issued each year by the FBI. Called the Financial Crimes Report, it lists results of investigations carried out by the FBI's Financial Crimes Section (FCS). The FCS is composed of the Asset Forfeiture/Money Laundering Unit, the Economic Crimes Unit, the Health Care Fraud Unit, the Forensic Accountant Unit, and the National Mortgage Fraud Team. The FCS oversees the investigation of financial fraud and supervises asset forfeitures from individuals engaged in such crimes.

Recent Responses to Corporate Crime

Very few corporate crooks were the recipients of truly meaningful sanctions in the past. Take the savings and loan scandal that occurred in the 1980s following the deregulation of those entities. Multiple bank executives looted their own banks of up to $473 billion, a sum many times greater than the losses from all the "regular" bank robberies in American history put together (Calavita & Pontell, 1994). Two of the biggest players in this scandal were sentenced to less than two years imprisonment for stealing $20 million in one case and $30 million in another (Reiman, 1998).

Things are beginning to change, however. As a result of Congressional hearings and public outcries following the scandals of the early 2000s, Congress passed and President George W. Bush signed into law the **Sarbanes-Oxley Act** (SOA) of 2002. This act authorized a huge increase in the SEC's budget to $776 million, and an additional 200 employees were hired to carry out the SOA mandates (American Institute of Certified Public Accountants, 2004, p. 6). The act and its provisions have enhanced the morale of the previously underfunded SEC, which now sees its role as more proactive rather than simply reactive (Burr, 2004). The SOA requires company chiefs to personally vouch for their company's financial disclosures, ensuring that they can no longer hide behind a "plausible deniability" ("I didn't know what was happening") defense. A comprehensive review of the effectiveness of the SOA on Fortune 500 companies by Brian Harte (2011) found that it has had a moderating effect on illegal corporate behavior.

A separate act, the **White-Collar Crimes Penalty Enhancement Act** of 2002, creates new securities offenses with significantly enhanced penalties. It also relaxes some procedural evidentiary requirements for prosecutors who formerly had to prove "willfulness" in white-collar cases (i.e., prove beyond a reasonable doubt that the defendant took some action knowing that it violated a specific law). Prosecutors now only have to show that defendants did what they did, period, which has always been the standard in other criminal cases ("ignorance of the law is no excuse"). Relaxed standards for proving obstruction of justice (and penalties of up to 20 years for conviction) are also included. This should make it easier for loyal and otherwise guiltless employees attempting to shield their employers to reveal what they know to investigators.

According to Lowell and Arnold (2003),

> Congress clearly intended to send a message to the law enforcement community to be tougher on violators of business law and regulations. Further, Congress's message will echo to prosecutors and sentencing judges who will avail themselves of the new SOA maximums or use previously available means to enhance maximum penalties. (p. 228)

SEC investigators and prosecutors are clearly taking advantage of the tools provided them by the SOA. One commentator remarked, "Today, prosecutors are driven to go after corporate fraud with an almost evangelical zeal" (Burr, 2004, p. 10). Sentencing judges also appear to be matching that zeal, perhaps indicating that the days of leniency for white-collar criminals are over. In July 2005, Bernard Ebbers, ex-CEO of WorldCom, was sentenced to 25 years in prison for his role in an $11 billion fraud; in June 2005, John Rigas, founder of Adelphia Communications Corporation, was sentenced to 15 years and his son Timothy to 20 years for their roles in yet another massive fraud; in September 2005, Tyco executives Dennis Koslowski and Dennis Swartz were sentenced to 8 and 25 years, respectively for multimillion dollar corporate fraud ; and in October 2006, Enron CEO Jeffrey Skilling was sentenced to 24 years and 4 months for his part in the massive Enron fraud. Finally, in June 2009, Bernard Madoff was sentenced to 150 years' imprisonment for his massive, $13 billion-plus Ponzi scheme.

While no criminal charges have been brought up to 2018, the subprime mortgage debacle that led to the housing bubble pop in 2007 was the worst financial crisis since the Great Depression. US Department of Housing and Urban Development policies designed to make home buying "more affordable" led to people taking on mortgages that they could not afford and subsequently lost, or they found themselves saddled with homes worth considerably less than they had paid for them (Leonnig, 2008). It all perhaps began in 1995 when the Clinton administration loosened housing loan rules by rewriting and vigorously enforcing the 1977 Community Reinvestment Act (CRA). The CRA put pressure on banks to lend to low-income borrowers ("No credit? No job? No problem!"). According to *The New York Times'* Steven Holmes (1999):

> Fannie Mae, the nation's biggest underwriter of home mortgages, has been under increasing pressure from the Clinton Administration to expand mortgage loans among low and moderate income people and felt pressure from stockholders to maintain its phenomenal growth in profits.

Who or what is ultimately to blame for the mess is literally anyone's guess. Economists on the right and the left have written millions of words contradicting one another, blaming either government policies or Wall Street greed. For instance, Thomas DiLorenzo (2007) wrote that the housing crisis was "the direct result of thirty years of government policy that has forced banks to make bad loans to uncreditworthy borrowers." Another point of view blames the entire thing on American capitalist "system exhaustion": "The financial crisis therefore represents the exhaustion of that paradigm rather than being the result of specific policy failures" (Pally, 2010, p. 33).

This crisis highlights the rancorous debates between left and right about the "proper" role of government in the American economy since the inception of the first regulatory agency. As Arnold and Stevens (2011) put it: "The experience with government sponsored agencies and moral hazard illustrates the danger of mixing economic interventions with social agenda" (p. 1072). The phrase *moral hazard* to which Arnold and Stevens refer is a kind of "heads I win, tails you lose" tendency to take unwarranted risks when costs are not borne by the party taking the risk, such as the banks that made risky mortgage loans—albeit initially reluctantly—but then could pass on that risk to the quasi-government mortgage agencies Fannie Mae and Freddie Mac. This is a case of privatizing the profit and socializing the risk, since it is the US taxpayer who bears the burden.

Because the issue is highly politicized, it is wise to consider the thoughts of someone who is both highly respected in the economic world and not American. Oonagh McDonald, a former Labour Party member of the British Parliament and its spokeswoman on financial matters, has written extensively on the issue and published a heavily documented book, *Fannie Mae and Freddie Mac: Turning the American Dream into a Nightmare* (2012). This book has become the Bible for those seeking to understand the largest white-collar crime (or rather series of crimes) in American history. McDonald's analysis, in a nutshell, is as follows:

> Clinton set the wheels in motion; Bush did little to stop the juggernaut of "affordable" or "subprime lending," which rolled on without any obstacles in its way. But when house prices began to fall and interest rates began to rise, almost half of all outstanding mortgages were revealed as subprime. When it all went wrong, politicians both in the US and elsewhere sought to deflect attention from their own actions by the ever-popular sport of

attacking and blaming the banks. Of course, many of the banks played their part as well, but the prime responsibility is a political one of seeking to increase home ownership at any price. (pp. 328–329)

Government's role in the scandal is not disputed: government-sponsored enterprises such as Fannie Mae and Freddie Mac largely control the American mortgage market, and the Clinton administration did set the ball rolling by practically mandating the distortion of normal lending procedures. However, as McDonald asserts, there is enough blame to go around. The person who made the most money out of the crisis was Fannie Mae CEO Franklin Raines. Raines made over $91 million between 1999 and 2004, $52.6 million of which came in the form of bonuses based on fraudulently reported profits (Gordon, 2008). Raines eventually had to pay back $24.7 million to settle a lawsuit, although most of this was paid by Fannie Mae insurance, not by Raines personally. Raines made his bogus bonuses the same way that Enron executives and other corporate crooks did, but neither he nor any other Fannie Mae executive has been criminally investigated. Apparently, there are people too big to jail (Raines was a friend of President Obama) and financial institutions too big to fail. Nevertheless, the people hurt most by the scandal were those whom the subprime loans were supposed to help. The words written by British novelist and philosopher C. S. Lewis long ago seem appropriate here: "Of all tyrannies, a tyranny exercised for the good of its victims may be the most oppressive" (1970, p. 292).

ENVIRONMENTAL LAW

Accompanying the increasing concern for justice in many areas of American life since the 1960s is a concern for environmental justice, one that is overseen by the EPA, the largest of the regulatory agencies just discussed. The EPA defines **environmental justice** as follows:

Environmental Justice is the fair treatment and meaningful involvement of all people regardless of race, color, national origin, or income with respect to the development, implementation, and enforcement of environmental laws, regulations, and policies. EPA has this goal for all communities and persons across this Nation. It will be achieved when everyone enjoys the same degree of protection from environmental and health hazards and equal access to the decision-making process to have a healthy environment in which to live, learn, and work.

United States Environmental Protection (nd) Environmental Justice. Agencyhttps://www.epa.gov/environmentaljustice

This definition is couched in due process terms, in that a clean and healthy environment is something due to everyone simply by virtue of sharing a common planet. Environmental justice is an ideal that is difficult to attain because everyone does not enjoy "the same degree of protection" from unhealthy environments, although the effort is being made through environmental laws and regulations.

The Development of Environmental Laws and Regulations

In the 1960s Lake Erie was considered "dead," the Cuyahoga River in Cleveland spontaneously burst into flames, and a number of other, similar events gave birth to the modern environmental movement. When the first Earth Day was held in 1970, it was clear that Americans had had enough of environmental degradation. Environmental laws existed before the 1960s, but the most effective protections were passed after the late 1960s. Beginning in 1969 with the signing into law of the National Environmental Policy Act (NEPA) and continuing through the 1970s with the Clean Air Act (1970) and the Clean Water Act (1972), the government began to put teeth into the public desire for a clean and healthy environment (Simonsen, 2007).

The NEPA's main requirement was that agencies in charge of new government projects submit environmental impact statements detailing their effects on the environment. Additional relevant acts that passed around this time included provisions regulating the handling and disposal of hazardous waste, the control of toxic chemicals, and the identification and cleanup of hazardous waste sites. These acts all provided for criminal prosecution and/or civil penalties for violations.

States and localities have also passed laws to protect the environment, modeled after federal laws. These laws and their enforcement vary widely, however, because local governments shape their laws around the types of businesses and industries within their borders (Epstein, 1998). For instance, if oil production is a major industry in a certain area, then that state and/or county's environmental laws will be focused on concerns over oil's use and the likelihood of leaks and waste oil being dumped into waterways or the soil.

Enforcement of Environmental Laws

Local police and prosecutors are not trained to enforce environmental laws and do not view such enforcement as a priority. Thus, the involvement of citizens, advocacy groups, and the media in reporting environmental abuses and pushing for prosecutions and cleanup has been vital. The EPA, the largest regulatory agency in the federal government, is charged with many duties, though it has tended to center its regulatory focus on the areas of air and water pollution and hazardous waste and chemicals (Burns & Lynch, 2004). The EPA divides its enforcement tasks into three areas: civil, cleanup, and criminal.

- *Civil enforcement*: Serves a number of important goals, including returning violators to compliance and deterring misconduct in others, eliminating or preventing environmental harm, and preserving a level playing field for responsible companies that abide by the laws.

- *Cleanup enforcement:* Deals with sites where there has been a release or the threat of a release of hazardous substances into the environment.

- *Criminal enforcement*: Used against the most serious environmental violations as well as those that include egregious negligence or conduct involving intentional, willful, or knowing disregard of the law.

Whether enforcement involves federal, state, or local laws and regulations, certain common problems confront enforcers. It is not always clear whether a violation is criminal or civil, and because the alleged violators/criminals provide jobs and taxes for the local community, regulatory agencies are often reluctant to enforce the laws fully. Corporate entities are often rich and powerful as well, and politicians frequently are elected with campaign funds largely donated by corporations.

Most federal and state regulations allow both civil and criminal enforcement, but with few exceptions, regulatory agencies tend to pursue civil rather than criminal penalties. The choice is related to the difficulty in prosecuting environmental crimes due to the frequent lack of evidence tying a corporate actor to the decision to commit the offending act. This, plus the frequent lack of the political will to enforce regulations, often results in offenses being punished with fines rather than with criminal sanctions (Burns, Lynch, & Stretesky, 2008). When the violator is a governmental entity, the reluctance to enforce regulations is likely tied to the fact that local governments cannot do anything to remedy the situation without resorting to unpopular tax increases.

Burns and Lynch (2004) note that support for environmental protection has waxed and waned across presidential administrations since 1970, when the EPA was created through executive order by President Richard Nixon. The Nixon administration had a largely positive influence on environmental regulation; the Ford administration was too short-lived to have much influence; the Carter administration, though sympathetic to environmental regulation, provided mixed messages by weighing the benefits of a pro-business versus a pro-environment stance. Burns and Lynch argue that the pro-business/anti-regulatory stance of the Reagan administration damaged the EPA, although it was under the Reagan administration that lead was removed from gasoline and the dangerous pesticide ethylene dibromide was removed from the market. President George H. W. Bush also had a mixed record on the environment, at one point pushing to strengthen the Clean Air Act but at another opening up wetlands for development. President Bill Clinton, though bringing hope of environmental reform into office, was a disappointment in that the EPA's research staff was reduced during his tenure.

President George W. Bush is considered the worst president regarding environmental issues. Bush

> reversed a campaign pledge to control carbon dioxide emissions from power plants; . . . announced that the U.S. would withdraw from the Kyoto Protocol on climate change; sought to open the Arctic National Wildlife Refuge to oil exploration; withdrew the EPA's new arsenic-in-drinking-water standards; and had the boundaries of 19 National Parks redrawn to encourage oil exploration. (Burns & Lynch, 2004, p. 95)

President Barack Obama entered office with the "greenest" credentials ever, although Bruce Walsh (2011) documents how he backtracked on many green issues after entering office. He did kill the Keystone XL pipeline, a multibillion-dollar project that the Canadian government describes as a "critical energy infrastructure project" that will "ensure energy security, job creation and stimulate the economy"

(TransCanada, 2012). This pipeline will bring crude oil from Canada to the United States. While killing the pipeline endeared President Obama again to environmentalists, if not to the unemployed and the folks lined up at the gas pump, President Trump resuscitated the project in early 2017 and has approved other such projects in his efforts to make the United States energy independent. This and other actions like cutting the budget and power of the EPA hardly endear President Trump to the greens.

Environmental Crime

Environmental crimes are primarily offenses committed by business interests, such as dumping tons of toxic waste in rivers, lakes, and oceans; failing to repair or prevent toxic mercury emissions from smokestacks; and including harmful chemicals (e.g., lead) in products such as lipstick and children's toys. Many of these corporate crimes have far-reaching health and safety effects that harm millions of people and other living creatures. Regardless of whether they are criminally or civilly prosecuted, defendants typically are tried under principles of strict liability (recall that strict liability is a legal doctrine relaxing the *mens rea* requirement and making persons responsible for damages their actions or products cause, regardless of any malignant intent). In fact, the classic strict liability case involved an environmental wrong when water from a man's textile mill reservoir overflowed and flooded the mine shafts of another man in nineteenth-century England (*Rylands v. Fletcher*, 1868).

The classic American case cementing use of the strict liability criteria for polluters is *United States v. Weitzenhoff* (1994). This case involved two managers of a Honolulu sewage treatment plant (Michael Weitzenhoff and Thomas Mariani) who were convicted of dumping nonbiodegradable waste into the ocean on 40 different occasions in violation of the Clean Water Act. Each defendant was sentenced to prison, and each subsequently appealed his conviction on the basis of statutory vagueness. The Ninth District Circuit Court denied their appeals, basically stating that regardless of the alleged vagueness of the statute, the defendants should have known what they were doing was wrong. The defendants then appealed their case to the US Supreme Court, but the Court denied certiorari, thus allowing the convictions to stand.

Despite the lesson of *Weitzenhoff*, the single biggest violators of the Clean Water Act according to a recent study using EPA data (Duhigg, 2009) are local governments with inadequate sewer systems. As populations have exploded in cities and suburbs, their infrastructure, like sewer systems, have not always expanded to accommodate this growth. Unlike corporations, these governmental entities are not making a profit off polluting, but they are polluting enough that hundreds of their citizens are sickened by waterborne illnesses.

> More than a third of all sewer systems . . . have violated environmental laws since 2006. . . . Thousands of other sewage systems operated by smaller cities, colleges, mobile home parks and companies have also broken the law. But few of the violators are ever punished. (Duhigg, 2009, p. A18)

The most spectacular and costly man-made environmental disaster in American history was the British Petroleum (BP) *Deepwater Horizon* oil blowout on April 20, 2010, that killed 11 men and spewed oil into the Gulf of Mexico for almost three months. In March 2012, BP agreed to the largest class-action lawsuit settlement in American history—$7.8 billion. At the time of writing, federal government prosecutors were deciding whether or not to file criminal charges against BP employees who may have given false information to regulators regarding risks associated with drilling in the Gulf of Mexico. BP eventually settled all suits for $4.5 billion in November of 2012.

As noted in chapter 1, we have evolved a "risk society" that is preoccupied with safety and the future and with the sense that we can control the future by attending to the dangers and hazards engendered by scientific and technological advances. We can only do this with law and regulation, but history has shown that the law is a sluggish creature, often requiring a kick to stir it. Social movements have arisen in response to the many environmental disasters of the twentieth century to provide that kick. Many other potential environmental disasters loom for the twenty-first century, so vigilance must be maintained. As always, the law is required to mediate the often-competing claims of businesses and environmentalists as tensions between economic and environmental concerns wax and wane. When the economy is buoyant, unemployment is down, and energy prices are low, everyone sympathizes with "the greens," but when the opposite situations obtain, environmental concerns are sacrificed to the needs of the economy.

SUMMARY

Civil law is law designed to address private wrongs and is composed of tort, contract, property, family, and juvenile categories. There are many differences between civil and criminal law, the most important being the lower "preponderance of evidence" standard of proof. Tort law is law regarding wrongs committed against private citizens, which also may be crimes that have already been prosecuted in criminal courts. A variety of tort categories mirror criminal categories (e.g., intentional versus negligent wrongs) as well as a similar variety of defenses to liability.

Tort reform is about the efforts of certain business interests to limit what they consider frivolous lawsuits and to place caps on punitive damages. Tort reform should lead to lower insurance premiums and more affordable services for consumers from those who currently pay huge premiums to cover lawsuits. On the other hand, punitive damages have a way of forcing businesses to be more careful about what they place on the market and ensuring that service providers closely monitor their work.

Property law is law about the rights of ownership or possession of personal (movables like furniture and automobiles), real (buildings, houses), and intellectual (ideas, songs, abstract creations) property. It also has to do with the responsible use of property and how it can be used, disposed of, given away, or inherited.

Contract law is law covering the conduct of business. A contract is a legally binding promise of one party to do or provide something to another party in exchange for a similar promise from the other party. A number of requirements must be met for a contract to be legal: two parties, capacity, assent, and legality. If the terms of a contract are not met, it is considered a breach of contract, for which the injured party can seek legal redress.

Family law has to do with such issues as the legal requirements for a valid marriage, the duties and responsibilities of the parties in the marriage, the dissolution of the marriage, and alimony and child support. The Defense of Marriage Act defined marriage as something that can only occur between opposite-sex partners. However, the Supreme Court has ruled the act to be unconstitutional and that gay marriage is permissible.

Administrative or regulatory law is public law dealing with the relationship of governmental administrative agencies' oversight of business. There has been a huge growth of administrative agencies since the birth of the country, with a particularly large increase taking place in the 1930s. This growth occurred against the sharp opposition of Republicans and businesses who saw agency regulation as unwarranted intrusion and the first step toward a communist-like planned economy. Democrats saw agency oversight as simply protecting public interests. A compromise was reached with the passage of the Administrative Procedure Act, which placed procedural constraints on agency oversight activities.

Administrative agencies have been empowered by Congress to create law, enforce it, and adjudicate it within their special area of expertise. If an agency uncovers violations within its oversight purview, it may require offending parties to cease and desist and may assess fines against them. Most such violations are settled informally, but quasi-judicial hearings may be held if they are not. If accused parties do not like the agency's ruling, they may take the case to civil court. Typically, however, these courts defer to agency rulings under the so-called Chevron deference rule.

Administrative investigation and adjudication is often the first step in uncovering corporate (white-collar) crime. If a corporation is found to be engaging in criminal activities (as opposed to regulatory violations), the administrative agency refers the case to the appropriate criminal justice agency for prosecution. Traditionally, white-collar criminals have been treated leniently compared to the treatment of ordinary street criminals, but with the economic scandals of the early 2000s, this began to change. In 2002, Congress passed the Sarbanes-Oxley Act and the White-Collar Crimes Penalty Enhancement Act, designed to provide the SEC and the criminal justice system with greater ability to investigate, prosecute, and punish white-collar crooks.

DISCUSSION QUESTIONS

1. How does civil law differ procedurally from criminal law?
2. In light of the different standards of proof in civil versus criminal law, would you favor a "preponderance of evidence" standard of proof in criminal trials over the "beyond a reasonable doubt" standard? Defend your position.
3. Discuss your opinion about tort reform; that is, should there be strict caps on punitive damages?
4. Do you favor gay marriage? Does its legality undermine the traditional opposite-sex marriage?
5. The tension between liberals and conservatives is evident in their respective opinions about the expansiveness of administrative law. In your opinion, where does public protection stop and unwarranted government intrusion begin?
6. Should corporate criminals be punished as severely as street criminals? Should there be massive fines for companies committing illegal acts? What if those fines bankrupt the company, resulting in the loss of hundreds of jobs?

CHAPTER TERMS

Administrative law
Administrative Procedure Act
Adverse possession
All-property model
Annulment
Bailment
Chevron deference
Civil law
Clear and convincing evidence
Common law marriage
Comparative negligence
Consent
Contract law
Contracts

Contributory negligence
Defense of Marriage Act
Dual-property model
Easement
Environmental justice
Family law
Fee simple absolute estate
Fee simple estate
Freehold estate
Immunity
Involuntary commitment
Negligence
No-fault divorce
Ordinary care
Plaintiff

Preponderance of the evidence
Property
Punitive damages
Res judicata
Sarbanes-Oxley Act
Specific performance
Tenancy in common
Tort law
Uniform Commercial Code
White-Collar Crimes Penalty Enhancement Act

References

American Institute of Certified Public Accountants. (2004). American Institute of Certified Public Accountants Summary of the Sarbanes-Oxley Act of 2002. Retrieved from http://www.aicpa.org/info/sarbanes_oxley_summary.htm

Arnold, T., & Stevens, J. (2011). Mixed agendas and government regulation of business: Can we clean up the mess? *University of Richmond Law Review, 45,* 1059–1089.

Burns, R., & Lynch, M. (2004). *Environmental crime: A sourcebook.* New York, NY: LFB Scholarly Publishing.

Burns, R., Lynch, M., & Stretesky, P. (2008). *Environmental law, crime and justice.* El Paso, TX: LFB Scholarly Publishing.

Burr, M. (2004, December). SEC gains power, prestige in post-Enron era. *Corporate Legal Times,* pp. 10–13.

Calavita, K., & Pontell, H. (1994). Savings and loan fraud as organized crime: Toward a conceptual typology of corporate illegality. *Criminology, 31,* 519–548.

Cohen, T. (2005). *Federal tort trials and verdicts, 2002–2003.* Washington, DC: Bureau of Justice Statistics.

Cohen, T., & Smith, S. (2004). *Civil trial cases and verdicts in large counties, 2001.* Washington, DC: Bureau of Justice Statistics.

Crain, N., & Crain, W. (2010). The impact of regulatory costs on small firms. Small Business Administration. Retrieved from https://www.sba.gov/advocacy/impact-regulatory-costs-small-firms

Crews, Jr., C. (2015). One nation, ungovernable? Confronting the modern regulatory state. In Boudreaux , D.(ed.) *What America's decline in economic freedom means for entrepreneurship and prosperity* (pp. 117-181). : Vancouver, BC: The Fraser Institute.

DiLorenzo, T. (2007). The government-created subprime mortgage meltdown. Retrieved from https://www.lewrockwell.com/2007/09/thomas-dilorenzo/the-government-created-subprime-mortgage-meltdown/

Duhigg, C. (2009, November 23). Sewers at capacity, waste poisons waterways. *The New York Times,* pp. A1, A18.

Dukeminier, J., & Krier, J. E. (1988). *Property* (2nd ed.). Boston, MA: Little, Brown.

Epstein, J. (1998). State and local environmental enforcement. In M. Clifford (Ed.), *Environmental crime: Enforcement, policy, and social responsibility* (pp. 145–168). Gaithersburg, MD: Aspen.

Federal Bureau of Investigation. (2010). 2009 Financial Crimes Report. Retrieved from http://www.fbi.gov/stats-services/publications/financial-crimes-report-2009

Fenster, M. (2005). The birth of a "logical system": Thurman Arnold and the making of modern administrative law. *Oregon Law Review, 84,* 69–146.

Friedrichs, D. (2001). *Law in our lives.* New York, NY: Oxford University Press.

Gallup Poll. (2015). Gay and lesbian rights. Retrieved from http://www.gallup.com/poll/1651/gay-lesbian-rights.aspx

Gordon, N. (2008, April 18). Franklin Raines to pay $24.7 million to settle Fannie Mae lawsuit. *Seattle Times.* Retrieved from http://www.seattletimes.com/business/franklin-raines-to-pay-247-million-to-settle-fannie-mae-lawsuit/

Harte, B. (2011). Illegal corporate behavior: Analyzing the effectiveness of the 2002 Sarbanes-Oxley Act. PhD dissertation, Trident University International, Cypress, CA. Retrieved from http://gradworks.umi.com/34/67/3467260.html

Hellinger, F., & Encinosa, W. (2006). The impact of state laws limiting malpractice damage awards on health care expenditures. *American Journal of Public Health, 96,* 1375–1381.

Holmes, S. (1999, September 30). Fannie Mae eases credit to aid mortgage lending. *The New York Times.* Retrieved from http://www.nytimes.com/1999/09/30/business/fannie-mae-eases-credit-to-aid-mortgage-lending.html

Insurance loss leaves doctors scrambling for coverage. (2003). *The Lancet, 362,* 376.

Kionka, E. (1988). *Torts.* St. Paul, MN: West Publishing.

Leonnig, C. (2008, June 10). How HUD mortgage policy fed the crisis. *The Washington Post.* http://www.washingtonpost.com/wp-dyn/content/article/2008/06/09/AR2008060902626.html?noredirect=on

Lewis, C. S. (1970). *God in the dock: Essays on theology and ethics.* Edited by W. Hooper. London, England: Wm. B. Eerdmans.

Lowell, A., & Arnold, K. (2003). Corporate crime after 2000: A new law enforcement challenge or déjà vu? *American Criminal Law Review, 40*, 219–240.

McDonald, O. (2012). *Fannie Mae and Freddie Mac: Turning the American dream into a nightmare.* New York, NY: Bloomsbury Academic.

Melone, A., & Karnes, A. (2003). *The American legal system: Foundations, processes, and norms.* New York, NY: Oxford University Press.

Mencimer, S. (2004, October). False alarm. *Washington Monthly.* Retrieved from http://www .washingtonmonthly.com/features/2004/0410.mencimer.html

Occupational Safety and Health Administration. (2005). OSHA facts—December 2004. Retrieved from http://www.osha.gov/as/opa/oshafacts.html

Pally, T. (2010). Americas exhausted paradigm: Macroeconomic causes of the financial crisis and great recession. *New School Economic Review, 4*, 15–43.

Reiman, J. (1998). *The rich get richer and the poor get prison* (5th ed.). Boston, MA: Allyn & Bacon.

Samuels, S. (2006). *Law, politics, and society.* Boston, MA: Houghton Mifflin.

Schleifstein, M. (2012). BP's $4.5 billion settlement of criminal charges includes at least $1.2 billion for Louisiana coastal restoration. *The Times-Picayune*, 16 Nov. 2012. Retrieved from https://www.nola.com/news/gulf-oil-spill/index.ssf/2012/11/bp_enters_ 45_billion_settlemen.html.

Schiller, R. (2005). "Saint George and the dragon": Courts and the development of the administrative state in twentieth-century America. *Journal of Policy History, 17*, 110–124.

Shepard, G. (1996). Fierce compromise: The Administrative Procedure Act emerges from New Deal politics. *Northwestern Law Review, 90*, 1557–1683.

Simonsen, C. (Ed.). (2007). *The essentials of environmental law* (3rd ed.). Upper Saddle River, NJ: Pearson/Prentice Hall.

TransCanada. (2012). The Keystone pipeline project. Retrieved from http://www .transcanada.com/keystone.html

US Attorney General's Committee. (1941). *Final report of the Attorney General's Committee on Administrative Procedure.* Washington, DC: US Government Printing Office.

Walsh, A. (1988). "The people who own the country ought to govern it": The Supreme Court, hegemony, and its consequences. *Law and Inequality, 5*, 431–451.

Walsh, A., & Ellis, L. (2007). *Criminology: An interdisciplinary approach.* Thousand Oaks, CA: SAGE.

Walsh, B. (2011, September 6). Is Obama bad for the environment? *Time Magazine.*

White House. (2006). Federal agencies & commissions. Retrieved from https://www .whitehouse.gov/1600/federal-agencies-and-commissions

Cases Cited

Chevron U.S.A., Inc. v. Natural Resources Defense Council, Inc., 467 U.S. 837 (1984)

City of Oakland v. The Oakland Raiders, 646 P.2d. 835 (1982)

Loving v. Virginia, 388 U.S. 1 (1967)

Lubitz v. Wells, 113 A.2d. 147 (1955)

National Cable & Telecommunications v. Brand X Internet Services, 545 U.S. 967 (2005)

National Labor Relations Board v. Bildisco & Bildisco, 465 U.S. 513 (1984)

Obergefell v. Hodges, 576 U.S. ___ (2015)

Pierson v. Post, 3 Cal. R. 175, 2 Am. Dec. 264 (1805)

Reynolds v. United States, 98 U.S. 897 (1878)

Rylands v. Fletcher, L.R. 3 H.L. 330 (1868)

Skinner v. State of Oklahoma, Ex. Rel. Williamson, 316 U.S. 535 (1942)

Sullivan v. O'Connor, 296 N.E.2d. 183 (1973)

Turner v. Safley, 482 U.S. 78 (1987)

United States v. Weitzenhoff, 35 F.3d 1275, 9th Cir. (1994)

United States v. Windsor, 570 U.S. (2013)

Zablocki v. Redhail, 434 U.S. 374 (1978)

CHAPTER 8

JUVENILE JUSTICE

Jon Venables and Robert Thomson came from severely deprived and abusive single-parent homes in Liverpool, England. On February 12, 1993, Jon and Robert, both then 10½ years old, abducted 2-year-old Jamie Bulger from a Liverpool shopping mall, beat him, sexually molested him, and killed him, leaving his body on train tracks to be mutilated. The abduction was caught on closed-circuit TV, and both boys were arrested and charged as adults with murder. The trial took place in an atmosphere of intense national rage and grief. Both boys were convicted and ordered to serve a minimum of 10 years, the first 8 years in a juvenile facility.

In 1999, the boys' lawyers appealed their case to the European Court of Human Rights (a supranational court with jurisdiction among all European Union countries) claiming that they had not received a fair trial. The court agreed, stating that the trial had taken place in a charged atmosphere and that the boys should not have been tried as adults. The boys were released in 2001 without serving one day in an adult prison. The British government paid an estimated $8 million to furnish them with new homes and identities (they had received numerous death threats). By way of contrast, the Bulgers were given only $15,000 in victim compensation.

Keep this case in mind as you read about juvenile behavior and early efforts to deal with it humanely. When you read about juveniles being transferred to adult court in the United States for far less heinous crimes, think about the contrast between American and European attitudes toward juvenile crime and punishment. How much more protection are juveniles entitled to? How far should the government go to protect them after release, if at all?

INTRODUCTION

This chapter addresses the history and current practices of juvenile justice in the United States. We will see that society has come a long way in its understanding and treatment of children and youths (collectively known as juveniles) since ancient times.

Our evolving understanding of childhood and the sometimes emotional turmoil of adolescence has led to a system of justice for juveniles that is different from the adult system. Juvenile justice today falls under the umbrella of civil rather than criminal law, and as such, there are a number of differences in the way that juvenile offenders are processed through the courts as compared with adult offenders. Juveniles who commit acts that are criminal when committed by adults are considered a separate class of offenders called **delinquents**. The term *delinquent* comes from the Latin for "to leave undone," and it conveys the notion that the juvenile has *not done* something he or she *was supposed to do* (behave lawfully) rather than has *done* something he or she *was not supposed to do* (behave unlawfully). This subtle difference reflects the presumably rehabilitative rather than punitive thrust of American juvenile justice.

WHAT IS JUVENILE DELINQUENCY?

Historically, juveniles have been subject to laws that make some actions illegal for them that are legal for adults (e.g., smoking, not obeying parents, and not attending school). Such acts are called **status offenses** because they apply only to individuals of a particular status—that of a juvenile—and to distinguish them from offenses that are violations of the criminal law. Status offenses are proscribed because juveniles are assumed to lack the requisite ability to appreciate the long-term consequences of their behavior and therefore need of protection from themselves. Acts such as smoking, drinking alcohol, and having sex can have negative effects that juveniles often fail to recognize. Acts such as disobeying parents and school truancy can seriously jeopardize juveniles' future acquisition of suitable social roles (Binder, Geis, & Bruce, 2001). If parents cannot or will not shield their children from harm, then operating under the ostensibly benign philosophy of juvenile justice, the juvenile system becomes a substitute source of discipline and training for responsible adulthood.

Status offenses constitute the largest proportion of juvenile offenses and thus consume an inordinate amount of juvenile courts' time and resources (Bynum & Thompson, 1999). For this and other reasons, some states have relinquished juvenile court jurisdiction over such acts to other social service agencies. In states that have not relinquished jurisdiction over status offenders, terms such as *child in need of supervision* or *person in need of supervision* tend to be used to distinguish status offenders from juveniles who have committed acts that are crimes when committed by adults (i.e., delinquents).

THE EXTENT OF DELINQUENCY

The public image of juvenile offenders tends to be fueled by sensationalized media accounts of atypical cases, such as the outburst of school shootings in Arkansas, Kentucky, and Oregon that occurred during the late 1990s (Lawrence & Mueller, 2003). However, juveniles do commit a disproportionate percentage of the Federal Bureau of Investigation's Uniform Crime Report Part I index crimes. According to the Office of Juvenile Justice and Delinquency Prevention (OJJDP, 2018), in 2017, law enforcement agencies in the U.S. made an estimated 809,700 arrests of persons under age 18, 59% less than the number of arrests in 2008. Juveniles accounted for 16.4 percent of Part I index violent crimes and 28.8 percent of Part I index property crimes. However, youths under 18 represent only about 6 percent of the American population (US Census Bureau, 2010) and thus are overrepresented about 2.5 times among violent offenders and about 4.5 times among property offenders.

Figure 8.1 presents a graph showing arrest rates by age in the United States in 1999. Although the height of the peak differs somewhat from year to year, the same pattern—that is, a sharp increase beginning around puberty that rises steadily until the mid-teens and then falls off—is present each year and in every country where arrest statistics are kept (Walsh & Ellis, 2007). There is thus something very special going on at this stage of life to account for this state of affairs.

No discussion of juvenile delinquency can proceed without noting that some degree of anti-social behavior is normative for juveniles. Youths are "feeling their oats" and seeking to cast off parental apron strings to become their own persons. During this period, the young are seeking their identities in an increasingly complex and confusing world and are asking themselves who they are, what their place in society is, and where they are going. The juvenile courts are thus dealing with individuals at a time in their lives when they are most susceptible to anti-social behavior. Individuals (especially males) who do *not* engage in some form of anti-social behavior are statistically in the minority (Moffitt & Walsh, 2003). Looking at data from 12 different countries, Junger-Tas (1996) concluded that delinquent behavior is a part of growing up and that the peak ages for different types of crimes were similar across all countries (14 to 15 years for vandalism, 16 to 17 years for property crimes, and 18 to 20 years for violent crimes).

This has always been so. Shakespeare's shepherd in *The Winter's Tale* expresses the wish that youth could be put to sleep between the ages of 10 and 23. "for there is nothing in between but getting wenches with child, wronging the ancientry, stealing, fighting" (Walsh, 2006, p. 399). Why this sharp rise in anti-social behavior has been a

Figure 8.1 Arrest Rates Per 100,000 in the United States by Age in 1999

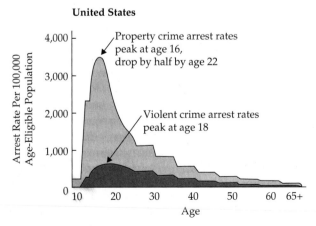

Source: L. Ellis and A. Walsh (2000). *Criminology: A global perspective.* Boston, MA: Allyn & Bacon, p. 109. Reprinted with permission.

constant across time and cultures has been something of a mystery to criminologists, who have long admitted that they cannot explain it by any known set of sociological or psychological variables (Gottfredson & Hirschi, 1990). However, work in the neurosciences over the past 15 to 20 years has thrown much light on the topic. We briefly discuss part of this evidence because, as we shall see, the courts are making some important decisions in juvenile justice influenced by neuroscience data on the juvenile brain (Garland & Frankel, 2006).

DEVELOPMENTAL FACTORS AND JUVENILE DELINQUENCY

The New York Academy of Sciences' 2003 conference on adolescent brain development provided some key messages that help us to understand adolescent behavior (White, 2004, p. 4):

> Much of the behavior characterizing adolescence is rooted in biology intermingling with environmental influences to cause teens to conflict with their parents, take more risks, and experience wide swings in emotion.

> The lack of synchrony between a physically mature body and a still maturing nervous system may explain these behaviors.

> Adolescents' sensitivities to rewards appear to be different than in adults, prompting them to seek higher levels of novelty and stimulation to achieve the same feeling of pleasure.

Puberty marks the onset of the transition from childhood to adulthood and is accompanied in males by a 10- to 20-fold increase in testosterone, a hormone linked to aggression and dominance seeking (Ellis, 2003). Neurotransmitters such as dopamine that excite behavior also increase during this period, while inhibitory transmitters such as serotonin decrease (Collins, 2004; Walker, 2002). The brain is undergoing a period of physical reorganization that slowly refines the neural circuitry to its adult form during this period as well (Walker, 2002). For instance, the prefrontal cortex is receiving its final coat of a fatty substance called myelin to insulate various brain structures that are important for the speedy electrochemical transmission of information. The prefrontal cortex is the brain's "CEO," serving functions such as modulating emotions from the brain's emotional centers and making reasoned judgments and plans. In a nutshell, the adolescent brain is immature, and as neuroscientist Richard Restak (2001) put it, "The immaturity of the adolescent's behavior is perfectly mirrored by the immaturity of the adolescent's brain" (p. 76).

The point is that there are *physical* reasons why adolescents do not evidence the same level of judgment that adults do and why they tend to assign faulty attributions to situations and to the intentions of others. A brain on "go slow" superimposed on a hormone-driven physiology on "fast forward" may explain why "teenagers often find it difficult to gauge the meanings and intentions of others and to experience more events as aversive during adolescence than they did as prepubescent children and will do so again as adults" (Walsh, 2002, p. 143). Around about the age of 22, when the brain reaches its adult state in most people, more adultlike personality traits emerge (McCrae et al., 2000, p. 183). To put this in the context of justice policy, by far the most successful "treatment" for delinquency is simply growing older.

It has long been known that the vast majority of youth who offend during adolescence desist and that only a small number continue to offend in adulthood. Terrie Moffitt (1993) calls the former adolescent-limited (AL) offenders and the latter life-course-persistent (LCP) offenders. LCP offenders begin offending prior to puberty and continue well into adulthood. They are saddled with neuropsychological and temperamental deficits that are manifested in low IQ, hyperactivity, inattentiveness, negatively emotionality, and low impulse control that arise from a combination of genetic and environmental effects on brain development. LCP offenders constitute only about 7 percent of all delinquents but are responsible for at least 50 percent of all delinquent acts and crimes. Moreover, LCP offenders tend to commit serious crimes. such as assault, robbery, and rape. whereas AL offenders tend to commit relatively minor offenses. such as petty theft (Moffitt & Walsh, 2003).

AL offenders, on the other hand, have developmental histories that place them on a prosocial trajectory that is temporarily derailed at adolescence. They are not burdened with the neuropsychological problems that weigh heavily on LCP offenders; they are "normal" youths adapting to the transitional events of adolescence and whose offending does not reflect any stable personal deficiencies. More teens than in the past are being diverted from their pro-social life trajectories because better health and nutrition has lowered the average age of puberty while the average time needed to prepare for participation in an increasingly complex economy has increased. These changes have resulted in about a 5- to 10-year maturity gap between puberty and entry into the job market. Thus, "adolescent-limited offending is a product of an interaction between age and historical period" (Moffitt, 1993, p. 692). It is against this backdrop that we discuss the history of and philosophy behind juvenile justice.

HISTORY AND PHILOSOPHY OF JUVENILE JUSTICE

While it may seem odd that the juvenile justice system is considered a branch of civil law, the reason for this will become clear as we discuss its historical development. Throughout much of history, young children have been considered not much different from property, and as such, civil law has been critical to the development of juvenile justice. Also important to our discussion is the concept of *culpability*, which describes the level to which persons are held legally responsible for their actions. The minimum legally defined age of criminal responsibility was defined at common law as 7 years (it is now 10 years in British common law) and is the age of responsibility in most states, but it ranges from 6 years in North Carolina to 10 years in Arkansas, Colorado, Kansas, Pennsylvania, and Wisconsin (Snyder, Espiritu, Huizinga, Loeber, & Petechuck, 2003, p. 2). The idea of reduced culpability for children is relatively new. Throughout much of history, no special allowances were made for children when it came to determining culpability and punishment, and there are records of children as young as six being housed in jails and prisons with adults and even being executed for relatively minor offenses (Schmalleger, 2003).

The social conception of children is a fundamental consideration in the study of juvenile justice. Historically, the control of children's behavior has been the responsibility of the family, particularly fathers. Children were considered the property of their fathers, who were invested with the authority to maintain discipline within the family as they saw fit. The ancient Romans used the term ***patria potestas*** (literally, "fatherly power") to describe the authority of the father over his family. He had power of life or death over his children and, as such, could sell them into slavery, abandon them, or even kill them, although punishments were sometimes prescribed for fathers who exercised their power arbitrarily (Binder et al., 2001). Because children held no special status in society, no special status was given to youthful offenders. Fathers were accountable for the actions of children under their control and were responsible for their punishment when they misbehaved.

Toward the end of the fourth century, there developed a trend toward limiting the power that fathers had over their children in Roman society, as the cultural ideal of ***paterna pietas*** ("fatherly love") became prominent. While this ideal did not dramatically change the nature of juvenile treatment, it did indicate a gradual shift toward a more benign method of attempting to control the behavior of the young. However, there were still no separate rules or regulations for children, no separate system to deal with youthful offenders, and few laws as to how much or what types of punishment a father could inflict upon his children.

Under the increasing influence of the Christian church during the Middle Ages, the brutal nature of the treatment of children gradually lessened. Church doctrine held that children under the age of seven could not be held responsible for spiritual transgressions because they had not yet reached the age of reason. The English courts of the period came to accept this doctrine and exempted children below this age from criminal responsibility as well. Additionally, they afforded special status to children between the ages of 7 and 14, during which time children could be held criminally responsible and treated as adults only if it could be shown that they were fully aware of the consequences of their actions. Fourteen was the cutoff age between childhood and adulthood for the purpose of assigning criminal responsibility because individuals were considered rational and responsible enough at this age to marry (Springer, 1987).

Institutional Control

Although parents retained the primary responsibility for the behavior of their children, the impetus toward greater state involvement had been in evidence since the formation of the English chancery courts (or courts of equity) in the thirteenth century. These courts adopted the doctrine of ***parens patriae***, which literally means "father of his country" or, more loosely but more correctly in a practical sense, "state as parent." *Parens patriae* gave the king, by virtue of his role as the symbolic father of all his subjects, the right to intercede and act in the best interest of the child or any other legally incapacitated persons such as the mentally ill. This philosophical shift in the treatment of juveniles meant that the state, not the parents, had the ultimate authority over children. It also meant that children who fell under the jurisdiction of the courts could be removed from their families if judged to be delinquent, abandoned, or in need of the care and protection that their parents were unwilling or unable to provide and placed in the custody of the state (Schmalleger, 2003).

The parental control model was not completely lost in the transition. In keeping with this model, children without parents or with inadequate ones were assigned to foster families through a system known as **binding out**. While the idea of binding out is the precursor of modern adoption, the practice was more akin to indentured servitude, since children were generally accepted only by families who could profit from their labor. Children whose parents could not control them or who were simply too poor to provide for them were apprenticed to richer families, generally land-owning farmers, who used them for domestic or farm labor. It was during this time that the first laws directed specifically at children were established, including laws that condemned begging and vagrancy (Sharp & Hancock, 1995).

The concern over vagrancy and laziness moved the English authorities to create workhouses in which "habits of industry" were to be instilled in their youthful residents, who were typically vagrants and beggars. The first one, opened in 1555, was a converted palace called Saint Bridget's Well, which was subsequently shortened to Bridewell. Despite its regal origins, Bridewell soon became a prisonlike institution. Nevertheless, it was considered so successful that in 1576 the English Parliament passed a law establishing **Bridewells**, or workhouses, in every English county (Whitehead & Lab, 1996). The idea behind the Bridewells was that youth were trainable and malleable, and if vagrant youths were removed from the negative influences of street life, they could be taught proper work habits and become contributors to society.

While originally established as training schools, Bridewells were soon filled with all types of problem children. It was not uncommon for parents to place their own children in these institutions in the hope that the experiences there would reform them and help them to develop a work ethic. The directors of these institutions often used the children as a cheap source of labor for their own economic gain as well, and were often cruel and harsh in their treatment of them (Krisberg & Austin, 1993).

Childhood in the United States

The British colonization of the United States provided an additional way to deal with delinquent youths, many of whom were sent from the Bridewells to the colonies as indentured servants, sometimes even without parental notification or support. Due to labor shortages in the colonies, many destitute and rebellious youth were promised wealth and happiness in the New World. They earned their passage to the colonies by agreeing to work for their employers for a specific term, usually four years, and were considered the legal property of their "owners" (Krisberg & Austin, 1993).

The economy in the United States took a downturn in the early 1800s, limiting opportunities available in the infant factory system of the northeastern United States for the increasing number of poor immigrants arriving in the country. Unemployment was rife during this period, and the streets of many big cities were cluttered with destitute and unwanted children who engaged in illegal activities to survive. The problem was particularly bad in large urban areas such as New York and Boston, which did not have the resources to deal with the rising number of juveniles requiring state supervision. At that time, children who were arrested for any anti-social act, including vagrancy and begging, were placed in the same jails as adult offenders.

In response to this situation, a number of concerned New York citizens formed a group known as the Society for the Prevention of Pauperism, later known as the Society for the Reformation of Juvenile Delinquents. The motivation for this group was the belief that the primary causes of criminal behavior were economic; therefore, if children were provided with food, shelter, and vocational training, they would choose to become productive citizens rather than thieves and beggars. Based on this assumption, and following the Bridewell model, the New York House of Refuge was established in 1825 to house orphans, beggars, vagrants, and juvenile offenders. Not long after, several other cities, counties, and states established their own homes for "the perishing and dangerous classes" as they were called (Binder et al., 2001, p. 202). The Society for the Reformation of Juvenile Delinquents described the goals of the House of Refuge and its image of delinquents as follows:

> The design of the proposed institution is, to furnish, in the first place, an asylum, in which boys under a certain age, who become subject to the notice of our police, either as vagrants, or homeless, or charged with petty crimes, may be received, judiciously classed according to their degree of depravity or innocence, put to work at such employments as will tend to encourage industry and ingenuity, taught reading, writing, and arithmetic, and most carefully instructed in the nature of their moral and religious obligations while at the same time, they are subjected to a course of treatment, that will afford a prompt and energetic corrective of their vicious propensities, and hold out every possible inducement to reformation and good conduct. (Hart, 1832, p. 21)

Children assigned to these houses were to remain there until those in charge determined that they were reformed, and criteria for admission were often arbitrary. For instance, parents could place their children in residence for such offenses as idle and disorderly behavior. Given this situation, it soon became clear that the courts would have to create standards for admission and control, which they did in *Ex Parte Crouse* (1838). (The term *ex parte* designates a hearing in the presence of only one of the parties to a case.) This case challenged the power of magistrates to remove children from their parents and send them to these institutions. The subject of the case, a child named Mary Ann Crouse, was placed in the Pennsylvania House of Refuge by her mother against the wishes of her

House of Refuge

father (Whitehead & Lab, 1996). Course's father argued that it was unconstitutional to incarcerate a child without a jury trial. Citing the *parens patriae* doctrine, the Pennsylvania Supreme Court ruled that parental rights are superseded by the "best interest of the child" doctrine, as those interests were viewed by the courts. This landmark decision brought the ideals of the English chancery courts as they pertained to juveniles to America, thus establishing *parens patriae* as settled law in American juvenile jurisprudence (del Carmen, Parker, & Reddington, 1998).

While the purpose of the Houses of Refuge was to train and care for children, in practice they looked very similar to the Bridewells. Children lived highly disciplined lives and worked at jobs that brought income to the institution. The indeterminate nature of children's residence allowed the institutions a great deal of latitude in their treatment of them. Throughout the nineteenth century, children placed in these institutions were exploited, worked long hours, often received little or no training, and were frequently mistreated (Whitehead & Lab, 1996).

The Child Savers

As the nineteenth century drew to a close, there emerged a growing discontent with government corruption and inefficiency among the rising and increasingly influential middle classes. This dissatisfaction generated a group of concerned individuals collectively referred to as **Progressives**, who called for the professionalization of public service. In the later part of the nineteenth century, a group of well-funded and highly educated liberal reformers (mostly females) known as the **Child Savers** began an ideological attack on the Houses of Refuge, which they saw as oriented toward punishment rather than rehabilitation. Central to their attack was the belief that juveniles could be molded into better citizens by religious instruction and training them to satisfy their basic needs through honest labor and thrift. Reformers argued that children should be deinstitutionalized and placed in settings that provided a more family-like atmosphere where they could be taught the value of hard work and social conformity. Most often, the type of intervention these reformers suggested for wayward children was their placement with farm families in the western United States. It was thought that since criminal environments breed criminals, a dramatic change to more wholesome surroundings was the best solution to the problem of juvenile delinquency. These farm families were often idealized as "God's reformatories" (Mennel, 1973).

The motives of many reformers may have been less than entirely altruistic, as they often held beliefs similar to those of the people who created the Bridewells in sixteenth-century England. Many reformers believed that the poor were innately criminal, that poverty was a sign of personal defects, such as laziness and feeblemindedness, and that the presence of destitute and vagrant children in neighborhoods contributed to their decline and, for this reason, it served the public interest to rid the city of them.

The Beginning of the Juvenile Courts

Regardless of their motives, the Child Savers created an impetus for change in the way that juvenile offenders were handled. It became increasingly obvious that the solutions applied by the criminal courts were not working with children; adult criminal courts were not equipped to apply the doctrine of *parens patriae* in a fashion consistent with the spirit of its philosophy. In 1899, Cook County, Illinois, enacted the first Juvenile Court Law providing for a separate court system for juveniles, and by 1945, every state in the union had established juvenile court systems (Hemmens, Steiner, & Mueller, 2003). In establishing these courts, the legislation created both a class of offenders separated by their age status and a nonadversarial courtroom process using civil law standards of proof—that is, "preponderance of evidence" rather than the more restrictive "beyond a reasonable doubt." Juvenile judges were afforded a great deal of latitude in determining how "the best interests of the child" were to be achieved. In principle, the juvenile court was supposed to emphasize an individualized approach to youthful offending, tailoring each case to the unique characteristics and needs of the child rather than simply matching sentences to offenses. In practice, however, it gave judges wide latitude to impose their own private views of morality on children.

The ideal (not necessarily the day-to-day practice) of the juvenile courts in the early twentieth century was best described in 1909 by Judge Julian Mack:

> The child who must be brought into court, of course, should be made to know that he is face to face with the power of the state, but he should at the same time, and more emphatically, be made to feel that he is the object of its care and solicitude. The ordinary trappings of the courtroom are out of place in such a hearing. The judge on the bench, looking down upon the boy standing at the bar, can never evoke a proper sympathetic spirit. Seated at desks, with the child at his side, where he can on occasion put his arm around his shoulder and draw the lad to him, the judge, while losing none of his judicial dignity, will gain immensely in the effectiveness of his work. (Small, 1997, p. 120)

This kind of judicial solicitude probably is no longer in evidence in any juvenile court in the land, where the judge, surrounded by all the trappings Judge Mack called "out of place," does indeed "look down upon the boy."

The creation of a separate system of justice for juveniles brought with it a set of terms (or euphemisms) describing the processing of children accused of committing delinquent acts that differentiated it from the adult system. These terms reflect the protective and rehabilitative nature of the juvenile system in contrast with the punitive nature of the adult system. To illustrate these differences, in Table 8.1, we follow Tony, age 19, and his younger brother, Craig, age 15, as they are processed through the adult and juvenile court systems after being apprehended for robbery in 1960. The italicized terms are the parallel terms used in their respective courts; for example, in Item 1, Tony is *arrested* and Craig is *taken into custody*. Tony receives all due process rights guaranteed to him by the Bill of Rights; Craig receives none of these because he is processed in accordance with civil law procedure (as we shall see, however, juveniles are now entitled to most due process rights). Craig receives the *solicitous protection* of the court under the *parens patriae* philosophy, which is cold comfort when he is similarly incarcerated against his will for longer than his brother, notwithstanding that it is in a *training school* rather than in a *prison* like Tony. Note that the age of majority (when one becomes an adult) was 21 in the 1960s.

Table 8.1 *Major Distinctions Between the Juvenile and Adult Systems in the United States*

Tony's Trip Through the Adult System	Craig's Trip Through the Juvenile System
1. Tony is *arrested* and taken to jail.	1. Craig is *taken into custody* and taken to the juvenile detention center.
2. The prosecutor seeks an *indictment* or *information* charging Tony with robbery.	2. The prosecutor *petitions the court* for an adjudication of delinquency.
3. The *defendant* (Tony) is *arraigned* and *pleads* guilty, not guilty, or no contest to the charge.	3. The *respondent* (Craig) receives a *hearing* and *admits or denies* the charge in the petition.
4. Tony pleads not guilty and goes to *trial*, which is an adversarial process open to the public.	4. Craig denies and receives an *adjudicatory hearing*, which is a nonadversarial process generally not open to the public.
5. The jury returns a verdict of *guilty* using the "beyond a reasonable doubt" standard.	5. The judge *adjudicates* Craig *delinquent*, generally using the "preponderance of evidence" standard of proof.
6. A *presentence investigation report* is written.	6. A *predispositional or social inquiry report* is written.
7. Tony is *incarcerated* in *prison* for five years.	7. Craig is *detained* in a *training school* for "the remainder of his minority" (age 21).
8. Tony is *paroled* after serving four years and is supervised by an adult probation/parole officer.	8. Craig is released at age 20 and receives *aftercare* under the tutelage of a juvenile probation officer.

JUVENILE WAIVER TO CRIMINAL COURT

Under certain circumstances, juveniles can be **waived** (transferred, or bound over) to adult criminal court, where they are subject to criminal prosecution and punishments. When juveniles are waived to criminal court, they lose their status as minors and become legally culpable for their alleged crime. The simple philosophy underlying juvenile waivers seems to be "Do adult crime, do adult time." A transfer to adult court is called a waiver because the juvenile court waives (relinquishes) its jurisdiction over the child in question to the adult system. Waivers are designed to allow the juvenile courts to transfer to a more punitive system those youths over a certain age who have committed particularly serious crimes or have exhausted the juvenile system's resources in trying to rehabilitate them.

Alarm and disenchantment eventually crystallized into a "get tough" philosophy in which every state allowed some form of waiver, and the practice increased by 400 percent in the 1980s over what it was in the 1970s (Steiner & Hemmens, 2003). Juveniles become increasingly more likely to be waived if they are chronic offenders approaching the upper age limit of their state juvenile court's jurisdiction. Note that only about 1.5 percent of juvenile cases nationwide are waived to the criminal courts (Schmalleger, 2003, p. 352).

There are three primary ways in which juveniles can be waived to criminal court:

Judicial waiver occurs when a juvenile court judge decides, according to his or her own discretion after a "full inquiry," that the juvenile should be transferred. At present, 48 states allow judicial discretionary waivers. Some states have mandatory waivers for some offenses, but the juvenile system is still involved in that juvenile judges must determine if the criteria for a mandatory waiver are met. A third form of waiver under this heading is the presumptive waiver. In this type, the burden of proof is on the juvenile to prove that he or she is amenable to treatment and therefore should not be waived, not on the prosecutor to prove that the child should be waived. This is similar to the burden of proof shift in criminal courts when the defendant claims insanity.

Prosecutorial discretion waiver or *direct file* allows prosecutors to file some cases in either juvenile or adult court. In such cases (usually limited by age and seriousness of the offense), the prosecutor can file the case directly with the adult court and bypass the juvenile court altogether. Fourteen states and the District of Columbia allow prosecutorial discretion waivers.

Statutory exclusion waiver or *legislative waiver* indicates instances in which state legislatures have statutorily excluded certain offenses (the most serious ones) from the juvenile courts for those over a certain age, which varies from state to state. These automatic waivers exist in 31 states.

The presumed social benefits of waivers (deterrence and reduction of crime) have not materialized. Studies have shown that juveniles waived to adult courts are more likely to recidivate than youths adjudicated for similar crimes in juvenile court, although we suspect that this is because the most delinquent-prone youths are waived (Butts & Mitchell 2000). Neither does a waiver necessarily guarantee a more punitive disposition. Waived juveniles who commit violent crimes are likely to be incarcerated, but juveniles waived for property and drug offenses often receive more lenient sentences than they would have in juvenile courts (Butts & Mitchell, 2000). It is easy to see how juries and adult court judges would be more reluctant to convict and/or send nonviolent minors to adult institutions than a juvenile judge would be to adjudicate them delinquent and send them to a juvenile institution.

Figure 8.2 Shows the case flow of 1,504,100 youths processed through the juvenile system in one year (Knoll & Sickmund, 2012). We see that only 55 percent of the juveniles taken into custody ("arrested") or otherwise referred to juvenile court were petitioned (formally charged), and only 1 percent were waived to adult court. Among those not petitioned, most had their cases dismissed, some were placed on informal probation (probation without a formal adjudication of delinquency, sometimes known as diversion), and some received "other sanction"—this could be something as minor as a written apology to something as serious as placement in a mental institution.

Figure 8.2 Flow of 1,504,100 Cases through the Juvenile Court System in a Typical Year

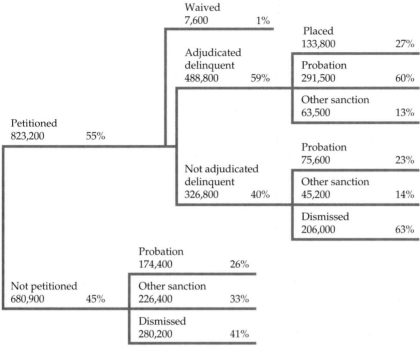

Source: C. Knoll & M. Sickmund (2012). *Delinquency cases in juvenile court, 2009.* Washington, DC: National Center of Juvenile Justice.

EXTENDING DUE PROCESS TO JUVENILES

Under the philosophy of *parens patriae*, juvenile courts viewed their mission as help-ing troublesome, neglected, or abandoned children overcome their difficulties, not punishing them. Yet children were being punished, and often in arbitrary ways that would not be tolerated in the adult system. Critics argued that the *parens patriae* doc-trine allowed too much latitude for courts to restrict the rights of juveniles. It also was argued that because the actual practice of juvenile corrections was still very similar to adult correctional practices at the time, in that it was punitive, and that since the courts could remove juvenile rights to liberty, juveniles should be afforded the same due process protections as adults. Nevertheless, in a number of early cases, state courts generally held that the doctrine of *parens patriae* was suitable and proper for the treatment of children and that any problems concerning juvenile court opera-tion were ones of implementation rather than of philosophy (Whitehead & Lab, 1996).

The US Supreme Court maintained a hands-off policy with regard to juvenile issues until 1948 in *Haley v. Ohio.* On October 14, 1945, a storekeeper in Canton, Ohio, was shot to death in his store by one of two boys. The petitioner, 15-year-old John

Harvey Haley, served as a lookout for these two older boys. Haley was not allowed to see his mother for five days after his arrest, and there was evidence that he was beaten by the police in long interrogation sessions during the course of which he confessed. He was subsequently sentenced to life imprisonment, partly on the basis of that confession. The issue before the Court was whether the due process clause of the Fourteenth Amendment prohibits the use of coerced confessions against juveniles. The Court ruled that the Fourteenth Amendment does prohibit the police from violating the due process clause in obtaining confessions from juveniles and that confessions obtained in this fashion are inadmissible in court.

Kent v. United States

The *Haley* case dealt with the actions of the police, not with the operation of the juvenile courts. In *Kent v. United States* (1966), we have the first instance in which the Supreme Court provided oversight to juvenile court proceedings, marking a steady shift away from the juvenile courts' traditional operating principle of *parens patriae.* Morris Kent first came to the attention of the juvenile court of the District of Columbia when he was 14 years old, charged with several burglaries and a purse-snatching. In 1961, when he was 16 years old, Kent broke into a woman's apartment, raped her, and stole her wallet. Fingerprints left at the scene identified him as the culprit, and during interrogation, he admitted several other similar offenses. Because of the seriousness of the offense and Kent's chronic delinquency, the juvenile judge waived the case to adult court for prosecution. The code of the District of Columbia allowed juvenile court judges to waive jurisdiction and transfer to adult criminal court children over the age of 16 charged with a serious crime after a "full investigation." The judge in the Kent case read "full investigation" to mean private consultation and reflection on police reports and the predisposition report. He held no hearing and denied Kent's counsel access to Kent's social service file.

The adult court found Kent not guilty of two counts of rape "by reason of insanity," and he was consigned to a psychiatric hospital (he was still there at the time of the Supreme Court hearing in 1966). However, he was found guilty of six counts of housebreaking and robbery, for which the judge sentenced him to 30 to 90 years in prison. Had Kent remained in juvenile court, he could have been sentenced to a maximum of five years (the remainder of his minority). Kent appealed, arguing that the waiver process had not included a "full investigation," no findings were made, no reasons were stated for the waiver, and counsel had been denied access to the files upon which the juvenile judge presumably relied to make the waiver determination. Kent's appeal to the US Court of Appeals was denied, and the case came before the US Supreme Court.

In the majority opinion remanding Kent's case to district court, Justice Abe Fortas called the waiver decision a "critically important stage" in the juvenile process and added that

> there is no place in our system of law for reaching a result of such tre-
> mendous consequences without ceremony—without hearing, without
> effective assistance of counsel, without a statement of reasons . . . . the
> admonition to function in a 'parental' relationship is not an invitation to
> procedural arbitrariness.

Justice Fortas also noted that under the philosophy of *parens patriae,* "there may be grounds for concern that the child receives the worst of both worlds: that he gets neither the protections accorded to adults nor the solicitous care and regenerative treatment postulated for children." The Court thus determined that juveniles must be afforded certain constitutional rights, and in doing so, it began formalizing the juvenile system into something akin to the adult criminal courts (Hemmens et al., 2003).

In re Gault

The *Kent* decision opened the door for a close inspection of juvenile courts by the Supreme Court, which heard a second case concerning the civil rights of juveniles one year later in *In re Gault* (1967). (The Latin phrase *In re* literally means "in the matter of" and is used in nonadversarial proceedings.) In 1964, 15-year-old Gerald Gault was taken into custody following a complaint by a neighbor that he had made lewd and indecent remarks during a phone call. The worst of these remarks were "Are your cherries ripe today?" and "Do you have big bombers?" (Butts & Mitchell, 2000, p. 176). For these obviously adolescent and relatively innocuous remarks, Gault was adjudicated delinquent and sentenced to a total of six years in the State Industrial School. An adult convicted of the same offense would have faced a fine of $5 to $50 and a maximum of 60 days in jail. The court never resolved the issue of whether Gault actually made the call because the alleged victim did not appear at the adjudicatory hearing.

The US Supreme Court used this case to establish five basic constitutional due process rights for juveniles: (a) the right to proper notification of charges, (b) the right to legal counsel, (c) the right to confront witnesses, (d) the right to privilege against self-incrimination, and (e) the right to appellate review, all of which had been denied to Gault. The Court determined that "failure to observe the fundamental requirements of due process has resulted in instances, which might have been avoided, of unfairness to individuals and inadequate or inaccurate findings of fact and unfortunate prescriptions of remedy." Justice Fortas took some robust stabs at the doctrine of *parens patriae* in this case, calling it a phrase that has "proved to be a great help to those who sought to rationalize the exclusion of juveniles from the constitutional scheme; but its meaning is murky and its historic credentials are of dubious relevance." He also likened the juvenile court's proceedings against Gault to a "kangaroo court."

It is important to note that in extending due process rights to juveniles and introducing more formalized procedures into juvenile courts, the major tenets of *parens patriae* have not been voided. What has changed is the previously almost unbridled discretion of juvenile authorities. The due process protections extended under *Gault* do not automatically apply in all cases, either; rather, they apply only in adjudication hearings likely to result in a juvenile's deprivation of liberty (Hemmens et al., 2003).

In re Winship

A third significant Supreme Court case involving the juvenile court is *In re Winship* (1970). In 1967, 12-year-old Samuel Winship was accused of stealing $112 from a woman's purse taken from a locker. Since the juvenile court system was developed from civil law, the standard of proof required for conviction was the civil system's "preponderance of the evidence." Winship was adjudicated delinquent in a New York court based on this standard and ordered to spend 18 months in a state training school. Winship appealed his case to the New York Supreme Court, which denied it on the grounds that a delinquent adjudication is not a conviction, that it affects no rights or privileges such as the right to vote or hold office, and that because juvenile proceedings are not criminal proceedings, there can be no deprivation of due process. (Perhaps in this decision we can appreciate Justice Fortas's point about the murkiness of *parens patriae* and how its collection of euphemisms can be used in ways far from being "in the best interests of the child.")

In Justice William J. Brennan's majority opinion reversing Winship's conviction, he noted that despite the euphemisms employed by the juvenile courts, a conviction is a conviction and deprivation of liberty is deprivation of liberty no matter what name the places of confinement go by. The Court ruled that when commitment to a secure facility is a possibility, the "beyond a reasonable doubt" standard of proof must extend to juvenile adjudication hearings even though juvenile proceedings are civil in nature.

McKeiver v. Pennsylvania

In 1968, 16-year-old Joseph McKeiver was charged with robbery, larceny, and receiving stolen goods. McKeiver was represented at the adjudication hearing by counsel, and he requested a jury trial, which was denied. Adjudicated delinquent and placed on probation, he lost all appeals in lower courts and eventually appealed to the Supreme Court. The sole issue before the Court in *McKeiver v. Pennsylvania* (1971) was "Do juveniles have the right to a jury trial during adjudication hearings?" The Court ruled that they do not, thus backing away somewhat from their due process momentum and reaffirming *parens patriae* to some extent. In delivering the Court's majority opinion, Justice Harry Blackmun wrote:

> The imposition of the jury trial on the juvenile court system would not strengthen greatly, if at all, the fact-finding function, and would, contrarily, provide an attrition of the juvenile court's assumed ability to function in a unique manner. It would not remedy the defects of the system . . . and would once again tend to place the juvenile squarely in the routine of the criminal process.

Justice Blackmun added that "[i]f in its wisdom, any State feels the jury trial is desirable in all cases or in certain kinds, there appears to be no impediment to installing a system embracing that feature." The Court did not rule that the states cannot provide juveniles with this due process right, only that they are not constitutionally required to do so.

Breed v. Jones

Breed v. Jones (1975) recommenced the Supreme Court's program of applying due process rights to juveniles. Seventeen-year-old Gary Jones, a chronic delinquent, was charged with armed robbery in 1970. A petition was granted alleging that Jones had committed the acts outlined therein, and an adjudicatory hearing was held on this matter. At the hearing, the judge found that the allegations in the petition were true (in effect, meaning that Jones was guilty) and continued the proceedings for a dispositional hearing upon completion of the predisposition report. At the disposition hearing, the judge ruled that Jones was not amenable to treatment available to the juvenile court and ordered him transferred (waived) to adult court.

Jones's counsel petitioned for a writ of habeas corpus before the juvenile court and then the California Court of Appeal, alleging a claim of double jeopardy in violation of the Fifth and Fourteenth Amendments. Both courts denied the petition, stating that jeopardy did not attach to his adjudicatory hearing. The case finally arrived at the Supreme Court, which in a unanimous decision declared that double jeopardy did, indeed, attach to Jones's adjudicatory hearing. Remember that although the adjudicatory hearing is nominally a civil process and not technically a trial, it is the functional equivalent of a trial in that a "finding of fact" against the respondent can result in a substantial loss of liberty. The Court essentially ruled that Jones was subjected to the burden of two trials for the same offense; therefore, the double jeopardy clause of the Fifth Amendment had been violated. Practically, the ruling meant that a waiver to adult court cannot occur after jeopardy attaches, and jeopardy attaches at the adjudicatory hearing when evidence is first presented.

Schall v. Martin

Gregory Martin, age 14, was arrested in 1977 and charged with armed robbery, assault, and possession of a weapon. Martin was held in detention pending adjudication because the court determined that he was at "serious risk" of further criminal activity if released. He was adjudicated delinquent after spending 15 days in detention. Martin's attorney filed a writ of habeas corpus challenging the constitutionality of preventative detention while awaiting a fact-finding hearing. The issue before the Supreme Court in *Schall v. Martin* (1984) was whether the preventative detention of a juvenile charged with a delinquent act is constitutional. The Court ruled that preventative detention of juveniles was constitutionally permissible because it serves a legitimate state interest in protecting both society and the juvenile from the risk of further crimes while awaiting a hearing. In effect, this ruling established that juveniles do not enjoy the right to bail consideration, and it reasserted the *parens patriae* interests of the state in promoting the best interests of the child.

Graham v. Florida

Another major juvenile case is *Graham v. Florida* (2010), in which 17-year-old Terrance Graham was sentenced to life in prison without possibility of parole. Graham had been convicted of robbery when he was 16 and placed on probation. He was subsequently arrested for an armed home invasion and admitted to several other armed robberies. The sentencing judge considered him to be highly dangerous and beyond rehabilitation. However, the Supreme Court overturned Graham's sentence. As Justice Anthony Kennedy wrote in the majority opinion:

> The Constitution prohibits the imposition of a life without parole sentence on a juvenile offender who did not commit homicide. A State need not guarantee the offender eventual release, but if it imposes a sentence of life it must provide him or her with some realistic opportunity to obtain release before the end of that term.

As a result, dozens of other juveniles sentenced to life without parole are now entitled to be resentenced.

Miller v. Alabama

The last relevant juvenile case to be examined is *Miller v. Alabama* (2012), in which Evan Miller, age 14, and another boy, after indulging in alcohol and marijuana, robbed, beat with a baseball bat, and killed a neighbor. The boys then returned later and set fire to the neighbor's trailer to destroy evidence. Miller and the other boy were convicted of murder and sentenced to life without possibility of parole. The Supreme Court's majority opinion held that mandatory life without parole for juveniles violates the Eight Amendment's prohibition on cruel and unusual punishment. *Miller* extended *Graham*, which had explicitly excluded murder, to include juvenile murderers. It is important to note that the Court did not invalidate all juvenile sentences of life without parole. It only ruled that they should not be mandatory and that judges must assess a juvenile's potential for rehabilitation and consider the youth's home environment, the circumstances of the offense, and how the youth's age might have influenced the perpetration of the criminal act.

THE JUVENILE DEATH PENALTY

The greatest moral issue associated with juvenile justice is application of the death penalty to individuals who committed their crimes when they were juveniles. From 1973 to 2003, a total of 22 juvenile offenders were executed in the United States, 13 (59 percent) of them in Texas (Streib, 2003). Note that the ultimate penalty has been applied only to persons who committed their murders when they were juveniles in particularly heinous and depraved ways. The issue has gone before the Supreme Court on four occasions.

The first was *Eddings v. Oklahoma* (1982). In 1977, Monty Lee Eddings, age 16, and several companions stole an automobile to run away from their homes. Sometime during the trip, Eddings was pulled over by an Oklahoma Highway Patrol officer. When the officer approached the car, Eddings shot and killed the officer with a shotgun. After Eddings was arrested and found guilty, the state presented three aggravating circumstances that it maintained warranted the death penalty. The judge allowed only Eddings's youthful age to be entered as a mitigating factor, rejecting others such as the abusive treatment he received at home. In vacating Eddings's death sentence, the Supreme Court ruled that in death penalty cases, the courts must consider any and all mitigating factors in deciding whether to impose the death sentence, although the Court did not rule on how judges should weigh the relevance of those factors.

The next such case was *Thompson v. Oklahoma* (1988). William Thompson, age 15, was one of four persons charged with the brutal murder of his former brother-in-law. All four persons were found guilty and sentenced to death. The Supreme Court granted certiorari to consider whether a sentence of death for a crime committed by a 15-year-old is cruel and unusual punishment. In effect, Thompson's attorney was asking the Court to draw the line at an age below which it was constitutionally impermissible to execute juveniles. Using the "evolving standards of decency that marks the progress of a maturing society," the Court drew the line at 16 years, hence sparing Thompson's life.

Stanford v. Kentucky (1989) involved even more heinous murder circumstances. Kevin Stanford, age 17, and his accomplice repeatedly raped and sodomized a female during and after their commission of a robbery at a gas station, after which they drove her to a secluded area where Stanford shot her in the face and in the back of the head. In a 5-4 decision, the Supreme Court ruled that if states choose to execute juveniles who were 16 or 17 at the time of the commission of their crimes, it was constitutionally permissible. The *Thompson* and *Stanford* cases taken together thus set the minimum age for the execution of juveniles at age 16.

There were certain indications in *Stanford* that some of the justices were anxious to revisit the juvenile death penalty issue again as soon as possible, and that their intention was to eventually rule it unconstitutional. Their opportunity came 16 years later, when they heard *Roper v. Simmons* (2005). Seventeen-year-old Christopher Simmons and two younger accomplices burglarized a home, kidnapped the owner, tied her up, beat her, and threw her alive off a high bridge into the river below to drown. Simmons had been saying to friends before the crime that he wanted to commit a murder and bragged about having done so afterward.

Simmons was sentenced to death for this crime, but his sentence was overturned by the Missouri Supreme Court. The state of Missouri then petitioned the US Supreme Court to reverse this. In a 5-4 decision, the Court decided to redraw the age line at 18 years, below which it was now constitutionally impermissible under the Eighth Amendment prohibition against cruel and unusual punishment to execute anyone. This case brought a blizzard of *amicus curiae* (literally, "friend of the court") **briefs**, which are presented to the Court arguing in support of one side or the other by interested parties not directly involved with the case. Parties filing amicus briefs in favor of Simmons included the European Union, the American and British Bar Associations, the American Medical and Psychological Associations, and 15 Nobel Prize winners. Six states filed amicus briefs in favor of Roper (superintendent of the prison in which Simmons was incarcerated), arguing in support of capital punishment for juveniles.

In writing the majority opinion, Justice Anthony Kennedy noted that the United States was the only country in the world that gives official sanction to the juvenile death penalty, and that such a penalty contravenes the United Nations Convention on the Rights of the Child, which every country in the world has ratified save Somalia and the United States. (As Justice Antonin Scalia noted in his dissent, however, whether all these countries honor the Convention in practice as well as on paper is open to question.) Kennedy also noted the neurological evidence of the immaturity of the adolescent brain but went to some length to announce that neither this information nor the opinion of the world community was controlling on the Court's decision.

Supreme Court decisions have to have at least the appearance of being based on constitutional grounds. Statements devoid of strictly legal reasoning are relegated to dicta (nonbinding explanatory statements). The Court cannot justify decisions with statements such as "the scientific evidence compels us" or "world opinion demands." This would be politics, not law. Thus, the majority opinion cited *Atkins v. Virginia*

(2002), in which the Court ruled that the execution of those who are mentally retarded constituted cruel and unusual punishment under the Eighth Amendment, because of the lesser degree of culpability attached to the mentally challenged, and noted that such reasoning should have even greater power when applied to juveniles. The Court also cited state legislation by noting that a national consensus against executing juveniles existed, as evidenced by the fact that a plurality of states (30) either barred execution for juveniles or banned the death penalty altogether. Finally, Justice Kennedy noted that UK laws were particularly relevant to the case given the English origins of the Eighth Amendment, and that UK law had banned the juvenile death penalty as cruel and unusual in 1930 and subsequently banned the death penalty in its entirety.

Figure 8.3 presents a summary of Supreme Court cases altering the nature of juvenile court proceedings from *Kent* (1966) to *Miller* (2005).

ERODING THE DISTINCTION BETWEEN ADULT AND JUVENILE COURT SYSTEMS

In their dissenting opinions in *Winship*, Justices Warren Burger and Potter Stewart complained that this decision, along with the *Kent* and *Gault* decisions, were eroding the differences between juvenile and criminal courts—in effect, that they were

Figure 8.3 Supreme Court Cases Altering the Nature of Juvenile Court Proceedings, 1966–2012

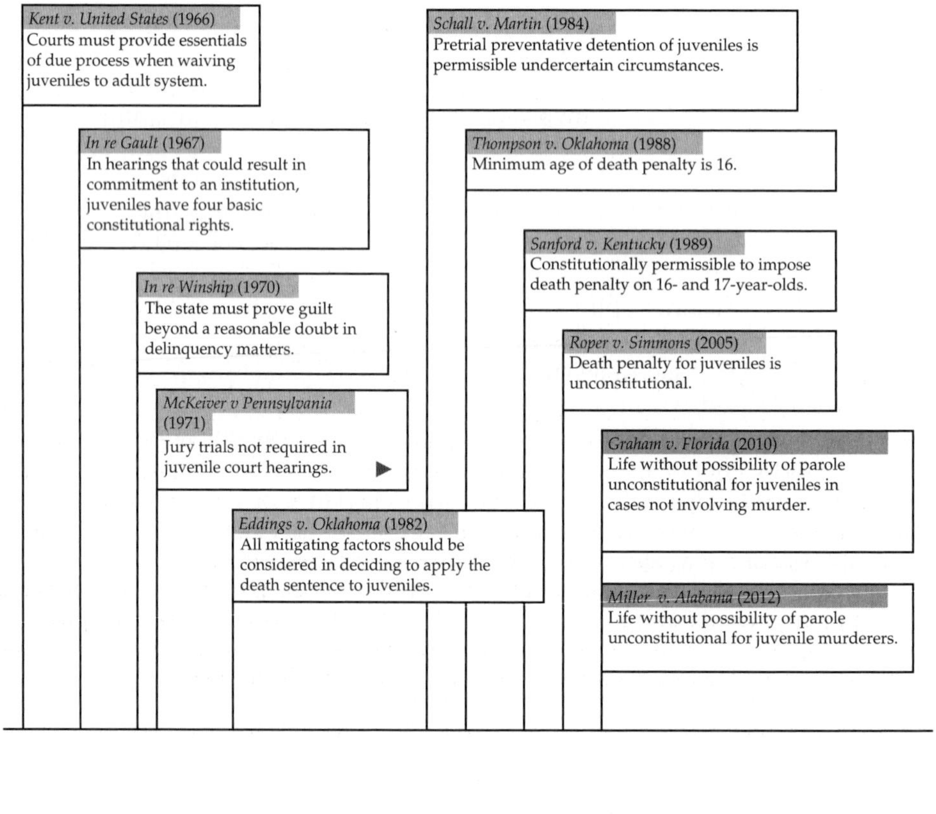

Kent v. United States (1966)
Courts must provide essentials of due process when waiving juveniles to adult system.

In re Gault (1967)
In hearings that could result in commitment to an institution, juveniles have four basic constitutional rights.

In re Winship (1970)
The state must prove guilt beyond a reasonable doubt in delinquency matters.

McKeiver v Pennsylvania (1971)
Jury trials not required in juvenile court hearings.

Eddings v. Oklahoma (1982)
All mitigating factors should be considered in deciding to apply the death sentence to juveniles.

Schall v. Martin (1984)
Pretrial preventative detention of juveniles is permissible undercertain circumstances.

Thompson v. Oklahoma (1988)
Minimum age of death penalty is 16.

Sanford v. Kentucky (1989)
Constitutionally permissible to impose death penalty on 16- and 17-year-olds.

Roper v. Simmons (2005)
Death penalty for juveniles is unconstitutional.

Graham v. Florida (2010)
Life without possibility of parole unconstitutional for juveniles in cases not involving murder.

Miller v. Alabama (2012)
Life without possibility of parole unconstitutional for juvenile murderers.

ISSUE HIGHLIGHT

Neuroscience and Young Brains: Less Guilty by Reason of Adolescence?

Ever since *Roper v Simmons* (2005), the issue has arisen about how much confidence we should put on neuroscience in determining the level of culpability of adolescents who commit horrendous crimes. Neuroscience arguments focus on the emotional irrationality of youthful conduct, but the law only requires guilty intent (*mens rea*), which asks only if a defendant rationally knew that a harmful act would result from one's actions. This raises the issue of how much blameworthiness we can ascribe to young offenders, and should they ever be tried as adults given they obviously are not? Should culpability be less or equal to what we ascribe to adults?

Less

Neuroscience has put the "juvenile" back in juvenile justice and vindicates both the presence of a separate juvenile system and what reformers have been saying for over two centuries. It is an exact science that proves the rational brain is undeveloped in juveniles while the emotional brain is on overdrive. This being the case, how can we possibly argue that juveniles should be held to the same level of culpability for their actions as adults? The adolescent brain is undergoing dramatic changes in ways that affect the young's ability to reason. They can't weigh the consequences of their decisions, nor can they delay gratification, in the same way that adults can because the reasoning process is freighted with too much emotion. The adult system places less culpability on "heat of passion" assaults and murders and considers low IQ (another brain-based factor) to be a mitigating factor. So if these "brain things" are mitigating factors for adults, why shouldn't the immature adolescent brain be considered a general mitigating factor for all juveniles? Thus, juveniles should be tried in juvenile court, where they have a chance of rehabilitation while their brains mature. We are not saying that mitigation on the basis of youth is an excuse, however, and trying them in juvenile court is not the same as absolving them of all responsibility. They must pay for their acts, but in a humane way according to what modern science tells us, and they should never be tried as adults and warehoused in adult prisons as irredeemably evil.

Equal

Neuroscience is not an exact science like physics or chemistry. It relies only on probabilistic generalizations about adolescents as a *class of individuals* from numerous brain scans; it is not very helpful in making highly individualized determinations about *specific* juveniles before the court. Thus, making inferences about specific individuals and his or her intentions from aggregate data derived from the group to which he or she belongs is a mistake. We may ask if Christopher Simmons's brain was any less mature at 17 years of age than millions of other adolescents who did not plan, execute, and brag about a horrendous crime. His planned actions were highly indicative of his ability to form the requisite *mens rea* and hardly indicative of impulsiveness. We know that people with low IQ (less than 70) lack understanding of the long-term consequences of their behavior, but low IQ is a known property of individuals and one that does not apply to Simmons. To argue that Simmons's crime, and many others like his, was a direct result of the normal maturational process that we all experienced is fallacious. Adolescence can be a trying time, but the overwhelming majority of us emerge from it without committing horrible crimes. To say that even the worst juvenile thugs must be retained in the juvenile system and kept locked up there only until adulthood is a risk that society should not have to take. Imagine a 17-year-old brutally raping and killing his 7-year-old neighbor, serving four years in juvenile detention, and then being released back into the community at age 21 supposedly "rehabilitated."

criminalizing juvenile courts. These rulings clearly have helped to create a juvenile court system that more closely reflects the procedural guidelines established in adult criminal courts. Juveniles have given up some benefits, such as the informality of solicitous treatment, a high level of confidentiality, and the sealing of their juvenile records, to gain others (formal due process rights). Only time will tell if this convergence of systems results in more just outcomes for juveniles than they received under unmodified *parens patriae*.

One interesting example of extending adult criminal standards to juveniles is the application of provisions of the 1996 Megan's Law to them. **Megan's Law** (named for Megan Kanka, age seven, who was kidnapped, raped, and murdered by a twice-convicted sex offender), requires law enforcement agencies in all 50 states to register sex offenders in their area. The law requires adjudicated delinquent sex offenders as well as convicted adult sex offenders to register with law enforcement agencies as sex offenders for the rest of their lives. Although most might agree that such a consequence is appropriate for a 17-year-old boy convicted of raping a toddler, but should it apply to a 12-year-old boy who moons a group of younger children or to a juvenile who grabs the breasts of a female classmate in the lunchroom? Megan's Law has been applied to cases such as these, thus making no distinctions between predatory sex offenders and incidents that we used to pass off as adolescent playfulness (Trivits & Repucci, 2002). Surely not all sex offenses are created equal, and to treat them as if they were trivializes the experiences of the truly brutalized while elevating the youthful peccadilloes to the point where any boy could be stigmatized for life. This is not meant to excuse the behaviors just described, or to belittle how the targets of those behaviors may have felt about their experiences; it is just a reminder of the principle of proportionality.

RESTORATIVE JUSTICE

Because of high levels of recidivism among juvenile and adult offenders as well as the skyrocketing costs of incarceration, alternative forms of dealing with them have emerged. One major innovation came from an Office of Juvenile Justice and Delinquency Prevention grant that called for strategic development of juvenile justice policies and models based on the philosophy that juvenile crime is a social problem best handled using a variety of social resources. One of the major consequences of this grant has been the application of *restorative justice* in juvenile corrections (and often in adult corrections as well) over the past quarter century (Bazemore & Umbreit, 1994).

Restorative justice may be defined as "every action that is primarily oriented toward justice by repairing the harm that has been caused by the act" and "usually means face-to-face confrontation between victim and perpetrator, where a mutually agreeable restorative solution is proposed and agreed upon" (Champion, 2005, p. 154). Though relatively new in Western correctional systems, it has been suggested that the concept is an ancient one, despite a multitude of competing histories and claims as to where it originated, what it was to accomplish, and how it was to achieve these goals (Sherman & Strang, 2002).

Much of the appeal of restorative justice, according to Kelly Richards (2005), is not so much attributable to the failure of other correctional philosophies, as some have claimed, but rather to the widespread acceptance of other concepts of contemporary culture, such as "self-help, New Age, therapy, and recovery" (p. 384). That is, the general cultural acceptance of the therapeutic "And how did that make you feel?" sentiment set the stage for the academic and correctional acceptance of restorative justice. The "healing" approach also gained impetus when various victim's rights movements emerged in the 1970s (Bazemore & Umbreit, 1994). Richards (2005) also follows many in asserting that the origins of restorative justice have been mythologized and romanticized by accounts that tend to resurrect images of the "noble savage" behaving in far more "civilized" (nonpunitive) ways than people in contemporary societies, and that advocates of restorative justice sometimes slip into viewing the offender as a victim.

All previous models, whether retributive or rehabilitative in orientation, were "offender driven" (i.e., how do we respond to the offender?) and ignored the needs of victims and the community. These older models held the legal position that the victim of a crime was the state and that the debt incurred by the offender was owed to society. Restorative justice defines crime and delinquency as offenses committed by one person against another, not against a bloodless state, and in doing so personalizes justice by engaging the victim, the offender, and the community in a process of *restoring* the situation to its preoffense status as far as possible. Thus, restorative justice gives equal weight to the needs of offenders, victims, and the community (Bazemore & Umbreit, 1994). The philosophy of restorative justice was formally endorsed by the American Correctional Association in 1994 and again in 2004 (Walsh, 2006).

Under the general philosophical rubric of restorative justice, a model for juvenile probation known as the *balanced approach* emerged. The balanced approach focuses on three equally important components for the sanctioning of juvenile offenders. First, juveniles are to be held accountable for their actions. Central to this notion is creating awareness among offenders regarding how their actions impact their victims and the community. In addition to the usual dispositional treatments, there is a greater focus on restitution and community service. The second component under the balanced approach is community protection. This element addresses directly the growing public fear of crime by focusing on community-based programming and surveillance designed to limit nonproductive time for juveniles while maintaining supervision levels. Examples of this ideal include midnight basketball programs and after-school programs. Both have shown success in providing "voluntary incapacitation" for participants (Mueller & Heck, 1997). The balanced approach also provides for the development of employment and educational skills for juvenile offenders through competency development programs.

An integral part of the restorative justice balanced approach is victim–offender reconciliation programs (VORPS). These programs bring offenders and victims together (voluntarily) in face-to-face meetings that are facilitated by a trained mediation counselor to iron out ways in which the offender can right the harm done to the victim. Victims are afforded the opportunity to let offenders know how their victimization has hurt them and affected their lives, and offenders are able to put a face to what was otherwise an abstract victim. These meetings may spark rehabilitative feelings of guilt and empathy in offenders who may never have previously experienced such feelings following their delinquent or criminal behavior. As part of the process, a contract is worked out between victim, offender, and mediator laying out what the offender has to do in order to repair the damage he or she has caused. This contract (usually involving monetary restitution and verbal and written apologies) is monitored for compliance by the mediator, who makes a report to the court if necessary. It is assumed that VORPS may assuage some of the rage and helplessness often felt by crime victims and thus lead to psychological closure for them. VORPS have been extremely successful, with one study reporting that 97 percent of victims involved express satisfaction (Coates, 1990). Similar positive results have been found in Britain, Canada, and Germany, with a few negative results muddying the water a bit (reviewed in Walsh, 2006).

As part of its overall mission, the Office of Juvenile Justice and Delinquency Prevention has embraced the balanced approach to restorative justice for juvenile offenders, and many states have followed suit (Carter, 2006; Lauen, 1997). Current juvenile justice policy ranges broadly from state to state. Several authors have suggested that the lack of continuity in juvenile treatment has led to a system with no common understanding of the developmental stages associated with children (Krisberg & Austin, 1993). Further, there clearly is no commonly accepted theory or philosophy about what causes juvenile delinquency, and policy therefore seems to be a hodgepodge of stopgap interventions sprinkled with crime control ideals (see Walker, 1998). Criminologists have constructed a variety of theories concerning human behavior and the causes of crime, but these causes are rarely addressed in modern juvenile justice policy—and perhaps they should not be, since they often are poles apart in their assumptions about human nature. However, if these theories can integrate the harder and more sophisticated data coming from the neurosciences (e.g., those earlier in this chapter) and from the biosocial sciences in general, we will have more cause for optimism.

Restorative justice is not meant to replace traditional methods of dealing with delinquents and criminals but rather to complement them. The method can be slotted into a graduated system of sanctioning that begins with restorative solutions and escalates into more coercive methods for offenders who persist in victimizing others (Braithwaite, 2006). For instance, with a first offender who has committed a minor crime, the strategy might be to treat the matter outside of the traditional justice system and entirely in restorative terms (mediated by a court official like a probation officer). This could be escalated to formal probation for a subsequent offense, then to electronic monitoring, and finally to incarceration if the offender persists. However, because restorative justice is about victims as well as offenders, restorative aspects may still be attached to specific cases even if the offender is incarcerated. As Sherman and Strang (2007) put it: "Offenders would be subjected to increasing constraints on their freedom if they persisted in crime, but they would always be encouraged to meet with their victims [if victims so desire] to explain their crime and offer to make amends" (p. 88).

How well does restorative justice work? The answer depends on what we want to accomplish and for whom. First and foremost, we want to reduce recidivism. The general consensus is that restorative justice works best for low-risk offenders with a capacity for empathy and remorse, but also that it can work well as a valuable entrée into other rehabilitative programs for higher-risk offenders that focus on criminogenic risk factors (Lilly, Cullen, & Ball, 2007). A study assessing the overall effects on recidivism from 32 different studies found that 72 percent reported restorative justice participants were less likely to recidivate than nonparticipants, although the effect was weak (Latimer, Dowden, & Muise, 2001). The same researchers found that among 13 studies testing victim satisfaction with the process, only one study reported victim dissatisfaction and, overall, that participating victims reported greater satisfaction with their case outcomes than nonparticipating victims. Of course, these findings must be viewed in terms of self-selection bias. That is, both victims and offenders take part in restorative processes on a voluntary basis and therefore are at least partially open to the goals of the process. Nevertheless, restorative justice is another weapon in the correctional armamentarium that although having only minor effects on most offenders, at least gives the previously neglected victims a voice in the justice process that they appear to appreciate.

SUMMARY

Juvenile justice stems from civil law, and as such, the commonalities between the two are readily visible. The juvenile system deals with both status offenses and delinquency: the former are applicable only to juveniles; the latter involves actions that are crimes if committed by an adult. Until recently, proof standards and courtroom procedures were much the same for both categories. However, recent Supreme Court decisions have created a juvenile justice system that more closely reflects the adult criminal justice system, especially in cases involving serious delinquent behavior.

Juveniles commit a disproportionate number of both property and violent crimes, and this has been true across time and cultures. Recent scientific evidence relates this situation to the hormonal surges of puberty juxtaposed with an adolescent brain undergoing myriad changes. Although most adolescents commit anti-social acts, only a small proportion continue to commit them after brain maturation is completed. This evidence was presented to the Supreme Court in a 2005 juvenile death penalty case.

The history of juvenile justice has three distinct periods. Originally, Western culture relied heavily on parents to control children. As society has changed, however, so have the expectations regarding juvenile delinquency. Institutional control of wayward youth was the model from the mid-1500s until the inception of the juvenile courts. In the United States, this occurred in the late 1800s and early 1900s. The juvenile court model, following the doctrine of *parens patriae*, continues today, but recently, there has been a movement away from the broad discretion formerly accorded to juvenile courts to a model that more closely reflects the constitutionally granted protections afforded to adult offenders. Much of this change has issued from the increased waivers of juveniles to adult courts and from the often-arbitrary control that juvenile justice authorities have exercised over juveniles.

The due process "revolution" in juvenile courts beginning with *Kent v. United States* (1966) is summarized in Figure 8.3. Some commentators deplore this trend as having criminalized the juvenile courts; others applaud it as assuring that juveniles are afforded due process rights and are not treated arbitrarily. *Parens patriae*, under which the "best interests of the child" are to be protected, has not disappeared altogether, and restorative justice is a promising compromise between the punitive approach of the adult courts and the sometimes overly protective nature of some juvenile courts in the past.

DISCUSSION QUESTIONS

1. How does the civil law differ procedurally from the criminal law in juvenile courts?
2. Discuss the development of childhood as a separate class of citizen in Western culture.
3. Discuss the doctrine of *parens patriae* in relation to the development of the juvenile court system in the United States.
4. Should the courts seriously consider the hormonal and neurological evidence as valid legal defenses reducing (but not eliminating) culpability for juveniles?
5. Do you agree with the majority opinion in *Roper v. Simmons* (2005)? Support your arguments with reference to Justice Kennedy's affirming opinion or Justice Scalia's dissenting opinion. Both opinions are available by typing the case name in any Web search engine.
6. Do you think that restorative justice is workable? If so, in what circumstances would and would it not be?

CHAPTER TERMS

Amicus curiae **briefs**
Binding out
Bridewells
Child savers
Delinquents
Judicial waiver
Megan's Law

Parens patriae
Paterna pietas
Patria potestas
Progressives
Prosecutorial discretion waiver
Restorative justice

Status offenses
Statutory exclusion
waiver
Waived

References

Bazemore, G., & Umbreit, M. (1994). *Balanced and restorative justice*. Washington, DC: Office of Juvenile Justice and Delinquency Prevention, US Department of Justice.

Binder, A., Geis, G., & Bruce, D. (2001). *Juvenile delinquency: Historical, cultural, and legal perspectives*. Cincinnati, OH: Anderson.

Braithwaite, J. (2006). Narrative and "compulsory compassion." *Law and Social Inquiry, 31*, 425–446.

Butts, J., & Mitchell, O. (2000). Brick by brick: Dismantling the border between juvenile and adult justice. In J. Butts & O. Mitchell, *National Institute of Justice 2000: Vol. 2. The nature of crime: Continuity and change*. Pp. 167–213 Washington, DC: National Institute of Justice.

Bynum, J., & Thompson, W. (1999). *Juvenile delinquency: A sociological approach*. Boston, MA: Allyn & Bacon.

Carter, K. (2006). Restorative justice and the balanced approach. In A. Walsh (Ed.), *Correctional assessment, casework, and counseling* (4th ed., pp. 8–11). Lanham, MD: American Correctional Association.

Champion, D. (2005). *Probation, parole, and community corrections* (5th ed.). Upper Saddle River, NJ: Prentice Hall.

Coates, R. (1990). Victim-offender reconciliation programs in North America: An assessment. In B. Galaway & J. Hudson (Eds.), *Criminal justice, restitution, and reconciliation* (pp. 125–134). Monsey, NY: Criminal Justice Press.

Collins, R. (2004). Onset and desistence in criminal careers: Neurobiology and the age–crime relationship. *Journal of Offender Rehabilitation, 39*, 1–19.

del Carmen, R., Parker, V., & Reddington, F. (1998). *Briefs of leading cases in juvenile justice*. Cincinnati, OH: Anderson.

Ellis, L. (2003). Genes, criminality, and the evolutionary neuroandrogenic theory. In A. Walsh & L. Ellis (Eds.), *Biosocial criminology: Challenging environmentalism's supremacy* (pp. 13–34). Hauppauge, NY: Nova Science.

Ellis, L., & Walsh, A. (2000). *Criminology: A global perspective*. Boston, MA: Allyn & Bacon.

Garland, B., & Frankel, M. (2006). Considering convergence: A policy dialogue about behavioral genetics, neuroscience, and law. *Law and Contemporary Problems, 69*, 101–113.

Gottfredson, M., & Hirschi, T. (1990). *A general theory of crime*. Stanford, CA: Stanford University Press.

Hart, N. (1832). *Documents relative to the House of Refuge, instituted by the Society for the Reformation of Juvenile Delinquents in the City of New-York*. New York, NY: Mahlon Day.

Hemmens, C., Steiner, B., & Mueller, D. (2003). *Significant cases in juvenile justice*. New York, NY: Oxford University Press.

Junger-Tas, J. (1996). Delinquency similar in Western countries. *Overcrowded Times, 7*, 10–13.

Krisberg, B., & Austin, J. (1993). *Reinventing juvenile justice*. Newbury Park, CA: SAGE.

Knoll, C., & Sickmund, M. (2012). *Delinquency cases in juvenile court, 2009*. Washington, DC: National Center of Juvenile Justice.

Latimer, J., Dowden, C., & Muise, D. (2001). *The effectiveness of restorative justice practices: A meta-analysis*. Ottawa, ON: Department of Justice Canada.

Lauen, R. (1997). *Positive approaches to corrections: Research, policy, and practice*. Lanham, MD: American Correctional Association.

Lawrence, R., & Mueller, D. (2003). School shooting and the man-bites-dog criterion of newsworthiness. *Youth Violence and Juvenile Justice, 1*, 330–345.

Lilly, J., Cullen, F., & Ball, R. (2007). *Criminological theory: Context and consequences*. Thousand Oaks, CA: SAGE.

McCrae, R., Costa, P., Ostendorf, F., Angleitner, A., Hrebickova, M., Avia, M., . . . Smith, P. (2000). Nature over nurture: Temperament, personality, and life span development. *Journal of Personality and Social Psychology, 78*, 173–186.

Mennel, R. (1973). *Thorns and thistles*. Hanover, NH: University of Hanover Press.

Moffitt, T. (1993). Adolescent-limited and life-course-persistent antisocial behavior: A developmental taxonomy. *Psychological Review, 100*, 674–701.

Moffitt, T., & Walsh, A. (2003). The adolescence-limited/life-course persistent theory and antisocial behavior: What have we learned? In A. Walsh & L. Ellis (Eds.), *Biosocial criminology: Challenging environmentalism's supremacy* (pp. 125–144). Hauppauge, NY: Nova Science.

Mueller, D., & Heck, C. (1997). The neutral-zone as one example of community wide problem solving. In Q. Thurman & E. McGarrell (Eds.), *Community policing in a rural setting*. Cincinnati, OH: Anderson. pp. 115–121.

OJJDP Statistical Briefing Book. Online. Available: https://www.ojjdp.gov/ojstatbb/crime/qa05101.asp?qaDate=2017. Released on October 22, 2018.

Restak, R. (2001). *The secret life of the brain*. Washington, DC: Joseph Henry Press.

Richards, K. (2005). Unlikely friends? Oprah Winfrey and restorative justice. *Australian and New Zealand Journal of Criminology, 38*, 381–399.

Schmalleger, F. (2003). *Criminal justice today* (5th ed.). Englewood Cliffs, NJ: Prentice Hall.

Sharp, P., & Hancock, B. (1995). *Juvenile delinquency: Historical, theoretical, and societal reactions to youth*. Englewood Cliffs, NJ: Prentice Hall.

Sherman, L., & Strang, H. (2007). *Restorative justice: The evidence*. London, England: Smith Institute.

Small, M. (1997). Juvenile justice: Comments and trends. *Behavioral Sciences and the Law, 15*, 119–124.

Snyder, H., Espiritu, R., Huizinga, D., Loeber, R., & Petechuck, D. (2003). *Prevalence and development of child delinquency.* Child Delinquency Bulletin Series. Washington, DC: US Department of Justice, Office of Juvenile Justice and Delinquency Prevention.

Springer, C. (1987). *Justice for juveniles.* Washington, DC: US Department of Justice, Office of Juvenile Justice and Delinquency Prevention.

Steiner, B., & Hemmens, C. (2003). Juvenile waiver 2003: Where are we now? *Juvenile and Family Court Journal, 54,* 1–24.

Streib, V. (2003). The juvenile death penalty today: Death sentences and executions for juvenile crimes, January 1, 1973–June 30, 2003. Retrieved from http://www.deathpenaltyinfo.org/juvdeathstreib.pdf

Trivits, L., & Repucci, N. (2002). Application of Megan's Law to juveniles. *American Psychologist, 57,* 690–704.

US Census Bureau. (2010). *Statistical abstracts of the United States.* Washington, DC: Author. Retrieved from http://www.census.gov/prod/2010pubs/03statab/vitstat.pdf

Walker, E. (2002). Adolescent neurodevelopment and psychopathology. *Current Directions in Psychological Science, 11,* 24–28.

Walker, S. (1998). *Sense and nonsense about crime and drugs: A policy guide* (4th ed.). Belmont, CA: Wadsworth.

Walsh, A. (2002). *Biosocial criminology: Introduction and integration.* Cincinnati, OH: Anderson.

Walsh, A. (2006). *Correctional assessment, casework, and counseling* (4th ed.). Lanham, MD: American Correctional Association.

Walsh, A., & Beaver, K. (2008). The promise of evolutionary psychology for criminology: The examples of gender and age. In J. Dunteley & T. Shackleford (Eds.), *Evolutionary forensic psychology.* Pp. 20–37 Oxford, England: Oxford University Press.

Walsh, A., & Ellis, L. (2007). *Criminology: An interdisciplinary approach.* Thousand Oaks, CA: SAGE.

White, A. (2004). *Substance use and the adolescent brain: An overview with the focus on alcohol.* Durham, NC: Duke University Medical Center.

Whitehead, J., & Lab, S. (1996). *Juvenile justice: An introduction.* Cincinnati, OH: Anderson.

Cases Cited

Atkins v. Virginia, 536 U.S. 304 (2002)

Breed v. Jones, 421 U.S. 517 (1975)

Eddings v. Oklahoma, 445 U.S. 104 (1982)

Ex Parte Crouse, 4 Whart. 9 (Pa. 1838)

Graham v. Florida, 560 U.S. 321 (2010)

Haley v. Ohio, 332 U.S. 596 (1948)

In re Gault, 387 U.S. 1 (1967)

In re Winship, 397 U.S. 358 (1970)

Kent v. United States, 383 U.S. 541 (1966)

McKeiver v. Pennsylvania, 402 U.S. 528 (1971)

Miller v. Alabama, 567 U.S. 460 (2012)

Roper v. Simmons, 543 U.S. 551 (2005)

Schall v. Martin, 104 U.S. 2403 (1984)

Stanford v. Kentucky, 492 U.S. 361 (1989)

Thompson v. Oklahoma, 487 U.S. (1988)

CHAPTER 9

THE LAW
AND
SOCIAL CONTROL

Frank Walters was knifed to death outside a London nightclub on October, 12, 2012; John Creeger was taken into custody for his murder three days later. Police were able to make the arrest (and subsequent conviction) of Creeger because the murder and Creeger's flight from the scene in a taxicab were caught on three of the many of closed-circuit TV (CCTV) cameras situated in London. Creeger's image was checked against thousands of faces in a database and quickly identified.

In 1890, a *Harvard Law Review* article expressed concerns about privacy issues emanating from the invention of photography. One wonders how the authors would react if resurrected into our post-9/11 world of wall-to-wall surveillance. It is estimated that an urban citizen in the United Kingdom is caught on camera an average of 300 times per day, and big cities in the United States are catching up. The rationale for this high-tech surveillance is the prevention and detection of crime, particularly terrorism. As the Creeger case testifies, CCTV cameras can be very useful in detecting crime, but to civil libertarians, it all smacks of Big Brother.

Then there is the USA Patriot Act, which has greatly enhanced the government's power to spy on its citizens in the name of deterring and detecting terrorists. All of this surveillance increases the sense of security for those who trust the government but decreases it for those who do not. Do we really care how many times a day we are caught on camera if the bad guys are caught on them too and brought to justice? What about our right to privacy? How much of it are we willing to give up in the name of safety? Benjamin Franklin once wrote, "Those who would give up an essential liberty for temporary security deserve neither." But then Franklin did not live in an age with weapons of mass destruction, Islamic terrorism, and rampant crime. When reading this chapter, consider the delicate balance between the government's power and responsibility to exercise social control and our constitutionally guaranteed right to privacy.

INTRODUCTION

If law has one overriding function, it is social control. This is evident in the central philosophical question in sociology: "How is society possible?" *Society* is a name we give to the product of countless interactions carried on by people living within some geographical and political boundary. These involve the energy of diverse individuals pursuing their personal interests in interaction with others pursuing their personal interests. This being so, it is not surprising that social life is rife with potential antagonism, conflict, and competition: rich against poor, environmentalist against developer, minority against majority, conservative against liberal, me against my neighbor, ad infinitum. As Thomas Hobbes told us long ago, if people are to live together peacefully, there must be some method for containing, organizing, or channeling human energy to produce cooperation and integration rather than conflict and disintegration. In other words, societies need the formal mechanism of social control that we call law.

WHAT IS SOCIAL CONTROL?

We define **social control** *as any action, either deliberate or unconscious, that influences conduct toward conformity, whether or not the persons being influenced are aware of the process.* The term *control* can be used as a noun to denote restriction and supervision and as a verb to denote regulation and restraint. The primary function of the law is to establish and maintain social control through a system of codified rules and regulations. Social control is a much broader concept than the law, however, because other informal mechanisms of social control, such as the informal socialization process that helps to develop our consciences, are more effective.

It is not only peaceful coexistence that makes society possible—it is peaceful and *predictable* coexistence. To the degree that members of a society abide by group rules and expectations, they will know with some degree of certainty what others will do in a variety of situations. Social life would be impossible without at least a modicum of predictability. To increase peace, predictability, and social unity, societies need mechanisms for minimizing nonconformity and deviance and for maintaining social order. Tolerance of nonconformity is a mark of a democratic society, but if such nonconforming behavior hammers too hard at the heart of deeply held standards of what is right and proper, if it jeopardizes our feelings of safety, security, propriety, and freedom, then those who conform to society's mores have a right to defend themselves against it.

A TYPOLOGY OF SOCIAL CONTROL

We may classify social control along two dimensions: direct versus indirect and formal versus informal. Direct control is coercive, and indirect control is persuasive and voluntary. Direct control is exemplified by the effect of a police officer—the uniformed symbol of law and control—on the behavior of those who are aware of the officer's presence. Those who might want to steal that CD or run that red light will not do so if they perceive the presence of the officer. People prevented from illegal behavior only by the threat of the officer are externally (directly) controlled. People who behave well regardless of the presence of an officer are controlled indirectly because they have internalized a belief in the rightness or wrongness of various acts. Indirect control is better than direct control because those who are directly controlled only can be trusted to behave well when they are being watched, but indirectly controlled individuals watch themselves. Of course, these two forms of control are not mutually exclusive; each supports and reinforces the other.

Informal control begins with the socialization process in which we internalize rules of proper conduct. Internalized rules provide us with an internal, self-regulating thermostat we call a conscience, which makes us feel guilty, anxious, and uncomfortable when we behave badly but happy and self-righteous when we behave well. Few of us are so self-controlled that we do not deviate from the norms of expected behavior at some time or another. Controls set us at odds with our hedonistic human nature; there is more truth than we are willing to acknowledge in the old saying "Everything I like is either illegal, immoral, or fattening." Plato (1960) made the same point more eloquently some 2,500 years ago: "The universal voice of mankind is always declaring that justice and virtue are honorable, but grievous and toilsome; and that the pleasures of vice and injustice are easy of attainment, and are only censored by law and opinion" (p. 47).

Being "censored by opinion" is informal censure—the merest raising of the eyebrows, the snub, the frown, the cold shoulder, the dressing down. This kind of control depends on whether we value the opinions and affections of others and on our range of significant others. Sometimes the power of significant others to control our behavior can play second fiddle to people and ideas we may never meet. The "stars" we see in movies and on athletic fields are much admired by the young, and many strive to emulate these heroes with whom they will never have direct contact.

Different kinds of socially harmful behaviors, such as drug use and sexually promiscuous behavior, are tired conventions among the Hollywood set, and through the influence of the media, they have done much to destigmatize—and perhaps even glamorize—these behaviors. Stigmatization is still a powerful social control (try lighting a cigarette in a nonsmoking area if you doubt this). Stigmatizing formerly acceptable behavior (e.g., smoking in public places) and destigmatizing the formerly unacceptable (e.g., unwed motherhood), certainly has contributed powerfully to dramatic changes in the prevalence of these behaviors over the past two or three decades.

Stigma and other informal means of social control usually suffice in societies that are homogeneous with respect to important social parameters, such as race, language, and religion, but they become less so in direct proportion to the growth of diversity along these dimensions, a fact that we have seen emphasized over and again by the great social and legal thinkers. Complex and heterogeneous societies also need social peace and predictability to function properly and may need alternative methods to get it. As informal controls prove inadequate, our vices are more likely to be censored by more formal means. Formal control is the kind of structured, impersonal control exercised by the state via the law.

THE LAW AS A SOCIAL CONTROL MECHANISM

Legal sociologist Donald Black (1976) put the relationship between formal and informal controls well when he stated that "law varies inversely with other forms of social control" (p. 107). In other words, as informal controls exercised by the family, church, school, and neighborhood weaken, increasing reliance is placed on formal legal controls.

Black gives the examples of juvenile law, which is less punitive than adult law in part because juveniles are subject to more informal controls by parents and teachers compared with adults. Black's proposition explains the greater legal intervention in families of juveniles where parental authority is weak or in families where fathers are absent. The tendency of juvenile authorities to retain juveniles from broken homes in custody and to release children from intact homes to the care of their parents is sometimes interpreted as unfairly discriminating against poor children while favoring children from intact homes. But in terms of Black's proposition about the inverse relationship between formal and informal controls, this practice makes sense. Juvenile authorities make calculations about the amount of control exercised over the child by informal means. If this amount is deemed inadequate, then legal controls are substituted for those from other sources that are lacking. In a very real sense, frequent and widespread use of the law to contain deviant behavior is a measure of the extent of how the more fundamental social institutions—family, church, and school—have weakened.

The fundamental distinctions between direct versus indirect and formal versus informal control allows us to bring the concept of social control more sharply into focus. These two dichotomies create four separate social control mechanisms: **direct/ formal**, **direct/informal**, **indirect/formal**, and **indirect/informal**. To illustrate these separate (but often significantly overlapping) mechanisms, we use an incident in Nathaniel Hawthorne's novel *The Scarlet Letter*, a book familiar to most students.

In this novel, Hester Prynne is found guilty of adultery and bearing a child out of wedlock by the authorities of the seventeenth-century Massachusetts Bay Colony. The colony is a very close-knit and homogeneous community, which means that there is strong and widespread agreement about the norms of acceptable behavior. Indicative of the seriousness with which Hester's behavior is viewed, among the various penalties discussed by women during her trial are branding with hot irons and death, "for the shame she has brought on us all." As far as the women are concerned, Hester violated the values that underlie the family, the very basis of society, and must be punished so that others are not tempted to do the same. Her judges sentence her to forever endure the scorn of her community by wearing a badge of shame on her dress—an elaborately embroidered letter *A*, labeling her as an adulteress. Her transgression is so great as to warrant the direct intervention of formal law, but her actual punishment is direct but informal "social" punishment—the reproach and ostracism of all who know of her shame. Figure 9.1 illustrates the social control typology.

Punishment and Deterrence

Citizens of the Massachusetts Bay Colony believed that sexual activity outside of marriage was such a serious offense that the norms forbidding it had been codified into law, and the law provided penalties for violations. The people viewed the

Figure 9.1 Social Control Typology Applied to Hester Prynne's Punishment

	Formal	Informal
Direct	Hester's arrest, trial and sentencing by agents of the state	Social shame and ridicule suffered by Hester
Indirect	The threat of legal sanctions perceived by onlookers ("it could happen to me")	Norms reinforced by viewing and participating in Hester's punishment

exercise of legal power against Hester as legitimate—that is, right and just *as defined by those affected by that power*. Thus, the legitimacy of any law (and, by extension, the power to enforce it) rests at bottom with those affected by the power, not those who exercise it.

Adultery, while still a crime carrying the possibility of imprisonment in twenty-one states and in the armed forces, no longer—rightly or wrongly—is considered any business of the state by the majority of Americans. Most American citizens would probably consider any enforcement of adultery statutes resulting in imprisonment of the participants to be an illegitimate use of state power today.

When people violate the rules of acceptable behavior, they usually feel guilty in proportion to the level of disapproval attached to the violation. But the internal restraints of guilt and anxiety are not always strong enough to allay deviant temptations, and some people lack effective internal restraints altogether. It has always been considered wise to augment internalized rules with the tangible experience of punishment. Just as praise and rewards express social approval and value, punishment expresses social condemnation. As Brubaker (1993) put it, "Punishment, like praise, publicly expresses our determinations of what people deserve" (p. 81). Hester's punishment functioned in her community to reaffirm and define the boundaries of acceptable behavior and thus was directed just as much at onlookers as at Hester herself. Those who witnessed her shame were reinforced in their belief in the correctness of the social norms, more so because they themselves participated in the various actions and gestures of ostracism and contempt that constituted Hester's punishment. Thus, the *direct and formal* control over Hester functioned simultaneously as a powerful *indirect and informal* control for others.

Deterrence has long been considered the primary function of punishment and is defined as the prevention of criminal acts by the use or threat of punishment. Deterrence may be either *specific* or *general*. **Specific deterrence** refers to the effect of the imposed punishment on the future behavior of the person who is punished. If the offender desists from future criminal activity, we say that the punishment worked; if he or she continues to engage in crime, we say that it did not. There is evidence that punishment (imprisonment) is not a significant deterrent for most offenders, although it does appear to have an impact on white-collar criminals and minor blue-collar offenders for whom there exist informal social controls (Siegel, 2006).

The influence of punishment on specific individuals being punished has a lot to do with the **contrast effect**, which is the difference between the circumstances of punishment and the offender's usual life. Incarceration is a nightmarish contrast for those who previously enjoyed the company of a loving family and the security of a valued career. For such people, the mere prospect of experiencing the embarrassment of public disgrace that threatens the families and careers of those who have invested time, effort, and emotional energy in acquiring and nurturing them is a strong deterrent. This is why having a strong stake in conformity is such a powerful mechanism of informal social control. On the other hand, for those lacking strong family ties and a commitment to a legitimate career, punishment has little effect because the disparity between the punishment and their normal lives is minimal. As Bob Dylan sang, "When you ain't got nothin', you got nothin' to lose."

General deterrence refers to the preventive effect of punishment on those who have witnessed but not personally experienced it (e.g., Hester Prynne's witnesses). Convicted and punished offenders serve as examples to the rest of us regarding what may happen if we violate the law. As Radzinowicz and King (1979) asserted:

> People are not sent to prison primarily for their own good, or even in the hope that they will be cured of crime. Confinement is used as a measure of retribution, a symbol of condemnation, a vindication of the law. It is used as a warning and deterrent to others. It is used, above all, to protect other people . . . from the offender's depredations. (p. 296)

Some may insist that our moral conscience and not the threat of punishment keeps us from committing criminal acts. Such a view invests the human conscience with an essence independent of its origins and maintenance. Conscience is the name we give to the internalized norms of our social groups admonishing us to conform to its obligations, and we feel anxious, guilty, and ashamed when we act contrary to those obligations. But how long would we feel these pangs of conscience and trust them to keep us in check were it not for Plato's censorship by "law or opinion"? Plato argued that it is only the real threat of punishment—physical, psychological, or both—that keeps any of us honest. As one wag has suggested, "Locks exist to keep honest folks honest; they present no problem for the dishonest." We may all have different thresholds for crossing the line from law-abiding to criminal behavior, but few of us are immune from doing so altogether.

To illustrate his point, Plato (1960, pp. 43–44) recounts the allegory of an honest shepherd named Gyges in Lydia. One day while wandering from the campsite, Gyges descends into an opening in the earth made by an earthquake and finds a gold ring. While sitting around the campfire that night with the other shepherds, he chances to turn the ring and becomes invisible. Upon turning it again, he reappears and notes with pleasure that he can disappear and reappear at will. Thus armed, Gyges goes to the royal palace, seduces the queen, and conspires with her to murder the king and usurp the throne. Plato asserts that given such an opportunity to be free of the prying and censorious eyes of others, to be free of both formal and informal social controls, "no man can be imagined to be of such an iron nature that he would stand fast in justice" (p. 44).

The anonymity of the modern city functions as a kind of ring of Gyges, rendering us "invisible" to the censorious judgments of others. As so many social theorists have pointed out, the city frees us from the social controls exercised by the close-knit communities of yesteryear. We have seen that the use of law as a social control mechanism varies inversely with the loss of more informal and effective methods of social control. To the extent that this is true, the use of law to control behavior becomes a measurable marker of the failure of other forms of control.

The failure of informal controls can be roughly gauged by comparing the size of the legal profession in the United States with those of other countries. Abadinsky (2003) tells us that more than 50,000 lawyers are admitted to the bar in the United States each year, and that the United States has one lawyer for every 345 people compared to one for every 1,220 in the United Kingdom and one for every 9,000 in Japan. Americans rely on law as an acceptable form of dispute resolution, and perhaps the number of lawyers in the United States is as much a sign of cultural evolution as it is of the lack of informal mechanisms of control. Americans continue to file millions of legal actions each year to keep each new batch of lawyers occupied. These legal actions involve everything from the Supreme Court hearing death penalty appeals to debtors and creditors fighting over a few dollars in small claims court.

Other Philosophies of Punishment

There are other philosophies of punishment besides deterrence. A philosophy of punishment involves justifying the imposition of a painful burden on unwilling subjects. When we justify something, we are providing reasons for doing it in terms of morality ("It's the right thing to do") and in terms of the goals we wish to achieve ("Do this, and we'll get that"). Legal scholars have traditionally identified four other major objectives or justifications for punishing criminals besides deterrence: retribution, incapacitation, rehabilitation, and reintegration.

Retribution

Retribution is the justification for punishment exemplified by the "eye for an eye" concept. It is a "just desserts" model that demands punishment match the degree of harm inflicted on victims: minor crimes deserve minor punishments, and more serious crimes deserve more serious punishment. This law the most honestly stated justification for punishment because it posits no secondary purpose, such as the reform of criminals or deterring them from further criminal behavior. California is among the states that have explicitly embraced this justification in their criminal codes (California Penal Code Sec. 1170a): "The Legislature finds and declares that the purpose of imprisonment for a crime is punishment" (Barker, 2006, p. 12).

Retribution as presently conceived is not Durkheimian revenge "that ceases only when exhausted." Rather it is constrained revenge curbed by proportionality and imposed by neutral parties bound by laws mandating respect for the rights of individuals against whom it is imposed. Logan and Gaes (1993) go so far as to claim that only retributive punishment "is an affirmation of the autonomy, responsibility, and dignity of the individual" (p. 252). By holding offenders responsible and blameworthy for their actions, we are treating them as free moral agents, not as mindless victims of fate.

Incapacitation

Incapacitation refers to the inability of incarcerated criminals to victimize people outside the prison walls. Its rationale is aptly summarized in James Q. Wilson's (1975) trenchant remark: "Wicked people exist. Nothing avails except to set them apart from innocent people" (p. 391). It goes without saying that incapacitation "works" while criminals are incarcerated. Elliot Currie (1999) uses robbery rates to illustrate, stating that in 1995 there were 135,000 inmates in state and federal institutions whose most serious crime was robbery and that each robber on average commits five robberies per year. Had these robbers been left on the streets, they would have been responsible for an additional 135,000 × 5 or 675,000 robberies in addition to the 580,000 actual robberies reported to the police in 1995. The morality and goals justification in this philosophy of punishment is simple social defense.

Rehabilitation

Rehabilitation means to restore or return to constructive or healthy activity. The rehabilitative goal is based on a medical model that used to view criminal behavior as a moral sickness requiring treatment. Today, this model views criminality in terms of "faulty thinking" and criminals as being in need of "programming" rather than "treatment." It is different from deterrence in that the goal of rehabilitation is to change offenders' attitudes so that they come to accept that their behavior was wrong, not to deter them by the threat of further punishment.

Reintegration

The goal of **reintegration** is to use the time that criminals are under correctional supervision to prepare them to reenter the free community as well to be as equipped to do so as possible. In effect, reintegration is not much different from rehabilitation, but it is more concrete and pragmatic, focusing on concrete programs such as job training rather than on psychological attitude change.

Table 9.1 presents a summary of the key elements of the punishment philosophies discussed in terms of justifications, strategies, focus, and their images of offenders. The commonality they all share is the prevention of crime.

Black's Styles of Social Control

Donald Black (1976, p. 5) identified four legal "styles" of social control: *penal, therapeutic, compensatory,* and *conciliatory*. Briefly, the **compensatory style** involves some breach of obligation resulting in an accused debtor and an alleged victim. The solution necessary to restore social harmony is payment of the debt. The **conciliatory style** usually involves a breach in a harmonious relationship between two people who are now disputants (e.g., husband and wife in a divorce suit). There is no necessary consideration of who is right or wrong, only concern for a fair and reasonable resolution of the problem. These two styles are dealt with elsewhere in this book in the context of civil law.

Our concern in this chapter is with the penal and therapeutic styles. The **penal style** is one in which a person has violated some aspect of the penal code (has

Table 9.1 *Summary of Key Elements of Different Punishment Philosophies*

	Retribution	Deterrence	Incapacitation	Rehabilitation	Reintegration
Justification	Moral: Just desserts	Prevention of further crime	Risk control and community protection	Offenders have correctable deficiencies	Offenders have correctable deficiencies
Strategy	None: Offenders simply deserve to be punished	Make punishment more certain, swift, and severe	Offenders cannot offend while in prison	Treatment to reduce offenders' inclination to reoffend	Concrete programming to make for successful reentry into society
Focus of Perspective	The offense and just desserts	Actual and potential offenders	Actual offenders	Offenders' faulty thinking patterns	Offenders' concrete needs to reintegrate into society
Image of offenders	Free agents whose humanity we affirm by holding them accountable	Rational beings who engage in cost–benefit calculations	People not to be trusted but to be constrained	Good people who have gone astray will respond to treatment	Ordinary folk who require and will respond to concrete help

Adapted with permission from M. Stohr, A. Walsh, & C. Hemmens. (2009). *Corrections: A text reader.* Thousand Oaks, CA: Sage.

committed a crime) and is thus subject to punishment. The **therapeutic style** is one in which a person's unacceptable conduct is considered "sick" and in need of treatment rather than the result of willful misbehavior deserving of punishment. These styles often overlap, such as when a convicted offender is deemed in need of psychiatric or substance abuse treatment. The penal style shares with the compensatory style the characteristic of being *accusatory* in that there is a victim and a wrongdoer. The therapeutic style shares with the conciliatory style the characteristic of being *remedial* (legal means are used to remedy a situation for which blame is not usually legally assigned).

The penal style of social control assigns blame to individuals for their actions and punishes them accordingly. The law assumes rational individuals engage in cost–benefit analysis ("How will I benefit from this behavior, and what might it cost me?") before they act. It follows from this rational view of human nature that the law must do what it can to tip the scale against criminal behavior by making the costs of a crime outweigh its benefits through punishing those convicted of criminal acts to a degree commensurate with the damage caused. This view invests criminals with a capacity for calculation exceeding that of most individuals but pays tribute to their capacity for moral responsibility.

Opposing this view are those who want to blame everyone and everything for crime—except the criminal. Such people question the efficacy, or even the morality, of punishment because for them, crime is "caused" by some factor in the environment (capitalism, racism, poverty, and so forth) that oppresses, degrades, and humiliates the underclass while ignoring the crimes of the rich and powerful. From this view-point, external forces determine the behavior of criminals; therefore, to punish them is to divert attention from the "true" causes of crime. Less radical advocates of this position stress personal characteristics of the typical criminal rather than some aspect of the social environment. For example, individuals with such characteristics as low IQ and impulsiveness are not likely to engage in rational cost–benefit analyses.

The personal and environmental factors just mentioned influence the probability of criminal behavior, but rightly or wrongly, the law acts *as if* criminal activity is the product of free choice. This is the only possible stance the law can take; it cannot wait for "root causes" of crime to be identified and eradicated before it responds. To the extent that our behavior is determined, punishment or the threat of punishment becomes part of the bundle of determinants, and as we have already said, the social control function of punishment is not confined to the person being punished.

SOCIAL CONTROL AND THE CRIMINAL JUSTICE SYSTEM

The criminal justice system—the machinery set up by the state to manage the criminal courts, law enforcement, and corrections—is the quintessential example of direct/formal social control, having been designed specifically for that purpose. The criminal justice system is the mechanism that enforces the laws deemed necessary for the safety and protection of society. The American criminal justice system is designed primarily to prevent injustice rather than to promote justice. In enforcing rules to prevent injustice, however, it simultaneously promotes justice. Yet the criminal justice system has come under much criticism both from conservatives (it "coddles criminals") and liberals (it is "discriminatory"). Conservatives would like to change the system by cracking down on criminals, increasing the severity of punishment, and eliminating so-called "legal technicalities" that sometimes allow factually guilty criminals to go free. The liberals' more optimistic view of human nature leads them to want to change the system in the direction of more reliance on rehabilitation, treatment programs, and use of community-based alternatives to prison (Walsh & Ellis, 2004).

IS THE UNITED STATES SOFT ON CRIME?

The belief that the United States is soft on crime is pervasive, but is it accurate? Not if our incarceration rate means anything. Figure 9.2 shows the incarceration rates per 100,000 population for selected countries in 2014 (Walmsley, 2015). Only Russia comes close to touching the US rate, and the closest any modern Western nation comes to the US rate is England and Wales, with a rate five times lower. American sentences also tend to be longer than those of other democracies (Siegel, 2006).

In fairness to the "soft on crime" view, the rate per 100,000 *citizens* incarcerated is not the same as the rate per 100,000 *criminals* incarcerated. Incarceration rates are

Figure 9.2 Incarceration Rates per 100,000 Population for Comparable Countries and Selected Other Countries in 2014

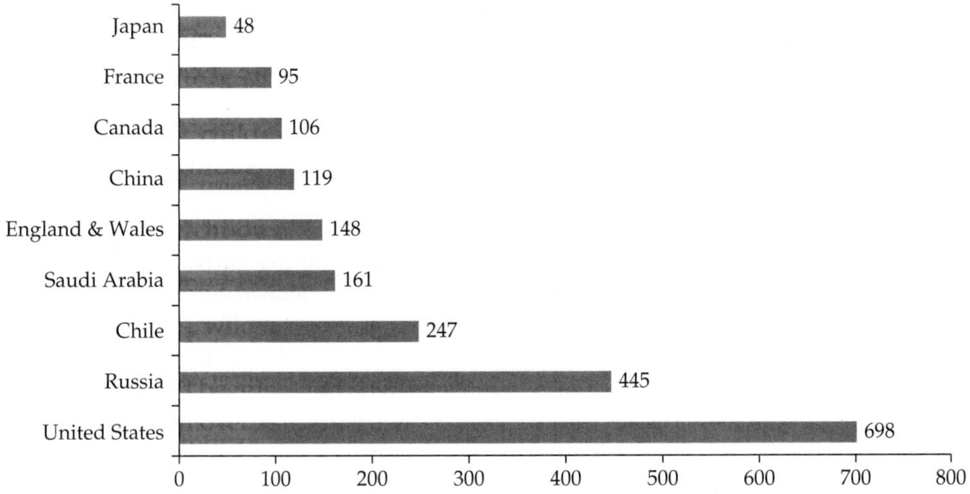

Source: Adapted from figures provided by Walmsley (2015). World Prison Population List.

determined by dividing the number of people incarcerated per 100,000 people (criminals and noncriminals alike) in the population. These calculations are useless for assessing the question at hand. We need to know the rate per 100,000 *criminals*, but we have no idea how many criminals there are in the United States, let alone in other countries. We can look at crime rates as a rough approximation, however. Mauer (2003) points out that our homicide rate is about five times that of England and Wales, which matches our five times greater incarceration rate. When it comes to property crimes, however, the US rate is about in the middle of the pack of nations (less than in Britain, for instance), yet burglars serve an average of 16.2 months in prison in the United States compared with 6.8 months in Britain and 5.3 months in Canada (Mauer, 2003). Compared to other democracies, then, we are probably hard on crime, but we are softer than authoritarian countries such as China or Saudi Arabia, which we discuss in chapter 14.

PLEA BARGAINING

The accused can mitigate the severity of punishment by cooperating with the prosecutor and engaging in **plea bargaining** (pleading guilty in exchange for a lighter sentence). About 90 percent of all felony suspects plead guilty rather than have their day in court (Siegel, 2006), which raises some legal and moral issues. Conservatives condemn plea bargaining as unwarranted leniency because criminals are punished for crimes that bear little resemblance to the ones actually committed. Liberals criticize plea bargaining because it coerces suspects to surrender their Sixth Amendment right to a trial, their Fifth Amendment privilege against self-incrimination, and their right to any subsequent appeal of their conviction (because they have admitted their guilt).

It would seem that plea bargaining offers something for everyone while leaving no one completely satisfied. Victims may be the least satisfied but have the benefit of certain conviction and at least some punishment for the offenders. The police enjoy a benefit from a plea bargain in that they are saved from numerous appearances in court. Judges and prosecutors benefit by the speedy and efficient clearing of cases, and the community as a whole saves the cost of a trial. Even criminals gain when their plea bargains result in more lenient treatment than they otherwise may have received. Thus, while the plea bargaining process draws a lot of criticism, the principal parties in the legal drama appear quite comfortable with it.

The parties most immediately involved—the prosecutor and the defendant—have the greatest incentive to use the plea bargain. The pressure on prosecutors with huge caseloads is great, and this may sometimes lead them to threaten defendants with dire consequences if they refuse to bargain. The Supreme Court upheld the constitutionality of such threats in *Bordenkircher v. Hayes* (1978). Paul Lewis Hayes had been indicted for forgery, a crime for which the maximum penalty in Kentucky was 10 years. The prosecutor offered to recommend five years if Hayes pled guilty, which he refused to do. The prosecutor then informed Hayes that he would seek a second indictment of him as a habitual offender if Hayes insisted on a trial. Hayes still refused, was indicted as a habitual offender, and sentenced to life imprisonment. An appeals court overturned Hayes's conviction as a habitual offender, but the US Supreme Court reaffirmed his conviction and declared that in the tit-for-tat world of plea bargaining, there was no element of punishment or injustice in what the prosecutor did because Hayes was free to accept or reject his offer.

It is not only prosecutors who may become vindictive about a defendant's refusal to accept a plea agreement. Judges have been accused of operating according to the "You take some of my time; I'll take some of yours" rule (Uhlman & Walker, 1980). No wonder that "experienced" defendants are anxious to bargain, but what about those who insist on their due process rights? "Such defendants may be viewed as disruptive, as lacking in any show of contrition and, therefore, deserving of more severe treatment. If convicted, they will receive sentences in excess of the norm" (Abadinsky, 2003, p. 229).

Although defendants who go to trial do receive more severe sentences if convicted, this is to be expected because these defendants are being sentenced for a more serious crime than are those who plead guilty to a reduced charge or for a specific sentence. Still, there appears to be an element of punishment attached to noncooperation. Adjusting for the effects of prior record, crime seriousness, and charge reduction, one study determined that defendants found guilty at trial were 4.76 times more likely to be imprisoned than those who pled guilty, and among those who went to prison, trial defendants received an average of 13.5 more months than plea defendants (Walsh, 1990a). We cannot say with certainty if these differences represent a penalty tacked on to the sentences of those defendants audacious enough to demand their constitutional rights, or whether it represents a reward in the form of leniency for those kind enough not to "waste" the court's time. However, the pressures to plea bargain show that those additional social control mechanisms exist even in contexts where one would think control is already maximized.

THE DEATH PENALTY DEBATE

The death penalty has been subjected to intense scrutiny over the past three decades. Given the social, political, and philosophical issues surrounding it, and particularly the finality of the sentence, it is reasonable that this ultimate form of social control should be hotly debated, although throughout much of our history, the death penalty has been considered a normal and legitimate form of punishment. It remains highly popular with the American public today, with the federal government and 31 of the 50 states retaining it as of 2018. The latest available Gallup Poll (October 2017) shows that 54 percent of Americans favor the death penalty while 41 percent oppose it (see Figure 9.3; Jones, 2018). Support for the death penalty goes up and down with crime rates. For instance, only 47 percent favored it in 1957, when the crime rate was extremely low, and 80 percent favored it in 1994, when crime rates were at their peak (Hatch & Walsh, 2016).

Legal opposition to the death penalty has revolved around the Eighth Amendment's prohibition of cruel and unusual punishment. Very few challenges to the penalty arose until the National Association for the Advancement of Colored People and the American Civil Liberties Union (ACLU) waged a joint attack on it beginning in the early 1960s. As a consequence of their efforts, pending executions throughout the country were suspended awaiting the Supreme Court's word on the matter. That word came down in *Furman v. Georgia* (1972), in which the Court decided that the death penalty per se was not unconstitutional but that the arbitrary and discriminatory way in which it was imposed did violate the Eighth Amendment.

Figure 9.3 Are You in Favor of the Death penalty for a Person Convicted of Murder?

Are you in favor of the death penalty for a person convicted of murder?

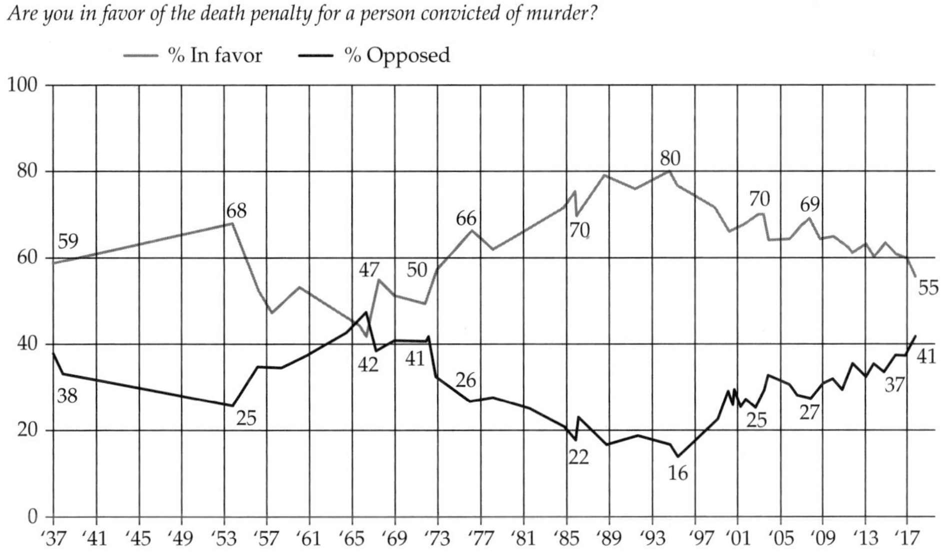

Source: Jones (2018).

Because the criteria for imposing the penalty, not the penalty itself, were found to be unconstitutional, death penalty states began the process of changing their sentencing procedures. Some states introduced the bifurcated (two-step) hearing process, with the first to determine guilt (the trial) and the second to impose the sentence with a full hearing of aggravating and mitigating circumstances that argue for or against imposition of the death penalty. Other states removed sentencing discretion and made the death penalty mandatory for certain types of homicide.

In *Gregg v. Georgia* (1976), the Supreme Court upheld the constitutionality of the bifurcated hearing, but on the same day, the Court also decided against mandatory death sentences in *Woodson v. North Carolina* (1976). Other noteworthy death penalty cases include *Coker v. Georgia* (1977), in which the Court struck down the death penalty for rape as "grossly disproportionate," and *Penry v. Lynaugh* (1989) and *Stanford v. Kentucky* (1989), in which the Court allowed the imposition of the death penalty on the mentally retarded and on juveniles, respectively. However, the Court reversed itself on Eighth Amendment grounds in the matter of the execution of the mentally retarded in *Atkins v. Virginia* (2002) and in the matter of executing juveniles in *Roper v. Simmons* (2005). In *Atkins*, six justices concluded that the overwhelming disapproval of the world community must be considered a relevant factor (although not a controlling one) in determining the imposition of capital punishment on mentally retarded individuals, and as we have seen, similar reasoning was apparent in *Simmons*. Much to the chagrin of constitutional conservatives such as the late Justice Antonin Scalia, the plurality of the Supreme Court seems to be increasingly respecting international *jus cogens* norms. A final case of interest is *Baze and Bowling v. Rees* (2008). Ralph Baze and Thomas Bowling were two Kentucky inmates who challenged the state's lethal injection method of execution as cruel and unusual. In a 7-2 decision, the Supreme Court ruled that lethal injection did not violate the Eighth Amendment.

The death penalty is carried out relatively rarely in the United States today. In early 2017, there were 2,905 prisoners under a sentence of death, and as shown in Figure 9.4, a total of 20 were executed in 2016 (Death Penalty Information Center [DPIC], 2017a). Of those under sentence of death, 42.3 percent were white, 41.8 percent black, 13.1 percent Hispanic, and 2 percent "other." Only 1.6 percent of death row inmates were women. Among people executed from 1977 to April 2017, 55.5 percent were white, 34.4 percent black, 8.2 percent Hispanic, and 1.6 percent other (DPIC, 2017).

Arguments Against the Death Penalty

Opponents of capital punishment view the death penalty as a barbaric anachronism that the United States shares with such countries as China and Iran. On this issue, we have distanced ourselves from countries most like ourselves in other respects and associated ourselves with countries holding values usually considered antithetical to ours. The United States is the only Western democracy that retains the death penalty. Japan, South Korea, India, Singapore, and Thailand are the only other democratic countries with the death penalty, although it is rarely used. The countries with the highest rates of executions—China, Iran, and Saudi Arabia—have repeatedly demonstrated their lack of respect for the dignity of

Figure 9.4 Executions in the United States 1976 to August 13, 2018

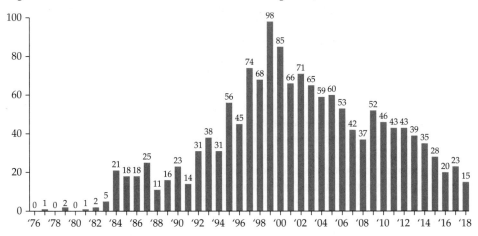

Source: Death Penalty Information Center. (2018). Facts about the death penalty.

human life, and opponents of capital punishment argue that our "evolving standards of decency" should preclude the United States from being associated with them in any way.

Proponents of capital punishment often cite its supposed deterrent effect, but opponents say that there is no sound evidence that it is a deterrent. Friedman (1984) points out that while capital punishment may function as a deterrent in societies that use it frequently, mercilessly, and without much legal ado, "[i]t cannot work well in the United States, where it is bound to be rare, slow, and controversial" (p. 214). Studies conducted to assess the issue "have failed to support the hypothesis that the death penalty is a more effective deterrent to criminal homicide than long-term imprisonment" (Radelet & Borg, 2000, p. 45). Given this reality, and if deterrence is the only rationale for capital punishment, then it is argued that we should join the other democracies and leave governmental killing of citizens to nondemocratic regimes. Even Russia and South Africa, our two closest incarceration rate competitors, have abandoned the practice (Radelet & Borg, 2000).

Not only does capital punishment not serve as a deterrent, say death penalty abolitionists, executions actually may "cause" a slight rise in the homicide rate due to the "brutalization effect" (Siegel, 2006). Advocates of the brutalization argument point to what they see as the contradictory message that is sent by the state killing people to teach other people that killing is wrong. The brutalization effect (if there actually is an effect) is said to have its influence on "fringe" killers through this message, which abolitionists interpret as saying that it is proper to kill someone who has wronged you (Hatch & Walsh, 2016). According to abolitionists, killing criminals puts a society sanctioning such treatment on the same moral level as the murderer.

Death penalty advocates often cite their belief that execution is cheaper than holding people in prison for life. Opponents point out that a sentence of death actually is more costly to the taxpayer financially than a sentence of life imprisonment without the possibility of parole. However, the DPIC (2015) cites a 2011 California study stating if the sentences of all prisoners on that state's death rows were commuted to life without parole, the state would save $130 million per year. The ACLU (see Hatch & Walsh, 2016) reports that there was a $1.1 million difference between the least expensive death penalty prosecution and trial, which cost $1.8 million, and the most expensive non–death penalty murder prosecution and trial, which cost $661,000. Think of how many public safety employees California could hire with the money it spends pursuing a goal it knows will be thwarted in all but the tiniest fraction of instances.

The most telling argument against capital punishment, one that must give pause to even its most ardent advocates, is the possibility of executing the innocent. The mere possibility of such an occurrence is abhorrent to abolitionists. Erroneous convictions in capital cases, while rare, occur more often than we would like to think. Careful research has turned up 350 convictions in capital cases up to 1988 that later were determined to have been erroneous, including cases in which "victims" later turned up alive and well (Radelet & Bedau, 1988). Later data from the DPIC (2015) reveal that 150 convicted people have been exonerated and freed from death row across the country since 1973. There are many instances of incompetent defense attorneys who miss potentially important evidence and even vindictive prosecutors who purposely hide exculpatory evidence from the defense (Albanese, 2005). Because such mistakes and illegalities occur, and since death is irreversible, the death penalty must be abolished, opponents maintain.

Yet another argument is that human life is sacred, and thus no person has the right to take any other person's life. To do so is to play God, who according to this argument has the sole right to decide when a person's life is to be ended. When the state steps in to kill convicted criminals, it is both denying the sanctity of life and playing God. This is why "leaders of Catholic, most Protestant and Jewish denominations are strongly opposed to the death penalty, and most formal religious organizations in the United States have endorsed statements in favor of abolition" (Radelet & Borg, 2000, p. 54).

Arguments Favoring the Death Penalty

Supporters of capital punishment agree that few convincing studies have demonstrated a deterrent effect of capital punishment in the United States. However, they argue that if the death penalty were imposed with greater certainty and frequency, we may be able to demonstrate such an effect. Additionally, the deterrence studies that have been conducted examine all homicides, but the majority of homicides are crimes of passion for which the death penalty is not an option. They say studies should be conducted only on the effect of capital punishment on homicides committed with deliberation and premeditation. These death penalty–eligible homicides are by definition crimes that the perpetrators have thought about (premeditated), and thus presumably have thought about the penalty as well.

Under conditions of uncertainty regarding either/or questions (God either exists or He does not; the death penalty either deters or it does not), we can only place our bets on the option that promises the most advantageous outcomes. *If* the death penalty deters and we choose to use it, we prevent the death of innocent victims. If we do not choose to use it, we will be party to the murders of those victims. If the death penalty *does not* deter and we choose to execute murderers, we have gained nothing, and the only cost we have sustained are the lives of those who deserved to die anyway. This cost–benefit assessment (what society stands to lose or gain under these conditions) places the burden of proof squarely on the shoulders of those who wish to abolish the death penalty, not on its proponents. In other words, society stands to gain more by retaining the death penalty *if* it deters than it stands to gain if the death penalty *does not* deter and we abolish it; thus, the onus must be on those who wish to deprive society of this alleged protection to prove their case more convincingly.

One study of the criminal activity of 39 convicted murderers *after* they had served their time for their murders found that between them, they had 122 arrests for serious violent crimes (including 7 additional murders), 218 arrests for serious property crimes, and 863 "other" arrests (DeLisi, 2005, p. 165). Had these 39 murderers been executed, much social harm in the form of pain, suffering, and economic loss would have been averted. Death penalty advocates may agree with abolitionists, however, that the same harms would have been averted had they been sentenced to life without parole.

Death penalty advocates also may agree that it is more costly to impose a sentence of death than one of life imprisonment but claim this is only because of the seemingly interminable appeal process. Limiting appeals and bringing the case quickly to closure would save taxpayers' money and perhaps also enhance the deterrent effect of the death penalty. The Supreme Court moved in the direction of placing limits on death penalty appeals in *Coleman v. Thompson* (1991), but we have seen little evidence that limitations have actually occurred. In fact, the time lapse between conviction and execution increased from an average of 14.4 months in the 1950s to an average of 122 months in 2000 and to 174 months (14.5 years) in 2010 (Snell, 2011).

Death penalty advocates reject the argument that use of capital punishment in the United States places the country on the same moral plane as the authoritarian countries using it. The moral equivalency of physically equivalent acts is not automatically valid. If someone restricts your freedom, binds you, and forcibly transports you to a place of captivity, it is called "kidnapping" and is a crime, but if a police officer does the same thing to you, it is called "arrest." The officer, as a legitimate holder of legal authority, is representing the moral order of society and is acting in its name, as is the state executioner. Arrest is a moral and legitimate social reaction to some immoral harm done to society. And the death penalty is also a moral and legitimate social reaction to an immoral act. Thus, death penalty advocates argue that the moral difference between *arrest* and *kidnapping* is the same as the moral difference between *execution* and *murder*.

Those who argue that the imposition of the death penalty is racially biased and therefore should be abolished erroneously conflate the justice, usefulness, and morality inherent in the death penalty with its maldistribution among those eligible to receive it (van den Haag, 1993). If the death penalty appears discriminatory, keep in mind that in *McClesky v. Kemp* (1987), the Supreme Court ruled that statistical aggregates do not per se establish a violation of the Eighth or Fourteenth Amendments in individual cases. Maldistribution is certainly unjust, but it does not make those who receive the death penalty any less deserving of it. The solution to biased sentencing is equity in sentencing, which implies neither the abolition nor the retention of capital punishment. Proponents of capital punishment argue that equity in sentencing (given similarly situated defendants, of course) should be achieved by imposing more death sentences, not by imposing the death penalty on no one (van den Haag, 1993).

The prospect of an innocent person being executed is troubling to proponents of capital punishment. However, the figure cited most often by abolitionists of 350 innocent convictions is misleading. Radelet and Bedau (1988) did indeed list 350 erroneous *convictions*, but only 25 of them actually were executed, and the 150 exonerated individuals reported by the DPIC (2015) were, after all, exonerated. Mistakes are made in all human activities, but before we give up any of them, we generally weigh the cost and benefits of doing so. Death penalty advocates believe the benefits of retaining this ultimate form of social control outweigh the benefits of abolishing it. Given more accurate evidence gathering and evaluating techniques (e.g., DNA testing) and greater scrutiny of the criminal justice system by the public, the media, and watchdog groups such as the Innocence Project (a nonprofit legal clinic that takes on postconviction cases dealing with DNA evidence), the likelihood of innocent defendants being executed today is much less than it has been in the past.

ISSUE HIGHLIGHT

Pathways to Wrongful Convictions

Unfortunately, people sometimes are convicted for crimes, including capital murder, that they did not commit. Federal Defender's Office investigator Virginia Hatch and her collaborator Anthony Walsh (2016) list the "big six" causes of wrongful convictions in their best-selling book, *Capital Punishment: Theory and Practice of the Ultimate Punishment.*

Eyewitness misidentification. People tend to trust eyewitness evidence, but it is the most unreliable form of evidence. A witness may not be telling the truth for any number of reasons. A witness also may be telling the truth as her or she sees it, but perception and/or memory may not be accurate. His or her recollection may be influenced by outside suggestion, such as police coaxing, or by their own subconscious desires to please investigators.

False confessions. False confessions are a major cause of wrongful convictions. For a variety of reasons such as mental illness, some people volunteer a confession to gain notoriety. For instance, Jon Karr claimed to have killed six-year old Jon Benet Ramsey in 1996, but DNA from the crime scene showed he could not have. Voluntary confessions are discovered in 27 percent of DNA exoneration cases. Other confessions called "compliant confessions" are prompted by stressful police interrogations in which a person may seek short-term relief by confessing.

Bad science. The use of improper or invalidated forensic science has been a contributing factor in about 50 percent of DNA wrongful conviction cases. This "bad science" is really "poorly used" or "insufficiently validated science" rather than bad per se, and it includes things such as fingerprint evidence, hair comparison/analysis, DNA analyses, and other forensic practices. Fingerprint evidence is not as foolproof as the movies make it out to be when we have partial or smudged prints. The same is true with manual examination of hair samples, although if the root is still attached, technicians can get better results by extracting DNA. However, even DNA evidence can be suspect if not meticulously handled. DNA testing is a complex process, and human beings make errors, take shortcuts, and even fudge data. A number of police labs have been found to falsify DNA results.

Snitch testimony. This is testimony by informants serving time or awaiting sentencing who make up stories to support the police or prosecutor's version in exchange for some consideration, such as a reduction in own sentences or charge dismissal. "If you can't do the time, just drop a dime" is the operational principle here, and it is a key issue in about 15 percent of DNA exonerations.

Ineffective defense counsel. Ineffective attorneys fail to investigate a client's alibi or pursue alternative suspects, fail to call forensics experts, may miss courts dates, or simply fail to grasp all of the legal nuances of the case. This is simply poor legal representation.

Prosecutorial misconduct. Typically, this involves the withholding of exculpatory evidence, the awareness and ignoring of witness perjury, and the improper use of evidence. Even with clear evidence of prosecutorial misconduct, prosecutors rarely are held accountable. A study of 381 cases reversed due to police and prosecutor misconduct found that not a single prosecutor was held accountable. When prosecutors are acting as advocates for the people, they enjoy absolute immunity from legal actions against them for any action in the furtherance of that advocacy.

THE LAW AND SOCIAL CONTROL OF POLITICAL DISSENT

A government's need to control extremes of political dissent is even more important than its need to control crime. The rights to free speech and assembly enshrined in the Bill of Rights imply the right to dissent, but there are limits to what even democracies will tolerate. All governments, regardless of political persuasion, wish to hold on to the reins of power and attempt to do so through various mechanisms of social control. However, there are important differences in these mechanisms among authoritarian, totalitarian, and democratic regimes. Authoritarian governments demand conformity to a single party line but not political participation, thus maintaining a distinction between public and private life. Penalties are extracted from citizens only for opposition, not for failing to contribute. Totalitarian regimes do not permit political neutrality, thus blurring the distinction between public and private lives. All must participate in the political process no matter how banal it is—such as the ritual of voting for unopposed candidates. Democracies maintain the distinction between public and private lives by encouraging, but not requiring, political participation and by allowing political plurality. Democratic governments thus exercise less control over political dissent than other forms of government.

This does not mean that democratic governments will allow all forms of political nonconformity, or that they do not attempt to maintain themselves in power. Although the law is a tool used by legitimate holders of political power to hold on to that power, if the reins of power are to be turned over to others, there are also rules to accomplish this in an orderly and peaceful manner. In democratic nations, power is transferred periodically between political parties whose legitimate claim to power is not challenged.

If, however, political entities outside of the mainstream, such as the American Communist Party, claim legitimacy and a place in the political power race, parties of established legitimacy generally view it as a threat to the social and political order. Both the Republican and the Democratic parties are in effect committed to the preservation of each other. When such threats are perceived, many different methods may be used to combat them, such as the force of arms, physical harassment, public opinion, and election laws that limit participation. One or all of these forms may be—and have been—used to counter threats to the political status quo in the United States.

It has been claimed that the United States, relative to other democracies, does not have a good reputation for tolerating political dissent. As Jethro Lieberman (1972) put it, "The United States has a long history of welcoming dissent in the abstract and punishing it in the concrete" (p. 74). And Seymour Lipset (1964) has written that "more than any other democratic country, the United States makes ideological conformity one of the conditions for good citizenship" (p. 321). Whether or why the United States is less politically tolerant than other democracies is not a question we explore here. Perhaps it is necessary for new nations lacking a long cultural heritage (and thus lacking a natural conformity born of tradition) to go to greater lengths to ensure political conformity through more formal controls in the same way that it uses law to ensure social conformity in the absence of strong informal controls. Any new political force that may be perceived as a threat to a growing feeling of national unity runs the risk of suppression. The ink was barely dry on the Constitution when the first new political force in the United States—the Democratic-Republican Party, or simply the Republican Party (this party was not the forerunner of the modern Republican Party, which was founded in 1854 as an antislavery party)—felt the sting of political suppression. The Republican Party had a number of its members prosecuted under the 1798 Sedition Act for criticizing the Federalist government. The act, however, had the effect of uniting the Republican Party and did much to gain Thomas Jefferson the presidency in the 1800 election (Brinkley, Current, Friedel, & Williams, 1991, p. 186).

Populist or "fringe group" third parties in the United States can be tolerated because they generally are wrapped around a single central issue (the gold standard, the federal deficit, and so forth), none of which seriously threatens the political, social, and economic status quo. However, parties such as the socialist and communist parties, which do threaten the status quo, especially when they achieve a significant following as they did in the early 1900s, are a different proposition. By 1919, the American Socialist Party had become a serious threat to established political power and became the target of extraordinary efforts to crush it. As Charles Dunn (1982) explains:

> After the Socialists won control of some thirty-two municipal governments, their headquarters in several cities were ransacked, their funds confiscated, their leaders jailed, and their newspapers denied mailing privileges. Winning candidates were even denied seats in state legislatures and Congress. (p. 234)

The combined effect of these tactics was to destroy socialism as a viable political alternative in the United States. Yet according to Dunn (1982, p. 235), the Federal Bureau of Investigation burglarized the offices of the Socialist Workers Party no less than 92 times from 1960 to 1966. What happened here to the rule of law, to free speech, and to other constitutional protections? Political scientist Michael Parenti (1977) answers: "When change threatens the rule, the rules are changed" (p. 203).

A more welcome method of destroying the appeal of threatening third parties is to co-opt what is most appealing about their political platforms. Milton and Rose Friedman (1980) noted long ago that almost every item on the economic platform of the American Socialist Party platform of 1928 has been adopted in the United States. Among the reforms and benefits the platform called for were the 40-hour work week, unemployment benefits, Social Security pensions, public works, legalization of trade unions, child labor laws, and the establishment of government unemployment offices. These and many other items in the platform have been so integrated into American life that few today would call them "socialist" or "un-American."

Wartime constitutes another period in which governments tend to forget such niceties as civil liberties, although they usually are careful to use the law to suppress them. President Woodrow Wilson's administration made far-reaching use of the law to assure political conformity after the United States entered World War I. The Espionage Act of 1917, which defined the term *espionage* very broadly, allowed the Post Office to confiscate any "seditious material." The Sabotage and Sedition Acts of 1918 made it illegal for anyone to publicly express opposition to the war or to criticize the president or Congress. The great majority of the American people apparently supported these acts as legitimate exercises of state power, since many citizens joined groups to root out those who criticized the war or high government officials. The main targets of these groups were the socialists and communists, who opposed the war on principle. The activities of these groups are summarized by Brinkley et al. (1991):

> [The American Protective League] . . . enlisted the services of 250,000 people, who served as "agents"—prying into the activities and thoughts of their neighbors, stopping men on the street and demanding to see their draft cards, opening mail, tapping telephones, and in general attempting to impose unity of opinion on their communities. Attorney General Thomas W. Gregory described them approvingly as a "patriotic organization." Other vigilante organizations—the National Security League, the Boy Spies of America, the American Defense Society—performed much the same function. (p. 678)

These patriotic snoops functioned as a form of grassroots social control. Any person, or any groups of persons, whose philosophy ran counter to the official line had to be extremely careful, for the eyes and ears of orthodoxy were everywhere. The situation described in the preceding quotation reminds us of the Hitler Youth, Germany's system of "block wardens" during the Nazi period, and Chinese "people's mediation committees" (see chapter 14). The big difference in America is that these conditions were temporary aberrations that sprang up in response to unusual circumstances. When the war was over, things more or less reverted to normal.

This return to normalcy did not apply to the continued threats to the American political order coming from communists and socialists, however. When the constitutionality of wartime legislation was challenged, the Supreme Court proved once again that the judiciary is situated firmly in the camp of the political status quo. In *Schenck v. United States* (1919), the Court upheld the constitutionality of the Espionage Act and set forth the famous "clear and present danger" test for determining when it is permissible to curtail First Amendment rights. In *Gitlow v. New York* (1925), the

Court, even while asserting the First Amendment right to freedom of speech and binding the states to it, upheld the conviction of Benjamin Gitlow, a socialist convicted of passing out seditious (anti-war) pamphlets in New York.

Cold wars as well as hot ones can move the government to feel that it is in "clear and present danger" and thus needs to defend itself by limiting freedom of speech. The Smith Act of 1940, the Internal Security Act of 1950, and the Communist Control Act of 1954 were attempts to control and destroy the American Communist Party. The Communist Control Act has never been tested before the Supreme Court. However, the Smith Act was declared constitutional in *Dennis v. United States* (1951), and a provision of the act making it a crime to belong to the Communist Party was upheld in *Scales v. United States* (1961). The Internal Security Act, which required the Communist Party to register with the attorney general as an agent of a foreign state, was upheld in *Communist Party v. Subversive Activities Control Board* (1961). Although a number of these rulings later were qualified, these decisions point to the political nature of the Supreme Court.

Threats to the nation tend to lead to greater state power, which the state rarely relinquishes after the threat is passed. Some have expressed the fear that passage of the **USA Patriot Act** on October 11, 2001, in response to the horrendous terrorist attacks of September 11, 2001, is the beginning of the end of American civil liberties. The act grants federal agencies greater authority to track and intercept private communications, gives greater powers to the Treasury Department to combat corruption and prevent money laundering, and creates new crimes, penalties, and procedures for use against domestic and foreign terrorists (Doyle, 2002). Others feel that if the Patriot Act prevents another 9/11, it is all right with them. After all, if you are not engaged in any of the preceding activities, what do you have to fear?

While no one suggests that law enforcement is interested in intercepting e-mail exchanges of chili recipes or listening to someone's call home asking for money, the ACLU fears that the Patriot Act's definition of "terrorism" has great potential for abuse. The ACLU claims that the definition is broad enough to encompass the activities of several legitimate activist groups, such as Greenpeace, Operation Rescue, and the Environmental Liberation Front, which often are thorns in the side of the "establishment," and that it could put participants at risk for the same enhanced criminal penalties and asset forfeitures applied to genuine terrorists (ACLU, 2002). Furthermore, the ACLU does not believe that innocents caught up in a net could seek relief from the courts because as Greenberg (1980) points out, "From the Alien and Sedition Acts during the administration of John Adams, up to the present, *the Supreme Court has never declared unconstitutional any act of Congress designed to limit the speech of dissidents*" (p. 357; emphasis in original).

Let us not be overly critical. Every nation has the right—indeed, the obligation—to protect and preserve those things it values from perceived threats. Certainly, many communists and socialists were imprisoned for their beliefs, and that is unconscionable in a democracy. However, challenges to the status quo in many other countries have been treated much more severely. The Soviet Union executed more than 6 million of its citizens who held favorable attitudes toward capitalism (Hosking, 1985). The current threat from Islamic terrorism may be just as dangerous, but the law has evolved a more tolerant attitude since the days of the communist threat.

No one has been prosecuted or persecuted for his or her written or spoken opposition to the Patriot Act, and no one is likely to be.

THERAPEUTIC SOCIAL CONTROL: LAW AND PSYCHIATRY

Among the institutions devoted to social control is the psychiatric hospital. Psychiatry and its concepts of mental health and mental illness are potentially means of achieving social control in conjunction with the legal system. By definition, a person who is mentally ill does not conform to the behavioral expectations of society and may be referred for treatment. This "medicalization of deviance" has many critics who stress the negative side, but we should not lose sight of its positive side. If non-conformity is causing serious disruptions of individuals' lives, or if the mentally ill are a danger to themselves or to others, then the state has a duty under the doctrine of *parens patriae* to intervene. Since the goal of psychiatry is to cure and control, not punish, it is the quintessential example of Black's therapeutic social control.

On the other hand, there is real danger in saying that "by definition, a person who does not conform to the behavioral expectations of the group is mentally ill." Psychiatric disorders have a definite organic basis, and no one would dispute that these people are in need of treatment. However, there are those, who consider the whole concept of *mental* illness to be bogus, a myth used to label socially disvalued behaviors (e.g., drunkenness, drug abuse, homosexuality, and belonging to organizations such as communist or socialist parties). Placing psychiatric labels on such behavior legitimizes the use of a form of social control called psychiatry (Jones, 2004). Vago (1991) illustrates the social control function of psychiatric hospitals:

> It is not surprising to find that many state mental hospitals include people who have committed trivial misdemeanors or who have not been convicted of any crime at all, but have been sent there for "observation." The police and courts may refer individuals whose behavior appears odd for psychiatric examination, and if they are found to be "insane," they can be confined in a mental hospital against their will for long periods, in some cases, for life. (p. 148)

The former Soviet Union made widespread use of psychiatric labeling to justify locking up dissidents in mental hospitals. The ideology of Soviet psychiatry has been stated as follows: "Personal mental adjustment is to be found in the submerging of one's wishes and desires to the needs of the group or society, in the assumption that society has rights against the individual and not vice-versa" (Horowitz, 1984, p. 230). The task of Soviet psychiatrists "was to identify and *treat* political dissent" (Grimm, 1977, p. 136). "Treatment" often consisted of the involuntary administration of drugs, and one could not be considered "cured" until deemed to be in conformity with political orthodoxy, deviation from which served as the sole definition of the "illness" in the first place. We are not talking about persons with a genuine inability to cope with the realities of everyday life but rather about people who voiced their opposition to the regime one time too many.

Responding to criticisms made by the American Psychiatric Association, Soviet psychiatrists defended themselves by suggesting that the Americans look to their own misuses of the art. Among the cases they cited were those of Ezra Pound, the poet, who criticized American involvement in World War II, and General Edwin Walker, an outspoken critic of American intervention in Central America, both of whom ended up in an insane asylum (Grimm, 1977). However, Ezra Pound actively assisted the enemy during World War II by broadcasting propaganda from Italy, and General Walker was released after only five days. Soviet psychiatrists also defended themselves on the grounds that their involvement saved "patients" from a worse fate in a prison camp. The ethical dilemma of where to place their loyalty (to the patient or the government) may apply to psychiatrists and psychologists everywhere when they are employed by the state. As is the case with their Russian counterparts, American mental health professionals see their role in the criminal justice system as humanitarian, standing as scientific, morally neutral buffers between a possibly mentally ill defendant and a nonscientific judiciary bent on punishing the sick and the well alike.

Others with less charitable views see American psychiatrists and psychologists as tools of the state providing scientific authority to legitimize the state's decisions (Jones, 2004). Researchers find it strange that almost all criminal defendants referred to mental health professionals by the courts end up with some sort of psychiatric label attached to them. Scheff (1964) and Walsh (1990b) found that all referrals in their respective samples received a label indicative of some form of mental illness. Either referring judges are remarkably adept at spotting psychiatric problems, or psychiatrists are remarkably adept at spotting what judges want and then supplying the appropriate label. Holman and Gaston (1987) found that clients referred by organizations that favored more severe labels (e.g., the courts) were more likely to receive more severe psychiatric labels than those referred by other organizations. This offers support for those who believe that mental health professionals paid by the state may unwittingly serve as agents of social control (Jones, 2004).

The idea that people who engage in deviant behavior are sick and require treatment is illuminated in the case of sex offenders. In 1997, the US Supreme Court upheld a Kansas statute (*Kansas v. Hendricks,* 1997) aimed at keeping certain sex offenders behind bars under civil commitment laws *after they have served their prison terms* if they demonstrate "mental abnormality" or "personality disorder." Leroy Hendricks had numerous arrests for molesting children of both sexes and admitted that he continued to experience "uncontrollable" sexual attraction to children. The Kansas statute paved the way for other states and the federal government to pass similar involuntary confinement laws. Prior to 1990, civil commitments were limited to those who were said to suffer from mental illness, but to cover sex offenders, several states have loosened their criterion for commitment to "mental abnormality" as opposed to "mental illness." The phrase "mental abnormality" can be used to cover any kind of behavior or thinking that we disapprove of, and its use is "reminiscent of Soviet policies that institutionalized dissidents" (Grinfeld, 2005, p. 2). Whatever your thoughts about sex offenders are, the *Hendricks* decision created a special category of individuals defined as "abnormal" who may be punished indefinitely for what they *might do* if released.

"NO TAXATION WITHOUT REPRESENTATION!": A CASE OF JUDICIAL SOCIAL CONTROL

Most people in the United States feel that the use of power to enforce rules is legitimate because the law itself is seen as legitimate. Even when obeying the law hurts, as in compliance with income tax laws, few people, though they curse and complain about their unfairness, deny that income tax laws are legitimate. Tax laws are legitimate because we know that taxes are necessary if the government is to function and provide the many services private citizens cannot supply for themselves. Legislative bodies constitutionally levy taxes, supposedly with the consent of the people. If the majority of the people do not consider those taxes legitimate, then mechanisms exist to replace the legislators most responsible for levying them. Thus, vesting the ability to tax in elected bodies is a precept vital for the democratic control of public institutions.

A violation of this precept occurred in Kansas City, Missouri, in 1983. Federal district court judge Russell Clarke had ruled that the Kansas City Municipal School District had been operating a de facto segregated school system (mainly as a result of "white flight" to the suburbs) and ordered it to remedy the situation as required by federal law. The remedy involved the building of so-called "magnet schools" that would attract white suburban students back to the inner city. The facilities in these magnet schools were described by Justice Anthony Kennedy in his dissent in the case (*Missouri v. Jenkins*, 1990):

> Every school would have a 2,000 square-foot planetarium; greenhouses and vivariums; a 25-acre farm with an air-conditioned meeting room for 104 people; a model United Nations wired for language translation; broadcast capable radio and television studios with an editing and animation lab; a temperature controlled art gallery; movie editing and screening rooms; a 3,500 square-foot dust-free diesel mechanics room; 1,875-square foot elementary school animal rooms for use in a zoo project; swimming pools; and numerous other facilities.

The Kansas City Municipal School District responded to Clarke's ruling by saying that it did not have the funds (an initial total exceeding $200 million) to implement the scheme. After certain considerations were made, Clarke ruled that it must find the money and ordered the school district's property tax levy raised from $2.05 to $4.00 per $100 of assessed property value, and then later to $4.96 (Gewertz, 2000). Thus, homeowners in the school district saw their property taxes double, with a further 24 percent added later, and all by judicial fiat—not even George III was that bold! (Among the "injuries and usurpations" listed against King George in the Declaration of Independence was that he imposed "taxes on us without our consent"; "No taxation without representation!" was the rallying cry of the American Revolution.)

Taking their case to the US Supreme Court, attorneys for the state of Missouri argued that surely the doubling of taxes by order of an unelected, life-tenured federal judge (more correctly, Clarke had ordered county commissioners to do so under pain of contempt of court) violates all fundamental precepts of democratic control; surely the ruling violated Article III of the Constitution laying out the boundaries of judicial power, and surely the due process clauses of the Fifth and Fourteenth Amendments were violated by depriving citizens within the Kansas City Municipal School District of property "without due process of law."

The Supreme Court, in a 6-3 decision, was not impressed by these arguments. In authoring the Court's opinion, Justice Byron White reiterated that the Kansas City Municipal School District was segregated, that *Brown v. Board of Education of Topeka* (1954; discussed in chapter 11) required desegregation, and that the *Brown* decision placed the onus on local authorities for solving the problems of segregation. Since the local authorities had not done so, it was then incumbent on the judiciary to implement the constitutional requirement of *Brown* via a **writ of mandamus** (a court order compelling a public official to do his or her duty) compelling the school district to levy taxes adequate for compliance. That the taxation remedy impacted homeowners within the district presented no problem of conscience to the Court because the ruling "places the responsibility for solutions to the problems of segregation upon those who have themselves created the problems," wrote Justice White. By fleeing to the suburbs, white homeowners were deemed to be responsible for segregation and thus should be financially responsible for the solution.

Justice Kennedy's scathing dissent considered the ruling an insult to all Americans who want the best for their children and who strive to obtain it by their own efforts. He also considered it to be the federal bullying of a local government and its people, a usurpation by one branch of government (the judiciary) of the powers constitutionally vested in another (the legislature) and a clear violation of due process:

> Perhaps the KCMSD's Classical Greek theme schools emphasizing forensics [the art or study of argumentative discourse] and self-government will provide exemplary training in participatory democracy. But if today's dicta become law, such lessons will be of little use to students who grow up to become taxpayers in the KCMSD.

By mid-1993, the price tag for these schools had exceeded the normal school budget by $1.3 *billion*, and at one point, 44 percent of the K-12 education budget was being spent on the 9 percent of students enrolled in the Kansas City and St. Louis magnet schools (Ciotti, 1998). And despite such funding, the magnet-school students were consistently outscored on all indices of academic achievement by pupils in Missouri's underfunded nonmagnet schools, and many magnet schools even lost state accreditation (Gewertz, 2000).

A second trip to the Supreme Court (*Missouri v. Jenkins II,* 1995)—based on Missouri's reluctance to provide large, across-the-board salary increases to magnet-school teachers given the continued failures of their students and again arguing that underachievement was not attributable to de facto segregation—found a more sympathetic ear. In this decision, the Court reasoned that school segregation was no longer *de jure* (by law), as it had been at the time of *Brown,* but was now the result of other social forces. The Court also reasoned that the state had done everything practicable to remedy the segregation problem and expressed its wish to see control of the schools back in the hands of local authorities. This case did not necessarily invalidate the 1990 ruling, however. Courts are reluctant to give the impression they are ignoring precedent and therefore narrowly tailor their opinions to the specific issue at hand while endeavoring in their dicta to make other intentions known. Even so, it was the beginning of the end of the 17-year magnet school experiment, which finally ended in 1999.

This case provides an example of the awesome power of the law to exert social control despite opposition by the overwhelming majority of citizens, which can be seen as a major dysfunction of the law. Social control by any number of means is a necessity in all societies. However, the agents of control from time to time may overstep the boundaries of legitimate power, and even legitimate power sometimes may be excessively and inappropriately applied. There are those who abhor and resist social control of any kind on ideological and/or temperamental grounds, but when social controls are consistent with norms of fairness and with human dignity, they exist for the benefit of us all. A society that does not hold its citizens to standards of decent behavior is a society in trouble, as is a society that allows judges or any other authority to use citizens and their resources as a means to an ideological end, as in the case of Judge Clarke and his social engineering.

SUMMARY

Social control is a necessary process that makes human existence relatively peaceful and predictable. It involves all those mechanisms that influence people to conform to the behavioral expectations of the social group through direct (coercive) or indirect (voluntary) means as well as formal or informal means. Informal means include any that make clear those observing our conduct disapprove of it (e.g., the social snub, ostracism, direct confrontation, and so forth). Formal means are those exercised by duly authorized agents of social control whose specific mandate is to control behavior (e.g., agents of the criminal justice system).

Most of us are controlled indirectly and informally, meaning that we rely on internalized norms of conduct (conscience) to regulate our behavior. As society becomes more complex and diverse, our conscience (our informal social control) is weakened. The more we are freed of voluntary and informal restraints on our behavior, the more our behavior is likely to be controlled by direct and formal means. The use of law to control citizen behavior is a measure of the moral strength or weakness of a society.

Violations of the law often result in punishment, which is supposed to have a deterrent effect (both on those experiencing the punishment and on those witnessing it), thus preventing future violations. Whether deterrence "works" depends on a host of factors, such as the strength of our conscience, how personally rewarding our transgressions are, what we have to lose if our transgressions are discovered, and our ability to recognize and weigh the costs and benefits of transgressions.

Among Black's four styles of social control are the penal and therapeutic styles. Although these styles often overlap, the former denotes the control exercised over those who have violated the criminal codes, while the latter denotes controls exercised over those who also have violated behavioral expectations but against whom blame has not been placed. Blame is assigned and punishment applied in the first instance because the offender is held responsible for his or her actions, but blame is withheld in the second instance because the controlee is considered mentally ill and in need of treatment rather than punishment.

The criminal justice system's reason for being is to exert social control. Many issues within this system are highly controversial, such as plea bargaining, the death penalty, and differential sentencing. The race issue looms large in the latter two issues, with some scholars supposing that the criminal justice system is racist and therefore that minority defendants are treated more harshly than white defendants. There is evidence both for and against the proposition that the criminal justice system is racist.

Suppressing political dissent is even more important to defenders of the status quo than suppressing crime. Even democracies have their ways to limit the political competition among parties, which are not too ideologically separate. The United States generally is considered less tolerant of political dissent than most other democracies. This intolerance is particularly in evidence during times of war or other threats from abroad, such as the communist threat. During such times, Congress often has passed legislation limiting the free speech and activities of political nonconformists. The Supreme Court never has declared any of this legislation unconstitutional.

Psychiatry is an effective form of "scientific" social control—what better way to control dissidents than to label them mad? This form of social control was practiced extensively in the former Soviet Union. Soviet psychiatrists often defended their conduct from the criticism of foreign psychiatrists by asserting that their "treatment" was a humanitarian alternative to the prison camp. Western psychiatrists defend themselves from accusations that they are the servants of the agents of social control by also citing humanitarian concerns. Certainly, psychiatry can be used for good purposes, but by its very nature, it is highly susceptible to misuse.

A particularly egregious example of social control by the judiciary was exercised by a federal judge in Kansas City, Missouri, in 1983. He ordered the doubling of property taxes in the Kansas City Municipal School District to fund so-called "magnet schools." These schools were viewed as a method of desegregating Kansas City schools by attracting white students from the suburbs to the many benefits that would be available at them. Issues of legality, fairness, and justice were brushed aside by the Court in favor of the one overriding concern—the implementation of *Brown v. Board of Education of Topeka*. These issues were discussed from the perspective of Justice Kennedy, who wrote the dissenting opinion.

DISCUSSION QUESTIONS

1. Name two or three factors that may contribute to decreased social cohesiveness. What, if anything, can we do to minimize their impact?
2. Was Hester Prynne's punishment justified for the sake of maintaining family values as the Puritans viewed them?
3. Do you think that most people (including yourself) would act as Gyges did if they had found such a ring?

4. What are your thoughts on the greater use of law in the United States to stifle political opposition than in other democratic countries? Do you think this situation is still true today?

5. After you have thought through all the arguments presented, both pro and con, on the death penalty, what is your position? Give your reasons.

6. What are your thoughts about *Missouri v. Jenkins* (1990)? Should a judge have that much power? What might have been an alternative solution to implementing *Brown v. Board of Education of Topeka*?

CHAPTER TERMS

Compensatory style
Conciliatory style
Contrast effect
Direct/formal social control
Direct/informal social control
General deterrence

Incapacitation
Indirect/formal social control
Indirect/informal social control
Penal style
Plea bargaining
Rehabilitation

Reintegration
Retribution
Social control
Specific deterrence
Therapeutic style
USA Patriot Act
Writ of mandamus

References

Abadinsky, H. (2003). *Law and justice: An introduction to the American legal system* (5th ed.). Upper Saddle River, NJ: Prentice Hall.

Albanese, J. (2005). *Criminal justice* (3rd ed.). Boston, MA: Pearson.

American Civil Liberties Union. (2002). How the USA Patriot Act redefines "domestic terrorism." Retrieved from http://www.aclu.org/national

Barker, V. (2006). The politics of punishing: Building a state governance theory of American imprisonment variation. *Punishment and Society, 8,* 5–32.

Black, D. (1976). *The behavior of law.* New York, NY: Academic Press.

Brinkley, A., Current, R., Freidel, R., & Williams, T. (1991). *American history: A survey.* New York, NY: McGraw-Hill.

Brubaker, S. (1993). In praise of punishment. In R. Monk (Ed.), *Taking sides: Clashing views on controversial issues in crime and criminology* (pp. 44–55). Guilford, CT: Dushkin.

Ciotti, P. (1998). Money and school performance: Lessons from the Kansas City desegregation experiment. *Policy Analysis, 298,* 1–25.

Currie, E. (1999). Reflections on crime and criminology at the millennium. *Western Criminology Review* 2. Retrieved from http://www.westerncriminology.org/documents/WCR/v02n1/currie/currie.html

Death Penalty Information Center. (2015). Innocence and the death penalty. Retrieved from http://www.deathpenaltyinfo.org/innocence-and-death-penalty

Death Penalty Information Center. (2018). Facts about the death penalty. Retrieved from http://www.deathpenaltyinfo.org/documents/FactSheet.pdf

DeLisi, M. (2005). *Career criminals in society.* Thousand Oaks, CA: SAGE.

Doyle, C. (2002). *The USA Patriot Act: A sketch.* Washington, DC: Congressional Research Service, Library of Congress.

Dunn, C. (1982). *American democracy debated.* Morristown, NJ: Scott, Foresman.

Durkheim, E. (1951). *The division of labor in society.* Glencoe, IL: Free Press.

Friedman, L. (1984). *American law: An introduction.* New York, NY: Norton.

Friedman, M., & Friedman, R. (1980). *Free to choose: A personal statement.* New York, NY: Harcourt Brace Jovanovich.

Gewertz, C. (2000, April 22). A hard lesson for Kansas City's troubled schools. *Education Week,* pp. 1–5.

Greenberg, E. (1980). *The American political system: A radical approach.* Cambridge, MA: Winthrop.

Grimm, R. (1977). Brain control in a democratic society. In W. Smith & A. Kling (Eds.), *Issues in brain/behavior control.* New York, NY: Spectrum Books.

Grinfeld, M. (2005). Sexual predator ruling raises ethical, moral dilemmas. *Psychiatric Times, 16,* 1–4.

Hatch, G., & Walsh, A. (2016). *Capital punishment: Theory and practice of the ultimate penalty.* New York, NY: Oxford University Press.

Hawthorne, N. (2003). *The Scarlet Letter.* Boston, MA: Hayes Barton Press.

Holman, J., & Gaston, R. (1987). Interorganizational influences on mental health diagnoses: A macro-level study of the labeling process. *Sociological Perspectives, 30,* 180–200.

Horowitz, A. (1984). Therapy and social solidarity. In D. Black (Ed.), *Toward a general theory of social control* (Vol. 1, pp. 211–250). New York, NY: Academic Press.

Hosking, G. (1985). *The first socialist society: A history of the Soviet Union from within.* Cambridge, MA: Harvard University Press.

Jones, E. (2004). Sexually violent predator laws: Psychiatry in service to a morally dubious enterprise. *The Lancet, 364,* 50–51.

Jones, J. (2018). U.S. death penalty support lowest since 1972. Gallup Poll. Retrieved from http://news.gallup.com/poll/221030/death-penalty-support-lowest-1972.aspx

Lieberman, J. (1972). *How the government breaks the laws.* Baltimore, MD: Penguin.

Lipset, S. (1964). The sources of the "radical right." In D. Bell (Ed.), *The radical right* (pp. 307–371). Garden City, NY: Anchor.

Logan, C., & Gaes, G. (1993). Meta-analysis and the rehabilitation of punishment. *Justice Quarterly, 10,* 245–263.

Mauer, M. (2003). *Comparative international rates of incarceration: An examination of causes and trends.* Washington, DC: The Sentencing Project.

Parenti, M. (1977). *Democracy for the few.* New York, NY: St. Martin's Press.

Plato. (1960). *The republic and other works.* Translated by B. Jowett. Garden City, NY: Dolphin.

Radelet, M., & Bedau, H. (1988). Fallibility and finality: Type II errors and capital punishment. In K. Haas & J. Inciardi (Eds.), *Challenging capital punishment: Legal and social science approaches* (pp. 91–112). Newbury Park, CA: SAGE.

Radelet, M., & Borg, M. (2000). The changing nature of death penalty debates. *Annual Review of Sociology, 26,* 43–61.

Radzinowicz, L., & King, J. (1979). *The growth of crime: The international experience.* Middlesex, England: Penguin Books.

Scheff, T. (1964). The societal reaction to deviance: Ascriptive elements in the psychiatric screening of mental patients in a Midwestern state. *Social Problems, 11,* 401–413.

Siegel, L. (2006). *Criminology* (9th ed.). Belmont, CA: Wadsworth.

Snell, T. (2011). *Capital punishment, 2010: Statistical tables.* Washington, DC: Bureau of Justice Statistics.

Uhlman, T., & Walker, N. (1980). He takes some of my time; I take some of his: An analysis of judicial sentencing patterns in jury cases. *Law and Society Review, 14,* 323–339.

Vago, S. (1991). *Law and society.* Englewood Cliffs, NJ: Prentice Hall.

van den Haag, E. (1993). The ultimate punishment: A defense. In M. Katsh (Ed.), *Taking sides: Clashing views on controversial legal issues.* Guilford. CT: Dushkin.

Walmsley, R. (2015). World prison population list (11th ed.). University of London. http://www.prisonstudies.org/sites/default/files/resources/downloads/world_prison_population_list_11th_edition_0.pdf

Walsh, A. (1990a). Standing trial versus copping a plea: Is there a penalty? *Journal of Contemporary Criminal Justice, 6,* 226–236.

Walsh, A. (1990b). Twice labeled: The effects of psychiatric labeling on the sentencing of sex offenders. *Social Problems, 37,* 375–389.

Walsh, A., & Ellis, L. (2004). Ideology: Criminology's "Achilles' heel?" *Quarterly Journal of Ideology, 27,* 1–25.

Wilson, J. (1975). *Thinking about crime.* New York, NY: Vintage.

Cases Cited

Atkins v. Virginia, 536 U.S. 304 (2002)

Baze and Bowling v. Rees, 553 U.S. 35 (2008)

Bordenkircher v. Hayes, 434 U.S. 357 (1978)

Brown v. Board of Education of Topeka, 347 U.S. 483 (1954)

Coker v. Georgia, 433 U.S. 584 (1977)

Coleman v. Thompson, 501 U.S. 722 (1991)

Communist Party v. Subversive Activities Control Board, 367 U.S. 1 (1961)

Dennis v. United States, 341 U.S. 494 (1951)

Furman v. Georgia, 408 U.S. 238 (1972)

Gitlow v. New York, 266 U.S. 652 (1925)

Gregg v. Georgia, 428 U.S. 153 (1976)

Kansas v. Hendricks, 138 U.S. 521 (1997)

McClesky v. Kemp, 481 U.S. 279 (1987)

Missouri v. Jenkins, 495 U.S. 33 (1990)

Missouri v. Jenkins II, 515 U.S. 70 (1995)

Penry v. Lynaugh, 492 U.S. 302 (1989)

Roper v. Simmons, 112 S.W. 3rd 397 (2005)

Scales v. United States, 367 U.S. 203 (1961)

Schenck v. United States, 249 U.S. (1919)

Stanford v. Kentucky, 492 U.S. 361 (1989)

Woodson v. North Carolina, 428 U.S. 280 (1976)

CHAPTER 10

THE LIMITS OF SOCIAL CONTROL: POLICING VICE

In 1996, Majed Al-Timimy, age 28, and Latif Al-Husani, age 34, two Iraqi refugees living in Lincoln, Nebraska, decided it was time that they were married. A fellow Iraqi refugee told Majed and Latif that he had two daughters who would make good wives that he wanted to marry off. His offer was gratefully accepted, and a Muslim cleric was flown in from Ohio to perform the joint ceremony. Everyone concerned was happy that the proceedings were done right, according to Iraqi Islamic custom. Some months after the wedding, however, one of the brides ran away. Her concerned husband dutifully reported it to the police, and at this point, American and Iraqi norms of morality clashed head on. The two brides Majed and Latif had married were only 13 and 14 at the time of their marriages. Individuals younger than 17 years cannot marry under Nebraska law, so the runaway report became a criminal confession. The girls' parents were arrested and charged with child endangerment, and Majed and Latif were arrested and charged with multiple counts of statutory rape.

The Iraqi community was shocked and outraged that these men were arrested and could face up to 50 years in prison simply for engaging in a marriage on which all parties had agreed. An Iraqi woman (who was herself married at age 12 in Iraq) interviewed by the police swore that both girls were excited and happy about the wedding. As we have seen, however, minors below the age of consent by definition cannot give consent. Because of the doctrine of strict liability, Majed and Latif's ignorance of Nebraska law meant nothing to the prosecutor, so they were charged, found guilty, and sentenced to four to six years in prison. They were paroled in 2000, with one of the conditions of their parole being that they have no contact with their "wives."

Were the actions of these men despicable and immoral child sex abuse or simply normal, unremarkable, marital sex with females who happened to be a little too young for contemporary American moral tastes? Why can something that is legally and morally permissible in one culture be severely punished in another? We discussed this question briefly in chapter 5, but we greatly extend it in this chapter in the context of so-called vice crimes. Most such crimes (or at least acts that are and/or have been defined as crimes) are sexual in nature, such as homosexuality, sodomy, pornography, and underage sex. The questions asked in this chapter include whether these actions are really harmful and, if so, then to whom and to what extent. We will see that the law has vacillated wildly on these issues, and we will learn how the law's reach has lengthened and shortened at various times in our history.

INTRODUCTION

A few years ago in Idaho, one of America's most libertarian ("Get the government off my back") states, a popular bumper sticker said: "Do it now before they make it illegal." This sticker nicely illustrates humanity's split personality with respect to things that may both attract and repel us. Being hedonistic, we seek a wide variety of sensual pleasures, but also being censorious with moral pretensions, we want to deny certain pleasures to others. If we are attracted to the forbidden, we keep it secret while openly condemning others who are similarly attracted: virtue is practiced in public, vice behind closed doors. This chapter focuses on the role of law in regulating vice crimes and asks what the limits of societal control over the individual should be. Many of the "vices" we examine are now, if not exactly virtues, legal, and in some cases supported by the majority (or a sizable minority) of the American people. They are examined only to illustrate the role of law in regulating ostensibly private conduct and how the law itself sometimes makes 180-degree turns on its previous stance in response to changing cultural values. These values can, of course, reverse direction again, and the law will once more be called upon to enforce them.

WHAT IS A VICE CRIME?

What constitutes "vice" varies significantly across time and cultures, as our opening vignette demonstrates. Those who are morally outraged by cultures that allow girls as young as 12 to marry and become sexually active may feel smug about the moral superiority of the United States, where presently no state has an age of consent of less than 16. Such has not always been the case, however. As Lawrence Friedman (2005) reminds us: "In 1885, no state had an age of consent above twelve—in the vast majority, the age was still ten (seven in Delaware!)" (p. 446). If that seems too distant, take the case of rock singer Jerry Lee Lewis, who in 1957 married his 13-year-old cousin, which was not too far out of the ordinary in the American South at the time (Baltakis, 2002). Lewis, who was 22 years old when he married, would find himself in prison today, but in 1957, his marriage was perfectly legal. This illustrates how the fickle sands of the law constantly blow this way and that over the moral terrain.

A **vice crime** is any consensual act that offends the moral standards of the community that has defined the act as worthy of condemnation and legal control. Vice crimes cover a smorgasbord of offenses, some of which have been variously called *public-order offenses, consensual offenses, victimless crimes,* or even *nuisance offenses.* Vice is the opposite of virtue, and in earlier times, proponents of criminalization asserted that such acts must be punished and suppressed simply because they are immoral. Opponents of criminalization countered on grounds of moral relativism. In modern times, however, the whole concept of morality is losing its cachet, so proponents of criminalization have turned to arguments based on harm—that is, vice should not necessarily be regulated because it is immoral but because it causes harm (Harcourt, 1999). People calling themselves progressives, liberals, or libertarians (and sometimes even conservatives) have turned to harm arguments to support decriminalization, but they focus on harms caused by *enforcing* vice laws rather than on harms caused by the prohibited acts.

Because of the shift of emphasis from morality to harm, a key term in our definition of a vice crime is *consensual*, meaning that the parties in the activity have freely agreed to take part in it because they find it pleasurable or rewarding in one way or another. Such acts include prostitution, gambling, illicit drug use, and adultery. Because these acts are consensual, some prefer to refer to them as *victimless*, since any harm that may arise from such activities accrues only to those who freely choose to engage in them. So if the law interferes with those engaging in such activities, it is, according to some, an unwarranted and patronizing infringement on their liberty.

This argument rests on something called the *harm principle*. This principle was addressed in chapter 5 when we examined the elements of a crime that the prosecutor must prove to obtain a guilty verdict. In that chapter, we noted that there could be no legal liability without harm, but in this chapter, we extend the discussion of harm to encompass social and philosophical issues. The issue of harm is central to a discussion of vice crimes in which questions are asked such as "Who is harmed?" "What is the nature of the harm?" and most important, "Is the harm caused by criminalizing the act worse than the harm caused by the act itself?"

The harm principle was best enunciated by the British philosopher John Stuart Mill in his famous essay *On Liberty*. Mill's conception of harm has been the basis for debating the limits of societal tolerance in academia and in the courts ever since its first publication in 1859. According to Mill (1913), the **harm principle** is as follows:

> The sole end for which mankind are warranted, individually or collectively, in interfering with the liberty of action of any of their number, is self-protection. That the only purpose for which power can be rightfully exercised over any member of a civilized community, against his will, is to prevent harm to others. His own good, either physical or moral, is not sufficient warrant. He cannot rightfully be compelled to do or forbear because it will be better for him to do so, because it will make him happier, because, in the opinion of others, to do so would be wise, or even right. . . . The only part of the conduct of anyone, for which he is amenable to society, is that which concerns others. In the part which merely concerns himself, his independence is, of right, absolute. Over himself, over his own body and mind, the individual is sovereign. (p. 6)

For Mill, then, you should enjoy the liberty to swing your arms in any and all directions, and the liberty to do so should be constrained by force of law only when your arms come too close to someone else's nose. This is one of the core principles of both libertarianism and liberalism. If you pull your arm out of joint swinging it, you have harmed only yourself, and that should be no one's business but your own because you did not victimize anyone—that is, your actions were victimless.

The term *victimless* is popular among advocates of vice decriminalization or legalization but also invites rancorous debate because vice crimes are far from victimless. (Mill recognized this and was by no means a radical libertarian.) Leaving aside the fact that vice participants are harming themselves, the real victims are often third-party innocents. The man who brings a sexually transmitted disease back to his wife after visiting a prostitute, the man who gambles away the family's money, and the woman who takes illicit drugs during her pregnancy are all causing great harm to many other people. Rather than being viewed as victimless, vice crimes are better conceived of as consensual *mala prohibita* acts that always have the potential for causing harm to people other than those actually engaging in them.

All vice offenses cause some harm, but the debate today revolves around the question of whether or not the harm caused is great enough to warrant siphoning off criminal justice resources that could be applied to more serious crimes and/or whether the harm is great enough to justify the state interfering with the privacy rights of citizens. For instance, adultery (sexual intercourse of a married person with someone other than his or her spouse) is an act of betrayal, which may cause untold hurt, pain, and anger in the spouse betrayed as well as damage to any children in the marriage. Adultery is so seriously disruptive to society (because the family is the basic institution of any society) that it has been considered a serious offense worthy of the death penalty by many cultures around the world in conformity with the Old Testament's Leviticus 20:10, which proclaims: "And the man that committeth adultery with another man's wife, even he that committeth adultery with his neighbor's wife, the adulterer and the adulteress shall surely be put to death." Adultery is still a capital crime in some Islamic countries, and it once was in England and the American colonies for a brief period in the seventeenth and eighteenth centuries though the death penalty was rarely carried out (Greenstein, 2004).

In the early part of the twentieth century, however, several cities instituted special "morals courts" to deal with adultery and fornication (sex between unmarried adults). No fewer than 500 such cases were prosecuted in Chicago's Morals Court in 1914 (Friedman, 2005, p. 569), but such courts disappeared after too many prominent citizens became candidates for prosecution. Adultery is still technically a crime in the United States, with some states mandating that only the married party be prosecuted and others mandating prosecution for both parties. In 2018, adultery was still a crime in 21 US states, punishable by a fine (a paltry $10 in Maryland) or even jail time (up to three years in Massachusetts), though in reality it carries very little threat of prosecution. With 21 percent of married men and 12.5 percent of married women admitting they have committed adultery at least once (Greenstein, 2004)—and these are just the honest ones—imagine the impact on both the criminal justice system and society as a whole if these laws were enforced with any semblance of vigor.

HOMOSEXUALITY AND SODOMY

In modern legal usage, **sodomy** is anal sex between two men *or* a man and a woman, although a number of anti-sodomy statutes in the United States and elsewhere have considered sodomy to be synonymous with homosexual conduct. In the 1920s, most states expanded the definition of sodomy to include fellatio (mouth–penis contact), and a few states also included cunnilingus (mouth–vagina contact) in their definition (Canaday, 2008). Interestingly, cunnilingus between two women was never considered a crime in English common law because lawmakers could not envision women doing such a thing. In an 1811 case from Scotland, the very thought was considered an "oxymoron" by the House of Lords (the upper house of the British Parliament), since "the crime here alleged has no existence" (Painter, 2005, p. 6).

As with adultery, the image of homosexuality and sodomy in Christianity, Judaism, and Islam arose from Leviticus 20:13, which says: "If a man also lie with mankind, as he lieth with a woman, both of them have committed an abomination: they shall surely be put to death; their blood shall be upon them." Sodomy is not mentioned in the passage, but it has been taken for granted that when two men "lieth" together, that is what they are doing. However, according to 10 history professors who submitted an *amicus curiae* brief in a sodomy case (recall that these "friends of the court" briefs are submitted by individuals or groups who are not a party to the case and who offer relevant information about the matter before the court), sodomy has *not* been considered historically to be synonymous with homosexuality (Chauncey et al., 2003). They gain support from early Christian writers such as St. Thomas Aquinas, who considered sodomy to "cover any genital contact intended to produce orgasm except penile–vaginal intercourse in an approved position" and/or sexual activity that "could not result in procreation regardless of the gender involved" (Chauncey et al., 2003, p. 5).

Throughout most of European history, same-sex sexual behavior was considered a sin to be dealt with by the ecclesiastical courts rather than a crime, although from time to time this was punctuated with secular interference and criminalized. In general, however, people who engaged in homoerotic behavior were seen not as a special class of people but rather as ordinary folks who engaged in "unnatural acts" (Canaday, 2008). It was not until 1869 that the term *homosexual* was coined and homosexuals began to be seen as a distinct category of persons (Burr, 1993), thus marking the beginning of the focus on the actors (homosexuals) rather than the act (sodomy). With the coining of the term and the classification of people into it, legal statutes began to equate sodomitic sex with homosexuality. As Chauncey and colleagues (2003) assert:

> Only in the late nineteenth century did the idea of the homosexual as a distinct category of person emerge, and only in the twentieth century did the state begin to classify and penalize citizens on the basis of their status as homosexuals. (p. 10)

The law's stance on homosexuality was also influenced by the rise of psychiatry in the mid to late nineteenth century. For many years, homosexuality was considered by the American Psychiatric Association (APA) to be a disease. Burr (1993) notes that "by the 1940s homosexuality was discussed as an aspect of psychopathic, paranoid, and schizoid disorders" (p. 2). Up to and during the 1940s, many states had draconian "treatment" strategies for homosexuals, with some gay males being subjected to such things as electric shock treatment, aversion therapy, castration, and in rare instances, lobotomies (an incision in the frontal lobe of the brain to sever certain nerve tracts) as well as hysterectomies for lesbians (Burr, 1993; Painter, 2005).

The APA removed homosexuality from its list of mental diseases in 1973. The APA now considers it to be a variant of human sexuality and has characterized it as a "sexual preference," which implies choice. Bringing choice into the debate suggests that things could be otherwise, enabling moralists to bombard homosexuals with religious exhortations and offers of counseling that would help them to see that their "choice" is the wrong one. The term most often used today, however, is *sexual orientation*, in recognition of the growing scientific consensus that the roots of homosexuality are biological (Savolainen & Lehmann, 2007). Homosexuals no more choose their sexual orientation than do heterosexuals: attraction to their own sex is part of their biological constitution and cannot be changed by religious exhortations or counseling any more than a heterosexual can be browbeaten into becoming a homosexual.

Despite the evolving tolerance for homosexuals in society and the growing respect for privacy rights, the majority of states still had anti-sodomy laws on their books through the 1990s, some exclusively targeting homosexual sodomy. With the onset of the AIDS epidemic in the 1980s, laws against homosexual conduct were enforced in the name of reducing harm, not moral repugnance. For instance, many cities closed gay bathhouses (where indiscriminate sexual activity took place with multiple partners) because of the potential harm associated with exchanging bodily fluids containing HIV, the virus that causes AIDS (Harcourt, 1999).

In 1986, the Supreme Court upheld the Georgia anti-sodomy law in *Bowers v. Hardwick* (1986). Michael Hardwick and another male were arrested after they were found engaging in mutual oral sex by a police officer who had entered Hardwick's apartment to serve a misdemeanor arrest warrant for an unrelated offense. The local prosecutor declined to press charges, but Hardwick sued the Georgia attorney general (Bowers), hoping to have the sodomy law declared unconstitutional. The case eventually wound up in the Supreme Court, with Hardwick claiming that his privacy rights had been violated (Carpenter, 2004). Using the rational-basis standard of review ("Is there a bona fide state interest served by the statute?"), the Court sided with Georgia, but the written opinions made it quite clear that the justices' moral inclinations had trumped evolving constitutional law. However, the decision could be considered more kindly in the context of the AIDS epidemic, which was creating a moral panic in the 1980s and was then considered exclusively a gay disease; it was even called "gay-related immune deficiency syndrome" at the time.

In 2003, a total of 18 states still had laws on the books forbidding consensual sodomy regardless of the sex of the partners or even marital status, and 4 other states had anti-sodomy laws aimed at homosexuals only. The Supreme Court overruled its *Bowers* decision in *Lawrence v. Texas* (2003) and invalidated all remaining sodomy statutes throughout the United States. In this case, John Lawrence and Tyron Garner were caught engaging in anal sex in Lawrence's apartment by a deputy sheriff responding to a false report of a "weapons disturbance" inside. They were arrested, convicted, and fined $200 each. The men appealed their conviction on privacy grounds and on Fourteenth Amendment equal protection grounds because the Texas law prohibited sodomy between same-sex partners but not between opposite-sex partners and was thus unconstitutional (Carpenter, 2004).

Justice Anthony Kennedy wrote the majority (6-3) opinion in *Lawrence*, and he turned again to international precedent, as he did when writing the opinion in *Roper v. Simmons* (2005) outlawing the death penalty for juveniles. He noted that the Court's reasoning in *Bowers* had "been rejected by the European Court of Human Rights [ECHR], and that other nations have taken action consistent with an affirmation of the protected right of homosexual adults to engage in intimate, consensual conduct." In referring to the ECHR, Kennedy brought up the fact that England and Wales had legalized consensual homosexual activity in 1967 and Scotland in 1980. In a case cited by Justice Kennedy (*Dudgeon v. The United Kingdom*, 1980), the ECHR invalidated Northern Ireland's sodomy laws on privacy and human rights grounds. Thus, *Lawrence* brought US law into conformity with laws governing privacy rights in other Western democracies.

The Law and Gay Rights Versus Religious Liberty

Recently, the United States has seen a two-part revolution with regard to homosexuality that has generated heated debate from the courthouse to the altar and beyond. First, people who were once classified as having a disease are now a quasi-protected category in the aftermath of Supreme Court's landmark rulings in *United States v. Windsor* (2013) and *Obergefell v. Hodges* (2015). The Civil Rights Act of 1964 lists the necessary characteristics of protected classes as having (a) a history of long-standing, widespread discrimination; (b) economic disadvantage; and (c) immutable characteristics (some characteristic that is beyond the person's control). While some deny homosexual individuals fit into this scheme, arguing that homosexuality is a behavior and not an "immutable characteristic" such as race or sex, we have seen that the hereditary link of homosexuality has long been established in science and is thus "immutable." Homosexuals have also faced widespread discrimination, so under the language of the 1964 Civil Rights Act, homosexuals do fit the requirements of a protected class.

The second part of the revolution involves the dissenting judges' concerns regarding religious liberty in the aftermath of *Obergefell v. Hodges* (2015). Justice Samuel Alito remarked that the decision "will be used to vilify Americans who are unwilling to ascent to the new orthodoxy." However, Alito was predicting a future that had already arrived. The intolerance, intimidation, and legal threats once aimed at homosexuals are now aimed at people with strong religious beliefs who think that marriage should be only between a man and a woman. These people have been the targets of threats, hate mail, and other forms of intimidation, and courts are increasingly penalizing them for refusing to violate their moral consciences. Steve Endean of the National Gay Rights Lobby calls an act of religious conscience that violates gay rights "a unique vile form of bigotry" (Laycock, 2014, p. 870). Such attacks are becoming commonplace as well. According to Andrew Koppelman (2014): "A standard—but unfair—rhetorical move within the gay rights movement is to treat all its adversaries as mindless bigots. . . . Fair or unfair, it is a move that is increasingly successful" (p. 939).

This "success" is odd because religion is the original protected category in the United States: the first white settlers came to America to escape state attacks on religious freedom. Religious freedom was so fundamental to the Founding Fathers that they enshrined it in the very first words of the Bill of Rights: "Congress shall make no law respecting an establishment of religion, or prohibiting the free exercise thereof." (The second clause is the free exercise clause of the First Amendment.)

As with all freedoms, however, there are exceptions. While government cannot interfere with religious beliefs, it can interfere with religious practices. The first Supreme Court decision interpreting the scope of the free exercise clause was in *Reynolds v. United States* (1878), in which the Court upheld George Reynolds's conviction for bigamy, which Reynolds claimed was an integral part of his Mormon faith. The Court indicated that bigamy was a crime under federal law and that to provide constitutional protection for any and all religion-based practices could open the door too wide. For instance, a religion that claimed exemption from paying individual income taxes for its members would lead to numerous feigned religious conversions and would, if granted, mean government support for that religion when the Constitution mandates government to maintain religious neutrality.

THE CONCEPT OF COMPELLING GOVERNMENT INTEREST

The accepted standard for weighing the government's interest against a constitutional right is that there must be a **compelling government interest** to do so. What is or is not "compelling" is defined from case to case using the strict scrutiny standard of review, and if the courts decide that a government interest is compelling, that interest must be achieved by the "least restrictive means" available. For instance, this standard has been used in cases involving the refusal by people to allow blood transfusions for children in medical need of them and any religious practice in prisons that would undermine prison security. The compelling government interest in such cases is obvious, and few would argue that religion should trump law in any of them. Each of these cases involved individuals engaging in actions that either were contrary to criminal law or could hurt or endanger others, which the state says they *must not* do. But what about the state mandating that people *engage* in some action contrary to their religious beliefs, such as facilitating a same-sex marriage or allowing a same-sex couple to adopt a child? Is this a legitimate exercise of state power? Chai Feldblum (2006) believes that it "is perfectly reasonable for a legislature not to provide any [religious] exemption that will cordon off a significant segment of society [homosexuals] from anti-discrimination prohibition" (p. 115).

In furtherance of this anti-discrimination goal, the City of Houston felt that the content of church sermons was a "compelling state interest" when in 2014 it subpoenaed the sermons of five pastors. These sermons urged congregants to exercise their rights to speak out against a city ordinance allowing transgender individuals to use either a male or a female bathroom. While the subpoenas were cheered by gay activists, the Texas Attorney General wrote to the city attorney that "your action is a direct assault on the religious liberty guaranteed by the First Amendment," adding that the "people of Houston and their religious leaders must be absolutely secure in their knowledge that their religious affairs are beyond the reach of the government" (Sanburn, 2014). Houston ultimately dropped the subpoenas, but its action raises the issue of what is or is not "beyond the reach of the government" when it comes to religion.

Changes in the secular definition of marriage have resulted in the collision of constitutional rights that pose seemingly irreconcilable demands. When religious organizations work for the welfare of children and, at the same time, accept taxpayer money to do so, there attaches an obligation to treat all comers equally. For people who have religions that do not accept the legitimacy of same-sex marriage, to comply with state demands means that they must violate religious doctrine, which they sometimes refuse to do. Religious organizations, motivated by religious principles, do much good in society for the needy, but they require leeway to do so in accordance with those same principles.

For instance, faced with conflicting demands from church and state over same-sex couple adoptions, in 2006 Catholic Charities of Boston announced it would no longer offer adoption services:

> Sadly, we have come to a moment when Catholic Charities in the Archdiocese of Boston must withdraw from the work of adoptions, in order to exercise the religious freedom that was the prompting for having begun adoptions many years ago. (Rutledge, 2008, p. 297)

Founded in 1727, Catholic Charities is the largest and oldest private organization ministering to the poor and needy, including abandoned or orphaned children in need of adoption. It placed far more Boston-area children—many of them difficult to place, such as children with physical or mental health problems or the offspring of mixed races—than any other adoption agency in Massachusetts (Rutledge, 2008). Other Catholic Charities across the nation also have either stopped providing adoption services or have scaled back their services in the face of the loss of public funds.

The issue is not limited to religious organization. It also extends to small businesses, many of which have been targeted legally for discriminating against homosexuals for reasons of religious conscience. For instance, in 2006 Vanessa Willock tried to hire Elane Photography for her same-sex wedding. Elaine Huguenin, co-owner of Elane Photography, refused on religious grounds. The New Mexico Human Rights Commission found that she was guilty of discrimination and in violation of the state's public accommodation law. That decision was upheld by the New Mexico Court of Appeals in June of 2012. Although New Mexico Supreme Court Justice Richard Bosson concurred with the majority opinion in *Elane Photography v. Willock* (2012), it did not sit well with him. In his opinion, Bosson stated:

> The Huguenins are not trying to prohibit anyone from marrying. They only want to be left alone to conduct their photography business in a manner consistent with their moral convictions . . . they are compelled by law to compromise the very religious beliefs that inspire their lives. Though the rule of law requires it the result is sobering.

The Huguenins were ordered to pay court costs and $6,637.94 in attorneys' fees to Willock. In 2014, the Supreme Court denied Elane Photography's petition for certiorari, letting the New Mexico ruling stand. Oddly enough, at this time New Mexico did not recognize same-sex marriage, only doing so in 2013.

In 2013, Barronelle Stutzman, a 70-year-old grandmother and owner of Arlene's Flowers, declined to provide flowers for a same-sex marriage for long-term customer and friend Robert Ingersoll because to do so was contrary to her faith. Ingersoll and the state of Washington filed discrimination suits against her. In February 2015, the court ruled that both the state and Ingersoll may collect damages and attorneys' fees from Stutzman personally and from her business. This ruling means that Stutzman may lose her business, her home, and her savings because she refused to violate her religious beliefs. Stutzman's attorney, Kristen Waggoner, commented on the ruling:

> The message of these rulings is unmistakable: the government will bring about your personal and professional ruin if you don't help celebrate same-sex marriage. Laws that are supposed to prohibit discrimination might sound good, but the government has begun to use these laws to hurt people—to force them to conform and to silence and punish them if they don't violate their religious beliefs on marriage. (Alliance Defending Freedom, 2015)

The U.S. Supreme Court sent Barronelle Stutzman's case back to the Washington Supreme Court in June of 2018, citing its hostility to religious liberty.

In 2013, Aaron and Melissa Klein, owners of Sweet Cakes by Melissa, refused to bake a wedding cake for a lesbian wedding, stating that it would violate their religious consciences. The Kleins, parents of five children, believed this decision was protected by their right to practice their religion as they see fit. The Oregon Bureau of Labor and Industries (OBLI) saw it differently and found that they had violated Oregon's anti-discrimination laws. The Kleins received many hate-filled e-mails and phone calls and shared a number of the e-mails with TV interviewers, one reading "You stupid bible thumping, hypocritical bitch. I hope your kids get really, really, sick and you go out of business." Wedding vendors became so harassed by gay rights groups that they stopped doing business with Sweet Cakes by Melissa, which had to close its doors. In 2015, the commissioner of the OBLI, Brad Avakian, ordered the Kleins to pay damages to the lesbian couple of $135,000. The Kleins refused to pay, but the state garnished all of the assets the Kleins had left (Hallowell, 2015).

The issue is often framed as a refusal to serve gays. Taylor Flynn (2010), for instance, finds herself "unnerved by proponents' failure to recognize the dignitary harm at the heart of public *refusals to serve* historically marginalized groups." She sees the issue as analogous to posting a "No gays served here!" sign and says "Such sign-posting is an embodiment of second-class citizenship" (p. 236; emphasis added). And so it would be, but the issue in each of these cases was not about serving gays. Defendants in each case had served gays many times. Elane Photography employed people who were homosexual, and Barronelle Stutzman of Arlene's flowers was a friend of the gay man who sued her and had served him multiple times.

The issue is rather one of *participating* in an event that contravenes religious identities. In no instance was the issue one of whether or not a same-sex couple can get married, have flowers at their ceremony, have their photos taken, or obtain a wedding cake. All of these goods and services are available in abundance from people anxious to provide them, including the defendants in these suits if doing so did not include endorsing a practice they consider wrong. The issue has thus become that the businesses owned by devout individuals must either violate their identities or face legal penalties and be driven out of business. Conform or withdraw from society was the counsel of outwardly gay Colorado Senator Pat Steadman when he said of people whose religion requires them to discriminate in the provision of their services: "Get thee to a nunnery and live there then. Go live a monastic life away from modern society" (Laycock, 2014, p. 871). This is the kind of intolerant message once aimed at homosexuals—"live your scandalous life if you must, but live it in the closet outside of mainstream society." David Benkof in the *Seattle Post-Intelligencer* (2008) quotes another intolerant senator:

> Openly gay Washington state Sen. Ed Murray, D-Seattle, and a representative of the largest Michigan gay-rights group, the Triangle Foundation, have both told me that people who continue to act as if marriage is a union between a man and a woman should face being fined, fired and even jailed until they relent.

CAN THE RIGHTS OF BOTH GAYS AND RELIGIOUS DISSENTERS BE PROTECTED?

Some see the battle between religious liberty and gay rights as a zero-sum battle: "Once the nation realizes that there will be a winner and a loser, then the only question is whether religious liberties and free speech rights should be repressed to promote legal recognition of same-sex relationships" (Lindevaldsen, 2010, p. 461). Others see the possibility of compromise. Thomas Berg (2010) is among those who maintain that the same arguments for recognizing gay marriage can be applied to protecting the rights of religious dissenters. He argues that

> both same-sex couples and religious believers claim that their conduct stems from commitments central to their identity: love and fidelity to a life partner, faithfulness to the moral norms of God—and that they should be able to live these commitments in a public way, touching all aspects of their lives. (p. 207)

Homosexuals claim a right beyond private behavior: the right to have their love and commitment publicly recognized in marriage. Likewise, religious people wish to live by the tenets of their faith in their public lives, not just in their places of worship.

There should be no winners and losers in these battles. The issue becomes one of determining if we can both recognize gay marriage and accommodate religious liberty without burdening either side because neither side can change. As Laycock and Berg (2013) state:

> No person who wants to enter a same-sex marriage can change his sexual orientation by any act of will, and no religious believer can change his

understanding of divine command by any act of will. . . . These things do not change because government says they must. (p. 4)

Betty Odgaard, another defendant in a same-sex marriage suit in Iowa, put it well:

> We hire and serve gays and lesbians . . . and we respect that good people disagree with our religious conviction against hosting a ceremony that violates our faith. We simply ask that the government not force us to abandon our faith or punish us for it. (Anderson & Ford, 2014, p. 4)

Anyone who takes the liberty claims of either gays or religious dissenters seriously must in good conscience weigh the claims of the other with equal seriousness.

A balanced approach that denies neither same-sex civil marriage nor the religious objector's refusal to participate in it seems appropriate. This is a position with which the American public appears to agree. A Gallup Poll (2014b) showed that 55 percent of Americans support same-sex marriage, more than double the 27 percent who supported it in 1996. A majority of Americans also now support the rights of gays to participate fully in civil life without interference from the state. At the same time, the American public does not want the state to interfere with the rights of religious people to live their lives in accordance with their religious consciences. This was evidenced by a Rasmussen Reports (2013) poll that found

> Americans draw a fine line when it comes to respecting each other's rights. If a Christian wedding photographer who has deeply held religious beliefs opposing same-sex marriage is asked to work a same-sex wedding ceremony, 85 percent of American adults believe he or she has the right to say no [8 percent disagreed and the remaining 7 percent were undecided or did not answer].

Examined through a lens of balanced burdens, the prima facie case for religious exception is straightforward: the burdens placed on the Catholic Church, Elane Photography, Arlene's Flowers, and Sweet Cakes by Melissa heavily outweigh the burden on gay couples. Thus, either the Catholic Church must relinquish its reason for being or a gay couple must seek another adoption agency; either a photographer, florist, or baker must face financial ruin in this life and perhaps (in their eyes) eternal damnation in the next, or gay couples must seek another vendor for their event. Whatever our view of religion, we have to realize that violating one's religious belief is qualitatively different from violating a secular belief. As John Garvey (1996) put it: "The harm threatening the believer is more serious (loss of heavenly comforts, not domestic ones) and more lasting (eternal, not temporary)" (p. 287).

Is there a "war on religion" taking place in America? Rod Dreher (2015) believes so: "Christians and other religious conservatives, who now understand that the left's culture warriors, having won the gay-rights conflict decisively, are determined to shoot the prisoners" (p. 32). Gay rights extremists may have such an agenda—and it is easy to see why given religion's long-standing opposition to the gay lifestyle—but it is doubtful that the courts have. Judges are merely following current law, which they must do despite any personal qualms they might have (witness Justice Bosson's distaste for the New Mexico ruling in *Elane Photography*). If law is the problem, then law is the answer in the form of providing religious exceptions to discrimination.

Over the history of the United States, the government has allowed many religious exceptions. Conscientious objectors have been excused from military duty; religious physicians cannot be made to perform abortions; during Prohibition, Catholics and Jews were allowed to serve wine at communion; Muslims cannot be required to transport alcohol; the Catholic Church can deny women ordination as priests; prison employees cannot be made to participate in executions of the condemned; and Amish parents may take their children out of school and provide them with vocational training rather than state-mandated academic education (Walsh, 2015). One can argue, of course, that these exceptions burden only the state and not the rights of individuals (with the possible exception of an abortion seeker or would-be female priest), but this ignores the problem for those required to violate their deeply held religious principles or lose their businesses and face legal penalties. It is intolerant to call these principles nothing but superstitious dogma or their adherents evil bigots. Whether one is gay, straight, or bisexual, or deeply religious, agnostic, atheist, or even anti-theist, one's innate sense of fairness should militate against the notion that anyone should be made to choose between their livelihood and their moral consciences.

Burwell v. Hobby Lobby Stores, Inc. (2014) points to a solution for mutual protection of rights. In this case, the Supreme Court ruled that the company Hobby Lobby does not have to provide contraceptive methods to its employees that violate the Christian beliefs of the company's owners. These contraceptives include the "morning-after pill" and certain intrauterine devices that are abortifacients (devices designed to end pregnancies rather than prevent them). The Court ruled that "closely held" corporation owners have religious rights under the **Religious Freedom Restoration Act** (RFRA) of 1993. Closely held corporations are businesses in which more than 50 percent of the value of stock is directly or indirectly owned by five or fewer individuals. The Court decided that the US Department of Health and Human Services' claim that Hobby Lobby must provide abortifacients does not hold because while the government has found "least restrictive means" that it has used for religious and nonprofit organizations, these have not been offered to closely held corporations. In this case, by "least restrictive means" the Court is saying that there are other ways of accessing the contraceptives in question that are less restrictive of religious liberty than the Department of Health and Human Services mandate. These include government provision of contraceptives, tax credits, or other financial support for those who want them.

The RFRA was passed unanimously in the US House of Representatives and by a vote of 97-3 in the US Senate and was signed by President Bill Clinton. The act mandates that the strict scrutiny standard of review be used when determining whether the free exercise clause has been violated. The law was passed as a barrier to growing government encroachment on religious liberty. Using the same logic exercised in *Burwell*, there are ways of accessing photographers, florists, and bakers without restricting the religious liberty of others. Further, Arlene's Flowers, Elane Photography, Sweet Cakes by Melissa, and numerous other small businesses across the country that have been similarly targeted are "closely held corporations." Indeed, they fit the definition far better than the much bigger Hobby Lobby, but in no instance has the least-restrictive-means criterion applied.

The reason is that in 1997, the Supreme Court, in *City of Boerne v. Flores,* held that the RFRA applies only to the federal government and not to the states. Responding to this ruling, 21 states have passed their own RFRAs, but Oregon and Washington, the two states involved in the flower and bakery cases, are not among them. New Mexico does have a RFRA, but it did not protect Elane Photography because the New Mexico Supreme Court held that it applied only to disputes in which a government agency was a party, as was the case in Oregon and Washington.

The gay rights/religious freedom issue is an important and extremely divisive one that the courts must resolve. The goal is to arrive at a just solution without re-sorting to coercive legal tactics that have profound negative effects on one side or the other. To be accepted, the policies promulgated must be widely regarded as just, necessary, and not destructive of anyone's fundamental values. Moral compromises have to be made in situations when not all the demands of either side can be met, for it would be unjust to disregard the demands of one side entirely to satisfy the demands of the other fully (Walsh, 2015).

ISSUE HIGHLIGHT

Transgender Bullying and Bathroom Laws

One of the major concerns in schools is the bullying of children considered "different." Bully-ing can reach the level of serious criminal acts if not nipped at the bud. On August 12, 2013, California Democratic Governor Jerry Brown signed of a law allowing transgender K through 12 students access to restrooms and locker rooms they choose regardless of their gender desig-nation. This led to both praise and outrage around the country as other states either followed suit or passed laws forbidding such a practice. Some see this as government control extending even into the restroom, while others see it as legitimate government protection of a minority group against bullying. Is this a good thing for transgender rights and bullying prevention, or a bad thing for safety and privacy in women's toilets and locker rooms?

Good

This law is without doubt a further step toward equality for LGBT people. We should move forward, stop putting people in little boxes, and embrace diversity and respect for individu-als who don't fit neatly into arbitrary, socially constructed categories of "male and female." Gender segregation in bathrooms and locker rooms is wrong simply because gender segre-gation is wrong. We pigeonhole people as "men" or "women" as if they are the only choices available when we know that gender is fluid. Transgendered students sit with other students in the classroom and lunchroom; why not also in the restroom and locker room? We believe that laws allowing people to choose the facilities they use will reduce the bullying and dis-crimination that transgender children suffer. With laws such as this, transgender students can live their lives as their self-identified gender and are likely to feel more accepted by others in society. Transgendered individuals do no simply "chose" to identify with the opposite sex an-ymore that cisgendered (people who identify with the sex they are assigned at birth) do; they are simply born in what their brains tell them is the wrong body.

Bad

The notion that the male or female sex is an arbitrary social construction is insane (we wonder if the medical profession has heard this gem of postmodernist nonsense). We agree that transgendered people do not chose to be that way, but with all that's going on in the world today, is there any more bizarre issue than who gets to do their business where? Transgender people are far less than 1 percent of the population, yet the safety and privacy of our children are put at risk for this absurdity. Yes, all students sit at the same desks and lunchroom chairs, but isn't the bathroom stall something a lot more private? What's to stop someone who looks like Grizzly Adams from claiming to be transgendered in order to enter female toilets and locker rooms as peeping toms? Do you want such men in *your* daughter's bathroom? If a person is truly transgendered (completely looks and acts in a way opposite of the sex he or she was born with), no one in the restroom would have the slightest idea that the person is anything other than what he or she looks like. Far from advancing LGBT rights, the heated opposition to such laws may work against them by amplifying an "us versus them" mentality.

PROSTITUTION AND COMMERCIALIZED VICE

Prostitution and commercialized vice is defined by the Federal Bureau of Investigation's (2004) *Uniform Crime Reports Handbook* as follows:

> The unlawful promotion of or participation in sexual activities for profit. To solicit customers or transport persons for prostitution purposes; to own, manage, or operate a dwelling or other establishment for the purpose of providing a place where prostitution is performed; or to otherwise assist or promote prostitution. (p. 142)

This offense thus covers people who sell their sexual services, those who recruit them, those who solicit clients for them, and those who house them. The common term for a procurer and panderer is *pimp* and for the keeper of a brothel is *madam*.

Prostitution may be succinctly defined as the provision of sexual services in exchange for money or other tangible reward, and a *prostitute* as a person who engages in prostitution as a source of income. Exchanging sexual favors for some other valued resource is as old as the species, and prostitution has long been referred to as the world's oldest profession. Attitudes about the "profession" throughout history have ranged from one extreme to the other. Some ancient societies employed prostitutes in temples of worship with whom worshipers "communed" and then deposited an offering into the temple coffers, just like Christians take bread and wine and contribute to the collection basket. The earliest-known writings on prostitution are contained in the Code of Hammurabi, in which prostitutes seemed to have enjoyed something of a privileged status: 6 of its 282 codes specifically mention the rights of prostitutes (King, 2009).

It was not unusual for many high-born women in ancient Greece who had fallen on hard times to become high-class courtesans, called *hetaerae*, who supplied their wealthy clients with stimulating conversation as well as sexual services. The lower classes had to content themselves with the brothel-based *pornae* or the prettier and more entertaining *auletrides*, who would make house calls (Bullough, 1976). This ancient Greek hierarchy of sex workers is mirrored in modern America, with the *hetaerae* working for elite escort services, *auletrides* working for less selective services, and the brothel prostitutes being the *pornae*. The only legal brothels in the United States are in certain counties of Nevada, where prostitution cohabits comfortably with other cherished vices, but de facto brothels probably exist in every city in the United States, often masquerading as massage parlors.

Prostitution has been regarded throughout much of American history as a "necessary evil." During the American Revolution, camp followers who serviced the sexual needs of the troops were tolerated, and the term *hooker* is apparently derived from the women who serviced the Union troops commanded by General Joseph Hooker during the Civil War (Hagan, 2008). Prostitutes were particularly active in the Old West, where women were a rare commodity. However, the scourge of venereal disease and the grip of Victorian morality marked a change in American attitudes during the latter part of the nineteenth century, at which time many jurisdictions criminalized prostitution. In 1910, the federal government became involved when Congress passed the White-Slave Traffic Act (also known as the Mann Act), prohibiting "white slavery" (prostitution) and making it a felony to transport females across state lines for immoral purposes.

The period between 1920 and 1940 was a one of "judicial enforcement of Victorian sexual norms," in which "most judges . . . adopted a tough stance toward prostitution and justified their actions based on their concern to preserve 'high moral standards'" (Harcourt, 1999, pp. 109–194). This stance is exemplified by the circumstances of the only prostitution case to come before the US Supreme Court (*Mortensen v. United States*, 1944). In 1940, the petitioners, Mr. and Mrs. Mortensen, were convicted of transporting women across state lines for immoral purposes under the Mann Act. The Mortensens, who ran a brothel in Grand Island, Nebraska, had traveled to Salt Lake City, Utah, accompanied by two of their prostitute employees. Although there was no evidence that the trip was anything other than a vacation to visit Mr. Mortensen's parents, all parties were convicted in district court. In 1944, the US Supreme Court overruled the convictions, stating that they were improperly charged under the Mann Act because all evidence showed that the journey in question was an innocent vacation.

In 1998, the Supreme Court avoided ruling on the legal status of prostitution by denying certiorari to an appeal made by a prostitute calling herself Jane Roe II and alleging that Florida's prostitution laws violated her "fundamental right to privacy" pursuant to the Court's "discovery" of privacy rights in *Griswold v. Connecticut* (1965) and *Roe v. Wade* (1973). Roe II's certiorari application was based on an Eleventh Federal District Court's affirmation of the Florida Supreme Court's decision that prostitution did not fall under the umbrella of privacy as currently understood (*Roe v. Butterworth*, 1997). The district court asserted that the state's rational interest in criminalizing prostitution was to protect the sanctity of marriage and that privacy is a concept that can apply only to fundamental rights implicit in the concept of ordered liberty.

What are the harms of prostitution, and are they sufficient to warrant state intervention? Most of the harms are obvious, ranging from the Continental Army's concern about the spread of venereal disease to the modern feminists' concern about the exploitation of women. Prostitutes do help spread deadly diseases, and they certainly are open to exploitation and violence perpetrated by their customers and their pimps. The seamy world of prostitution also is closely related to the drug market, other forms of serious criminality, neighborhood blight, and the exploitation of children.

Perhaps the worst exploitation is that of trafficking women (and even children) from poor countries to work in the brothels of rich nations. Some of these women come knowing what they are getting into, but most others are duped, coerced, or forced. Even so-called voluntary migrants are forced to sell themselves into the quasi-slavery of prostitution due to the poverty and lack of opportunities in their countries of origin (Raymond, 2003). Some make the argument that legalizing or decriminalizing prostitution would eliminate many of these problems, while others say that doing so would make them worse.

Should Prostitution Be Decriminalized/Legalized?

As sordid as we may feel that prostitution is, it has always been with us and presumably always will be. If we cannot stop it, perhaps we should legalize it or decriminalize it. When the Greek lawmaker Solon (638–559 BCE) legalized and taxed it, he was widely praised by the citizenry:

> Hail to you Solon! You bought public women [prostitutes] for the benefit of the city, for the benefit of the morality of a city that is full of vigorous young men who, in the absence of your wise institution, would give themselves over to the disturbing annoyance of better women. (Durant, 1939, p. 116)

Along with the open availability of prostitutes providing its "vigorous young men" safe outlets for their urges, the taxes on prostitution also enabled Athens to build the temple to Aphrodite, the goddess of love. Legalizing prostitution thus means that it becomes a legitimate occupation and that the state can regulate (licensing brothels and prostitutes, determining where they can be located, requiring regular health checkups, etc.) and tax it, as currently is done in Nevada. In other words, legalization refers to the use of law to control prostitution by determining the legal conditions under which it can operate.

The Netherlands provides an example of a country that has legalized prostitution. All parties—prostitutes, pimps, procurers, and customers—are legally sanctioned as long as they remain in prescribed areas. The downside, and it is a truly obnoxious downside, is that various studies have found that about 70 percent of Dutch prostitutes are trafficked in from poorer countries because legalization has greatly expanded the demand for a variety of "exotic" females (Raymond, 2003). There is no evidence that legalization has stemmed trafficking in the Netherlands; rather, it has tended to increase it. Figure 10.1 from the US Immigration and Customs Enforcement shows the extent of human trafficking worldwide, mostly to fuel the sex trade.

Decriminalization, on the other hand, simply means the removal of laws against prostitution without imposing regulatory controls on it. This is a kind of "blind eye" stance toward prostitution. Decriminalization also is the stance favored by the American Civil Liberties Union and prostitution rights groups such as COYOTE (Call Off Your Old Tired Ethics), who oppose legalization since it requires regulation and further stigmatizes the "profession" (Weitzer, 1999). The tolerance of massage parlors by the police (and, evidently, the public) constitutes de facto decriminalization in the United States. Decriminalization basically means business as usual for prostitutes, and it saves many millions of taxpayers' dollars not expended on arresting, prosecuting, and punishing women, most of whom are in the "business" because they perceive few alternatives or who may have been forced into it by pimps on whom they rely for love, protection, and drugs (Tutty & Nixon, 2003).

The United Kingdom is an example of a country that has decriminalized prostitution. There, women are not penalized for selling sexual favors, but all third-party activities, such as pimping, procuring, and in any way living off "immoral earnings," are criminalized. A prostitute may not solicit in the street, so the police target their re-

Figure 10.1 Thumbnail Sketch of Human Trafficking

Source: From US Customs and Immigration Enforcement. (2013). Human Trafficking.

sources exclusively on controlling street prostitution. For a prostitute to be strictly legal, that individual must work independently, and for the place of business not to be considered a brothel, the prostitute must employ no more than a maid and/or receptionist (West, 2000). Whether prostitution is legalized or decriminalized, however, one inevitable upshot has always been an increase in demand as more men come to see it as no big deal ("It's legal, so it must be okay") or to engage in it because there is no longer risk of arrest.

A third option is practiced by Sweden. The Swedes have decriminalized prostitution but also maintained laws criminalizing the purchasing of prostitutes' services. If a prostitute and the john (customer) are caught engaging in sex, the john is arrested and the prostitute sent on his or her way. Since many customers are married or otherwise respectable members of society, an arrest experience has a very large deterrent effect. An American study of arrested johns found that only 18 out of 2,200 men arrested for soliciting were arrested again for soliciting over a four-year period—a remarkably low recidivism rate of only 0.8 percent (Weitzer, 1999).

PORNOGRAPHY/OBSCENITY

Although the terms *pornography* and *obscenity* are used interchangeably in everyday speech, they are different concepts in law. In concurring with the majority of the US Supreme Court when overturning the conviction of a theater manager for showing an erotic French movie called *The Lovers* that the courts of Ohio had deemed obscene, Justice Potter Stewart famously declared that he could not define obscenity, "[b]ut I know it when I see it" (*Jacobellis v. Ohio*, 1964). The courts certainly have had difficulty wrestling with what constitutes pornography/obscenity, and although we all "know it when we see it," we still need reasonable definitions in order to proceed. We define **pornography** as the depiction of sexual behavior in pictures, writing, film, or other material intended to cause sexual arousal. **Obscenity** is a legal term for any subcategory of pornography that is not constitutionally protected, such as child pornography. Pornography is related to prostitution and literally means "the writings of whores." We can think of consumers of pornography as vicariously engaged in prostitution, since they are using the material to assist their sexual arousal and the actors depicted in the pornography have been paid to facilitate that arousal.

We have certainly traversed far on the moral seas since 1960, when the book *Lady Chatterley's Lover* was banned in Britain and the United States because of its sexually explicit language. The courts agreed that the book was obscene, but the bans were lifted in both countries because it also was considered to have redeeming literary qualities. Because of the publicity surrounding the case, the book became an instant bestseller, but certainly not for its "redeeming literary qualities." Today, the objectionable language in the book is heard dozens of times in movies and in many rap songs, which are arguably musical pornography (think of Lil' Wayne grabbing his crotch as he sings the chorus of his hit record "I Wish I Could Fuck Every Girl in the World"). Photographer Robert Mapplethorpe even had a museum exhibition funded by National Endowment for the Arts featuring homoerotic pictures that included one man urinating into the mouth of another. The exhibit was widely defended by cultural mandarins as art, prompting some to quip that the difference between art and pornography is a government grant.

The guiding common law principle historically has been the so-called Hicklin test, derived from the English case *Regina v. Hicklin* (1868). In this case, the court ruled that the law can ban anything that "depraves and corrupts those whose minds are open to such immoral influences and into whose hands a publication of this sort might fall." This rule held if any part of a book fit the ruling, even if that book had literary merit. The Hicklin test prevailed until obscenity was more strictly defined as material whose dominant theme appeals to the prurient interest of the average person according to contemporary community standards (*Roth v. United States*, 1957).

In *Miller v. California* (1973), the Supreme Court reaffirmed that obscenity is not protected speech and offered a way to define it. The Court established the so-called **Miller Test**, which specifies that to be considered obscene (a) the material must appeal to prurient interests as determined by the "average person" applying "contemporary community standards," (b) it must describe-illustrate sexual activity in a "patently offensive" way, and (c) it must lack any serious literary, artistic, scientific, or political value. This is a truly fuzzy definition that permits everything and nothing, depending on what a local jury or court considers prurient, patently offensive, and lacking in serious value, thus making the distinction between obscenity and pornography meaningless.

Pornography in all its forms has been strongly criticized by religious leaders and conservatives as eroding moral standards by representing deviant sexuality as normal and by separating sex from love and marriage. Feminists criticize pornography as an evil that is insulting and demeaning to women, a mechanism by which cultural meanings of sexuality and women are distorted, a cause of rape and child molestation, and exploits the lowest moral depths of those who make it and those who consume it. At the same time, however, feminists tend to oppose most forms of censorship, and most feminists, according to Beverly Brown (2007), oppose sexual morality as "the other of liberalism [i.e., sexual morality is a conservative value]" (p. 78).

Defenders of pornography claim that it does not cause *direct* harm and, according to the harm principle, that only direct harm should be prohibited (this argument is analogous to the *causation* principle, i.e., the legal or proximate cause as opposed to the factual or "but for" ultimate cause discussed in chapter 5). This argument notwithstanding, we punish imprudent acts all the time according to their potential for harm. People driving drunk or recklessly do not cause any direct harm most times they do so, but they are punished if caught by the traffic cop because the *potential* for harm is always present and that potential is what justifies state intervention.

Rather than contending with harm claims, defenders of pornography have shifted their emphasis to the freedom of speech clause of the First Amendment. Thanks to the existing national appetite for pornography, they also have deep pockets with which to fight any acts, laws, or ordinances designed to curb their trade (according to a CNBC program *Porn: Business of Pleasure*, which aired on September 5, 2009, porn profits are at least $13 billion a year in the United States). The pornographers have won practically all their battles, other than those involving child pornography, based on free speech arguments. In a famous pornography case heard by the US Seventh Circuit Court of Appeals (*American Booksellers Association, Inc. v. Hudnut*, 1984) that invalidated an Indianapolis, Indiana, anti-pornography ordinance passed explicitly on the basis of the harm it does, Judge Frank Easterbrook wrote:

> [We] accept the premises of this legislation [that pornography causes harm]. Pornography is a systematic practice of exploitation and subordination based on sex which differentially harms women. The bigotry and contempt it produces, with the acts of aggression it fosters, harm women's opportunities for equality and rights. Yet this simply demonstrates the power of pornography as speech. All of these unhappy effects depend on mental intermediation. Pornography affects how people see the world, their fellows, and social relations.

In other words, while the court agreed that pornography is harmful, it is harm that clearly "demonstrates the power of pornography as speech." The First Amendment thus becomes a sort of verbal jujitsu by which the strength of the harm argument is turned against itself. Judge Easterbrook's statement that the "unhappy effects" of pornography depend on "mental mediation" reflects the legal/factual distinction in the causation principle and essentially means that those effects must first clear the sieve of individual interpretation, and it is this thought process that constitutes speech. Even child pornography is not outside the protection of the First Amendment as long as the images presented are "virtual" (i.e., computer-generated) rather than real children (*Ashcroft v. Free Speech Coalition*, 2002). Thus, freedom of speech trumps harm.

There is one harm claim, however, that is difficult to reconcile with the actual data—namely, that pornography causes rape. This is the most serious of the harm claims, and it is epitomized by the feminist slogan "Pornography is the theory, rape the practice." According to longitudinal data from the various National Crime Victimization Surveys conducted by the Bureau of Justice Statistics (2009), however, there has been a steady and significant drop in self-reported rape victimization that roughly coincides with the emergence of explicit pornography in the late 1960s and early 1970s. Another study looking at rape rates and growth in the release of hard-core pornography titles from 1988 to 2005 found that rape rates decreased by 80 percent (from 2.5 per 1,000 women to 0.5 per 1,000) while porn titles increased 550 percent (Ferguson & Hartley, 2009). No one claims that the easy availability of pornography has *caused* a substantial drop in rape in the United States, but at the same time, those who claim a causal relationship between rape and pornography do not welcome these data. It should be noted that these are nationally aggregated data, and by no means do they disprove the claim that some individuals have been motivated to rape women or molest children by pornography. It all depends on Judge Easterbrook's "mental mediations."

Free speech is our most valuable freedom and must be protected by any means. The free speech clause of the First Amendment is both the foundation of and the crown jewel of the Bill of Rights, without which all the other rights contained therein would be impotent. The question is: "How far should the free exercise of this right be allowed to go?" There is abundant evidence that the Founding Fathers meant the clause to cover political and religious speech but were very much opposed to obscenity (Stone, Seidman, Sunstein, & Tushnet, 1999, p. 189). As we are frequently reminded, however, the Constitution is a living document that evolves with the times. Opponents of the death penalty are ever willing to remind us that "evolving standards of decency" should no longer permit us to execute murderers. By the same token, those who are convinced that morality is an important social cement might consider the law's current stance on pornography as indicative of society's "evolving standards of *in*decency." Many who oppose pornography aver that too much emphasis has been placed on the protection of individual rights and not enough on the rights of that collection of individuals we call "society." British lawmaker Patrick Devlin's (1965) position is reminiscent of sociologist Émile Durkheim's concern about the role that shared morality plays in social solidarity:

> The law exists for the protection of society. It does not discharge its function by protecting the individual from injury, annoyance, corruption, and exploitation; the law must protect also the institutions and the community of ideas, political and moral, without which people cannot live together. Society cannot ignore the morality of the individual any more than it can his loyalty; it [society] flourishes on both and without either it dies. (p. 22)

Note that we cannot, from this position, use the argument that if someone takes offense at pornography, then he or she should close the book, turn off the television, avoid the movie, or avert the eyes because the harm claim is a general one about society as a whole, not any one individual. We also should note that in no country is free speech an absolute. In the United States, we limit many kinds of speech and expression, including libel, false advertising, advertising content, speech intended to incite panic or riot, blackmail/extortion notes, threatening letters, as well as a few other incidences, and we do so on the basis of the harm principle. Indeed, the courts have upheld ordinances against billboards and the like containing explicit advertising for pornography, leading to the curious situation that the law allows more regulation of the advertising of the product than of the product itself.

ABORTION

Few issues more strongly divide modern America and raise more hackles than the abortion issue, and no other moral issue has engaged the courts to the extent that abortion has. Analogies such as comparing abortion to the Holocaust on one side and characterizing its prohibition as slavery on the other abound at the zealous extremes of the debate. Such hyperbole makes it difficult to offer a definition without causing offense to one side or the other. We offer a definition of abortion here that is as value neutral as we can make it: **abortion** is the intentional termination of a pregnancy by the removal or expulsion of an embryo/fetus from the uterus resulting in its death. Some individuals view this "termination" as simply a medical procedure analogous to removing a tumor, while others see it as the murder of an unborn child.

When abortion was prohibited in the United States, it was considered a vice crime, although it hardly fits those parts of the standard definition of vice that describe it as a pleasurable experience people habitually seek to repeat. There is nothing pleasurable about the abortion experience, and surely no one wants to repeat it. The terms *victimless* and *consensual* for describing the act also are problematic and bring angry outcries from abortion opponents. Pro-life advocates maintain that the embryo/fetus/potential human being/human being (take your pick of the descriptors) is very much a victim, although it cannot complain to the law about it. Kaplan (1988) asserts that the term *consensual* is no better than *victimless*, since "it merely underscores that the fetus, which the foes of abortion regard as a human being, has not consented to anything" (p. 153). This leaves us with having to assume that abortion has been characterized as a vice crime because of its link with illicit sex or perhaps to prevent it from falling into a more serious category, such as murder or manslaughter, during the years when it was legally prohibited (Stuntz, 2000).

As long as women have become pregnant without having the support of a committed mate, they have sought abortions. In the ancient world, abortion was induced by a variety of herbal potions or physical means such as pressure applied to the abdomen by binding or hitting, jumping from considerable heights, or lifting heavy weights. As with sodomy and prostitution, attitudes regarding abortion have fluctuated across the centuries. The first laws regulating abortion are found in the Code of Hammurabi, which stipulated fines for causing "miscarriage" (King, 2009). In the

Middle Ages and into the nineteenth century, abortion during the early stages of pregnancy was generally accepted in Western Europe, with exceptions from time to time and place to place. The point at which it became prohibited was at the *quickening*, or the first discernible movement of the fetus, which usually occurs around the fourth month of pregnancy. In the late nineteenth century, however, public opinion about abortion changed. In 1869, the Roman Catholic Church prohibited abortion under any circumstances for its members.

The attitude toward those who performed abortions generally was more severe than that toward those sought abortions, as is illustrated by the case of Eleanor Beare in England, who was indicted in 1732 for "destroying the Foetus in the Womb of Grace Belfort, by putting an iron instrument up into her body, and thereby causing her to miscarry" (*Rex v. Beare*, 1732). Counsel for the Crown opened his case with the following statement:

> Gentlemen . . . the Misdemeanor for which the Prisoner stands indicted, is of a most shocking Nature; to destroy the Fruit in the Womb carries something in it so contrary to the natural Tenderness of the Female Sex, that I am amazed how ever any Woman should arrive at such a degree of Impiety and Cruelty, as to attempt it in such a manner as the Prisoner has done, it has really something so shocking in it, that I cannot well display the Nature of the Crime to you: It is cruel and barbarous to the last degree.

At the instigation of religious leaders and the American Medical Association, by the turn of the twentieth century every state prohibited abortion at any stage of pregnancy except when a woman's life was at risk (Garrow, 1998). Enforcement was slack, however, and various estimates put the number of illegal abortions performed at around 1 million per year in the 1960s (Rosenberg, 1991). Many of these abortions were performed by either shady or reformist physicians, but many also were performed in dangerous and unsanitary conditions by any individual claiming expertise in such matters. Because of the conditions under which they were performed, an estimated 5,000 women died each year from illegal abortions (Stuntz, 2000). Publicity surrounding the plight of these women created a growing opposition to abortion laws, and after *Griswold*, the stage was set to challenge abortion laws in the Supreme Court on privacy grounds.

By 1973, a total of 17 states had amended their laws to allow abortion under certain conditions (rape, incest, health risks), but most still had restrictive laws. In *Roe v. Wade* (1973), the Supreme Court gave women the right to unlimited access to abortion in the first trimester (thus back to the old common law rule about the quickening), allowed states to regulate abortion in the second trimester, and permitted states to prohibit it in the third trimester unless the life or health of the mother was at risk. In the case of *Doe v. Bolton* (1973), which was argued on the same day as *Roe*, the Supreme Court, in invalidating Georgia's abortion laws, ruled that a woman may obtain an abortion after *viability* (the point at which the fetus is able to survive outside the womb) only if it was necessary to protect her health.

Ever since the *Roe* and *Doe* (both pseudonyms) decisions, the Court has been fine-tuning abortion law. In 1980, it upheld the Hyde Amendment, which restricted Medicaid funding for abortions to cases of rape or incest (*Harris v. McRae*, 1980); in

1989, it upheld a Missouri statute banning the use of public facilities and employees to perform abortions, as well as the requirement that physicians test for fetal viability beginning at 24 weeks of pregnancy (*Webster v. Reproductive Health Services*, 1989). These decisions were seen by pro-choice advocates as retreats from the promise of *Roe*. On the other hand, in *Planned Parenthood v. Danforth* (1976), the Court overturned a Missouri law that required married women to obtain their husband's consent before having an abortion, and in *Hodgson v. Minnesota* (1990), it invalidated a law requiring that both parents be informed before a minor could obtain an abortion. These rulings were viewed by pro-lifers as violating paternal and parental rights, respectively.

In *Planned Parenthood of Southeastern Pennsylvania v. Casey* (1992), the Court overturned the trimester scheme it introduced in *Roe* by upholding a Pennsylvania act requiring (a) a woman seeking an abortion to give "informed consent" after being provided with information about the possible risks and complications involved and to notify her spouse of her intentions, (b) minors to have parental consent, and (c) a 24-hour waiting period before obtaining the abortion. There also was a provision imposing reporting requirements on abortion facilities. In other words, it was now permissible for states to regulate abortion before as well as after fetal viability.

Nothing splits the two opposing camps more bitterly than the issue of partial-birth abortion, which is done by partially extracting the fetus, collapsing the skull, and extracting the brain. After Nebraska defined this as "killing the child" and made it a felony, an abortion physician named LeRoy Carhart challenged the law as unconstitutional in *Stenberg v. Carhart* (2000). The Court agreed with Carhart and struck down the Nebraska law. According to Justice Stephen Breyer, "All those who perform abortion procedures using that method must fear prosecution, conviction, and imprisonment [which places] an undue burden upon a woman's right to make an abortion decision." The depth of feeling that this form of abortion brings out can be gauged by Justice Antonin Scalia's scathing dissent: "The notion that the Constitution of the United States . . . prohibits the States from simply banning this visibly brutal means of eliminating our half-born posterity is quite simply absurd."

As a result of the *Stenberg* decision, Congress entered the fray by passing the Partial-Birth Abortion Ban Act of 2003. This act contained the following two research findings crucial to the promulgation of the act:

1. A moral, medical, and ethical consensus exists that the practice of performing a partial-birth abortion—an abortion in which a physician delivers an unborn child's body until only the head remains inside the womb, punctures the back of the child's skull with a sharp instrument, and sucks the child's brains out before completing delivery of the dead infant—is a gruesome and inhumane procedure that is never medically necessary and should be prohibited.

2. Rather than being an abortion procedure that is embraced by the medical community, particularly among physicians who routinely perform other abortion procedures, partial-birth abortion remains a disfavored procedure that is not only unnecessary to preserve the health of the mother but in fact poses serious risks to the long-term health of women and, in some circumstances, their lives. As a result, at least 27 states banned the procedure, as did Congress, which voted to ban the procedure during the 104th, 105th, and 106th Congresses.

As a result of this act, a number of states, including Nebraska, reinstituted partial-birth abortion bans. The same Dr. LeRoy Carhart who was the petitioner in *Stenberg v. Carhart* was then joined by other abortion providers in challenging the constitutionality of the act. After a round of appeals in lower courts, the case eventually found its way to the Supreme Court as *Gonzales v. Carhart* (2007). The Court found that the Partial-Birth Abortion Ban Act passed constitutional muster. In this case, the Court did not overturn *Stenberg* but, rather, distinguished it from *Gonzales* (recall that when a court "distinguishes," it is saying that although the present case is similar to a prior case, the prior case is not overruled because of significant differences between the prior and present cases). The Court held that the Nebraska statute at issue in *Stenberg* was more ambiguous than the later federal statute in *Gonzales*. Legal cynics among us might say that the real difference that "distinguished" *Stenberg* from *Gonzales* was the replacement of moderate Justice Sandra Day O'Connor with conservative justice Samuel Alito, since both cases were 5-4 decisions. This once again illustrates how the theoretically neutral law serves practical ideological positions.

The partial-birth issue may be responsible for significantly changing the attitudes of Americans about abortion over the past 15 years. In 2001, as Figure 10.2 shows, 48 percent of Americans considered themselves pro-choice and 42 percent considered themselves pro-life. In 2016 there was almost an even split between pro-lifer (46 percent) and pro-choice (47 percent). There are relatively few people at the moral extremes, however. Only 27 percent thought that abortion should be legal under any circumstances, and only 22 percent thought that it should be illegal in all circumstances (Saad, 2016). It seems that many pro-choice Americans hold this view only for pragmatic reasons, since 47 percent of all Americans polled in one survey viewed abortion as morally wrong versus 43 percent who viewed it as morally acceptable.

Figure 10.2 Public Opinion on Abortion: 2001–2016

With respect to the abortion issue, would you consider yourself to be pro-choice or pro-life?

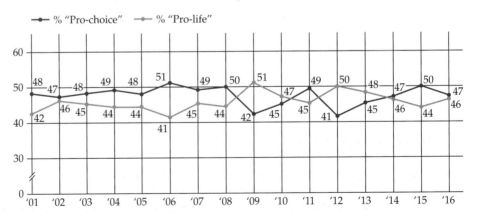

Given these figures and recent court decisions, we may well see a return to pre–*Roe v. Wade* abortion laws if the Supreme Court decides that abortion is entirely a matter for the individual states.

If we leave out the bitter issue of "termination" versus "killing" (which is impermissible for the pro-life side, since the status of the fetus/child is precisely, and possibly the only, issue at hand), we may ask what other harms are involved. A number of studies have shown that women who undergo an abortion are significantly more likely to be diagnosed with a range of mental disorders, such as clinical depression, substance abuse, bipolar disorder, and suicidal ideation (Cougle, Reardon, & Coleman, 2003; Fergusson, Horwood, & Ridder, 2006), although other sources claim that the risk of these harms is low (American Psychological Association, 2005).

One particularly contentious "benefit" of legalized abortion, according to a study conducted by Donohue and Levitt (2001) that managed to upset liberal pro-choice advocates ("It smacks of eugenics and racism") as well as conservative pro-lifers ("The idea that something positive can come from abortion is bizarre"), is that it contributed significantly to the large reduction in crime in the United States. Those authors summarized their study as follows:

> Crime began to fall roughly 18 years after abortion legalization. The 5 states that allowed abortion in 1970 experienced declines earlier than the rest of the nation, which legalized in 1973 with *Roe v. Wade*. States with high abortion rates in the 1970s and 1980s experienced greater crime reductions in the 1990s. In high-abortion states, only arrests of those born after abortion legalization fell relative to low-abortion states. Legalized abortion appears to account for as much as 50 percent of the recent drop in crime. (p. 379)

The essence of this argument is that were it not for legalized abortion, many thousands of unwanted children would have been born, and that this "unwantedness" is a major predictor of criminality. Unwanted children are likely to grow up in poor, single-parent homes and are at significant risk for abuse and neglect. Additionally, legal abortion reduced the size of the birth cohort, resulting in fewer young males to victimize others when they grow up. Although this argument has intuitive appeal (fewer children born into criminal environments obviously means less crime down the road), it also is possible that legalized abortion actually increased the number of unwanted children because as abortion rates were going up, so was the rate of births to unmarried mothers (Lykken, 1995). In other words, the legal availability of abortion granted females license to engage more freely in unprotected sex.

ALCOHOL AND ILLICIT DRUGS

Ben Franklin, arguably the wisest of our Founding Fathers, once wrote: "Beer is proof positive that God loves us and wants us to be happy." Franklin was not alone in praising the Almighty for the gift of alcohol. The ancient Egyptians credited the god Osiris with inventing beer, the ancient Chinese considered it a gift from heaven, and the Babylonians and Indians are among the ancients who worshiped wine goddesses

(McGovern, 2003). Humans certainly have a fondness for ingesting substances that alter their moods: we swallow, gulp, sniff, inhale, and inject with such relish that it suggests sobriety is a difficult state to tolerate. But among all the diverse substances used to change our moods, alcohol is definitely the favorite route to Franklin's happy state. We drink to loosen our tongues, to be sociable, to liven up our parties, to feel good, to sedate ourselves, and to anesthetize the pains of life. With the help of alcohol, we can reinvent ourselves as superior beings: the timid become bold, the tongue-tied become loquacious, and the shy become confident.

If alcohol is God's gift to humanity, its abuse is humanity's gift to Satan. Of all mood-altering substances, alcohol is the one most directly linked to crime, especially violent crime (Martin, 2001). At least 70 percent of American prison inmates (Wanberg & Milkman, 1998) and 60 percent of British inmates (McMurren, 2003) are alcohol and/or drug addicted. Police officers spend more than half of their active time on alcohol-related offenses, and about one-third of all arrests in the United States are for alcohol-related offenses (Mustaine & Tewkesbury, 2004). About 75 percent of robberies and 80 percent of homicides involve a drunken offender and/or victim, and about 40 percent of other violent offenders in the United States had been drinking at the time of their offense (Martin, 2001). The US Department of Health and Human Services (2009) estimates the annual cost of alcohol abuse to society to be a staggering $185 billion ($244 billion in 2009 updated for inflation). According to Alcohol Alert (2009), an organization dedicated to reducing drunk driving, there were 15,387 alcohol-related traffic fatalities on US highways in 2007, constituting 37 percent of all fatal traffic accidents.

Another major problem is the number of neurological disorders that result from mothers drinking while pregnant, known as *fetal alcohol spectrum disorders* (FASD), the most serious of which is *fetal alcohol syndrome* (FAS). The prevalence of FASD in the United States is around 1 percent of live births (Manning & Hoyme, 2007). FAS has a number of readily identifiable physical abnormalities associated with it, since prenatal alcohol exposure adversely effects the migration and hookup of neurons in vital brain areas in the developing fetus (Goodlett, Horn, & Zhou, 2005). The behavioral symptoms of FAS include low IQ; hyperactivity; impulsiveness; poor social, emotional, and moral development; and a highly elevated probability of alcoholism (Jacobson & Jacobson, 2002). Each of these deficits is linked to high levels of criminal offending independent of FAS, but individuals with FAS are almost always saddled with them all. Many other problems are associated with alcohol as well, but the problems addressed here are evidence enough that alcohol is the cause of more obvious harm than all of the other vice crimes combined.

Taming the Beast in the Bottle

Children and adults of both sexes in premodern Europe drank beer simply because it was safer to drink than water, which in those unsanitary days had to be boiled before it could be consumed (McGovern, 2003). Beer was also less potent (about 1 percent alcohol, compared to most of today's beers, which average around 3.5 percent), so most of the problems associated with alcohol abuse arose from strong liquor, such as gin and rum. The first recorded attempt at the prohibition of alcohol in North America was made by the Massachusetts Colony in 1657 and was aimed only at those products, not at beer (Blue, 2004). However, throughout the history of colonial and post-colonial America, there have been efforts to prohibit all kinds of alcohol use, both for health and moral reasons (because it was associated with saloons in which gambling, prostitution, and violence were ever present).

Although the stirrings of temperance movements had existed since the American Revolution, the first to have any real impact was the Massachusetts Society for the Suppression of Intemperance, formed in 1828. By the time of the Civil War, 13 states had passed laws prohibiting the sale of alcohol, with several other states considering it (Augst, 2007). After the Civil War, the United States saw a rapid increase in prohibitionist sentiment. The Prohibition Party was founded in 1869 and the Women's Temperance Union in 1874, and in 1881, Kansas became the first state to outlaw the sale of alcohol in its constitution. Enforcement of prohibitionist laws was left primarily to the informal but effective methods of religious individuals, such as Carrie Nation, a bulldog of a woman who led others of her ilk into saloons with a Bible in one hand and a battle-axe in the other to do "God's work" by laying waste to "murder mills, hell holes, and the donkey bedmates of Satan" (Carver, 1999, p. 31).

The sentiment for prohibition grew to a crescendo with the entry of the United States into World War 1 in 1917 because many of the most prominent breweries had German names, such as Schlitz and Pabst. That same year, Congress approved a resolution for a constitutional amendment prohibiting the production, sale, transportation, or importation of alcoholic beverages in the United States and sent it to the states for ratification. Ratification was completed in 1919, and in January 1920, the Eighteenth Amendment became effective. The amendment was supplemented by the Volstead Act of 1919, and together, they constituted what became known as **Prohibition**. The Volstead Act defined intoxicating liquor as anything containing more than 0.5 percent alcohol and allowed a certain amount of wine and/or cider of that potency to be made at home. Despite Prohibition's rapid passage, greased by anti-German sentiment, it was nevertheless "the fruit of a century-long series of temperance movements springing from deep roots in the American reform tradition" and a culture that "was deeply hostile to alcohol" (Blocker, 2006, p. 233).

That "deep hostility to alcohol" might be better characterized as a deep hostility to other people's use. The public's thirst for alcohol, no longer served by legitimate breweries and the neighborhood bar, was now quenched at a higher price by organized crime and the neighborhood speakeasy. Even President Warren Harding, who was publically a "dry" (pro-Prohibition), served liquor at White House social functions and thus, like thousands of other Americans, was privately a "wet" (Stuntz, 2000). Yet in 1928, Americans elected staunch Prohibitionist Herbert Hoover over Al Smith, who was just as staunchly anti-Prohibition. Support for Prohibition waned after the 1929 stock market crash, which produced the Great Depression. Its opponents claimed that Prohibition was costing the government millions of dollars in its enforcement efforts and at the same time causing it to lose millions in revenue.

The economic argument won the day, and in December 1933, the Twenty-First Amendment repealed the Eighteenth Amendment, making it the only amendment to be repealed by the ratification of another. Thus ended the "noble experiment" aimed at stopping the evils of drink, reducing crime, emptying the prisons, lowering the tax burden, and improving health. Instead, it had done quite the opposite, allowing organized crime to flourish and corrupt countless government officials, producing more dangerous and potent homemade brews, filling the prisons, and gnawing at government revenue.

Illicit Drugs

The manufacture, sale, and abuse of nonprescription drugs such as cocaine and heroin remains the only behavior addressed in this chapter that is not currently legal, quasi-legal, or so tolerated that it is de facto legal. Alcohol is a legal and socially acceptable way of drugging ourselves today, but the use of what once fell under the umbrella term of *narcotics* is not. This was not always the case, for many of the drugs now banned have been legitimately used in religious rituals, for medical treatment, and for recreation around the world and across the ages. There is a reference to the opium poppy as "the plant of joy" in Mesopotamia from around 3000 BCE, and the early Egyptians used opium in their religious ceremonies (Davenport-Hines, 2002).

At the turn of the twentieth century, most drugs now considered illicit were widely used in the United States and around the world with minimal or nonexistent regulation (Wodak, 2007). Sigmund Freud was an avid consumer of cocaine and ecstatic about its medicinal properties. With the public not fully aware of the dangers of addiction, many substances were openly advertised and sold as cures for all sorts of aliments and for refreshing "pick-me-ups." The most famous of these refreshments was Coca-Cola, which until 1903 was made with the coca leaf (used to process cocaine) and kola nuts (hence the name). Many medicines on the market contained cocaine (e.g., Cocaine Toothache Drops), and others, such as Mother Barley's Quieting Syrup, used to soothe infants and children, contained laudanum, which was essentially opium.

Attitudes toward drug use in America gradually began to change as physicians and lawmakers came to understand more fully the addictive powers of many of these substances. Although earlier federal and state acts had aimed at specific practices and substances (e.g., opium smoking in opium dens), the **Harrison Narcotics Act** of 1914 was the benchmark act for changing America's attitudes toward drugs. According to Richard Davenport-Hines (2002), "By the early 1920s, the conception of the addict changed from that of a middle-class victim accidentally addicted through medicinal use, to that of a criminal deviant using narcotics (or stimulants) for pleasure" (p. 14). Although the Harrison Act initially reduced the number of addicts (estimated at around 200,000 in the early 1900s), it also spawned criminal black-market operations and, ultimately, many more addicts. Three years after the passing of the act, a Congressional report found: "The 'dope peddlers' appeared to have established a national organization, smuggling the drugs in through seaports or across the Canadian or Mexican borders. . . . The wrongful use of narcotic drugs has increased since the passage of the Harrison Act" (Casey, 1978, p. 11).

Drugs hijack the brain and produce more powerful, rapid, and predictable effects on its pleasure centers than alcohol. The Drug Enforcement Administration (2003, p. 13) estimates that 5 million Americans suffer from drug addiction and that about 55 percent of today's youth have used some form of illegal substance. Addiction is not an invariable outcome of drug use any more than alcoholism is an invariable outcome of drinking. But among those who experiment with drugs are some who are genetically predisposed to develop addiction, just as others are "sitting ducks" for alcoholism (Robinson & Berridge, 2003).

The Office of National Drug Control Policy (2014) issues an annual report by its Arrestee Drug Abuse Monitoring Program showing the percentage of arrestees testing positive for illicit drugs. Figure 10.3 shows the percentage in five major cities between the years 2007 and 2013. (This excellent reporting program was discontinued in 2014 due to budget cuts, making Figure 10.3 its last.) The figure makes it starkly clear that drugs are intimately related to criminal activity. Drug abuse does not appear to *initiate* a criminal career, but it does increase the extent and seriousness of one. As Menard, Mihalic, and Huizinga (2001) explain:

> Initiation of substance abuse is preceded by initiation of crime for most individuals (and therefore cannot be a cause of crime). At a later stage of involvement, however, serious illicit drug use appears to contribute to continuity in serious crime, and serious crime contributes to continuity in serious illicit drug use. (p. 295)

The link between drugs and crime is driven largely by their illegality, not by their pharmacological effects. Violence induced by illicit drug use is rare compared with violence induced by alcohol and is most likely to occur *after* the effects of the

Figure 10.3 Percentage of Arrestees Testing Positive for Illicit Drugs in Five Major Cities, 2007–2013

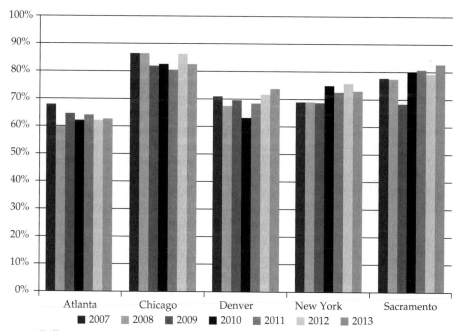

■ 2007   ■ 2008   ■ 2009   ■ 2010   ■ 2011   ■ 2012   ■ 2013

* Differences between each year and 2013 are significant at the 0.05 level or less.

drugs have worn off, leaving the users stressed, irritable, and paranoid. Just as the underworld stepped in to supply the demand for alcohol during Prohibition, it steps in today to supply drugs. The real link between drugs and violence is associated with "traditionally aggressive patterns of interaction within the system of drug distribution and use" (Goldstein, 1985, p. 497). In other words, violence is an integral part of "doing business"—the growing, processing, transporting, and selling of drugs and the bribery and corruption of law enforcement officials and politicians. A number of terrorist groups are financing their operations through lucrative drug trafficking.

On the streets of the United States, drug violence is most closely linked with gang battles for control of territory (control of drug markets). The National Institute of Justice (1991) estimated that in 1988, about 80 percent of the homicides in the District of Columbia were drug-related, and the dramatic increase in homicides beginning in the mid-1980s has been attributed to the emergence of crack cocaine and the subsequent recruitment of armed and dangerous young males to sell it (Blumstein, 1995). Crimes such as shoplifting, burglary, robbery, and prostitution are often committed by addicts to finance the high cost of their drugs.

The criminalization of acts such as sodomy and abortion generated many court cases challenging the legality of the statutes forbidding them, indicating that a significant portion of the population believe that such statutes overstep the bounds of government control of private behavior. No Supreme Court cases have challenged states' right to criminalize illicit drugs, however, which probably indicates widespread agreement that the manufacture and sale of such substances is morally wrong and is the cause of much harm. The use of illicit drugs clearly is very harmful to individuals, their families, and society (Nutt, King, Saulsbury, & Blakemore, 2007). What is even more clear is that the "war on drugs," just like Prohibition, is the cause of more harm than it prevents. Most countries have abandoned their own wars on drugs today and reverted to harm-reduction policies (i.e., policies aimed solely at minimizing harm). The United States is among only a handful of countries that reject harm-reduction programs favored by agencies such as the World Health Organization and the United Nations Children's Fund (Wodak, 2007). Such programs involve syringe-exchange programs, drug-substitution programs (e.g., methadone for heroin), and most important, decriminalizing drug use. According to Alex Wodak (2007), "No country which has started harm reduction programs has ever regretted that decision and then reversed their commitment" (p. 61).

The Opioid Epidemic

It seems that every decade endures an epidemic of some kind of drug: LSD in the 1960s, cocaine in the 1970s, crack in the 1980s, meth in the 1990s and early 2000s. Today, however, we have the worst epidemic of all—the opioid epidemic. These opioids include both illegal ones such as, heroin and legal ones such as fentanyl. Approved by the Food and Drug Administration for use as an analgesic (pain reliever) and anaesthetic, fentanyl often is sold and manufactured illicitly. It is a synthetic opioid that is 100 times more powerful than morphine and about 30 times stronger that heroin (US Department of Health and Human Services, 2018). The problem is that too many people are using it to numb the pain of empty lives, and too many

Figure 10.4 The Opioid Epidemic by the Numbers

 **THE OPIOID EPIDEMIC** BY THE NUMBERS

IN 2016...

 116
People died every day from opioid-related drug overdoses

 11.5 m
People misused prescription opioids[1]

 42,249
People died from overdosing on opioids[2]

 2.1 million
People had an opioid use disorder[1]

 948,000
People used heroin[1]

 170,000
People used heroin for the first time[1]

 2.1 million
People misused prescription opioids for the first time[1]

17,087
Death's attributed to overdosing on commonly prescribed opioids[1]

 19,413
Deaths attributed to overdosing on synthetic opioids other than methadone[2]

 15,469
Deaths attributed to overdosing on heroin[2]

 504 billion
In economic costs[2]

Source: U.S. Department of Health and Human Services. (2018). What Is the U.S. Opioid Epidemic?

are ending up numbing themselves permanently. As Figure 10.4 indicates, in 2016 more people died from overdosing on opioids in the United States (about 115 each day) than from homicide and automobile accidents combined, with synthetic and commonly prescribed drugs accounting for more than twice the deaths from heroin overdoses. Other commonly prescribed opioids that often lead to deadly overdoses are oxycodone (e.g., OxyContin®), and hydrocodone (e.g., Vicodin®)

Andrew Sullivan writes: "No other developed country is as devoted to the poppy [from which opioids are synthesized] as America. We consume 99 percent of the world's hydrocodone and 81 percent of its oxycodone. We use an estimated 30 times more opioids than is medically necessary for a population our size" (2018). Why this situation obtains is anyone's guess, but many have blamed America's profit-driven health care system, which is unique among highly developed countries (Kolodny et al., 2015; Sullivan, 2018). Pharmaceutical companies aggressively market these opioids to doctors who, under so-called "managed care" regimes, are told to manage patient care quickly and efficiently. It is so much quicker and efficient to hand patients complaining of pain a bottle of pills than to provide a full workup and prescribe a long and expensive alternative treatment. Sullivan (2018) tells us that a $3 medicaid co-pay of opioid pills can be sold on the streets for as much as $10,000, and this has turned many a middle-class patient into a drug dealer. Unlike the crack epidemic, for instance, the opioid epidemic did not lead to an increase in violent crime, at least until physicians, now aware of the addictive nature of these drugs, started limiting their prescriptions. Addicts then turned to heroin and the deadly synthetic fentanyl, and the whole chess game between dealers and law enforcement is now heading toward yet another stalemate.

Others have said that the problem goes far beyond an addictive or pharmacological one and is more a moral or spiritual issue. With family stability collapsing, fatherless homes increasing, and the number of people with no religious affiliation rising, more and more people are experiencing a profound disconnect and spiritual emptiness for which opiates have always been seen as a solution. This is something that law and law enforcement cannot fix. As Sullivan (2018) points out, Karl Marx once said that religion is the opiate of the people, but things have done a 180-degree turn and opiates have become the religion of the people. Sullivan also quotes a verse by the poet William Brewer that sums up the tragic shift poetically:

> Where once was faith,
> there are sirens: red lights spinning
> door to door, a record twenty-four
> in one day, all the bodies
> at the morgue filled with light.

The Future of Drug Regulation

The behaviors addressed in this chapter illustrate the limits of using the law for social control. As any economist will attest, efforts to prohibit exchanges that are mutually consensual and rewarding are doomed to failure. Criminalizing such acts really is an exercise in morality politics, in which legislative bodies respond to the publically held values of segments of the population who consider the acts to be perverse. As we pointed out at the beginning of this chapter, however, private behavior often diverges dramatically from public statements about that behavior. History is replete with examples of evangelical ministers caught in adultery or cavorting with prostitutes, with macho opponents of gay rights cruising gay bars, and even presidents or future presidents of the United States drinking or sampling illicit drugs when those substances were illegal. Legislative bodies and courts are thus responding to a level of opposition against a variety of vices that simply is not there.

This is not to deny the harms inherent in the various vice crimes, but we have to realize that many social problems have no solutions, only trade-offs. Advocates of either legalizing or decriminalizing a particular vice are not promoting it; they are simply recognizing the trade-off nature of trying to deal with it so that it causes the least amount of harm. Presumably, not even the most addicted person would recommend drug use as a good and desirable thing, but given the fact that drugs are here to stay and there are always people who will abuse them, the question really is one of a cost–benefit analysis of continuing the war versus seeking peace and compromise.

We are repeating many of the mistakes of Prohibition with the war on drugs, such as providing organized crime with a lucrative market, the corruption of officials, huge increases in imprisonment rates, many deaths from adulterated products, and recruitment of our children by addicts who sell to them in order to finance their own addiction. It may be that economic arguments will win the day, as they did with Prohibition, and lead us along the path many other modern nations have trod to combat the scourge of drugs. Redefining alcohol prohibition as an issue of economics and corruption helped to repeal this well-meaning moral experiment. The moral argument vis-à-vis drugs cuts both ways, however. Is it more moral to punish the use of admittedly bad substances or to minimize their harmful effects by dealing with them so that they do the least amount of harm?

SUMMARY

Although the law is designed to control deviance, it occasionally bites off more than it can chew. This chapter addressed some of those behaviors that seem impervious to any legal threats that a democratic government can make. Acts that have been defined as vice crimes are rewarding to those who engage in them, just as ordinary crimes such as robbery are. The major difference is that vice crimes are *mala prohibita*, in that both parties have freely consented to engage in them because it is mutually rewarding, whereas crimes like robbery are *mala in se*.

Based on John Stuart Mill's harm principle, vice crimes are defended as acts that should be beyond the reach of the law, since they are said to be consensual or "victimless." However, many vice crimes can be extremely harmful, and thus the debate is not about harm/no harm but about the ratio of harms caused by vice to the amount of harms caused by trying to enforce bans on it. Some vice crimes, such as fornication and adultery, are so widespread that any serious attempt to enforce prohibitions against them is just not possible. In fact, trying to regulate vice is so difficult, expensive, and opposed by the public that the manufacture and sale of addictive drugs is the only vice discussed in this chapter that remains meaningfully criminalized.

Historically, sodomy was considered to be any sex act meant to result in orgasm other than sex for reproductive purposes, but in the late nineteenth century, it came to mean primarily homosexual sexual activity. With the American Psychiatric Association's changing attitudes about homosexuality (evolving from a disease, to a choice, to a biological given), the remaining anti-sodomy statutes of all states were ruled unconstitutional in *Lawrence v. Texas* in 2003.

The new secular definition of marriage and homosexuals gaining quasi-protected category status has led to a clash of fundamental rights. Religious owners of small businesses are being forced by the state to provide services that facilitate gay marriage in violation of their faith. The issue is not one of serving gays, which they are all willing to do, but one of actively participating in the wedding by taking photographs and inscribing cakes with images of gay couples. The state should not be in the business of enforcing the rights of one group fully while ignoring completely the rights of the other, so religious exceptions could be the solution.

Prostitution has had a checkered existence in the United States. It has been alternatively viewed as a necessary evil (in towns with few women) to being damned as a destroyer of marriages and a carrier of disease and death. The arguments about prostitution have revolved around legalization or decriminalization. Legalization means that the state can regulate and tax it; decriminalization simply means that it is just another activity of no interest to the state. Although prostitution is technically illegal everywhere in the United States except Rhode Island and parts of Nevada, it is tolerated in almost every community as long as prostitutes stay off the street.

Pornography is legal in the United States, protected by the First Amendment; obscenity is not. However, where the line between them is, or even whether such a line even exists, is debatable. The test for obscenity outlined in *Miller v. California* (1973) clearly fits almost all products and activities readily available by mail, DVD, cable TV, the Internet, and even live sex shows. The courts have agreed that pornography is harmful but also that this very harm is what qualifies it as speech, and it therefore is protected. The immense amount of money spent on pornography/obscenity testifies to its popularity, which leads those of a more communitarian bent to decry the moral decline of the United States.

Abortion is the former vice crime that incites the most heated debate. In 2009, the pro-life and pro-choice factions were about evenly divided in the United States and still are. Abortion was allowed by common law up until the time of the detection of the first fetal movement (the quickening), but by the turn of the twentieth century, every state prohibited it except when the woman's life was at risk. Because of the alarming rate of illegal abortions that led to death, public opinion about abortion began to change in the 1960s. In 1973, the Supreme Court gave women the right to abortion in the first trimester and allowed the states to regulate it in the second trimester and to prohibit it during the third unless the life or health of the mother was at risk. The biggest issue today is that of partial-birth abortion, a brutal method of abortion that the US Congress has forbidden by an act the Supreme Court has upheld.

Alcohol is so popular and ubiquitous today that it is difficult to realize it was once considered as evil as narcotics in the United States and prohibited. Few people would dispute that alcohol abuse causes more harm than perhaps all the other vices combined, but this, plus the fact that alcohol is perfectly legal today, points dramatically to the difficulties in trying to control it legally. The prohibition of the manufacture, sale, and consumption of alcohol in 1920 ushered in a wild decade of criminal activity during which gangs battled for the control of the illicit alcohol market. In fact, Prohibition actually made worse practically all of the problems it was supposed to solve. We are arguably repeating the mistakes of Prohibition with today's "war on drugs." Many other democracies are dealing with their drug problem by treating it as a medical rather than a criminal problem, and they aim at minimizing the undoubted harm of drugs.

DISCUSSION QUESTIONS

1. Why are many people hypocritical about vice (i.e., publically condemning but privately practicing)?
2. Is the harm principle alone sufficient to determine the illegality of an act?
3. Discuss how the gay rights versus religious liberty issue might be resolved. Is it a zero-sum game in which either gay rights or religious liberty must be

trampled on? If so, which is more fundamental, and which needs more legal protection?

4. Make an argument for or against the proposition that requiring religious people to participate in same-sex marriage arrangement against their will is involuntary servitude forbidden by the Thirteenth Amendment.
5. Give reasons why prostitution should or should not be legalized or decriminalized.
6. In what sense can pornography be considered speech protected by the First Amendment?
7. Give the reasons you are pro-choice or pro-life.
8. Should the United States decriminalize/legalize drugs? What do you think would be the consequences of doing so?

CHAPTER TERMS

Abortion
Compelling government interest
Harm principle
Harrison Narcotics Act

Miller test
Obscenity
Pornography
Prohibition
Prostitution

Religious Freedom Restoration Act
Sodomy
Vice crime

References

Alcohol Alert. (2009). 2007 drunk driving statistics. Retrieved from http://www.alcoholalert.com/

Alliance Defending Freedom. (2015). Wash. floral artist's home, savings at risk of state seizure after court ruling. Retrieved from http://www.alliancedefendingfreedom.org/News/Detail?ContentID=83837

American Psychological Association. (2005). APA Briefing Paper on the impact of abortion on women. Retrieved from http://www.rcrc.org/pdf/APA%20document.pdf

Anderson, R., & Ford, L. (2014, April). Protecting religious liberty in the state marriage debate. Backgrounder no. 2891. Retrieved from http://www.heritage.org/research/reports/2014/04/protecting-religious-liberty-in-the-state-marriage-debate

Augst, T. (2007). Temperance, mass culture, and the romance of experience. *American Literary History, 19*, 297–323.

Baltakis, A. (2002). Jerry Lee Lewis and his marriages: An excuse to attack rock and roll. *Journal of American Culture, 25*, 51–56.

Benkof, D. (2008, May 28). Why California gays shouldn't celebrate state court ruling. *Seattle Post Intelligencer.* Retrieved from http://www.seattlepi.com/local/opinion/article/Why-California-gays-shouldnt-celebrate-state-1273942.php

Berg, T. C. (2010). What same-sex marriage and religious-liberty claims have in common. *Northwestern Journal of Law and Social Policy, 5*, 206–235.

Blocker, J. (2006). Did prohibition really work? Alcohol prohibition as a public health innovation. *American Journal of Public Health, 96*, 233–243.

Blue, A. (2004). *The complete book of spirits: A guide to their history, production and enjoyment.* New York, NY: HarperCollins.

Blumstein, A. (1995). Youth violence, guns, and the illicit-drug industry. *Journal of Criminal Law and Criminology, 86*, 10–36.

Brown, B. (2007). Pornography and feminism: Is law the answer? *Critical Quarterly, 34*, 72–82.

Bullough, V. (1976). *Sexual variance in society and history*. Chicago, IL: University of Chicago Press.

Burr, C. (1993, March). Homosexuality and biology. *The Atlantic Monthly*, pp. 47–65.

Canaday, M. (2008, September 16). The strange history of sodomy laws. *The Nation*. Retrieved from http://www.alternet.org/story/99092/the_strange_history_of_sodomy_laws

Carpenter, D. (2004). The unknown past of *Lawrence v. Texas. Michigan Law Review, 102*, 1464–1527.

Carver, F. (1999). With Bible in one hand and battle-axe in the other: Carrie A. Nation as religious reformer and self-promoter. *Religion and American Culture, 9*, 31–65.

Casey, E. (1978). History of drug use and drug users in the United States. Schaffer Library of Drug Policy. Retrieved from http://www.druglibrary.org/schaffer/History/CASEY1.htm

Chauncey, G., N. Cott, J. D'Emilio, E. Freedman, T. Holt, J. Howard, . . . L. Kerber. (2003). Amicus brief of history professors in the matter of *John Geddes Lawrence and Tyron Garner v. State of Texas*. Retrieved from www.findlaw.com

Cougle, J., Reardon, D., & Coleman, P. (2003). Depression associated with abortion and childbirth: A long-term analysis of the NLSY cohort. *Medical Science Monitor, 9*, 105–112.

Davenport-Hines, R. (2002). *The pursuit of oblivion: A global history of narcotics*. New York, NY: W. W. Norton.

Devlin, P. (1965). *The enforcement of morals*. Oxford, England: Oxford University Press.

Donohue, J., & Levitt, S. (2001). The impact of legalized abortion on crime. *Quarterly Journal of Economics, 116*, 379–420.

Dreher, R. (2015). Traditional Christians under siege. *Time, 185*, 13: 32.

Drug Enforcement Administration. (2003). *Drugs of abuse*. Arlington, VA: US Department of Justice.

Durant, W. (1939). *The life of Greece*. New York, NY: Simon & Schuster.

Federal Bureau of Investigation. (2004). *Uniform Crime Reports handbook*. Washington, DC: US Government Printing Office.

Feldblum, C. (2006). Moral conflict and liberty: Gay rights and religion. *Brooklyn Law Review, 72*, 61–123.

Ferguson, C., & Hartley, R. (2009). The pleasure of the moment . . . the expense damnable? The influence of pornography on rape and sexual assault. *Aggression and Violent Behavior, 14*, 323–329.

Fergusson, D., Horwood, L., & Ridder, E. (2006). Abortion in young women and subsequent mental health. *Journal of Child Psychology and Psychiatry, 47*, 16–24.

Flynn, T. (2010). Clarion call or false alarm: Why proposed exemptions to equal marriage statutes return us to a religious understanding of the public marketplace. *Northwestern Journal of Law and Social Policy, 5*, 236–259.

Friedman, L. (2005). *A history of American law*. New York, NY: Simon & Schuster.

Gallup Poll. (2017). Abortion. https://news.gallup.com/poll/1576/abortion.aspx

Gallup Poll. (2014b). Same-sex marriage support reaches new high at 55%. Retrieved from http://www.gallup.com/poll/169640/sex-marriage-support-reaches-new-high.aspx

Garrow, D. (1998). *Liberty and sexuality: The right to privacy and the making of* Roe v. Wade. Berkeley: University of California Press.

Garvey, J. (1996). Anti-liberal argument for religious freedom. *Journal of Contemporary Legal Issues, 7*, 275–291.

Goldstein, P. (1985). The drugs/violence nexus: A tripartite conceptual framework. *Journal of Drug Issues, 15*, 493–506.

Goodlett, C., Horn, K., & Zhou, F. (2005). Alcohol teratogenesis: Mechanisms of damage and strategies for intervention. *Developmental Biology and Medicine, 230*, 394–406.

Greenstein, J. (2004). Sex, lies and American tort law: The love triangle in context. *Georgetown Journal of Gender and the Law, 1*, 723–762.

Hagan, F. (2008). *Introduction to criminology* (6th ed.). Thousand Oaks, CA: SAGE.

Hallowell, B. (2015, December 31). Lawyer for Christian bakers who were forced to pay nearly $137,000 to lesbian couple reveals most shocking element of the case. *The Blaze* http://www.theblaze.com/stories/2015/12/31/lawyer-for-christian-bakers-who-were-forced-to-pay-nearly-137000-to-lesbian-couple-reveals-most-shocking-element-of-the-case/

Harcourt, B. (1999). The collapse of the harm principle. *Journal of Criminal Law and Criminology, 90*, 109–194..

Jacobson, J., & Jacobson, S. (2002). Effects of prenatal alcohol exposure on child development. *Alcohol Research and Health, 26*, 282–286.

Kaplan, J. (1988). Abortion as a vice crime: A "what if" story. *Law and Contemporary Problems, 51*, 151–179.

King, L. W. (Trans.). (2009). Hammurabi's code of laws. Retrieved from http://prostitution.procon.org/sourcefiles/Hammurabi.pdf

Kolodny, A., Courtwright, D., Hwang, C., Kreiner, P., Eadie, J., Clark, T., & Alexander, G. (2015). The prescription opioid and heroin crisis: a public health approach to an epidemic of addiction. *Annual review of public health, 36*, 559–574.

Koppelman, A. (2015). Theorists, get over yourselves: A response to Steven D. Smith. *Pepperdine Law Review, 41*, 937–942.

Laycock, D. (2014). Religious liberty and the culture wars. *University of Illinois Law Review, 14*, 839–880.

Laycock, D., & Berg, T. (2013). Protecting same-sex marriage and religious liberty. *Virginia Law Review, 99*, 1–9.

Lindevaldsen, R. (2010). Fallacy of neutrality from beginning to end: The battle between religious liberties and rights based on homosexual conduct. *Liberty University Law Review, 4*, 425–463.

Lykken, D. (1995). *The antisocial personalities.* Hillsdale, NJ: Lawrence Erlbaum.

Manning, M., & Hoyme, H. (2007). Fetal alcohol syndrome disorders: A practical clinical approach to diagnosis. *Neuroscience and Biobehavioral Review, 31*, 230–238.

Martin, S. (2001). The links between alcohol, crime and the criminal justice system: Explanations, evidence and interventions. *American Journal on Addictions, 10*, 136–158.

McGovern, P. (2003). *Ancient wine: The search for the origins of viniculture.* Princeton, NJ: Princeton University Press.

McMurren, M. (2003). Alcohol and crime. *Criminal Behavior and Mental Health, 13*, 1–4.

Menard, S., Mihalic, S., & Huizinga, D. (2001). Drugs and crime revisited. *Justice Quarterly, 18*, 269–299.

Mill, J. (1913). *On Liberty.* London, England: Longmans, Green.

Mustaine, E., & Tewksbury, R. (2004). Alcohol and violence. In S. Holmes & R. Holmes (Eds.), *Violence: A contemporary reader* (pp. 9–25). Upper Saddle River, NJ: Prentice Hall.

National Institute of Justice. (1991). *Annual report on adult arrestees: Drugs and crime in America's cities.* Washington, DC: US Department of Justice.

Nutt, D., King, L., Saulsbury, W., & Blakemore, C. (2007). Development of a rational scale to assess the harm of drugs of potential misuse. *The Lancet, 396*, 1047–1053.

Office of National Drug Control Policy. (2014). ADAM II 2013 annual report. Retrieved from http://www.whitehouse.gov/sites/default/files/ondcp/policy-and-research/adam_ii_2013_annual_report.pdf

Painter, G. (2005). The sensibilities of our forefathers: The history of sodomy laws in the United States. Retrieved from http://www.glapn.org/sodomylaws/sensibilities/introduction.htm

Rasmussen Reports. (2013). 85% think Christian photographer has right to turn down same-sex wedding job. Retrieved from http://www.rasmussenreports.com/public_content/business/general_business/july_2013/85_think_christian_photographer_has_right_to_turn_down_same_sex_wedding_job

Raymond, J. (2003). Ten reasons for *not* legalizing prostitution and a legal response to the demand for prostitution. *Journal of Trauma Practice, 2*, 315–332. Retrieved from http://www.prostitutionresearch.com/laws/000022.html

Robinson, T., & Berridge, K. (2003). Addiction. *Annual Review of Psychology, 54*, 25–53.

Rosenberg, G. (1991). *The hollow hope: Can courts bring about social change?* Chicago, IL: University of Chicago Press.

Rutledge, C. (2008). Caught in the crossfire: How Catholic Charities of Boston was victim to the clash between gay rights and religious freedom. *Duke Journal of Gender, Law & Policy, 15*, 297–314.

Saad, L. (2016). Americans attitudes toward abortion unchanged. Retrieved from http://www.gallup.com/poll/191834/americans-attitudes-toward-abortion-unchanged

Sanburn, J. (2014, October 17). Houston's pastors outraged after city subpoenas sermons over transgender bill. *Time*. Retrieved from http://time.com/3514166/houston-pastors-sermons-subpoenaed/

Savolainen, V., & Lehmann, L. (2007). Genetics and bisexuality. *Nature, 445*, 158–159.

Stone, G., Seidman, L., Sunstein, C., & Tushnet, M. (1999). *The First Amendment*. New York, NY: Aspen Law and Business.

Stuntz, W. (2000). Self-defeating crimes. *Virginia Law Review, 86*, 1871–1899.

Sullivan, A. (2018, February 20). The poison we pick. *New York Magazine*. Retrieved from http://nymag.com/daily/intelligencer/2018/02/americas-opioid-epidemic.html

Tutty, L., & Nixon, K. (2003). Selling sex? It's really like selling your soul. Vulnerability to and the experience of exploitation through child prostitution. In K. Gorkoff & J. Runner (Eds.), *Being heard: The experience of young women in prostitution* (pp. 29–45). Black Point, NS: Fernwood.

US Department of Health and Human Services. (2009). Updating estimates of the economic costs of alcohol abuse in the United States. Center for Substance Abuse Treatment. Retrieved from http://www.maine.gov/dhhs/osa/pubs/us/2009/costoffset.pdf

US Department of Health and Human Services. (2018). What is the U.S. opioid epidemic? Retrieved from https://www.hhs.gov/opioids/about-the-epidemic

US Immigration and Customs Enforcement. (2013). Human trafficking. Retrieved from http://www.ice.gov/human-trafficking

Walsh, A. (2015). Tragic choices in ideological battles: Gay rights versus religious freedom. *Journal of Religion and Society, 17*, 1–26.

Wanberg, K., & Milkman, H. (1998). *Criminal conduct and substance abuse treatment: Strategies for self-improvement*. Thousand Oaks, CA: SAGE.

Weitzer, R. (1999). Prostitution control in America. *Crime, Law, and Social Change, 32*, 83–102.

West, J. (2000). Prostitution: Collectives and the politics of regulation. *Gender, Work, and Organization, 7*, 106–118.

Wodak, A. (2007). Ethics and drug policy. *Psychiatry, 6*, 59–62.

Cases Cited

American Booksellers Association, Inc. v. Hudnut, 475 U.S. 1001 (1986) and 98 F. Supp. 1316 (S.D. Ind. 1984)

Ashcroft v. Free Speech Coalition, 535 U.S. 234 (2002)

CHAPTER 11

LAW, SOCIAL CHANGE, AND THE CLASS STRUGGLE

In February 1932, future British Prime Minister Winston Churchill was knocked down by a cab as he crossed Fifth Avenue in New York. Churchill had a flask of whiskey on his person, which made this great man a criminal in the United States. This strange state of affairs existed because of the National Prohibition Act, passed in 1919 to enforce the Eighteenth Amendment's prohibition of the manufacture, sale, or importation of alcoholic beverages. Temperance and abstinence movements had existed for decades before this based on the fact that unbridled drinking was the cause of many of society's problems, particularly crime. In passing the act, lawmakers were responding to demands for change in an important area of social life. Activists of all persuasions agitate for change, and sometimes lawmakers put their stamp of approval on their goals by passing acts and making favorable judicial decisions.

The intention, of course, was to severely limit drinking and thus to limit the evils associated with it. Unfortunately, good intentions often have unintended consequences that few people see beforehand. What the US Congress did in 1919 was give every petty criminal gang in the country a green light to unlimited expansion and riches. In many ways, it literally kick-started organized crime in the United States and ushered in a decade of gang wars and widespread corruption. Prohibiting alcohol made it more exciting to imbibe it in the speakeasies that sprang up everywhere. In a number of cases, people were poisoned by bad liquor, and there was apparently no letup in incidents of spousal or child abuse.

Given that what lawmakers do may "misfire" in many ways, is there a danger in using law to regulate morality? The risk was clear during Prohibition, but are we doing the same thing today by criminalizing drugs such as marijuana and cocaine? What are the limits of law in producing social change? Does law lead or follow? More important, what are the *principled* limits of law in social change? These are some of the questions to keep in mind as we examine the role of law in social change.

INTRODUCTION

In chapter 10, we discussed so-called vice crimes and society's efforts to control them. When a society experiences frequent violations of its normative standards and its capacity or willingness to control this deviance is limited, social change may occur, and the boundaries of acceptable behavior may be redefined and redrawn. In chapter 10, we saw that changes of this nature occur frequently as American society defines and redefines what it considers acceptable behavior. Every time society decides that the formerly unacceptable is now acceptable or the formerly acceptable is now unacceptable, it is engaging in social change. The changes discussed in chapter 10 revolved around personal and moral issues, such as pornography and abortion; this chapter deals with broader issues of a social, political, and economic nature, particularly the struggle of the working classes for justice.

WHAT IS SOCIAL CHANGE?

Social change may be defined as any relatively enduring alteration in social relationships, behavior patterns, values, norms, and attitudes occurring over time. Some changes may seem trivial, but they may aggregate and interact with other trivial as well as nontrivial changes to produce patterns of behavior and values that can appear grotesquely alien to individuals born in an earlier period. Because of the sheer complexity of modern societies and the intricate interaction of their component parts, each small change generates its own momentum, gathering speed in a chain reaction as each change generates even more change. The sheer pace of modern social change can leave some of us giddy and confused, alienated and afraid.

There was a time in history when people lived out their lives with nary a hint of social change. Norms, customs, values, and practices endured essentially intact through each individual's short journey from cradle to grave. Small and isolated cultures are like small and isolated gene pools—they tend toward equilibrium. Ideas are "inbred" and produce only small mutations from the standard ideas available; there are only so many permutations possible from a limited pool of either genes or ideas. As mentioned in chapter 1, for much of human history, large-scale social changes usually originated outside the culture and came in the form of wars, invasions, famines, pestilence, and changes in climate, but rarely from within the culture itself. Such cultural continuity is psychologically comforting, conferring as it does a sense of meaning and stability on the lives of people experiencing it. The comfort of habit is one of the reasons that many people resist change, even if it may be desirable on moral grounds, and occasionally enlist the law in their endeavors to do so.

Those who most stoutly resist social change are usually those who profit most from society as it exists or who feel most psychologically threatened by change. Changes such as the emergence of legalized pornography and abortion in the 1970s may be resisted because "it's just not right," meaning that the change is perceived as being at odds with traditional values. Tensions occur when the pressures of change collide with established norms, and these tensions occasionally lead to the emergence of prejudice and intolerance. Most social changes, however, tend to work themselves out without serious conflict, and most changes that do generate conflict usually are resolved in courts of law in modern societies.

THE LAW AS A CAUSE OF SOCIAL CHANGE

Historically, the law has played only a minor role in social change compared with other causes, but its role has increased hugely over the past two centuries. The law is mostly reactive rather than proactive in social change; that is, it reacts to social forces rather than sets such forces in motion. At other times, however, the law, as an independent source of power, functions as the instrument of social change. There is a tendency to view law as a barrier to change because it consists for the most part of norms and customs that have been codified, and norms and customs, almost by definition, are resistant to change. Indeed, the very slowness of social change in preindustrial society is what made custom a sufficient basis for formal systems of law. But is custom a sufficient basis in a modern society? And if not, what will replace it, and what does it mean for social change? The tension inherent in these questions was well put over a century ago by the Conservative British Prime Minister Benjamin Disraeli:

> The great question is, not whether you should resist change which is inevitable, but whether that change should be carried out in deference to the manners, the customs, the laws, and the traditions of the people, or in deference to abstract principles and arbitrary and general doctrines. (Ashford, 1990, p. 46)

To understand Disraeli's point about laws and traditions versus abstract principles, contrast the French (1789) and Russian (1917) revolutions (1917) with the English (1688) and American (1776) revolutions. The first two were driven by abstract theories, appealed to the heart with stirring shibboleths of equality, tried to wipe the slate clean of everything that went before, but ended up trading one form of despotism for another. They produced bloody reigns of terror driven by the belief that human nature can be molded by force and fiat and led to the guillotine, mass executions, and gulags. The English and American revolutions were driven by attempts to restore the old order in deference to the traditions of law and the customs of Anglo-Saxon culture. They also produced change, but they did not throw out the baby with the bath water. Both eschewed utopianism and abstract theories, produced the English and American Bill of Rights, respectively, and balanced political power.

When the law no longer enjoys an organic relationship with custom, society is in the process of cultural fracture (Bonsignore et al., 1989). Those who think this way believe that the use of law to generate social change is wrong and self-defeating unless that law is a natural extension of social custom. The law is supposed to be close to the heartbeat of the people, a palpable manifestation of their moral sentiments. If law is to be an instrument of change, it should involve limiting the removal of some specific defect, not chasing utopian dreams of social perfection. This is a conservative view of the law and one that tends to be held by those who call for a return to traditional values and for laws supporting and enforcing them. Such a call may be laudable in a less diverse society than the United States, but many feel that returning to traditional values in this country means returning to the customs of white Anglo-Saxon America—which may be fine if one is white, Christian, and heterosexual.

This should not be construed as a condemnation of the mainstream cultural traditions of the United States. They are still laudable and meaningful, and they have produced a wealthy and decent society where rights and liberty are honored more than in the vast majority of nations around the world. But many Americans were never part of this cultural tradition to begin with, so they may not support a "return" to it. The United States today is a heterogeneous stew of many different cultural traditions and customs, which means that American law, if it is to be perceived as fair, cannot be based on the customs and morality of just one group. Non–European American groups tend to look at the role of law quite differently, hoping that it can be used as a valid tool to change custom, not defend it. For them, law should be responsive to the injustices suffered by them, and it should legislate and enforce social reforms. In other words, law based on universalistic principles of justice, not the customs of one particular subset of society that are defended by positivist law, should regulate social behavior. As the law becomes more involved in social life, however, it faces major challenges, chief among which is how to preserve it without offending cultural pluralism. That is, the law built on Anglo-American moral traditions must validate itself by effecting principles of justice in ways that are understood and appreciated by all minority groups as well as the mainstream.

SOCIAL MOVEMENTS, THE LAW, AND SOCIAL CHANGE

There is a reciprocal relationship between law and social change. Sometimes social conditions give rise to changes in the law, and sometimes changes in the law give rise to changes in social conditions. We must remember that law is not an isolated phenomenon; it is an integral and inextricable part of culture and society. This is perhaps more true of the United States than any other country. As long ago as 1835, the French philosopher and political commentator Alexis de Tocqueville (1945) noted that nearly all American politicians are trained in the law, that legal language and attitudes saturate American culture, and that almost any issue of any importance sooner or later becomes a "subject for judicial debate" (pp. 330–331).

We may consider the role of law in social change to be most often facilitative rather than causative; that is, it serves as a conduit guiding the progress of some reform that is already in the works for other reasons. Those "other reasons" almost invariably involve organized groups of ordinary people making realistic claims on their government to advance their collective interests. When enough people are involved in this process, we call it a social movement. A classic definition of a **social movement** is that of Charles Tilly (1984), who defined it as

> a sustained series of interactions between powerholders and persons successfully claiming to speak on behalf of a constituency lacking formal representation, in the course of which those persons make publicly visible demands for changes in the distribution or exercise of power, and back those demands with public demonstrations of support. (p. 306)

Law provides a very important part of the terrain for social movements to exploit when pursuing their goals because most social movements rely on claims of rights denial to frame their grievances. Few things are more powerful in recruiting and mobilizing individuals, and in creating a common identity, than to sharpen their sense of rights deprivation. As Frances Zemans (1983) asserts: "What the populace actually receives from government is to a large extent dependent upon their willingness and ability to assert and use the law on their own behalf" (p. 694). In other words, only when the wheel squeaks will it get some oil. But the law can turn a deaf ear to the squeak, so it is up to individuals in the movement to crank up the volume by extralegal means. As Wilson and Cordero (2006) put it: "Combining rights consciousness with a bill of rights and a willing and able judiciary improves the outlook for a rights revolution, but material support for sustained pursuit of rights is still crucial" (p. 327). This extralegal "material support" refers to tactics employed by various social movements, which include media campaigns, strikes, protest marches, and other forms of disruptive tactics that reach the ears of politicians and judges and may persuade them to apply the legal oil can.

The contentious politics of social movements pursuing rights and other interests depend to a large extent on democracy, since dissent in nondemocratic societies is rarely tolerated. As we have previously noted, conflict is actually functional in a democratic society because it is a way in which rightful claims of justice are brought to the fore and recognized. Charles Tilly (2004), perhaps the foremost modern theorist of social movements, claims: "Democratization promotes the formation of social movements" (p. 36). In other words, democracy not only tolerates dissent in the form of social movement, it also promotes it. Tilly goes on to say that social movements as we know them had their origins in early eighteenth-century Britain and the United States, and that the British anti-slavery movement has some claim to be the first social movement. Before there was a free press and other methods by which information could be shared quickly with many others, and before there was an independent judiciary, social movements intended to address grievances were unlikely to go anywhere without resorting to widespread violence. Tilly (2004) makes a case for the American Revolution as a series of small social movements for limited reforms being largely ignored until they coalesced into violent revolution.

Once a social movement is observed successfully making its rights claim, other previously silent groups are aroused in what has been called a "contagion effect" (McCann, 2006, p. 26). There is an ebb and flow of contagion effects depending on the historical period, with some periods being much more "contagious" than others. As we shall see, the period between 1953 and 1986 was particularly active when the US Supreme Court under Chief Justices Earl Warren and Warren Burger was responsive to justice claims. Think of the cascade of legislation and court cases that rode in on the coattails of demands by minorities, women, and gays over the past 50 or 60 years. Law legitimized many of their demands in specific and rational ways, and it provided sanctioning provisions for those who would deny them. Law functions to legitimize change, to smooth the way, and to grease the squeaky wheels of opposition to change. Examples of the role of law (both as a block and a facilitator) in the success or failure of social movements are dispersed throughout this book. The century-long fight for workers' rights is featured in this chapter. The rights of gays and lesbians are addressed in chapters 7 and 10, abortion rights in chapter 10, women's rights in chapter 12, and minority racial/ethnic rights in chapter 13. Figure 11.1 illustrates the typical relationship between law and social change with some important examples. The relationship can be viewed as a series of social demands (inputs) flowing into legislatures and courts to be digested and coming out the other end as law (outputs).

BRITISH LAW AND THE AMERICAN REVOLUTION

Anyone reluctant to credit the law with much of a role in social change might ponder the possibility that were it not for a number of British legal decisions in the eighteenth century, the American colonies may have remained loyal to the mother country. Most of us are aware of the many pieces of British legislation following the French and Indian Wars. Many of those laws were designed to make the American colonists pay their share of the expense of that war, which was, after all, fought to defend them. These included the Mutiny Act of 1765 (requiring colonists to provision and maintain the army), the Sugar Act of 1774 (designed to eliminate illegal sugar trade between

Figure 11.1 Flowchart Illustrating Typical Role of Law in Social Change

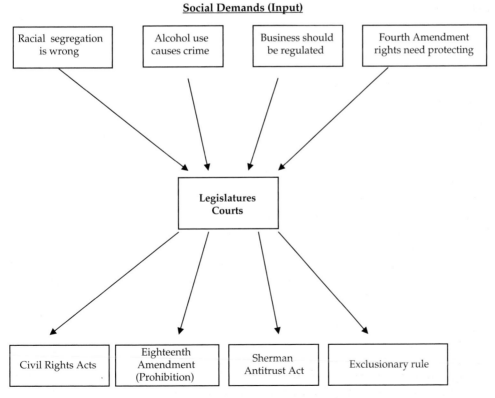

the colonies and the French and Spanish West Indies), and the Stamp Act of 1765 (imposed a tax on every printed document in the colonies). Colonists used British law to oppose these acts; serving on grand juries, they refused to return indictments against violators.

The **Proclamation Act** of 1763 was particularly galling to many prominent colonists. This act forbade white settlement west of the Appalachians in conformity with a British peace treaty with the Ottawa Indians. Powerful land speculators such as George Washington, William Crawford, and Benjamin Franklin had invested heavily in the Ohio Valley, which the Proclamation ceded to Native Americans. This did much to cause many of these speculators "to favor an independent American government, which might look more kindly on their real estate plans" (Woodin, 1974, p. 43).

In addition to these legislative acts, several judicial rulings also may have contributed to the fracture between Britain and the American colonies. Two famous slavery cases—*Somerset v. Stewart* (1772) and *Joseph Knight v. Wedderburn* (1778), which were heard in England and Scotland, respectively—may have been instrumental in propelling the more reluctant southern states into the revolution (Parrillo, 2003). The *Somerset* case involved a slave named James Somerset who was taken to England by his Virginian master, Charles Stewart. Somerset escaped, was captured again, and then held aboard ship for transportation to Jamaica. Lord Chief Justice Mansfield issued a writ of habeas corpus preventing Somerset's departure from England and requiring Stewart to present him to the court. The legal issue involved was whether or not a slave can be considered free because of his sojourn on free soil. Justice Mansfield declared that he could, and in doing so, he berated slavery as so odious that "whatever inconveniences, therefore, may follow from the decision, I cannot say this case is allowed or approved by the law of England; and therefore the black must be discharged" (Klingberg, 1968, p. 39).

Mansfield's decision applied only to England, Wales, and Ireland, but it set the precedent for *Knight*, decided in 1778. *Knight* had the effect of outlawing slavery from every part of the British Isles and by extension, many jurists of the time believed, throughout the British Empire (this did not actually occur until 1833). Such a possibility, if enforceable, would have been unacceptable to the southern American colonies whose way of life rested heavily on slavery. According to Donnelly (2006), these cases were "the starting point for the falling dominos that led to the abolishment of slavery, and [to] affirmative action in the United States" (p. 40). We cannot know for sure the part these two decisions actually played in the subsequent events, but they do point to the "ripple" effect of law on so many aspects of human life.

As noted earlier, unlike the revolutions in France and Russia, the American Revolution was quite a legal affair; in fact, "The American Revolution was a reluctant uprising staged by men who were exceptionally dedicated to the English constitution" (Johnson, 2006, p. 3). The reluctance to part from the ways of their forefathers was well voiced by Thomas Jefferson in 1775: "Believe me, dear Sir: there is not in the British Empire a man who more cordially loves a union with Great Britain than I do. But, by the God that made me, I will cease to exist before I yield to a connection on such terms as the British Parliament propose" (Hazelton, 1970, p. 19). Many revolutionaries took the position that the separation from Britain was a legal separation and that the Declaration of Independence was a political bill of divorce based on legal grounds found in the English constitution (Johnson, 2006). The principle that the constitution, not the monarch, is sovereign was settled in the Glorious Revolution of 1688. The offenses charged against George III (as Thomas Jefferson noted, parliament, not George, was the culprit because the monarch's power was severely limited by the Glorious Revolution) in the Declaration of Independence were all offenses against British legal principles. The rebellious colonists reasoned that since the sovereignty of the law over the monarch had been established, and since George III was now placing himself above the law, they had a legal right to revolt. In the minds of many of the leading figures of the American Revolution, they were loyal to the precedent established by the Glorious Revolution of their forefathers in England (Johnson, 2006).

LAW AND SOCIAL ENGINEERING IN THE FORMER SOVIET UNION

The history of the Soviet Union provides an excellent contrast with the United States to discuss the role of law in social change. The history of prerevolutionary Russia shows that the law can delay, if not altogether stifle, the "natural" tides of social change. That Czarist Russia failed to survive is a vindication of conservative philosopher Edmund Burke's dictum that "[a] state without the means of some change is without means of its conservation" (Ashford, 1990, p. 46). After the fall of the czar and the formation of the Soviet Union in 1922, rather than using law to stifle social change, the Soviets used it to force social change. These changes and attempted changes provide the best case example available for examining the strengths and weaknesses of law as a vehicle of social change.

A student of the history and political development of the United States is well advised to study the US Constitution, which has served as a set of guiding principles for the role of law in social change throughout American history. A study of Soviet constitutions (there have been five since 1918) and subsequent Russian constitutions would not yield similar benefits, for it would be difficult to discover general legal principles that would help the reader to understand Soviet society. The various Soviet constitutions have been longer and more detailed (the 1977 version had 173 articles) than the US Constitution (7 original articles and 27 amendments). The 27 amendments to the US Constitution have occurred over more than 200 years; the Russian constitution (the one that existed prior to Boris Yeltsin's new democratic constitution) had been amended, on average, once a day from 1990 to the enactment of the new Constitution of the Russian Federation in December 1993 ("Stalin or Yeltsin?", 1993). The Russian constitution allowed Vladimir Putin to seek and overwhelmingly win a fourth term as president. There is nothing "unconstitutional" about this since the Russian constitution was intended to enable presidential power. Any rights outlined in the Russian constitution are not guaranteed by law, a strong judiciary, or independent political parties, but by the power of the Russian president.

We may consider these Soviet and subsequent Russian constitutions to be preeminently political weapons changed on a whim rather than documents enunciating society's organizing principles. Nevertheless, although the Russian state subordinates the rule of law to politics, the five Soviet constitutions and present Russian constitution serve the purposes of all **constitutions**, which are the following:

Legalize the existing political order and legitimize its ideology.

Provide a framework for the administration of government.

Regulate social and institutional behavior.

Enumerate national goals and aspirations.

The Russian experience shows that written constitutions are not a guarantee of political freedom. Nevertheless, Soviet leaders went to great lengths to make Soviet policy-making conform to formal rationality processes so that their social experiments would be perceived in the West as legitimate (Hosking, 1985). Officially, the legal process in the Soviet Union was conducted in conformity with Weber's formal rationality, but in reality, it conformed more with substantive irrationality, the substance provided by Marxist ideology. Legal decisions often were made by revolutionary tribunals on an ad hoc basis to conform to the will of the Communist Party (Reichel, 2005). The use of vague concepts like "counter-revolutionary" and "enemy of the people" allowed the creation of "instant" offenses not designated as crimes in any penal code (*ex post facto* laws). Such practices are expressly forbidden in common law but justified by the Soviets as necessary to preserve the revolution.

A cliché often heard is that "You can't legislate morality." The American experiences with such attempts, discussed in chapter 10, tend to support this cliché. However, one would not find much support for such a position in the former Soviet Union. The Soviets viewed law as a force for social change that could and would mold the attitudes and behaviors of the people in any way the government deemed appropriate. The ultimate goal was the "dictatorship of the proletariat," in which such bourgeois (middle-class) vestiges as law would not be needed. Recall from chapter 1 that Marx considered law to be nothing more than the codified ideology of the ruling class; in the Soviet utopia, there would be no ruling class and therefore no need for law.

During the early days of the Soviet Union, Western concepts of law were thrown out in favor of **Soviet legalism**, a principle defined as "strict and unflinching observance and fulfillment of Soviet laws by all organs of the socialist state and public organizations, institutions and all citizens, in all circumstances, and at all times" (Barry & Barner-Barry, 1978, p. 135). One of the most significant attempted changes involved the family. Because the family is the transmitter, defender, and modeler of the old order, if it is destroyed, society as it is presently constituted is destroyed. The Soviets were committed to destroying the "bourgeois family," declaring it was based on the "paternalistic" notion of property-based marriage that exploited women. To destroy the family, the party passed legislation making divorce and abortion available on demand, legitimized unmarried cohabitation, and encouraged "free love" as the "essence of communist living" (Hazard, Butler, & Maggs, 1977, p. 470).

These laws had devastating consequences. "Free love" combined with quick and easy divorce resulted in hundreds of thousands of fatherless children roaming the streets who "formed into gangs, attack[ing] and rob[bing] people in the street, or even invad[ing] and ransack[ing] apartment blocks" (Hosking, 1985, p. 213). When the

Soviets assessed the damage, they quickly reversed themselves and wrote pro-family laws extolling the family and the sanctity of marriage, denouncing divorce, and praising the joys of parenthood. Thus, the formerly reviled became the praised, and the formerly praised (e.g., "free love") was redefined and reviled as "bourgeois."

Overall, the Soviet experience points to both the power and the limits of law to induce social change. Large-scale and wholesale changes can be written into law, but lacking the legitimacy of custom, they may have to be enforced by strong police tactics. Law is a much more efficient instrument of social control and social change if it relies on legitimacy rather than brute coercion. The fact that the Soviet authorities did a 180-degree turn on family law points out that law follows as well as leads social change, even in totalitarian systems.

THE US SUPREME COURT AND SOCIAL CHANGE

Law has been characterized by Talcott Parsons (1977) as an "intellectual stepchild" of sociologists engaged in studying social change (p. 11). Parsons was puzzled by this neglect because he saw law as the "single most important key to understanding problems of social integration" and, by extension, social change (p. 52). The ultimate source of law in the United States is the Constitution, but as Chief Justice Charles Evans Hughes's famous dictum makes clear, "The Constitution is what the Supreme Court says it is." Thus, the Supreme Court is the ultimate legal authority in the United States, and to the extent that constitutional law is the source of social change, the Court is the source of that change. As phrased by Weinberg and Weinberg (1980): "[T]he Supreme Court's role has been central to the relationship between law and social change" (p. 261). In examining the record of the Supreme Court, we find much that supports both the conflict and the consensus theories of law, for the Court has issued a number of rulings that both prevented and generated important social change. We first examine how the Court has used its power to prevent the working classes from achieving social and economic justice and then how it has used the same power to generate justice in many noneconomic spheres of American life.

Dynamic and Constrained Views of the Supreme Court's Power

In his very influential book *The Hollow Hope*, Gerald Rosenberg (1991) took a social science and historical scalpel to the idea that Supreme Court decisions are powerful proximate causes of events that follow. He presented two views on the extent of the Court's ability to induce social change: the dynamic and the constrained.

The **dynamic view** maintains that the Court can be more effective than other government institutions in bringing about social change because it is free of election concerns and thus can act in the face of public opposition. Supreme Court justices are unelected and tenured for life, so they cannot be removed from office by public disapproval of their actions as politicians can. Likewise, individuals and groups who may be disadvantaged in the legislative process coming before the Court in pursuit of just social change do so on the basis of constitutional issues regardless of their "connections or position" (Rosenberg, 1991, p. 23).

The **constrained view** avers that the Supreme Court per se can rarely produce significant social change because of three important constraints. The first constraint is the bounded nature of constitutional rights. Only a limited number of issues can come before the Court, but this constraint can be overcome by ample case precedent in the general direction of the proposed change. For instance, the right to privacy "discovered" by Justice William Douglas under the penumbra of the Bill of Rights in *Griswold v. Connecticut* (1965) granting access to birth-control devices was used to grant abortion rights in *Roe v. Wade* (1973). The second constraint is that the Court lacks the necessary independence from the other branches of government, which means that the Court must rely on the cooperation of those branches to enforce its rulings. Overcoming this constraint necessitates the support of a large segment of Congress and of the executive branch. The third constraint is that the Court lacks the tools to develop policies and implement decisions for significant change. This constraint may be overcome with public support (or at least low levels of public opposition).

Rosenberg received both criticism and support for his position. He is not saying that courts do not matter. They matter greatly; where would defendant's rights be without *Miranda v. Arizona* (1966) and *Mapp v. Ohio* (1961)? He is merely saying that social and political events are more salient and that courts have an *indirect* effect on change, as we will see in chapter 13. Another supporter of this view wrote: "Neither the canonical nor the anti-canonical constitutional decisions of the Supreme Court have produced the wonderful results or horrible evils sometimes attributed to them" (Graber, 2011, p. 34). (*Canonical* decisions are "landmark" decisions widely considered to have been decided correctly; *anti-canonical* decisions are reviled and widely considered to have been decided wrongly.)

Rosenberg simply reminds us that the judicial process operates at the intersection of law and politics and thus is not the all-powerful institution that some think it to be. It is indeed difficult to find a case in which the Supreme Court ruled in favor of major social change where the three constraints had not been overcome in the ways that Rosenberg suggests. The Court does lack the tools to implement its rulings and relies on the other branches to provide those things for it. Like most dichotomies, however, this one may be drawn too rigidly; sometimes the Court's rulings can reflect the dynamic view and sometimes the constrained view. To the extent that the Court reflects dynamism by altering political dynamics in accordance with its rulings, it relies on one very important resource: legitimacy.

The Legitimacy Basis of the Court's Power

Constrained by its lack of the power of the purse (legislative branch) and the sword (executive branch), the Supreme Court must rely more on the power of legitimacy to gain compliance than either of the other two branches. **Legitimacy** is the ability to command compliance with rules despite the lack of objective means to compel it. Weber (1968) used the term *authority* to refer to this kind of legitimate power, and he proposed three ideal types: *traditional, charismatic,* and *rational-legal*. Any of these three types is considered sufficient in itself to confer legitimacy, but the Supreme Court enjoys them all. Given that Supreme Court justices are neither elected by nor accountable to the people, it is important that we examine this idea of legitimacy upon which the power of the Court ultimately rests. Whether we think of the Court as an almost divinely inspired creator and guardian of American rights (Taylor, 1990) or as "at once the most powerful, and the most irresponsible of all the men in the world who govern other men" (Rodell, 1955, p. 4), the concept of legitimacy is central to our understanding of it.

Woven as it is into the fabric of American history, the Court is legitimized by **traditional authority**. Established by Article III of the Constitution, it is almost as old as the Republic itself, and it is as difficult to imagine the United States without the Supreme Court as it is to imagine Great Britain without the monarchy. Tradition has a powerful hold on the psychology of people; they obey traditional authority because it is often invested with a kind of quasi-divine inspiration and perhaps because "it has always been there." Unless something very seriously wrong with the institution is brought to public attention, there is rarely any questioning of traditional authority.

Traditional authority may be maintained even in the face of criticism if it is buttressed by **charismatic authority**, a form of authority "generated by exceptional, unusual, and even quasi-supernatural qualities attributed to individuals or institutions" (Corbin & Walsh, 1988, p. 76). Robert Taylor (1990), who describes the Supreme Court as "a priesthood that governs," paints a rather dramatic picture of the process of the justices' decision making and of the awesome consequences of those decisions. Note that all this occurs after the Court has decided for itself, in true autocratic manner, which of the numerous petitions brought before it that it wants to hear.

> No public hearings are then held, only arguments for the various sides, and these are strictly timed and can, at the Court's pleasure, be dispensed with altogether. Then follows secret deliberations . . . and finally, the promulgation of an entirely new law, valid across the nation and virtually immune to repeal. A law may upset the established customs and practices of an entire culture; it may abruptly make criminal conduct legal . . . or render criminal what has previously been permitted; or it may force upon lower jurisdictions policies radically at odds with those that have the support of the people and with what had been long established there—and all this without warning . . . as in the most rigid despotism. (p. 42)

Taylor (1990) is not criticizing the Court for its alleged despotism; on the contrary, he feels that the Court provides us with opportunities to exercise our "needs" for deference and servility, "to bow down to persons and things" (p. 41). The Court's legitimacy does rest to some extent on the quasi-religious myths and symbols associated with it and with the Constitution. Myths and symbols are designed to arouse such feelings of worshipful reverence in the beholder. The legitimizing effect is more in evidence when these aloof justices in their marble palace interpret the Constitution than when they are dealing with issues of statutory construction: "Just as the magisterial statements of the Papacy are more compelling for Roman Catholics when they come *ex cathedra*, the Supreme Court's rulings may have more legitimacy when symbolically connected to the US Constitution" (Corbin & Walsh, 1988, p. 77).

The refusal of the Court to allow television cameras behind the "purple curtain," their refusal to grant interviews, and their affected, haughty, and imperious demeanor (compare their demeanor with that of members of Congress during the State of the Union address) all contribute to that special impression of priestly "otherworldliness." Some feel that the Court should divest itself of its aura of myth, mystery, and arrogance:

> Since the isolation treasured by most of the justices mutes the Court's voice in national politics, we urge, as a start, that the Court give up its haughty posture and begin making serious attempts to relate to the American public. (Levine & Becker, 1980, p. 273)

Notwithstanding the fact that the last thing in the world the Court is designed to do is "relate to the American public," if the fiction of the Court were to be exposed, "it would soon raise questions of legitimacy, and thus undermine both the Court and the impact of its decisions" (Cox, 1981, p. 206).

The final form of legitimizing authority is **rational-legal authority**. Beneath all the priestly garb and symbolism, the Court's authority is preeminently rational-legal, which is authority derived from rules rationally and legally enacted. The Supreme Court is provided for in Article III of the Constitution, but just how far its power was intended to stretch is a matter of contention. Some legal scholars assert that the Framers of the Constitution intended some form of judicial review of the constitutionality of federal and state legislation, while others contend that it is clear that the Framers never meant the Court to have the power to void acts of Congress. As we have seen, the Court itself did not assert the power of judicial review until Chief Justice John Marshall explored the Court's power in this regard in *Marbury v. Madison* in 1803.

Legal scholars may argue all they want about the constitutionality of judicial review, but as Rosenberg (1991) reminded us, the Court could not void anything without the cooperation of the other two branches of government. This cooperation is forthcoming because the other branches find the Court to be more useful than a nuisance. As we saw earlier, legislative bodies often are confronted with "touchy" subjects that they would rather not deal with in a decisive manner, and therefore deal with such issues by legislation so vague and ambiguous that no clear use can be made of it. They are only too pleased to allow judges, who do not need to worry about reelection, to "interpret" legislation and thus to engage in judicial lawmaking. This de facto abdication of legislative bodies from their proper role as lawmakers, and the concomitant usurpation of that role by the judiciary, is seen by many as a major threat to the validity of the American political system, which is supposed to be one in which those who govern are accountable to the governed (Lewis, 1999).

The Supreme Court's Swing Voter: The Most Powerful Person in the United States?

Recent Supreme Court decisions lend more support to the dynamic model of Supreme Court power than to the constrained model. Readers will notice the name of Justice Anthony Kennedy constantly appearing as writing the majority opinion in many of the recent landmark decisions involving controversial social issues such as gay marriage. Although no one justice has any more voting power over another, Justice Kennedy, as the only political centrist on the Court, had the so-called "swing vote" on divisive social issues and was dubbed by many media pundits as the "most powerful man in America." Despite protestations to the contrary, the Court is a highly politicized institution whose decisions are better predicted by the ideology of the majority than by any analysis of the Constitution. The Court currently has four solid liberals in Justices Breyer, Ginsburg, Sotomayor, and Kagan and four solid conservatives in Justices Gorsuch, Kavanaugh, Thomas, and Alito. Justice Roberts has swung leftward on some recent issues, and now that Justice Kennedy has retired, perhaps the swing voter will be Justice Roberts. The votes of consistently liberal and conservative justices simply cancel each other out in ideologically infused cases, meaning that the only opinion that really matters is that of the swing voter. This single vote has more import than the 435 representatives and the 100 senators at the federal level combined, plus all other state and local legislators. In fact, when it comes to divisive social issues, the only person in this nation of 320-plus million people whose opinion counts most of the time is the swing voter's.

This sounds like the definition of despotism found in most dictionaries. This is troubling to many people. French lawyer and political philosopher Charles-Louis Montesquieu articulated a tripartite mode of governance whose separate powers were to serve as checks and balances to one another. He "argued that a state of political liberty would not exist if any of the three branches of government—executive, legislative, or judicial—arrogated to itself powers belonging to another branch" (Mendenhall, 2018, para. 10). The federal judiciary is the only branch to engage in such violations of the separation of powers mandate, striking down congressional acts and executive orders on whatever constitutional grounds they can muster if a majority of the Court does not like them. Court rulings them become the "law of the land," but lawmaking is the constitutional prerogative of legislators whose laws the courts are supposed to merely apply. This is the vision of separated powers that the Founders framed for the three branches of government. Each branch has a duty to show proper deference to the others, but it is up to each to ascertain its own level of deference. This issue engages the question of how the Constitution is to be interpreted.

ISSUE HIGHLIGHT

The Electoral College: Should It Be Abolished?

The 2016 presidential election raised the issue (as did some previous elections) of the usefulness of the Electoral College. Established in 1788 by Article II of the US Constitution, the Electoral College was a compromise between electing the president by Congress only or by popular vote only. It was supposed to be comprised of educated and wise electors, but today, it has become is a formality that ratifies the result of the states they represent. Because Donald Trump won the majority of electoral votes but lost the popular vote, many Democrats have called for elimination of the College. Should it be?

Yes

The Electoral College is an anachronism of a bygone age when most people were uneducated and unable to get necessary information to make informed decisions. The original electors were supposedly highly informed men free from political bias, but electors are now selected by the political parties and are expected to vote along party lines. Several voting laws limiting direct democracy in the Constitution, such as only white males being allowed to vote, have been discarded, so why not the Electoral College? This antiquated system ignores the will of the people. Hillary Clinton received 2.9 million more votes nationwide than Donald Trump, but Trump won the Electoral College by 77 more votes than Clinton, which is inherently anti-democratic. Trump is now the President of the United States despite being supported by fewer American voters than Clinton. This is the fifth time in our history that we have a president who did not win the popular vote. The Electoral College system is also tainted because it gives too much power to the so-called "swing states" such that presidential candidates devote too much time to these battleground states with the most electoral votes, such as Florida and Ohio. At the same time, they ignore states they can count on, such as California for the Democrats and Texas for the Republicans, as well as small states with few electoral votes, such as Idaho and Wyoming. If we could elect our presidents based on a national popular vote without the Electoral College, every American's vote would hold equal weight and the will of the majority of American people would be honored.

No

The Electoral College was founded to prevent states with larger populations from having undue influence, and to protect Americans from the risk of a "tyranny of the majority" whereby the voices of the masses can drown out those of minorities. The Framers founded a Constitutional *Republic* with certain inalienable rights, not a democracy of the omnipotent majority that can impose its will on the minority. Clinton's popular vote win came overwhelmingly from a single left-wing state, California ; Trump's votes came from the heartland states where voters wanted no part of the elitist leftist agenda. The proof of the latter is that the voters gave an unprecedented number of Congressional seats, governorships, and legislative bodies to the Republicans. A system of popular vote would marginalize people in rural communities and small cities as candidates pandered to areas with high population densities. Because candidates need electoral votes from multiple regions of the country, they can build campaign platforms with a truly national focus. Democrats tend to forget that Hillary won a popular majority in only 13 states and the District of Columbia, but Trump won the majority in 23 states. In 1992, President Bill Clinton won the electoral vote while receiving just 43 percent of the popular vote, and we did not see Democrats (or the Republicans) calling for the abolition of the Electoral College at that time; Democratic outrage is highly selective. In the final analysis, it is impossible to say that Trump would have lost if the election were based on the popular vote because the election simply was not conducted that way. If it were, both candidates would have campaigned in the "safe states" of the other and induced Californian Republicans and Texas Democrats to get out and vote in larger numbers. Finally, we have to ask ourselves if we want a president who is elected by virtue of winning one or two big states, or do we want one who is elected by narrower margins in a variety of states?

Interpreting the Constitution: Strict Constructionism or Living Document?

The heated and sometimes hostile Senate interrogations of Supreme Court nominees that we witness on television bring to the fore the question of the scope and limitations of judicial power. Conservative presidents tend to nominate justices who believe that the Court's task is to take the Constitution as it finds it. **Strict constructionism** asserts that judges must not place their own interpretations on the Constitution, even if by adhering to this philosophy the consequences would be personally abhorrent to them. A strict constructionist is a constitutional fundamentalist in the same sense as those who believe in the literal and unerring truth of the Bible are religious fundamentalists. In deciding a case, the strict constructionist looks for "original intent," meaning that he or she will peruse relevant material in an effort "to discover what the collective intention of the Framers was on disputed matters of interpretation" (Dworkin, 1985, p. 38). With sufficient historical data and insight, it is presumed that he or she will discover the true intent of the Framers.

A Supreme Court dominated by strict constructionists would have very little role in social change, opponents claim, because by adhering to original intent, the Court would be the captive of eighteenth-century thinking. This leads to an interesting hypothetical question: Since slavery, at least implicitly, was recognized as legitimate under the Constitution (Article I, Section 2), would slavery still be a fact of American life if its legality had been ruled on by successive strict constructionist Courts throughout American history? The Court put its stamp of approval on slavery in *Scott v. Sandford* in 1857, and because strict constructionists supposedly take the Constitution as they find it no matter how personally repugnant they may believe slavery to be, slavery would still be with us if the rulings of the Supreme Court were all that mattered.

Strict constructionists would not be disturbed by the specter we have raised and would find it absurd. Slavery would no more be present in the United States than it would in any other Western society. Constructionists would point out that important equity (justice) issues are the proper domains of Congress, not the Supreme Court. Congress can amend the Constitution in ways that accord with contemporary views of decency and morality, but until it does so, constructionists argue, the justices are bound to find in the Constitution only that which is there. Chief Justice Roger Taney put it this way in *Scott*:

> If any of its [the Constitution's] provisions are deemed unjust, there is a mode described in the instrument itself by which it may be amended; but while it remains unaltered, it must be construed now as it was understood at the time of its adoption.

It was the executive branch's Emancipation Proclamation of 1863, legally cemented by the legislative branch's passage of the Thirteenth Amendment in 1865, that made slavery illegal, not a judicial ruling of unconstitutionality. When the demands of justice rise above the demands of law, it is the legislature that should break the chains of law, not the judiciary. Constructionists understand how difficult it is to discover any kind of original intent or to be a servant to literal interpretations of the Constitution as though it were somehow of divine origin, but they believe that any stance other than strict constructionism leads to judicial activism. **Judicial activism** is a term used pejoratively when judges make rulings that critics perceive as based on a particular ideological agenda rather than on the law. Activist justices have found all sorts of ideas lurking in the penumbras of the Constitution that the Framers could never have imagined, and this is what irks strict constructionists. Even back in the early 1800s,

Thomas Jefferson wrote of the Marshall Court: "The Constitution is a mere thing of wax in the hands of the judiciary, which they may twist and shape into any form they please" (Tucker, 1837, p. 473). More modern critics of judicial activism, such as former Chief Justice William Rehnquist, say that it means judicial governance, which is a clear violation of the Constitutional separation of powers (Rehnquist, 1976). In his dissenting opinion in *United States v. Windsor* (2013) discussed in chapter 7, Justice Antonin Scalia also made plain his distaste for the Court's usurpation of the proper role of a democratically elected Congress to make law and its violation of the principle of the separation of powers:

> This case is about power in several respects. It is about the power of our people to govern themselves, and the power of this Court to pronounce the law. Today's opinion aggrandizes the latter, with the predictable consequence of diminishing the former. We have no power to decide this case. And even if we did, we have no power under the Constitution to invalidate this democratically adopted legislation. The Court's errors on both points spring forth from the same diseased root: an exalted conception of the role of this institution in America.

"Judicial activism" is often viewed as synonymous with the point of view that the Constitution *should be* a "living, breathing document" to be contemporaneously and not historically interpreted. While strict constructionists tend to be political conservatives, adherents of a "living" Constitution tend to be liberals. A living constitution is usually termed *lex non scripta* (literally, "law not written") and is exemplified by the common law constitutions of the United Kingdom and Canada (Walters, 2001). What makes these constitutions "living" is the fact that they are collections of documents and traditions added to over the centuries, and their flexibility makes them quickly responsive to evolving conditions and concerns. But there are those who maintain that the Framers of the US Constitution explicitly set out to produce a document that was a great deal more rigid than that of their British cousins: "The 'living, breathing' British constitution was no safeguard of American liberties" (Woods, 2004, p. 13). In any case, the Constitution is in many ways unavoidably "living," since it was purposely and necessarily written as generalities by men who probably knew it would have to be interpreted by others in different times confronted with issues the Framers could not envision. All that strict constructionists can hope for is that it does not become so "flexible" that it cannot stand straight.

Whether we view a Court ruling as conforming to the original intent of the Framers or as an example of judicial activism depends, in truth, on how it accords with our views on the matter. If the Court's ruling agrees with our opinions, then we may believe the justices correctly interpreted the Constitution; if it does not, we may angrily dismiss it as judicial activism. Depending on the issue and the ruling (whose ox is being gored), either liberals or conservatives may accuse the justices of voting their ideological biases (being judicial activists), and of course, both sides would be correct. Few legal scholars are naïve enough to believe that personal ideology does not strongly and sometimes decisively affect a justice's ruling. Should anyone doubt it, consider the 5-4 ruling strictly along ideological lines that effectively gave the disputed presidential election of 2000 to George W. Bush in *Bush v. Gore* (2000).

THE SUPREME COURT AND THE CLASS STRUGGLE

An extreme concentration of wealth leads inevitably to de facto plutocracy (the rule of the wealthy) functioning beneath the surface of the official government regardless of its political philosophy. Extreme concentrated wealth defiles the very ideas of justice and democracy, for it gives the wealthy far more influence on the political process than their numbers warrant. This fact has been recognized by all democratic governments, and they have responded to demands for democratic social change in three important ways: (a) they have encouraged working class efforts to form unions so that business interests can be confronted on a more equal footing, (b) they have ameliorated harsh exploitation by regulating the activities of business, and (c) they have sought to redistribute wealth by the implementation of a system of progressive income tax (Galloway, 1982). These equity efforts have been resisted everywhere by the wealthy classes and their political parties but nowhere else in the democratic world more successfully than in the United States, where the Supreme Court has assiduously guarded their interests. This clash of interests is what is addressed under the rubric of the American class struggle.

Many think of the Supreme Court justices as servants to the Constitution, as priests are the servants of the gospels. If this is the case, then the ideological composition of the Court should not matter, but of course, it does: presidents are not known for appointing justices who are hostile to their ideology. In fact, presidents are aware there is nothing they may do short of asking Congress to declare war that has such far-reaching effects on the nation than the appointment of a Supreme Court justice. The ideological composition of the Court is in many ways more important than the content of the "gospel" because the justices not only interpret what is written there, but often do so in ways diametrically opposed to the interpretations offered by previous Courts. As Michael Parenti (1977) put it:

> There is an old saying that the devil himself can quote the Bible for his own purposes. The Constitution is not unlike the Bible in this respect, and over the generations Supreme Court Justices have shown an infernal agility in finding constitutional justification for the continuation of almost every inequity and iniquity, be it slavery or segregation, child labor or the sixteen-hour day, state sedition laws or federal assaults on the First Amendment. (p. 251)

It is unnecessary to be more critical of the Founding Fathers than to say that they showed no pronounced enthusiasm for democracy. For many historians and political scientists, John Jay's (the first chief justice of the Supreme Court) prophetic statement—"The people who own the country ought to govern it"—exemplified the predominant sentiment of those at the Constitutional Convention, where the main issue appeared to be whether people or property should rule (Walsh, 1988). According to Richard Hofstadter (1948), "The men who drew up the Constitution in Philadelphia in 1787 had a vivid Calvinistic sense of human evil and damnation and believed with Hobbes that men are selfish and contentious" (p. 3). A corollary of this is that human nature is not to be trusted, and thus democracy is not to be trusted unless limited by boundaries advantageous to men of position and property. Analyses of the characters and philosophies of the Founding Fathers, as well as of the Constitution itself, lead many authorities of all political persuasions to view the Constitution as first and foremost an economic document favoring the moneyed classes. Galloway (1982) and Parenti (1980) cite many statements by Framers such as James Madison, John Adams, and Alexander Hamilton regarding their image of the "class struggle," a struggle that was very real to them.

"Scratch a believe in judicial supremacy," wrote Max Lerner (1939, p. 474), "and like as not you will find someone with a bitterness about democracy. The two are as close as skin and skeleton." Between 25 and 32 of the 40 delegates at the Constitutional Convention favored judicial review in one form or another (Dunn, 1978). Why did so many delegates favor such an anti-democratic method of settling disputed matters? Conflict theorists might cite the Golden Rule ("Those with the gold make the rules"). Having important decisions made by unelected officials based on an inherently conservative document safeguards privileges. If elected officials made the ultimate decisions, they might be swayed by public opinion, which may not necessarily be the opinions of the moneyed classes. Perhaps the untimely occurrence of the populist Shays' Rebellion (a six-month-long armed insurrection among Massachusetts farmers led by Revolutionary War veteran Captain Daniel Shays) that occurred just prior to the signing of the Constitution in 1787 crystallized the anti-democratic sentiments of the Framers. This occurrence probably goaded them into taking preemptive action against any future populist movements (Richards, 2003).

A less cynical interpretation is that the Declaration of Independence and the Constitution were radically democratic documents by the standards of the time and reveal that the Founding Fathers were at least procedural and principled democrats. The great statesman Winston Churchill (1974) had the following to say about the Declaration of Independence:

> We must never cease to proclaim in fearless tones the great principles of freedom and the rights of man which are the joint inheritance of the English-speaking world and which through Magna Carta, the Bill of Rights, the Habeas Corpus, trial by jury, and the English common law find their most famous expression in the American Declaration of Independence. (p. 7288)

The Founding Fathers foresaw the problems of unfettered democracy and applied some restraints to it; these restraints protect the rights of minorities of all kinds, not just the rights of the economically privileged. After all, the United States is a republic—a representative or indirect form of democracy—and not a democracy. An unfettered democracy would allow those at the bottom half of the economic heap to vote themselves a larger portion of the wealth of those on the top half and would find a political party to facilitate their aims. Any government that robs Peter to pay Paul will always have Paul's support, which is the kind of situation the Founders wisely guarded against (Sowell, 1999). They were very much aware of British historian Alexander Tyler's words, written about the time the US Constitution was adopted in 1787:

> A democracy cannot exist as a permanent form of government. It can only exist until the voters discover that they can vote themselves largesse from the public treasury. From that moment on, the majority always votes

for the candidates promising the most benefits from the public treasury with the result that a democracy always collapses over loose fiscal policy, always followed by a dictatorship. (quoted in Seidman, 1975, p. 30)

The informed conservative view may be summarized as acknowledging that the moneyed classes have benefited most from Constitutional protection but deemphasizing this in favor of pointing out how racial and ethnic minorities have benefited from its protection as well. Further, by protecting the "moneyed classes," we are protecting the successful from the resentful who would tax then out of existence, thus ultimately hurting everyone.

The Fourteenth Amendment and Business Interests

The Constitution may not be a tool of the "ruling class," but it has always been a bastion for the upper classes of society. In its battle to protect the economic elite from the demands of workers, the Court has relied heavily on Article I, Section X of the Constitution, which forbids states to pass any laws "impairing the obligation of contracts." The first use of this clause was in 1810 in *Fletcher v. Peck*, which involved wealthy New England speculators who bribed members of the Georgia legislature in 1795 to make land grants to them. When the conspiracy was uncovered, a later Georgia legislature rescinded the earlier legislation.

John Peck had sold some of the land in question to Robert Fletcher. The issue before the Supreme Court was whether the contract between Fletcher and Peck could be invalidated by Georgia. The Court ruled that the Georgia legislature could not annul contracts or grants made by previous legislative acts. Thus, rich speculators were able to keep the land in what Galloway (1982) called a "classic rich–poor issue" (p. 40). The members of the Court who set the obligation of contract precedent are described by Leo Pfeffer (1965): "All were members or representatives of the propertied, creditor classes, and all believed that the purpose of government was to protect the rights of property against the covetous depredations of the lower classes" (p. 41).

Although there were a number of other such "contract" cases, we move forward to a further milestone in the history of the Supreme Court's defense of the status quo: passage of the Fourteenth Amendment in 1868. This amendment was passed by a Republican-controlled Congress in response to discriminatory Black Codes passed by southern states during Reconstruction (see chapter 13) and designed to protect the most deprived and vulnerable members of our society (the newly freed slaves). However, the Court soon found ways to use it to protect rich business interests against the working class. The relevant section of the amendment is Section I, which reads "nor shall any state deprive any person of life, liberty, or property, without due process of law; nor deny any person within its jurisdiction the equal protection of the laws."

The Supreme Court viewed the Fourteenth Amendment as requiring state conformity with the Bill of Rights in economic matters. As Abadinsky (2003) put it, "Slowly, and over a long period of time, the Court began to apply these rights to the states. Ironically, they served to protect conservative business interests against legislative enactments designed to improve the conditions of workers" (p. 65). The absurd suggestion that the US Congress was thinking primarily about protecting corporations when it framed the Fourteenth Amendment was first made by a lawyer for the railroad industry in an 1886 case that is otherwise uninteresting: "Chief Justice Waite in *Santa Clara Co. v. Southern Pacific R. R. Co.* simply announced this doctrine, and corporations have been blessed and protected ever since" (Deloria & Wilkins, 1999, p. 52).

After the precedent was set, the courts no longer needed to rely on criminal conspiracy laws to suppress labor unions and other working-class organizations. Criminal conspiracies meant trials, and trials often meant juries composed of men sympathetic to the worker's struggle. Business interests could now seek judicial injunctions against strikes with relative ease, and union members disobeying such an injunction would soon find themselves in jail for contempt of court. This method of dealing with the "union rabble" circumvented the usual legal method of settling disputes and saved business much time and money. The courts were able to use the Fourteenth Amendment in this way by defining *person* very broadly as any body of people, such as a corporation, and *property* to include business profits. By interpreting the Fourteenth Amendment in this way, the courts opened the floodgates to a tide of judicial attacks on state laws that attempted to govern wages, hours, and safety provisions for workers on the grounds that such laws violated employers' "property rights."

The activity of labor unions and of Coxey's army (an army of unemployed workers who marched on Washington demanding job creation in the 1890s) conjured up the ghosts of Shays' Rebellion in the minds of the moneyed classes. Here again were the "great unwashed" making demands on government. Ideologically, they could not have chosen a worse time to press their claims. The "gay '90s" were saturated with the ideas of social Darwinism and Adam Smith's "invisible hand." These two philosophies coalesced as *laissez-faire* economics, which was strongly supported by the Supreme Court under Chief Justice Melville Fuller, who held the position from 1888 to 1910. For about a 40-year period after 1889, the Court invalidated 50 acts of Congress and about 400 state laws designed to help workers (Abadinsky, 2003). Essentially the Court struck down any and all legislation designed to introduce justice into the workplace.

The skill of the Court in interpreting legislation for means opposite to those presumably intended is evident in its rulings under the **Sherman Antitrust Act**. Passed by Congress in 1890, the act was designed to place controls on business. Few of the legislators who voted for the act expected or even wanted it to have any effect, but it was popular with the electorate who voted them in or out of office. Legislators thought they could rest easy that the courts would undo the damage their act had wrought to the power of privilege (Brinkley, Current, Freidel, & Williams, 1991), and the courts did not disappoint them.

The Court used the Sherman Antitrust Act as a hammer to pound the working class rather than to control business monopolies. In *United States v. E.C. Knight* (1895), the Court ruled that the Sherman Act controlled only commerce, that manufacturing was not commerce, and that therefore manufacturing monopolies did not violate the act. In *In re Debs* (1895), the Court upheld the conviction and imprisonment of Eugene Debs, leader of the American Railway Union, for violating a court injunction ordering the union to halt the famous Pullman strike of 1894. Thus, in a remarkable display of doublespeak, *on the same day* that the Court ruled in *Knight* that manufacturing was not commerce (manufactured goods have to be sold, transported, and distributed, and by definition, that is commerce), it ruled in *Debs* that trade unionism was! In *Adair v. United States* in 1908, the Court invalidated a federal law outlawing "yellow dog" contracts (contracts forced on employees requiring them to promise not to join a union as a condition of employment), saying that they violated "freedom of contract." The Sherman Act was again invoked against the unions in *Loewe v. Lawlor* (1908), when the Court ruled that the act forbade secondary boycotts by labor unions and upheld high damage payments against the union.

The late nineteenth and early twentieth centuries were replete with decisions that drove home the privileged position of business in American society. The Court appeared to be legitimizing the law of the jungle: the weak must bear the consequences of their weakness, the strong may enjoy the consequences of their strength, and the state should not be in the business of protecting even women and children from the predations of the entrepreneurial class. In *Lochner v. New York* (1905), for instance, the Court struck down maximum-hours legislation for bakers who were being forced by employers to work up to 16 hours each day. The Court ruled that such legislation denied employers liberty of contract. In *Hammer v. Dagenhart* (1918), the Court struck down federal legislation aimed at child labor reform, which would have cost business dearly, on the grounds that the law went beyond congressional power to regulate interstate commerce, and in *Adkins v. Children's Hospital* (1923), it struck down an act of Congress setting minimum wages for women and children as an unconstitutional violation of freedom of contract.

These cases are a small sample of the many anti–working class rulings of the Court during this period. In *no* case where the interests of the rich business classes were opposed to the interests of the working classes did the Court find in favor of the latter. A series of decisions in the 1930s even succeeded in undermining much of President Franklin Roosevelt's effort to ameliorate the effects of the Great Depression. The most significant of these decisions came in *Schechter Poultry Corp. v. United States* (1935), a unanimous decision that ruled Roosevelt's National Recovery Act unconstitutional. In *Louisville Bank v. Radford* (1935), the Court invalidated the Frazier-Lemke Act, which severely restricted the ability of banks to repossess farms when owners defaulted on their mortgage. Finally, in *United States v. Butler* (1936), the Court threw out the Agricultural Adjustments Act, which imposed a tax on processing farm products. The proceeds of the tax were to be paid to farmers in order to reduce crop production and thus artificially increase the prices of farm products by decreasing their supply.

In short, the Supreme Court was able to stifle what was seen by New Dealers as progressive social change for so long that the United States lagged behind most other industrial democracies in passing legislation benefiting workers by as many as 75 years (Walsh, 1988). However, the fact that the United States finally legalized trade unions and enacted many hours, wages, and safety bills points out that even an institution as powerful as the Supreme Court cannot buck pressures demanding social change indefinitely.

In defense of the Supreme Court's position on President Roosevelt's policies, a large number of modern economists argue that his New Deal actually extended and exacerbated the Great Depression, which was easing up under the influence of the free market before Roosevelt's programs were initiated (e.g., Cole & Ohanian, 2004). Opponents of the New Deal at the time saw it as vastly expanding the power of

This cartoon from the *Los Angeles Times* relates to the United Mine Workers strike in 1919 in which 400,000 coal workers walked out in defiance of a court order. With supplies of America's primary fuel running low came growing public calls for government intervention. The strike ended after five weeks with a 14 percent raise for the miners.

the federal government and granting Roosevelt almost dictatorial power. Even the most liberal member of the Court in 1935, Justice Louis Brandeis, had the following to say about the huge expansion of federal power under Roosevelt after the *Schechter Poultry* case: "This is the end of this business of centralization, and I want you to go back and tell the President that we are not going to let this government centralize everything. It's come to an end" (Pritchard & Thompson, 2009, p. 875). Another justice, James McReynolds, wrote: "If it were not for the Court this country would go too far down the road to Socialism ever to return" (Pritchard & Thompson, 2009, p. 875). Thus, Supreme Court cases often are decided with the "bigger picture" in mind rather than on the narrow issues involved in the cases themselves.

Perhaps fearful of an increase in riotous behavior during the Great Depression, Congress finally stripped the federal courts of their power to issue injunctions against labor unions engaged in labor disputes (although the courts have since reasserted this power) in the 1932 Norris–La Guardia Act. In 1935, Congress went one step further with passage of the National Labor Relations Act, also known as the Wagner Act, which legalized labor unions and required employers to engage in good-faith collective bargaining. The Wagner Act was declared constitutional in 1937 in *National Labor Relations Board v. Jones and Laughlin Steel Corporation*. The Court's turnabout in this case was perhaps motivated by President Roosevelt's anger at "judicial legislators" and his proposed plan to "pack" the Court. As wags of the time were fond of saying, the shift in the Court's attitude was "[t]he switch in time that saved nine." Of the Court's behavior during the period of the New Deal, Robert Jackson (1941; who was shortly to become a Supreme Court justice himself) wrote that "the basic grievance of the New Deal was that the Court has seemed unduly to favor private economic power and always to find ways of circumventing the efforts of popular government to control or regulate it" (p. xii).

The Court's partiality for business interests has not been so blatantly obvious since this period, although a number of scholars have noted that labor laws in the United States provide fewer protections against exploitation, injury, illness, job protection, and unemployment than the laws of the dozens of other industrial nations. Human Rights Watch, the largest human-rights organization based in the United States, has frequently declared that US labor laws are grossly at odds with international human rights laws (Acuff & Friedman, 2006).

Two more recent cases demonstrate this point. In *Allied Structural Steel v. Spannous* (1978), the Court prohibited the state of Minnesota from requiring companies who leave the state to insure pension payments to retired employees, and in *National Labor Relations Board v. Bildisco & Bildisco* (1984), it held that companies could unilaterally breach collective bargaining contracts without waiting for rulings of bankruptcy judges if those companies found such contracts to be "burdensome." This was an invitation for companies all over the United States to engage in union busting, which many gratefully accepted (see Walsh, 1988, for a review).

We have thus far looked at two sides of the triangle of reform activities that popularly elected governments have used to try to thwart excessive concentrations of wealth and power in one class: legalizing unions and regulating the activities of the rich. The redistribution of wealth via a progressive income tax system constitutes the third side of the triangle. Prior to instituting a system of income tax, the money to run the federal government (except during times of war) came mainly from the sale of federal lands and from customs taxes. As society became more complex and the United States became a world power with all the responsibilities that come with such status, the old methods of acquiring operating funds were insufficient. Consequently, Congress passed an act imposing the federal income tax. The Supreme Court struck the act down as unconstitutional in *Pollock v. Farmer's Loan and Trust Company* (1895). Although the burdened taxpayer of today may applaud such a decision, governments must be funded if they are to function. (Congress subsequently passed the Sixteenth Amendment in 1913 making federal income tax constitutional.) Thus, in three important cases heard in 1895 (*Pollock, E.C. Knight,* and *Debs*), the Court struck blows to each of the three principle reform activities employed by democratic governments everywhere.

A more charitable way of looking at the Supreme Court's role during this period is that it acted like the English judges in the early periods of the evolution of common law. As we saw in chapter 2, English judges became so rigidly wedded to the letter of the law that decisions often were made that grossly violated standards of equity, necessitating the developments of separate courts of equity. The various decisions involving economic issues make it plain that the Court dispensed law rather than justice during the period reviewed thus far. The justices became somewhat more sensitive to equity issues after the 1930s.

SOCIAL JUSTICE, EQUALITY, AND FREEDOM: A DEBATE

Has the so-called class struggle ended? What is equality and social justice? The concept of equality has many positive connotations carried over from the great struggles of previous centuries for legal and political equality. We have reached a point in the United States where all individuals, classes, and races are guaranteed equality before the law, but some want to go beyond this to demand **social justice**, a concept that its proponents define as economic equality. This issue engages people with seemingly irreconcilable differences. On the current scene, we have Occupy Wall Street types on one side of the barricade demanding more government involvement and higher taxes and Tea Partiers on the other demanding exactly the opposite. The French philosopher Voltaire once noted that "equality is at once the most natural and the most chimerical thing in the world: natural when it is limited to rights, unnatural when it attempts to level goods and power" (Durant, 1952, p. 245). Legal and political equality are natural equalities due to us by virtue of our humanity, and there is no justification for exceptions. No one denies the desirability of equality in this sense. Equality of "goods and power" is unnatural for Voltaire because it defies the Aristotelian notion of treating equals equally and unequals unequally according to relevant differences; that is, people's "goods and power" should depend on what they merit by virtue of their talent and effort.

Here, we present the arguments for and against social justice as its supporters and opponents make them.

The Argument for Social Justice

The ideal of social justice demands that we go beyond legal and political equality to embrace equality of "goods and power" regardless of so-called "talent and effort." Talent and effort are part of what John Rawls (1971; discussed in chapter 1) calls a "superior character," although he did not believe that anyone should be allowed to benefit from it:

> The assertion that a man deserves the superior character that enables him to make the effort to cultivate his abilities is equally problematic; for his character depends in large part upon fortunate family and social circumstance for which he can claim no credit. (p. 104)

Parents provide their offspring with both a suite of genes and an environment that sets them on developmental trajectories quite independent of anything those offspring may do. These trajectories are heavily influenced by their genes and environments, which lead to different cognitive and temperamental traits that aid or hinder their efforts in the job market. Given this, we can neither praise nor blame them for what they can or cannot accomplish. Karl Marx also believed that people should not be granted license to benefit from their superior abilities because

> one man is superior physically or mentally and so supplies more labor in the same time. . . . This *equal* right is an unequal right for unequal labor. It is, *therefore, a right of inequality in its content, like every right.* (Green, 1983, p. 439)

Sawhill and Morton (2007) couch this point in terms of fairness: "people are born with different genetic endowments and are raised in different families over which they have no control, raising fundamental questions about the fairness of even a perfectly functioning meritocracy" (p. 4). Thus, capitalist meritocracy is unfair, since under the principles of distributive justice "superior" people will receive more benefits as a result of being blessed with a natural superiority they did nothing to deserve. Natural talents and the benefits derived from them belong to society, not to the person who is lucky enough to have them and, as the principle of social justice assets, their fruits must be shared equally.

There has been a class war in America, and the rich have won. The Congressional Budget Office (2011) reports that the real after-tax income growth for the top 1 percent of the population from 1979 to 2007 was 278 percent, and for those in the 81st to 99th percentile, it was 65 percent. For those in the lowest quintile, it was 18 percent, with 28 percent in the second lowest quintile, 35 percent in the middle quintile, and 43 percent in the fourth quintile. We consider such inequality as revolting, equality to be the greatest good, and agree with Rose, Lewontin, and Kamin (1984), who state: "We share a commitment to the prospect of the creation of a more socially just—a socialist—society" (p. ix). Although opponents are quick to point out that all "Marxist" societies that have existed have not been successful, it may be noted that those societies were corruptions of true Marxism, which has yet to be tried.

Recall from chapter 1 that individuals in John Rawls's hypothetical "original position" were charged with developing a social system under a "veil of ignorance" regarding the talents and characteristics they would bring to it. Rawls maintained that under such conditions, all individuals would accept the principle of equality as a prime facie obligation, and we on the progressive side agree. Rawls's theory separates distributive justice from the capitalist notion of just deserts by which people are rewarded according to their contribution; that is, a merit-based reward system: "The principles of justice that regulate the basic structure and specify the duties and obligations of individuals do not mention moral desert, and there is no tendency for distributive shares to correspond to it" (1971, p. 311). Inequality is acceptable only if it is to the advantage of the worst-off individuals in society. This is Rawls's "difference principle," which states that the most just distribution of wealth maximizes the wealth of the lowest income group. Michael Sandel (2004) calls this principle "a powerful even inspiring vision of equality" (p. 156). Who could possibly disagree?

The Argument Against "Social Justice" as Defined by the Left

There are many who do, in fact, disagree; somehow the left has gotten to define what social justice means. For those who disagree, inequality is not valued, but is seen as the natural outcome of free individuals in a spontaneous competitive system and any attempt to interfere with it is considered a major threat to freedom. Thus, fairness is integral to justice—but what does it mean to be fair? Fairness appeals to our moral sentiments because it is a process by which we expect to "make things right." Although we may feel sorry for individuals burdened with disabilities they did nothing to create and would like to make it right for them, having sympathy for such individuals does not tell us how their position in life coheres with the moral issue of fairness. Surely it is unfair to say that talented people should *not* be allowed to enjoy the fruits of their talents.

Fairness is an issue saturated with contradictory notions. We all praise it, but we differ as to when we believe its promise has been fulfilled. Some view it as an equal opportunity *process*, whereas others see it as equality of *outcome*, or close to it. The fairness of the process can be guarded to a great extent by law, but no power on earth can guarantee equal outcomes unless we grant that entity unlimited power and that entity has unlimited wisdom. We consider unequal outcomes fair if the process is fair, and the process is fair if everyone is subjected to the same rules and judged by the same standards. With the rules of the game and the standards of judgment held constant, the only things that vary are the qualities that individuals bring to it, and only God Almighty can be blamed for the diversity of human talents. Fairness has nothing to do with it, as Nobel Prize–winning economist Friedrich Hayek (1976) points out:

> The manner in which the benefits and burdens are apportioned by the market mechanism would in many instances have to be regarded as very unjust *if* it were the result of a deliberate allocation to particular people. But this is not

the case. Those shares are the outcome of a process the effect of which on particular people was neither intended nor foreseen by anyone. (p. 64)

The income gains reported by the Congressional Budget Office do not alarm us. It is a good bet that much of the income gained by the lower income quintiles came from the entrepreneurial skills of those in the upper quintiles. Business is the life blood of any nation, and to paint it as a bad guy is envious naïveté. According to a study by the Cato Institute, roughly 80 percent American millionaires are the first generation of their family to be rich, starkly illustrating that people do not stay in the same income quintile all their lives (Tanner, 2011). Being poor in America is a transient thing—a snapshot taken in a given year—but the issue too often is framed as a fixed condition in which population quintiles always contain the same people. According to Hacker (2006), most people in the United States (about 58 percent) will experience poverty for at least a period of one year during their lives, and the US Census Bureau reports that only about 12 percent of the population is in poverty at any one time and only about 2 percent of the population is in poverty two or more years (Iceland, 2003). Poverty for most Americans is thus a short-term blip in their lives, and surely the entire history of the world shows that the free market system is the only way out of that condition.

Dreamers on the other side of the fence say that they want a "just socialist society," that a "true" Marxist/socialist society has not been tried, and they admit that all such societies have been "unsuccessful." This is a massive understatement; they have not only been unsuccessful—they have been nightmares. (How many more mass executions, gulags, and walls and minefields enclosing the proletariat in their egalitarian paradises do we need before concluding that such societies were not corruptions but inherent in Marxist doctrine? Rose et al. (1984) need reminding of Einstein's definition of idiocy—that is, "Doing the same thing over and over and expecting a different outcome." Even the "soft" socialism of Western Europe is learning to appreciate Margaret Thatcher's trenchant observation that "[t]he trouble with socialism is that sooner or later you run out of other people's money."

We agree that a society concerned with justice must do what it can to make things better for those plagued with misfortune by providing a safety net (welfare for the truly needy, Medicaid, social security, etc.). On the other hand, a society concerned with *liberty* knows that nature does not produce a state of equality, and to try to artificially produce one would involve a powerful state apparatus to force one group (the productive taxpayer) to further the goals of another (the tax consumer) without the former's consent. It is wrong to assume that individual talent is a social property: I did not obtain my talents at your expense, nor did you obtain yours at mine. The quest for "social justice" is a dangerous utopian dream leading to totalitarianism. As Friedman and Friedman (1980) put it:

> A society that puts equality—in the sense of equality of outcome—ahead of freedom will end up with neither equality nor freedom. The use of force to achieve equality will destroy freedom, and the force, introduced for good purposes, will end up in the hands of people who use it to promote their own interests. (p. 148)

Anyone who doubts this knows nothing of human nature.

THE SUPREME COURT'S ROLE IN INDUCING SOCIAL CHANGE

Despite the best efforts of the Supreme Court to maintain the economic status quo, social change has been a hallmark of the American society since its beginnings. The newly formed United States was too big, too empty, too wild, and too ambitious to be constrained overly much by the niceties of law, and the settlement of this land was far less orderly and "law driven" than the settlement of Canada (Hagan & Leon, 1977). Nevertheless, the law has played an active role in molding what was once a collection of semi-autonomous, bickering, and sometimes warring states into a single, unified, and mighty nation. As for the role of the Supreme Court (when the Court had just seven justices), as far back as the 1820s the aristocratic French commentator Alexis de Tocqueville (1945) claimed, "The peace, the prosperity, and the very existence of the Union are vested in the hands of seven Federal judges" (p. 156). This doubtless exaggeration contains some truth because the Supreme Court continually expanded the power of the federal government relative to that of the individual states and thus served as a nation builder.

Bringing the Country Together Through Case Law

A number of important pre–Civil War Supreme Court cases did much to mold a common national identity. In these cases, the Court took the words of Article VI of the Constitution (the supremacy clause) and put them into practice. The **supremacy clause** reads, in part, "the authority of the United States shall be the supreme law of the land; and all judges in every state shall be bound thereby, anything in the Constitution or laws of any State to the contrary notwithstanding."

In *Fletcher v. Peck* (1810; discussed earlier), the Court set the stage for its jurisdiction over state legislatures, an exercise in power stoutly resisted by the states. The Court further cemented its power in *Martin v. Hunter's Lessee* (1813), which involved a Virginia statute allowing the state to confiscate land owned by British Loyalists. The father of the petitioner, Philip Martin, had his land confiscated under this law. The Supreme Court ruled in favor of Martin, but Virginia refused to obey the ruling, arguing that the Court had no right to review state legislation. With the matter going before the Court again, the justices ruled that under Article VI of the Constitution, the Court had the final word over all federal *and* state courts, a decision that was to become the keystone of federal judicial power (Goldinger, 1990).

In *McCulloch v. Maryland* (1819), the Marshall Court "set down the classic statement of the doctrine of national authority" (McClosky, 1960, p. 66). The case posed two questions: (a) Could the US Congress charter a national bank (the Bank of the United States), and (b) if so, could the states tax it? Congress had chartered such a bank, and Maryland had taxed it in accordance with what that state considered to be its sovereign right. The Court ruled that Congress could charter such a bank and that the individual states could not tax it. In making this ruling, the Court had provided for an instrument of national economic stability while at the same time limiting the sovereignty of the states vis-à-vis the federal government.

In *Gibbons v. Ogden* (1824), the powers of the federal government were again pitted against those of the states. The basic issue in this case was whether Congress alone, or Congress and the states, could regulate interstate commerce. The Court ruled that while the individual states had the power to regulate commerce within their own borders, they had no power to regulate interstate commerce. Only the US Congress, it was declared, had the constitutional authority to do so. According to Brinkley and colleagues (1991), "the lasting significance of *Gibbons v. Ogden* was that it freed internal transportation from the restraints of the states and thus prepared the way for the unfettered economic development of the nation by private capitalism" (p. 268).

The combined impact of the Court's rulings in *Fletcher*, *Martin*, *McCulloch*, and *Gibbons* did much to integrate and unite the states and to generate feelings among Americans of being citizens of the *United* States as well as citizens of their individual states. Opposing this tide of national unity, however, was a surge of disunity generated by the existence of slavery in the South. Chief Justice Roger Taney was a believer in states' rights in an era when such issues were mostly linked to the increasingly sensitive issue of slavery. In *Scott v. Sandford* (1857), the Supreme Court ruled that slaves were property and that owners of property could not be deprived of it without "due process of law." This meant that Congress had no authority to pass laws depriving persons of their property, and thus the Missouri Compromise of 1820, which banned slavery in certain territories, was unconstitutional. This decision hardened positions on both sides of the slavery issue and helped to set the stage for the Civil War. (*Scott* is discussed more fully in chapter 13.)

Whatever role the decision may have played in bringing on the Civil War, it played a major one in giving the presidency to Republican Abraham Lincoln in the 1860 election. Northern and southern Democrats were bitterly divided over the decision, and each ran its own separate candidate in the election. Lincoln won 39.8 percent of the popular vote while the Democrats won 47.6 percent, divided between 29.5 percent for northern Democrat Stephen Douglas and 18.1 percent for southern Democrat J. C. Breckinridge (Brinkley et al., 1991, p. 401). The *Scott* decision did not "cause" the Civil War, but it did undermine federalist sentiment generated under the Marshall Court in favor of states' rights sentiment.

From the *Scott* decision of 1857 up to 1937, Court decisions had little or no effect on social change. As we have seen, during this period it appeared to have only the preservation of the status quo on its mind. But in 1937, the Court upheld Washington State's minimum wage law in *West Coast Hotel Co. v. Parrish*, which marked the first time that the Court had ruled in favor of the working class in a case where the interests of that class were opposed to those of the owner class. As Goldinger (1990) put it:

> Implicit in this reversal was the willingness of a majority of the Court to accept government authority to act to protect the general welfare of society— and to withdraw the Court from any role as the censor of economic legislation. (p. 42)

The Activism of the Warren and Burger Courts

The Court became a major catalyst of social change under the leadership of Chief Justice Earl Warren (1953–1969). In chapter 6, we discussed the activism of these courts in terms of criminal procedure rights, so we limit our discussion here to noncriminal matters. One of the most famous of all Supreme Court cases was *Brown v. Board of Education of Topeka* (1954). This case is canonical and has been called "the single most honored opinion in the Supreme Court's opus" (Balkin, 2001, p. 11). Race relations in the United States up to this time were governed by the "separate but equal" doctrine enunciated by the Court in the anti-canonical *Plessy v. Ferguson* (1896). The Court ruled in *Brown* that the *de jure* (by law) segregation of the races upheld as constitutional in *Plessy* violated the equal protection clause of the Fourteenth Amendment and thus was unconstitutional. In his written opinion, Justice Warren stated, "We conclude that in the field of public education the doctrine of 'separate but equal' has no place. Separate educational facilities are inherently unequal." Although the case dealt only with school segregation, it prepared American society for integration in all areas of social life (Mawdsley, 2004).

The *Brown* ruling provoked massive resistance on the part of the southern states, and by the fall of 1957, less than one-fourth of the affected southern school districts had even begun efforts to desegregate (Mawdsley, 2004). Governor Orval Faubus of Arkansas even went so far as to call out the Arkansas National Guard in an attempt to prevent integration. This open defiance of federal authority, as well as the danger posed to black children, forced a reluctant President Dwight Eisenhower (an opponent of desegregation) to dispatch federal troops to Arkansas in order to facilitate the enrollment of black children in schools (Balkin, 2001).

Writing of the impact of *Brown*, Rose (1967) states:

> If there had ever been a doubt . . . that a United States Supreme Court decision can change social behavior and social institutions, the implementation undertaken by the federal courts of the *Brown v. Board of Education* decision of 1954, should have dispelled it quickly. (p. 126)

Although the *Brown* decision was explicitly limited to segregation in the schools, in effect it invalidated all forms of de jure segregation. (See the impact of *Brown* on taxpayers in *Missouri v. Jenkins* [1990], discussed in chapter 9, and additional historical context to *Brown* in chapter 13). *Brown* showed once again how powerful the Court is, notwithstanding its lack of purse and sword. Its ruling was upheld despite the massive resistance of the overwhelming majority of southern whites; despite the resistance of southern governors, congressmen, and senators; and despite the pro-segregationist attitudes of the president of the United States. The will of the Court prevailed because it symbolizes the power of the Constitution as interpreted by it. As we shall see in chapter 13, however, there was considerable pressure brought to bear on the Court from the outside, including the federal government, in favor of *Brown*.

Cases that resulted in social changes of a sometimes profound nature coming from the Warren Court and the subsequent Court under Chief Justice Warren Burger (1969–1986) are too many to recount (most of the cases composing the "due process revolution" came out of Warren and Burger Courts but impacted only the criminal justice system and had limited effect on social change). Two important cases, however, hit at the heart of the most deeply held values of many Americans. In 1962, the Court banned prayer in public schools in *Engel v. Vitale*, and in 1973, it legalized abortion in *Roe v. Wade*. The *Engel* decision resulted in a firestorm of public protest, calls to impeach Justice Warren, and many suggestions (though no formal proposals) that it should be overruled by Congress with a constitutional amendment (Starr, 2002, p. 95). Many public schools continued to broadcast prayers over their public address system for years after the ruling. These systems have long since fallen silent, though, and the issue rarely generates any major steam today.

On the other hand, the Burger Court's decision in *Roe v. Wade* continues to polarize Americans into pro-life and pro-choice factions. Nevertheless, an increase in favorable attitudes toward abortion rights were in evidence up until 2009, at which time more Americans considered themselves pro-life (48 percent) than pro-choice (45 percent; see the discussion in chapter 10). Although both decisions were opposed by the majority of Americans at the time of the decisions, even in the 1980s it was already evident that the majority of Americans supported many of the principles enunciated in them (Barnum, 1985). Over time, these rulings have become institutionalized (the establishment of a pattern of norms accompanied by state provisions for their enforcement), which facilitates public acceptance of them, particularly among younger members of the public who have not lived in a time when school prayer was acceptable and abortion unacceptable. The ability to affect such changes in public attitudes over time underlines the legitimacy-conferring power of the Supreme Court (this is not to deny that a significant number of Americans oppose abortion and favor prayer in school). As Adamany (1973) says, to confer legitimacy is to "create acceptance of policy among those who oppose or who are neutral about its substance and heighten acceptance among those already committed to its content" (p. 807). Adamany's statement sums up for us the essence of the role of law in effecting social change, a role that is likely to become more important as society grows even more complex and ethnically diverse.

SUMMARY

Social change is an inevitable and constant phenomenon in modern societies. It comes from many sources, and although it is welcomed by some, others stoutly resist it. Both those who favor and those who oppose certain changes often utilize the law in their struggles. Those who oppose change tend to view the law as arising from the customs and norms of their ancestors; therefore, law is the repository of much conventional wisdom. Those who agitate for change, however, tend to view the law as the promoter and protector of universalistic principles of justice. Although the law is not as important as many other factors in generating social change, there is often a reciprocal relationship between the law and social change: sometimes the law causes change in society, and sometimes social change causes changes in the law. As society becomes still more complex, there will be an even greater role for law in the social change process.

Law played an important part in the birth of the United States. Many British Parliamentary acts were stoutly resisted by the American colonists, including the Proclamation Act, which prevented many leading figures in the American Revolution from realizing financial gains from lands ceded by the British to the Indians. Certain anti-slavery decisions in British courts may also have affected the decision of some of the southern states to opt for independence. Even though the American Revolution was a revolution, many of its stated principles were "legal" in the sense that the colonists justified their actions by appealing to British legal principles.

The extensive changes in postrevolutionary Russia provide examples of both the power and the limitations of law as a tool of social change. The changes in Russian society were truly revolutionary, and their implementation often required the use of terror tactics as well as law. The Soviet family was marked for particularly radical changes, which were duly accomplished. However, these changes proved disastrous, and family laws were changed again. The Soviets had no qualms about frequently changing the law whenever it suited them to do so.

In the United States, the Supreme Court has been a major player both in facilitating and thwarting social change. The Court relies on the myths and symbols that surround it to generate legitimate authority, and hence power, and has been called "a priesthood that governs." The Court often governs—via judicial review of legislation—because decision-making has been defaulted to them by legislators who, unlike the justices, are accountable to the people. There is much debate among legal scholars regarding judicial activism, with strict constructionists asserting that the judiciary should stick to the letter of the Constitution and constitutional liberals having a more favorable view of judicial activism.

The Supreme Court, especially for the first 150 years of its existence, was very active in preserving the privileges of the wealthy class. Under one constitutional guise or another, it consistently thwarted attempts by popularly elected legislators to better the lot of the working class, even using legislation (e.g., the Fourteenth Amendment and the Sherman Antitrust Act) against the very people it was designed to help. The Court consistently attacked the triangle of reforms—encouragement of unions, regulations on the activities of the owner class, and progressive taxation—that democratic governments everywhere have enacted in attempts to generate social justice. In response to President Roosevelt's "Court packing" threat, the Court moved away somewhat from its anti-progressive stance, although a bias in favor of the privileged is often observed in the Court's decisions today.

The issue of social justice shows how far apart different ideological segments can be on moral issues. Those on the left (at least, the most radical wing of the left) appear to value equality above all else. Those on the right (as well as more moderate liberals) maintain that to try to implement equality of outcome as opposed to equality of opportunity would destroy both freedom and economic incentive.

The Supreme Court, in addition to its role in stifling social change vis-à-vis class relationships, has played an important role in generating change. In a series of decisions between 1810 and 1824—*Fletcher v. Peck, Martin v. Hunter's Lessee, McCulloch v. Maryland,* and *Gibbons v. Ogden*—the Court greatly enhanced federal power over the states and in doing so contributed to the unity of the nation. However, the issue of slavery addressed in the *Scott* case reversed this trend toward national unity and indirectly led to the Civil War.

The Court became a major catalyst for social change under Chief Justice Earl Warren in the 1950s and 1960s. *Brown v. Board of Education of Topeka* prefaced a series of activist cases in the area of race relationships and criminal justice. Extending to the present time, the Supreme Court continues to either shock or delight Americans as it legitimizes the formerly forbidden and illegitimizes the formerly permitted.

DISCUSSION QUESTIONS

1. Do you think that a major purpose of the law should be to generate social change, as it is in socialist law? What positive and negative (in your opinion) social changes have taken place in the United States due to law rather than "natural" change?
2. What is the major difference between the stance of the government of the former Soviet Union and the stance of the government of the United States toward their respective constitutions?
3. Do you believe that the US Supreme Court should function according to the ideals of strict constructionism or of a "living, breathing" constitution?
4. In your opinion, has the Supreme Court done more harm or more good for the average person in the United States over the last 200 years?
5. Are you pro– or anti–social justice as defined in the debate in this chapter?

CHAPTER TERMS

Charismatic authority	Proclamation Act of 1763	Soviet legalism
Constitutions	Rational-legal authority	Strict constructionism
Constrained view	Sherman Antitrust Act	Supremacy clause
Dynamic view	Social change	Traditional authority
Judicial activism	Social justice	
Legitimacy	Social movement	

References

Abadinsky, H. (2003). *Law and justice: An introduction to the American legal system.* Upper Saddle River, NJ: Prentice Hall.

Acuff, S., & Friedman, S. (2006, June 28). A new assault on worker's rights. *Mother Jones.* Retrieved from http://www.motherjones.com/politics/2006/06/new-assault-workers-rights

Adamany, D. (1973). Legitimacy, realigning elections, and the Supreme Court. *Wisconsin Law Review, 3,* 780–846.

Ashford, N. (1990). Michael Oakshott and the conservative disposition. *Intercollegiate Review, 25,* 39–50.

Balkin, J. (2001, November 9). Is the "Brown" decision fading to irrelevance? *Chronicle of Higher Education,* pp. 11–12.

Barnum, D. (1985). The Supreme Court and public opinion: Judicial decision making in the post New Deal period. *Journal of Politics, 47,* 652–666.

Barry, D., & Barner-Barry, C. (1978). *Contemporary Soviet politics.* Englewood Cliffs, NJ: Prentice Hall.

Bonsignore, J., Katsh, E., d'Errico, P., Pipkin, R., Arons, S., & Rifkin, J. (1989). *Before the law: An introduction to the legal process.* Boston, MA: Houghton Mifflin.

Brinkley, A., Current, R., Freidel, R., & Williams, T. (1991). *American history: A survey.* New York, NY: McGraw-Hill.

Churchill, W. (1974). The sinews of peace: Address at Westminster College, Fulton, Missouri (March 5, 1946). In R. James (Ed.), *Winston S. Churchill: His complete speeches, 1897–1963* (Vol. 7) pp. 7285-7293. New York, NY: Chelsea House.

Cole, H., & Ohanian, L. (2004). New Deal policies and the persistence of the Great Depression: A general equilibrium analysis. *Journal of Political Economy, 112,* 779–816.

Congressional Budget Office. (2011). *Trends in the distribution of household income between 1979 and 2007*. CBO Publication no. 4031. Washington, DC: Author.

Corbin, A., & Walsh, A. (1988). The US Supreme Court and value legitimacy: An experimental approach with older Americans. *Sociological Inquiry, 58*, 75–86.

Cox, A. (1981). The Court as a legitimate institution. In S. Ulmer (Ed.), *Courts, law, and judicial processes* (pp. 203–227). New York, NY: Free Press.

de Tocqueville, A. (1945). *Democracy in America*. New York, NY: Vintage.

Deloria, V., & Wilkins, D. (1999). *Tribes, treaties, and constitutional tribulations*. Austin: University of Texas Press.

Donnelly, S. (2006). Reflecting on the rule of law: Its reciprocal relations with rights, legitimacy, and other concepts and institutions. *Annals of the American Academy of Political and Social Sciences, 603*, 37–53.

Dunn, C. (1978). *American democracy debated*. Morristown, NJ: Scott Foresman.

Durant, W. (1952). *The story of philosophy*. New York, NY: Simon & Schuster.

Dworkin, R. (1985). *A matter of principle*. Cambridge, MA: Harvard University Press.

Friedman, M., & Freidman, R. (1980). *Free to choose: A personal statement*. New York, NY: Harcourt Brace Jovanovich.

Galloway, R. (1982). *The rich and the poor in Supreme Court history*. Greenbrae, CA: Paradigm Press.

Goldinger, C. (1990). *The Supreme Court at work*. Washington, DC: Congressional Quarterly.

Graber, M. (2011). Hollow hopes and exaggerated fears: The canon/anti-canon in context. *Harvard Law Review, 125*, 33–39.

Green, M. (1983). Marx, utility, and right. *Political Theory, 11*, 433–446.

Hacker, J. (2006). *The great risk shift: The new insecurity and the decline of the American dream*. New York, NY: Oxford University Press.

Hagan, J., & Leon, J. (1977). Philosophy and sociology of crime control: Canadian–American comparisons. *Sociological Inquiry, 47*, 181–208.

Hayek, F. (1976). *Law, legislation and liberty* (Vol. II). London, England: Routledge.

Hazard, J., Butler, W., & Maggs, P. (1977). *The Soviet legal system*. Dobbs Ferry, NY: Oceana.

Hazelton, J. (1970). *The Declaration of Independence: Its history*. New York: Da Capo Press.

Hofstadter, R. (1948). *The American political tradition*. New York, NY: Vintage.

Hosking, G. (1985). *The first socialist society: A history of the Soviet Union from within*. Cambridge, MA: Harvard University Press.

Iceland, J. (2003, July). Dynamics of economic well-being: Poverty 1996–1999. US Census Bureau. Retrieved from http://www.census.gov/prod/2003pubs/p70–91.pdf

Jackson, R. (1941). *The struggle for judicial supremacy*. New York, NY: Alfred A. Knopf.

Johnson, H. (2006). The rule of law in the realm and the province of New York: Prelude to the American Revolution. *History, 91*, 3–26.

Klingberg, F. (1968). *The anti-slavery movement in England*. New York, NY: Archon.

Lerner, M. (1939). *Ideas are weapons*. New York, NY: Viking Press.

Levine, J., & Becker, T. (1980). Toward and beyond a theory of Supreme Court impact. In L. Weinberg and J. Weinberg (Eds.), *Law and society: An interdisciplinary introduction* (pp. 270–277). Lanham, MD: University Press of America.

Lewis, F. (1999). *The context of judicial activism: The endurance of the Warren Court legacy in a conservative age*. Lanham, MD: Rowman & Littlefield.

Mawdsley, R. (2004). A legal history of Brown and a look at the future. *Education and Urban Society, 36*, 245–254.

McCann, M. (2006). Law and social movements: Contemporary perspectives. *Annual Review of Law and Social Science, 2*, 17–38.

McClosky, R. (1960). *The American Supreme Court*. Chicago, IL: University of Chicago Press.

Mendenhall, A. (2018). How much legislative power do judges really have? *Intercollegiate Review* Online. Retrieved from https://home.isi.org/how-much-legislative-power-do-judges-really-have?

Parenti, M. (1977). *Democracy for the few.* New York, NY: St. Martin's Press.

Parenti, M. (1980). The Constitution as an elitist document. In R. Goldwin & W. Schambra (Eds.), *How democratic is the Constitution?* (pp. 39–58). Washington, DC: American Enterprise Institute.

Parrillo, V. (2003). *Strangers to these shores: Race and ethnic relations in the United States.* Boston, MA: Allyn & Bacon.

Parsons, T. (1977). Law as an intellectual stepchild. *Sociological Inquiry, 47,* 11–58.

Pfeffer, L. (1965). *This honorable Court.* Boston, MA: Beacon Press.

Pritchard, A., & Thompson, R. (2009). Securities law and the New Deal justices. *Virginia Law Review, 95,* 841–926.

Reichel, P. (2005). *Comparative criminal justice systems* (4th ed.). Upper Saddle River, NJ: Prentice Hall.

Rehnquist, W. (1976). The notion of a living constitution. *Texas Law Review, 693,* 401–415.

Richards, L. (2003). *Shays' Rebellion: The American Revolution's final battle.* Philadelphia: University of Pennsylvania Press.

Rodell, F. (1955). *Nine men: A political history of the Supreme Court from 1790 to 1955.* New York, NY: Random House.

Rose, A. (1967). School desegregation: A sociologist's view. *Law and Society Review, 2,* 125–140.

Rose, S., Lewontin, R., & Kamin, J. (1984). *Not in our genes: Biology, ideology, and human nature.* New York, NY: Viking Penguin.

Rosenberg, G. (1991). *The hollow hope: Can courts bring about social change?* Chicago, IL: University of Chicago Press.

Sandel, M. (2004). *Justice: What is the right thing to do?* New York, NY: Farrar, Straus and Giroux.

Sawhill, I., & Morton, J. (2007). *Economic mobility: Is the American dream alive and well?* Washington, DC: Economic Mobility Project.

Seidman, L. (1975). The economy and public policy. *Presidential Studies Quarterly, 5,* 28–31.

Sowell, T. (1999). *The quest for cosmic justice.* New York, NY: Free Press.

Stalin or Yeltsin? (1993, March/April). *Economist,* pp. 13–14.

Starr, K. (2002). *First among equals: The Supreme Court in American life.* New York, NY: Warner.

Tanner, M. (2011), The real "1 Percent." Cato Institute. Retrieved from https://www.cato.org/publications/commentary/real-1-percent

Taylor, R. (1990). The American judiciary as a secular priesthood. *Free Inquiry, 10,* 37–43.

Tilly, C. (1984). Social movements and national politics. In C. Bright & S. Harding (Eds.), *Statemaking and social movements* (pp. 297–317). Ann Arbor: University of Michigan Press.

Tilly, C. (2004). *Social movements, 1768–2004.* Boulder, CO: Paradigm Press.

Tucker, G. (1837). *The life of Thomas Jefferson* (Vol. II). London, England: Charles Knight.

Walsh, A. (1988). "The people who own the country ought to govern it": The Supreme Court, hegemony, and its consequences. *Law and Inequality, 5,* 431–451.

Walters, M. (2001). The common law constitution in Canada: Return of *lex non scripta* as fundamental law. *University of Toronto Law Journal, 51,* 91–141.

Weber, M. (1968). *Economy and society.* New York, NY: Bedminster.

Weinberg, L. S., & Weinberg, J. W. (1980). *Law and society*: Lanham, MD: University Press of America.

Wilson, B., & Cordero, J. (2006). Legal opportunity structures and social movements: The effects of institutional change on Costa Rican politics. *Comparative Political Studies, 39,* 325–351.

Woodin, G. (1974). *The shady side of America.* New York, NY: Ace Books.

Woods Jr, T. (2004). *The politically incorrect guide to American history.* New York: Regnery Publishing.

Zemans, F. (1983). Legal mobilization: The neglected role of the law in the political system. *American Political Science Review, 77,* 690–703.

Cases Cited

Adair v. United States, 208 U.S. 616 (1908)

Adkins v. Children's Hospital, 261 U.S. 525 (1923)

Allied Structural Steel v. Spannous, 438 U.S. 234 (1978)

Brown v. Board of Education of Topeka, 349 U.S. 294 (1954)

Bush v. Gore, 531 U.S. 98 (2000)

Engel v. Vitale, 370 U.S. 421 (1962)

Fletcher v. Peck, 6 Cranch 87 (1810)

Gibbons v. Ogden, 9 Wheaton 1 (1824)

Griswold v. Connecticut, 381 U.S. 479 (1965)

Hammer v. Dagenhart, 247 U.S. 251 (1918)

In re Debs, 158 U.S. 564 (1895)

Joseph Knight v. Wedderburn, How. St. Tr. 1 (1778)

Lochner v. New York, 198 U.S. 45 (1905)

Loewe v. Lawlor, 208 U.S. 274 (1908)

Louisville Bank v. Radford, 295 U.S. 255 (1935)

Mapp v. Ohio, 367 U.S. 643 (1961)

Marbury v. Madison, 1 Cranch 137 (1803)

Martin v. Hunter's Lessee, 1 Wheaton 304 (1813)

McCulloch v. Maryland, 17 U.S. 316 (1819)

Miranda v. Arizona, 384 U.S. 436 (1966)

Missouri v. Jenkins, 495 U.S. 33 (1990)

National Labor Relations Board v. Bildisco & Bildisco, 465 U.S. 513 (1984)

National Labor Relations Board v. Jones and Laughlin Steel Corporation, 301 U.S. 1 (1937)

Plessy v. Ferguson, 163 U.S. 537 (1896)

Pollock v. Farmer's Loan and Trust Company, 157 U.S. 601 (1895)

Roe v. Wade, 410 U.S. 113 (1973)

Santa Clara County v. Southern Pacific Railroad Company, 118 U.S. 394 (1886)

Schechter Poultry Corp. v. United States, 295 U.S. 495 (1935)

Scott v. Sandford, 60 U.S. 393 (1857)

Somerset v. Stewart, 98 Eng. Rep. 499 (1772)

United States v. Butler, 297 U.S. 1 (1936)

United States v. E.C. Knight, 156 U.S. 1 (1895)

United States v. Windsor, 570 U.S. _774_ (2013)

West Coast Hotel Co. v. Parrish, 300 U.S. 397 (1937)

CHAPTER 12

WOMEN AND THE LAW

by Mary K. Stohr

Although Alice Porter was fired from her job at Acme Linen in Livonia, North Carolina, for "excessive absenteeism" and "poor work performance," in reality she was fired because she got pregnant and had a child. Her company gave her two weeks' maternity leave, charging it to her vacation time. Unfortunately, her child had a number of minor health problems that necessitated Alice's absence from work to tend to his needs. No law protected Alice from Acme firing her unless the company specifically stated that it was because she became pregnant (she would be protected then by the Pregnancy Discrimination Act). To make matters worse, her husband left her and her children (four in all) and remained under- or unemployed on purpose to avoid paying child support, and she only had 13 months of welfare benefits. It seemed that Alice and her children were headed for a life of poverty, a status in which women outnumber men more than two to one.

If Alice lived in most other democracies, she would have been guaranteed by law up to 11 months maternity leave at 90 percent of her salary, and afterward, she would have her former employment back without loss of seniority or social allowances. These, and many other rights such as maternity allowances (a lump sum to cover costs of new child), family allowance (weekly sum paid per child regardless of need), and subsidized day care are guaranteed by Article II of the United Nations Convention on the Elimination of all Forms of Discrimination Against Women (UNCEFDW; see Table 12.1 later in this chapter).

The UNCEFDW recognizes that because of the biological differences between the sexes, women will always be treated worse than men unless the law intervenes and compensates for those differences. Only women can bear children, which leads to economic or even physical vulnerability, and men's greater aggression and physical strength gives them the ability to dominate and abuse women. Ask yourself, as you read this chapter, if strictly equal treatment of men and women is just. Men do not have to put their careers on hold to become parents, so why should women be punished for what they cannot help? And make no mistake, they are punished if they are treated in sex-neutral ways. The UNCEFDW mandates compensatory equality laws, not sex-neutral laws. As you read this chapter, decide whether or not you agree.

INTRODUCTION

This chapter explores how women and girls have been treated by the legal system from ancient times to the present. We trace the influence of patriarchy and how it has shaped legal practices throughout history. We show how it established a barrier against the struggle for suffrage and equality for women and girls in the nineteenth and twentieth centuries in the United States. The role of feminist legal theory, gendered law, and women's increasing involvement in the courts are explored. Because there are many forces aligned to thwart justice and equality for women, it is critical to consider how gender influences the dispensation of rights and liberties, especially if we are interested in a different and more highly evolved world in the twenty-first century. We begin with feminist legal theory to become familiar with how various feminist scholars might analyze and evaluate the issues discussed in this chapter.

FEMINIST LEGAL THEORY

Feminism is a set of theories and strategies for social change that takes gender as its central focus in attempting to understand social institutions, processes, and relationships. It is both a social movement and a worldview of which the law is but a part, albeit a part that feminists believe can be used to right the inequities of gender. Feminist legal theory, or **feminist jurisprudence**, is simply the practice of examining and evaluating the law from a feminist perspective. For feminist legal theorists, the law is the codification of a culture's normative practices that are deeply masculine in nature, since they reflect male visions, realities, and goals. Because all known societies have been controlled by men, the law, insofar as it has been applied to gender relationships and issues, has been the written embodiment of patriarchy.

Patriarchy literally means "rule of the father" and is a term used to describe any social system that is male dominated at all levels, from the family to the highest reaches of government, and supported by the belief of overall male superiority. A patriarchal society is one in which "male" traits, such as competitiveness, aggressiveness, autonomy, and individualism, are lauded and "female" traits, such as intimacy, connection, cooperation, and nurturance, while appreciated, are downplayed (Grana, 2002). Patriarchy occupies the same despised place among most feminist scholars that capitalism occupies among Marxists. The owners of the means of production (the *bourgeoisie*) are the oppressors in Marxist theory; the owners of the means of *re*production (owners of women and girls) are the oppressors in feminist theory. This does not mean that women are powerless in a patriarchy, only that the most powerful roles in most sectors of society are held predominantly by men. Feminists believe that law is a mirror of patriarchal society and that it has been used to devalue and disenfranchise women. Patriarchies (essentially every society to various degrees) have used the law as a gender control mechanism to assure male domi-nance over women and girls, largely by claiming female incompetence and demon-izing female sexuality.

Feminist jurisprudence is split by two major debates: the reformist/radical and the sameness/difference debates (Burchard, 2006). Reformist feminists tend to be lib-erals who want to retain but reconfigure the current legal system so that it recognizes women as equal to males. Radical feminists see the present system as so corrupted by patriarchy that it must be abandoned and replaced with one that is free of biases.

The sameness/difference debate revolves around the issue of whether women should be treated equally with males due to the sameness of the sexes or treated differently based on relevant differences between the sexes. In essence, this debate is about whether women are better off if they are treated by the law as men are treated or better off if the law acknowledges the obvious differences between the sexes and treats women with these differences in mind (Grana, 2002). As one femi-nist scholar put it, "To some, the law was unjust in its unequal treatment of equals, whereas for others its injustice lay in its equal treatment of unequals" (Haney, 2000, p. 646). Sameness feminists accused their difference feminist sisters of trying to rep-licate prefeminist protectionist arguments (women need special protection because they are weak and helpless). Difference feminists accused their sameness sisters of being blind to obvious biological differences and to the plight of women who suffer the consequences of those differences (e.g., pregnant women in the workforce being held to the same attendance and performance standards as men).

This "damned if you do, damned if you don't" impasse led to a compromise posi-tion that asserts the law must accept relevant gender differences but should focus on their consequences rather than on the differences per se. As Burchard (2006) argues, "Rights should be based on needs [e.g., paid maternity leave and the guarantee of reemployment afterwards], and if women have needs that men do not, that should not limit their rights." Or as Baer (1999) put it, "Law can treat men and women alike where they are alike and different where they are different" (p. 55). In some cases, the law has done this; in others, it has not, as we shall see.

WOMEN AND LAW IN HISTORY: THE BIRTH OF MISOGYNY AND OTHER TRIUMPHS

Early Greek society was somewhat ambivalent about the status of women. Early Greek accounts of creation begin with an earth goddess who is mother to all, with few males of power present (Coole, 1993). After earth mated with sky and the lineage that produced Zeus was created, the subordination of the female goddesses began as male gods assumed the mantle of rationality and wisdom and women were faulted for the world's woes. The Greek myth of Pandora's box mirrors the biblical myth of Eve's apple. Pandora, the first woman on earth, had been given a box by Zeus, which she was not to open under any circumstance. But Pandora opened the box, in which all evil had been contained, and evil spread around the earth. Myths such as this pro-vide a subtle underpinning for **misogyny**—the hatred, devaluation, and ridicule of women, and an ideology that justifies and maintains men's subordination of women.

Homer's tales of approximately 800 BCE featured traditional roles for women as domestic servants, baby-makers, and sexual booty in times of war, although there was some recognition of women's intelligence and strength in overcoming their trials (Coole, 1993). Plato and Aristotle regarded women as inferior to men, with women thought of as the body and men as the soul. Women's appropriate sphere was the home; for men, it was the world. Life for women in the Athens of the time was enclosed and controlled for the comfort and pleasure of wealthier men. In Sparta, by contrast, because of its emphasis on breeding, women had more public lives, and property was communally owned. But in general, the laws governing women in ancient Greece were repressive: women possessed few rights or liberties, and their worth was little valued.

High-status women were able to achieve some power and voice in politics when the Greek city-states were more authoritarian and hierarchical than when they were ostensibly republics (Hillard, 1992). Perhaps this is because when the rights and liberties of men are circumscribed in autocracies, their political status may sink to that of women. Aristocratic women may wield a certain amount of power in autocratic societies because of their wealth and their positions as wives and mothers of powerful men.

Cicero, a prominent Roman politician who lived in the first century BCE, wrote that the proper place for the woman was at home as the subordinated wife of her husband and that she was to be excluded from the most important sacrifices and rites (Cicero, 1985). This opinion was codified in the *Twelve Tables,* which decreed that women were subordinate to male guardianship and were to remain as minors in either their father's or their husband's households (Cicero, 1985).

Similarly, in the medieval European feudal system, women were subordinate and homebound. They were allowed to own and dispose of property only if no male relative was in the picture (Grana, 2002). Among the lower classes, women's lives were freer but harder, as they and their menfolk had to scramble for survival. Church theology reinforced the belief that women were and should be subordinate to their husbands because this was their "natural" state ordained by God (Coole, 1993). Female submission to their husbands in everything is ordered in the Bible in Ephesians 5:22–24, Colossians 3:18, Titus 2:5, and 1 Peter 3:1. The apostle Paul declares that the function of women is to sexually gratify men (1 Corinthians 7:1–2) and that men were made for the glory of God and women for the glory of men (1 Corinthians 11:3–9).

Renaissance writers in the fifteenth century saw women as more virtuous and less worldly than men. Women were not to be involved in the world outside the home, not because they were evil (as had been assumed in the Middle Ages) but because the world was evil. Thus, women were counseled to maintain the home and to avoid the corruption of public affairs (Coole, 1993). The sixteenth-century Reformation and the emergence of Protestantism reinforced domestic patriarchy. In Tudor England (1485–1603), women had almost no rights under either secular or religious law. They were expected to be silent, obedient, and chaste and not allowed to participate in public life. Women were homebound, uneducated, and restricted from involvement in the worlds of politics, art, and academia. What labors they were allowed to engage in were little noticed and even less appreciated. Some women were privately well educated, however, and others inherited wealth when there were no male relatives (Pollock, 2006).

English philosophers Thomas Hobbes and John Locke conceded some rights to women, such as the right to possessions acquired before marriage, but they still considered women as naturally inferior to men in all matters (Coole, 1993). Women could negotiate contracts with their husbands, but given the political and economic realities, it was unlikely that they would. When reading philosophers of this period, the reader is struck by how invisible women were.

While French philosopher Jean-Jacques Rousseau demanded equality for all men, he expressly denied it for women. He believed that women could not be citizens because they did not possess the ability to reason or judge (Coole, 1993). Rousseau believed that the proper sphere for women was the private home and the proper sphere for men was the public square. It was only in the public sphere that voices could be raised in unison and heard, and only when voices were heard could demands for rights and liberties be acknowledged. Dixon (1992) reviews the acceptable roles and attitudes that women were allowed throughout history:

> Most societies do have a legitimate public role for women, but it is usually one without the most prestigious kind of power and tends to be an extension of the society's private construction of the feminine—such as a benevolent super-mother, bestowing largesse and concern on subjects; a pious wife or daughter performing a sacral function; the lady of impeccable virtue, producing perfectly pedigreed heirs. These acceptable images carry great rewards for the women involved. But the image is fragile and the first lady who tries to assume real power beyond the prescribed sphere is immediately subject to virulent attack that turns the acceptable icon upside down; ungovernable selfishness, impurity, and whorishness are the inverse of feminine generosity, piety, and chastity. (p. 219)

Mary Wollstonecraft (1792/1967), an early English feminist writing in *A Vindication of the Rights of Woman*, argued that we cannot know what the natural abilities of women to reason are until they are taught the same things as men. She noted that women's education and training had not been geared toward a role of citizenry and responsibility in the public sphere and that their physical appearance was emphasized to the detriment of their intelligence and strength. Wollstonecraft further argued:

> Men complain, and with reason, of the follies and caprices of our sex, when they do not keenly satirize our headstrong passions and groveling vices. Behold, I should answer, the natural effect of ignorance! The mind will ever be unstable that has only prejudices to rest on, and the current will run with destructive fury when there are no barriers to break its force. Women are told from their infancy, and taught by the example of their mothers, that a little knowledge of human weakness, justly termed cunning, softness of temper, *outward* obedience, and a scrupulous attention to a puerile kind of propriety, will obtain for them the protection of man; and should they be beautiful, everything else is needless, for, at least, twenty years of their lives. (pp. 49–50)

She then makes the point that women should be educated for their own development and because they are the ones who will educate future generations. If girls were allowed to mature mentally as boys were, Wollstonecraft argued, we would find as much intellect and reason among them as we do among men.

THE RELATIVE VALUE OF CITIZENS:
THE STRUGGLE FOR WOMEN'S SUFFRAGE

Due to women such as Wollstonecraft, women began to accrue legal rights through-out the nineteenth century in the same way other undervalued persons did. In the United States, voting rights were first extended to lower-class white males under the Jacksonian reforms of the 1820s and 1830s. They were then extended by law to black males under the Fifteenth Amendment. Despite the Fourteenth Amendment's declaration that "[a]ll persons born or naturalized in the United States, and subject to the jurisdiction thereof, are citizens of the United States and of the State wherein they reside" and that no state should "deny to any person within its jurisdiction the equal protection of the laws," this basic right of citizenship was denied to women. For all practical purposes, women appear to have not been included in the definition of "person" for the purposes of allowing them their rights.

Notably, before the American Revolution, some colonies had allowed unmarried women with property to vote, but none of the new state constitutions, with the exception of New Jersey, allowed women to exercise this right (Sachs & Wilson, 1978). In 1807, however, the New Jersey constitution was amended to rescind women's suffrage. It is a tragic irony that a country founded on the ideals of democracy explicitly denied it to women, minority men, and initially, to white males without sufficient property.

The conception of common law that formed the basis for the US system of juris-prudence decreed that adult women were not allowed to be fully functioning adults. In his *Commentaries on the Laws of England*, which formed the basis for common law in this country, Blackstone (1765–1769) made known his belief that women were essen-tially chattel. Under the system of **coverture**, a married couple became one person, and that person was, of course, the man. A married woman had no legal rights or obligations separate from those of her husband, and her whole existence was merged into that of her husband. Dusky (1996) asserts that coverture

> would later be compared to slavery, in that it effectively stripped married women of any legal rights except the right to be prosecuted for heinous crimes. . . . In general married women could not own land, retain their own wages, enter into contracts, or sue anybody. (pp. 252–253)

Our Founding Fathers paid little heed to the pleas of the Founding Mothers for the vote or other citizenship rights. When asked in a letter by his wife Abigail in 1776 to "remember the ladies" when liberties and rights were accorded, John Adams (who was to become the second president of the United States) replied that "I cannot but laugh . . . you are so saucy. . . . Depend on it, we know better than to repeal our mas-culine systems" (Dusky, 1996, p. 253). Abigail had been asking only that women not be at the mercy of tyrannical husbands, as common law allowed. Thomas Jefferson, the author of the Declaration of Independence and third president of the United States, concurred with Adams, writing, "Even were our state a true democracy there would still be excluded from our deliberations women, who, to prevent deprivations of morals and ambiguity of issues, should not mix promiscuously in gatherings of men" (Dusky, 1996, p. 254). When Jefferson wrote in the Declaration "We hold these

Truths to be self-evident, that all Men are created equal," he really did mean *men*, and then only property-owning *white* men.

Thus, when Elizabeth Cady Stanton called for the right to vote for women at the 1848 woman's rights convention in Seneca Falls, New York, some of the other delegates were surprised and thought such a demand unreasonable (Dusky, 1996). Most male politicians, and most citizens of both sexes at the time, still viewed women as too emotional, ignorant, and unpredictable to make rational decisions (Bailey, 2006). Later in the century when the Fourteenth and Fifteenth Amendments were ratified, giving black men the vote, women's request that the word *sex* be added to the Fourteenth Amendment so that they too could vote was denied. Sojourner Truth, a famous black female orator of the time, lamented that granting black men the right to vote without giving the same right to black women would lead to continued domestic oppression of women (Dusky, 1996).

The reluctance to give women the right to vote at the national level did not deter several western states from allowing them to vote in state elections (Whittick, 1979). The Wyoming territory gave women the vote in 1869. and Utah did so in 1870. When both territories were admitted to the Union as states, these rights were confirmed. Colorado (1893) and Idaho (1896) also granted women the right to vote. Despite these advances at the state level in the West, the rest of the country did not follow suit until the ratification of the Nineteenth Amendment in 1920. When women did finally secure voting rights, it was only after a long-fought battle that spanned the globe and required the allegiance of diverse groups.

For instance, Susan B. Anthony and 14 other women were prosecuted for voting illegally in 1872 (Dusky, 1996). At her trial, Anthony argued that women could not be tried without a jury of their peers and that under a male-dominated judicial system, she had no voice because she had no vote. When the judge instructed the jury to find her guilty, they did. She was fined $100 and court costs. She never had to pay the fine or serve time in jail after her trial, however, as her lawyer, against Anthony's will, bailed her out. Further, the judge refused to enforce the fine because he did not want her jailed. These actions (bailing her out and refusing to enforce her fine) were taken because there was concern that if she did spend time in jail, she could appeal the decision to the Supreme Court using a writ of habeas corpus (Sachs & Wilson, 1978).

The first case relating to women's voting rights to make its way to the US Supreme Court was *Minor v. Happersett* (1874), in which Virginia Minor claimed that Reese Happersett had violated her rights by refusing to register her as a voter in Missouri. A unanimous Court rejected Minor's argument, stating that

> [n]o argument as to woman's need of suffrage can be considered. We can only act upon her rights as they exist. It is not for us to look at the hardship of withholding. Our duty is at an end if we find it is within the power of a State to withhold. Being unanimously of the opinion that the Constitution of the United States does not confer the right of suffrage upon any one, and that the constitutions and laws of the several States which commit that important trust to men alone are not necessarily void, we affirm the judgment.

In 1902, Elizabeth Stanton, Susan B. Anthony, and Carrie Chapman Catt, all from the United States, organized an International Woman Suffrage Conference in

Washington, DC, to which five countries sent delegates. Before the next meeting of the conference in 1904 in Berlin, Anthony, Catt, and Anita Augspurg developed the following principles for conference attendees in their Declaration of Principles:

> That men and women are born equally free and independent members of the human race; equally endowed with intelligence and ability, and equally entitled to the free exercise of their individual rights and liberty.

> That the natural relation of the sexes is that of interdependence and cooperation, and that the repression of the rights and liberty of one sex inevitably works injury to the other, and hence to the whole race.

> That in all lands, those laws, creeds, and customs which have tended to restrict women to a position of dependence; to discourage their education; to impede the development of their natural gifts, and to subordinate their individuality, have been based on false theories, and have produced an artificial and unjust relation of the sexes in modern society.

> That self-government in the home and the State is the inalienable right of every normal adult, and the refusal of this right to women has resulted in social, legal, and economic injustice to them, and has also intensified the existing economic disturbances throughout the world.

> That governments which impose taxes and laws upon their women citizens without giving them the right of consent or dissent, which is granted to men citizens, exercise a tyranny inconsistent with just government.

> That the ballot is the only legal and permanent means of defending the rights to the "life, liberty and the pursuit of happiness" pronounced inalienable by the American Declaration of Independence, and accepted as inalienable by all civilized nations. In any representative form of government, therefore, women should be vested with all political rights and privileges of electors. (Whittick, 1979, p. 32)

At the time of the conference in 1904, New Zealand and Australia were the only sovereign nations that had given women the right to vote, so the Declaration was considered quite radical and not likely to garner support from most governments (Whittick, 1979). The major achievement of this conference was the establishment of the International Woman Suffrage Alliance, with Carrie Chapman Catt serving as its first president.

Subsequent congresses of the Alliance from 1906 to 1914 saw it grow to delegates from 24 nations. By the 1910 meeting, supportive men's alliances in some European countries also were sending delegates, who would return to their native lands after the conferences and agitate for the vote and other rights for women. Their form of agitation depended on the local politics and propensities of their respective countries but included reaching out to progressive politicians and party machines as well as campaigning door to door among the voters.

In Great Britain, women age 30 and older were given the right to vote in 1918 after much lobbying of members of Parliament (Whittick, 1979). In the United States, New York, Michigan, Oklahoma, and South Dakota, in addition to the previously mentioned western states, had already granted female suffrage. Most other European countries that had not already granted female suffrage followed the British example in the 1920s and 1930s. Sadly, Susan B. Anthony died in 1906 without having been recognized as a full citizen with voting rights (Dusky, 1996). In view of the long suffrage struggle that had preceded World War I and of women's invaluable contributions to the war effort, it became inevitable that suffrage would be achieved. After much struggle by feminists in the United States, women were given their right to vote in 1920 with the ratification of the Nineteenth Amendment, which reads: "The right of citizens of the United States to vote shall not be denied or abridged by the United States or by any State on account of sex." This is the first and only time that the US Constitution explicitly recognizes that there is another sex—women. Carrie Chapman Catt, one of this country's most prominent fighters for women's rights, once remarked about the woman's suffrage movement:

British Suffragettes Annie Kennedy and Christabel Pankhurst

> To get that word *male* out of the Constitution, cost the women of this country 52 years of pauseless campaign; 56 state referendum campaigns; 480 legislative campaigns to get state suffrage amendments submitted; 47 state constitutional convention campaigns; 277 state party convention campaigns; 30 national party convention campaigns to get suffrage planks in the party platforms; 19 campaigns with 19 successive Congresses to get the federal amendment submitted, and the final ratification campaign.
>
> Millions of dollars were raised, mostly in small sums, and spent with economic care. Hundreds of women gave the accumulated possibilities of an entire lifetime, thousands gave years of their lives, hundreds of thousands gave constant interest and such aid as they could. It was a continuous and seemingly endless chain of activity. Young suffragists who helped forge the last links of that chain were not born when it began. Old suffragists who helped forge the first links were dead when it ended. (Dworkin, 1993, pp. 19–469).

WOMAN AS HUMAN AND PERSON

The lesser value for women and girls held for much of human history was reflected in Western (and other) traditions of legal thought in which women and girls were regarded as property (Bailey, 2006). If a woman is property, then she can be bought, sold, traded, and replaced whenever convenient. She exists only in relation to her husband, father, and brothers, as a wife, daughter, and sister—but not as an autonomous person. If she maintains her "place," marries, and is obedient, then she is a "Madonna" to be placed on a pedestal and protected by men from the predations of other men. If she does not marry or is widowed, divorced, or abandoned, then she is likely to be regarded as a "whore" and be subject to rape, persecution, and harassment (Ollenburger, 1998).

Matilda Joslyn Gage (1893/1980), a militant humanist activist for women's suffrage in the nineteenth century, was one of the first individuals to campaign for the separation of church and state. She claimed that US law was actually canon (church) law, and that the church had purposefully worked for the complete subjugation of women. She made so many other dubious claims—such as that prehistoric humans lived in matriarchal (female-ruled) systems, that women were responsible for many ideas (e.g., the cotton gin) that men stole, and that the witch hunts of the fifteenth through eighteenth centuries resulted in about 9 million deaths—that she destroyed much of her hard-won credibility. However, many of the points she made about witchcraft and the responses to it are worth noting:

That women were chiefly accused.

That men believing in woman's inherent wickedness, and understanding neither the mental nor the physical peculiarities of her being, ascribed all her idiosyncrasies to witchcraft.

That the clergy inculcated the idea that woman was in league with the devil, and that strong intellect, remarkable beauty, or unusual sickness were in themselves proof of this league. Catholics and Protestants yet agree in holding women as the chief accessory of the devil. (Gage, 1893/1980, p. 112)

Moreover, the church was motivated to conjure up witches and then condemn them because the killing of a witch released her family property to the church and to its prosecutors and judges (Gage, 1893/1972).

RAPE AND OTHER MISOGYNOUS ATROCITIES

Laws against rape and the beating of women and girls historically have been more focused on the property rights of male owners than on the suffering of the female victims (Ollenburger, 1998; Wilson & Daly, 1992). As Brownmiller (1975) documents in her classic book *Against Our Will*, the rape of women and girls throughout history has been tied to their status as property. When that property became damaged (i.e., the loss of virginity), it was not the woman who was legally recognized as suffering a loss but her owner (i.e., father or husband); thus, it was he who had to be compensated for the "damaged goods" now in his possession. As Brownmiller (1975) puts it:

Ancient Babylonian and Mosaic law was codified on tablets centuries after the rise of formal tribal hierarchies and the permanent settlements known as city-states. Slavery, private property and the subjugation of women were facts of life, and the earliest written law that has come down to us reflects this stratified life. Criminal rape, as a patriarchal father saw it, was a violation of the new way of doing business. It was, in a phrase, the theft of virginity, an embezzlement of his daughter's fair price on the market. (p. 18)

If a woman was not a virgin, then male rape concerns revolved less around "property damage" and more about her supposed behavior surrounding the crime. Men asked themselves questions such as how willingly the victim participated, if she had led her attacker on by provocative dress or actions, and whether she resisted with sufficient vigor. Under the Code of Hammurabi, a raped married woman might be drowned along with her attacker if her husband no longer wanted her, and the ancient Hebrews would stone both rapist and victim because her complicity in the act was assumed (Brownmiller, 1975).

The efforts of feminists to obtain some legal protection against physical and sexual abuse in marriage are also linked to the conception of women as the subordinate property of men (Morash, 2006). Resistance by the courts to such efforts reflects the belief that a man has a right to do what he will with his own property (i.e., wife and daughters).

Seventeenth-century judges only upheld the murder conviction of a man who beat his wife to death with a pestle [a large heavy club used for pounding and grinding wheat] because a pestle was a deadly weapon, not an appropriate instrument of correction. (Clark, 1992, p. 188)

Early American common law also recognized the "rule of thumb," which stated that a man had a right to beat his wife as long as the stick he used was no bigger in circumference than his thumb. The "rule of thumb" derives from English common law, but in 1868, a North Carolina judge in *State v. Rhodes* was still affirming this right of the husband to beat his wife.

A wife's subjugation to the authority of her husband approached that of everyone's subjugation to the sovereignty of the monarch in early English common law, as the existence of a crime called **petite treason** attests. If a husband killed his wife, the crime was simply a murder punishable by hanging. However, if a wife killed her husband, her very own "sovereign," the seriousness of the crime was elevated to that of treason (albeit, only a "little" treason), for which the punishment was burning at the stake (McIntyre, 1995).

Wives across the globe have been punished severely for the crime of adultery, but men generally have not (Morash, 2006; Wilson & Daly, 1992). The gender-based criminalization of adultery in most countries reflects the proprietary interest that men have in their wives. The reasoning behind this asymmetry is given by eighteenth-century English philosopher Samuel Johnson: "the man imposes no bastards upon his wife" (Allman, 1994, p. 134). In other words, if a wife should willingly mate with another man, the paternal source of offspring is in question (Johnson seems to overlook the fact that an adulterous man may impose "bastards" on some other man). If a wife should be raped, then it is better from this perspective that she be injured seriously so that her unwillingness to engage in the extramarital sex be made clear (Wilson & Daly, 1992).

Things are not very different in some parts of the world even today. Islamic laws state that a woman accusing a man of rape must produce four Muslim male witnesses as evidence or potentially face charges of false accusation, for which she may receive 80 lashes. She also may face charges of adultery, for which she may be stoned to death if she is married. If the rape victim is unmarried and cannot produce the almost-impossible evidence, she receives 100 lashes for adultery. Such draconian measures admittedly occur only rarely (for few risk further victimization by reporting the rape) and then only in countries practicing fundamentalist shari'a law, such as Sudan, Nigeria, Iran, Saudi Arabia, and Bangladesh (International Society for Human Rights, 2006).

Srdja Trifkovic (2005) further reveals the position of women in many Islamic societies and the extent to which they are controlled:

> The relegation of women to such an inferior position deprives Islamic societies of the talents and energies of half its people . . . it also entrusts the other half's crucial early years of upbringing to undereducated and downtrodden mothers. The idea of "love" is removed from those men's understanding of sexuality, which is too often reduced to hurting others by violence. Gross mutilation of little girls, known as clitorectomy [cutting off the clitoris] and rampant in Muslim Africa, and to a lesser extent in Arabia, is the direct result of a culture that deems female orgasm as indecent and threatening, because it implies mutuality. (p. 9)

ISSUE HIGHLIGHT

"Me Too" And "Time's Up" Movements and Their Relevance to Women in the Legal Profession

In 2017 and 2018, the "Me Too" movement grew out of the Harvey Weinstein scandal in Hollywood and spread to all sectors of the American economy. "Me Too" refers to the widespread sexual and gender harassment that mostly women experience from their primarily male supervisors, coworkers, and clients. On social media or in other interactions, one woman would explain her experience, and the common refrain from others would be "that happened to me too!"

Sexual and gender harassment has existed as long as men and women have worked together, and it has been litigated, sometimes successfully, by women in American courts for decades. The "Me Too" movement and the exposure of complaints by multiple women (this exposure is often referred to as the parallel "Time's Up" movement) about high-profile men in politics, the entertainment industry, all kinds of businesses (particularly the tech industry), and the public sector has underlined the fact that sexual and gender harassment have not disappeared and are widespread in some workplaces and broadly tolerated in others.

Women in the legal profession have been far from immune from sexual and gender harassment. As they entered the profession in larger numbers during the mid to late 1900s, women had to fight for admittance to law schools and for job placement. Once situated in their jobs, they still faced harassment by their colleagues and clients and when in court (Young Lawyer Editorial Board of The American Lawyer, 2018). Some legal scholars report that sexual or gender harassment in the legal profession may be as much as 20 percent higher than is typical for other workplaces (Grossman, 2018). "And in law firms, we will find that number to be a little bit higher; sometimes, as high depending on the study as 60 percent or 2/3rd who have either been victimized or been very close to it. So from everything we know again; data, anecdote survey, qualitative interviews, it looks like the problem in law firm is always a little bit worse than it is in most other places" (Grossman, 2018). In response to the "Me Too" and "Time's Up" movements and the sheer amount of harassment they have exposed, including that perpetrated by lawyers, in February 2018 the American Bar Association (ABA) policy-making body recommended that employers "in the legal profession . . . prohibit, prevent and promptly redress sexual harassment and retaliation claims, including adopting measures to ensure that the heads of law firms be informed of financial settlements to resolve claims" (ABA, 2018, para. 1).

WOMEN'S WORK AND OTHER LEGAL MATTERS

Laws seeking to treat people differently based on immutable characteristics such as race or national origin must pass the most stringent of constitutional tests (strict scrutiny), and the state must prove a compelling state interest. As we saw in chapter 3, unlike other immutable characteristics, gender has not been considered a suspect classification. Until the latter part of the twentieth century, laws treating men and women differently were evaluated by the rational basis test, meaning that because no suspect classification is implicated, a state may enact legislation impacting that class of persons if there is a rational basis for the legislation. Under the rational basis test standard of review, state actions are presumed to be valid and rarely are struck down.

In 1971, the US Supreme Court added the intermediary scrutiny standard of review and defined sex/gender as a quasi-suspect classification. A law passes constitutional muster under this standard only if the Court finds that it is *substantially related* to an important government purpose. The case before the Court was *Reed v. Reed* (1971) and involved an Idaho statute declaring that if a minor died intestate (i.e., without leaving a legal will), then a male parent executor is preferred over a female parent executor if both claim to be equally entitled to act as such. The Court reversed the ruling of the Idaho Supreme Court by stating that arbitrarily favoring equally qualified persons on the basis of a classification violated the equal protection clause of the Fourteenth Amendment.

In many sex-based distinction cases since then, the courts have turned to the sex/gender roles occupied by women and men by virtue of biological and cultural imperatives. Obviously, only women can bear children, and women tend to be the caregivers in any society. The courts would be remiss if they did not give full weight to these facts when applying the constitutional measuring rod to sex-based legislation. For instance, the Supreme Court apparently did just that when it upheld the Immigration and Naturalization Service's (INS) practice of making it easier for foreign-born children of female US citizens to acquire American citizenship than for foreign-born children of male US citizens (*Nguyen v. INS*, 2001). The Court agreed with the INS that there is (generally, of course) a stronger bond between mothers and children than between fathers and children and that children need their mothers more. The *Nguyen* ruling satisfies difference feminists by recognizing relevant sex differences, but sameness feminists are upset because *Nguyen's* reliance on gender stereotypes of different parenting roles for men and women harms both, and threatens a return to the era when laws and policies based on women's "proper" roles were used to justify restricting their participation in economic and political life. (National Women's Law Center, 2001, p. 1)

The first wave of the feminist movement concentrated on achieving voting rights for women, while the second wave focused on other basic rights and liberties, such as property, educational and employment opportunities, and "outing" male violence against women and children (Brenner, 1996). Many of these changes did not occur until the 1970s when the feminist movement, following on the heels of the civil rights movement, experienced a resurgence. After *Reed,* Supreme Court decisions in *Frontiero v. Richardson* (1973) and *Duren v. Missouri* (1979) established that women could administer estates, were entitled to equal benefits from the government, and had the right to serve on juries (Dusky, 1996). Interestingly enough, the second woman appointed to the Supreme Court, Ruth Bader Ginsburg, was instrumental in litigating these landmark cases when she served as the head of the American Civil Liberty Union's Women's Rights Project in the 1970s and early 1980s (Dusky, 1996).

There was a little-known period in early American history when some white women were accorded more rights than they previously had been or were to experience again until the twentieth century (Sachs & Wilson, 1978). Because of the shortage of women and labor during the early colonial period, free white women were afforded rights to own and dispose of their own property and to operate a business. Sachs and Wilson (1978) report that during this period in Philadelphia, "women engaged in roughly 30 different trades ranging from essential to luxury services," including "silversmiths, tin-workers, barbers, bakers, fish picklers, brewers, tanners, ropemakers, lumberjacks, gunsmiths, butchers, milliners, harnessmakers, potash manufacturers, upholsterers, printers, morticians" (p. 70). After the Revolutionary War, however, women were pushed back into the home, and their liberties in the areas of work, community, property ownership, and the ability to exercise control of their deceased husband's property were curtailed.

THE UNCEFDW AND THE EQUAL RIGHTS AMENDMENT

International standards have recognized that gender roles are not arbitrary "stereotypes" and have endeavored to protect women's participation in economic and political life at the same time. Table 12.1 reproduces Article 11 of the **United Nations Convention on the Elimination of All Forms of Discrimination Against Women** (UNCEFDW), which was passed by the United Nations General Assembly in 1979. The Convention became an international treaty in 1981 after the 20th country ratified it. Notice that the ideas in UNCEFDW support difference feminists rather than sameness feminists.

The UNCEFDW guarantees women the same kinds of rights (and then some) that feminists of both genders have been striving to introduce in the United States with the **Equal Rights Amendment** (ERA) since it was first introduced to Congress

Table 12.1 *Article 11 of the United Nations' Convention on the Elimination of All Forms of Discrimination Against Women*

1. States Parties shall take all appropriate measures to eliminate discrimination against women in the field of employment in order to ensure, on a basis of equality of men and women, the same rights, in particular:

(a) The right to work as an inalienable right of all human beings;

(b) The right to the same employment opportunities, including the application of the same criteria for selection in matters of employment;

(c) The right to free choice of profession and employment, the right to promotion, job security and all benefits and conditions of service and the right to receive vocational training and retraining, including apprenticeships, advanced vocational training and recurrent training;

(d) The right to equal remuneration, including benefits, and to equal treatment in respect of work of equal value, as well as equality of treatment in the evaluation of the quality of work;

(e) The right to social security, particularly in cases of retirement, unemployment, sickness, invalidity and old age and other incapacity to work, as well as the right to paid leave;

(f) The right to protection of health and to safety in working conditions, including the safeguarding of the function of reproduction.

2. In order to prevent discrimination against women on the grounds of marriage or maternity and to ensure their effective right to work, States Parties shall take appropriate measures:

(a) To prohibit, subject to the imposition of sanctions, dismissal on the grounds of pregnancy or of maternity leave and discrimination in dismissals on the basis of marital status;

(b) To introduce maternity leave with pay or with comparable social benefits without loss of former employment, seniority or social allowances;

(c) To encourage the provision of the necessary supporting social services to enable parents to combine family obligations with work responsibilities and participation in public life, in particular through promoting the establishment and development of a network of child-care facilities;

(d) To provide special protection to women during pregnancy in types of work proved to be harmful to them.

3. Protective legislation relating to matters covered in this article shall be reviewed periodically in the light of scientific and technological knowledge and shall be revised, repealed or extended as necessary.

in 1923. Not until 1972, however, was the ERA passed by Congress and finally sent to the states for ratification. The ERA never received the votes of the 38 states required to amend the Constitution, though, and so went into a state of hibernation. There are concerted efforts underway to resurrect the ERA in several states. Ironically, the passage of the Twenty-Seventh Amendment in 1992 concerning pay raises for Congress*men* provided much of the impetus for the new ERA push. The Twenty-Seventh Amendment actually went to the states for ratification in 1789, which was 203 years before it was ratified (Held, Herndon, & Stager, 1997). Thus, there is no time limit for the ratification of an amendment once introduced.

Why do we need the ERA in a time when women have all the civil, political, and social rights that men enjoy? The problem is that these rights have been won with legislation and court decisions that, with the exception of the right to vote, can be ignored, inconsistently applied, or even rescinded at any time. The passage of the ERA would rest these rights on the solid bedrock of the Constitution and thus provide the courts with consistent and unequivocal principles with which to confront gender-equity issues. The standard of review in such cases would be elevated to strict scrutiny, and sex/gender would become a suspect classification. Finally, with the passage of the ERA, American women may begin to realize some of the benefits outlined in Article 11 of the UNCEFDW.

DOMESTIC VIOLENCE

Domestic violence is a problem disproportionately affecting women that only relatively recently has been addressed by the law (remember the "rule of thumb" discussed previously). **Domestic violence** refers to any abusive act (physical, sexual, or psychological) that occurs within a domestic setting. Domestic violence is the most prevalent form of violence in the United States, with most of it being intimate partner violence (IPV; Tolan, Gorman-Smith, & Henry, 2006). IPV is overwhelmingly committed by males against females (see Figure 12.1), although when females commit such violence, they are more likely to use a weapon to equalize the size and strength difference between the sexes (Smith & Farole, 2009). Evidence from around the world indicates that IPV is driven primarily by male sexual jealousy and suspicion of infidelity (Lepowsky, 1994).

Studies based on DNA evidence find that between 1 percent and 30 percent (depending on the culture or subculture) of children are fathered by someone other than the presumed father (Birkenhead & Moller, 1992). The threat of infidelity is thus real, which suggests that IPV should be most common in environments where infidelity is most likely. Such environments would be those in which marriages are most precarious, where moral restrictions on pre- and extramarital sexual relationships are weakest, and where out-of-wedlock birth rates are highest. Indeed, it is consistently found in victimization surveys that women in the lowest income group are approximately five times more likely to be victims of domestic violence than women in the highest income groups (Catalano, 2007).

Although not limited to the lower classes, domestic violence is most prevalent among competitively disadvantaged males (Graham-Kevan & Archer, 2009). Such males have low mate value because they have less to offer in terms of resources or prospects of acquiring resources, which tends to make their mates less keen to maintain the relationship and more likely to seek other partners. These males may turn to violently coercive tactics to prevent partner's defection. Figure 12.1 provides a nationwide "snapshot" of some demographics associated with domestic violence in 2003.

In response to calls to "do something" about domestic violence, the **Violence Against Women Act** was passed as part of the Violent Crime Control and Law Enforcement Act of 1994. It is a federal law that serves as a nationwide model of response to domestic violence and provides funding for programs to train professionals involved in various aspects of domestic violence, such as police officers,

Figure 12.1 Highlights of the 2003 Report on Intimate Partner Violence

Demographic characteristic	Percent of intimate partner violence—	
	Victims	**Defendants**
Total	100%	100%
Gender		
Male	14%	86.3%
Female	86.0	13.7
Race/Hispanic origin		
White non-Hispanic	37.1%	33.6%
Black non-Hispanic	26.4	33.5
Hispanic	33.6	30.8
Other non-Hispanic	2.8	2.0
Age at offense		
17 or younger	2.7%	0.2%
18–24	26.1	24.2
25–34	34.9	34.8
35–54	34.0	38.2
55 or older	2.3	2.6

Note: Among the 3,750 cases of intimate partner violence, data on a defendant's gender were reported for 99.4%; race/Hispanic origin for 85.6%; age for 99.2%. Data on a victim's gender were reported for 100% of cases; race/Hispanic origin for 94.5%; age for 94.4%.

Source: E. Smith & D. Farole, (2009). *Profile of intimate partner violence cases in large urban counties.* Washington, DC: Bureau of Justice Statistics.

victim advocates, judges, and prosecutors. The act provides yet another example of the dynamic interplay between the law and social movements—in this case, the various women's movements of the 1970s and 1980s.

One of the tactics the law has used against domestic violence is to implement mandatory arrest and no-drop prosecution requirements. These requirements seemed to be the panacea after a series of experiments in 1982 showed that mandatory arrest resulted in a significant reduction in repeat calls compared to other methods of dealing with the situation (Durlauf & Nagin, 2011). Unfortunately, this has not been the situation across the board. Subsequent experiments in different neighborhoods showed that mandatory arrest reduced further incidents of IPV in middle-class neighborhoods due to its shaming effect, but in inner-city neighborhoods, it actually increased incidents of IPV because arrest had the result of angering rather than shaming perpetrators (Durlauf & Nagin, 2011).

WOMEN'S REPRESENTATION IN THE LEGAL PROFESSION

Women's admittance into the legal profession has been fraught with struggle and hardship. Clearly, major victories have been achieved in the admittance of women to law schools and legal practice, while some obstacles to women's full participation remain. As Martin and Jurik (1996) indicate:

> The obstacles faced by women justice workers are part of larger organizational and social patterns that construct and support women's subordination to men. Women in fields numerically dominated by men face many barriers: exclusion from informal work cultures, hostility expressed at the international level, organizational policies that promote gender segregation, differential assignments, and sexual harassment. The confluence of these barriers produces lower pay and slower advancement for women in these fields. (p. 2)

These obstacles to admittance to the legal profession were based on a long tradition of excluding women from it, even though some women in colonial America performed quasi-legal work. For instance, Margaret Brent, a well-connected and capable woman, was the executor of the estate of the governor of the Maryland colony in 1638 (Morello, 1986). Brent was from a wealthy family in England who settled in Maryland and made her fortune in real estate. As part of her duties as executor, she handled claims against the estate in court, settled an impending riot by soldiers who had a hefty claim against it, and appeared before the assembly asking for a vote and a voice. Despite her success and obvious ability, she was denied a vote and eventually left Maryland for Virginia, where she settled until her death on an estate she called "Peace" (Morello, 1986, p. 7).

Other women in colonial America also were tangentially involved in court processes affecting themselves and others, primarily property matters and estates to which they had some claim. Morello (1986) notes that in 1783, a black slave woman named Elizabeth Freeman successfully argued in a Massachusetts court for her freedom. Another black woman, Lucy Terry Prince, was the first woman to argue before the Supreme Court in a 1795 case involving a land dispute (Morello, 1986). But because women were essentially barred from clerkships with lawyers (a primary means of entering the profession before the proliferation of law schools), admittance to law schools, and state bar exams, it was difficult, if not impossible, for them to practice law until the latter half of the nineteenth century. Even then, however, women did not practice law in any meaningful numbers until the latter half of the twentieth century (Bernat, 1992; Friedman, 1993).

Underpinning this exclusion from legal practice was the belief that feminine characteristics were not suited for the practice of law, which required rationality and an objective and unemotional demeanor. Women were viewed as lacking in the requisite logical capacity and as overly subjective and emotional. It would, of course, have been incongruent with women's citizenship status in the seventeenth, eighteenth, and nineteenth centuries to be able to practice law when they did not have the legal status of citizens.

Despite these obstacles, a few women were admitted to the study of law and to the bar in the latter half of the 1800s. In 1869, two white women (Arabella Babb Mansfield in Iowa and Myra Bradwell in Illinois) passed the bar. When Bradwell applied to practice law, she was twice denied by the Illinois Supreme Court, the first time because she was married and coverture applied and the second time just because she was a woman (Friedman, 1993). Bradwell appealed to the US Supreme Court (*Bradwell v. Illinois*, 1873), which upheld the right of Illinois to deny her admission to legal practice. Justice Joseph Bradley's opinion was that

> [c]ivil law, as well as nature herself, has always recognized a wide difference in the respective spheres and destinies of man and woman. The paramount destiny and mission of women are to fulfill the noble and benign offices of wife and mother. This is the law of the Creator.

Arabella Mansfield: First Female Lawyer in the United States

By the time of *Bradwell v. Illinois*, however, Arabella Mansfield had been admitted to the bar in Iowa in 1869, although she did not practice law, opting for a career in college teaching and administration. Nevertheless, Mansfield holds the distinction of being the first female lawyer in the United States.

Two other white women, Lemma Barkeloo and Phoebe Cousins, were admitted to Washington University Law School in 1869 (Bernat, 1992, 1996). One year later, Ada Kepley, a white woman, graduated from the University of Chicago Law School, and the first black woman, Charlotte Ray, graduated and was admitted to the bar in 1872. In 1870, a white woman, Esther Morris, was appointed as a justice of the peace in a mining camp in Wyoming (Spohn, 1990). Despite these gains, it was not until 1918 that women were allowed to join the American Bar Association and not until 1920 that women were admitted to the bar in all states. It was not until 1928 and 1950 that Columbia University and Harvard Law Schools, respectively, admitted women. Many other elite schools restricted admittance for almost as long (Martin & Jurik, 1996).

Morello (1986) reports that Harlan Fiske Stone, once a dean of the school of Columbia Law School and later a Supreme Court justice, had not permitted women to register as students when he was there. Morello also found that in the 1940s, "Roscoe Pound threw a woman visitor out of his class because he did not believe in teaching law to women," and that on "Ladies Day" at Harvard in the 1950s, female students were allowed to "recite on one specially selected day each semester and then only for the amusement of the professor and the male members of the class" (Morello, 1986, p. xiv). Supreme Court Justice Ginsburg, the second woman appointed to that court, reported that even though she had graduated at the top of her class (she tied for first) from Columbia Law School in 1959, she had no job offers and was forced to take a clerkship for a federal judge (Meyers, 2004).

By the 1970s, women were finally being admitted to law schools and to the practice of law in larger numbers (Law School Admission Council, 2005; Martin & Jurik, 1996).

These increases may not have occurred at all but for the agitation by the second wave of feminists or without the passage of the 1972 amendment Title VII to the Civil Rights Act of 1964 and the Equal Employment Opportunity Act of 1972 (Harrington, 1994; Spohn, 1990). Title VII forbade discrimination in employment based on sex unless there was a bona fide occupational qualification. Also in 1972, Title IX of the Higher Education Act was passed, constraining the ability of law schools to discriminate based on sex through the threat of losing federal financial assistance (Martin & Jurik, 1996). Suddenly, the last vestiges of the formal legal barriers to admittance to law and its practice came tumbling down for women.

According to the Law School Admission Council (2005), the nonprofit organization that administers the Law School Admissions Test, as of 2005 about half of the applicants to American law schools were women. The *Princeton Review: The Best Law Schools, 1998 Edition,* reported that in the mid-1990s, 44 percent of students entering law schools were women (Hollander & Tallia, 1997). These figures represent major increases from even the 1970s, when only 10 percent of applicants to law schools were women (Law School Admission Council, 2005). In a preliminary analysis of the female student experience at Harvard Law School, Neufeld, Sanders, and Wilk (2004) found that women had a different experience in law school than men. The authors found that women were less confident in their legal skills and less likely to apply for law review than men, and more women than men indicated that they hoped to work for a nonprofit or a legal services organization. In contrast, more men expected to work in prestigious law firms or businesses. The authors also noted that women constituted 28 percent of all faculty and administrators of law schools, 16 percent of all tenured law school professors, 8 percent of all deans, and 12.9 percent of all partners in law firms. Overall, women comprised 24 percent of those working in the legal profession. Linda Hirshman, a philosophy professor at Brandeis University (see Gest, 2001), noted that about 20 law schools had female deans and one-fifth had female full professors in 2001.

Women's careers in the legal profession have shifted over time. Traditionally, federal judgeships, a much-sought-after prize for many public service–minded lawyers, have gone to men. Over the years, however, US presidents have been increasingly more willing to nominate and appoint women. As of 2004, President Bill Clinton held the record for female appointments to judgeships, at 104 in his two terms, which is almost three times the number of women appointed by President George H. W. Bush in his one term (36) or President George W. Bush in his first term (33), and over four times the number of women appointed by President Ronald Reagan in either of his terms (Maguire & Pastore, 1998; Meyers, 2004). According to Supreme Court Justice Ruth Bader Ginsburg, President Carter in the 1970s first broke the barrier to the appointment of women with 40 federal judgeships at a time when only 6 women then held such positions (Meyers, 2004).

Clearly, women at the turn of the millennium had made great inroads into the legal profession (Law School Admission Council, 2005), although barriers to full participation were yet to be removed. Today, there are still far fewer women serving as judges, partners in prestigious law firms, and law school faculty than expected, given their numbers in the profession (Hollander & Tallia, 1997; Meyers, 2004). This disparity can be explained in part by the fact that many women may choose to adopt a "mommy track" when they have children. Therefore, women lawyers are more likely to choose to work fewer hours, adopt more flexible schedules, and/or take a leave of absence when their children are young. Men are less likely to make such a choice. Some disparity also likely is due to latent sexist perceptions about the abilities and propensities of women. In the 1970s, female law students had to sue to end discriminatory hiring practices by law firms (e.g., *Kohn v. Royall, Koegel, and Wells* [1973]), and in the 1980s, they had to sue their own law firms to be allowed to make partner (e.g., *Hishon v. King and Spalding* [1984]). Such issues remain unresolved (Hollander & Tallia, 1997; Martin & Jurik, 1996).

Today, women outperform men in undergraduate grade point average and do as well as men in medical, business, and other graduate/professional programs, but not as well as men in law school. Some scholars report that female students claim differential treatment in law school, as they are not called on in class and their questions and input are often ignored (Hollander & Tallia, 1997). Some of the top-ranked law schools, such as Yale and Harvard, do not even score in the top 100 schools in terms of female representation on faculties, law reviews, and student bar associations (Hollander & Tallia, 1997).

In general, women have gained equal footing in terms of sheer numbers of those involved in law careers and in the evaluations of their job satisfaction vis-à-vis their male colleagues. In her study of the perceptions of 424 female and male attorneys, Hall (1995) found that they "share similar work values, career orientations, and perceptions of work. Both genders were relatively satisfied with their work because they valued the most positive aspects of their jobs" (p. 121). She did find perceptions of fewer promotional opportunities among women attorneys and that this affected their job satisfaction. Hall (1995) explained that women did not rate their own chances of promotion lower but rather the chances of other women being lower.

Pollitz Worden (1997) surveyed 553 private criminal defense attorneys in Georgia and found that men and women were in basic agreement on values: "although male respondents express more extreme advocacy of due process and defendants' rights, women and men differ little in their attitudes toward punishment issues and cynicism regarding defendants" (p. 1). Thus, much like research on job satisfaction, job enrichment, job commitment, stress, and work values in policing and corrections (Stohr, Lovrich, & Mays, 1997; Stohr, Lovrich, & Wood, 1996), women and men in the legal profession tend to be more similar than dissimilar.

THE BIAS STUDIES

Despite some similarities in experiences on the job, latent discriminatory attitudes permeate America's courtrooms. In a review of more than 30 state gender-bias studies, Hemmens, Strom, and Schlegel (1998) found the following:

> In theory, all persons involved in court proceedings are supposed to be treated equitably. A number of states have conducted studies which indicate that in actuality men and women receive differential treatment in court. As is the case in many aspects of American society, women are

most often victims of gender bias. Female litigants face an uphill battle in pursuing their cases in both civil and criminal courts. (p. 22)

Such bias is manifested in the beliefs, perceptions, and practices of the courtroom actors and clients. In cases of domestic violence, the California Task Force found that a majority of the male courtroom personnel (53 percent) thought that claims of abuse by female victims were "exaggerated" (Hemmens et al., 1998). Massachusetts attorneys reported that judges sometimes wondered aloud what victims did to deserve beating. Wisconsin and Minnesota attorneys reported that a victim's willingness to press charges determined whether a prosecution would go forward in many cases, despite the fact that the state was the aggrieved party and could prosecute regardless of victim involvement. In task force studies done in Nevada, New Mexico, Nebraska, Washington, Michigan, and Missouri, approximately 30 percent to 50 percent of court actors reported that women were prevented in some way from effectively pursuing court orders to protect themselves from their abusers.

Hemmens and colleagues (1998) indicate that in sexual assault cases, several gender-bias studies revealed perceptions among a number of court actors that victims of these crimes have less credibility with judges and jurors than victims of other crimes. If the victim in a sexual assault knew the offender, the offense is regarded as "less serious" and treated that way. Courtroom actors report that the sexual history of the victim often is allowed in such cases despite its irrelevance to the issue of consent.

Gender-bias studies in several states reflect perceptions of disparity in treatment in divorce, marital property, and child support that disadvantage women and children (Hemmens et al., 1998). In some states, between 30 percent to 60 percent of courtroom actors believe that men are awarded a disproportionate share of the marital property by predominately male judges in divorce cases.

Reported bias is also found in the treatment of female attorneys and judges (Hemmens et al., 1998). Female attorneys report that male judges or attorneys accord them less credibility than their male counterparts, make comments about their appearance, or subject them to sexist remarks or jokes. Female attorneys indicate that they are regarded as "bitches" if they respond as aggressively as male attorneys and are less likely to be hired or selected than similarly qualified men. Hemmens and colleagues (1998) conclude by recognizing the extent of the gender bias and by making a recommendation that education be used to reduce it:

> The implication of gender bias is that women are still not being viewed as equal to their male counterparts. Although current laws and affirmative action plans have furthered women's equality, they cannot by themselves change the attitudes of individuals. It is the individual attitudes that require change if gender bias is to be eradicated. . . .
>
> The task force reports on gender bias provide strong evidence that gender bias exists in all aspects of the court system, and in virtually all courts. The reports also indicate that there is a wide variation in the perception of the existence of bias, depending on the gender of the observer. Remedying gender bias requires convincing those most often guilty of it that they are acting in a biased fashion. If this can be accomplished, a major step will have been taken. (p. 40)

LAW, EQUALITY, AND JUSTICE

As we have discussed, there has been a concerted effort by feminists over the centuries to force the law to recognize women both as people and as equal citizens entitled to all the rights and privileges that such status entails. In modern secular democracies, legal status as citizens has for the most part been achieved, as has access to all avenues of higher education in the law. What feminist scholars are now debating is the extent to which further justice can be achieved through the use of the courts and whether equality with men necessarily involves justice for women. Perhaps the best option at present would be for the US Congress to ratify and implement the provisions of the UNCEFDW, a much easier process than a constitutional amendment.

As we have seen, the law is androcentric (male centered), so efforts to decide issues affecting females as victims of males are likely to be stymied by the male view of what women are or should be. For instance, because women continue to be culturally defined by the old "Madonna/whore" dichotomy, rape trials often see court actors sexualizing women's bodies and failing to focus on the assault (Smart, 1989). Smart also argues that the law has been used to control women's bodies, such as by requiring parental consent to obtain an abortion.

A corollary to this view is the one proposed by Carol Gilligan (1982) that women and men are basically different and that the law as it is currently written and practiced reflects masculine values of competitiveness, aggressiveness, and male logic. She writes:

> As we have listened for centuries to the voices of men and the theories of development that their experience informs, so we have come more recently to notice not only the silence of women but the difficulty in hearing what they say when they speak. Yet in the different voice of women lies the truth of an ethic of care, the tie between relationship and responsibility, and the origins of aggression in the failure of connection. (p. 171)

Gilligan would propose that as more women enter the profession of the law, it, as well as the courts, will begin to reflect more feminine values, such as cooperation, support, and care. This shift will not necessarily mean the demise of the rule of law, but it may mean there will be more *justice* in its practice.

Mackinnon (1993) also recognizes the differing frameworks that men and women experience and are shaped by but argues that a new jurisprudence and a new relationship between life and law is needed. Law should be fashioned so that there is a basic equality in treatment and protection; however, to effectuate justice, law and legal procedures also must recognize the female experience, the female reality, and the female voice. Therefore, laws that truly work to protect women's and girls' abilities, access, rights, and liberties, as they do men's, will not be wholly neutral, just as laws are not and have not been neutral in conception or practice, both as Mackinnon argues and our review of history has indicated. As we have found throughout the history of humankind, law and juridical practice have been conceived and practiced in such a way that they have disadvantaged girls and women. In the future, let it not be so.

BUILDING UNDERSTANDING

Imagine a world where one gender holds the vast majority of powerful political and corporate positions and controls most of the wealth, a world where law either forbids the involvement of the "powerless gender" in politics or business and/or more informal controls, imposed by the culture, family, and work requirements, bar access to powerful positions and attainment of wealth. Imagine a world where positions in the criminal justice systems and lawmaking are largely dominated by this powerful gender as well.

Imagine the "weaker gender" being cloistered in strict Islamic countries, not allowed to own or dispose of property or to speak freely without harassment, threat of violence, or actual assault by religious adherents; totally dominated by the other gender; not believed when testifying independently in court; or not allowed to walk about, eat in restaurants, go to the theater, or go shopping without an escort and being shrouded with clothing. Imagine places such as India and China where the less-valued gender survives early childhood at a much lower rate than the valued male gender because of abandonment or infanticide.

Imagine that in America there is a state where members of this "insignificant gender" are sometimes married to men who already have several wives and are kept in poverty and not educated so that they cannot escape the abuse of themselves and their children in these marriages. Although the behavior of these men is widely known and violates the law of Utah and the Mormon Church to which they align themselves, only recently have the authorities taken meaningful steps to prosecute them.

Imagine a world where religious groups such as the Catholics and Church of Jesus Christ of Latter-Day Saints exclude this "less worthy gender" from real positions of leadership in the church (elders, priests, bishops), or where Southern Baptists admonish the "less capable gender" to submit to the leadership and guidance of the wiser and more-capable-of-leadership gender. Or try to conceive of societies where one gender commits the vast majority of physical and sexual assaults and murders and members of "a "victimized gender" are victims as children and as adults, a world in which the "less violent" gender is told to stay inside, not to travel alone, and to worry from childhood on about how to avoid rape and abuse from family members, friends, and strangers. Imagine a world where "a blamed gender" is routinely told that they asked for their own abuse or are condemned because they do not leave their abusers in their traditional family when they and their children have few resources to do so and current cultural values do not support it.

Imagine a world where children and adults of the "object gender" have their bodies prostituted or trivialized in strip and topless clubs, brothels, and in print, video, and other media. This occurs even though such pornographic depictions have been tied to the sexual abuse and denigration of the suffering of the "object gender." In some Asian countries, children and adults of this gender are sold into prostitution for unscrupulous foreign members of the more abusive gender.

Can you imagine such a sexist world? Would it be possible for you to conceive of this "powerless," "weaker," "less valued," "insignificant," "less worthy and capable," "victimized," "blamed," and "object" gender as being male? If not, then why not? Why is there not a general sense of outrage that these appellations do, indeed, apply to women and girls right now in *our* world? The fact that many are not even concerned about such injustice for females is itself the strongest evidence of the prevalence and acceptability of injustice and privilege in our world.

SUMMARY

Feminist jurisprudence evaluates the law from a critical feminist perspective, noting that it is a system of control devised by men for men. All societies throughout history have been patriarchies in which women have been disadvantaged. Feminist scholars disagree, however, on how the situation can be put right. They split primarily along reformist/radical and sameness/difference lines.

Full social and legal justice for women are hard-won prizes that have yet to be fully realized in many countries, including the United States. The ability to participate completely as citizens and to have the freedom to self-determine how one will live and negotiate in this world are not liberties that girls or women have been able to assume as their right. Such freedoms were not self-evident for women, nor did the Founders intend that they be. As Elizabeth Cady Stanton stated, to the extent that such rights have finally been accorded, it has been at great cost in time, money, and lives of courageous feminist women and men.

At the same time that Western women have achieved some legal standing, however, they continue to struggle against the more informal strictures that permeate homes, workplaces, courtrooms, and churches. These informal strictures limit women's and girls' opportunities and shape their perceptions of themselves as less capable, able, and wise than men and boys. The repercussions of such perceptions about women and girls are stark and clear. History tells us that the abuse of women and girls arises out of a perception of their inferiority as human beings. Therefore, we might reasonably assume that those persons and entities engaged in perpetuating such perceptions also are, indirectly or directly, fostering the denigration of females and limiting their potential as human beings. Necessarily, these limitations on half the human population are crippling the ability of our culture to advance and flourish as it might.

A parallel issue for justicians is whether justice can mean the same thing in an environment with patriarchal overtones. Should justice be differential, as Gilligan (1982) argues in light of the special needs, backgrounds, and propensities of women? Or does justice require an adherence to equal treatment of men and women under the law, as Mackinnon (1993) would have it? If we have learned anything, we should know that as a country, we will be engaged in resolving such social and legal justice issues well into the twenty-first century.

DISCUSSION QUESTIONS

1. Why do you think that women and girls generally are valued less than men and boys?
2. What central figures were involved in gaining the vote for women in the United States, and how long did it take?

3. Why do you think the western states were quicker in granting suffrage to women than the eastern states?
4. Who was Mary Wollstonecraft, and what did she argue?
5. How is the practice of rape tied to the conception of women and girls as property?
6. What do the findings of the studies by Hall (1995) and Pollitz Worden (1997) tell us about how women and men perceive their jobs as lawyers?
7. What were the general conclusions of the gender-bias studies on courts by Hemmens and colleagues (1998)?

CHAPTER TERMS

Coverture
Domestic violence
Equal Rights Amendment
Feminist jurisprudence

Misogyny
Patriarchy
Petite treason
United Nations Convention on the

Elimination of All Forms of Discrimination Against Women
Violence Against Women Act

References

Allman, W. (1994). *The Stone Age present*. New York, NY: Simon & Schuster.

American Bar Association (2018). ABA adopts new policy to combat sexual harassment in the legal workplace. *ABA*. Retrieved from https://www.americanbar.org/news/abanews/aba-news-archives/2018/02/aba_adopts_new_polic.html

Baer, J. (1999). *Our lives before the law: Constructing a feminist jurisprudence*. Princeton, NJ: Princeton University Press.

Bailey, F. (2006). Images of women. In A. Merlo & J. Pollock (Eds.), *Women, law, and social control* (pp. 32–46). Boston, MA: Allyn & Bacon.

Bernat, F. (1992). Women in the legal profession. In I. Hoyer (Ed.), *The changing roles of women in the criminal justice system: Offenders, victims, and professionals* (2nd ed., pp. 307–322). Prospect Heights, IL: Waveland Press.

Bernat, F. (1996). Book review of *America's first woman lawyer: The biography of Myra Bradwell* by J. Friedman. *Women & Criminal Justice, 7*, 94–97.

Birkenhead, T., & Moller, A. (1992, July). Faithless females seek better genes. *New Scientist*, pp. 34–38.

Blackstone, W. (1765–1769). *Commentaries on the law of England*. 4 vols. London, England: Routledge.

Brenner, J. (1996). The best of times, the worst of times: Feminism in the United States. In M. Threlfall (Ed.), *Mapping the women's movement* (pp. 17–72). London, England: Verso.

Brownmiller, S. (1975). *Against our will: Men, women and rape*. New York, NY: Simon & Schuster.

Burchard, M. (2006). Feminist jurisprudence. In *The Internet encyclopedia of philosophy*. Retrieved from http://iep.utm.edu/j/jurisfem.htm

Catalano, S. (2007). *Intimate partner violence in the United States*. Washington, DC: Bureau of Justice Statistics.

Cicero, M. (1985). *On the commonwealth*. New York, NY: Macmillan.

Clark, A. (1992). Humanity or justice? Wifebeating and the law in the eighteenth and nineteenth centuries. In C. Smart (Ed.), *Regulating womanhood: Historical essays on marriage, motherhood and sexuality* (pp. 187–220). London, England: Routledge.

Coole, D. (1993). *Women in political theory: From ancient misogyny to contemporary feminism* (2nd ed.). Boulder, CO: Lynne Rienner.

Dixon, S. (1992). Conclusion: The enduring theme. Domineering dowagers and scheming concubines. In B. Garlick, S. Dixon, & P. Allen (Eds.), *Stereotypes of women in power: Historical perspectives and revisionist views* (pp. 209–226). New York, NY: Greenwood Press.

Durlauf, S., & Nagin, D. (2011). Imprisonment and crime: Can both be reduced? *Criminology & Public Policy, 10,* 13–54.

Dusky, L. (1996). *Still unequal: The shameful truth about women and justice in America.* New York, NY: Crown.

Dworkin, A. (1993). Against the male flood: Censorship, pornography, and equality. In P. Smith (Ed.), *Feminist jurisprudence* (pp. 19–38). New York, NY: Oxford University Press.

Friedman, J. (1993). *America's first woman lawyer: The biography of Myra Bradwell.* Buffalo, NY: Prometheus Books.

Gage, M. (1980). *Woman, church and state: The original expose of male collaboration against the female sex.* Watertown, MA: Persephone Press. (Original work published 1893.)

Gest, T. (2001). Law schools' new female face. *U.S. News and World Report.* Retrieved from http://www.usnews.com

Gilligan, C. (1982). *In a different voice: Psychological theory and women's development.* Cambridge, MA: Harvard University Press.

Graham-Kevan, N., & Archer, J. (2009). Control tactics and partner violence in heterosexual relationships. *Evolution and Human Behavior, 30,* 445–452.

Grana, S. (2002). *Women and (in)justice: The criminal and civil effects of the common law on women's lives.* Boston, MA: Allyn & Bacon.

Grossman, J. (2018). Sexual harassment in the legal profession. *Lawyer-2-Lawyer.* Retrieved from https://legaltalknetwork.com/podcasts/lawyer-2-lawyer/2017/12/sexual-harassment-in-the-legal-profession/

Hall, D. (1995). Job satisfaction among male and female defense attorneys. *Justice System Journal, 18,* 121–137.

Haney, L. (2000). Feminist state theory: Applications to jurisprudence, criminology, and the welfare state. *Annual Review of Sociology, 26,* 641–666.

Harrington, M. (1994). *Women lawyers: Rewriting the rules.* New York, NY: Alfred A. Knopf.

Held, A., Herndon, S., & Stager, D. (1997). Why the Equal Rights Amendment remains legally viable and properly before the states. *William & Mary Journal of Women and the Law, 3,* 113–136.

Hemmens, C., Strom, K., & Schlegel, E. (1998). Gender bias in the courts: A review of the literature. *Sociological Imagination, 35,* 22–42.

Hillard, T. (1992). On the stage; behind the curtain: Images of politically active women in the late Roman republic. In B. Garlick, S. Dixon, & P. Allen (Eds.), *Stereotypes of women in power: Historical perspectives and revisionist views* (pp. 37–64). Westport, CT: Greenwood Press.

Hollander, D., & Tallia, R. (1997). *The Princeton Review: The best law schools.* New York, NY: Random House.

International Society for Human Rights. (2006). Shariah law, adultery and rape. Retrieved from http://www.steinigung.org/artikel/shaia_adultery_rape.htm

Law School Admission Council. (2005). Think about law school. Retrieved from http://www.lsac.org

Lepowsky, M. (1994). Women, men, and aggression in egalitarian societies. *Sex Roles, 30,* 199–211.

Mackinnon, C. (1993). Toward feminist jurisprudence. In P. Smith (Ed.), *Feminist jurisprudence* (pp. 449–466). New York, NY: Oxford University Press.

Maguire, K., & Pastore, A. (Eds.). (1998). *Sourcebook of criminal justice statistics, 1997.* Washington, DC: US Department of Justice.

Martin, S., & Jurik, N. (1996). *Doing justice, doing gender.* Thousand Oaks, CA: SAGE.

McIntyre, L. (1995). Law and the family in historical perspective: Issues and antecedents. *Marriage and Family Review, 21,* 5–30.

Meyers, L. (2004, July 1). Justice Ruth Bader Ginsburg weighs in on women's progress in the legal profession—and what kept them out for so long. *Cornell News.* Retrieved from http://www.news.cornell.edu/stories/2004/07/justice-ruth-bader-ginsburg-womens-progress-law

Morash, M. (2006). *Understanding gender, crime, and justice.* Thousand Oaks, CA: SAGE.

Morello, K. (1986). *The invisible bar: The woman lawyer in America, 1638 to the present.* New York, NY: Random House.

National Women's Law Center. (2001). *The Supreme Court and women's rights: Fundamental protections hang in the balance.* Washington, DC: Author.

Neufeld, A., Sanders, C., & Wilk, K. (2004). A study of women's experiences at Harvard Law School. Paper presented at Taking Stock: Women of All Colors in Law School Conference, New York. Retrieved from http://www.aals.org

Ollenburger, J. (1998). *Sociology of women: The intersection of patriarchy, capitalism, and colonization.* Upper Saddle River, NJ: Prentice Hall.

Pollitz Worden, A. (1997). Gender and professional values in the criminal bar. *Women and Criminal Justice, 8*(3), 1–28.

Pollock, J. (2006). Gender, justice, and social control. In A. Merlo & J. Pollock (Eds.), *Women, law, and social control* (pp. 3–31). Boston, MA: Allyn & Bacon.

Sachs, A., & Wilson, J. (1978). *Sexism and the law: A study of male beliefs and legal bias in Britain and the United States.* New York, NY: Free Press.

Smart, C. (1989). *Women, crime and criminology: A feminist critique.* London, England: Routledge and Kegan Paul.

Smith, E., & Farole, D. (2009). *Profile of intimate partner violence cases in large urban counties.* Washington, DC: Bureau of Justice Statistics.

Spohn, C. (1990). Decision making in sexual assault cases: Do black and female judges make a difference? *Women and Criminal Justice, 2,* 83–101.

Stohr, M., Lovrich, N., & Wood, M. (1996). Service v. security concerns in contemporary jails: Testing behavior differences in training topic assessments. *Journal of Criminal Justice, 24,* 437–448.

Stohr, M., Lovrich, N., & Mays, G. (1997). Service v. security focus in training assessments: Testing gender differences among contemporary women's jail correctional officers. *Women and Criminal Justice, 9,* 65–85.

Tolan, P., Gorman-Smith, D., & Henry, D. (2006). Family violence. *Annual Review of Psychology, 57,* 557–583.

Trifkovic, S. (2005, January). Islam and women: *The Christian Science Monitor's* distortion and the reality. *Chronicles Magazine.* Retrieved from http://www.chroniclesmagazine/News/Trifkovic05/NewsST010305.html

Whittick, A. (1979). *Woman into citizen.* Santa Barbara, CA: ABC-Clio.

Wilson, M., & Daly, M. (1992). The man who mistook his wife for chattel. In J. Barkow, L. Cosmides, & J. Tooby (Eds.), *The adapted mind: Evolutionary psychology and the generation of culture* (pp. 289–326). New York, NY: Oxford University Press.

Wollstonecraft, M. (1967). *A vindication of the rights of woman.* New York, NY: Norton. (Original work published 1792).

Young Lawyer Editorial Board of The American Lawyer (2018). This Is What Sexual Harassment in the Legal Industry Looks Like. *The American Lawyer.* Retrieved from https://www.law.com/americanlawyer/2018/02/28/yl-board-this-is-what-sexual-harassment-in-the-legal-industry-looks-like/?slreturn=20180404140130

Cases Cited

Bradwell v. Illinois, 83 U.S. 130 (1873)

Duren v. Missouri, 439 U.S. 357, 364 (1979)

Frontiero v. Richardson, 411 U.S. 677 (1973)

Hishon v. King and Spalding, 467 U.S. 69 (1984)

Kohn v. Royall, Koegel, and Wells, 496 F2d 1094 (1973)

Minor v. Happersett, 88 U.S. 162 (1874)

Nguyen v. INS, 533 U.S. 53 (2001)

Reed v. Reed, 404 U.S. 71 (1971)

State v. Rhodes, 61 N.C. 453 (1868)

CHAPTER 13

RACIAL MINORITIES AND THE LAW

Kevin O'Malley was born in 1964 in Toledo, Ohio, just three months after his parents emigrated from Ireland. Jake Paterson was born in the same year, 300 years after his ancestors were dragged from Africa to these shores in chains. With identical Law School Admission Test scores, both young men applied to the prestigious University of Michigan law school in 1986. Kevin was denied because his score was at the 55th percentile for white applicants (the cutoff was the 60th percentile), but Jake was admitted because his score placed him at the 90th percentile for black applicants.

Affirmative action is a way of trying to put things right for the Jakes of America, but is it right to do it at the expense of the Kevins? Jake's ancestors may have been wronged, but not by Kevin's ancestors. Kevin's father was a line worker in a glass factory and Jake's an assistant high school principal, so need did not enter the law school's decision. Do different standards for different races drive wedges between them? Haven't we defined race-based treatment in the past as racism? Doesn't the paternalism inherent in preferential treatment imply inferiority, and doesn't it fly in the face of the American values of meritocracy and self-reliance? The Constitution is about individual rights, not group rights, so how is affirmative action justified?

One of the justifications is that schools and neighborhoods are reseg-regating, taking us back to a divided nation of mutually hostile groups. Do we want that, and if not, how else can we achieve racial harmony and social equality? The worst abuses of affirmative action, such as racial quotas and different standards, have all but gone. Supreme Court decisions in 2003 out-lawed awarding admission "points" based on race but allowed race to be taken into account if (a) there is an important state interest (e.g., a diverse workforce) involved and (b) there is no other way to achieve the goal. In 2014, the Court ruled that the states can ban affirmative action programs, so perhaps it has seen its day unless a later, more liberal Court rules otherwise. As you read this chapter, think about whether affirmative action is the final step in acknowledging the wrong we have done to minorities in the past or if it perpetuates racist ideas of inferiority.

INTRODUCTION

The nation that was to become the United States has been bedeviled by race almost from the moment the first white settlers landed in the New World. The presence of Native American Indians, the odious practice of slavery, and the immigration of peoples from the Asian continent virtually assured that racial relations would be contentious and require continual actions of the law to settle the multitude of issues that arise in a multiracial/multiethnic society. These issues arose (and still arise) as people of different racial/ethnic groups whose collective identities differ from that of the dominant group have understandably demanded recognition of their status as equal citizens before the law and effective representation in the decision-making institutions of our society.

The United Nations Declaration on Minorities insists that the rights of minorities can exist only within the framework of democracy (Wheatley, 2003). By its very nature, democracy is responsive to "the will of the people"—that is, the will of the majority of the people. "The greatest good for the greatest number" is a noble principle in a racially homogeneous society, but in a diverse society such as the United States, the relationship between the majority will and individual rights for *all* people is problematic. This is where an independent judiciary, free of the politician's need to be responsive to those who elect him or her, should step in and apply rules of law and justice that may be at odds with the popular "will." As Immanuel Kant put it, "for law to be legitimate it must enjoy the united and consenting will of all [not just the majority]" (Wheatley, 2003, p. 510).

To expect the courts to transcend the social and political contexts in which they are embedded is to harbor an overly romanticized vision. The courts can only go so far if they are not supported by the legislative and executive branches of government. Historically, in cases concerning minority rights, the Supreme Court almost inevitably sided with what the majority of the people in the United States want—to keep minority group members "in their place" and to affirm the superiority of the white race. Even when state and federal legislation had been passed granting minorities certain rights, the Supreme Court justices often saw it as their duty to rule that legislation unconstitutional. However, things changed considerably after the civil rights movements among blacks, women, and gays in the 1960s, and the courts are now prone to favoring minorities over majorities in many cases.

AFRICAN AMERICANS

Slavery and the Law

Slavery is as old as human history, and few practices instituted by human beings are more repulsive. It is still practiced in a variety of forms in a number of African Islamic countries today (Murphy, 2014). American slavery evolved from the English practice of indentured servitude, a system in which people could pay off their debts by working for an employer for a fixed number of years. People who wished to emigrate to the American colonies could indenture themselves in exchange for passage. The courts could also indenture criminals to private or public employers for their crimes. The relationship between employer and indentured was one of master and servant rather than of employer and employee in the modern sense. After a certain period of time, usually seven years, indentured servants were released and given 50 acres of land to start their own businesses. Most indentured servants in the colonies were white, but many were black and had the same rights as whites—to be freed upon serving their time.

The first African slaves were brought by Dutch traders to Jamestown, Virginia, in 1619. Because slavery was illegal under English common law, the slaves were assimilated into the system of indentured servitude rather than sold into slavery (Wood, 1970). Among those first arrivals was a man who took the name of Anthony Johnson. After serving his period of indenture, Johnson became the first free African and first African landowner in America. He eventually became the owner of 250 acres, the master of five indentured servants (four whites and one black), and the plaintiff in a case laying the groundwork for legal slavery in North America.

The case *Johnson v. Parker* occurred in March 1655 in Virginia. The previous year, a black indentured servant named John Casor claimed that his owner, the aforementioned Anthony Johnson, illegally held him past his term of indenture. Robert Parker, a white neighbor, told Johnson that if he did not release Casor, he would testify to this fact in court. Fearing loss of his lands for violating the law of indenture, Johnson freed Casor, and then Castor indentured himself to Parker for seven years. After a destructive fire on his tobacco plantation, Johnson sought to rebuild and needed help, so he sued Parker for Casor's return. A Montgomery County court ruled for Johnson, declaring that Parker was illegally detaining Casor from his rightful master and, as a consequence, Johnson could legally hold Casor "for the duration of his life" (Wood, 1970, p. 48). Although there were previous cases of both blacks and whites being sentenced to lifetime servitude for crimes they had committed, Casor became the first person to be declared a legal slave in a civil case in the colonies. As Goldsmyth, Radford, Jones, Hawkins, & Russell (1916, p.235) put it: "No earlier record has been found of judicial support given to slavery in Virginia except as punishment for crime" (p. 235). It is ironic that an African became the legal owner of a slave according to the ruling of a civil court that laid the legal groundwork for slavery in what would become the United States of America.

The terms *slavery* or *slave* do not appear in the US Constitution. In fact, it is sometimes claimed that the Declaration of Independence and the Constitution contain language that can be interpreted as having outlawed slavery (Wiecek, 2000). Such claims invoke the phases reminiscent of natural law in those documents such as "inalienable rights" to buttress their arguments. Others claim that the English case of *Somerset v. Stewart* (1772; see chapter 11) should have been followed and all slaves freed because "the precedent had become part of American common law" (Wiecek, 2000, p. 2452).

Anthony Johnson: The First Legal Slave Holder in North America

Had the *Somerset* precedent been followed, slaves would have been freed and the Civil War avoided. Or as Barnard (2005) put it:

> Whereas they [the Constitutional Framers] could have followed English common law, colonial charters, colonial courts, and the principles that stated they themselves, as Whites, could not be enslaved, they chose instead to compromise these principles for the sake of political support and regional peace. (p. 129)

On the other hand, the Constitution contains language clearly supporting slavery. Article I, Section 9 affirms the rights of the southern states to allow "the migration or importation of such persons as any of the States now existing shall think proper to admit." Article I, Section 2 refers to "free Persons" and "three-fifths of all other Persons." Slaves were included in the count only for the purpose of improving the representation of the southern states in the House of Representatives. Finally, Article IV, Section 2 states:

> No person held to service in one State, under the Laws thereof, escaping into another shall, in Consequence of any law or Regulation therein, be discharged from such Service of Labor, but shall be delivered up on claim of the Party whom such service or Labor be due.

The need to placate the southern states and claims of property rights clearly trumped both natural law and *Somerset*, and the die was set for 200-plus years of court battles aimed at securing the status of "we the people" for African Americans.

The *Amistad* Case

An important moral step in the direction of securing this status was the *Amistad* case, which may be familiar to students from the 1997 movie of the same name. In 1839, African slaves being transported to Cuba aboard the Spanish ship *Amistad* revolted and killed all but two of their captors, whom they needed to navigate the ship back to Africa. The navigators took the ship to New York instead, where the remaining Africans were captured and held while the courts decided what should become of them. The case of the African captives, led by Sengbe Pieh, who has gone down in American history as Joseph Cinque, attracted attention from abolitionists anxious to gain moral support for the abolition of slavery and from southern slaveholders fearful of the impact a court decision would have on the institution of slavery. Cinque and his fellow captives were represented by former president of the United States John Quincy Adams, who argued for them before the Supreme Court. A federal district court judge had previously ruled in favor of Cinque, but pro-slavery President Martin Van Buren ordered the prosecutor to appeal to the Supreme Court.

Adams argued that the Africans had been kidnapped and held against their will and thus had every right to act in any way necessary to secure their freedom. The contesting claim came from the Spanish government, which wanted them tried for murder and piracy, a claim with which Van Buren sympathized. Adams argued for the Africans' freedom on the basis of the natural law principles found in the Declaration of Independence while at the same time claiming that his moral argument had no bearing on the slavery interests of the southern states. The Court agreed with him, ordering the "kidnapped Africans" released and returned to Africa.

According to Howard Jones (2002), although the Africans had been freed on a strictly legal basis (their capture was in violation of an Anglo-Spanish treaty against the slave trade), "it left the public impression that the American judicial system had dealt a severe blow to slavery by exalting the sanctity of freedom" (p. 25). He further stated that the decision "constituted a landmark ruling against slavery" because "black people had brought suit on behalf of their rights as human beings and, whether on the basis of law or morality, went free." *United States, Appellants v. The Libellants and Claimants of the Schooner Amistad* (1841) exacerbated the bitter feelings between slave and nonslave states and helped to cement their respective attitudes about slavery.

The *Dred Scott* Case

In 1857, the chief justice of the US Supreme Court, Roger Taney, who was openly pro-slavery, saw his chance to rectify the "damage" to the institution of slavery caused by the *Amistad* case in *Scott v. Sandford*. Dred Scott was born into slavery in St. Louis, Missouri. Under the **Missouri Compromise** of 1820, Missouri was the only slave state formed from the territory gained by the Louisiana Purchase. Scott was sold by his first owners to John Emerson, an army physician who took him to Illinois, a free state, and then to the free Wisconsin territory.

Scott and his wife Harriet returned to St. Louis with Emerson in 1840, ending a seven-year sojourn in free territory. In 1846, Scott petitioned for his freedom based on his stay in free territory. Such petitions were not unusual in Missouri and were mostly successful for slaves who had sojourned in free states. Court rulings in such cases typically were based on *Somerset*, which as Wang (2002) reminds us ruled "that the status of 'slave' was so contrary to the common law and natural law that it could not be supported by specific positive legislation" (p. 31). The impact of *Somerset* was somewhat undermined by an 1827 English case (*The Slave, Grace*) in which the High Court ruled "that once a slave returned to a slave jurisdiction then the law of England would no longer be in force and his status would again be determined by the laws of the slaver jurisdiction" (Wang, 2002, p. 32). The Missouri courts took little notice of this case at this time, but it was cited in concurring opinions in the subsequent *Scott v. Sandford* case argued before the US Supreme Court.

A Missouri district court awarded Scott his freedom in 1850, but Irene Emerson (John's widow) appealed to the Missouri Supreme Court. Irene's brother, John Sanford (his name was misspelled in *Scott v. Sandford*) now acted on her behalf. Unfortunately for Scott, a number of significant political changes had taken place in the meantime. Northern and southern states were again embroiled with the issue of whether slavery should be allowed in the new territories acquired by the United States in the Mexican-American War, and pro-slavery Thomas Benton had become a US senator for Missouri. This combination of events led the Missouri Supreme Court in 1852 to reverse the lower court decision, and it did so explicitly on political rather than legal grounds.

Lawyers for Scott then decided to take the case to the US Supreme Court on the basis that the case was a dispute between citizens of different states (Sanford lived in New York and Scott in Missouri). At issue was far more than securing Scott's freedom; the case was really about securing a Supreme Court ruling on the status of slavery. Justice Taney's decision contained his opinion that under Article III of the Constitution, no black person, even if free, could be a citizen of the United States and thus could not bring suit in the federal courts. The Court could have simply denied certiorari to Scott and let the Missouri decision stand, but it plainly wanted to use the case to make a pronouncement on slavery because the issue was tearing at the heart of the nation (McClosky, 1994).

The Court ruled that blacks were "altogether unfit to associate with the white race either in social or political relations; and so far inferior, that they have no rights which the white man was bound to respect" (Abadinsky, 2003, p. 62). Scott's claim to have been free because of his sojourn in free territory was denied because the Court said that Congress had limited jurisdiction in the territories (lands that were not yet granted statehood) and therefore could not forbid slavery in them. The claim also ran afoul on Fifth Amendment grounds that barred the law from depriving anyone of their property (as a slave, Scott was "property") without due process of law. Thus, although the issue was not before it, the Court also ruled the Missouri Compromise unconstitutional.

The constitutionality of the Missouri Compromise was a moot point in 1857, since Congress had already repealed it with the passage of the **Kansas-Nebraska Act** of 1854, which opened up areas of the West to slavery. This act was widely interpreted at the time as a precursor to legalizing slavery throughout the United States, and it precipitated its own "mini" civil war between pro-slavery and anti-slavery factions in "bleeding Kansas" (Brinkley, Current, Freidel, & Williams, 1991, p. 392). What the Supreme Court had done in *Scott* was to put its stamp of approval on slavery. Some also saw the ruling as settling the issue of slavery and thus ending the movement toward sectionalism between the North and the South. Of course, it had the opposite effect, and it took the Civil War to finally put an end to slavery.

As far as Scott himself, he did achieve his freedom in 1857, when the sons of his first owner purchased it for him. Sadly, he died 16 months later (Wang, 2002).

Emancipation and the Reconstruction Period

The American Civil War (which began April 12–13, 1861) was fought to preserve the Union, not to free the slaves. Of course, slavery was a major factor leading up to the war, making it almost inevitable. The northern and southern economies and cultures had diverged in a number of fundamental ways because of slavery. The industrial North opposed slavery primarily because of the fear that its spread would imperil the economic position of free white workers, and the agricultural South supported it because slavery was the very foundation of its economy.

As the war progressed, the North began to see its objective as freeing the slaves as well as preserving the Union. This objective had a military as well as a moral purpose because the South relied heavily on slaves to man the factories, farms, mines, and shipyards, and a proclamation of emancipation would sow discontent and mutiny among them. Abraham Lincoln's **Emancipation Proclamation** was first issued in September 1862 as a "preliminary" proclamation warning that if the rebellious states did not end the fighting and join the Union by January 1, 1863, all slaves in those states would be freed. Of course, the Confederacy did not end the fighting and the Emancipation Proclamation was issued as promised. The Proclamation did not free slaves in slave states loyal to the Union, since that might have driven them into the arms of the Confederacy. The final proclamation was issued in January 1863.

To forestall any postwar effort to have the Emancipation Proclamation ruled unconstitutional as a simple military order (remember: only Congress, not the executive branch, can make law), President Lincoln pressed Congress to pass the Thirteenth Amendment, banning slavery within the United States and territories, which it did in 1865. The amendment legally ended slavery in America after 200 years. By this time, however, almost all slaves had been freed by other means, such as state legislation or federal compensation to slave owners.

Blacks fared better in the immediate aftermath of the Civil War, during the period known as **Reconstruction** (reestablishment and reorganization of the seceded southern states). However, they were not prepared to succeed in white society even if they had been welcomed into it. Legally released from bondage, some did not leave their former masters, and others were left with nothing but the clothes on their backs and a few meager possessions. The federal government made attempts to help the emancipated slaves by keeping troops in the South to protect them and by establishing the **Freedman's Bureau**, which provided former slaves with food, clothing, schools, and even land that had been abandoned or confiscated. With federal troops to protect them, for a short time "[s]outhern blacks voted in extraordinary numbers, electing hundreds of black officeholders. Black jury service was common; streetcars were generally desegregated; and blacks finally gained access to public education" (Klarman, 2004, p. 10).

Nevertheless, many southern jurisdictions were seeking to recreate slavery in new, legal forms that came to be known as the **Black Codes**. The codes were enacted under the assumption that blacks would not work unless compelled to do so. These codes controlled, restricted, and inhibited the movements and behavior of ex-slaves almost as totally as slavery itself had. Codes authorized local authorities to arrest unemployed blacks and to fine them for vagrancy. These vagrancy laws supplied white enterprises with a plentiful supply of black laborers because blacks arrested on any pretext had the "choice" of paying a fine or working for an employer who paid his or her fine. The employer could then work the unfortunate "vagrant without compensation until he had repaid the debt to the employer's satisfaction" (Clarke, 1998, p. 69). Justices of the peace and law enforcement officers literally made their living arresting and sentencing "vagrants," and those who paid their fines made handsome profits from their labor.

Congress struck back at the Black Codes by passing the Fourteenth Amendment in 1868, which declared that all persons born or naturalized in the United States were citizens of both the United States and of the state in which they live. Congress still left the question of suffrage for blacks to the individual states, but both northern and southern states were very reluctant to grant it. In response to this reluctance, Congress passed the Fifteenth Amendment in 1870, granting suffrage to African American males. Section 1 of this amendment reads, "The right of citizens of the United States to vote shall not be denied or abridged by the United States or by any State on account of race, color, or previous condition of servitude."

The Emergence of Jim Crow Laws

Jim Crow laws were essentially any state or federal laws that enforced the segregation of the races. According to C. Van Woodward (1974), the origin of the term *Jim Crow* lies in an 1832 song-and-dance routine of the same name. The philosophical underpinning of these laws was **racism**, a form of bigotry more insidious than other forms such as xenophobia and ethnocentrism. The latter forms involve fear and dislike of out-groups and attitudes of in-group superiority, but those attitudes may be eased by contact and assimilation. Racism, however, is not alleviated by contact and assimilation because its victims are not despised and persecuted because they have had little contact with their persecutors but, usually, because they have had too much. Jim Crow racism thus was a combination of overt bigotry, a belief in the innate inferiority of blacks, and support for legal and normative segregation of the races (Bobo and Kluegel, 1997).

In response to increasing Jim Crowism, Congress passed the Civil Rights Act of 1875 stipulating that all persons were entitled to full access and enjoyment of all accommodations and facilities in public places. Despite this act, blacks were routinely denied access to such facilities, which led to five cases from five states coming before the Supreme Court and collectively referred to as the *Civil Rights Cases* (1883). In those cases, the Court ruled that the Fourteenth Amendment protected blacks only from state discrimination, not from discrimination by businesses and individuals. It also ruled that the Civil Rights Act was unconstitutional because it sought to control the legislative power of the individual states, thereby violating the Tenth Amendment, which reserves all powers not granted to the federal government to the states.

Following this decision, southern states began enacting sweeping legislation stipulating complete separation of the races in all spheres of life. Some states under Democratic control even enacted statutes such as the poll tax and literacy tests in efforts to disenfranchise (take away the right to vote from) blacks. By the 1890s, virtually all forms of integration had disappeared in the South (Klarman, 2004, p. 11).

Segregation, Disenfranchisement, and the *Plessy* and *Williams* Cases

Most states were not overly troubled with granting *civil* rights (the right to sue, engage in contracts, own property, and so on) to blacks but balked at granting them *political* rights (the right to vote, hold political office, or serve on juries) and, most of all, *social* rights (the right to mingle with whites in any capacity). Although social rights were less important than civil and political rights in a practical sense, the lack of them was more objectionable to blacks because it marked them as inferior and unfit to come into close proximity to whites. In common with many other states, Louisiana passed a statute decreeing that all railroad companies must provide separate but equal accommodations for black and white passengers as part of efforts to legally keep the races separate.

In 1892, a committee of mixed-race (black, white, and American Indian) Creoles calling themselves the *Comite des Citoyens* (citizen's committee) decided to test this statute by arranging for Homer Plessy to sit in a whites-only railroad car and to inform the conductor that, according to Louisiana law, he was "colored." In fact, Plessy was seven-eighths white and was physically indistinguishable from a white person (Davis, 2002). This did not matter, however, because one was either "pure" white or nonwhite, a simple racial dichotomy to which the *Comite des Citoyens* objected. Plessy was arrested, refused to identify his race, was found guilty, and then appealed his case to the Supreme Court.

The issue before the Court in *Plessy v. Ferguson* (1896) was the reasonableness of the Louisiana statute; that is, in passing this bill, did the legislature act with reference to the traditions and customs of the people of Louisiana? Plessy's lawyers argued that the Fourteenth Amendment outlawed race as a legal distinction, that race was only a social construction, and that because of this, no law could exist to classify anyone into a distinct racial category. The Court disagreed, ruling that "separate but equal" laws were not repugnant to the Fourteenth Amendment because they did not impact the legal equality of the races. It also dismissed Plessy's claim that race did not exist as "absurd"; Justice Henry Brown, delivering the opinion, stated:

> We consider the underlying fallacy of the plaintiff's argument to consist in the assumption that the enforced separation of the two races stamps the colored race with a badge of inferiority. If this be so, it is not by reason of anything found in the act, but solely because the colored race chooses to put that construction upon it. (Klarman, 2004, p. 21)

The Supreme Court thus placed its stamp of approval on states' efforts to deny social rights to blacks.

Two years after *Plessy*, the Court heard an important case regarding states' efforts to disenfranchise blacks. The Fifteenth Amendment prohibited the states from denying males the right to vote based on race, so the issue for southern states became how to deny blacks the vote without seeming to do it on that basis. Two methods were the poll tax and the literacy test. These methods reduced the black vote by 62 percent by the 1890s. They also reduced the white vote by 26 percent, but this was alleviated somewhat with the passage of "grandfather clauses," allowing anyone whose ancestors had voted to vote as well (Brinkley et al., 1991). The constitutionality of these obvious shenanigans was tested in *Williams v. State of Mississippi* in 1898.

In 1896, African American Henry Williams was indicted for the crime of murder by a grand jury composed entirely of white men. Williams claimed that the way in which the jury was summoned, selected, and charged violated the Fourteenth Amendment in that it systematically excluded blacks and resulted in a biased, all-white jury. Williams thus challenged the literacy tests used to exclude blacks from serving on juries as well as from voting. The Court interpreted the tests as excluding blacks on the basis of literacy, not race, because the tests also excluded illiterate whites not covered by grandfather clauses. Thus, the tests did not violate the Fourteenth or Fifteenth Amendments. Determining voter eligibility standards was ruled to be within the prerogative of the individual states under the Tenth Amendment.

Evidently, the Court was willing to let the southern states do as they pleased with respect to voting standards as long as they did not violate the exact letter of the Fourteenth or Fifteenth Amendments. And so *Plessy* and *Williams* were sown into the patchwork of the southern states' Jim Crow laws that stripped blacks of the rights they had gained during Reconstruction. Disenfranchisement was so effective that by "the turn of the century the last black Congressman left office, and virtually all black people in the south were disenfranchised" (Pinkney, 1969, p. 30).

Lynching and Black Protest

Two black leaders emerged in this era of robust Jim Crowism with radically different ideas about how blacks should respond: Booker T. Washington and W. E. B. DuBois. Washington implied that black "deficiencies" rather than white discrimination were responsible for their condition and that they should appease whites by keeping their distance and engaging in hard (manual) work. This point of view was applauded by whites as a vindication of their own views, but blacks understandably did not accept it. The chief opponent of Washington's philosophy was DuBois, who counseled that blacks should aspire to higher education, not be content with manual work, and agitate for the restoration of their rights.

With the help of progressive whites, DuBois founded the **National Association for the Advancement of Colored People** (NAACP) in 1910. The most pressing issue for the NAACP at this time was the sadistic practice of lynching. According to the Constitutional Rights Foundation (2005), between 1892 and 1968, a total of 4,743 persons (over 70 percent of them black) were lynched in the United States. Black soldiers who had fought "to make the world safe for democracy" in World War I noted the irony in that slogan upon their return to the United States. This resulted in a rise in black militancy and in NAACP membership, but it also precipitated a violent white backlash. In the aftermath of the war, there was a revival of the Ku Klux Klan (KKK), numerous white race riots, and an increase in lynching from 36 cases in 1917 to 76 in 1919 (Klarman, 2004). Although many states had anti-lynching laws, the federal government did not. In 1918, Republican Missouri Congressman Leonidas Dyer introduced the Dyer Anti-Lynching Bill in Congress, but it was halted by a Democratic filibuster in the Senate. Another anti-lynching law known as the Gavagan Bill was again killed by Democratic filibusters in the Senate (Constitutional Rights Foundation, 2005). Incredibly, the federal government did not pass an anti-lynching law until the passage of the 1968 Civil Rights Act.

The most significant test of the 1968 act came in 1981, when the Federal Bureau of Investigation (FBI) was called in to investigate the lynching of Michael Donald. Donald was chosen as a victim at random because of the anger of two young white men at a jury's failure to convict a black man for the murder of a white police officer. The FBI arrested James Knowles, who confessed to the murder and testified against his co-conspirator, Henry Hays, the son of the second-highest-ranking KKK member in Alabama. Knowles was sentenced to life imprisonment; Hays was sentenced to death and executed in 1997. Hays was the first white man since 1913 to be executed for murdering a black man. The Southern Poverty Law Center filed a civil suit on behalf of Michael's mother, and an all-white jury found the KKK culpable for the death of Michael Donald and ordered punitive damages of $7 million. To comply with this order, the KKK had to hand over all its assets and skulk off into virtual oblivion (Spartacus Educational, 2005).

"We Shall Overcome"

World War II signaled the beginning of the end of Jim Crow. Many blacks migrated from the South to fill the vacancies left by military draftees in northern factories flush with orders for war-related materials. Being confronted with less white animosity than they had endured in the South, blacks became less subservient and more demanding of their basic rights. These demands, coupled with a growing belief among whites that the demands were justified, led to a series of executive, legislative, and judicial actions that began digging Jim Crow's grave, although he was still far from dead. The executive orders began with President Franklin Roosevelt's Fair Employment Practices Committee and President Harry Truman's Commission on Higher Education and the latter's ordering of full integration in the armed forces (D'Sousa, 1995). Significantly, these orders were in response to growing black militancy (e.g., a threatened march on Washington in 1941 in support of integration in the workplace) rather than on any real executive concern with black issues (Brinkley et al., 1991).

The first significant post–World War II Supreme Court ruling on black rights came in *Smith v. Allwright* (1944). Some states in the South held all-white primaries, legally justifying it by declaring the Democratic Party to be a "volunteer organization." The Texas Supreme Court had declared the Democratic Party of Texas to be such an organization, enabling county election official S. S. Allwright to deny Lonnie Smith the right to vote in the 1940 Texas Democratic primary. Allwright claimed that under the ruling made in the *Civil Rights Cases* of 1883, the Court had no power to influence private (nonstate) discrimination. The Court disagreed, ruling that the practice violated the Fifteenth Amendment because primaries are conducted under state statutory authority.

According to Klarman (2004), "*Smith v. Allwright* launched a revolution in politics in the urban South" because the "NAACP constantly threatened registrars and party officials with criminal liability if they defied *Smith*" (pp. 454–458). As in any endeavor, success breeds success, so in many ways the *Smith* decision in 1944 paved the way for the most important civil rights case of the twentieth century, *Brown v. Board of Education of Topeka* (1954), which ended racial segregation in American schools.

The *Brown* decision provoked a violent backlash in the South and ushered into power politicians who ran on platforms accusing their opponents of being "soft on race," just as many current politicians accuse their opponents of being soft on crime. Several cases related to the ruling (including *Brown v. Board of Education of Topeka II* in 1955) occurred in the face of numerous efforts on behalf of various schoolboards to circumvent the ruling. Only 23 black children—a mere 0.001 percent of black schoolchildren—were in schools with white children in the South prior to *Brown*; in the two years afterward, that figure was 0.13 percent; and 10 years later (1963–1964), the proportion was only 1.2 percent (Rosenberg, 1991).

Why was there such massive resistance to *Brown* relative to the minimal resistance generated by *Smith*? As indicated earlier, granting social rights to black citizens was at the top of the hierarchy of white fears. Exercising civil and political rights mixes the races only briefly for a definite purpose, but exercising social rights might do so at an unacceptably intimate level. Even during Reconstruction, all southern schools were segregated, even as black males voted in large numbers. In the late

1940s, a plurality of Southerners supported the rights of blacks to vote and to attend professional and graduate schools with whites, while at the same time they "ferociously resisted grade school desegregation" (Klarman, 2004, p. 456).

Congressional Activity

The picture changed dramatically after Congress passed the **Civil Rights Act of 1964**. This act gave federal officials both the power to bring desegregation suits on behalf of individuals and the power to withhold federal funds to school districts practicing racial discrimination. Unlike the miniscule changes following *Brown*, 91.3 percent of Southern black schoolchildren were in desegregated schools by 1972–1973 (Rosenberg, 1991, p. 50). Thus, the legislative branch, with its power of the purse, had a much deeper impact than the judicial branch. Judicial rulings can always be ignored, wrongly interpreted, or willfully "misinterpreted," thus necessitating further legal battles and long delays, whereas the legislative branch has the ability to withhold funds almost immediately upon being made aware of a violation of its rulings.

A similar situation existed relative to voting rights after *Smith v. Allwright* (1944). Prior to this ruling, only 5 percent of southern blacks of voting age were registered to vote, and after the ruling, in 1947, only 12 percent were registered. However, the US Congress passed the **Voting Rights Act of 1965**, and things changed dramatically. This act provided for federal supervision of county voter registration sites and prohibited the use of literacy tests. (The poll tax had been declared unconstitutional by the Twenty-Fourth Amendment in 1964.) Following the passage of this act, the percentage of voting-age blacks in the South who were registered to vote had risen to 66.9 percent by 1970 (Rosenberg, 1991, p. 61).

The Supreme Court upheld the constitutionality of the 1964 Civil Rights Act in *Heart of Atlanta Motel v. United States* (1964) and the Voting Rights Act in *South Carolina v. Katzenbach* (1966). In its rulings, the Court used language 180 degrees from the language used to render similar legislative efforts unconstitutional in previous cases, indicating that the Court responds to the political and social pressures of the moment more than it cares to acknowledge.

The Cold War and International Pressure

Smith and *Brown* gave legitimacy, support, and impetus to black protest movements and precipitated an unprecedented level of activism. Demonstrations, marches, and sit-ins all over the South and the often vicious police responses to them were viewed across the United States through the medium of television. Watching this go on day after day generated a lot of white sympathy for the black cause, just as the novel *Uncle Tom's Cabin* had done for abolitionist sentiment over a century before. The big difference in the *Brown* case was that the audience was international as well as national, and international opinion was no longer irrelevant to American politicians.

The United States emerged from World War II as a superpower with an ideology based on the ideals of democracy and free enterprise. The Soviet Union also arose from the war as a superpower but with communist ideals of one-party rule and state control of the economy. It was inevitable that the two countries would become enemies, but fortunately for the world at large, the so-called **Cold War** (which lasted from the end of World War II until 1989) was fought only with propaganda and proxy wars. The United States and the Soviet Union were competing for "the hearts and minds of men" on the world stage, and the "Negro problem" proved to be a profound embarrassment for the United States as well as a powerful propaganda weapon for the Soviet Union (Dudziak, 2000).

The US government's efforts to polish its image had a large impact on civil rights policies. The State Department strongly urged civil rights reforms, and President Truman's controversial order desegregating the military was defended because segregation was "damaging to our country's reputation with millions of people around the world" (Klarman, 2004, p. 183). Even though President Dwight Eisenhower's segregationist sentiments were well known, his government attorneys filed an amicus brief in *Brown* specifically arguing that school segregation should be invalidated, not on moral grounds but because "racial discrimination furnishes grist for the Communist propaganda mill" (Klarman, 2004, p. 299). The government in fact filed briefs in almost all racial civil rights cases coming before the Supreme Court during the period, urging it to view the issue through a Cold War lens (Dudziak, 2000).

AMERICAN INDIANS

The Early Years

Every minority group in America (and elsewhere) has a story of discrimination to tell, and the history of white malfeasance against American Indians is at least as horrific as that practiced against African Americans. By most accounts, it was even worse because the United States, *as a matter of official policy*, practiced both physical and cultural genocide against the American Indians (Parrillo, 2003). According to Aguirre and Turner (1998), "If we need an index of discrimination against Native Americans, a 10-fold drop [from their numbers prior to white expansion into their territories] in the size of the population is as good as any" (p. 105). The size of the Indian population before colonization in what is now the United States has been estimated to be between 6 and 10 million, divided into approximately 300 culturally and linguistically distinct tribes (Parrillo, 2003). Much of that culture and most of those languages have been lost.

Early colonial relationships between whites and Indians ranged from peaceful coexistence to distrust and hostile confrontations. Hostilities increased as white settlers encroached more and more on Indian territories. Westward expansion saw the waxing and waning of white stereotypes of Indians. Early settlers greatly admired the Indians as "noble savages," with a "nobility of character" (D'Sousa, 1995, p. 85). As white settlers moved west and encountered Indian opposition, the image of the "screaming, savage red man" emerged. Indians were enslaved in all 13 colonies, with a 1708 Carolina settlement census showing 2,900 African slaves and 1,400 Indian slaves (French, 2003). Indians proved more difficult than Africans to maintain in slavery, however, and the practice of Indian slavery soon disappeared.

The practice of physical genocide against the Indians began early. The Massachusetts colony, for instance, paid cash bounties for Indian scalps, and many whites found the practice lucrative (Parrillo, 2003). The Indians were still a powerful force to be reckoned with, however, and both the French and the British courted them during the French and Indian War (1754–1761). With the defeat of the French and the threat of war with a growing confederation of powerful Indian tribes under the Ottawa chief, Pontiac, the British government issued the Proclamation Act of 1763. As we saw in chapter 11, the Proclamation Act forbade any further white settlement beyond the Appalachians; it also proclaimed that any land purchases from Indians without a representative of the royal government present at the proceedings would be illegal. This essentially established the British government as the protector of Indian rights and the Indian tribes as its wards. As we also have seen, a number of historians consider this act a contributing cause of the American Revolution, although it was to become a template of the United States' own stance toward the Indians (Parrillo, 2003).

In 1787, the Continental Congress passed the **Northwest Ordinance**, which provided for a survey of what was then the Northwest Territories (lands bounded by the Great Lakes, the Mississippi and Ohio rivers, Canada, and Pennsylvania) with regard to future white settlement. The Northwest Ordinance gave Congress rather than the states the sole right to trade with the Indians. Although the ordinance promised to act in good faith toward the Indians, all of the territories were areas that had been made off limits by the 1763 Proclamation Act.

In laying out the powers of the Congress, Article I, Section 8 of the US Constitution specifically recognizes the quasi-independent status of the Indians: the Congress shall thus have power "[t]o regulate commerce with foreign nations, and among the several States, and with the Indian tribes." The **Treaty of Fort Pitt** (the first of about 350 treaties made with the Indians) also implicitly recognized the sovereignty of the Indian nations and assured them that the United States had no designs on Indian lands (Wildenthal, 2003). This status began to change as land-hungry whites moved West and legal challenges began to arrive at the portals of the US Supreme Court.

The Marshall Trilogy: Defining Indian Status

New definitions of Native American sovereignty emerged in three Supreme Court cases that have come to be known as the **Marshall Trilogy** (named after Chief Justice John Marshall). Although the first of these cases, *Johnson v. McIntosh* (1823), was a land ownership dispute between whites, the Court used it to define the relationship of the federal government to the Indian nations. Joshua Johnson had purchased Indian land in 1773 under the legitimate authority of the British government, and William McIntosh purchased land from the United States in 1818, part of which overlapped Johnson's purchase. By all rules of law, Johnson should have prevailed, but the Court used the case to justify whittling away at Indian rights, violating "Euro-American individual property rights to place itself in a superior political position relative to tribal nations who were not even parties to the dispute" (Wilkins, 1997, pp. 31–32).

This "superiority" was enunciated by Chief Justice Marshall in an argument that has come to be known as the **Discovery Doctrine**. This doctrine asserted that the European power that "discovered" an area of the Western hemisphere is deemed to have sovereignty over it to the exclusion of other European powers and indigenous peoples. Chief Justice Marshall stated that discovery gave the discovering nation and its successor, the United States, "an exclusive right to extinguish the Indian titles of occupancy, either by purchase or conquest" (Wilkins, 1997, p. 368). The Court also asserted that Indians are merely "occupants" of the land, and only "in possession" of it at the pleasure of the United States.

The next case in the trilogy, *Cherokee Nation v. Georgia* (1831), further clarified the legal status of the Indian nations. The Cherokees were one of the so-called five "civilized tribes" (the others were Choctaw, Chickasaw, Creek, and Seminole) whose lifestyle had become virtually indistinguishable from that of whites, even to the point of having a written constitution and owning black slaves. Unfortunately, their land was within the state of Georgia, which had been annexing it and asserting its authority over the Cherokee. Georgia's claims were buoyed by the 1830 **Indian Removal Act** that called for the removal of all Indians in the southeastern states to "Indian territory," an area that is now Oklahoma. The Cherokee Nation petitioned the Supreme Court for relief, citing its sovereign status as a foreign nation and its treaties with the federal government to that effect. The Court ruled that the Cherokee Nation was not a foreign nation with sovereign rights and thus did not have control of their lands, nor did it have standing to approach the Court as a court of original jurisdiction because only sovereign political entities may do so. It further ruled that the Cherokee Nation was a "domestic dependent nation" whose relationship to the government was that of ward to guardian.

The Cherokees won a legal victory, however, in *Worcester v. Georgia* (1832), the third case in the trilogy (Samuel Worcester was a white missionary and a willing defendant in a test case against Indian removal and for Indian sovereignty). The Court defined the Cherokee in this case as a "distinct community" within the parameters of the original definition as a domestic dependent nation in which the laws of Georgia did not apply. This ruling established the doctrine that the federal government and not the individual states had authority in Indian affairs, but Georgia's encroachment on Cherokee lands continued without federal interference. Upon hearing of the Court's ruling, President Andrew Jackson is reported to have said, "John Marshall has rendered his decision, now let him enforce it" (Parrillo, 2003, p. 250).

The Period of Removal and Physical Genocide

Under the Indian Removal Act, Indians all over the Southeast were rounded up and marched at gunpoint to Indian Territory (Oklahoma). In 1838–1839, the Cherokees were marched over 1,000 miles in the dead of winter, losing 25 percent of their number to death along the way (French, 2003). This event became known as the Trail of Tears and was the first of a long series of such trails or "long walks" suffered by Indian tribes across the country as the United States pursued its policy of Manifest Destiny. See Figure 13.1 for the routes the various tribes took to Indian Territory.

Manifest Destiny was the ideological justification for the Mexican-American War (1846–1848), the annexation of Texas, the Gadsden Purchase (portions of what is today Arizona and New Mexico), and the resolution of the dispute with the British over the Pacific Northwest territories. These territorial acquisitions brought many more Indian tribes, such as the Apache, Navaho, and Nez Perce, within the orbit of white American power.

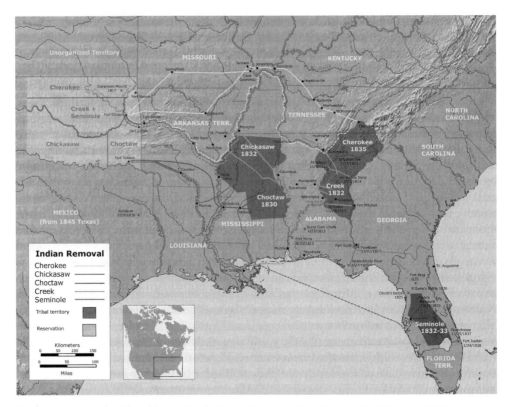

Figure 13.1 Map of the Route of the Trails of Tears (Indian Removal): 1836 and 1839

In the year before the Cherokee Trail of Tears, the Dakota Sioux were expelled from 35 million acres of rich agricultural land east of the Mississippi River in exchange for promises of later payment. The money hallmarked for payment was instead used to assist white settlement on the land while many Sioux died from starvation and disease in their new lands (French, 2003). The Dakota Sioux were moved farther west in 1851, again without the promised payment, which precipitated an Indian uprising. After being defeated, the Sioux were moved to Nebraska, where they replaced the Spotted Tail Sioux, who in turn replaced the Ponca Tribe, who were removed to Oklahoma.

This chain of events led to a significant federal court case resulting from a chief of the Ponca Tribe named Standing Bear illegally leaving the Oklahoma reservation. The two major issues in *Standing Bear v. Crook* (1879) were whether Indians had the right to leave the reservation and whether Indians were persons. General George Crook had asserted that Indians were not persons, and thus Standing Bear had no rights to petition the court for a writ of habeas corpus questioning the conditions of his arrest. The court ruled in favor of Standing Bear on both counts, stating that "an Indian is a person within the meaning of the law of the United States." According to French (2003), this ruling "elevated Indians from the status of feral animals with bounties on their heads to 'persons,' albeit not equal to the white man," and it signaled "the beginning of the end of physical genocide and forced the federal government to now focus on the destruction of Indian cultures instead of Indians per se" (p. 13).

The Assimilation Period and Cultural Genocide

The period of physical genocide on the Great Plains was marked by the wholesale destruction of the buffalo herds. This was mostly the doing of private enterprise, but it was encouraged by the government: given the almost total dependency of the Plains Indians on the buffalo, elimination of the herds would lead to the destruction of the Indians. And it was the loss of the buffalo more than the losses suffered in the various wars that led to the Plains Indians reluctantly moving onto the reservations, where their cultures could be systematically eroded.

In 1871, Congress passed an act ending treaty-making with the Indians, stating that henceforth all Indian matters would be handled by legislation (previous treaties would remain in effect unless Congress abolished them). Indian matters would thereafter be decided unilaterally by whites. The Supreme Court endorsed the right of Congress to abrogate Indian treaties in the *Cherokee Tobacco* case (1871), which upheld the federal government's right to tax Cherokee tobacco sales in violation of an 1866 treaty. The termination of treaty-making clearly stamped Indians as wards of the government and ushered in an era known as the **assimilation period**, which lasted until 1934.

Assimilation is a process of "outsiders" becoming integrated into the larger culture by adopting its values, attitudes, and practices. For the Indians, it meant giving up their cultures and becoming "civilized" and "Christianized." The agency in charge of these assimilative efforts was the **Bureau of Indian Affairs** (BIA), which was first established by the War Department in 1824. During the assimilation period, the BIA became responsible for all aspects of Indian life, such as providing food and other resources, running schools, dispensing justice, and most important in the opinion of society, eliminating "heathen" and "godless" (i.e., nonwhite) practices.

Initially, Indians dispensed their own justice for crimes committed by Indians against other Indians on the reservation. In *Ex Parte Crow Dog* (1883), the Supreme Court upheld this principle in reversing a federal district court conviction of Crow Dog, who had been charged with the slaying of another Indian in Indian country. The BIA was among those who objected to this ruling, and in response, Congress passed the **Major Crimes Act** of 1885. This act extended federal criminal jurisdiction over Indians, or any other person, in Indian country. The original seven offenses in this act became the "index crimes" published yearly in the FBI's Uniform Crime Reports (French, 2003). The Supreme Court upheld the constitutionality of the Major Crimes Act in *United States v. Kagama* (1886), further weakening Indian autonomy and strengthening the BIA.

The single biggest push toward the destruction of Indian cultures was probably the enactment of the **General Allotment Act** (also called the **Dawes Act**) of 1887. This act provided for the division of reservation lands into tracts that were to be allotted to individual members of the tribe in parcels of 160 acres each for a period of 25 years. Any land left over after the allotment would go to the United States and be sold, with the money "held in trust" by the US government. Individuals who were able to make a success of their allotments over the 25-year period would be awarded title to the land and American citizenship. Few Indians became the self-reliant farmers the act had hoped to create. Few had the background required for farming, and there also was cultural opposition to tearing up sacred ground. Additionally, whites succeeded in getting many Indians to sign over the land to them (Parrillo, 2003).

Many tribes, especially the five "civilized tribes," actively resisted this transparent attempt to destroy the communal underpinnings of their cultures and were able to avoid it for a while. In response to this "intransigence," in 1898 Congress passed an act that imposed allotment of Indian lands in Oklahoma, which had been specifically designated as Indian Territory, and severely curtailed the governing powers of the five tribes. As the Commissioner of Indian Affairs Thomas Morgan made plain in 1890, the Dawes Act had

> become the settled policy of the government to break up reservations, destroy tribal relations, settle Indians upon their own homesteads, incorporate them into the national life, and deal with them not as nations or tribes or bands, but as individual citizens. (Virginia Archive, ND), 2005)

From the time of the Dawes Act to 1934, the Indians lost approximately two-thirds of their lands to whites (McLemore, 1983).

Indians who attempted to assimilate, however, found it difficult. Some states had Jim Crow laws for Indians as well as blacks, with separate facilities and sections in theaters and other establishments labeled "Whites," "Colored," and "Indian" (US Department of Justice, 2005a), and they were denied citizenship. When John Elk, for instance, left his tribe, settled in Omaha, Nebraska, and tried to register to vote, he was rejected. In a landmark case, the Supreme Court rejected Elk's claim of his Fifteenth Amendment voting rights in *Elk v. Wilkins* (1884), stating that Indians were still in a state of "pupilage" and that the question of Indian citizenship would have to be decided by the Congress and "not for each Indian for himself" (Wildenthal, 2003, p. 28).

The legal status of Indians hit its lowest point in *Lone Wolf v. Hitchcock* (1903). This case involved the government opening up land in Oklahoma defined as "surplus" by the Dawes Act to white settlement. The land in question was occupied by the Comanche and Kiowa tribes, who naturally objected. Whites were settling the land even as the case wound its way to the Supreme Court. A unanimous Court rejected the Indian claim in upholding Congress's "plenary" (i.e., absolute or complete) power to abrogate treaties in "times of emergency," although Congress had claimed no such emergency and the Court was unable to articulate one. In effect, the *Lone Wolf* ruling legitimized theft and was a clear violation of the taking clause of the Fifth Amendment, which requires just compensation for property taken for public use.

The Beginning of the End of Cultural Genocide (with a Few Backward Steps)

Congress finally conferred American citizenship on all Indians in the **Indian Citizenship Act** of 1924. Ten years later, in a radical turnaround government policy, the Roosevelt administration enacted the **Indian Reorganization Act** of 1934. This act ended the practice of cultural genocide; encouraged Indians to revive their languages, religions, and customs; ended the allotment system; permitted reconsolidation of the individual plots into communal tribal lands; and gave preferences to Indians in gaining employment with the BIA. Nevertheless, tribal governments were pressured to adopt white-style political institutions, which generated internal tribal divisions, and the Interior Department still had the power to approve or reject tribal laws (Wildenthal, 2003).

In 1953, Congress decided that it was time to terminate federal supervision of Indian tribes as soon as practical and passed a series of acts that are collectively known as the policy of **termination**. This policy apparently was meant to be pro-Indian and designed to fully assimilate them into mainstream American life by encouraging individuals to leave reservations and move to urban areas. However, it had devastating consequences for terminated tribes. Federal funds for the running of reservations were promptly cut off, hospitals and other facilities shut down, tribes disintegrated, and the reservations themselves became counties of the states in which they were located and subject to state control and taxes. Although this supposedly accorded every individual Indian the same legal rights that whites enjoyed, it eliminated tribal sovereignty and law. The termination policy had the opposite effect of what was intended, in that it deprived the Indians of the resources they needed to become independent while at the same time eroding tribal sovereignty.

Because of its unpopularity among the Indians and its negative consequences, efforts to implement termination had all but ended by the 1960s, and the policy was officially renounced at President Richard Nixon's insistence by the **Indian Self-Determination Act** of 1975. Part of the government's turnaround may be laid at the door of increasing Indian militancy after the founding of the **American Indian Movement** in 1968. The period between 1968 and the passage of the Self-Determination Act in 1975 saw the occupation of Alcatraz Island by about 600 Indians for a period of 18 months, the 10-week armed standoff with the FBI at Wounded Knee on a Sioux reservation, the occupation of the BIA headquarters, and the "Trail of Broken Treaties" march on Washington, DC. As was the case with black activism, these actions brought wide national and international exposure and sympathy to the Indian cause.

ASIAN AMERICANS

Asians (we focus here only on the Chinese and Japanese because they are the largest groups and arrived first) have suffered a great deal of prejudice and discrimination in the United States also. Chinese immigrants came to the United States voluntarily, and immediately upon arrival, they became the targets of legal and extralegal harassment. They were subjected to special taxes; barred from holding land or citizenship; and beaten, lynched, and driven out of towns all across the West. The conditions of their employment (sometimes referred to as the "coolie trade") often amounted to "a new system of slavery" (Kitano & Daniels, 1995, p. 22). The Chinese also were subjected to stereotypes not much different from those applied to blacks: "They were accused of living in filth, harboring disease, being heathens, and, worst of all, being less than human. Their sexual habits were compared to those of animals; questions of character and honesty were constantly raised" (Kitano & Daniels, 1995, pp. 183–184).

The Chinese first started arriving in the United States as sojourners (immigrants who intended to eventually return home) after gold was discovered in California in 1848. Although previous legislative efforts to limit immigration from "undesirable" European countries by individual states had been ruled unconstitutional, Congress passed the **Chinese Exclusion Act** of 1882 without legal challenge. However, many Chinese still managed to enter the United States through loopholes (notably by falsely claiming US relatives). The Exclusion Act was repealed by Congress in 1943, and at the same time, the Chinese were granted naturalization rights and immigration quotas (Kitano & Daniels, 1995).

Although some states sometimes granted immigrant Chinese and Japanese naturalized citizenship, a California circuit court ruled *In re Ah Yup* (1878) that only individuals of European or African origins were eligible to become citizens. The state of California even attempted to bar American-born Wong Kim Ark from reentering the United States under the Chinese Exclusion Act after he had made a short trip to China. This resulted in a landmark Supreme Court ruling that the government could not deny citizenship to anyone born in the United States (*United States v. Wong Kim Ark*, 1898). This did not mean that foreign-born Asians could become naturalized citizens; in fact, the Supreme Court explicitly stated that they could not in *Ozawa v. United States* (1922).

Asian Americans were allowed a greater level of assimilation than African Americans and had even been allowed into integrated schools by the early 1900s. The worst act of discrimination against any Asian group occurred in 1942, one month after the Japanese attack on Pearl Harbor. In response to this attack, President Franklin Roosevelt issued Executive Order 9066 authorizing the evacuation and relocation of people of Japanese ancestry. This order was justified as a "military necessity," but very few of the many more numerous "enemy aliens" of German or Italian origin were likewise rounded up. More than 110,000 Japanese (most of them second- or third-generation Americans) were sent to camps or "relocation centers" across the Western states and forced to live under harsh physical and psychological conditions (Parrillo, 2003).

Was it constitutional to imprison native-born Americans without trial even if the United States was at war with the country of their ancestry? The American Civil Liberties Union had been looking for a test case to answer this question and found one in Fred Korematsu, a second-generation American who was arrested for remaining illegally in an area deemed vulnerable to espionage and placed on five years' probation. In *Korematsu v. United States* (1944), the Supreme Court ruled 6-3 that although internment was constitutionally suspect, it was justified during circumstances of wartime "emergency and peril" and that the government's need to protect against espionage outweighed Korematsu's rights. In another internment ruling (*Ex Parte Endo*, 1944) handed down on the same day, however, the Court unanimously ruled that the government could not continue to detain a citizen, Mitsuye Endo, whom the government conceded was loyal to the United States.

The Endo case began the release of all detainees and the beginning of the struggle for redress. A 1948 act brought internment victims about 10 percent of what they had lost through their "relocation." Korematsu's original indictment was voided and his conviction reversed by a federal district court in 1983 (Daniels, 2002). In 1988, each surviving detainee was awarded a tax-free payment of $20,000 and a formal government apology for violating their rights because of racial prejudice (Parrillo, 2003).

HISPANICS

According to the US Census Bureau (Humes, Jones, & Ramirez, 2011), there were 50.5 million Hispanics in the United States in 2010. At 16 percent of the population, Hispanics are the largest minority group in the United States. Until fairly recently, however, they have been a "silent minority," which may be why few people can identify circumstances, issues, and struggles associated with this group while most educated people have at least some knowledge of the struggles faced in the past by African Americans, American Indians, and Asian Americans. One of the reasons we have not seen major civil rights efforts on the scale of the black civil rights movement is that Hispanic group reference has tended to be to national origin—Cuba, Mexico, Puerto Rico, and so on—rather than to a homogeneous "Hispanic" category (Johnson, 2005a). The black/white categories have largely defined race relations in the United States, and acceptance as "white" has been the major concern for Hispanics (Blanton, 2006).

The "whiteness" of Hispanics was determined by a Texas immigration case *In re Rodríguez* (1897). The issues at stake were Hispanic voting rights and who could become a US citizen. Mexican-born Rodríguez had been a resident of Texas for 10 years before he applied for citizenship, which automatically confers voting rights. Under the law of the time, only whites and blacks could be citizens, and since Rodríguez was neither white nor black, he did not qualify. There were efforts afoot in Texas at the time to disenfranchise Texas-born Mexican Americans, so the case became important in this respect as well. Primarily because of the constraints of a treaty ending the Mexican-American War (see later discussion), Rodríguez was declared white and granted citizenship and voting rights, a decision that also put an end to disenfranchisement efforts (Calavita, 2007).

ISSUE HIGHLIGHT

Should Sanctuary Cities Be Denied Federal Funding?

A number of cities across the country are "sanctuary cities," which refers to cities that refuse to cooperate with federal requests to detain arrested "undocumented immigrants" or "illegal aliens" (what we chose to call them reveals our politics). Some argue that sanctuary cities should not receive federal funding because they are refusing to enforce federal immigration laws. Should these funds be withheld?

Yes

Sanctuary cities are defying US Code § 1373 stating that "a Federal, State, or local government entity or official may not prohibit, or in any way restrict, any government entity or official from sending to, or receiving from, the Immigration and Naturalization Service information regarding the citizenship or immigration status, lawful or unlawful, of any individual." The federal government has the sole responsibility for defending the borders of the United States and should not be prevented from doing so by local governments. While we realize that most illegal aliens are not a direct threat to public safety, an enormous amount of crime is committed by a portion of them. The most notorious case was that of Juan Lopez-Sanchez, who murdered Kate Steinle in 2015. Lopez-Sanchez had seven felony convictions in the United States and had been deported five times, yet San Francisco refused to detain him for Immigration officials. Not only this, illegals (to call them "undocumented workers" is like calling the street-corner dope dealer an "undocumented pharmacist") consume billions of taxpayer dollars in various goods and services, such as health care, food stamps, and housing subsidies. Twelve states actually allow illegals to obtain a state driver's license. Illegal aliens can then use these licenses to illegally vote in major elections, and if they do, they will vote Democrat because that is the party of tax and spend. Many people who want to come to the United States legally—educated people who can benefit this country—may have to wait years to do so, and that's unfair when those here illegally and with little education get to stay. Finally, if these cities don't have to obey laws that protect the safety, security, and sovereignty of the United States, why should the rest of us?

No

Forget the US Code; the right of the states to enact their own policies is protected by the Tenth Amendment that states: "The powers not delegated to the United States by the Constitution, nor prohibited by it to the States, are reserved to the States respectively, or to the people." The Constitution says nothing about immigration. Conservatives are all for states' rights until they collide with an issue they support. While the Lopez-Sanchez case is extremely sad, most sanctuary cities would not have released him back on the streets. Sanctuary cities exist to protect undocumented immigrants from federal immigration laws, which often target them indiscriminately and deport people who have lived in the US since childhood and have committed no crimes. Yes, undocumented immigrants use goods and services provided by the taxpayer. However, many pay taxes themselves, and many more would if they were granted legal status. Allowing undocumented immigrants access to a driver's license encourages them to behave responsibly and perhaps obtain auto insurance. If they do vote "illegally," it gives them a feeling of belonging, and if they vote Democrat, then they are, like everyone else, voting their interests. As for those who want to come here legally, we fail to see how the undocumented immigrants we are trying to protect on humanitarian grounds can only come here if they "can benefit this country." That seems to be an especially selfish position.

The Mexican-American War and the Treaty of Guadalupe Hidalgo

The origin of Hispanic civil rights concerns began with the Mexican-American War fought between 1846 and 1848. The primary cause of this war was the admittance of Texas to the United States in 1845, although the call of Manifest Destiny can be heard in the background (Hietala, 2003). Texas won its independence from Mexico in 1836, and although Mexican President General Antonio López de Santa Anna (albeit with the metaphorical gun to his head) acknowledged Texan independence by signing treaties to that effect, Mexico still considered Texas to be part of its territory. The Mexican-American War concluded militarily with the defeat of Mexico and the occupation of Mexico City and politically with the **Treaty of Guadalupe Hidalgo**. This treaty ceded over 525,000 square miles of territory to the United States (present-day Texas, Arizona, California, Nevada, New Mexico, and Utah, as well as parts of Colorado, Kansas, and Wyoming; San Miguel & Valencia, 1998). The extent

Figure 13.2 Territory Acquired by the United States Under the Treaty of Guadalupe Hidalgo and the Gadsden Purchase

of these territories can be seen on the map (dark lines) in Figure 13.2. The United States compensated Mexico with $18.25 million (worth $597.3 million in 2018) for the territory and assumed a $3.25 million ($106.40 million in 2018) debt the Mexican government owed to American citizens (Noel, 2011). The shaded territory at the bottom of Arizona and New Mexico in Figure 13.2 is the Gadsden Purchase from Mexico in 1853 for $10 million ($327 million in 2018).

With the conquest of these new territories, approximately 80,000 Mexicans came under US authority and were granted US citizenship if they desired it; only 1,000 refused in favor of retaining Mexican citizenship (Noel, 2011, p. 436). Mexican Americans therefore were granted citizenship before any other minority group, but despite this and their classification as "white," Hispanics have had their share of discriminatory treatment in the United States. The Treaty of Guadalupe Hidalgo guaranteed Mexicans living in the conquered territories "the free enjoyment of their liberty and property" and the right to retain their language co-equal with English as an official language. Yet there was no love for Mexicans among large portions of the Anglo population. For instance, in 1846 Illinois Congressman Orlando Ficklin described them as "barbarous and cruel, a sordid and treacherous people . . . destitute of noble impulses" (Hietala, 2003, p. 210).

A number of the Mexicans living in the conquered territories were holders of land grants either from Spain or from Mexico after its independence from Spain in 1821. The Treaty of Guadalupe Hidalgo guaranteed that these land grants would be honored, but California required all grant holders to produce their titles for confirmation. The California Land Commission confirmed 604 of the 813, but some proved to be problematic for a variety of reasons (Gates, 1958). If titles could not be confirmed, the land was taken by the state and became available to homesteaders under the federal Homestead Act, which provided free farmland of up to 160 acres of undeveloped federal land west of the Mississippi. Most of this land was acquired by Anglo homesteaders and was widely seen by Mexican Americans as an illegal confiscation (Gates, 1958). However, the US Supreme Court in *Van Reynegan vs. Bolton* (1877) ruled in favor of the descendents of Mexican land grant claimants, and many homesteaders (Anglo and Mexican) on disputed lands were evicted without any compensation for improvements they had made (Gates, 1958).

Push and Pull: Invitation and Exile

The United States has had a long history of welcoming Hispanics at one time and expelling them at another. Throughout the late 1800s and early 1900s, Mexican Americans were employed by large agricultural enterprises in southern California. The Mexican government routinely implored its citizens to remain in Mexico where their labor was needed, yet many factors both "pushed" Mexicans out of Mexico and "pulled" them into the United States. The Mexican Revolution of 1910–1920, combined with the abject poverty of Mexico, resulted in as many as 500,000 refugees crossing the border into the welcoming arms of American agricultural and mining interests as sources of cheap labor (Romo, 1975).

During the economic crisis and high unemployment during the Great Depression, however, state governments passed legislation barring the employment of aliens on projects funded by governments. This had a big impact on Mexican Americans, both citizens and noncitizens, because no distinction was made between them. The federal government embarked on a program of repatriation of aliens back into Mexico, along with their American-born children (according to US law, American-born citizens cannot be "repatriated" because the term means "return to one's native land"). During this period, the Mexican government also enticed Mexicans back home to develop that country's hinterland, and thousands returned voluntarily (Balderrama & Rodríguez, 1995). According to Kevin Johnson (2005b, p. 2), however, about 1 million persons of Mexican descent were forcibly removed from the United States during this period.

Another about-turn occurred in 1942, brought on by the severe labor shortages in the United States during World War II. The need for workers to replace Americans serving in the military prompted the American and Mexican governments to craft a series of agreements that resulted in the **Bracero Program** (Spanish for "strong-arm"). In effect from 1942 to 1964, this program called for the importation of temporary contract laborers from Mexico to the United States. Only fit individuals were recruited, and many who did not qualify for the program entered the United States illegally, much to the chagrin of Mexican farmers who saw their crops rotting in the fields due to the loss of workers. To stem the tide of illegal emigration, Mexico deployed the military along its border with the United States and made it a crime, punishable by two to five years' imprisonment and a 10,000-peso fine, to leave Mexico without proper authorization (Hernandez, 2006). Many illegals did leave, however, and were actually preferred hires by employers because of the red tape and costs involved with the Bracero Program (farmers had to pay the costs of transporting *braceros* from Mexico and ensure their return at the expiration of their contract).

Yet another reversal occurred in 1954 with **Operation Wetback**. The Mexican economy was suffering serious losses due to workers fleeing to the United States; thus, Operation Wetback was a cooperative American-Mexican effort to stem the tide of illegal immigrants. About 1 million undocumented workers were rounded up in the United States in 1954 and handed over to Mexican authorities at the border or to Mexican deportation ships in American ports (Hernandez, 2006). Once back in Mexico, many deportees were forcibly removed hundreds of miles into the interior and often had to submit to forced labor (Hernandez, 2006). To save their Mexican workers, many American employers "dried out" their "wetbacks" by going through the process of legalizing them via the Bracero Program (Garcia, 1980). The Bracero Program ended in 1964.

Segregation, Jury Representation, and Voting Rights

As mentioned previously, Hispanics have faced many of the same problems as other minority groups in the United States, although they are neither as well known nor as momentous. Nevertheless, many of the legal battles fought by Hispanics set the stage for the battles fought by other groups. For instance, with respect to school segregation, a case involving Hispanics (*Mendez et al. v. Westminster School District et al.*, 1946, 1947) was heard seven years before the *Brown* decision involving African Americans. California law at the time authorized segregated schools for Asians but did not do so for Mexican Americans, although segregation was a de facto practice in many California schools. The federal court did not rule on the constitutionality of segregation per se but did rule that the segregation of Mexican Americans was invalid because the law did not authorize it. Presumably, the case would have been decided differently had the plaintiffs been Asian Americans (Johnson, 2005a).

In terms of voting rights in Texas, the issue was not one of barring Hispanics from voting but rather of concocting a redistricting scheme that would dilute the impact of the Hispanic vote. In *White v. Regester* (1973), the Supreme Court ruled that the legislative districts within each state must reflect population demographics and not preexisting political boundaries if those boundaries were the result of gerrymandering (manipulating geographic boundaries to include or exclude certain groups to achieve desired electoral results). In its ruling, the Court noted that a proposed reapportionment plan "contained constitutionally impermissible deviations from population equality, and that the multimember districts provided for Bexar and Dallas Counties invidiously discriminated against cognizable racial or ethnic groups."

As we have seen, however, Hispanics had not been viewed as a "cognizable racial or ethnic group" but rather as white. In a landmark case involving jury representation, the US Supreme Court extended Fourteenth Amendment rights to Mexican Americans in *Hernandez v. Texas* (1954). This case involved the murder of Jose Espinosa by Pedro Hernandez, who was convicted by an all-Anglo jury in Jackson County, Texas. Hernandez's lawyers demonstrated that no Mexican American had been on a jury there for more than 25 years. In a unanimous ruling, the Court held that the Fourteenth Amendment rights extend to all racial/ethnic groups and ordered Hernandez retried (he was subsequently reconvicted by a jury of his peers). In effect, the Court ruled that Hispanics are a separate racial/ethnic group. The Court's ruling stated: "The State of Texas would have us hold that there are only two classes—white and negro—within the contemplation of the Fourteenth Amendment. The decisions of this Court do not support this view" (Johnson, 2005a, p. 173). According to Johnson (2005a), *Hernandez* was the first time that the "Supreme Court recognized the discrimination against Mexican Americans in social life" (p. 199).

Beginning in the early 1980s, the Mexican government reversed its previous policy and urged its citizens to migrate to the United States and send money back home to support families (Lauderdale, 2011). Since this time, there has been a massive influx of Mexican immigrants, both legal and illegal. Traditionally, immigration to the United States has been mostly European. In 1960, the vast majority of immigrants to the United States were still from Europe or Canada, but in 2000, there were more immigrants from Mexico (7,841,000) than from Canada and all European countries combined (Huntington, 2009). According to the former general counsel for the Immigration and Nationalization Service, James Walsh (2005), both the Mexican government and Mexican drug cartels have a vested interest in the failure of the United States to secure its borders. For the Mexican government, it is a safety valve relieving the pressure of overpopulation, undereducation, and unemployment, as well as a source of income as billions of dollars are sent back into Mexico. The Mexican government even prints a "Migrant Guide" instructing its nationals how to avoid detection and successfully enter the United States (Walsh, 2005). The drug cartels also love America's porous borders (and their government's efforts to make them more so) because it makes smuggling their product into the country easier.

In response to this huge influx of illegal immigrants, in 1994 the citizens of California passed Proposition 187, also known as the *Save Our State* initiative. This initiative prohibited illegal aliens from obtaining social services such as health care and public education, with the expectation that this would prevent more illegal immigration and even drive some back across the border. Backers of the proposition bill pointed out that a National Research Council report showed a $2.6 billion deficit (determined by the difference between what illegal immigrants paid in taxes and what they consumed in social benefits and criminal justice costs) in California in 1997 (Rubenstein, 2012). The law based on the proposition was found to be unconstitutional by a federal judge, who ruled that it infringed on the federal government's exclusive jurisdiction over immigration matters despite the fact that it was the lack of federal action to stem the tide that had initiated the proposition. The chaos, poverty, corruption, and inability of the Mexican government to rule in many areas of that country (having ceded power to drug lords) led some to consider Mexico a "failed state" (Lauderdale, 2011). And if it is not already, according to Justin Raimondo (2014), it is rapidly becoming so:

> While the cartels shoot half of Mexico, and terrorize the other half, it seems they've been getting a helping hand in Washington, whose "law enforcement" agencies knowingly allowed sophisticated firearms to be smuggled across the border, into Mexico. As BATF special agent John Dodson told the House Oversight Committee: *This is not a matter of some weapons that had gotten away from us or allowing a few to walk so that we could follow them to a much larger significant target. Allowing loads of weapons that we knew to be destined for criminals was the plan. This was the mandate.*

If Mexico is a failed state, we can expect even more illegal immigration from there.

Because of their traditionally relatively small population prior to the 1980s and their concentration in the Southwest, Hispanics were late in forming a powerful civil rights organization akin to the NAACP. The main group that appears to be spearheading Hispanic interests at the moment most loudly is the Movimiento Estudiantil Chicano de Aztlan (MEChA; Chicano Student Movement of Aztlan). This is a radical group whose constitution (Article II, Section 1) states that it accepts any member who believes in and works for "the liberation of AZTLAN, meaning self-determination of our people in this occupied state and the physical liberation of our land." *Aztlan* refers to the territory conquered and purchased from Mexico in the nineteenth century that MEChA and other Latino groups would like to reclaim. They call this the *reconquista* (reconquest) and claim that this will happen when Hispanics outnumber all other groups in the area. Prominent members of this group include Los Angeles Mayor Antonio Villaraigosa and California Congressman Raul Grijalva.

Ironically, the Mexican claim to the territory is the weakest of all claimants. It rests on having had control of the territory before the United States, but the Mexican government controlled this territory for a mere 27 years (1821–1848) after wresting it from Spain, which had controlled it for 279 years (1542–1821). If "being first" is the basis for claiming the territory, then the Native American tribes have by far the strongest claim.

HOW FAR HAVE WE COME?

Racial civil, political, and social equality for all groups is now a fact enshrined in the law of the land and accepted by all but the most reactionary racists. As Bobo and Kluegel (1997) put it, "Most whites now endorse integration in principle and reject discrimination, preferring instead equal treatment regardless of race" (p. 93). Between 1967 and 1993, blacks won mayoral races in 87 cities across the United States, mostly because of white support—in two-thirds of these cities, blacks were a minority of the population (Thernstrom & Thernstrom, 1997). W. E. B. DuBois would be astounded at the progress blacks made in the hundred years after the founding of the NAACP. There have been two successive African American secretaries of state, two Supreme Court justices, and countless other blacks in high-ranking positions in the government, military, business, education, and all other spheres of life. DuBois would be even more astounded to hear that a black man named Barack Hussein Obama, "whose name shouts its Third World otherness" (Harris & Davidson, 2009, p. 2), was twice elected to the office of president of the United States. Obama garnered over 95 percent of the black vote, but he could not have won without substantial white support. In fact, he received more of the white vote in the 2008 election than Democratic candidate John Kerry received in the previous presidential election, and he even received the majority of the white vote in states such as Vermont (68 percent) and Oregon (60 percent; Caswell 2009). Numerous pundits have even claimed that Obama won the race precisely *because* he is black (Ansolabehere & Stewart, 2009). Obama's razor-thin résumé and his association with radicals who frequently voiced anti-American sentiments, such as Jeremiah Wright, Bill Ayers, Bernadine Dohrn, and Michael Pfleger, would have been more than enough to sabotage the campaign of any white candidate.

DuBois would also be amazed to discover that not only are his people not denied access to prestigious occupations, but because of affirmative action programs, they actually are accorded preferential treatment and consequently have moved into those occupations at a more rapid rate than whites (Wilson, Sakura-Lemessy, & West, 1999). He would see that we have a national holiday celebrating the life of Martin Luther King, Jr.—and that Dr. King is the only individual of any race so honored, since even George Washington has been absorbed into a generic Presidents' Day.

DuBois would be disappointed to find that there is a greater percentage of African Americans in poverty than any other racial group, but his hard-headed philosophy of self-help would preclude him from blaming this on white society (Gabbidon, 2001). He would weep with joy to hear African American economist Glen Loury (1995) say that "we are the most privileged, empowered people of African descent anywhere on the globe" (p. 200) and another African American economist, Walter Williams (2002), say that "blacks spend enough money each year to make us, if we were a nation, the 14th richest" (p. 2). Finally, he would be most gratified to hear historians tell him that although the law has done its part in assuring equal rights, the black activism that he himself set in motion, coupled with international pressure, must take most of the credit.

Although we noted that affirmative action is essentially dead, it appears to be quite healthy in federal employment. A US Office of Personnel Management (2011) study showed that blacks were massively overrepresented in all 22 federal agencies and in 16 of 17 federal executive departments. While constituting just over 10 percent of the US workforce, blacks comprise 24 percent of the employees at the Treasury and Veteran's Affairs; 28 percent at the State Department; 37 percent at the Department of Education; 38 percent at Housing and Urban Development; 42 percent at the Equal Opportunity Commission; 53 percent at the Government Printing Office; 44 percent and 50 percent, respectively, at the quasi-government organizations Fannie Mae and Freddie Mac; and 81 percent of the Court Services and Offender Supervision Agency (US Office of Personnel Management, 2011). The latter lists 100 percent of its first-level managers, 81 percent of its mid-level managers, and 63.1 percent of its senior-level managers as black (US Equal Employment Opportunity Commission, 2009).

Native Americans have also made great strides in their quest for equality. Indians are certainly less sovereign today than they were before Europeans "discovered" the Americas, but they are far more so than was the case 100 years ago. According to Indian activist John Tahsuda (2003), since the passage of the Indian Self-Determination Act, we have seen refinement of self-determination policies to the point that it has become self-governance with "nearly complete control over federal programs" (p. 562). Since then, federal and Supreme Court rulings have almost always been in favor of Indians. For instance, in *United States v. Sioux Nations of Indians* (1980), the Court ruled that the Sioux were entitled to compensation of over $100 million for the seizure of the Black Hills in 1877, and numerous other such rulings have favored Indians rights when they were opposed by individual, corporate, or state or federal government interests.

The major exceptions have been the denial of criminal (*Oliphant v. Suquamish Indian Tribe*, 1978) and civil (*Nevada v. Hicks*, 2001) jurisdiction over non-Indians in Indian country. The rationale for this is that the Indian Civil Rights Act of 1968 applied most of the Bill of Rights to Indians with exceptions that respected Indian tribal sovereignty but, in doing so, denied some rights to individuals. The act allows the establishment of tribal religions, but it does not require tribal criminal justice systems to provide attorneys for indigent offenders or to provide the right to a jury trial in civil cases (Indian Civil Rights Act, 1968). By submitting to the overall sovereignty of the United States, the tribes must deal with non-Indian citizens in a manner acceptable to American law.

Compared to other racial groups, there are relatively few Chinese (3.8 million) or Japanese (1.3 million) in the United States today (US Census Bureau, 2011), giving them less political "muscle" than most other minorities. Despite this lack, they have gone from being loathed as the "yellow peril" to being lauded as the "model minority." Compared with whites, Asian Americans today have a higher median family income, are more likely to be married and to have a college degree, and are less likely to be divorced (Reeves & Bennett, 2003). Overall, Asians have assimilated into American culture well, with relatively minimal legal conflict.

It is too early to assess the progress of Hispanics in the United States. They have been (and are) the targets of discrimination as the labor needs of American business have waxed and waned over the years. Unlike other immigrant groups, the illegal status of many Hispanics may stymie efforts to assimilate into mainstream American culture in the same way that previous immigrant groups have.

This brief overview of the law as applied to minority issues in the United States may tend to give the reader a jaundiced view of the law. There is much grist for the conflict view of law in this chapter. We have seen the Supreme Court put its imprimatur on slavery, segregation, the unilateral abrogation of treaties, forced assimilation, the denial of Indian sovereignty and the appropriation of their lands, and Japanese American internment. In the past, the courts have functioned primarily as a tool to legitimize the policies of the other two branches of government rather than as a separate branch designed to temper their excesses. In more recent years, however, minorities, women, and the working class have been able to use the law to resist their domination, but in each case, it was activism (conflict) that provided the impetus. This conflict ranged from Rosa Parks's simple refusal to give up her seat on a Detroit bus to the worldwide propaganda conflict between the capitalist West and the communist East. Overall, depending on one's politics or the reach of one's vision about what government and its laws can accomplish, progress in obtaining civil rights for all inhabitants of the United States may be seen as lying anywhere on a continuum between "a rousing success" and "still a long way to go."

SUMMARY

The United States has had a troubled racial history that the law has struggled to come to terms with. The issue of slavery and its aftermath has kept all three branches of government busy crafting executive orders, legislative acts, and judicial rulings. The *Amistad* case provided some support for the abolition of slavery in the United States, but the *Dred Scott* case put the Supreme Court's stamp of approval on slavery, was interpreted by some as its approval of the expansion of this system, and hardened the respective stances of the northern and southern states.

The Civil War and the Emancipation Proclamation put an end to slavery, and Congress made its abolition law with passage of the Thirteenth Amendment. The lot of the newly freed slaves appeared to have improved greatly during the Reconstruction period, a time in which the federal government, through the Freedman's Bureau, protected the lives and rights of African Americans. However, the southern states tried to re-create slavery under the notorious Black Codes, denying blacks many rights. Congress struck back by passing the Fourteenth Amendment, declaring blacks to be citizens of the United States, and the Fifteenth Amendment, granting blacks suffrage rights.

Plessy v. Ferguson (1896) and *Williams v. Mississippi* (1898) challenged racial segregation and black disenfranchisement, respectively. The Supreme Court ruled in *Plessy* that "separate but equal" laws did not violate the Fourteenth Amendment, and in *Williams*, it ruled that voting eligibility standards are the prerogative of the individual states under the Tenth Amendment. These two rulings effectively stripped blacks of the rights that they had gained in the Reconstruction period.

The early part of the twentieth century saw the founding of the NAACP to combat the prejudice and discrimination aimed at blacks, especially the cruel practice of lynching. After World War II, things began to improve considerably: we saw the beginning of the end of segregation, and Congress passed the sweeping Civil Rights Act of 1964 and the Voting Rights Act of 1965. Much of this impetus came from the activism of blacks themselves, whose struggles were beamed around the world via television. And much of the success of this activism came from efforts on the part of the government to polish its image with the international community as it struggled with the Soviet Union during the Cold War for the hearts and minds of Third World nations. Whatever the impetus, there is no doubt that the situation of blacks in the United States has improved greatly over what it was 100 years ago.

American Indians have endured efforts to destroy them both physically and culturally. Such efforts began early in our history as white settlers increasingly encroached on Indian territory. The government of the United States took over the role of the British as the "guardians" of the Indians, a position enunciated in the so-called Marshall Trilogy of cases in the 1830s. In these cases, the Supreme Court ruled that Indian tribes were not sovereign nations, that they were only in possession of the lands that they occupied at the pleasure of the United States, and that they were "domestic dependent nations" under the sovereignty of the United States. After this, many Indian tribes were forcibly removed to Indian Territory (Oklahoma), and many Indians died on these long treks from their homelands. A Supreme Court ruling that Indians were "persons" moved the government to attempt to assimilate them into American society by inculcating white American values to "civilize" and "Christianize" them. These efforts had the effect of destroying much of Native American culture. Gradually, the federal government exerted more and more control over the Indian nations while still denying them citizenship rights.

The Indian Reorganization Act of 1934 encouraged Indians to resurrect their languages and their culture, but the termination policies of the 1950s almost destroyed tribal sovereignty again. Termination policies ended with the Indian Self-Determination Act of 1975 in response to the obvious failure of the policies and to increasing Indian militancy, led by the American Indian Movement. Since that time, the government (including the courts) has done much to improve the condition of the Indians, who have now regained almost complete sovereignty.

Asian Americans arrived relatively late in America and have been few in number. Thus, they have not generated a history of discrimination at the same level of African Americans and Indians. Nevertheless, they have suffered ill treatment, beginning with efforts to exclude Chinese from the country as "undesirables." Both Chinese- and Japanese-born immigrants were denied citizenship for many years, a denial that the Supreme Court ruled constitutional. Japanese Americans were interned in relocation camps after the Japanese attack on Pearl Harbor.

Hispanic legal issues have not been of the same magnitude as those of other groups, primarily because they have endeavored to be accepted as white and had voting rights before any other minority group. The biggest issue with respect to Hispanics today is the issue of illegal immigrants, as millions try to cross the border every year to escape the grinding poverty and drug wars in Mexico and to obtain the benefits available in the United States.

DISCUSSION QUESTIONS

1. Should the Founding Fathers have followed the precedent regarding slavery in *Somerset v. Stewart* (1772)? Why or why not?
2. We saw that the Supreme Court in *Scott v. Sandford* (1857) was very concerned about the danger that an anti-slavery ruling might tear the country apart. However, as it turned out, the pro-slavery ruling did so. Do you think that doing the just thing, regardless of what one thinks the consequences may be, is always preferable to doing the expedient thing?
3. Discuss whether the southern states' circumventions of the Thirteenth, Fourteenth, and Fifteenth Amendments point to the inability of the law to effect social change in the face of concerted opposition?
4. Could the United States have expanded "from coast to coast" in ways that would not have meant the mistreatment of the Indians?
5. Do Hispanics have a valid claim to the territory conquered/purchased by the United States? If so, does Spain also have a valid claim, since Mexico took it from her? What about the Indians from whom Spain took the land?
6. How important has militant activism on the part of oppressed groups been in gaining them rights relative to legal action? If militant activism is that important, why did the various Indian wars, slave uprisings, and violent worker strikes of the nineteenth century not produce positive results?

CHAPTER TERMS

American Indian Movement	Black Codes	Chinese Exclusion Act
Assimilation period	Bracero Program	Civil Rights Act of 1964
	Bureau of Indian Affairs	Cold War

Dawes Act
Discovery Doctrine
Emancipation
Proclamation
Freedman's Bureau
General Allotment Act
Indian Citizenship Act
Indian Removal Act
Indian Reorganization
Act

Indian Self-
Determination Act
Jim Crow laws
Kansas-Nebraska Act
Major Crimes Act
Marshall Trilogy
Missouri Compromise
National Association
for the Advancement of
Colored People

Northwest Ordinance
Operation Wetback
Racism
Reconstruction
Termination
Treaty of Fort Pitt
Treaty of Guadalupe
Hidalgo
Voting Rights Act of 1965

References

Abadinsky, H. (2003). *Law and justice: An introduction to the American legal system* (5th ed.). Upper Saddle River, NJ: Prentice Hall.

Aguirre, A., & Turner, J. (1998). *American ethnicity: The dynamics and consequences of discrimination.* Boston, MA: McGraw-Hill.

Ansolabehere, S., & Stewart, C. (2009, January/February). State of the Nation: Amazing race: How post-racial was Obama's victory? *Boston Review.* Retrieved from http://www .bostonreview.net/Ansolabehere-amazing-race.

Balderrama, F. & Rodríguez, R. (1995). *Decade of betrayal: Mexican repatriation in the 1930s.* Albuquerque: NM: University of New Mexico Press.

Barnard, Y. (2005). Better late than never: A takings clause solution to reparations. *Washington & Lee Journal of Civil Rights & Social Justice, 12,* 109–151.

Blanton, C. (2006). George L. Sanchez, ideology and whiteness in the making of Mexican American civil rights movement. *Journal of Southern History, 72,* 569–604.

Bobo, L., & Kluegel, J. (1997). Status, ideology, and dimensions of whites' racial beliefs and attitudes: Progress and stagnation. In S. Tuch & J. Martin (Eds.), *Racial attitudes in the 1990s: Continuity and change* (pp. 93–120). Westport, CT: Praeger.

Brinkley, A., Current, R., Freidel, F., & Williams, T. (1991). *American history: A survey.* New York, NY: McGraw-Hill.

Calavita, K (2007). Immigration law, race, and identity. *Annual Review of Law and Society, 3,* 1–20.

Caswell, B. (2009). The presidency, the vote, and the formation of new coalitions. *Polity, 41,* 388–407.

Clarke, J. (1998). *The lineaments of wrath: Race, violent crime, and American culture.* New Brunswick, NJ: Transaction.

Constitutional Rights Foundation. (2005). "The hands of persons unknown": Lynching in America. Retrieved from http://www.crf-usa.org/brown-v-board-50th-anniversary/ hands-of-persons-unknown.html

Daniels, R. (2002). *Koramatsu v United States* revisited: 1944 and 1983. In A. Gordon-Reed (Ed.), *Race on trial: Law and justice in American history* (pp. 112–129). New York, NY: Oxford University Press.

Davis, T. (2002). Race, identity, and the law: *Plessy v Ferguson.* In A. Gordon-Reed (Ed.), *Race on trial: Law and justice in American history* (pp. 61–76). New York, NY: Oxford University Press.

D'Sousa, D. (1995). *The end of racism: Principles for a multiracial society.* New York, NY: Free Press.

Dudziak, M. (2000). *Cold War civil rights: Race and the image of American democracy.* Princeton, NJ: Princeton University Press.

French, L. (2003). *Native American Justice*. Chicago, IL: Burnham.

Gabbidon, S. (2001). W. E. B. DuBois: Pioneering American criminologist. *Journal of Black Studies, 31*, 581–599.

Garcia, J. (1980). *Operation Wetback: The mass deportation of Mexican undocumented workers in 1954*. Westport, CT: Greenwood Press.

Gates, P. (1958). Adjudication of Spanish-Mexican land grants in California. *Huntington Library Quarterly, 21*, 213–236.

Goldsmyth, S., Radford, J., Jones, D., Hawkins, P., & Russell, J. H. (1916). Colored Freemen as slave owners in Virginia. *The Journal of Negro History, 1*, 233–242.

Harris, J., & Davidson, C. (2009). Obama: The new contours of power. *Race and Class, 50*, 1–19.

Hernandez, K. (2006). The crimes and consequences of illegal immigration: A cross-border examination of operation wetback, 1943–1954. *Western Historical Quarterly, 37*, 421–444.

Hietala, T. (2003). *Manifest design: American exceptionalism and empire*. Ithaca, NY: Cornell University Press.

Humes, K., Jones, N., & Ramirez, R. (2011). *Overview of race and Hispanic origin*. Washington, DC: US Census Bureau.

Huntington, S. (2009). The Hispanic challenge. *Foreign Policy*. Retrieved from http://foreignpolicy.com/2009/10/28/the-hispanic-challenge/

Indian Civil Rights Act. (1968). 25 U.S.C. §§ 1301–03. Washington, DC: US Government Printing Office.

Johnson, K. (2005a). *Hernandez v. Texas*: Legacies of justice and injustice. *Chicano-Latino Law Review, 25*, 153–200.

Johnson, K. (2005b). The forgotten "repatriation" of persons of Mexican ancestry and lessons for the "war on terror." *Pace Law Review, 25*, 1–26.

Jones, H. (2002). The impact of the *Amistad* case on race and law in America. In A. Gordon-Reed (Ed.), *Race on trial: Law and justice in American history* (pp. 14–25). New York, NY: Oxford University Press.

Kitano, H., & Daniels, R. (1995). *Asian Americans: Emerging minorities*. Englewood Cliffs, NJ: Prentice Hall.

Klarman, M. (2004). *From Jim Crow to civil rights: The Supreme Court and the struggle for racial equality*. New York, NY: Oxford University Press.

Lauderdale, M. (2011). The dying elephant: Prelude to a failed state. *Professional Development, 14*, 36–46.

Loury, G. (1995). *One by one from the inside out: Essays and reviews on race and responsibility in America*. New York, NY: Free Press.

McClosky, R. (1994). *The American Supreme Court*. Chicago, IL: University of Chicago Press.

McLemore, S. (1983). *Racial and ethnic relations in America*. Boston, MA: Allyn & Bacon.

Murphy, L. T. (2014). Blackface abolition and the new slave narrative. *Cambridge Journal of Postcolonial Literary Inquiry, 1*, 93–113.

Noel, L. (2011). "I am American": Anglos, Mexicans, Natives, and the national debate over Arizona and New Mexico statehood. *Pacific Historical Review, 80*, 430–467.

Parrillo, V. (2003). *Strangers to these shores: Race and ethnic relations in the United States*. Boston, MA: Allyn & Bacon.

Pinkney, A. (1969). *Black Americans*. Englewood Cliffs, NJ: Prentice Hall.

Raimondo, J. (2014). Is Mexico a failed state? Looks like it. Retrieved from http://original.antiwar.com/justin/2014/10/19/is-mexico-a-failed-state/

Reeves, T., & Bennett, C. (2003). *The Asian and Pacific Islander Population in the United States: March 2002*. Washington, DC: US Department of Commerce, Economics and Statistics Administration, US Census Bureau.

Romo, R. (1975). Response to Mexican Immigration, 1910–1930. *Aztlan, 6*, 173–195.

Rosenberg, G. (1991). *The hollow hope: Can courts bring about social change?* Chicago, IL: University of Chicago Press.

Rubestein, E. (2012). Remembering Proposition 187. *The Social Contract, 22,* 3–7.

San Miguel, G., & Valencia, R. (1998). From the Treaty of Guadalupe Hidalgo to Hopwood: The educational plight and struggle of Mexican Americans in the Southwest. *Harvard Educational Review, 68,* 363–377.

Spartacus Educational. (2005). Lynching. Retrieved from http://www.spartacus.schoolnet.co.uk/USAlynching.htm

Tahsuda, J. (2003). Economic self-determination: Federal policies promoting development of reservation economies. *New England Law Review, 37,* 559–563.

Thernstrom, S., & Thernstrom, A. (1997). *America in black and white: One nation indivisible.* New York, NY: Simon & Schuster.

US Census Bureau. (2011). *Asian/Pacific American heritage month.* Washington, DC: US Government Printing Office.

US Department of Justice. (2005a). Civil rights and Native Americans. Retrieved from http://www.policyalmanac.org/culture/archive/native_americans.shtml

US Department of Justice. (2015). Introduction to federal voting rights laws. Retrieved from http://www.justice.gov/crt/introduction-federal-voting-rights-laws-1

US Equal Employment Opportunity Commission. (2009). Court Services and Offender Supervision Agency. Retrieved from http://www.eeoc.gov/federal/reports/fsp2009/csosa.cfm

US Office of Personnel Management. (2011). The federal workforce. Retrieved from https://www.opm.gov/policy-data-oversight/diversity-and-inclusion/reports/feorp2011.pdf

Virginia Archive (nd). American Indian education in Virginia. http://www.virginiaindianarchive.org/exhibits/show/american-indian-education-in-v/education-2---indian-schools/hampton-institute

Walsh, J. (2005). Los Estados Unidos de Americo. *The Social Contract, 16,* 75–78.

Wang, X. (2002). The *Dred Scott* case. In A. Gordon-Reed (Ed.), *Race on trial: Law and justice in American history* (pp. 26–47). New York, NY: Oxford University Press.

Wheatley, S. (2003). Deliberative democracy and minorities. *European Journal of International Law, 14,* 507–527.

Wiecek, W. (2000). Somerset's case. In L. Ley & K. Karst (Eds.), *Encyclopedia of the American Constitution* (Vol. 5, pp. 2451–2452). New York: Macmillan.

Wildenthal, B. (2003). *Native American sovereignty on trial.* Santa Barbara, CA: ABC-Clio.

Wilkins, D. (1997). *American Indian sovereignty and the U.S. Supreme Court.* Austin: University of Texas Press.

Williams, W. (2002). *The devil made me do it.* Retrieved from http://www.mugu.com/cgi.bin/Upstream

Wilson, G., Sakura-Lemessy, I., & West, J. (1999). Reaching the top: Racial differences in mobility paths in upper-tier occupations. *Work and Occupations, 26,* 165–186.

Wood, W. (1970). The illegal beginning of American Negro slavery. *American Bar Association Journal, 56,* 45–49.

Woodward, C. Van. (1974). *The strange career of Jim Crow.* New York, NY: Oxford University Press.

Cases Cited

Brown v. Board of Education of Topeka, 347 U.S. 483 (1954)

Brown v. Board of Education of Topeka II (Brown II), 349 U.S. 294 (1955)

Cherokee Nation v. Georgia, 30 U.S. 1 (1831)

Cherokee Tobacco, 78 U.S. 616 (1871)

Civil Rights Cases, 109 U.S. 3 (1883)

Elk v. Wilkins, 112 U.S. 94 (1884)

Ex Parte Crow Dog, 109 U.S. 556 (1883)

Ex Parte Endo, 323 U.S. 243 (1944)

Heart of Atlanta Motel v. United States, 379 U.S. 241 (1964)

Hernandez v. Texas, 347 U.S. 475 (1954)

In re Ah Yup, 1 F. Cas. 223 (1878)

In re Rodríguez, 81 F. 337 (W.D. Tex. 1897)

Johnson v. McIntosh, 21 U.S. (8 Wheat.) 543 (1823)

Johnson v. Parker, Northampton County Order Book (1655–1668)

Korematsu v. United States, 323 U.S. 214 (1944)

Lone Wolf v. Hitchcock, 187 U.S. 553 (1903)

Mendez et al. v. Westminster School District et al., 64 F.Supp. 544 (C.D. Cal. 1946)

Mendez et al. v. Westminster School District et al., 161 F.2d 774 (9th Cir. 1947)

Nevada v. Hicks (99–1994), 533 U.S. 353 (2001)

Oliphant v. Suquamish Indian Tribe, 435 U.S. 191 (1978)

Ozawa v. United States, 260 U.S. 178 (1922)

Plessy v. Ferguson, 163 U.S. 538 (1896)

Scott v. Sandford, 60 U.S. 393 (1857)

Smith v. Allwright, 321 U.S. 649 (1944)

Somerset v. Stewart, 98 Eng. Rep. 499 (1772)

South Carolina v. Katzenbach, 383 U.S. 301 (1966)

Standing Bear v. Crook, 25 F. Cas. 695 (1879)

The Slave, Grace, 2 Hagg. Admir. (G.B.) 94 (1827)

United States, Appellants v. The Libellants and Claimants of the Schooner Amistad, 40 U.S. 518 (1841)

United States v. Kagama, 118 U.S. 375 (1886)

United States v. Sioux Nations of Indians, 448 U.S. 371 (1980)

United States v. Wong Kim Ark, 169 U.S. 649 (1898)

Van Reynegan vs. Bolton, 95 U.S. 33 (1877).

White v. Regester, 412 U.S. 755 (1973)

Williams v. State of Mississippi, 170 U.S. 213 (1898)

Worcester v. Georgia, 31 U.S. 515 (1832)

CHAPTER 14

COMPARATIVE LAW: LAW IN OTHER CULTURES

Over a 10-day period in September 1993, Michael Peter Fay, an 18-year-old American living in Singapore, went on a rampage in which he vandalized at least 18 cars, among various other acts. Fay pled guilty to two (out of 53) counts and was sentenced to a fine, jail time, and six lashes of a rattan cane. Many Americans applauded Singapore and opined that this tiny country could teach us a thing or two about dealing with obnoxious teenagers. Others were appalled at what they considered barbaric treatment of a juvenile and thanked God that we do not whip our miscreants in this country anymore. Whatever people's opinions may have been on the matter, if they had one, they were thinking about comparative law.

Although whipping is a common penalty in Singapore, it became a hot political issue in the United States because Fay, an American, was involved. Twenty-four US senators signed a letter condemning the sentence and appealing for clemency. Singaporeans resented such interference, many pointing out that Singapore is a safe and orderly society while the United States is mired in crime. Many other commentators in both the United States and Singapore pointed to differences in the legal penalties as causes for the differences in crime between the two countries. Although both are common law countries, Singapore very much values the crime control model over the American due process model, and its defenders note that America pays the price for its liberal attitudes in crime and general mayhem. This is what comparative law is all about: How do two or more legal systems differ and how are they similar, and what are the consequences of those differences?

Would the United States be a safer and more civic-minded country if it adopted a Singaporean attitude toward crime? Perhaps, but are we willing to go that far? If so, how about going further and cutting off the hands of thieves and executing adulterers, as is done in some Islamic countries that are even safer than Singapore? These are some of the things to think about when we read about other systems and ask, "Why don't we do that?"

INTRODUCTION

All societies, from the smallest tribe to the most populous and complex, develop rules for assuring peace, order, predictability, and cultural survival. These rules and their application may differ enormously from society to society and reflect both a particular culture's history and its present social, political, and economic practices, philosophies, and ideals. This chapter briefly introduces law as it is understood in societies other than the United States. There are many advantages to studying a familiar subject from a different point of view. As mentioned in the preface, it has been said that if you only know your own culture, you do not know your own culture—and we completely agree. After all, we cannot know what "up," "tall," and "no" mean without knowing what "down," "short," and "yes" mean. We are not implying that other legal systems are directly the opposite of our system in the United States. What we are saying is that knowledge other legal systems provides a new understanding and appreciation of our own and better equips us to identify both its strengths and its weaknesses.

LAW IN PRELITERATE BANDS AND TRIBES

There are still a few hundred thousand people in the world today who live in the kinds of simple hunter-gatherer, horticultural, and herding societies that all our ancestors lived in 10,000 to 50,000 years ago. These societies have no written language and thus are collectively referred to as *preliterate* societies. We have defined a crime as a violation of a criminal statute, and criminal statutes, by definition, must be written down. Since these societies have no written language and hence no statutes, can people living in preliterate societies commit crimes? Technically speaking, they cannot, but they certainly can and do commit acts that are the equivalent of crimes as defined by statutes in literate societies. People in these societies obviously cannot commit acts such as tax evasion, securities fraud, embezzlement, and carjacking, but they can commit homicide and theft. Some of these preliterate cultures have homicide rates that are truly astounding when compared with the average rate of about 7.5 per 100,000 in the United States over the past two decades. For example, the Agta, a hunting and gathering society inhabiting an island in the Philippines, have an estimated homicide rate of 326 per 100,000; the Yanomamo of South America, 165.9; and the !Kung of South Africa, 29.3 (Ellis & Walsh, 2000). When evaluating these rates, however, we must remember that all of these societies exist in very unhealthy environments lacking even the most rudimentary medical facilities and thus even minor injuries can be life-threatening.

Even though preliterate societies lack written codes of conduct, social control is of central concern to all organized groups, and people living in these cultures are ruled by customs as rigid and inviolable as any law. Bands are small groups (typically between 50 and 100 members) of hunters and gatherers, and tribes are larger groups (anywhere from a few hundred to many thousands) who augment hunting and gathering with agriculture.

Just as there are no written laws in preliterate societies, there are no formal agents of social control, such as police or judges. These societies have no need for such people because everyone usually knows everyone else to some extent, and thus everyone is exposed to the informal pressures toward conformity that can be brought to bear by other members. There also is the marked absence of resource inequalities in such simple societies and therefore less envy and motivation to take what is not one's own. Whenever there are proscribed and prescribed acts, however, and sanctions that flow from them are sustained by authority, there is law.

The Inuit people inhabiting northern Canada, Alaska, Greenland, and Siberia provide a good example of social control among bands. The most common crimes among the Inuit when they lived in nomadic bands were murder (very rare) and adultery. Why? There was very little worth stealing among the Inuit that was not readily available to all, so property crime was rare. Lacking formal means of redress for offended parties, the Inuit relied on self-redress. Self-redress involved the aggrieved party killing the offender, but this would set in motion a chain reaction of interfamily murders, as it does in some preliterate societies where homicide rates are extremely high. Such blood feuds seriously undermine the viability of band societies unless revenge murders can be carried out in such a way that the killer's identity is not blatantly obvious.

One alternate tactic that avoided bloodshed and vendettas was a unique kind of mechanism of self-redress among the Inuit called the **song duel**, which involved the participants hurling sung insults at one other. These duels were so important that it was not uncommon for both parties to hire talented composers to write their songs, just as an American might hire an attorney. The duelists would "sing their insults while weaving and dancing in front of each other, and to emphasize their jibes they butt heads" (Kidder, 1983, p. 15). The duel was witnessed by an applauding and hissing crowd, which declared one of the parties the winner on the basis of how thoroughly he had humiliated his opponent. This decision by the peers of both parties was intended to conclude the matter just as finally as a jury or judicial decision does in developed societies. However, neither party was found "guilty" or "not guilty," nor were they forced to pay compensation. The ridicule was seen as a way to restore social relationships fractured by the wrongdoing.

The use of nondeadly duels to settle serious grievances is common among band societies, but the absence of specialized and formal agents of social control does not preclude a group response to an offender on occasion. Ostracism and banishment are terrible punishments in band societies, for they signal social and possibly physical death in the harsh and hostile environments often inhabited by bands. For intractable offenders (that small percentage of psychopathic offenders who exist in any society, regardless of how close-knit it may be), the Inuit may rely on some member of the band quietly pushing the offender off the ice to drown when no one else is looking (Lykken, 1995).

In modern times, as the Inuit have moved into permanent settlements, traditional social control mechanisms have become less effective, and Inuit customary law has been replaced by the formalized laws of the nations in which those settlements are located. Large settlements populated by a mixture of people from different regions provide more opportunities for different types of crimes, and these crimes are dealt with through formal social control by police and courts (Inuit Women's Association of Canada, 2006). The changes in Inuit mechanisms of social control exemplifies Émile Durkheim's concept of the movement from mechanical to organic solidarity discussed in chapter 1.

Tribes, which are larger and more complexly organized than bands, have more intricate methods of social control. Because the tribe is much larger than the band, leadership and social control become more precisely defined. The Huron of southern Ontario serves as our example of tribal social control. In the past, each Huron clan (a small subunit of a tribe based on kinship) was represented at a tribal council headed by a civil chief whose primary duty was to mediate disputes. Murder, theft, witchcraft, and treason were the major crime categories recognized by the Huron. Prior to the arrival of the white man's law, the Huron provided for self-redress for murder of a relative, but like the Inuit, they also feared the chain-reaction nature of blood feuds. Murders (and assaults) usually were settled by fines payable not by the offender himself but by his clan. Because the murderer had burdened them with a fine, his clan kin would respond negatively by ridiculing and insulting him. Such is the power of shame and dishonor in preliterate societies that this form of punishment sometimes resulted in the offender taking his own life. Fines were not levied on thieves; the recovery of stolen property and the shaming of the thief was considered punishment enough.

Whereas murder, assault, and theft were private wrongs against the individual, witchcraft and treason were crimes against the tribe. These crime categories often were used as "catch-all" categories to eliminate a few persistently extreme deviants and undesirables. The punishment for these crimes was death. Executions could only be ordered by a council of chiefs and, in the case of execution for witchcraft, only with the consent of the offender's clan. Given this proviso, we can assume that anyone executed for "witchcraft" had exhibited truly reprehensible behavior over a long period of time and that no one mourned his or her passing (Wright & Fox, 1978).

As with the Inuit, Huron law has been modernized. The Huron now live under the laws of the jurisdictions in which they reside (the United States and Canada) but have their own systems of law and enforcement within their reservations. The following are the stated legal goals of the Huron of Fulton, Michigan (Huron Tribal Court, 2014):

- To develop a judicial system that meets the judicial needs of both the tribal community and its government.

- To provide a forum for the resolution of all disputes under tribal law arising in law and equity.

- To provide due process and equal protection to all persons.

- To promote Tribal self-government, community development, and the human potential of all persons.

- To develop judicial institutions and judicial tools that reflect the band's culture, traditions, and values.

This brief discussion of band and tribal law illustrates and emphasizes how customs deemed vital to group solidarity and survival are maintained. These customs or laws are binding obligations on all members of the social group, and if any member fails to live up to the group's behavioral expectations, he or she is subjected to pressure from the group utilizing various mechanisms to right the wrong. These mechanisms can be something as incomprehensible to us as the song duel among the Inuit or as understandable as the fine among the Huron. It is important to understand, however, that both mechanisms produce the same result—the shaming of the offender, the reinforcement of the moral rightness of the custom in the minds of group members, and the return of social tranquility.

LAW IN THE MODERN WORLD: THE FOUR TRADITIONS

There are four main traditions of law in the world today: *civil law, common law, Islamic law,* and *socialist law* (Reichel, 2005). Of course, there are numerous systems of law in the world, each unique in many respects, but just about all of them are related to some degree to one of these four. Some legal systems, due to the legacy of conquest and/or colonization and sometimes voluntary borrowing, are hybrids of one or more of these traditions, with indigenous elements also thrown into the mix. Even among members of the same legal tradition, there are many specific differences, such as between England and the United States within the common law tradition or between France and Germany within the civil law tradition. Space limitations force us to explain non–common law systems primarily by noting how they differ from American common law. These same limitations also require us to narrow our discussion of these different systems to one representative nation. Figure 14.1 shows the representation of the various legal traditions in the world today.

Common Law

As we have seen, the common law tradition originated in England, and its influence spread around the world, mainly through British colonization. India is the world's most populous common law country, although Indian law is liberally sprinkled

Figure 14.1 Percentages of World's Nations Employing the Four Legal Traditions

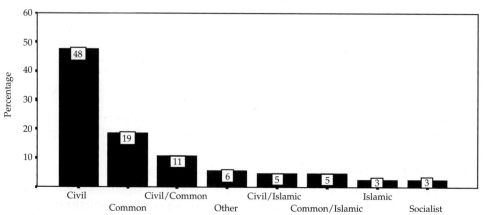

Source: Adapted from percentages provided by Reichel (2005).

with indigenous Hindu law. In addition to the widespread British influence, various aspects of the common law tradition have spread to formerly American-occupied countries such as the Philippines, Japan, and Italy, where common law procedural principles were superimposed on a basically civil law structure. No system of law is imported whole, however, and Britain's daughter countries—the United States, Canada, Australia, and New Zealand—along with England itself have often found it necessary to depart from some specific common law practices to varying degrees without violating its general principles. Nevertheless, it remains the major source of modern criminal law in all English-speaking countries except Scotland and South Africa, both of which employ hybrids of common and civil law (Fairchild & Dammer, 2001), although it has had limited influence outside English-speaking countries. Only countries either colonized or defeated in war by Britain or the United States have imported the common law, whereas many have imported civil law. Friedman (1977) explains that this is probably because "the civil law is neat; it is compactly packaged for export. The common law is cumbersome, unsystematic; to import it, is like carrying groceries home in one's hands without a shopping bag or net" (p. 47).

Historical Aspects of Common Law

The origin of the English common law is traditionally traced to the Norman conquest of England in 1066. Prior to the Norman invasion, English law was a mixture of ancient custom, Church law, and remnants of Roman and Germanic law. The principles and applications of these laws varied greatly from one area to another within England. Powerful feudal lords, who often settled their disputes by combat, determined the law of the land. Because these lords relied on combat, and because their subjects had few rights, law as we know it was not considered necessary. After the Norman invasion, William the Conqueror and his royal successors set out to provide the English with a law common to all (hence the term *common law*), both as a means both to unify England and to increase royal power at the expense of the feudal lords.

Norman kings did not seek to impose alien laws on the Anglo-Saxon English. The common law was fashioned from local customs and practices, shaped and formalized by judicial decisions based on the facts they had before them. These decisions ultimately became the basis for future judicial decisions for judges confronted with similar cases in what became known as the doctrine of precedent. Eventually, these decisions, as well as the arguments made by lawyers involved in the cases, were written down and circulated for review by other judges and lawyers. Thus, much of the English common law is "judge-made," or case law, which has evolved over the centuries in response to the problems of the common person. In a very real sense, common law represents the crystallization of custom as it existed at the time of its inception.

Basic Features of Common Law

Although we discussed common law at length in chapter 3, certain basic features require repeating in order that we may have a basis for comparing other legal traditions to it. Common law is distinguished from other systems of law in five important ways: (a) its unwritten nature, (b) its respect for precedent, (c) its adversarial procedures, (d) its use of grand and petit juries, and (e) its extensive use of judicial review.

These distinguishing features should be viewed as differences in degree rather than in terms of absolute differences existing in one tradition and not in others. We briefly elaborate on these features next.

1. *Common law is unwritten.* When we say that common law is unwritten, we do not mean that it is literally not written down or that it lacks precision of meaning. Common law has a long history of producing revered documents stressing the rule of law since the Magna Carta in 1215. The term *unwritten* is used to distinguish its origin in the customs of the people as formalized by judges from the written or statutory laws of the civil tradition, which were imposed on citizens from above. Common law, however, has long surrendered its lawmaking role to legislative statutes and codified criminal law while maintaining its role in procedural law. It is in the United States that judges retain a modicum of the old lawmaking role rather than in England, where the laws of Parliament (unlike those of the US Congress) are not subject to judicial review.

2. *Common law respects precedent.* Common law's respect for precedent flows from its origin as case law, which reflects the accumulated wisdom of generations of judicial decisions. Precedent operates in vertical and horizontal dimensions. The vertical dimension means that lower courts in their deliberations should always consider decisions made by higher courts, and the horizontal dimension means that courts at the same level should maintain consistency in their interpretations of the law. The doctrine of precedent allows predictability, consistency, and rationality in common law.

3. *Common law is adversarial.* The adversarial nature of common law stems from the "trial by combat" method of settling disputes in medieval times. In an adversarial system, both the prosecution and the defense are expected to vigorously pursue their self-interest (a "victory" for the state or for its client). Judges in common law countries, particularly the United States, function as disinterested referees, making sure that the opposing sides follow the legal rules. Judges do not control the flow of information to the court, generally do not question suspects or witnesses, and do not pass judgments of guilty or not guilty (a bench trial is an exception). Judges in other legal traditions play a much more active role.

4. *Common law uses grand and petit juries.* Indictment by grand jury and trial by petit jury are cherished procedures in common law countries. Traditionally, juries were viewed as bodies of citizens interposing themselves between the power of the state and the accused. The expense of grand juries, as well as the various criticisms laid against them, led to their abolition in England and Canada and to their decreased use in the United States. Likewise, many practical considerations have led to reduced use of trial juries than was previously the case. The extensive use of plea bargaining, the legality of non-unanimous jury decisions, and the use of six-person juries in some states under certain circumstances make the jury less central in common law today.

5. *Common law uses judicial review.* Judicial review refers to the judiciary's examination of the legality of the actions and decisions of executive and

administrative officers of the government as well as appellate review of lower court decisions. The scope of judicial review is limited to various degrees in different common law countries. For instance, the US Supreme Court can rule any state or federal law unconstitutional, but no judicial power in Britain can overrule a Parliamentary act. The Supreme Court of Canada is beginning to evolve along the lines of its American counterpart, although Canada's fear of judicial lawmaking applies the brakes to excessive judicial interference in legislative business (Thompson, 1985). Judicial review of criminal cases from the lower courts follows roughly similar lines in all common law countries.

Civil Law

As we see from Figure 14.1, civil law is the most pervasive legal tradition in the world, used by almost half of the world's nations. The civil law tradition is sometimes called continental law, or code law, to avoid confusion with the civil branch of law in common law countries. Variations of it are found in all countries of Western Europe except England, Wales, and Ireland; all Central and South American countries; many former non-British African colonies; and a number of Asian countries (Fairchild & Dammer, 2001). Former Warsaw Pact nations such as Poland and Hungary, as well as Russia, have reverted to civil law systems. As within common law, the civil law tradition encompasses a variety of systems that differ on many specifics due to its unique developmental history in each country. Some Scandinavian countries often classified as belonging to civil law tradition have systems that are a lot like civil law in some respects but a lot like common law in others. Thus, this four-way classification of legal traditions is somewhat arbitrary in a number of cases (Reichel, 2005).

Historical Origins of Civil Law

Civil law has a longer history of development than common law. Although its development is not as centered on one country as the development of common law (i.e., on England), it probably owes its greatest debt to ancient Rome and nineteenth-century France and Germany. The first historical example of a written code of laws can be traced back to the edicts of King Hammurabi's Code. More relevant to the development of modern civil law is early Roman law, beginning with the Laws of the Twelve Tables, a compilation of rules regulating family, economic, and religious conduct, written around 450 BCE. A further advance in Roman law did not occur for almost another 1,000 years, when the Emperor Justinian published the *corpus juris civilis*, or Code of Justinian, in 533 CE. Modern civil law owes most to the *Code Civil des Français* (Napoleonic Code) published in 1804, for it became the blueprint for all subsequent civil law codes. This code contains 400 codes of law and 14,000 pieces of legislation on all topics from criminal codes to the conduct of marriage.

Basic Features of Civil Law

The basic features of civil law are almost mirror opposites of the features of common law, although the two systems are not so far apart in practice as this statement might imply. The important historical difference between code law and common law is that historically, the former has been developed after a major social upheaval that eliminated previous political regimes. The impetus for such sweeping change usually is a deep distrust and hatred of the previous status quo. For instance, French civil law developed after the French Revolution disposed of the hated *ancien régime*, and socialist law arose after the Russian Revolution overthrew the czar and all the old ways he stood for. The American Revolution produced no such drastic changes in the common law. The American revolutionaries had many complaints against their mother country, but they did not have a disdain for her traditions and institutions. Any differences between American and British common law have evolved slowly and in response to the differing needs of the two nations.

Our discussion of civil law centers on the French system, which comes closest to the civil law prototype. A very basic philosophical difference between the American and French legal systems, particularly criminal law, is that American law, like American political ideology, emphasizes individualism whereas French political ideology and social traditions emphasizes communitarian, and even paternalistic, values. The American criminal justice system emphasizes the rights of the accused; the French system may be characterized as a crime control system emphasizing the rights of the victimized community (Reichel, 2005). The core components of civil law are as follows.

1. *Civil law is written rather than unwritten.* As opposed to common law's slow accumulation of case law derived from decisions based on local customs, the Napoleonic Code and its successors are all codes of conduct (statutes) written from above and imposed on citizens and subjects below. These codes are binding because they have been written down at the behest of some powerful authority (e.g., Hammurabi, Justinian, or Napoleon), not because they are necessarily customary. In other words, writing the codes or principles of conduct down *creates* them in a civil law system, but writing them down in a common law system *reveals* the codes or principles that already exist in custom (Rogoff, 2014).

The comparison of principles may be overdrawn. Most law in common law countries today is code (statutory) law based on legislative fiat rather than case law. Codes in common law countries differ in one important aspect from their counterparts in civil law countries, however. In common law countries, they are viewed as *supplementing* previous law rather than abolishing it, which emphasizes the evolutionary nature of common law. In civil law countries, new codes *replace* previous law, which emphasizes the revolutionary nature of civil law. It should also be noted that the legal prescriptions and proscriptions outlined in the various civil law codes were mostly consistent with the norms and customs that prevailed at the time of their publication, so in this sense of codifying custom, civil law is not too different from common law or from any of the other legal traditions.

2. *Precedent is not officially recognized.* The doctrine of precedent emphasizes common law's ethos of tradition and slow evolutionary change and provides for flexibility by allowing judges to "make law" using their *un*precedented rulings and responses to legal issues in cases containing unique circumstances. This flexibility is not possible in civil law systems because, theoretically, the

codes laid down in civil law are complete the day they are enacted and are not subject to judicial review. As such, there is no need to refer to past cases for guidance; the code itself is all the guidance needed. In practice, however, no code is so complete as to provide unambiguous guidance in all matters coming before the courts, and civil law judges often refer to and rely on case law and thus precedent (Abadinsky, 2003). The two main differences between common and civil law stances toward precedence is that in civil law, precedence is not binding and is the tool of last resort.

3. *Civil law is inquisitorial rather than adversarial.* This is the primary distinguishing feature of civil law vis-à-vis common law. The term *inquisitorial* conjures up images of the Spanish Inquisition, torture, and the notion that the accused is assumed guilty unless he or she can prove innocence, all of which is untrue. The **inquisitorial system** is a system of extensive investigation, interviews, and interrogations carried out in civil law countries to ensure that an innocent person is not subjected to trial (Terrill, 2014). The term *inquisition* should be thought of as denoting "inquiry," as the term *adversarial* denotes "contest." The inquisitorial focus is on truth and not so much on procedure, so many of the procedural protections afforded suspects in common law countries either do not exist or exist in modified form.

This does not mean that the system runs roughshod over individuals. Article 9 in the *Déclaration des droits de l'homme et du citoyen* (Declaration of the Rights of Man and of the Citizen) specifically states: "As all persons are held innocent until they shall have been declared guilty, if arrest shall be deemed indispensable, all harshness not essential to the securing of the prisoner's person shall be severely repressed by law." The French practice of providing attorneys for indigent defendants precedes the practice in the United States by more than half a century. It may even be more protective in some senses. For instance, to protect the accused from adverse publicity, criminal investigations are conducted in secret. No names or other information pertaining to the case are released to the press unless or until the investigation leaves authorities with little doubt that they have a strong case against the accused. These and other such protections have led more than one comparative legal scholar to voice the opinion that civil law is more protective of the innocent and that common law is more protective of the guilty (Fairchild & Dammer, 2001; Maechling, 1993). This suggests that civil law procedure is more likely to arrive at the truth and serve the purpose of justice than is common law procedure.

This "truth-seeking" is accomplished by an active judicial supervision of evidence gathering and active judicial participation in the investigation of the suspect and the crime and by a cooperative rather than adversarial spirit among all participants. After the police make an arrest, the case is referred by the prosecutor to an investigating judge (*juge d'instruction*), who is the key person in the system. He or she directs the police investigation, proceeds with indictments, leads searches and hearings, and appoints experts if they are needed. French defense lawyers do not have access to the file until after the indictment of their client. A body called "the investigating chamber" monitors detentions of suspects and the decisions of the investigating judge.

In an adversarial system in which the outcome may rest on the relative skills of attorneys, defendants able to bear the costs of good attorneys and related investigatory costs (expert witnesses and the like) have a significant advantage over less wealthy defendants. Such inequalities are much less relevant in a judge-controlled inquisitorial system in which judges call expert witnesses on behalf of both sides. *All* relevant evidence as to the guilt or innocence of the accused is considered, including his or her character and hearsay evidence, and nothing is automatically excluded because of so-called technicalities. The only exception to this is when evidence or confessions are obtained via physical or legal threats (Reichel, 2005).

The intensive pretrial investigation minimizes the likelihood that an innocent person will be brought to trial, but it also implies a strong presumption of guilt if the investigation does lead to a trial. In France, a trial is more a public review of case facts and a consideration of mitigating and aggravating circumstances for the purposes of sentencing than a forum for determining guilt or innocence. Thus, although a French *investigation* takes place under the presumption of innocence, a French *trial*, in a sense, takes place with an unspoken presumption of "probably guilty." Civil law practitioners often argue that the presumption of innocence is necessary under common law because the investigation stage is not as thorough as it is under civil law (Rogoff, 2014).

Civil law advocates tend to view the various legal rights afforded to common law defendants as both unnecessary and constraining in the search for truth. American advocates of civil law argue that such rights have limited applicability to the modern United States because they were grounded in efforts to prevent abuses prevalent during medieval times. For instance, it often is argued that the Fifth Amendment prohibition against self-incrimination speaks of being *compelled* to do so via use of torture to extract confessions, but according to Maechling (1993), it is used today as a ploy allowing the accused to evade responding to valid questions put to him or her by the police and prosecution.

Needless to say, a "truth-seeking" system could not operate without the input of the "star" of the show—the accused. Nevertheless, French defendants may refuse to answer questions or cooperate with the investigation because they are only expected (not required) to cooperate. French defendants are advised of their right to remain silent during pretrial proceedings, but because of the presumption that all parties involved in a case will cooperate in the investigation, it does not have the same force of meaning as in common law (Rogoff, 2014). Remaining silent during civil law trial proceedings may be legally considered as evidence of guilt, unlike in common law countries where jurors must not draw negative conclusions from a defendant's silence.

4. *Civil law traditionally has made little use of juries.* In France, juries are used only in serious criminal cases, and they do not have exactly the same role as in common law countries. Civil law juries consist of three professional judges and nine laypersons (Rogoff, 2014). Civil law jurors can question witnesses and the accused and receive defense and prosecution summations. Trial judges are not investigating judges but rather what are called *juge des libertes et de la detention* (judge of freedom and detention; Terrill, 2014). Judges are active participants in trials and see their job as seeking the truth by directly

questioning suspects, witnesses, and other trial participants. Civil law advocates see no problem with this because judges in these countries are highly trained civil servants who owe their positions to education and experience, not political patronage. In essence, civil law judges play, to various degrees, all of the roles played in common law systems by judges, investigators, prosecutors, defense attorneys, and jury members.

In a jury trial, all jurors, judges, and laypersons alike are allowed to question witnesses and the accused. Jury deliberations are doubtless dominated by the professional judges on whom the laypersons must rely for explanations of law, but guilt or innocence is determined by a secret ballot in which each of the 12 votes is of equal importance. A verdict requires agreement of at least 8 of the 12 jurors rather than unanimity. If the verdict is guilty, voting begins immediately on the penalty that the defendant should receive. In common law countries, there is almost always at least 30 days between verdict and sentence to allow authorities (probation officers) to conduct a presentence investigation. This investigation is needed because sentences are imposed in light of information not usually admitted during trial in a common law country as well as on the basis of legally relevant factors (crime seriousness and prior record). The French trial, however, involves judging the character of the defendant as well as the facts of the crime and his or her criminal record, so sentencing deliberations can proceed immediately following the verdict (Terrill, 2014).

5. *Judicial review is used sparingly.* There is not one but three Supreme Courts in France. The **Cour de Cassation** is supreme in criminal and civil matters, the **Conseil d'Etat** in administrative matters, and the **Conseil Constitutionnel** in constitutional matters. Up until 2010, there was no judicial review of legislative statutes in most instances. The French equivalent to the US Supreme Court in terms of dealing with constitutional issues is the *Conseil Constitutionnel* (the Constitutional Council). It used to be the case that this entity was unique among national supreme courts in that it was outside the judicial system as a *council*, not a court hearing cases forwarded to it from lower courts. The council's main function was to rule on the constitutionality of *proposed* legislation, not legislation already in effect, when requested to do so by the executive or legislative branches of government (Rogoff, 2014).

The Constitutional Council gradually has become a fully functional court since the constitutional reforms of 2008. It is now possible for any citizen to raise an issue of unconstitutionality (a petition called a *question prioritaire constitutionelle*) before a lower court, which is reviewed by the relevant Supreme Court (*Cour de Cassation* or *Conseil d'Etat*). If either of these courts decides that the matter is constitutionally relevant, it submits it to the Constitutional Council, which is required to settle the matter within three months (Creelman, 2010). This has drastically increased the council's workload. Also increasing the burden have been added requests from the executive and legislative branches to review pending laws for constitutionality, to avoid the risk that they will later be overturned. Ann Creelman (2010) notes, "In a commentary published in *Le Monde* on August 1, 2010, Cécile Prieur stated that the Constitutional Council has been 'transformed into a Supreme Court'" (p. 3).

It remains to be seen how far the Constitutional Council will travel down this road in the face of the deep distrust the French have for "judicial governance." The French have rejected American-style judicial review because they believe that important decisions affecting large numbers of people should be made by legislators elected by and accountable to the voters, not by appointees with lifetime tenure who are shielded from the wrath of the people. In civil law countries, courts generally are obliged to follow the statutes as written, and judges do not have the power to evaluate them. In the United States, however, the content of a statute is not fully established legally until it has been so construed by the courts. Some civil law countries tend to view the practice of judicial review of legislation as inherently anti-democratic and a violation of the principle of separation of powers. In other civil law countries, such as Germany, Italy, and Austria, the judicial power to void legislation is as great as in the United States, although the limited job tenure of the judges serving on those courts (Constitutional Council members hold the job for nine years), as well as a civil law "hands-off" tradition, tends to blunt the kind of judicial activism exercised by the US Supreme Court. Figure 14.2 illustrates the French court system.

Figure 14.2 French Court Systems: Judicial and Administrative

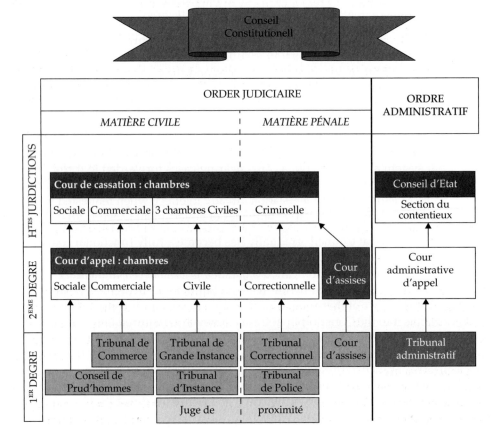

Judicial decisions involving criminal matters as well as private and commercial disputes are appealable to higher courts and then to the court of last resort, the *Cour de Cassation* (*cassation* means "to break" or "to smash"). The *Cour de Cassation* sits in six chambers, each with 15 judges (Rogoff, 2014). As the term implies, its function is to "smash" erroneous decisions made by lower courts. However, the decisions of the court, while authoritative, are not binding on the lower courts in the way that appellate decisions are in common law countries. Also, unlike common law appellate courts, whose function is to rule only on points of law, civil law appellate courts in France and in some other countries can rule on matters of both law and fact. In some instances, an appeals court may hold a new trial if new evidence is brought before it, and it can increase or decrease a criminal sentence upon appeal (Abadinsky, 2003). Neither of these options is available to appeals courts in common law countries.

French law recognizes three offense categories: *crimes, delicts,* and *contraventions*. This classification determines which court in France's three-tiered system of criminal courts will hear the case. **Crimes** (major offenses for which the penalty can be from five years to life imprisonment) are tried in *assize* **court**, the only court that uses juries; **delicts** (less serious offenses for which the penalty can be up to five years) are tried in **correctional court** (*tribunal correctionnel*); and contraventions (minor offenses with a maximum penalty of two months in jail) are tried in **police court** (*tribunal de police*; Terrill, 2014).

Although we have been positive about French civil law, primarily because it is more of a truth-seeking system than the common law, there is potential for abuse as in any system. The investigation into a crime is so thorough that it often takes a long time, during which the accused typically is held in custody without bail. Additionally, bail is granted infrequently in France, both because the country operates under a crime control model and because the accused is expected to be available to help with the inquiry. And by the time a case gets to trial, everyone involved basically knows what is going to happen because the trial is more a forum for a review of the *known* facts (of which all parties are aware) than a forum for fact *finding*. The system is one of professional bureaucracy that lacks the same measure of lay participation favored by common law countries. The expectation of cooperation on the part of the defendant, and the negative conclusions that judge and jurors can draw if he or she does not cooperate, is something that an American due process purist finds alarming.

Socialist Law

Socialist law originated in 1917 with the Russian Revolution and establishment of the Union of Soviet Socialist Republics (USSR). The collapse of the USSR saw the end of socialist law in Russia and its former Eastern European satellites, but variants continue to exist in China, North Korea, Vietnam, and Cuba. Socialist law is based on Marxist/Leninist ideology, and it is the only system of law that considers itself a temporary anachronism devoted to its own demise. Marxist ideology envisioned the eventual "withering away" of the state and an ensuing "dictatorship of the proletariat" in which law would not be needed. Socialist law emphasizes communal values over individual rights and is a low-tolerance, crime control model rather than a due process model. This concept of law is best exemplified by Marxist statistician Karl Pearson in an essay titled "The Moral Basis of Socialism," published in 1887:

> The legislation or measures of police, to be taken against the immoral and anti-social minority, will form the political realization of Socialism. Social-ists have to inculcate that spirit which would give offenders against the State short shrift and the nearest lamp-post. Every citizen must learn to say with Louis XIV, *"L'etat c'est moi!"* [I am the state!]. (Walsh, 2009, pp. 244–245)

The origin of such illiberal attitudes is that "archaic" concepts of individual rights and procedural limitations on state power had purchase only as long as the state and the individual were distinct entities and at odds with one another. In a socialist society, the state and the laws that support it would "wither away," and whatever would be construed as the "state" thereafter would become one with and inseparable from the individual (*L'etat c'est moi!*). Thus, individuals would not be in need of bourgeois proce-dural protections. Indeed, procedural rights are conspicuously absent in contemporary socialist legal systems under the principle of the oneness of the state and the individual.

Since the demise of the USSR, Russia has moved closer to traditional civil law. This leaves China as the largest and most important country with a socialist legal system, although it is evolving into a uniquely Chinese form. As Mo Zhang (2010) put it: "In 1997, the ruling Communist Part of China made it a goal to establish a 'socialist legal system with Chinese characteristics'" (p. 2). There were certain signs that China would embrace some form of democracy since its embrace of capitalist economics, but in 2017, China's Communist Party cleared the way for President Xi Jinping to stay in power indefinitely. China is thus moving toward becoming more totalitarian rather than less.

Chinese Socialist Law

Ancient Chinese philosopher Confucius (551–479 BCE) expressed the attitude toward law that has pervaded Chinese thinking for centuries when he wrote, "The superior man is concerned with virtue; the inferior man is concerned with law" (Fairchild & Dammer, 2001, p. 78). Because of the Confucian influence emphasizing informal discussion, mediation, and compromise to resolve disputes, some scholars maintain that Imperial China (221 BCE to 1911 CE) never developed a sound rational-formal legal system in the Weberian sense (Situ & Liu, 1996). Others point to the **Ch'ing Code** of 1646, which contained 436 statutes and specified 4,000 offenses for which punishment was prescribed, as ample evidence that Chinese law has always been at least substantively rational—that is, "guided by general rules or principles other than that of the law itself" (Marsh, 2000, p. 283).

1. *Chinese law is written, and precedent is not recognized.* During the rule of Mao Zedong (1949–1976), the Chinese legal system borrowed heavily from the Soviet legal codes. The present system of Chinese law was established in 1954, but it was 1979 before China's first code of criminal law and procedure (the Ch'ing Code contained no formal procedural rules) was adopted (Davidson & Wang, 1996). Under this new code of criminal procedure, the Chinese judiciary began to exercise a small measure of independent power (Situ & Liu, 1996). In

common with civil law, judges can only apply the law; they cannot make it. Judges have even less independence than French judges; thus, precedent in the sense of applying judge-made law has no place in the Chinese system. However, unlike the strictly worded formalism of the penal codes of common and civil law traditions, Chinese law has always had a high degree of flexibility in both substance and procedure.

2. *The Chinese system is inquisitorial and adversarial.* The Chinese system has both inquisitorial and adversarial aspects, but its emphasis is squarely on the inquisitorial process. Until 1996, the system did not operate under the presumption of innocence at either the investigatory or the trial phase, and the burden of proof rested squarely on the accused. Under the new codes, there is an assumption of innocence, and defense attorneys can now challenge the prosecutor's case (Lu & Miethe, 2002). However, China still stresses confession, contrition, and eventual reintegration of the defendant back into the community, which shows that Confucian ideals have not been completely lost. Historically, Chinese courts have placed so much emphasis on confession that they do not even allow defendants to know what evidence is to be presented against them. Any such disclosure would taint the voluntary nature of a confession because if defendants were to confess guilt after being made aware of the evidence against them (as in an American plea bargain negotiation), they would merely be acknowledging the obvious and remorse would be hard to gauge (Reichel, 2005). Amnesty International (2005) claims that torture is still sometimes used in China as a means of obtaining confessions, which if true hardly points to their "voluntariness."

The accused in China have the right to defend themselves in court, to hire a lawyer, or to entrust their defense to a relative or lay advocate. The court may appoint an advocate at its discretion, but with only about 170,000 lawyers in all of China in 2010 (about one lawyer per 12,000 citizens versus one per 265 citizens in the United States), they are hard to come by (Weihua, 2012).

Chinese advocates do not support their clients in the Western sense of vigorously seeking to establish their innocence or arguing technical points of law. The function of the advocate is to see that procedural law is observed (the relative leeway allowed in its interpretation notwithstanding) during processing of the defendant and to argue for leniency before sentencing. This may be because, as Lu and Miethe (2002) point out, "the stronger the defense[,] the more severe the punishment is likely to result" (p. 271).

In addition, according to a 2004 Congressional Executive Commission on China report, anything other than minimal advocacy could be risky for defense attorneys. This report claims that Chinese prosecutors harass defense attorneys by threatening them with criminal prosecution for "evidence fabrication." Evidence fabrication is an article of the Chinese criminal code and is defined as evidence that a defense attorney relies on that is later shown to be false. It is not necessary to show that defense attorneys knew the evidence to be false in order to obtain a conviction. The evidence fabrication code specifically targets defense lawyers, and Chinese attorneys have understandably come to view defense work as a "high-risk activity" (Congressional Executive Commission on China, 2004, para. 4). In Lu and Miethe's (2002) study of 237

Chinese theft cases, no defense attorney maintained his or her client's innocence, but all made pleas for leniency.

3. *Chinese law uses a quasi-jury system.* Because of China's Confucian heritage, there has been a long tradition of informal social control via the sanctioning mechanisms available to **people's mediation committees** that are organized in work and neighborhood groups (Fairchild & Dammer, 2001). Every adult in China belongs to one or more of these groups, and thus strong pressures toward conformity are everywhere. When citizens go beyond violating norms to committing crimes, laypersons are also involved in the formal justice system. A criminal trial in China may be held in front of what is known as a **collegial bench** composed of one to three professional judges and two to four laypeople's assessors (Reichel, 2005). Although assessors have a vote as to the verdict in a case, they are highly unlikely to disagree with the professional judges (Fairchild & Dammer, 2001).

In May 2005, the Chinese initiated a new jury system that has been praised as a step forward by many civil rights advocates. There are many differences between the American idea of jurors and jury service and this new system, however. According to Chinese news sources ("Jurors to Help," 2005), many Chinese have applied to serve as lay jurors for a five-year term, notwithstanding the fact that they are compensated monetarily only if they are not regularly employed. Candidates must be over 23 years old, have two years or more of college, and be of good health and sound morality. The stated intention is to make these jurors more independent of professional judges and to "help build a more 'democratic, open, and just authoritative judiciary'" ("Jurors to Help," 2005, para. 13). As previously mentioned, however, Xi Jinping's ascension to lifetime and absolute ruler of China does not bode well for any kind of independent judiciary.

As in the civil tradition, the Chinese trial is held mainly to review the facts and to consider sentencing options. The judges, the prosecutor, and the victim or victim's representatives may all interrogate the defendant, who does not have the right to remain silent. Following the interrogation phase is the debate phase, in which the defendant may debate the judges, the prosecutor, or the victim. Upon termination of the debate, the defendant is allowed to make a final statement before the judges retire to deliberate. As in civil law, the trial panel decides both the verdict and the punishment by majority vote. Unlike the civil system, difficult cases may be submitted to an adjudication committee whose decision is binding on the trial panel.

China is the world's leader in the number of executions each year. The death penalty may be applied for 55 different offenses (down from 68 before 2011), including murder, rape, economic crimes committed by high-level officials, and counterrevolutionary offenses. According to the Chinese human rights organization, Dui Hua (2018), there were at least 2,000 executions in China in 2016, but because the actual number is a state secret, it could be many more. The 2,000 figure is still over 30 times more executions than occurred in the United States (39) in the same year, and 23 times greater when adjusting for population size (Hatch & Walsh, 2016). The average length of time a person sentenced to death waits until execution in China is two months (Dui Hua, 2018), as opposed to 15 years in the United States (Hatch & Walsh, 2016).

There are two types of death sentence: immediate and delayed. A delayed sentence involves a two-year suspension of sentence during which defendants must show that they are reformed. If a person is considered rehabilitated, the sentence usually is changed to a long period of incarceration; if not, he or she is executed. An immediate sentence is carried out within seven days of imposition of the penalty. Such a sentence is imposed when in the court's opinion the defendant is beyond rehabilitation. Execution is by a single shot at the base of the skull, or more recently by lethal injection (Dui Hua, 2018). Penal sanctions in China are characterized by the use of "reeducation" and forced labor camps with the stated function of resocializing inmates to rid them of "politically incorrect" thoughts and behaviors.

4. *Judicial review is limited.* Although politically China is not a federal system, Chinese courts are hierarchically structured at national, provincial (state), county, and local levels, as they are in the United States. At the top of the hierarchy is the **Supreme People's Court** (SPC). The functions of the SPC are to handle cases affecting the entire country, supervise lower-level courts, interpret statutes, and provide explanations and advisory opinions to judicial and political bodies. The SPC is unlike the US Supreme Court in three important ways: (a) it is answerable for its actions to a Standing Committee of the Chinese Communist Party, (b) it offers advisory opinions, and (c) it does not hear cases forwarded to it from lower courts (Davidson & Wang, 1996). Its American counterpart is answerable to no one, refuses to render advisory opinions, and is kept busy by appeals forwarded from the lower courts, which constitute the vast majority of its business. Figure 14.3 shows the hierarchical structure of Chinese courts.

The next highest rung in the ladder is the **Higher People's Court** (HPC), which operates at the provincial level and is analogous to an American state supreme court. The HPC hears cases affecting the entire province in which it is located and appeals from lower courts, particularly death-sentence appeals. One strange function of the HPC is to hear cases in which foreigners have committed crimes or in which Chinese citizens have committed crimes against foreigners (Felkenes, 1989). The movie *Red Corner*, starring Richard Gere as American entrepreneur Jack Moore accused of killing a Chinese woman, illustrates the functioning of the HPC.

The **Intermediate People's Court** has exactly the same duties as the HPC at the prefecture (multicounty) level. The one major difference is that it is a court of original jurisdiction for cases involving serious crimes in the prefecture, such as murder, rape, robbery, and aggravated assault.

The **Basic People's Court** (BPC) operates at the county level and is analogous to the American district (felony) court. The BPC is the workhorse of the Chinese system and handles a variety of criminal and civil cases that would be shared by district and municipal courts in the United States. The BPC also directs the work of people's mediation committees, which are informal dispute resolution committees.

There is higher judicial review of the outcome of a trial, with both the defendant and the prosecutor having the right to one appeal. The appeals court, consisting of three to five judges, reviews both the law and the facts of the case. The court

Figure 14.3 Chart of Hierarchy of Chinese Courts

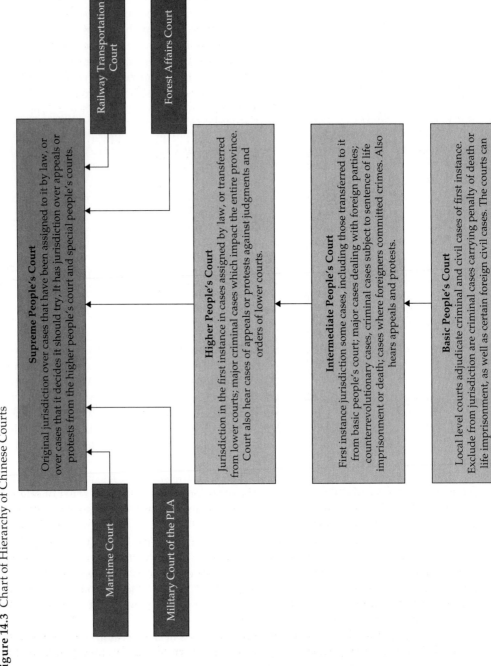

may return the case to the original court for retrial, modify the original judgment, decrease or reaffirm the sentence on appeal from the defendant, or increase or reaffirm it on appeal from the prosecutor (Davidson & Wang, 1996). The prosecutor's right to appeal a "not guilty" verdict reveals the lack of the right to be free of double jeopardy in China.

Given that the purpose of socialist law is to further the interests of the revolution by legalizing its dictates, Chinese judges have had no part in reviewing the constitutionality of legislation passed by the Chinese Communist Party. Even the judges on the SPC are appointed by and answerable to the Standing Committee of the Chinese Communist Party. However, according to Taisu Zhang (2012): "Despite enormous political and institution constraints, the Chinese judiciary seems to be advancing . . . towards greater judicial independence, legal professionalism, and perhaps even some power of constitutional review" (p. 3). Much of this would seem to be inevitable as China becomes economically modernized and more and more enmeshed in international affairs, where legal expertise becomes vital. On the other hand, the Chinese Communist Party appointed a party bureaucrat, Wang Shengjun, with no legal training as president of the SPC in 2008, perhaps indicating a desire to maintain the party's ideological grip on the court. This is indicated by Wang's speeches in which he refers to the "three supremes": "the supremacy of the Party, the supremacy of popular interests [incorporating popular opinions into judicial decisions], and the supremacy of the constitution and law" (Zhang, 2012, p. 4). Note that the supremacy of the Party comes first and constitutional law comes last, quite the reverse of the way the American judiciary would put it.

Nevertheless, international pressures given impetus by membership in the World Trade Organization (WTO) have moved China to promise to reform its judiciary by making it more independent and granting it the power to review administrative law (Mei-Ying Hung, 2004). Note that this involves only review of administrative law, the predictability and fairness of which are needed for participation in the WTO. Nevertheless, WTO membership has placed China's entire legal system under international scrutiny that may eventually bring about political reforms, without which any real legal reforms are highly unlikely (Mei-Ying Hung, 2004).

Islamic Law

Islamic law exists mainly in Middle Eastern Arabic countries, most of northern Africa, and in the Pakistani and Bangledeshi regions of the Indian subcontinent. Each Islamic country is different, and just as socialist law countries vary in their adherence to Marxism, Islamic countries vary in the level of their adherence to strict Qur'anic interpretations. Fundamentalist Iran insists on strict adherence to the Qur'an in theory but in practice is more pragmatic, and Turkey has gone further than any other Islamic country in secularizing its laws. Saudi Arabia serves as our model nation illustrating Islamic law because the Qur'an has served as Saudi Arabia's constitution since the birth of that nation in 1926.

In Saudi Arabia, the Qur'an functions as a constitution, laying out general principles that must be interpreted and applied to a variety of specific cases. Saudi Arabia's constitution is stated in Article One of the Basic Law of 1992: "The Kingdom of Saudi Arabia is a sovereign Arab Islamic State. Its religion is Islam. Its constitution is Almighty God's Book, The Holy Qur'an, and the Sunna of the Prophet." Saudi Arabia adopted a secular abridged constitution called *Nizam* (Basic Law) compiled from administrative records and royal decrees in 1992. This document fulfills some functions of a constitution, but it is secondary to the Qur'an, contains no guarantees of rights, and is applicable mainly to administrative matters (United Nations Developmental Programme, 2005).

1. *Islamic law is written.* **Islamic law** has its origins in the collected revelations and thoughts of the Prophet Muhammad contained in Islam's Holy Book, the Qur'an (Koran). The Qur'an and its companion book containing the statements and deeds of the Prophet, the **Sunna**, contain numerous moral precepts relating in a general way to all aspects of life, but it is not per se a legal code. The generality of the Qur'an's moral precepts necessitates their augmentation by the commentary of legal scholars and case law. Guiding this Islamic jurisprudence, as well as providing supplements to and clarifications of the Qur'an, is a collection of sayings and actions of the Prophet Muhammad called the **Hadith**. What emerges from the Qur'an, case law, and scholarly commentaries is called **shari'a**, "the path to follow."

Three key factors distinguish Islamic law from the other three traditions. First, Islamic law claims to be based on direct revelation from God and as such is unchangeable and binding on all people. Second, it attempts to regulate the behavior and thought processes of the individual on practically all matters. Islamic law is thus a theocratic (religious) system as opposed to the other, secular legal traditions. It is total in its scope, and it requires total and unqualified submission to the will of Allah as that is laid out in the Qur'an. Third, it neither requires nor finds it desirable to achieve uniformity of law. The lack of recourse to generalized principles of law has led some Western commentators to consider it a system of ad hoc justice akin to informal dispute resolution rather than a rational and predictable system of law as we know it in the West (Abadinsky, 2003).

2. *Islamic law is a hybrid inquisitorial/adversarial system in which precedent is absent and no use is made of juries.* Like the Chinese system, Saudi Arabian law is a hybrid of the inquisitorial and adversarial systems, with strong emphasis on the former. Although the system contains few procedural rules, suspects have the right to confront their accusers and are assumed innocent until proven guilty. Criminal court proceedings in Saudi Arabia are very informal by Western standards. The judge, or *qadi* (or *khadi*), hears cases and makes decisions based on his own distillation of the facts and the testimony before him and on the principles of Islamic justice as he sees them. He is not bound by precedent, not even his own, or by the decisions of higher courts. Anderson (1959) tells an anecdotal story of a conversation between Muhammad, the prophet of Islam, and a *qadi* in Yemen relating

how the *qadi* would make a legal decision with the tools provided by Islamic law:

"On what," Muhammad is said to have asked, "will you base your judgments?"
  "On the Book of God," the Qadi replied.
  "But suppose there is nothing therein to help you?"
  "Then," said the Qadi, "I will judge by Sunna of the Prophet."
  "But suppose there is nothing there, either, to help you?"
  "Then I will follow my own opinion," the Qadi is supposed to have replied; and Muhammad is said to have thanked the Almighty that He had Vouchsafed him such a worthy emissary. (p. 13)

Wiechman, Kendall, and Azarian (2005) applaud this, stating that "common law is filled with precedents, rules, and limitations which inhibit creative justice. Judges under Islamic law are free to create new options and ideas to solve new problems associated with crime" (p. 2). This "creative," arbitrary judging is exactly what Western systems have tried to curtail since Beccaria's appeal in the eighteenth century for predictability and equity in sentencing.

Crime and Punishment

Before we proceed further with the court process, it is necessary in this tradition first to discuss crimes and their punishment, which is the fourth aspect of Islamic law that differentiates it from other systems. Unlike other legal systems that categorize the seriousness of crimes and the punishment they engender by the severity of the damage they cause to the victim and/or to society, Islamic law characterizes offenses by the types of punishment they engender. If a punishment is prescribed by the Qur'an, it tends to be more severe than if it is not, regardless of the seriousness of the crime as Westerners might view it.

Islamic law has three classifications of crime: *hudud, quesas,* and *ta'azir.* **Hudud** (the plural of *hadd,* or "fixed penalty" crime) crimes and the penalties attached to them are considered God prescribed, and no judge or legislative body can alter the penalty for them (Souryal, Potts, & Alobied, 1994). *Hudud* crimes and their penalties (in parentheses) are adultery (death); fornication (whipping—80 lashes); false accusation of any of the foregoing crimes (whipping—100 lashes); alcohol consumption (whipping—varies; death is possible after a third offense); apostasy—conversion from Islam to some other faith (death); theft (amputation of hand); and robbery (amputation of alternate-side hand and foot). A publication called *Information Pack for British Prisoners in Saudi Arabia* issued to British nationals by the British embassy in Saudi Arabia informs prisoners what the British government can and cannot do for them and how to apply for a transfer to a British prison. The following two sentences tell the chilling story of what they may expect if convicted:

Criminal law punishments in Saudi Arabia include public beheading, stoning, amputation and lashing. The Saudi courts impose a number of severe physical punishments. The death penalty can be imposed for a wide range of offences including murder, rape, armed robbery, repeated drug use, apostasy, adultery, witchcraft and sorcery and can be carried out by beheading with a sword, stoning or firing squad, followed by crucifixion. (British Foreign Office, 2013, p. 9)

The appearance of witchcraft and sorcery in this list seems strange to Western eyes. However, a 60-year-old Saudi woman was beheaded for witchcraft in 2011, and many others are charged with these offenses. According to Dawn Perlmutter (2013), Western reporters saw it as a "catch-all" charge covering anyone who has offended the authorities by exercising freedom of speech and never considered that the victim actually was practicing witchcraft as it is viewed in Islam. Perlmutter (2013) states that the belief in witchcraft, sorcery, magic, ghosts, and demons is widespread among all social classes in the Muslim world and is

> manifested in the theological concept of *jinn*, inhabiting the entire sphere of the Muslim occult. Furthermore, magical beliefs can constitute an existential and political threat to Islamic religious leaders, provoking severe punishments and strict prohibitions of any practice not sanctioned by their authority. (p. 73)

The Qur'an does not specify a punishment for witchcraft or sorcery, and thus they are punished as *ta'azir* crimes.

Hudud crimes are heard by a panel of three judges. There are variations in these sentences according to circumstance and social status. For instance, adultery carries the death penalty only for married persons; single persons receive 100 lashes. Typically, only males are executed for apostasy, but they may be given three days to repent (under torture if necessary); females are imprisoned and may be lashed each day until they repent. A free person receives 80 lashes for drinking alcohol, and slaves get 40 (Fairchild & Dammer, 2001). Human rights groups strongly oppose Saudi Arabia's system of justice, citing vague laws, arbitrary arrests, flogging and long detention without trial, and torture to obtain confessions (International Commission of Jurists, 2002).

Unlike other legal systems for which the rules of evidence remain the same for every crime, Islamic law maintains higher standards for *hudud* crimes. This curiosity means that because theft is a *hadd* crime and murder is a *quesas* crime, theft demands stricter rules of evidence than murder. A conviction for a *hadd* crime requires either a confession or the eyewitness testimony of at least two adult males (sometimes two women may substitute for one male) who must be Muslims of impeccable character (Terrill, 2014). Such requirements would certainly tend to minimize convictions for many crimes that take place in private, as most acts of adultery, sodomy, and fornication presumably do. These evidentiary requirements may have been purposely designed to make conviction virtually impossible for most *hudud* crimes because of the harshness of the punishment. Indeed, it is considered commendable when witnesses do *not* come forward so that the accused can settle the matter privately with God (Reichel, 2005).

ISSUE HIGHLIGHT

Cultural Relativism and Moral Judgments

Cultural relativism is a core concept of cultural anthropology that maintains all cultures are of equal value and must be respected in their own right. Conflicting moral beliefs are not to be considered judgmentally as right or wrong or good and bad, but rather viewed from a neutral perspective. To judge another culture by one's own cultural standards is considered ethnocentric. Others maintain there are universal standards of morality and human rights that should be respected. The UN Commission on Human Rights (UNCHR) has the mandate of promoting that respect. We have seen the barbaric punishments in Saudi Arabia for acts that aren't even crimes elsewhere and the promiscuous use of the death penalty in China. Should these countries be condemned, or should they be respected as different but equal?

Respected

Cultural practices can be considered justly good in one culture and justly bad in another; to assert otherwise is to insist that there are concrete moral truths when in reality they are just abstractions. Since absolute moral truths do not exist, no culture (or its practices) can be objectively better than another. Moral relativism maintains that cultural approval is what makes an action right; the morality of a certain action can only be determined by appealing to the culture that commends it. We abhor many practices of countries like Saudi Arabia and would not want them practiced here, but that's because we were raised to believe in American ideas of right and wrong. Yet right and wrong are dictated completely by the culture, especially its religion, and any act or practice of any culture should be evaluated by taking this into account. Criticisms of countries such as Saudi Arabia show a lack of tolerance and respect for both its religion and its cultural practices, which the vast number of Saudi Arabians surely want preserved and respected. How would we like it if the Saudis condemned the United States (and they do) for its drug and alcohol problems, its pornography, its crime, and its sexual permissiveness? When the UNCHR criticizes female circumcision, it fails to see that it is understood in those cultures where it is practiced as an ancient, symbolic act that denotes a rite of passage embedded in culturally important beliefs about purity, sexuality, and fertility. Demanding that all cultures comply with universal standards of right and wrong is intolerant cultural imperialism.

Condemned

We are realists about moral truths; they exist because they have observable consequences when they are respected or when they are violated. Just because they are abstractions does not mean that they are not real. No one has ever seen other abstractions such as intelligence, empathy, or happiness, but we see those instantiated in humans every day. Relativists like to say that there are no objective truths, but isn't asserting that there are no objective truths itself an assertion of objective truth? To say that no culture is better than any other is to turn a blind eye to the millions of souls who want to leave their culture and come to Western ones where their human rights are respected. We don't see traffic going the other way either because common people with their common sense know that all cultures are not equal. To deny universal standards of human decency is to imply that some humans are less entitled to human rights simply because of where they live. No amount of political correctness can excuse the Holocaust, the execution of homosexuals for being what they are, or the execution of women for "inappropriate" dress. A structure of moral absolutism applied universally is warranted in the face of such cultural barbarity. If there are no standards for deciding among conflicting moral beliefs, then discussions of morality are relegated to descriptive and non-normative discourse, which amounts to intellectual laziness hiding behind the mask of tolerance of diversity. Many cultures in the world remain centuries behind in their thinking about human rights. The universality of human rights is widely accepted by many nations, but the influence of cultural relativism and multiculturalism undermines that noble notion.

Quesas means "equal harm" or "retaliation," and this classification includes crimes committed against individuals rather than against God. Penalties for these crimes are based on the "eye for an eye" principle. These crimes are serious ones, such as murder and assault and battery, but they are crimes for which the Qur'an does not specify a penalty. Thus, penalties of these crimes can be negotiated or even forgiven by the victim or the family of the victim in exchange for *diyya* ("blood money"). In the case of murder, the *diyya* for killing a Muslim male is about $80,000 for accidental deaths and $106,666 for purposeful murder. A woman is worth only one-half of a man in the Islamic tradition, so the *diyya* for killing a Muslim woman is one-half that of a man. The *diyya* for killing non-Muslims depends on the victim's religion. The family of a murder victim can demand execution, and its wishes are honored by the government.

Ta'azir ("discretion" or "deterrence") crimes typically include consumption of pork, bribery, provocative dress, "wifely disobedience," and traffic offenses for which the imposition of punishment is discretionary. Penalties may range from a dressing down by the judge, a short prison sentence, or some form of light corporal punishment. Because the purpose of punishment for these crimes is discretionary (not determined by the Qur'an or by the wishes of victims or their families), a number of other, more serious crimes can be considered *ta'azir*. One such crime is sodomy (homosexual anal sex). Although not a *hadd* crime, sodomy is considered to be basically the same thing as adultery and is punished as such. Homosexual conduct is a capital crime for males, but it carries a penalty of 100 lashes for females (El-Awa, 1982).

Because only evidence in the form of witnesses and/or confession can be the basis of conviction for a *hadd*, and because the convicted may withdraw his confession (repeated four times), *hudud* crimes are the least likely to result in the death penalty (Peiffer, 2005). Acts similar to *hudud* crimes may be tried as a *quesas* or *ta'azir* crime to assure conviction and punishment. Whether the crime is a *quesas* or *hadd* depends on the circumstances. Murder would be punished as a *hadd* crime if it was committed during some other *hadd* crime, such as robbery or an act of terrorism (because terrorism is

Dira Square in Riyadh Dira Square in Riyadh, the capital city of Saudi Arabia, is the site of public amputations and beheadings. It has been macabrely nicknamed "Chop-Chop Square" by foreign residents.

"waging war against God and his Apostle" and making or spreading "corruption on earth").

This leaves only guaranteed death sentences for *ta'azir* crimes. *Ta'azir* crimes carrying the death penalty are mostly drug-related (the death penalty is mandatory for drug smuggling) and terrorism but also include sorcery, heresy, or "spying for infidels." Because there is little uniformity in Islamic law, judges have discretion to ignore the *hudud/ta'azir* distinction in order to impose any sentence they wish. Peiffer (2005) points to one case of robbery, which is a *hadd* crime for which amputation is prescribed as a punishment. In this case, the judge sentenced two robbers to death by treating the robbery as a *ta'azir* crime, even though no one had been hurt and the money was returned. A major function of appeals courts in other legal traditions is to try to ensure uniformity of the law, but because legal uniformity is not a concern in the Islamic tradition, in Saudi Arabia these courts exist only to hear appeals against sentences imposed by lower courts. Such appeals, heard by panels of three to five judges, are particularly likely to occur for sentences of death, stoning, or amputation (Reichel, 2005). The appellate court must review these sentences but does not review either the law or the facts; rather, it "merely ensures that the judge paid sufficient attention to the point of objection" (Peiffer, 2005, p. 521).

According to Amnesty International (2014), Saudi Arabia "officially" executed 79 people in 2013, although many secret executions are suspected to have occurred as well. Taking this official figure, there is a rate of 2.724 executions per million, which is over 21 times the US rate of 0.124 per million in 2013 (Hatch & Walsh, 2016). Saudi Arabia is behind only China, North Korea, Iraq, and Iran in the proportion of its people it executes.

Saudi Arabian law does not normally allow legal representation in a trial, preferring that the accused speak for themselves. This is not as bad as it sounds because prosecutors do not subject the accused to skillful cross-examination, nor is there any jury to be swayed by emotional testimony. The *qadi* is the sole finder of guilt or innocence, and he may not even have to concern himself with either fact or law due to the practice of oath-taking in Islamic courts. If the crime in question is a *hadd*, the offended individual is responsible for bringing a complaint against the offender. Since few cases of adultery or burglary are likely to take place in front of two (burglary) or four (adultery) witnesses, oath-taking has a central role in most trials. A series of initial statements (not made under oath) may be made by both parties in the dispute regarding various aspects of evidence and character for the *qadi* to evaluate. The climax of the trial comes when one of the parties challenges the other to swear an oath that he is telling the truth. Which party challenges and which swears is decided by the *qadi*. Whoever swears the oath wins the case, for there is no opportunity to rebut or challenge the oath. If a person declines to swear the oath, and this occurs with some regularity, he automatically surrenders the case. There is no punishment for perjury because those who falsely swear will be punished in the next life (Wiechman, Azarian, & Kendall, 1995).

3. *Judicial review is limited to certain crimes only.* After judgment is rendered by the **Musta'galah** (ordinary courts) or **Kubra** (high courts) for *ta'azir* crimes (in the first instance) or for *hudud or quesas* crimes (in the second instance), the appeals process may come into play. Death sentences are appealable only

for a *ta'azir* crime and may be filed up to 30 days after conviction. Because *hudud* crimes are prescribed by the Qu'ran and thus are inviolable in theory, they cannot be appealed, although pardons and stays have been granted by the king. However, even the king cannot reduce the punishment for *hudud* crimes, and pardons are based only upon doubt about guilt. A death sentence for a *quesas* murder may be appealed to a victim's family only, who may then "pardon" the offender for blood money; there is no possibility for government-issued pardon for such crimes.

Saudi Arabian judges typically have degrees in shari'a law, and sometimes a postgraduate qualification from the Institute of Higher Judiciary in Riyadh. The legal education of these judges is entirely religious (based on the Qu'ran and the Hadith), with no reference to any kind of secular procedural and evidentiary concerns (Terrill, 2014). Neither blacks (10 percent of the Saudi population) nor women can be judges (Alahmed, 2013). Due to the lack of generalized principles of law, Saudi judges have almost unlimited discretion to render decisions based on their own distillation of the facts and the principles of religion.

The formal head of the Saudi judicial system is the king of Saudi Arabia, but on a day-to-day level, the Ministry of Justice actually presides over it. This ministry is not a court per se; it is rather an administrative body, a source of pardons, and a final body of appeal that determines if verdicts have been rendered in conformity with shari'a. Since shari'a is based on the word of God as written in the Qu'ran, the final word as to correct interpretation (a form of constitutional review in Saudi Arabia's case) rests in the hands of religious rather than secular authorities. Because the Qu'ran does not envision conflict between the interests of the rulers and the ruled, and because the law is of divine origin and valid for all time, there can be no provision for judicial review of governmental actions (Fairchild & Dammer, 2001).

THE FOUR TRADITIONS AND THE RULE OF LAW

A useful way of making comparisons among the four legal traditions is the degree to which the rule of law is present. Recall from chapter 2 that the rule of law has three important principles: (a) there is *recognition* of fundamental principles and values stressing human dignity and value, (b) values and principles are articulated and *formalized* in writing and contained in revered documents, and (c) substantive laws and administrative procedures are *implemented* to hold the state and its agents to those fundamental values and principles. As we have seen, the rule of law is a restraint on the state and its agents preventing them from exercising arbitrary power.

Next, we consider how the representative nations of the three non–common law traditions stack up in terms of their adherence to the rule of law with reference to the indices of civil liberties quantified by Freedom House (2018) and the Economist Intelligence Unit (2018). Both indices use up to 60 different indicators to examine many aspects of freedom and democracy across the world, but we are concerned only with each country's civil liberties score as a proxy for where they lie on Packer's due process/crime control continuum discussed in chapter 2 (see Figure 14.4). Freedom House

Figure 14.4 Representative Countries Compared on the Due Process-Crime Control Continuum and on their Democracy Scores (Numbers under Flags)

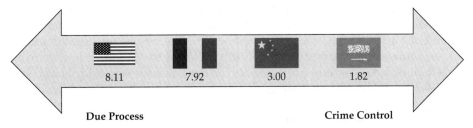

Due Process   Crime Control

ranks countries on a scale of 0 through 100, with 100 indicating the highest level of civil liberty. The Economist Intelligence Unit ranks countries zero through 10, with 10 indicating the highest civil liberty score. For comparison purposes, the United States is rated 89 by Freedom House and 7.98 by the Economist Intelligence Unit on civil liberties (Norway was ranked highest, with 9.873, and North Korea last, with 1.08).

In 2018, France ranked just below the United States with a score of 7.80 on the Economist index, and just above the United States on the Freedom House index with a score of 90. Saudi Arabia and China scored 1.93 and 3.10, respectively on the Economist index and 10 and 15, respectively on the Freedom House index.

The fundamental principles and values of France are articulated in the 1789 document **Declaration of the Rights of Man and of the Citizen** and in the 1958 **Constitution of the Fifth Republic**. France unquestionably exhibits the first two elements of the rule of law. When addressing the third element, we must be careful of legal ethnocentrism. The French do lack due process protections as Americans view them. These protections, however, are viewed by the French as protecting the guilty at the expense of the innocent, and the French have their own procedures for holding agents of the state responsible for implementing their revered values and principles. France does not lack due process procedures; it simply has different ones aimed more solidly (as the French see it) at punishing the guilty and freeing the innocent and thus more in conformity with the principles of justice.

One of the authors of this book (Walsh) was teaching in France and studying the French criminal justice system after the O. J. Simpson trial verdict (discussed in chapter 7). The verdict was a major source of conversation between him and representatives of the French criminal justice system, all of whom expressed total inability to understand the logic of either the process or the verdict. This confusion makes it clear that France and the United States have very different ideas about "civil liberties." The French criminal justice professionals made it very clear why many legal people in civil law countries "find the common law to be crude, unorganized, and culturally inferior" (Reichel, 2005, p. 156).

Islamic law recognizes fundamental values and principles, and those values and principles have been committed to writing in the Qur'an. Thus, Islamic law conforms to the first two requirements of the rule of law. However, the provision of procedures for implementing those values and principles has not been a major concern in Islamic law. Some Islamic countries that have secularized their laws provide moderate due process rights, but states that maintain strict shari'a have no procedures to review the acts of their government and its agents and to hold them accountable. Turkey seemed to be the one Islamic country to extend civil liberties, especially when trying to obtain entry into the European Union, but since the failed coup of 2016, Recep Tayyip Erdoğan has moved the country back in the direction of Shari'a. The lack of procedural rules is the result of Muslims' Qur'anic duty to give allegiance to the existing civil authority regardless of how just or unjust it may be. It is assumed that Allah will punish unjust actions in due course. Islamic law thus does not operate under the rule of law because its written principles and values are not backed by formal procedures for holding the government accountable to them. Socialist law is different from the other three traditions in that it fails to meet any of the criteria for operating under the rule of law. In fact, the rule of law is absent by design in socialist law because it subordinates itself to social policy and does not even recognize any fundamental values and principles that could be written down to serve as the basis for holding authorities accountable. As we have seen, there are certain procedural rules under socialist law, but these are followed or not followed according to the needs of the state at that moment. China has legislated various reforms since it joined the WTO, but how or if they will be implemented under Xi Jinping's "lifetime presidency" remains to be seen. China was rated a 6 on civil liberties by Freedom House (better than Saudi Arabia) and 3.0 by the Economist Intelligence Unit.

It is interesting to note that each of our representative nations opposes American-style judicial review of governmental actions but for vastly different reasons. The French oppose judicial review because it thwarts the will of the people as expressed by the legislature but nevertheless are moving rapidly toward it, as we have seen. The Chinese oppose judicial review because it interferes with the wishes of the Communist Party, and the Saudis oppose it because the law is the word of God and thus cannot be amended by any mere mortal. Judicial review (albeit at different levels) of substantive and procedural criminal law is, however, an integral part of all modern common and civil law systems, regardless of whether or not judicial review of legislation is permitted in a given country.

To conclude, France is a modern democratic nation that functions under the rule of law. On the other hand, both China and Saudi Arabia are traditional autocratic systems. Both are ruled *by* law because there is no other way a nation can survive. However, being ruled *by* law is not the same as functioning under the rule *of* law. Rule *by* law unencumbered by anything as inconvenient as respect for universal human rights brings with it only a stifling constraint of liberty; the rule *of* law implies a liberating constraint. Put otherwise, the rule *of* law implies that the government serves the law, whereas rule *by* law implies that the law serves the government.

THE CONVERGENCE OF SYSTEMS

As the world becomes more complex and interdependent, its cultures will converge more and more, which probably means that the various legal systems will become more similar in all places. One of the most positive trends in criminal law around much of the world is an increased concern for individual rights and the rule of law. The interpenetration of cultures means widespread exposure to the methods that other countries use to settle disputes and to define and punish criminals. Such exposure will inevitably lead to cross-fertilization and, perhaps, a better balance between individual and community rights than has heretofore existed. This trend was already in evidence nearly 40 years ago when Merryman (1969) wrote:

> In a sense, it can be said that the evolution of criminal procedure in the last two centuries in the civil law world has been away from the extremes and abuses of the inquisitorial system, and that the evolution in the common law world during the same period has been away from the abuses and excesses of the accusatorial [adversarial] system. The two systems, in other words, are converging from different directions toward roughly equivalent mixed systems of criminal procedure. (p. 134)

Does this convergence also apply to the socialist and Islamic traditions? It is becoming more difficult for individual nations to participate in the community of nations without conducting themselves according to rational-formal law. The need for uniformity in commercial law is already in evidence. China's acceptance on paper of the international community's "suggestions" on civil rights reforms upon its entry in the WTO is a case in point. Countries in the Islamic tradition that have strongly pursued modernization have discouraged the use of Islamic law, and despite the zealous embrace of Islamic fundamentalism by Iran, that country has not totally abandoned the civil law aspects of its system. Because Islam forbids certain business practices (i.e., payment of interest), even Saudi Arabia has had to make concessions to the exigencies of international trade and banking (Fairchild & Dammer, 2001).

There are, of course, also substantial cultural barriers to convergence in areas other than commercial law. Only greater secularization of Islamic nations will temper the harsh criminal code of shari'a as well as extend human rights to women, religious minorities, and gays in those countries. Unfortunately, at the time of writing, such rights appear to be decreasing rather than increasing, as shari'a law is experiencing a robust resurgence in many Islamic countries around the world (Freedom House, 2018), which essentially means a retreat from the rule of law. The same can be said of China, which appears to be moving further away from human rights rather than closer.

The establishment of supranational courts such as the **International Court of Justice**, also known as the World Court, situated in The Hague, Holland, and the European Court of Human Rights, situated in Strasbourg, France, provides further evidence for the convergence of systems. The judicial body of the United Nations, the World Court rules on international law, although nations often see fit not to abide by its rulings if those are not in their national interest. Given the lack of an executive mechanism to enforce its rulings, we might ask if the World Court is truly a court in the traditional sense.

The European Court of Human Rights, which is the court of final appeals among the nations of the European Union, does find its rulings respected by the member nations. Now that the United Kingdom is leaving the European Union, all member nations are civil law nations. Because of a great deal of cross-fertilization among the various traditions, there is much that is "civil" about the American system and much that is "common" among civil law countries. There will probably always be some differences in legal systems from society to society, however. The trajectory of modernism and international legal conformity will clash with the reluctance to dispense with deep-seated cultural beliefs in many nations, especially those with legal traditions based on religious prescriptions, leaving the study of comparative law an interesting one for many years to come.

SUMMARY

Even the simplest of societies need rules to live by, whether or not those rules are written down and formalized as law. Band and tribal cultures rely mostly on informal methods of enforcing rules, such as shame and ridicule, which are very effective in small-scale social groups where everyone knows everyone else.

There are four main traditions of law in the world today, and we examined them in terms of how the three non–common law traditions differed from common law, focusing on France (civil law), China (socialist law), and Saudi Arabia (Islamic law). Civil law is the most common legal tradition (48 percent of nations), followed by common law (19 percent), with Islamic and socialist law next (each with 3 percent). The remaining nations have mixtures of the four traditions.

Civil law and socialist law arose out of the French and Russian Revolutions, respectively, and represent the complete abandonment of the status quo as it existed prior to those events. This is contrasted with common law, which has evolved piecemeal over the centuries without any major traumatic breaks. We noted that the French civil law tradition differs from common law in several ways. The French legal system has been characterized as a "truth-seeking" system in which all sorts of evidence is admissible and in which the innocent are more likely to be set free and the guilty found guilty than is the case in a common law system.

Socialist law is a system of law that is subordinate to the social policy goals of the ruling communist party and under which suspects are granted very few due process rights. Since the breakup of the Soviet Union and the Russian rejection of communism, the major socialist law country remaining today is China. The Chinese system places emphasis on confession and reintegration into the community. Defendants are not told of the evidence against them; they usually defend themselves in court by the debate process; and the prosecutor can appeal a "not guilty" verdict. A large number of crimes in China carry the death penalty, and the number of criminals executed annually in China exceeds the number from any other country from which data are available.

Islamic law is based on the Qur'an, the Islamic holy book, and the Sunna, which together comprise the shari'a, "the path to follow." Islamic law is a theocratic system, and Saudi Arabia has adopted the Qur'an as its constitution and insists on strict adherence to its principles. Rather than categorizing crimes according to the degree of damage done to the individual or society, Islamic law categorizes them by the punishment for them prescribed in the Qur'an.

There are three broad classes of crimes—*hudud, quesas,* and *ta'azir. Hudud* crimes carry the most severe penalties, which cannot be changed by man since they are prescribed by God. Because no penalty is prescribed for murder (a *quesas* crime) in the Qur'an, it is possible to receive a more lenient sentence for murder than for crimes such as adultery, sodomy, or apostasy, all of which carry the death penalty. Because of the severity of the penalty for such crimes, standards of evidence are said to be extremely high, and it often is preferred that a person accused of such a crime settle the matter privately with God. Oath-swearing is the major means of deciding a case in a Saudi court, which has few formal legal rules.

In terms of how our representative nations followed the rule of law, we found that France offers extensive protections to the accused, although they are somewhat different from those offered in the United States. Saudi Arabia conforms to the first two principles of the rule of law but fails on the third (laws and procedures to hold the state and its agents accountable). China fares poorly on all three elements of the rule of law, although there are indications that the concept of due process may be taking hold there.

As the various nations of the world become more economically integrated, we can expect to see a degree of convergence of legal systems. This has been going on for some time because of legal cross-pollination. There is fairly universal agreement that economic advancement requires a rational-formal legal system, and many nations formerly not employing such a system are doing so, if only in the area of commercial law thus far. The various supranational courts that have sprung up over the past century also will tend to move disparate systems closer to each other over time.

DISCUSSION QUESTIONS

1. Why would the practice of shaming as it occurs in preliterate cultures work, or not work, in the United States to deter crime?
2. Would civil law as exemplified in the French system work in the United States? Are there any aspects of the French system you would like to see incorporated into American law?
3. What is the major advantage of civil law over common law, and what is the major disadvantage? Look at the question from both due process and crime control perspectives.
4. Do you think it would be an improvement over our current legal system if we adopted a theocratic system based on the Bible and made the Bible our constitution?
5. If you are guilty of a capital offense, would you rather be tried in Saudi Arabia or China?
6. Because adherence to international laws and courts necessarily means surrendering some aspects of national sovereignty, should the United States pay any attention at all to World Court decisions that run counter to its interests?

CHAPTER TERMS

Assize court
Basic People's Court
Ch'ing Code
Code Civil des Français

Collegial bench
Conseil Constitutionnel
Conseil d'Etat

Constitution of the Fifth
Republic
Corpus juris civilis
Correctional court

Cour de Cassation
Crimes
Declaration of the
Rights of Man and of the
Citizen
Delicts
Hadith
Higher People's Court
Hudud
Inquisitorial system

International Court of
Justice
Intermediate People's
Court
Islamic law
Kubra
Musta'galah
Nizam
People's mediation
committees

Police court
Qadi
Quesas
Shari'a
Socialist law
Song duel
Sunna
Supreme People's Court
Ta'azir

References

Abadinsky, H. (2003). *Law and justice: An introduction to the American legal system.* Upper Saddle River, NJ: Prentice-Hall.

Alahmed, A. (2013, March 15). The execution of the Saudi seven. *Foreign Policy.* Retrieved from http://www.foreignpolicy.com/articles/2013/03/15/The_execution_of_the_Saudi_Seven

Amnesty International. (2005). *Death penalty: 3,977 executed in 2004.* London, England: Author.

Amnesty International. (2014). *Death sentences and executions: 2013.* Retrieved from http://www.amnestyusa.org/research/reports/death-sentences-and-executions-2013

Anderson, J. (1959). *Islamic law in the modern world.* Westport, CT: Greenwood Press.

British Foreign Office. (2013). Information pack for British prisoners in Saudi Arabia. Retrieved from https://www.gov.uk/government/.../saudi-arabia-prisoner-pack. https://www.gov.uk/government/uploads/system/uploads/attachment_data/file/452341/Saudi_Arabia_Prisoner_Pack_2015_final_July_2015.pdf

Congressional Executive Commission on China. (2004). Defense lawyers turned defendants: Zhang Jianzhong and the criminal prosecution of defense lawyers in China. Retrieved from http://www.cecc.gov/publications/issue-papers/defense-lawyers-turned-defendants-zhang-jianzhong-and-the-criminal

Creelman, A. (2010, October). US-style judicial review for France? *Primerus,* 1–3.

Davidson, R., & Wang, Z. (1996). The court system in the People's Republic of China with a case study of a criminal trial. In O. Ebbe (Ed.), *Comparative and international criminal justice systems* (pp. 139–153). Boston, MA: Butterworth-Heinemann.

Dui Hua. (2018). Criminal justice. Retrieved from https://duihua.org/wp/?page_id=136

Economist Intelligence Unit. (2018). Democracy index 2017: Free speech under attack https://pages.eiu.com/rs/753-RIQ-438/images/Democracy_Index_2017.pdf

El-Awa, M. (1982). *Punishment in Islamic law: A comparative study.* Indianapolis, IN: American Trust Publishers.

Ellis, L., & Walsh, A. (2000). *Criminology: A global perspective.* Boston, MA: Allyn & Bacon.

Fairchild, E., & Dammer, H. (2001). *Comparative criminal justice systems.* Belmont, CA: Wadsworth.

Felkenes, G. (1989). Courts, sentencing, and the death penalty in the PCR. In R. Troyer, J. Clark, & D. Rojek (Eds.), *Social control in the People's Republic of China* (pp. 141–158). New York: Praeger.

Freedom House (2017). Populists and autocrats: The dual threat to global democracy https://freedomhouse.org/report/freedom-world/freedom-world-2017

Friedman, L. (1977). *Law and society: An introduction.* Englewood Cliffs, NJ: Prentice-Hall.

Hatch, G., & Walsh, A. (2016). *Capital punishment: The theory and practice of the ultimate penalty.* New York, NY: Oxford University Press.

Huron Tribal Court. (2014). Tribal court. Retrieved from http://nhbpi.com/sovereignty/tribal-court/

International Commission of Jurists. (2002). Saudi Arabia. Retrieved from www.icj/news.multi.php.mot=

Inuit Women's Association of Canada. (2006). *The Inuit way: A guide to Inuit culture*. Ottawa, ON: Author.

Jurors to help to decide court verdicts. (2005, April 24). *China Daily*, p. 1. Retrieved from http://www.chinadaily.com.cn/english/doc/2005-04/25/content_437095.htm

Kidder, R. (1983). *Connecting law to society*. Englewood Cliffs, NJ: Prentice-Hall.

Lu, H., & Miethe, T. (2002). Legal representation and legal processing in China. *British Journal of Criminology, 42*, 267–280.

Lykken, D. (1995). *The antisocial personalities*. Hillsdale, NJ: Lawrence Erlbaum.

Maechling, C. (1993). The adversarial system should be replaced. In M. Biskup (Ed.), *Criminal justice: Opposing viewpoints* (pp. 35–42). San Diego, CA: Greenhaven.

Marsh, R. (2000). Weber's misunderstanding of traditional Chinese law. *American Journal of Sociology, 106*, 281–302.

Mei-Ying Hung, V. (2004). China's WTO commitment on independent judicial review: Impact on legal and political reforms. *American Journal of Comparative Law, 52*, 77–132.

Merryman, J. (1969). *The civil law tradition: An introduction to the legal systems of Western Europe and Latin America*. Stanford, CA: Stanford University Press.

Peiffer, E. (2005) The death penalty in traditional Islamic law and as interpreted in Saudi Arabia and Nigeria. *William & Mary Journal of Women and the Law, 3*, 507–539.

Reichel, P. (2005). *Comparative criminal justice systems: A topical approach* (4th ed.). Upper Saddle River, NJ: Prentice-Hall.

Rogoff, M. (2014). *French constitutional law*. (2nd Ed.) Durham, NC: Carolina Academic Press.

Situ, Y., & Liu, W. (1996). An overview of the Chinese criminal justice system. In O. Ebbe (Ed.), *Comparative and international criminal justice systems* (pp. 125–137). Boston, MA: Butterworth-Heinemann.

Souryal, S., Potts, D., & Alobied, A. (1994). The penalty of hand amputation for theft in Islamic justice. *Journal of Criminal Justice, 22*, 249–265.

Terrill, R. (2014). *World criminal justice systems: A comparative survey*. New York, NY: Routledge.

Thompson, W. (1985). *Canada 1985*. Washington, DC: Stryker-Post.

United Nations Developmental Programme. (2005). Programme for governance in the Arab region. Retrieved from http://www.pogar.org/countries/constitution.asp?cid=16

Walsh, A. (2009). *Biology and criminology: The biosocial synthesis*. New York, NY: Routledge.

Weihua, C. (2012). Too many lawyers spoil the law. *China Daily*. Retrieved from http://www.chinadaily.com.cn/opinion/2011-02/15/content_12011698.htm

Wiechman, D., Azarian, M., & Kendall, J. (1995). Islamic courts and corrections. *International Journal of Comparative and Applied Criminal Justice, 19*, 33–46.

Wiechman, D., Kendall, J., & Azarian, M. (2005). *Islamic law: Myths and realities*. Retrieved from http://muslim-canada.org/Islam_myths.htm

Wright, B., & Fox, V. (1978). *Criminal justice and the social sciences*. Philadelphia, PA: W. B. Saunders.

Zhang, M. (2010). The socialist legal system with Chinese characteristic: China's discourse for the rule of law and a bitter experience. *Temple International & Comparative Law Journal, 24*, 2–19.

Zhang, T. (2012). Pragmatic court: Reinterpreting the Supreme People's Court of China. *Columbia Journal of Asian Law, 25*, 1–61.

CONSTITUTION OF THE UNITED STATES OF AMERICA

We the People of the United States, in Order to form a more perfect Union, establish Justice, insure domestic Tranquility, provide for the common defense, promote the general Welfare, and secure the Blessings of Liberty to ourselves and our Posterity, do ordain and establish this Constitution for the United States of America.

Article. I.

Section. 1.

All legislative Powers herein granted shall be vested in a Congress of the United States, which shall consist of a Senate and House of Representatives.

Section. 2.

The House of Representatives shall be composed of Members chosen every second Year by the People of the several States, and the Electors in each State shall have the Qualifications requisite for Electors of the most numerous Branch of the State Legislature.

No Person shall be a Representative who shall not have attained to the Age of twenty five Years, and been seven Years a Citizen of the United States, and who shall not, when elected, be an Inhabitant of that State in which he shall be chosen.

Representatives and direct Taxes shall be apportioned among the several States which may be included within this Union, according to their respective Numbers, which shall be determined by adding to the whole Number of free Persons, including those bound to Service for a Term of Years, and excluding Indians not taxed, three fifths of all other Persons. The actual Enumeration shall be made within three Years after the first Meeting of the Congress of the United States, and within every subsequent Term of ten Years, in such Manner as they shall by Law direct. The Number of Representatives shall not exceed one for every thirty Thousand, but each State shall have at Least one Representative; and until such enumeration shall be made, the State of New Hampshire shall be entitled to choose three, Massachusetts eight, Rhode-Island and Providence Plantations one, Connecticut five, New-York six, New Jersey four, Pennsylvania eight, Delaware one, Maryland six, Virginia ten, North Carolina five, South Carolina five, and Georgia three.

When vacancies happen in the Representation from any State, the Executive Authority thereof shall issue Writs of Election to fill such Vacancies.

The House of Representatives shall choose their Speaker and other Officers; and shall have the sole Power of Impeachment.

Section. 3.

The Senate of the United States shall be composed of two Senators from each State, chosen by the Legislature thereof for six Years; and each Senator shall have one Vote.

Immediately after they shall be assembled in Consequence of the first Election, they shall be divided as equally as may be into three Classes. The Seats of the Senators of the first Class shall be vacated at the Expiration of the second Year, of the second Class at the Expiration of the fourth Year, and of the third Class at the Expiration of the sixth Year, so that one third may be chosen every second Year; and if Vacancies happen by Resignation, or otherwise, during the Recess of the Legislature of any State, the Executive thereof may make temporary Appointments until the next Meeting of the Legislature, which shall then fill such Vacancies.

No Person shall be a Senator who shall not have attained to the Age of thirty Years, and been nine Years a Citizen of the United States, and who shall not, when elected, be an Inhabitant of that State for which he shall be chosen.

The Vice President of the United States shall be President of the Senate, but shall have no Vote, unless they be equally divided.

The Senate shall chuse their other Officers, and also a President pro tempore, in the Absence of the Vice President, or when he shall exercise the Office of President of the United States.

The Senate shall have the sole Power to try all Impeachments. When sitting for that Purpose, they shall be on Oath or Affirmation. When the President of the United States is tried, the Chief Justice shall preside: And no Person shall be convicted without the Concurrence of two thirds of the Members present.

Judgment in Cases of Impeachment shall not extend further than to removal from Office, and disqualification to hold and enjoy any Office of honor, Trust or Profit under the United States: but the Party convicted shall nevertheless be liable and subject to Indictment, Trial, Judgment and Punishment, according to Law.

Section. 4.

The Times, Places and Manner of holding Elections for Senators and Representatives, shall be prescribed in each State by the Legislature thereof; but the Congress may at any time by Law make or alter such Regulations, except as to the Places of chusing Senators.

The Congress shall assemble at least once in every Year, and such Meeting shall be on the first Monday in December, unless they shall by Law appoint a different Day.

Section. 5.

Each House shall be the Judge of the Elections, Returns and Qualifications of its own Members, and a Majority of each shall constitute a Quorum to do Business; but a smaller Number may adjourn from day to day, and may be authorized to compel the Attendance of absent Members, in such Manner, and under such Penalties as each House may provide.

Each House may determine the Rules of its Proceedings, punish its Members for disorderly Behaviour, and, with the Concurrence of two thirds, expel a Member.

Each House shall keep a Journal of its Proceedings, and from time to time publish the same, excepting such Parts as may in their Judgment require Secrecy; and the Yeas and Nays of the Members of either House on any question shall, at the Desire of one fifth of those Present, be entered on the Journal.

Neither House, during the Session of Congress, shall, without the Consent of the other, adjourn for more than three days, nor to any other Place than that in which the two Houses shall be sitting.

Section. 6.

The Senators and Representatives shall receive a Compensation for their Services, to be ascertained by Law, and paid out of the Treasury of the United States. They shall in all Cases, except Treason, Felony and Breach of the Peace, be privileged from Arrest during their Attendance at the Session of their respective Houses, and in going to and returning from the same; and for any Speech or Debate in either House, they shall not be questioned in any other Place.

No Senator or Representative shall, during the Time for which he was elected, be appointed to any civil Office under the Authority of the United States, which shall have been created, or the Emoluments whereof shall have been increased during such time; and no Person holding any Office under the United States, shall be a Member of either House during his Continuance in Office.

Section. 7.

All Bills for raising Revenue shall originate in the House of Representatives; but the Senate may propose or concur with Amendments as on other Bills.

Every Bill which shall have passed the House of Representatives and the Senate, shall, before it become a Law, be presented to the President of the United States: If he approve he shall sign it, but if not he shall return it, with his Objections to that House in which it shall have originated, who shall enter the Objections at large on their Journal, and proceed to reconsider it. If after such Reconsideration two thirds of that House shall agree to pass the Bill, it shall be sent, together with the Objections, to the other House, by which it shall like-wise be reconsidered, and if approved by two thirds of that House, it shall become a Law. But in all such Cases the Votes of both Houses shall be determined by Yeas and Nays, and the Names of the Persons voting for and against the Bill shall be entered on the Journal of each House respectively. If any Bill shall not be returned by the President within ten Days (Sundays excepted) after it shall have been presented to him, the Same shall be a Law, in like Manner as if he had signed it, unless the Congress by their Adjournment prevent its Return, in which Case it shall not be a Law.

Every Order, Resolution, or Vote to which the Concurrence of the Senate and House of Representatives may be necessary (except on a question of Adjournment) shall be presented to the President of the United States; and before the Same shall take Effect, shall be approved by him, or being disapproved by him, shall be repassed by two thirds of the Senate and House of Representatives, according to the Rules and Limitations prescribed in the Case of a Bill.

Section. 8.

The Congress shall have Power To lay and collect Taxes, Duties, Imposts and Excises, to pay the Debts and provide for the common Defence and general Welfare of the United States; but all Duties, Imposts and Excises shall be uniform throughout the United States;

To borrow Money on the credit of the United States;

To regulate Commerce with foreign Nations, and among the several States, and with the Indian Tribes;

To establish an uniform Rule of Naturalization, and uniform Laws on the subject of Bankruptcies throughout the United States;

To coin Money, regulate the Value thereof, and of foreign Coin, and fix the Standard of Weights and Measures;

To provide for the Punishment of counterfeiting the Securities and current Coin of the United States;

To establish Post Offices and post Roads;

To promote the Progress of Science and useful Arts, by securing for limited Times to Authors and Inventors the exclusive Right to their respective Writings and Discoveries;

To constitute Tribunals inferior to the supreme Court;

To define and punish Piracies and Felonies committed on the high Seas, and Offences against the Law of Nations;

To declare War, grant Letters of Marque and Reprisal, and make Rules concerning Captures on Land and Water;

To raise and support Armies, but no Appropriation of Money to that Use shall be for a longer Term than two Years;

To provide and maintain a Navy;

To make Rules for the Government and Regulation of the land and naval Forces;

To provide for calling forth the Militia to execute the Laws of the Union, suppress Insurrections and repel Invasions;

To provide for organizing, arming, and disciplining, the Militia, and for governing such Part of them as may be employed in the Service of the United States, reserving to the States respectively, the Appointment of the Officers, and the Authority of training the Militia according to the discipline prescribed by Congress;

To exercise exclusive Legislation in all Cases whatsoever, over such District (not exceeding ten Miles square) as may, by Cession of particular States, and the Acceptance of Congress, become the Seat of the Government of the United States, and to exercise like Authority over all Places purchased by the Consent of the Legislature of the State in which the Same shall be, for the Erection of Forts, Magazines, Arsenals, dock-Yards, and other needful Buildings;—And

To make all Laws which shall be necessary and proper for carrying into Execution the foregoing Powers, and all other Powers vested by this Constitution in the Government of the United States, or in any Department or Officer thereof.

Section. 9.

The Migration or Importation of such Persons as any of the States now existing shall think proper to admit, shall not be prohibited by the Congress prior to the Year one thousand eight hundred and eight, but a Tax or duty may be imposed on such Importation, not exceeding ten dollars for each Person.

The Privilege of the Writ of Habeas Corpus shall not be suspended, unless when in Cases of Rebellion or Invasion the public Safety may require it.

No Bill of Attainder or ex post facto Law shall be passed.

No Capitation, or other direct, Tax shall be laid, unless in Proportion to the Census or enumeration herein before directed to be taken.

No Tax or Duty shall be laid on Articles exported from any State.

No Preference shall be given by any Regulation of Commerce or Revenue to the Ports of one State over those of another; nor shall Vessels bound to, or from, one State, be obliged to enter, clear, or pay Duties in another.

No Money shall be drawn from the Treasury, but in Consequence of Appropriations made by Law; and a regular Statement and Account of the Receipts and Expenditures of all public Money shall be published from time to time.

No Title of Nobility shall be granted by the United States: And no Person holding any Office of Profit or Trust under them, shall, without the Consent of the Congress, accept of any present, Emolument, Office, or Title, of any kind whatever, from any King, Prince, or foreign State.

Section. 10.

No State shall enter into any Treaty, Alliance, or Confederation; grant Letters of Marque and Reprisal; coin Money; emit Bills of Credit; make any Thing but gold and silver Coin a Tender in Payment of Debts; pass any Bill of Attainder, ex post facto Law, or Law impairing the Obligation of Contracts, or grant any Title of Nobility.

No State shall, without the Consent of the Congress, lay any Imposts or Duties on Imports or Exports, except what may be absolutely necessary for executing it's inspection Laws: and the net Produce of all Duties and Imposts, laid by any State on Imports or Exports, shall be for the Use of the Treasury of the United States; and all such Laws shall be subject to the Revision and Control of the Congress.

No State shall, without the Consent of Congress, lay any Duty of Tonnage, keep Troops, or Ships of War in time of Peace, enter into any Agreement or Compact with another State, or with a foreign Power, or engage in War, unless actually invaded, or in such imminent Danger as will not admit of delay.

Article. II.

Section. 1.

The executive Power shall be vested in a President of the United States of America. He shall hold his Office during the Term of four Years, and, together with the Vice President, chosen for the same Term, be elected, as follows:

Each State shall appoint, in such Manner as the Legislature thereof may direct, a Number of Electors, equal to the whole Number of Senators and Representatives to which the State may be entitled in the Congress: but no Senator or Representative, or Person holding an Office of Trust or Profit under the United States, shall be appointed an Elector.

The Electors shall meet in their respective States, and vote by Ballot for two Persons, of whom one at least shall not be an Inhabitant of the same State with themselves. And they shall make a List of all the Persons voted for, and of the Number of Votes for each; which List they shall sign and certify, and transmit sealed to the Seat of the Government of the United States, directed to the President of the Senate. The President of the Senate shall, in the Presence of the Senate and House of Representatives, open all the Certificates, and the Votes shall then be counted. The Person having the greatest Number of Votes shall be the President, if such Number be a Majority of the whole Number of Electors appointed; and if there be more than one who have such Majority, and have an equal Number of Votes, then the House of Representatives shall immediately chuse by Ballot one of them for President; and if no Person have a Majority, then from the five highest on the List the said House shall in like Manner chuse the President. But in chusing the President, the Votes shall be taken by States, the Representation from each State having one Vote; a quorum for this purpose shall consist of a Member or Members from two thirds of the States, and a Majority of all the States shall be necessary to a Choice. In every Case, after the Choice of the President, the Person having the greatest Number of Votes of the Electors shall be the Vice President. But if there should remain two or more who have equal Votes, the Senate shall chuse from them by Ballot the Vice President.

The Congress may determine the Time of chusing the Electors, and the Day on which they shall give their Votes; which Day shall be the same throughout the United States.

No Person except a natural born Citizen, or a Citizen of the United States, at the time of the Adoption of this Constitution, shall be eligible to the Office of President; neither shall any Person be eligible to that Office who shall not have attained to the Age of thirty five Years, and been fourteen Years a Resident within the United States.

In Case of the Removal of the President from Office, or of his Death, Resignation, or Inability to discharge the Powers and Duties of the said Office, the Same shall devolve on the Vice President, and the Congress may by Law provide for the Case of Removal, Death, Resignation or Inability, both of the President and Vice President, declaring what Officer shall then act as President, and such Officer shall act accordingly, until the Disability be removed, or a President shall be elected.

The President shall, at stated Times, receive for his Services, a Compensation, which shall neither be increased nor diminished during the Period for which he shall have been elected, and he shall not receive within that Period any other Emolument from the United States, or any of them.

Before he enter on the Execution of his Office, he shall take the following Oath or Affirmation:—"I do solemnly swear (or affirm) that I will faithfully execute the Office of President of the United States, and will to the best of my Ability, preserve, protect and defend the Constitution of the United States."

Section. 2.

The President shall be Commander in Chief of the Army and Navy of the United States, and of the Militia of the several States, when called into the actual Service of the United States; he may require the Opinion, in writing, of the principal Officer in each of the executive Departments, upon any Subject relating to the Duties of their respective Offices, and he shall have Power to grant Reprieves and Pardons for Offences against the United States, except in Cases of Impeachment.

He shall have Power, by and with the Advice and Consent of the Senate, to make Treaties, provided two thirds of the Senators present concur; and he shall nominate, and by and with the Advice and Consent of the Senate, shall appoint Ambassadors, other public Ministers and Consuls, Judges of the supreme Court, and all other Officers of the United States, whose Appointments are not herein otherwise provided for, and which shall be established by Law: but the Congress may by Law vest the Appointment of such inferior Officers, as they think proper, in the President alone, in the Courts of Law, or in the Heads of Departments.

The President shall have Power to fill up all Vacancies that may happen during the Recess of the Senate, by granting Commissions which shall expire at the End of their next Session.

Section. 3.

He shall from time to time give to the Congress Information of the State of the Union, and recommend to their Consideration such Measures as he shall judge necessary and expedient; he may, on extraordinary Occasions, convene both Houses, or either of them, and in Case of Disagreement between them, with Respect to the Time of Adjournment, he may adjourn them to such Time as he shall think proper; he shall receive Ambassadors and other public Ministers; he shall take Care that the Laws be faithfully executed, and shall Commission all the Officers of the United States.

Section. 4.

The President, Vice President and all civil Officers of the United States, shall be removed from Office on Impeachment for, and Conviction of, Treason, Bribery, or other high Crimes and Misdemeanors.

Article. III.

Section. 1.

The judicial Power of the United States shall be vested in one supreme Court, and in such inferior Courts as the Congress may from time to time ordain and establish. The Judges, both of the supreme and inferior Courts, shall hold their Offices during good Behaviour, and shall, at stated Times, receive for their Services a Compensation, which shall not be diminished during their Continuance in Office.

Section. 2.

The judicial Power shall extend to all Cases, in Law and Equity, arising under this Constitution, the Laws of the United States, and Treaties made, or which shall be made, under their Authority;—to all Cases affecting Ambassadors, other public Ministers and Consuls;—to all Cases of admiralty and maritime Jurisdiction;—to Controversies to which the United States shall be a Party;—to Controversies between two or more States;—between a State and Citizens of another State;—between Citizens of different States;—between Citizens of the same State claiming Lands under Grants of different States, and between a State, or the Citizens thereof, and foreign States, Citizens or Subjects.

In all Cases affecting Ambassadors, other public Ministers and Consuls, and those in which a State shall be Party, the supreme Court shall have original Jurisdiction. In all the other Cases before mentioned, the supreme Court shall have appellate Jurisdiction, both as to Law and Fact, with such Exceptions, and under such Regulations as the Congress shall make.

The Trial of all Crimes, except in Cases of Impeachment, shall be by Jury; and such Trial shall be held in the State where the said Crimes shall have been committed; but when not committed within any State, the Trial shall be at such Place or Places as the Congress may by Law have directed.

Section. 3.

Treason against the United States, shall consist only in levying War against them, or in adhering to their Enemies, giving them Aid and Comfort. No Person shall be convicted of Treason unless on the Testimony of two Witnesses to the same overt Act, or on Confession in open Court.

The Congress shall have Power to declare the Punishment of Treason, but no Attainder of Treason shall work Corruption of Blood, or Forfeiture except during the Life of the Person attainted.

Article. IV.

Section. 1.

Full Faith and Credit shall be given in each State to the public Acts, Records, and judicial Proceedings of every other State. And the Congress may by general Laws prescribe the Manner in which such Acts, Records and Proceedings shall be proved, and the Effect thereof.

Section. 2.

The Citizens of each State shall be entitled to all Privileges and Immunities of Citizens in the several States.

A Person charged in any State with Treason, Felony, or other Crime, who shall flee from Justice, and be found in another State, shall on Demand of the executive Authority of the State from which he fled, be delivered up, to be removed to the State having Jurisdiction of the Crime.

No Person held to Service or Labour in one State, under the Laws thereof, escaping into another, shall, in Consequence of any Law or Regulation therein, be discharged from such Service or Labour, but shall be delivered up on Claim of the Party to whom such Service or Labour may be due.

Section. 3.

New States may be admitted by the Congress into this Union; but no new State shall be formed or erected within the Jurisdiction of any other State; nor any State be formed by the Junction of two or more States, or Parts of States, without the Consent of the Legislatures of the States concerned as well as of the Congress.

The Congress shall have Power to dispose of and make all needful Rules and Regulations respecting the Territory or other Property belonging to the United States; and nothing in this Constitution shall be so construed as to Prejudice any Claims of the United States, or of any particular State.

Section. 4.

The United States shall guarantee to every State in this Union a Republican Form of Government, and shall protect each of them against Invasion; and on Application of the Legislature, or of the Executive (when the Legislature cannot be convened), against domestic Violence.

Article. V.

The Congress, whenever two thirds of both Houses shall deem it necessary, shall propose Amendments to this Constitution, or, on the Application of the Legislatures of two thirds of the several States, shall call a Convention for proposing Amendments, which, in either Case, shall be valid to all Intents and Purposes, as Part of this Constitution, when ratified by the Legislatures of three fourths of the several States, or by Conventions in three fourths thereof, as the one or the other Mode of Ratification may be proposed by the Congress; Provided that no Amendment which may be made prior to the Year One thousand eight hundred and eight shall in any Manner affect the first and fourth Clauses in the Ninth Section of the first Article; and that no State, without its Consent, shall be deprived of its equal Suffrage in the Senate.

Article. VI.

All Debts contracted and Engagements entered into, before the Adoption of this Constitution, shall be as valid against the United States under this Constitution, as under the Confederation.

This Constitution, and the Laws of the United States which shall be made in Pursuance thereof; and all Treaties made, or which shall be made, under the Authority of the United States, shall be the supreme Law of the Land; and the Judges in every State shall be bound thereby, any Thing in the Constitution or Laws of any State to the Contrary notwithstanding.

The Senators and Representatives before mentioned, and the Members of the several State Legislatures, and all executive and judicial Officers, both of the United States and of the several States, shall be bound by Oath or Affirmation, to support this Constitution; but no religious Test shall ever be required as a Qualification to any Office or public Trust under the United States.

Article. VII.

The Ratification of the Conventions of nine States, shall be sufficient for the Establishment of this Constitution between the States so ratifying the Same.

THE AMENDMENTS

The Preamble to the Bill of Rights

Congress of the United States begun and held at the City of New York, on Wednesday the fourth of March, one thousand seven hundred and eighty nine.

THE Conventions of a number of the States, having at the time of their adopting the Constitution, expressed a desire, in order to prevent misconstruction or abuse of its powers, that further declaratory and restrictive clauses should be added: And as extending the ground of public confidence in the Government, will best ensure the beneficent ends of its institution.

RESOLVED by the Senate and House of Representatives of the United States of America, in Congress assembled, two thirds of both Houses concurring, that the following Articles be proposed to the Legislatures of the several States, as amendments to the Constitution of the United States, all, or any of which Articles, when ratified by three fourths of the said Legislatures, to be valid to all intents and purposes, as part of the said Constitution; viz.

ARTICLES in addition to, and Amendment of the Constitution of the United States of America, proposed by Congress, and ratified by the Legislatures of the several States, pursuant to the fifth Article of the original Constitution.

AMENDMENT I

Congress shall make no law respecting an establishment of religion, or prohibiting the free exercise thereof; or abridging the freedom of speech, or of the press; or the right of the people peaceably to assemble, and to petition the Government for a redress of grievances.

AMENDMENT II

A well regulated Militia, being necessary to the security of a free State, the right of the people to keep and bear Arms, shall not be infringed.

AMENDMENT III

No Soldier shall, in time of peace be quartered in any house, without the consent of the Owner, nor in time of war, but in a manner to be prescribed by law.

AMENDMENT IV

The right of the people to be secure in their persons, houses, papers, and effects, against unreasonable searches and seizures, shall not be violated, and no Warrants shall issue, but upon probable cause, supported by Oath or affirmation, and particularly describing the place to be searched, and the persons or things to be seized.

AMENDMENT V

No person shall be held to answer for a capital, or otherwise infamous crime, unless on a presentment or indictment of a Grand Jury, except in cases arising in the land or naval forces, or in the Militia, when in actual service in time of War or public danger; nor shall any person be subject for the same offence to be twice put in jeopardy of life or limb; nor shall be compelled in any criminal case to be a witness against himself, nor be deprived of life, liberty, or property, without due process of law; nor shall private property be taken for public use, without just compensation.

AMENDMENT VI

In all criminal prosecutions, the accused shall enjoy the right to a speedy and public trial, by an impartial jury of the State and district wherein the crime shall have been committed, which district shall have been previously ascertained by law, and to be informed of the nature and cause of the accusation; to be confronted with the witnesses against him; to have compulsory process for obtaining witnesses in his favor, and to have the Assistance of Counsel for his defence.

AMENDMENT VII

In Suits at common law, where the value in controversy shall exceed twenty dollars, the right of trial by jury shall be preserved, and no fact tried by a jury, shall be otherwise re-examined in any Court of the United States, than according to the rules of the common law.

AMENDMENT VIII

Excessive bail shall not be required, nor excessive fines imposed, nor cruel and unusual punishments inflicted.

AMENDMENT IX

The enumeration in the Constitution, of certain rights, shall not be construed to deny or disparage others retained by the people.

AMENDMENT X

The powers not delegated to the United States by the Constitution, nor prohibited by it to the States, are reserved to the States respectively, or to the people.

AMENDMENT XI (1795)

The Judicial power of the United States shall not be construed to extend to any suit in law or equity, commenced or prosecuted against one of the United States by Citizens of another State, or by Citizens or Subjects of any Foreign State.

AMENDMENT XII (1804)

The Electors shall meet in their respective states and vote by ballot for President and Vice-President, one of whom, at least, shall not be an inhabitant of the same state with themselves; they shall name in their ballots the person voted for as President, and in distinct ballots the person voted for as Vice-President, and they shall make distinct lists of all persons voted for as President, and of all persons voted for as Vice-President, and of the number of votes for each, which lists they shall sign and certify, and transmit sealed to the seat of the government of the United States, directed to the President of the Senate;—The President of the Senate shall, in the presence of the Senate and House of Representatives, open all the certificates and the votes shall then be counted;—The person having the greatest number of votes for President, shall be the President, if such number be a majority of the whole number of Electors appointed; and if no person have such majority, then from the persons having the highest numbers not exceeding three on the list of those voted for as President, the House of Representatives shall choose immediately, by ballot, the President. But in choosing the President, the votes shall be taken by states, the representation from each state having one vote; a quorum for this purpose shall consist of a member or members from two-thirds of the states, and a majority of all the states shall be necessary to a choice. And if the House of Representatives shall not choose a President whenever the right of choice shall devolve upon them, before the fourth day of March next following, then the Vice-President shall act as President, as in case of the death or other constitutional disability of the President. The person having the greatest number of votes as Vice-President, shall be the Vice-President, if such number be a majority of the whole number of Electors appointed, and if no person have a majority, then from the two highest numbers on the list, the Senate shall choose the Vice-President; a quorum for the purpose shall consist of two-thirds of the whole number of Senators, and a majority of the whole number shall be necessary to a choice. But no person constitutionally ineligible to the office of President shall be eligible to that of Vice-President of the United States.

AMENDMENT XIII (1865)

Section 1.

Neither slavery nor involuntary servitude, except as a punishment for crime whereof the party shall have been duly convicted, shall exist within the United States, or any place subject to their jurisdiction.

Section 2.

Congress shall have power to enforce this article by appropriate legislation.

AMENDMENT XIV (1868)

Section 1.

All persons born or naturalized in the United States, and subject to the jurisdiction thereof, are citizens of the United States and of the State wherein they reside. No State shall make or enforce any law which shall abridge the privileges or immunities of citizens of the United States; nor shall any State deprive any person of life, liberty, or property, without due process of law; nor deny to any person within its jurisdiction the equal protection of the laws.

Section 2.

Representatives shall be apportioned among the several States according to their respective numbers, counting the whole number of persons in each State, excluding Indians not taxed. But when the right to vote at any election for the choice of electors for President and Vice-President of the United States, Representatives in Congress, the Executive and Judicial officers of a State, or the members of the Legislature thereof, is denied to any of the male inhabitants of such State, being twenty-one years of age, and citizens of the United States, or in any way abridged, except for participation in rebellion, or other crime, the basis of representation therein shall be reduced in the proportion which the number of such male citizens shall bear to the whole number of male citizens twenty-one years of age in such State.

Section 3.

No person shall be a Senator or Representative in Congress, or elector of President and Vice-President, or hold any office, civil or military, under the United States, or under any State, who, having previously taken an oath, as a member of Congress, or as an officer of the United States, or as a member of any State legislature, or as an executive or judicial officer of any State, to support the Constitution of the United States, shall have engaged in insurrection or rebellion against the same, or given aid or comfort to the enemies thereof. But Congress may by a vote of two-thirds of each House, remove such disability.

Section 4.

The validity of the public debt of the United States, authorized by law, including debts incurred for payment of pensions and bounties for services in suppressing insurrection or rebellion, shall not be questioned. But neither the United States nor any State shall assume or pay any debt or obligation incurred in aid of insurrection or rebellion against the United States, or any claim for the loss or emancipation of any slave; but all such debts, obligations and claims shall be held illegal and void.

Section 5.

The Congress shall have the power to enforce, by appropriate legislation, the provisions of this article.

AMENDMENT XV (1870)

Section 1.

The right of citizens of the United States to vote shall not be denied or abridged by the United States or by any State on account of race, color, or previous condition of servitude.

Section 2.

The Congress shall have the power to enforce this article by appropriate legislation.

AMENDMENT XVI (1913)

The Congress shall have power to lay and collect taxes on incomes, from whatever source derived, without apportionment among the several States, and without regard to any census or enumeration.

AMENDMENT XVII (1913)

The Senate of the United States shall be composed of two Senators from each State, elected by the people thereof, for six years; and each Senator shall have one vote. The electors in each State shall have the qualifications requisite for electors of the most numerous branch of the State legislatures.

When vacancies happen in the representation of any State in the Senate, the executive authority of such State shall issue writs of election to fill such vacancies: *Provided*, That the legislature of any State may empower the executive thereof to make temporary appointments until the people fill the vacancies by election as the legislature may direct.

This amendment shall not be so construed as to affect the election or term of any Senator chosen before it becomes valid as part of the Constitution.

AMENDMENT XVIII (1917)

Section 1.

After one year from the ratification of this article the manufacture, sale, or transportation of intoxicating liquors within, the importation thereof into, or the exportation thereof from the United States and all territory subject to the jurisdiction thereof for beverage purposes is hereby prohibited.

Section 2.

The Congress and the several States shall have concurrent power to enforce this article by appropriate legislation.

Section 3.

This article shall be inoperative unless it shall have been ratified as an amendment to the Constitution by the legislatures of the several States, as provided in the Constitution, within seven years from the date of the submission hereof to the States by the Congress.

AMENDMENT XIX (1920)

Section 1.

The right of citizens of the United States to vote shall not be denied or abridged by the United States or by any State on account of sex.

Section 2.

Congress shall have power to enforce this article by appropriate legislation.

AMENDMENT XX (1933)

Section 1.

The terms of the President and the Vice President shall end at noon on the 20th day of January, and the terms of Senators and Representatives at noon on the 3d day of January, of the years in which such terms would have ended if this article had not been ratified; and the terms of their successors shall then begin.

Section 2.

The Congress shall assemble at least once in every year, and such meeting shall begin at noon on the 3d day of January, unless they shall by law appoint a different day.

Section 3.

If, at the time fixed for the beginning of the term of the President, the President elect shall have died, the Vice President elect shall become President. If a President shall not have been chosen before the time fixed for the beginning of his term, or if the President elect shall have failed to qualify, then the Vice President elect shall act as President until a President shall have qualified; and the Congress may by law provide for the case wherein neither a President elect nor a Vice President shall have qualified, declaring who shall then act as President, or the manner in which one who is to act shall be selected, and such person shall act accordingly until a President or Vice President shall have qualified.

Section 4.

The Congress may by law provide for the case of the death of any of the persons from whom the House of Representatives may choose a President whenever the right of choice shall have devolved upon them, and for the case of the death of any of the persons from whom the Senate may choose a Vice President whenever the right of choice shall have devolved upon them.

Section 5.

Sections 1 and 2 shall take effect on the 15th day of October following the ratification of this article.

Section 6.

This article shall be inoperative unless it shall have been ratified as an amendment to the Constitution by the legislatures of three-fourths of the several States within seven years from the date of its submission.

AMENDMENT XXI (1933)

Section 1.

The eighteenth article of amendment to the Constitution of the United States is hereby repealed.

Section 2.

The transportation or importation into any State, Territory, or Possession of the United States for delivery or use therein of intoxicating liquors, in violation of the laws thereof, is hereby prohibited.

Section 3.

This article shall be inoperative unless it shall have been ratified as an amendment to the Constitution by conventions in the several States, as provided in the Constitution, within seven years from the date of the submission hereof to the States by the Congress.

AMENDMENT XXII (1951)

Section 1.

No person shall be elected to the office of the President more than twice, and no person who has held the office of President, or acted as President, for more than two years of a term to which some other person was elected President shall be elected to the office of President more than once. But this Article shall not apply to any person holding the office of President when this Article was proposed by Congress, and shall not prevent any person who may be holding the office of President, or acting as President, during the term within which this Article becomes operative from holding the office of President or acting as President during the remainder of such term.

Section 2.

This article shall be inoperative unless it shall have been ratified as an amendment to the Constitution by the legislatures of three-fourths of the several States within seven years from the date of its submission to the States by the Congress.

AMENDMENT XXIII (1961)

Section 1.

The District constituting the seat of Government of the United States shall appoint in such manner as Congress may direct:

A number of electors of President and Vice President equal to the whole number of Senators and Representatives in Congress to which the District would be entitled if it were a State, but in no event more than the least populous State; they shall be in addition to those appointed by the States, but they shall be considered, for the purposes of the election of President and Vice President, to be electors appointed by a State; and they shall meet in the District and perform such duties as provided by the twelfth article of amendment.

Section 2.

The Congress shall have power to enforce this article by appropriate legislation.

AMENDMENT XXIV (1964)

Section 1.

The right of citizens of the United States to vote in any primary or other election for President or Vice President, for electors for President or Vice President, or for Senator or Representative in Congress, shall not be denied or abridged by the United States or any State by reason of failure to pay poll tax or other tax.

Section 2.

The Congress shall have power to enforce this article by appropriate legislation.

AMENDMENT XXV (1967)

Section 1.

In case of the removal of the President from office or of his death or resignation, the Vice President shall become President.

Section 2.

Whenever there is a vacancy in the office of the Vice President, the President shall nominate a Vice President who shall take office upon confirmation by a majority vote of both Houses of Congress.

Section 3.

Whenever the President transmits to the President pro tempore of the Senate and the Speaker of the House of Representatives his written declaration that he is unable to discharge the powers and duties of his office, and until he transmits to them a written declaration to the contrary, such powers and duties shall be discharged by the Vice President as Acting President.

Section 4.

Whenever the Vice President and a majority of either the principal officers of the executive departments or of such other body as Congress may by law provide, transmit to the President pro tempore of the Senate and the Speaker of the House of Representatives their written declaration that the President is unable to discharge the powers and duties of his office, the Vice President shall immediately assume the powers and duties of the office as Acting President.

Thereafter, when the President transmits to the President pro tempore of the Senate and the Speaker of the House of Representatives his written declaration that no inability exists, he shall resume the powers and duties of his office unless the Vice President and a majority of either the principal officers of the executive department or of such other body as Congress may by law provide, transmit within four days to the President pro tempore of the Senate and the Speaker of the House of Representatives their written declaration that the President is unable to discharge the powers and duties of his office. Thereupon Congress shall decide the issue, assembling within forty-eight hours for that purpose if not in session. If the Congress, within twenty-one days after receipt of the latter written declaration, or, if Congress is not in session, within twenty-one days after Congress is required to assemble, determines by two-thirds vote of both Houses that the President is unable to discharge the powers and duties of his office, the Vice President shall continue to discharge the same as Acting President; otherwise, the President shall resume the powers and duties of his office.

AMENDMENT XXVI (1971)

Section 1.

The right of citizens of the United States, who are eighteen years of age or older, to vote shall not be denied or abridged by the United States or by any State on account of age.

Section 2.

The Congress shall have power to enforce this article by appropriate legislation.

AMENDMENT XXVII (1992)

No law, varying the compensation for the services of the Senators and Representatives, shall take effect, until an election of representatives shall have intervened.

APPENDIX B
STUDENT-FRIENDLY LEGAL WEBSITES

Findlaw.com: http://www.findlaw.com
One of the best sites but tends toward "legalese."

Law Guru: http://www.lawguru.com
Perhaps the best site because of its links to other search engines.

Duhaime's Law Dictionary: http://www.duhaime.org.diction.htm
Good definitions (and more) of all legal terms.

Everybody's Law Dictionary: http://www.nolo.com/dictionary/worldindex.cfm
Legal definitions in plain English.

Alabama Law Review: http://www.law.ua.edu/lawreview
Provides full-text articles free of charge.

American University International Law Review: https://digitalcommons.wcl.american.edu/auilr/
This journal provides international legal perspectives.

American University Law Review: https://digitalcommons.wcl.american.edu/aulr/
Some full-text articles available free of charge. This is America's oldest and largest legal journal.

Cardozo Law Review: http://cardozolawreview.com/
Provides full-text articles free of charge.

Indiana Law Journal: http://ilj.law.indiana.edu/
Some full-text articles available free of charge.

US Supreme Court: http://www.supremecourtus.gov
Provides up-to-date access to Court decisions and many other items relevant to the Court.

Law and Society Association: http://www.lawandsociety.org/
Includes many interesting posted items as well as access to the journal link to its JSTOR journal.

GLOSSARY

Abortion: The intentional termination of a pregnancy by the removal or expulsion of an embryo/fetus from the uterus resulting in its death.

Actus reus: Meaning "a guilty act," it refers to the three forms of the criminal act: (1) voluntary bodily movements, (2) an omission in the face of a duty to act, and (3) possession.

Adequate provocation: A killing that occurs after such provocation, as the law deems sufficient, that could cause even a reasonable person to react violently.

Administrative law: A body of law (also known as regulatory law) created by administrative agencies under the powers granted to them by Congress.

Administrative Procedure Act: This 1946 act established the procedural standards federal agencies must follow when adjudicating violations of administrative law.

Administrative regulations: Forms of legislation that under certain circumstances may have the force of law.

Adverse possession: Legal doctrine that allows someone to take the real property of another if they have used it openly and continuously for a period of time.

Affirmative defenses: Defenses in which the defendant has the burden of production and the burden of persuasion.

Aggravated assault: An unlawful attack by one person on another for the purpose of inflicting severe or aggravated bodily harm.

Alford plea: A plea in which the defendant enters a guilty plea but at the same time officially denies having committed the crime to which he or she is pleading.

Alibi: When the defendant asserts that he or she is not the person who committed the act charged or a claim that the state has failed to meet its burden of proof on a particular element of the offense charged.

All-property model: A family law model for dividing property after a divorce; states using this model equally divide all jointly held property regardless of when it was acquired.

American Indian Movement (AIM): Radical activist Indian organization founded in 1968.

Amicus curiae **briefs:** Briefs presented to the court arguing in favor of one side or the other by interested parties not directly involved with the case.

Annulment: A legal determination that a valid marriage never existed between the parties.

Appellate jurisdiction: The power of the court to review a decision of a lower court.

Arraignment: A formal hearing before a felony court where defendants are again informed of the charges against them and advised of their rights.

Arson: Setting fire to a structure with the intent to burn the structure, either in whole or in part.

Article III Courts: Those courts established by Congress pursuant to its authority to create "inferior" or lower courts under Article III of the US Constitution.

Articles of Confederation: The 1781 document that was the first attempt at creating a unified United States.

Assimilation period: Period in which the US government attempted to integrate the Indians into white society by "civilizing" and "Christianizing" them.

Assize court: French court in which the most serious crimes are tried.

Attempt: Trying but failing to commit a crime is punishable as an attempt. For liability to attach, there must be proof of a specific intent to commit a criminal act and some steps taken in furtherance of the criminal act.

Attenuation exception: An exception to the exclusionary rule (or its "fruit of the poisonous tree" offshoot) stating that illegal evidence is admissible if it is attenuated (weakened) by it being sufficiently remote from the initial illegality.

Bailment: The temporary transfer of possession of personal property to another for a particular purpose.

Bar associations: groups of lawyers who attempted to regulate the practice of law.

Bar examination: A test a lawyer must take and pass to be eligible to practice law in a given state. Each state has its own bar association and bar examination; passage of the bar exam in one state does not allow a person to practice law in other states.

Basic People's Court: Chinese court analogous to American district (felony) court.

Battery: unjustified, offensive, and intentional physical contact.

Beliefs: Ideas we have about how the world operates and what is true and false.

Bill of Rights: The first 10 Amendments to the US Constitution.

Bills of attainder: Legislation imposing punishment without trial.

Binding out: The practice of assigning children to foster parents as indentured servants.

Black Codes: Various legal codes enacted by the southern states to control, restrict, and inhibit the movements and behavior of ex-slaves.

Booking: An administrative procedure that involves making an entry in the police blotter at the station indicating the just-arrested suspect's name, time of arrest, and offense and the taking of the suspect's fingerprints and photograph.

Bracero Program: Program calling for the importation of temporary contract laborers from Mexico to the United States.

Bridewells: Early English institutions for housing and training youthful offenders.

Burden of production: The duty to produce evidence. In every criminal case, the prosecution must introduce evidence showing the defendant, in all likelihood, committed the crime with which he or she has been charged.

Bureau of Indian Affairs (BIA): Agency responsible for all aspects of Indian life, especially during the assimilation period.

Burglary: Must be an unlawful entry accompanied by the present intent to commit another crime once inside. It may occur at all hours of the day and in virtually any structure, not just dwellings.

Casebook approach: The teaching of law by reading appellate court opinions.

Castle doctrine: An exception to the general rules of self-defense stating that persons attacked in their home need not retreat from a potentially deadly invasion and/or attack.

Causation: The legal principle that the criminal act is the act that is the cause of the harm. There are two types of causation: factual and legal.

Challenge for cause: A challenge in which a valid reason for wanting to dismiss a potential jury member is shown to the court's satisfaction. Usually involves demonstrating that a potential juror cannot be unbiased or impartial.

Charismatic authority: A type of authority underlain by mythical, quasi-supernatural qualities.

Chevron deference: The principle enunciated by the US Supreme Court that courts must defer to agency interpretations of their own laws.

Child Savers: Liberals whose goal was to reform the juvenile justice system.

Chinese Exclusion Act: An 1882 act barring Chinese from immigrating to the United States.

Ch'ing Code: Early (1646) Chinese law code containing many statutes and offenses.

Civil law: The area of common law regulating the conduct of private parties and their relationships.

Civil Rights Act of 1964: Sweeping Congressional act that ensured civil, political, and social rights for blacks.

Clear and convincing evidence: A standard of proof in civil law that falls between the usual *preponderance of evidence* and criminal law's *beyond a reasonable doubt*.

Code Civil des Français: Also known as the Napoleonic Code. It became the blueprint for all subsequent civil law codes.

Code of Hammurabi: The first known legal code.

Cold War: Period from the end of World War II to 1989. A propaganda war "fought" largely between the United States and the Soviet Union.

Collegial bench: Comprises one to three professional judges and two to four laypeople assessors who sit in judgment of Chinese individuals accused of serious crimes.

Common law: A common law system was developed in England by the thirteenth century. Common law was judge-made law. That is, it was law created by judges as they heard cases and settled disputes.

Common law marriage: A legally binding marriage despite the absence of legal documents. Allowed in only a handful of states today.

Comparative negligence: A legal doctrine that attempts to apportion the responsibility for negligent conduct among the parties involved.

Compelling government interest: Compelling-state-interest is a legal test to determine the constitutional validity of a law. Under this test, the government's interest is balanced against the individual's constitutional right to be free of the law in question.

Compensatory style: A form of social control in which some person or group has accused another person or group of breaching an obligation and brings the matter before the courts seeking compensation.

Complaint: An accusation on a formal document that may be filled out by an officer or a private citizen accusing a specified person or persons of committing a specified act or acts. If an arrest is made first, a complaint will be sworn out afterward, usually by the arresting officer. The complaint serves as the charging document for the preliminary hearing.

Complicity: Sets forth the situations where more than one person may be held liable for criminal activity. Complicity still requires all the elements of criminal liability (intent, act, harm, and causation) but allows liability to attach to someone else's conduct.

Conciliatory style: A form of social control using the law to remedy a breach in a formerly harmonious relationship. Blame is not usually assigned in such matters.

Concurrence: The union of the criminal act (*actus reus*) and criminal intent (*mens rea*).

Conflict perspective: Perspective emphasizing that conflict mostly characterizes society, in which resources are limited and people seek to maximize their interests.

Confrontation clause: Portion of the Sixth Amendment tht states that the accused has the right "to be confronted with the witnesses against him"—that is, to challenge via cross-examination any witnesses hostile to him or her.

Conseil Constitutionnel: France's constitutional court determining constitutionality of *proposed* legislation only.

Conseil d'Etat: The Supreme Court of France.

Consensus perspective: A perspective emphasizing that consensus mostly characterizes society, where being part of a shared culture contributes to social stability.

Consent: A defense to some crimes in which a person granting consent is harmed. A claim of consent must demonstrate that it was voluntary, knowing, and intelligent.

Consent to search: A search conducted pursuant to consent is not a search for Fourth Amendment purposes—that is, the Fourth Amendment simply does not apply.

Conspiracy: An agreement between two or more people for the purpose of committing a crime.

Constitution: A document that legalizes the existing political order and legitimizes its ideology, provides a framework for the administration of government, regulates social and institutional behavior, and enumerates national goals and aspirations.

Constitution of the Fifth Republic: The French Constitution.

Constrained view: A view of the US Supreme Court that maintains it can rarely produce significant social change because its practical powers are limited.

Contract law: A form of civil law governing the conduct of business, which deals with the enforceability of private agreements between individuals and between organizations.

Contracts: Legally enforceable promises.

Contrast effect: The contrast between the circumstances of punishment suffered and an offender's usual life; the greater the contrast, the greater the deterrent effect.

Contributory negligence: A legal rule now mostly out of favor that states if an injured party was in any way partially responsible for his or her injuries, he or she was barred from collecting from the tortfeasor.

Conviction: Result of a criminal trial in which the person accused has been found or has pleaded guilty.

Corpus delicti: Refers to the five elements of criminal liability, each of which must be established beyond a reasonable doubt.

Corpus juris civilis: Roman legal code also known as the Code of Justinian.

Correctional court: French courts trying crimes carrying up to five years in prison.

Cour de Cassation: France's highest appeals court hearing criminal cases.

Courts of Chancery: Early English courts in which judges were directed to view each case as unique, to be flexible and empathetic, and to think in terms of *standards* of fairness rather than *rules* of law.

Coverture: A legal term that describes the legal subsuming of the female person into the male person in marriage.

Crime: An act that is prohibited by law.

Crime control model: Criminal justice model emphasizing community protection from criminals and that civil liberties can only have meaning in a safe, well-ordered society.

Criminal homicides: Unlawful killings. There are three forms of criminal homicide: murder, manslaughter, and negligent homicide.

Critical legal studies: Also known as critical legal theory, this is a radical school of thought that claims law is politics by other means, or a way the "privileged classes" maintain their favored place in society and to "legitimately" keep the working class down.

Custody: When the suspect has been subjected to a formal arrest or equivalent restraints on his freedom of movement.

Dawes Act: See "General Allotment Act."

Declaration of the Rights of Man and of the Citizen: Revolutionary document integrated into the French constitution.

Defense: A response made by a defendant to the complaint that if successful allows the defendant to avoid criminal liability.

Defense of Marriage Act: A 1996 federal act defining marriage as a contract into which only people of opposite sexes can enter.

Delinquents: Minors who commit acts that are crimes when committed by adults.

Delicts: In the French criminal justice system, delicts are similar to the less serious felonies in the American system. They carry a maximum penalty of up to five years in prison and are tried in correctional court.

Detention: A **detention** occurs when a reasonable person, viewing the particular police conduct as a whole and within the setting of all the surrounding circumstances, would have concluded that the police in some way had restrained his or her liberty so that the person was not free to leave

Dicta: Legal or nonlegal arguments that are used to support the decision but that do not constitute precedent.

Direct/formal social control: Social control via the direct formalities of law (i.e., punishment legally applied to the transgressor).

Direct/informal social control: Social control via the informal application of stigma applied to the transgressor.

Discovery Doctrine: Chief Justice John Marshall's doctrine asserting white sovereignty over the Indians by virtue of being heir to the European power that "discovered" America.

Disorderly conduct: A catch-all phrase that has been held to include acts as diverse as public drunkenness, vagrancy, playing loud music, and fighting.

Distributive justice: The form of justice concerned with how a political entity such as a nation distributes its resources.

Diversity of citizenship: When the opposing parties in a lawsuit are from different states.

Domestic violence: Any abusive act (physical, sexual, or psychological) that occurs within a domestic setting.

Double jeopardy: The legal principle that states a jurisdiction may not (a) prosecute someone again for the same crime after the person has been acquitted, (b) prosecute someone again for the same crime after the person has been convicted, and (c) punish someone twice for the same offense.

Dual-property model: A family law model for dividing property after a divorce; states using this model equally divide all held jointly property that was acquired during the marriage.

Dual sovereignty doctrine: Under the dual sovereignty doctrine, a person can be prosecuted in both federal and state court for the same offense or in the courts of different states for the same offense if certain circumstances surrounding the offense occurred in more than one state.

Due process: A set of instructions informing agents of the state how they must proceed in their investigation, arrest, questioning, prosecution, and punishment of individuals who are suspected of committing crimes; a principle binding the state to follow certain procedures designed to protect individual rights before it may deprive individuals of life, liberty, or property.

Due process clause: Portion of the Fourteenth Amendment which says no state shall deprive a person of life, liberty, or property without "due process of law," Interpreted by the Supreme Court as prohibiting states from abridging certain individual rights. Many of these rights are included in the Bill of Rights.

Due process model: Concerned primarily with the protection of individual privacy. It emphasizes the importance of the formal legal process as a means of ensuring mistakes are kept to a minimum, and it operates on the presumption of innocence.

Durham rule: This rule is met when the act was caused by the defendant's mental illness.

Dynamic view: A view of the US Supreme Court maintaining that it can be more effective than other government branches in bringing about social change because it is free of election concerns and can act in the face of public opposition.

Easement: A limited right to use another's real property for a specific purpose and time period.

Emancipation Proclamation: Executive proclamation issued in 1863 by Abraham Lincoln, freeing all slaves in the United States.

Entrapment: A defense to criminal liability in which the defendant asserts he or she committed the crime only because the government encouraged them to do so. According to the US Supreme Court, it occurs when (a) the crime is the result of "the creative activity" of law enforcement and (b) the prosecutor cannot prove beyond a reasonable doubt that the defendant was "independently predisposed" to commit the crime.

Environmental justice: The fair treatment and meaningful involvement of all people, regardless of race, color, national origin, or income, with respect to the development, implementation, and enforcement of environmental laws, regulations, and policies.

Equal protection clause: Interpreted to preclude states from making unequal, arbitrary distinctions between people. It does not ban reasonable classifications, but it does prohibit classifications that are either without reason or based on race or gender.

Equal Rights Amendment: A proposed amendment to the US Constitution that would guarantee women certain rights.

Equity: A concept akin to *fairness* or *justice* that served as the basis of the Courts of Chancery in England.

Establishment clause: The first clause of the First Amendment, which forbids the government from creating a state religion.

Evolutionary perspective: Perspective of natural law that considers it to be natural because it flows from the evolved nature of the species.

Ex post facto laws: Criminalizing acts already completed but not previously forbidden by the penal law.

Exclusionary rule: A judicially created remedy for violations of the Fourth Amendment, it provides that any evidence obtained by the government in violation of the Fourth Amendment guarantee against unreasonable searches and seizures is not admissible in a criminal trial to prove guilt.

Excuse defense: One in which defendants admit that what they did was wrong but argue that under the circumstances they were not responsible for the improper conduct.

Execution of public duties: Agents of the state, such as police officers or soldiers, are permitted to use reasonable force in the lawful execution of their duties. This defense allows the use of deadly force under the proper circumstances and allows police to engage in activities that are otherwise criminal (e.g., posing as a drug dealer) if they are doing so as part of their law enforcement efforts.

Extortion: A taking of property accomplished by the threat of future harm to person, property, or reputation.

Factual cause: The idea that "but for" the actor's conduct, the harm would not have occurred. It is an initial act that sets a series of other acts in motion that leads to some harm. Factual causation is a necessary, but not a sufficient, element for the imposition of criminal liability. A legal cause also must exist.

False consciousness: In Marxist philosophy, the acceptance of a belief system among the working class that is contrary to their class interests.

Family law: The set of laws involving marriage, child custody, and other issues arising in personal relationships.

Fee simple absolute estate: An interest in real property that does not revert to the original owner.

Fee simple estate: An interest in real property that ends when the person dies, at which time the interest reverts to the original owner of the property.

Felony: A crime for which the possible punishment includes a sentence of imprisonment for at least one year.

Felony murder rule: A rule in which an individual may be held liable for an unintended killing that occurs during the commission of a dangerous felony, such as robbery or rape. There is no requirement of intent to either kill or inflict serious injury. It is enough if the person was engaged in what is considered a dangerous felony, or a felony in which serious injury is a reasonably foreseeable outcome. In most states, felony murder is treated as second-degree murder.

Feminist jurisprudence: The practice of examining and evaluating the law from a feminist perspective.

Forgery: False legal writing or altering of an existing legal document.

Formal irrationality: Legal decisions based on formal rules but not based on reason or logic.

Formal rationality: Legal decisions based on formal rules and on reason and logic.

Forms: Refers to Plato's belief that the objects and ideas in the world are only imperfect representations of the archetypal objects and ideas in the real world.

Freedman's Bureau: During the Reconstruction period, a bureau set up by the federal government to provide former slaves with food, clothing, schools, and other requirements.

Freehold estate: One wherein a person owns a piece of property as distinguished from only a right to use property (as in a rental agreement).

Fruit of the poisonous tree: An appendage to the exclusionary rule that dictates any evidence indirectly gained by an illegal police action must be excluded.

Fundamental rights: Rights that the US Supreme Court has determined are "essential to the concept of ordered liberty."

General Allotment Act (or Dawes Act): Act dividing up reservation lands into allotments given to individual Indians as part of the assimilation process.

General deterrence: The supposed preventive effect of punishment on those who have witnessed it but not experienced it.

General jurisdiction: When a court has the authority to hear a variety of cases rather than being limited to only a particular type of case.

Geographical jurisdiction: The authority of courts to hear cases that arise within specified boundaries, such as a city, county, state, or country.

Good faith exception: The exclusion of evidence obtained by police who have not knowingly violated the Fourth Amendment and who relied in "good faith" on other actors in the criminal justice system does not serve the purpose of deterring police misconduct, the primary goal of the exclusionary rule.

Grand jury: A group of citizens who listen to the case presented by a prosecutor and determine whether there is sufficient evidence to grant an indictment.

Habeas corpus: A document challenging the legality of a person's detention.

Hadith: A collection of sayings and actions of the Prophet Muhammad providing supplements to and clarifications of the Qur'an. Also a guide to Islamic jurisprudence.

Harm: The injury to another as a result of the act.

Harm principle: A principle first enunciated by John Stuart Mill stating that people should enjoy any and all liberties, even those harmful to themselves, as long as their behavior does not cause harm to others.

Harrison Narcotics Act: A 1914 act regulating drug use in the United States that was the benchmark act for changing America's attitudes toward drugs.

Hierarchical jurisdiction: The division of responsibilities and functions among the various courts.

Higher People's Court: Chinese court analogous to an American state supreme court.

Hudud: The most serious crimes under Islamic doctrine, for which the penalties attached are considered God prescribed; no judge or legislative body can alter the penalty for them.

Immunity: In law, the concept that some people (judges for actions that fall within the purview of judicial duties) or entities (sovereign states) are immune from legal prosecution for their actions.

Incapacitation: A philosophy of punishment justified by the inability of incarcerated criminals to victimize people outside the prison walls.

Inchoate crimes: Crimes that occur in preparation for an offense. Inchoate means "to begin" or "to partially put into operation."

Incorporation: Interpreting the due process clause of the Fourteenth Amendment, which says no state shall deprive a person of life, liberty, or property without "due process of law," as prohibiting states from abridging certain individual rights. Many of these rights are included in the Bill of Rights, hence these rights were included (or incorporated) in the definition of due process.

Independent source exception: Whereby evidence may be admitted if knowledge of that evidence is gained from a source that is entirely independent from a source tainted by police illegality

Indian Citizenship Act: Act granting US citizenship to Indians in 1924.

Indian Removal Act: An 1830 act mandating the removal of all Indians in the southeastern states to "Indian territory" (now the state of Oklahoma).

Indian Reorganization Act: A 1934 act that ended the practice of cultural genocide and encouraged Indians to revive their languages, religions, and customs.

Indian Self-Determination Act: A 1975 act ending the termination policy of the 1950s.

Indictment: A document formally charging the defendant with a crime that is handed down by a grand jury after hearing the evidence presented by the prosecutor.

Indirect/formal social control: Social control via the threat of legal sanctions perceived by individuals who have not transgressed the law.

Indirect/informal social control: Social control by reinforcing norms.

Inevitable discovery exception: An exception to the exclusionary rule that permits the introduction of illegally obtained evidence if the police can demonstrate they would have discovered the evidence by legal means anyway.

Information: A substitute for an indictment in which charges against a defendant are filed directly with the court by the prosecutor, thus bypassing the grand jury.

Initial appearance: The first court appearance by a suspect/defendant, which takes place in a municipal or justice of the peace court. It is here that suspects are informed of their constitutional rights and the nature of the charges against them and a bail decision is made.

Inquisitorial system: Investigatory criminal justice system characterized by cooperation between all parties in an effort to reach the truth.

Insanity: A legal term to describe mental illness and a defense to criminal liability in most jurisdictions. People who are found by the jury to be insane are not liable for their actions because they lack *mens rea*. There are several different tests for insanity, depending on the jurisdiction.

Intermediate People's Court: Chinese court that carries out the same functions as the higher people's court at the prefecture (multicounty) level. The major difference is that it is a court of original jurisdiction for cases involving serious crimes, such as murder and rape.

Interrogation: Interrogation occurs (a) when police are asking questions the answers to which may incriminate and (b) in circumstances in which the police, through their actions, create the "functional equivalent" of an interrogation.

International Court of Justice: Also known as the World Court, the judicial body of the United Nations. Deals with legal disputes among United Nations member states.

Involuntary commitment: The use of legal means to commit someone to a mental institution against his or her will.

Involuntary manslaughter: A criminal homicide where an unintentional killing results from a reckless act.

Irresistible impulse test: When a defendant could not control his or her conduct.

Islamic Law: A theocratic system of law based on the Qur'an, the Sunna, and shari'a.

Jim Crow laws: Any state or federal laws that enforced the segregation of the races in various areas of American life.

Judicial activism: Accusation made against judges when it is believed they have decided a case based on principles other than constitutional ones.

Judicial review: The power of the courts to examine a law to determine whether it is constitutional.

Judicial waiver: The transfer of a juvenile to criminal court as decided by a juvenile court judge at his or her own discretion after a full inquiry into the matter.

Jurisdiction: The legal authority or power of a court to hear, pronounce on, and decide a case.

Jury consultants: Experts hired by attorneys to help them determine what type of person is more likely to favor their side.

Justice: According to Aristotle, "justice consists of treating equals equally and unequals unequally according to relevant differences."

Justification defense: One in which the defendant admits he or she is responsible for the act that occurred but claims that under the circumstances the act was not criminal.

Kansas-Nebraska Act: Repealed the Missouri Compromise and opened up areas of the West to slavery.

Kubra: The high courts in Islamic law that hear serious (*hudud*) offenses.

Language: The words used to explain concepts, including legal concepts.

Larceny: The unlawful taking and carrying away of another's personal property with the intent to permanently deprive the rightful owner of its possession. Includes taking by stealth, by force, by fraud, and by false pretenses.

Law: A written body of general rules of conduct applicable to all members of a defined community, society, or culture, which emanate from a governing authority and which are enforced by its agents using the imposition of penalties for their violation.

Legal cause: Also referred to as proximate cause. The proximity in time between the accused's actions and the ultimate degree of harm caused to the victim. The question often asked in such cases is "for which act does it seem fair and just to hold the actor accountable?" Consequences of an act that are not reasonably foreseeable to the actor are "intervening causes" and may serve to relieve the actor of criminal liability.

Legal realism: The study of legal decision-making. It explores how law is applied and the implications of that application—that is, not law "as written" but law "as practiced."

Legislation: Statutes passed by the legislature (state or federal).

Legitimacy: The ability to command compliance with rules despite the lack of objective means to compel it.

Limited jurisdiction: Those courts that deal with the less serious offenses and civil cases. These courts are referred to by a variety of names, including justice of the peace court, magistrate's court, municipal court, and county court. These lower courts handle a wide variety of matters, including minor criminal cases, traffic offenses, violations of municipal ordinances, and civil disputes under a certain amount, usually $1,000.

Magna Carta: The "Great Charter" of 1215 limiting the power of the English sovereign and asserting certain rights on the part of the barons.

Major Crimes Act: An 1885 act that extended federal criminal jurisdiction over Indians and other persons in Indian country.

Mala in se **crimes:** Crimes that are universally condemned because they are inherently evil.

Mala prohibita **crimes:** Crimes that are defined as bad simply because they are forbidden.

Malice aforethought: An intentional, premeditated (planned) killing.

Manslaughter: voluntary: An intentional killing that occurs either (a) under a mistaken belief that self-defense required the use of deadly force or (b) in response to adequate provocation while in the sudden heat of passion; involuntary: a criminal homicide where an unintentional killing results from a reckless act.

Marshall Trilogy: Three US Supreme Court cases that defined the legal status of Native American sovereignty.

Mechanical solidarity: According to Durkheim, the form of social solidarity found in pre-modern societies.

Megan's Law: A federal law enacted in 1996 that requires law enforcement agencies in all 50 states to register sex offenders in their area.

Mens rea: Literally, "guilty mind." Liability generally does not attach based on action alone; some sort of guilty mind also must exist.

Miller test: A test specifying what material must be to be considered obscene: (a) the material must appeal to prurient interests as determined by the "average person" applying "contemporary community standards," (b) it must describe/illustrate sexual activity in a "patently offensive" way, and (c) it must lack any serious literary, artistic, scientific, or political value.

Misogyny: The hatred, devaluation, and ridicule of women.

Missouri Compromise: An 1820 act admitting Missouri into the union as a slave state but restricting the spread of slavery in certain other areas of the Louisiana Purchase territories.

Mistrial: A situation in which a trial is terminated because of a legal error that occurs during the trial that unfairly prejudices the defendant. A new trial may be held at a later date.

M'Naghten rule: The first, and still most common, test for insanity. Under it, a defendant is not criminally liable if he or she did not know either what he or she was doing or that it was wrong. Also known as the right-wrong test.

Model Penal Code: In relation to modern criminal law, it sets forth four levels of intent: purposeful, knowing, reckless, and negligent.

Motion: A request made to the court asking it for something, such as granting a continuance, suppressing evidence, or dismissing the case.

Motive: The cause or reason why an act is committed.

Movables: Personal property; property not permanently connected to the land.

Murder: A killing that occurs (a) purposefully, (b) knowingly, or (c) recklessly under circumstances exhibiting extreme indifference to human life. First-degree murder encompasses those killings that are deliberate and premeditated. Second-degree murder includes any killings that are intentional but not premeditated or planned.

Musta'galah: Type of court in Islamic law that hears minor (*ta'azir*) offenses.

National Association for the Advancement of Colored People (NAACP): Founded in 1910 by W. E. B. DuBois to advance the causes of African Americans.

Natural law: A theory or philosophy of law often contrasted with positive law and maintaining that there is a law that is either God-given or flows from the evolved nature of *Homo sapiens*.

Naturalistic fallacy: The fallacy of confusing what *is* with what *ought* to be.

Negligence: A failure to act with the appropriate level of care.

Negligent homicide: An unintentional killing in which the defendant should have known that he or she was creating a substantial risk of death by his or her conduct, which itself deviated from the ordinary level of care owed to others.

Nizam: Abridged secular Saudi Arabian constitution applicable mainly to administrative matters. It is secondary to the Qur'an and contains no bill of rights.

No-fault divorce: Divorce granted without assigning fault for the breakup of the marriage.

Nolo contendere: A plea in which the defendant accepts whatever punishment the court would impose on a guilty defendant but refuses to admit liability. Also referred to as a "no contest" plea. It is frequently used by defendants who fear being exposed to civil liability for their criminal misdeeds (a guilty plea would so expose them).

Norm: The action component of a value or a belief that prescribes and proscribes behavior as acceptable or unacceptable.

Northwest Ordinance: Provided for a survey of the Northwest Territories and gave the US Congress rather than the states the sole right to trade with Indians.

Obscenity: A legal term for any subcategory of pornography that is not constitutionally protected, such as child pornography.

Open fields: Refers to everything that is *not* defined as being within the curtilage.

Operation Wetback: A 1954 cooperative American/Mexican effort to stem the tide of illegal immigrants into the United States.

Ordinary care: The level of care required to avoid committing a negligent act and being civilly liable in tort law.

Organic solidarity: According to Durkheim, the form of social solidarity found in modern societies.

Original jurisdiction: The power of the court to hear the case initially.

Original position: John Rawls's version of Hobbes's and Locke's precontractual state of nature.

Overbreadth doctrine: A criminal law violates the overbreadth doctrine when it fails to narrowly define the specific behavior to be restricted.

Parens patriae: The obligation of the state to care for people in need of care and protection, such as children and the mentally ill.

Paterna pietas: Literally, "father love."

Patria potestas: Literally, "fatherly power": the power of the father over his family.

Patriarchy: A system whereby males are promoted and supported over females.

Penal style: Style of social control attained by punishing violators of the criminal law.

People's mediation committees: Committee of individuals organized in work and neighborhood groups to ensure rule conformity.

Peremptory challenge: One for which no reason need be given. While challenges for cause are unlimited, peremptory challenges are usually limited to a certain number. The US Supreme Court has held that peremptory challenges may not be used to exclude potential jurors on the basis of race (*Batson v. Kentucky*, 1986) or gender (*J.E.B. v. Alabama*, 1994).

Personal jurisdiction: The authority of the court over the person.

Petit jury: The trial jury.

Petite treason: A charge made under early common law against women who murdered their husbands. It was considered worse than an ordinary murder because the wife had committed it against her "sovereign master."

Plain view doctrine: Exception to the exclusionary rule. "Objects falling in the plain view of an officer who has a right to be in a position to have that view are subject to seizure."

Plaintiff: Person alleging that the defendant has harmed him or her in some way and who seeks damages for the injury.

Plea: The defendant's response to the charge against him or her.

Plea bargaining: Process in which the defendant in a criminal case pleads guilty in exchange for a more lenient sentence than he or she would otherwise face.

Police court: Lowest-level French trial court for crimes with a maximum penalty of two months in jail.

Pornography: The depiction of sexual behavior in pictures, writing, film, or other material intended to cause sexual arousal.

Positive law: Human-made law arising from social norms; contrasted with natural law.

Precedent: The decision of a court that governs the court issuing the decision and any lower courts in subsequent cases.

Preliminary hearing: The second step in the trial process, after the initial appearance. Here, the magistrate determines if there is probable cause to believe that an offense was committed and that it was the defendant who committed it. If probable cause is established, the defendant is "bound over" for trial. The preliminary examination is a formal adversarial proceeding conducted in open court. The US Supreme Court has defined it as a "critical stage" of the prosecution, which means the defendant has a right to have his or her lawyer present.

Preponderance of the evidence: The standard of proof in civil cases.

Privilege against self-incrimination: The right of criminal defendants not to be forced to testify against themselves.

Probable cause: A legal concept referring to the amount of proof a police officer must have to search or arrest someone.

Procedural defense: Defense in which it is claimed that somewhere along the line in processing the case, the criminal justice system violated the defendant's due process rights. These defenses include double jeopardy, denial of a speedy trial, and use of illegally seized evidence.

Procedural law: The rules the state must follow when investigating suspects or prosecuting someone who has committed a crime. It comprises the rules that govern the manner in which the state may go about depriving an individual of his or her liberty.

Proclamation Act: A 1763 act passed by the British Parliament forbidding white settlement in America west of the Appalachians.

Progressives: A nineteenth-century group of liberal reformers who argued for the professionalization of public service.

Prohibition: A name given to the combination of the Eighteenth Amendment and the Volstead Act of 1919 outlawing the manufacture and sale of alcohol in the United States.

Property: The right of ownership or possession of an item, which may be real, personal, or intangible.

Prosecutorial discretion waiver: Type of waiver (also known as a *direct file*) allowing prosecutors to file certain juvenile cases in either juvenile or adult court.

Prostitution: The provision of sexual services in exchange for money or other tangible reward. A *prostitute* is a person who engages in prostitution as a source of income.

Proximate cause: The legal principle that the criminal act is the one that is the most significant and that it seems fair and just to hold the actor accountable for his or her actions.

Punitive damages: Monetary awards beyond compensation that are designed to punish the defendant and to deter others.

Qadi (or *khadi*): Islamic judge.

Quesas: In Islamic law, serious non-*hadd* crimes for which punishment is not prescribed in the Qur'an.

Racism: A belief in the innate inferiority of persons of another race and discriminatory behavior consistent with that belief.

Rape: Carnal knowledge of a female forcibly and against her will.

Rational basis review: A less restrictive basis of judicial review used when neither a fundamental right nor a suspect classification is implicated in enacted legislation. Legislation must have a rational basis.

Rational-legal authority: A form of authority derived from rules rationally and legally enacted.

Reasonable expectation of privacy: A Fourth Amendment provision that applies to areas where persons have a reasonable expectation of privacy. There are subjective and objective components: (a) a subject must have a subjective expectation of privacy, and (b) society must view that expectation as reasonable.

Reasonableness clause: The portion of the Fourth Amendment that the US Supreme Court has interpreted to allow searches without warrants, provided there exist both probable cause and an exigent circumstance (meaning a critical or urgent situation) that justifies the failure to obtain a warrant.

Reconstruction: A period of reestablishment and reorganization of the seceded southern states after their defeat in the Civil War.

Rehabilitation: A philosophy of punishment that seeks to restore criminals to constructive activity through treatment programs designed to change thinking patterns.

Reintegration: A philosophy of punishment based on concrete programming, such as job training and education, designed to prepare criminals to reenter the free community as well equipped as possible to avoid committing future crimes.

Religious Freedom Restoration Act (RFRA): A federal law enacted in 1993 mandating that the strict scrutiny standard of review be used when determining whether the free exercise clause has been violated.

Res judicata: Civil law analogue of the prohibition against double jeopardy. Once a case has been through all possible appeals, it is decided forever.

Restitutive justice: According to Durkheim, the form of justice found in modern societies.

Restorative justice: An approach to criminal justice aiming to repair the harm done with an agreeable restorative solution.

Retreat doctrine: A doctrine stating that a person must retreat rather than use deadly force in a situation if doing so is possible without endangering the person's life.

Retribution: The justification for punishment exemplified by the "eye for an eye" concept; punishment must match the degree of harm inflicted on the victim.

Right–wrong test: Also known as the M'Naghten rule, or test for insanity in criminal courts. It is met if a defendant did not know either what he or she was doing or that it was wrong.

Risk society: A society organized in response to internally manufactured risks.

Robbery: The taking or attempted taking of anything of value from the care, custody, or control of a person or persons by force or threat of force or violence and/or putting the victim in fear.

Rule of four: A US Supreme Court rule that requires only four of the nine justices need to vote to accept a petition for a writ of certiorari for it to be issued—even though it takes five of nine justices for a majority to decide the case.

Rule of law: The principle that law, not men, govern and that no one is above the law.

Sarbanes-Oxley Act: Act passed by Congress in 2002 designed to crack down on white-collar crime.

Search: The examination of an individual's house, person, or effects to discover items related to criminal activity.

Search incident to arrest: Deals with the scope of the search; includes anywhere on the person and the "lunge area," or immediate vicinity of the suspect.

Seizure: The exercise of dominion or control by the police over a person or item.

Self-defense: A defense to criminal liability that states people may use force to repel an imminent, unprovoked attack in which they reasonably believed they were about to be seriously injured. The defendant may only use as much force as is necessary to repel the attack.

Shari'a: In Islam, "the path to follow"; rules of conduct revealed by Allah.

Sherman Antitrust Act: Passed by Congress in 1890 and designed to place controls on business.

Social change: Any relatively enduring alteration in social relationships, behavior patterns, values, norms, and attitudes occurring over time.

Social contract: Hypothetical contract between individuals creating a state that could protect them from predation and exploitation.

Social control: Any action that influences conduct toward conformity, whether or not the persons being influenced are aware of the process.

Social justice: A leftist concept that basically demands economic equality in addition to legal and political equality.

Social movement: A sustained series of interactions between power holders and persons claiming to speak on behalf of a constituency lacking formal representation, making publicly visible demands for changes in the distribution or exercise of power, and backing those demands with public demonstrations of support.

Socialist law: System of law based on Marxist principles and developed in the former Soviet Union. Socialist law subordinates the rule of law to the requirements of the state.

Socratic method: A method of teaching the law wherein the professor asks the law student a series of questions intended to force the student to identify key legal principles and doctrines and to apply them to hypothetical situations.

Sodomy: Anal sex between two people of either sex. An expanded definition includes fellatio (mouth–penis contact) and sometimes cunnilingus (mouth–vagina contact).

Solicitation: The intent to induce another to commit a crime.

Song duel: Method of restoring peace among the Inuit peoples through the perpetrator of a crime and the victim hurling singsong insults at one another.

Soviet legalism: Strict and unflinching observance and fulfillment of Soviet laws by all organs of the socialist state and public organizations, institutions and all citizens, in all circumstances, and at all times.

Special needs of law enforcement exception: A series of exceptions to the search warrant requirement. It is applied in cases that are a mixture of criminal investigation and conduct by other public agencies not related to the police. Examples include searches of students by school authorities, searches of closely regulated businesses, and searches of probationers and parolees.

Specific deterrence: The supposed preventative effect of imposed punishment on the future behavior of the person punished.

Specific performance: In civil law, when a court orders someone to do (or not do) something.

Standing: When a person has the right to bring legal action by virtue of being personally harmed.

Standing exception: Exception to the exclusionary rule under which a person must have the legal right to claim violation of his or her rights by virtue of being personally harmed by police illegality.

Standing mute: When a defendant refuses to enter a plea of any kind. In these instances, the court enters a "not guilty" plea on behalf of the defendant, thus preserving the constitutional right to trial.

Stare decisis: The legal basis for adhering to precedent; literally, "let the decision stand."

Status offenses: Noncriminal offenses such as truancy and ungovernable that apply only to individuals whose status is that of a juvenile.

Statute: Legislative enactment or bill.

Statutory exclusion waiver: An automatic waiver (also called a legislative waiver) applied when state legislatures have statutorily excluded serious offenses from the juvenile courts based on age.

Stop and frisk: Involves a police officer stopping people in public and questioning them as to their identity and activity, followed in some circumstances by a limited "pat-down" search of their outer clothing.

Strict constructionism: A philosophy maintaining that judges must seek to discover and adhere to the "original intent" of the Framers of the US Constitution when making decisions.

Strict liability: Imposes accountability without proof of criminal intent in situations where society deems it fair to do so, such as violations of drug and alcohol sales laws; liability without consideration of the intent of the defendant.

Strict scrutiny review: A rigorous standard of review exercised by the courts for cases involving legislation curtailing fundamental rights or a suspect classification.

Subject matter jurisdiction: The authority conferred on a court to hear a particular type of case.

Substantial capacity test: When the defendant lacks substantial capacity to appreciate the wrongfulness of his or her conduct or to know how to control it.

Substantive due process: A constitutional principle holding that in addition to procedural rights, the law must protect substantive rights, such as the right to possess or to say or do certain things.

Substantive irrationality: Legal decisions on a case-by-case basis without a set of legal principles.

Substantive law: Defined by statute, it prescribes (what we should do) and proscribes (what we should not do) various types of conduct.

Substantive rationality: Legal decisions on a case-by-case basis with a set of rules.

Sunna: Companion book to the Qur'an containing numerous moral precepts relating to all aspects of Islamic life.

Supremacy clause: A clause in the US Constitution stating that the authority of the United States (not the individual states) shall be the supreme law of the land.

Supreme People's Court: China's highest court. Deals with important national matters and appeals from lower courts.

Symbols: A concrete physical manifestation that "stands for" an abstraction.

Ta'azir: In Islamic law, *ta'azir* offenses are "rehabilitation" offenses, such as eating pork or dressing provocatively, for which punishment is discretionary and lenient by Islamic standards.

Technology: The totality of the knowledge and techniques a people employ to create the material objects of their sustenance and comfort.

Tenancy in common: Exists when multiple parties share equally in the ownership or possession of real property.

Termination: Policy aimed at terminating federal supervision of Indian tribes in the 1950s.

Therapeutic style: Style of social control aimed at those considered in need of treatment rather than punishment; a remedial style.

Tort law: The body of civil law associated with harm caused to plaintiffs by the action or inaction of defendants.

Traditional authority: A type of authority that rests on long-standing usage and custom.

Transcendentalism: A philosophy emphasizing the primacy of the spiritual over the material (the spirit transcends the material).

Transcendentalist perspective: A perspective on natural law that law originates in some transcendental realm (e.g., God) and must be followed by all.

Transferred intent: Applies to situations where a person intended to harm A but in error harmed B.

Treaty of Fort Pitt: First treaty made with the Indians. It implicitly recognized the sovereignty of the Indian nations and assured them that the United States had no designs on Indian lands.

Treaty of Guadalupe Hidalgo: Treaty that ended the Mexican-American War and ceded over 525,000 square miles of territory to the United States.

Trial de novo: Literally, "a new trial." A trial held as if no prior trial has been held. Often used as an appeal from small claims courts.

Uniform Commercial Code: A code of law concerning contracts designed to standardize trade and contract practices among merchants and businesses.

Uniform Crime Reports (UCR): The Federal Bureau of Investigation's annual report of crimes committed in the United States. It comprises Part I and Part II offenses. The UCR defines eight crimes (murder, rape, robbery, aggravated assault, burglary, larceny/theft, motor vehicle theft, and arson) as Part I offenses. Part II offenses are a mixture of *mala prohibita* offenses and less serious *mala in se* offenses.

United Nations Convention on the Elimination of All Forms of Discrimination Against Women: United Nations charter designed to accomplish what its title implies. The United States is one of the few countries that have not ratified the Convention.

Unlawful assembly: Disorderly conduct in a group setting; includes groups assembled in public without the necessary permits, as well as riots.

USA Patriot Act: Act passed in response to 9/11 terrorist attacks against the United States that expanded the authority of law enforcement to fight terrorism.

Values: Normative standards shared by the culture about what is good and bad, correct and incorrect, moral and immoral, normal and deviant.

Veil of ignorance: A concept in Rawls's theory of justice that asks what kind of society people would endeavor to make if they were completely ignorant of their future place in it (i.e., forced to choose behind the veil of ignorance).

Venire: Latin for "to cause" or "to make come" (to the courthouse). Prospective jurors are examined by the judge and/or the attorneys for the prosecution and defense to determine whether they have any bias, prejudice, or interest that would prevent them from being impartial.

Vicarious liability: The imputation of accountability from one person to another, usually the individual's superior.

Vice crime: Any consensual act that offends the moral standards of the community that has defined the act as worthy of condemnation and legal control.

Violence Against Women Act: Federal act first passed in 1994 providing for funding for training programs for professionals involved in various aspects of domestic violence, such as police officers, victim advocates, judges, and prosecutors.

Void for vagueness: A statute is void for vagueness if it fails to clearly define both the act prohibited and the appropriate punishment in advance.

Voir dire: Latin for "to speak the truth." Refers to the process of questioning potential jurors to determine whether they are fit to serve on a jury.

Voluntary manslaughter: An intentional killing that occurs either (a) under a mistaken belief that self-defense required the use of deadly force or (b) in response to adequate provocation while in the sudden heat of passion.

Voting Rights Act of 1965: Act providing federal supervision of voter registration sites and prohibiting the use of literacy tests.

Waived: Term used to describe a juvenile being transferred (waived) from juvenile to adult court because of the seriousness of the crime.

Warrant clause: The portion of the Fourth Amendment stating that all warrants must be based on probable cause and must describe the place to be searched or the person to be seized with "particularity."

White-Collar Crime Penalty Enhancement Act: Act passed in conjunction with the Sarbanes-Oxley Act. It enhanced penalties for white-collar crimes and relaxed evidentiary rules for prosecuting them.

William Blackstone: English judge and philosopher whose *Commentaries on the Laws of England* organized common law into the structure it has today.

Writ of certiorari: An order to the lower court to send the record of the case up to the US Supreme Court.

Writ of mandamus: A court order compelling a public official to do his or her duty.

TABLE OF CASES

PHOTO CREDITS

Chapter 1

Page 12: Wikimedia Commons. Found here: https://upload.wikimedia. org/wikipedia/commons/9/98/ Sanzio_01_Plato_Aristotle.jpg

Page 13: The Miriam and Ira D. Wallach Division of Art, Prints and Photographs: Print Collection, The New York Public Library. "Thomas Hobbes" The New York Public Library Digital Collections. http://digitalcollections.nypl.org/ items/510d47df-fe43-a3d9-e040-e00a18064a99

Page 15: Portrait of John Locke, by Sir Godfrey Kneller. Oil on canvas. 76x64 cm. Britain, 1697. Source of Entry: Collection of Sir Robert Walpole, Houghton Hall, 1779.

Page 17: https://commons.wikimedia.org/ wiki/File:Max_Weber_1894.jpg

Page 17: http://www.marxists.org/ glossary/people/d/pics/durkheim.jpg

Page 17: John Jabez Edwin Paisley Mayall

Chapter 2

Page 31: Jongleur100

Page 36: © Marie-Lan Nguyen/ Wikimedia Commons

Page 46: Ackermann's Microcosm of London (1808–11); Microcosm of London

Page 50: Wikimedia Commons. Found here: https://commons.wikimedia.org/ wiki/File:Cesare_Beccaria_ 1738-1794.jpg

Page 51: Wikimedia Commons. Found here: https://commons.wikimedia.org/ File:Edward_coke.jpg

Chapter 3

Page 60: Cleveland Division of Police

Page 62: The Miriam and Ira D. Wallach Division of Art, Prints and Photographs: Print Collection, The New York Public Library. "Sir William Blackstone." The New York Public Library Digital Collections. 1657. http://digitalcollections.nypl.org/ items/510d47da-2788-a3d9-e040-e00a18064a99

Page 65: Wikimedia Commons. Found here: https://commons.wikimedia. org/wiki/File:James_Madison.jpg

Page 84: Wikimedia Commons. Found here: https://commons.wikimedia. org/wiki/File:John_Marshall_by_ Henry_Inman,_1832.jpg

Chapter 4

Page 91: Wikimedia Commons. Found here: https://commons.wikimedia. org/wiki/File:Justice_William_O_ Douglas.jpg

Page 94: Photo by Paul Sakuma-Pool/ Getty Images

Page 96: Fred Schilling, Collection of the Supreme Court fo the United States

Page 99: Fred Schilling, Collection of the Supreme Court of the United States

Page 104: Wikimedia Commons. Found here: https://commons.wikimedia. org/wiki/File:The_Jury_by_John_ Morgan.jpg

Chapter 5

Page 121: Image reproduced with the permission of The American Law Institute

Page 127: Hulton Archive/Getty Images

Page 130: The American Law Institute: http://2013am.ali.org/agenda.cfm

Chapter 6

Page 145: Photo credit: Highbrowmagazine.com

Page 148: Polk County Today. Image can be found here: http:// www.polkcountytoday.com/ arrest103109.html

Page 153: Screenshot from 'The Beginning of the End' the permiere episode of Lost (season 4), image found here: http://lostpedia.wikia. com/wiki/File:LAPD-Hurley_ interrogation.jpg

Page 157: Collection of W. J. Sawchuck

Chapter 8

Page 212: Found on Wikimedia Commons here: https:// commons.wikimedia.org/wiki/ File:N.Y._House_of_Refuge_ (NYPL_Hades-255948-430967).jpg

ALSO found in the NY Public Library, here: https:// digitalcollections.nypl.org/ items/510d47da-fa00-a3d9-e040- e00a18064a99

Chapter 10

Page 281: United States Immigration and Customs Enforcement (2013). Human trafficking. ICE Blue Campaign. Here: https:// www.ice.gov/es/factsheets/ dhs-blue-campaign#

Chapter 11

Page 326: Wikimedia commons. Found here: https://commons. wikimedia.org/wiki/File: Keeping_warm.jpg

Chapter 12

Page 348: Wikimedia commons. Found here: https://commons.wikimedia. org/wiki/File:Annie_Kenney_and_ Christabel_Pankhurst.jpg

Page 358: Wikimedia Commons. Found here: https://commons.wikimedia.org/ wiki/File:Arabella_mansfield.jpg

Chapter 13

Page 371: From Today I Found Out, found here: http:// www.todayifoundout.com/ index.php/2013/08/the-first-legal- slave-owner-in-what-would-become- the-united-states-was-a-black-man/

Chapter 14

Page 428: Wikimedia Commons. Found here: https://commons.wikimedia.org/ wiki/File:Dira_Square.JPG

INDEX

The letter *f* following a page number denotes a figure, the letter *d* denotes a glossary term and *m* denotes a map.